SOURCES FOR *CULTURES OF THE WEST*

SOURCES FOR *CULTURES OF THE WEST*

VOLUME 1: TO 1750

EDITED BY

Clifford R. Backman
BOSTON UNIVERSITY

OXFORD
UNIVERSITY PRESS

Oxford University Press is a department of the University of Oxford.
It furthers the University's objective of excellence in research, scholarship,
and education by publishing worldwide. Oxford is a registered trade mark
of Oxford University Press in the UK and in certain other countries.

Published in the United States of America by Oxford University Press
198 Madison Avenue, New York, NY 10016, United States of America.

For titles covered by Section 112 of the US Higher Education Opportunity
Act, please visit www.oup.com/us/he for the latest information about
pricing and alternate formats.

CIP data is on file at the Library of Congress

ISBN 9780197670804

CONTENTS

NEW TO THIS EDITION

The Fourth Edition of *Sources for Cultures of the West* includes fifteen new sources:

4.6   Lysias, "Against Eratosthenes," CA. 400 BCE
6.5   Sulpicia Severa, Six Poems
8.7   *The Corpus of Roman Law*
12.10   Benvenuto Cellini, *Autobiography*, 1558–1563
15.6   Daniel Defoe/Captain Charles Johnson, "The Life of Anne Bonny," 1724
15.7   The Absolutist Regimes
16.6   Germaine de Staël, *Memoirs*
17.2   Olympe de Gouges, *Declaration of the Rights of Woman and of the Female Citizen*, 1791
22.10   Pope Pius IX, *The Syllabus of Errors*, 1864
23.7   Francis Galton, "Africa for the Chinese," 1873
26.6   Victims of the Shoah
27.1   Simone Weil, "The Love of Religious Practices," 1950
27.8   Decolonization around the World
28.13   Hélène Cixous, "The Laugh of the Medusa," 1975
29.11   Vladimir Putin, "On the Historical Unity of Russians and Ukrainians," 2021

HOW TO READ A PRIMARY SOURCE

Sources for Cultures of the West is composed of two hundred primary sources. A primary source is any text, image, or other source of information that gives us a firsthand account of the past by someone who witnessed or participated in the historical events in question. Although such sources can provide significant and fascinating insight into the past, they must also be read carefully to limit modern assumptions about historical modes of thought. Here are a few elements to keep in mind when approaching a primary source.

AUTHORSHIP

Who produced this source of information? A male or a female? A member of the elite or of the lower class? An outsider looking *in* at an event or an insider looking *out*? What profession or lifestyle does the author pursue, which might influence how they are recording their information?

GENRE

What type of source are you examining? Different genres—categories of material—have different goals and stylistic elements. For example, on the one hand, a personal letter meant exclusively for the eyes of a distant cousin might include unveiled opinions and relatively trivial pieces of information, like the writer's vacation plans. On the other hand, a political speech intended to convince a nation of a leader's point of view might subdue personal opinions beneath artful rhetoric and focus on large issues like national welfare or war. Identifying genre can be useful for deducing how the source may have been received by an audience.

AUDIENCE

Who is reading, listening to, or observing the source? Is it a public or private audience? National or international? Religious or nonreligious? The source may be geared toward the expectations of a particular group; it may be recorded in a language that is specific to a particular group. Identifying audience can help us understand why the author chose a certain tone or why they included certain types of information.

HISTORICAL CONTEXT

When and why was this source produced? On what date? For what purposes? What historical moment does the source address? It is paramount that we approach primary sources in context to avoid anachronism (attributing an idea or habit to a past era where it does not belong) and faulty judgment. For example, when considering a medieval history, we must account for the fact that in the Middle Ages, the widespread understanding was that God created the world and could still interfere in the activity of humankind—such as sending a terrible storm when a community had sinned. Knowing the context (Christian, medieval, views of the world) helps us to avoid importing modern assumptions—like the fact that storms are caused by atmospheric pressure—into historical texts. In this way, we can read the source more faithfully, carefully, and generously.

BIAS AND FRAMING

Is there an overt argument being made by the source? Did the author have a particular agenda? Did any political or social motives underlie the reasons for writing the document? Does the document exhibit any qualities that offer clues about the author's intentions?

STYLISTIC ELEMENTS

Stylistic features such as tone, vocabulary, word choice, and the manner in which the material is organized and presented should also be considered when examining a source. They can provide insight into the writer's perspective and offer additional context for considering a source in its entirety.

Clifford Backman
Boston University

SOURCES FOR *CULTURES OF THE WEST*

CHAPTER 1

WATER AND SOIL, STONE AND METAL: THE FIRST CIVILIZATIONS

1.1 SHAMASH HYMN, CA. 2000–1600 BCE

Shamash, or Šamaš, the Babylonian sun-god of justice, is the subject of this two-hundred-line ode. Depicted as the god of gods, Shamash rules everything, all the way from the lesser divinities to the daily practices of mortal merchants. In fact, the density of economic references in this religious hymn corresponds to an economic boom during this era. Consider how the hymn depicts the powerful god's concern for the moral welfare of his devotees.

Šamaš, at your arising mankind bows down, [. . .] every land.
Illuminator, dispeller of darkness of the *vault* of the heavens,
Who sets aglow the *beard* of light, the corn field, the life of the land.
Your splendour covers the vast mountains,
Your fierce light fills the lands to their limits.
You climb to the mountains surveying the earth,
You suspend from the heavens the circle of the lands.
You care for all the peoples of the lands,
And everything that Ea [god of wisdom], king of the counsellors, had created is entrusted to you.

Whatever has breath you shepherd without exception,
You are their keeper in upper and lower regions.
Regularly and without cease you traverse the heavens,
Every day you pass over the broad earth. . . .
In the underworld you care for the counsellors of Kusu, the Anunnaki,
Above, you direct all the affairs of men,
Shepherd of that beneath, keeper of that above,
You, Šamaš, direct, you are the light of everything. . . .
Among all the Igigi there is none who toils but you,

From Wilfred G. Lambert, *Babylonian Wisdom Literature*. Winona Lake, IN: Eisenbrauns, 1996 (1960), pp. 127–37.

None who is supreme like you in the whole
    pantheon of gods.
At your rising the gods of the land assemble;
Your fierce glare covers the land.
Of all the lands of varied speech,
You know their plans, you scan their way.
The whole of mankind bows to you,
Šamaš, the universe longs for your light. . . .
You stand by the traveller whose road is
    difficult,
To the seafarer is dread of the waves you
    give [. . .]
It [is you] who patrol the unseen routes,
You constantly tread paths which confront
    [Šamaš] (alone).
You save from the storm the merchant carrying
    his capital,
The [. . .] who goes down to the ocean you equip
    with wings.
You point out settling-places to refugees and
    fugitives,
To the captive you point out routes that (only)
    Šamaš knows. . . .
A man who covets his neighbour's wife
Will [. . .] before his appointed day.
A nasty snare is prepared for him [. . .]
Your weapon will strike at him, and there [will
    be] none to save him.

. . .

The merchant who practises trickery as he holds
    the corn measure,
Who weighs out loans (or corn) by the minimum
    standard, but requires a large quantity in
    repayment,
The curse of the people will overtake him before
    his time,

If he demanded repayment before the
    agreed date, there will be guilt upon
    him. . . .
The honest merchant who weighs out loans
    (of corn) by the maximum standard, thus
    multiplying kindness,
It is pleasing to Šamaš, and he will prolong his
    life.
He will enlarge his family, gain wealth,
And like the water of a never failing spring [his]
    descendants will never fail. . . .
The progeny of evil-doers will [fail.]
Those whose mouth says "No"—their case is
    before you.
In a moment you discern what they say;
You hear and examine them; you determine the
    lawsuit of the wronged.
Every single person is entrusted to your hands;
You manage their omens; that which is perplexing
    you make plain.
You observe, Šamaš, prayer, supplication, and
    benediction,
Obeisance, kneeling, ritual murmurs, and
    prostration.
The feeble man calls you from the hollow of his
    mouth,
The humble, the weak, the afflicted, the poor,
She whose son is captive constantly and
    unceasingly confronts you. . . .
Which are the mountains not clothed with your
    beams?
Which are the regions not warmed by the
    brightness of your light?
Brightener of gloom, illuminator of darkness,
Dispeller of darkness, illuminator of the broad
    earth.

STUDY QUESTIONS

1. Which specific groups is Shamash enjoined to thwart? Why?
2. How might the hymn be read as a warning to the living *lugals* in Sumerian culture?

1.2 "POEM OF THE RIGHTEOUS SUFFERER,"
CA. 2000–1600 BCE

This religious lament was recorded in cuneiform (a pictographic, or picture-based, language written with a stylus in clay that was developed ca. 3000 BCE) by the Babylonians, who dominated the Near East in the third and second millennia BCE. The concept of a broken bond between man and the gods, which is mourned here, was absorbed from the great Sumerian culture that preceded the Babylonian Empire. The poignant, bitter lament reveals an individual trying to comprehend the absence and silence of the god Marduk, who promises prosperity and joy to those who pray to him, despite the individual's adherence to traditional religious rite.

My god has forsaken me and disappeared,
My goddess has failed me and keeps at a distance.
The benevolent angel who (walked) beside [me]
    has departed,
My protecting spirit has taken to flight, and is
    seeking someone else.
My strength is gone; my appearance has become
    gloomy;
My dignity has flown away, my protecting made
    off. . . .
The king, the flesh of the gods, the sun of his
    peoples,
His heart is enraged (with me), and cannot be
    appeased.
The courtiers plot hostile action against me,
They assemble themselves and give utterance to
    impious words. . . .
They combine against me in slander and lies.
My lordly mouth have they held as with reins,
So that I, whose lips used to prate, have become
    like a mute.
My sonorous shout is [reduced] to silence,
My lofty head is bowed down to the ground,
Dread has enfeebled my robust heart. . . .
If I walk the street, ears are pricked;
If I enter the palace, eyes blink.
My city frowns on me as an enemy;
Indeed my land is savage and hostile.

My friend has become foe,
My companion has become a wretch and a
    devil. . . .
As I turn round, it is terrible, it is terrible;
My ill luck has increased, and I do not find the
    right.
I called to my god, but he did not show his face,
I prayed to my goddess, but she did not raise her
    head.
The diviner with his inspection has not got to the
    root of the matter,
Nor has the dream priest with his libation
    elucidated my case.
I sought the favour of the *zaqīqu*-spirit, but he did
    not enlighten me;
And the incantation priest with his ritual did not
    appease the divine wrath against me.
What strange conditions everywhere!
When I look behind, there is persecution,
    trouble.
Like one who has not made libations to his god,
Nor invoked his goddess at table,
Does not engage in prostration, nor takes
    cognizance of bowing down;
From whose mouth supplication and prayer is
    lacking,
Who has done nothing on holy days, and
    despised sabbaths,

From Wilfred G. Lambert, *Babylonian Wisdom Literature*. Winona Lake, IN: Eisenbrauns, 1996 (1960), pp. 33–41.

Who in his negligence has despised the gods' rites,
Has not taught his people reverence and worship,
But has eaten his food without invoking his god,
And abandoned his goddess by not bringing a
  flour offering,
Like one who has grown *torpid* and forgotten his
  lord,
Has frivolously sworn a solemn oath by his god,
  (like such an one) do I appear.
For myself, I gave attention to supplication and
  prayer:
To me prayer was discretion, sacrifice my rule.
The day for reverencing the god was a joy to my
  heart;
The day of the goddess's procession was profit
  and gain to me.
The king's prayer—that was my joy,
And the accompanying music became a delight
  for me.
I instructed my land to keep the god's rites,
And provoked my people to value the goddess's
  name.
I made praise for the king like a god's,
And taught the populace reverence for the palace.

I wish I knew that these things were pleasing to
  one's god!

What is proper to oneself is an offence to one's god,
What in one's heart seems despicable is proper to
  one's god.
Who knows the will of the gods in heaven?
Who understands the plans of the underworld gods?
Where have mortals learnt the way of a god?
He who was alive yesterday is dead today.
For a minute he was dejected, suddenly he is
  exuberant.
One moment people are singing in exaltation,
Another they groan like professional mourners.
Their condition changes like opening and
  shutting (the legs).
When starving they become like corpses,
When replete they vie with their gods.
In prosperity they speak of scaling heaven,
Under adversity they complain of going down to
  hell.

I am *appalled* at these things; I do not understand
  their significance.

STUDY QUESTIONS

1. In what sense has the *lugal* failed to fulfill his role as protector?
2. What is the responsibility of the gods to this worshipper, and what can he do if the gods renege on the contract?

1.3 "TALE OF SINUHE," EARLIEST MANUSCRIPT
CA. 1800 BCE

This Egyptian story recounts the adventures of Sinuhe, a member of a princely entourage, who has fled his homeland yet longs to return. This tale, which may be a historical account, describes Sinuhe's departure; a copy of the kingly decree calling him home is repeated; and his safe return culminates in the promise that he will be buried among his own people. Consider how Sinuhe's identity is intertwined with his proximity to his homeland.

R. B. Parkinson, *The Tale of Sinuhe and Other Ancient Egyptian Poems 1940–1640 BC* (Oxford World Classics). Oxford: Oxford University Press, 1997. Reproduced with permission of the Oxford University Press through PLSclear.

I travelled southwards.
I did not plan to reach this Residence,
expecting strife would happen;
I did not think to live after him.

. . .

Thirst's attack overtook me,
and I was scorched, my throat parched.
I said, "This is the taste of death."
But I lifted up my heart, and gathered my limbs
    together,
as I heard the noise of cattle lowing, caught sight
    of Syrians,
and a leader of theirs, who had once been
in Egypt, recognized me.
Then he gave me water,
while he boiled milk for me.
I went with him to his tribe,
and what they did was good.
Country gave me to country.
I set out for Byblos; I got to Qedem.
I had spent half a year there,
when Amunenshi carried me off.
He was the ruler of upper Retjenu,
and he told me, "You'll be happy with me,
for you'll hear the speech of Egypt."
He said this, knowing my character
and having heard of my understanding,
and the Egyptians who were with him there
had vouched for me.
Then he said to me, "Why did you
    come here?
Has anything happened in the Residence?"
Then I said to him, "It's that the Dual King
    Sehotepibre
has gone to the horizon,
and how this all happened is unknown."
But I spoke in half-truths.
"I have come from the expedition to the Libyan
    land:
it was reported to me, and my heart failed
and carried me off on the ways of flight.
I had not been talked of, and my face had not
    been spat upon;

I had heard no reproaches; my name had not
    been heard in the herald's mouth.
I do not know what brought me to this country—
    it is like a plan of God."

. . .

Now, he is a God who is peerless,
before whom no other exists.
He is a lord of understanding, excellent of plans,
    effective of orders;
coming and going are by his command.
He subjugates the countries.
His father stayed within his palace,
and he reported to him that what he had
    ordained was done.
Now he is a hero, active with his strong arm,
a champion without compare,
seen descending on barbarians, approaching the
    combat.
He curbs horns, weakens hands;
his foes cannot marshal troops.
He is vengeful, a smasher of foreheads;
close to him no one can stand.
He is far-striding, destroying the fugitive;
there is no end for the man who shows him his
    back.
He is firm-hearted at the moment of forcing
    retreat.
He turns back again and again; he shows not his
    own back.
He is stout-hearted, seeing the masses;
he allows no rest around his heart.

. . .

He is a lord of kindness, great of sweetness.
Through love he has conquered.
His city loves him more than its own
    members;
it rejoices at him more than at its God.
Men and women pass by, exulting at him.
He is a king, who conquered in the egg,
his eyes on it from birth.
He makes those born with him plentiful.
He is unique, God-given.
How joyful this land, since he has ruled!

He extends its borders.

. . .

And he said unto me, "Well, Egypt is certainly
      happy,
knowing of his success.
But look, you are here,
and you will stay with me; I shall do you good."
He placed me at the head of his children.
He joined me to his eldest daughter.
He had me make my choice of his country,
from the choicest of what was his,
on his border with another country.
It was a good land,   '
called Iaa.
Figs were in it, and grapes;
its wine was more copious than its water;
great its honey, plentiful its moringa-oil,
with all kinds of fruit on its trees.
Barley was there, and emmer, and numberless
      were its cattle of all kinds.
Now, what came to me as a favourite was great.
He appointed me the ruler of a tribe
of the choicest of his country.

. . .

I spent many years there,
and my children became heroes,
each man subjugating his tribe.

. . .

in his heart I attained high regard;
he loved me, knowing my valour.
He placed me at the head of his children, having
      seen the strength of my arms.

. . .

For now God has acted so as to be gracious to one
      with whom He was offended,
whom He led astray to another country.
Today, He is satisfied.
A fugitive takes flight because of his surroundings;
      but my reputation is in the Residence.
A creeping man creeps off because of hunger; but
      I give bread to my neighbour.
A man leaves his land because of nakedness; but I
      have bright linen, white linen.
A man runs off because of lack of someone to
      send; but I am plentiful of serfs.

Good is my house, spacious my dwelling place,
      and memory of me is in the palace.
Whatever God fated this flight—be gracious, and
      bring me home!
Surely You will let me see the place where my
      heart still stays!
What matters more than my being buried
in the land where I was born?
This is my prayer for help, that the good event
      befall,
that God give me grace!
May He act in this way, to make well the end of
      someone whom He made helpless,
His heart sore for someone He compelled to live
      in a foreign country!

. . .

COPY OF THE DECREE BROUGHT TO THIS HUMBLE SERVANT ABOUT HIS BEING BROUGHT BACK TO EGYPT:

"Horus Living-of-Incarnations;
Two Ladies Living-of-Incarnations;
Golden Horus Living-of-Incarnations;
Dual King Kheperkare;
Son of Re Senwosret
—may he live for all time and eternity!
Royal Decree to the Follower Sinuhe:
Look, this decree of the king is brought to you
to inform you that your roving through
      countries,
going from Qedem to Retjenu,
country giving you to country,
was at the counsel of your own heart.
What had you done, that you should be acted
      against?
You had not cursed, that your speech should be
      punished.
You had not spoken in the officials' council, that
      your utterances should be opposed.
This idea carried off your heart—
it was not in my heart against you.

. . .

Return to Egypt!

And you will see the Residence where you grew
up,
kiss the earth at the Great Portal,
and join the Friends.
For today you have already begun to be old, have
lost your virility,
and have in mind the day of burial,
the passing to blessedness.

A night vigil will be assigned to you, with holy
oils
and wrappings from the hands of Tayet.
A funeral procession will be made for you on the
day of joining the earth,
with a mummy case of gold,
a mask of lapis lazuli,
a heaven over you, and you placed in a hearse,
with oxen dragging you,
and singers going before you.

. . .

Your death will not happen in a foreign
country;
Asiatics will not lay you to rest;
you will not be put in a ram's skin when your
coffin is made.
This is too long to be roaming the earth!
Think of your corpse—and return!

. . .

This flight which your humble servant made—
I had not planned it. It was not in my heart.
I had not thought of it. I know not what parted
me from my place.
It was like the nature of a dream,
like a Delta man seeing himself in Elephantine,
a man of the marshy lagoons in Southern
Egypt.
I had no cause to be afraid; no one had run after
me.
I had heard no reproaches; my name had not
been heard in the herald's mouth.
Only—that shuddering of my limbs,
my feet hastening,
my heart overmastering me,
the God who fated this flight dragging me away!
I was not presumptuous before,

for a man respects him who is acknowledged by
his land,
and the Sungod has put respect for you
throughout the land,
and terror of you in every country.
Whether I am at home,
whether I am in this place—
it is you who veils this horizon of mine.
The sun shines for love of you;
the water of the river
is drunk when you wish;
the air of heaven
is breathed when you say.

. . .

I was given the house of a Governor,
such as belongs to a Friend.
Many craftsmen were building it,
all its trees were freshly planted.
Meals were brought to me from the palace,
three and four times a day,
as well as what the royal children gave,
without making a moment's ceasing.
A pyramid of stone was built for me,
in the midst of the pyramids.
The masons who construct the pyramid measured
out its foundations;
the draughtsman drew in it;
the overseer of the works which are in the burial
grounds busied himself with it.
All equipment to be put in a tomb shaft—
its share of these things was made.
I was given funerary priests;
a funerary demesne was made for me,
with fields in it and a garden in its proper place,
as is done for a Chief Friend.
My image was overlaid with gold,
and its kilt with electrum.
It is his Majesty who has caused this to be done.
There is no other lowly man for whom the like
was done.
I was in the favours of the king's giving,
until the day of landing came."

So it ends, from start to finish,
as found in writing.

STUDY QUESTIONS

1. How does the document draw attention to international relations in Middle Kingdom Egypt and the general view of outsiders in this culture?
2. Why do the gods of Egypt take special responsibility for the Nile and in what terms do they exercise that power?

1.4 *EPIC OF GILGAMESH*, 1800–600 BCE

A heroic epic about King Gilgamesh of Uruk (in modern Iraq), this work is one of the earliest surviving works of literature, from the origins of civilization in Mesopotamia. Accompanied by his friend Enkidu, Gilgamesh embarks on adventures and interacts personally with the gods. After the death of Enkidu as punishment for Gilgamesh's rejection of the goddess Ishtar, the protagonist turns his focus toward immortality. The epic's flood narrative is often compared with the biblical tale of Noah.

[Of him who] found out all things, I [shall te]ll the land,
[Of him who] experienced everything, [I shall tea]ch the whole.
He searched (?) the lands (?) everywhere.
He who experienced the whole gained complete wisdom.
He found out what was secret and uncovered what was hidden,
He brought back a tale of times before the Flood.
He had journeyed far and wide, weary and at last resigned.
He engraved all toils on a memorial monument of stone.
. . .
The story of that man, Gilgamesh, who went through all kinds of sufferings.

He was superior to other kings, a warrior lord of great stature,
A hero born of Uruk, a goring wild bull.
He marches at the front as leader,
He goes behind, the support of his brothers,
A strong net, the protection of his men,
The raging flood-wave, which can destroy even a stone wall.
Son of Lugalbanda, Gilgamesh, perfect in strength,
Son of the lofty cow, the wild cow Ninsun.
He is Gilgamesh, perfect splendor,
Who opened up passes in the mountains,
Who could dig pits even in the mountainside,
Who crossed the ocean, the broad seas, as far as the sunrise.
Who inspected the edges of the world, kept searching for eternal life,

From *Myths from Mesopotamia: Creation, the Flood, Gilgamesh, and Others*. Edited by Stephanie Dalley. New York: Oxford University Press, 1989, pp. 50–6, 71, 74, 77–84, 86–8, 95, 100–1, 107–19, 123–4. Reproduced with permission of the Oxford University Press through PLSclear.

Who reached Ut-napishtim the far-distant, by
  force.
Who restored to their rightful place cult centres
  (?) which the Flood had ruined.
There is nobody among the kings of teeming
  humanity
Who can compare with him,
Who can say "I am king" beside Gilgamesh.
Gilgamesh (was) named from birth to fame.
Two-thirds of him was divine, and one-third
  mortal.

. . .

He had no rival, and at his *pukku*
His weapons would rise up, his comrades have to
  rise up.
The young men of Uruk became dejected in their
  private [quarters(?)].
Gilgamesh would not leave any son alone for his
  father.
Day and night his [behavior(?)] was overbearing.
He was the shepherd (?)[]
He was their shepherd (?) yet []
Powerful, superb, [knowledgeable and expert],
Gilgamesh would not leave [young girls alone],
The daughters of warriors, the brides of young
  men.
The gods often heard their complaints.
The gods of heaven [] the lord of Uruk.
  "Did [Aruru (?)] create such a rampant wild
    bull?
  Is there no rival? At the *pukku*
  His weapons rise up, his comrades have to rise
    up.
  Gilgamesh will not leave any son alone for his
    father.
  Day and night his [behaviour (?)] is
    overbearing.
  He is the shepherd of Uruk the Sheepfold,
  He is their shepherd, yet []
  Powerful, superb, knowledgeable [and expert],
  Gilgamesh will not leave young girls [alone],
  The daughters of warriors, the brides of young
    men.
  Anu often hears their complaints."
They called upon great Aruru:
  "You, Aruru, you created [mankind (?)]!

Now create someone for him, to match (?) the
  ardour (?) of his energies!
  Let them be regular rivals, and let Uruk be
    allowed peace!"
When Aruru heard this, she created inside herself
  the word (?) of Anu.
Aruru washed her hands, pinched off a piece of
  clay, cast it out into open country.
She created a [primitive man], Enkidu the warrior:
  offspring of silence (?), sky-bolt of Ninurta.
His whole body was shaggy with hair, he was
  furnished with tresses like woman,
His locks of hair grew luxuriant like grain.
He knew neither people nor country; he was
  dressed as cattle are.
With gazelles he eats vegetation,
With cattle he quenches his thirst at the watering
  place.
With wild beasts he presses forward for water.

. . .

Gilgamesh spoke to him, to the hunter,
  "Go, hunter, lead forth the harlot Shamhat,
  And when he approaches the cattle at the
    watering place,
  She must take off her clothes and reveal her
    attractions."

. . .

Then wild beasts arrived at the water; they
  satisfied their need.
And he, Enkidu, whose origin is the mountain,
(Who) eats vegetation with gazelles,
Drinks (at) the watering place with cattle,
Satisfied his need for water with wild beasts.
Shamhat looked at the primitive man,
The murderous youth from the depths of open
  country.
  "Here he is, Shamhat, bare your bosom,
  Open your legs and let him take in your
    attractions!
  Do not pull away, take wind of him!
  He will see you and come close to you.
  Spread open your garments, and let him lie
    upon you,
  Do it for him, the primitive man, as women do.
  Then his cattle, who have grown up in open
    country with him, will become alien to him.

His love-making he will lavish upon you!"
Shamhat loosened her undergarments, opened
    her legs and he took in her attractions.
She did not pull away. She took wind of him,
Spread open her garments, and he lay upon her.
She did for him, the primitive man, as
    women do.
His love-making he lavished upon her.
For six days and seven nights Enkidu was aroused
    and poured himself into Shamhat.
When he was sated with her charms,
He set his face towards the open country of his
    cattle.
The gazelles saw Enkidu and scattered,
The cattle of open country kept away from his
    body.
For Enkidu had stripped (?); his body was too clean.
His legs, which used to keep pace with (?) his
    cattle, were at a standstill.
Enkidu had been diminished, he could not run as
    before.
Yet he had acquired judgment (?), had become
    wiser.
He turned back (?), he sat at the harlot's feet.
The harlot was looking at his expression,
And he listened attentively to what the harlot
    said.
The harlot spoke to him, to Enkidu,
    "You have become [profound] Enkidu, you
        have become like a god.
    Why should you roam open country with wild
        beasts?
    Come, let me take you into Uruk the
        Sheepfold,
    To the pure house, the dwelling of Anu and
        Ishtar,
    Where Gilgamesh is perfect in strength,
    And is like a wild bull, more powerful than
        (any of) the people."
She spoke to him, and her speech was acceptable.
Knowing his own mind (now), he would seek for
    a friend.
. . .
They stood at the edge of the forest,
Gazed and gazed at the height of the pines,
Gazed and gazed at the entrance to the pines,

Where Humbaba made tracks as he went to and fro.
The paths were well trodden and the road was
    excellent.
They beheld the Pine Mountain, dwelling-place of
    gods, shrine of Irnini.
The pines held up their luxuriance even on the
    face of the mountain.
Their shade was good, filling one with happiness.
Undergrowth burgeoned, entangling the forest.
. . .
He struck (?) (his) head (?), and matched him [].
They stirred up the ground with the heels of their
    feet,
Sirara and Lebanon were split apart at their
    gyrations,
White clouds grew black,
Death dropped down over them like a fog.
Shamash summoned up great tempests against
    Humbaba,
South Wind, North Wind, East Wind, West Wind,
    Moaning Wind,
Gale, *šaparziqqu*-Wind, *imhullu*-Wind, . . . -Wind
Asakku, Wintry Wind, Tempest, Whirlwind,
Thirteen winds rose up at him and Humbaba's
    face grew dark.
He could not charge forwards, he could not run
    backwards.
Thus the weapons of Gilgamesh succeeded
    against Humbaba.
. . .
He washed his filthy hair, he cleaned his gear,
Shook out his locks over his back,
Threw away his dirty clothes and put on fresh
    ones.
He clothes himself in robes and tied on a sash.
Gilgamesh put his crown on his head
And Ishtar the princess raised her eyes to the
    beauty of Gilgamesh.
    "Come to me, Gilgamesh, and be my lover!
    Bestow on me the gift of your fruit!
    You can be my husband, and I can be your
        wife.
    I shall have a chariot of lapis lazuli and gold
        harnessed for you,
    With wheels of gold, and horns of
        elmēšu-stone."

. . .

Gilgamesh made his voice heard and spoke,
He said to Ishtar the princess,
    "What could I give you if I possessed you?
    I would give you body oil and garments,
    I would give you food and sustenance.
    Could I provide you with bread fit for gods?
    Could I provide you with ale fit for kings?"

. . .

Which of your lovers [lasted] forever?
Which of your masterful paramours went to
    heaven?
Come, let me [describe (?)] your lovers to you!
He of the sheep (?) [. . .] knew him:
For Dumuzi the lover of your youth
You decreed that he should keep weeping year
    after year.
You loved the colourful *allallu*-bird,
But you hit him and broke his wing.
He stays in the woods crying "My wing!"
You loved the lion, whose strength is complete,
But you dug seven and seven pits for him.
You loved the horse, so trustworthy in battle,
But you decreed that he should gallop seven
    leagues (non-stop),
You decreed that he should be overwrought and
    thirsty,
You decreed endless weeping for his mother
    Sililu.
You loved the shepherd, herdsman, and chief
    shepherd
Who was always heaping up the glowing ashes for
    you,
And cooked ewe-lambs for you every day.
But you hit him and turned him into a wolf,
His own herd-boys hunt him down
And his dogs tear at his haunches.
You loved Ishullanu, your father's gardener,
Who was always bringing you baskets of dates.
They brightened your table every day;
You lifted your eyes to him and went to him.
"My own Ishullanu, let us enjoy your strength,
So put out your hand and touch our vulva!"
But Ishullanu said to you,
"Me? What do you want of me?
Did my mother not bake for me, and did I not eat?

What I eat (with you) would be loaves of
    dishonor and disgrace,
Rushes would be my only covering against the
    cold."
You listened as he said this,
And you hit him, turned him into a frog (?),
Left him to stay amid the fruits of his labours.
But the pole (?) goes up no more, [his] bucket
    goes down no more.
And how about me? You will love me and then
    [treat me] just like them!"
When Ishtar heard this,
Ishtar was furious, and [went up] to heaven.
Ishtar went up and wept before her father Anu,
Her tears flowed before her mother Antu.
    "Father, Gilgamesh has shamed me again and
        again!
    Gilgamesh spelt out to me my dishonour,
    My dishonour and my disgrace."
Any made his voice heard and spoke,
He said to the princess Ishtar,
    "Why (?) didn't you accuse Gilgamesh the king
        for yourself,
    Since Gilgamesh spelt out your dishonour,
    Your dishonour and your disgrace?"
Ishtar made her voice heard and spoke,
She said to her father Anu,
    "Father, please give me the Bull of Heaven, and
        let me strike Gilgamesh down!
    Let me . . . Gilgamesh in his dwelling!
    If you don't give me the Bull of Heaven,
    I shall strike (?) []
    I shall set my face towards the infernal
        regions,
    I shall raise up the dead, and they will eat the
        living,
    I shall make the dead outnumber the living!"

. . .

At the snorting of the Bull of Heaven a chasm
    opened up, and one hundred young men of
    Uruk fell into it,
Two hundred young men, three hundred young
    men.
At its second snorting another chasm opened up,
    and another hundred young men of Uruk fell
    into it,

Two hundred young men, three hundred young
   men fell into it.
At its third snorting a chasm opened up,
And Enkidu fell into it.
But Enkidu leapt out. He seized the Bull of
   Heaven by the horns.
The Bull of Heaven blew spittle into his face,
With its thick tail it whipped up its dung.
. . .
Then Gilgamesh, like a but[cher (?)] heroic and []
Plunged his sword in between the base of the
   horns and the neck tendons.
When they had struck down the Bull of Heaven
   they pulled out its innards,
Set them before Shamash,
Backed away and prostrated themselves before
   Shamash.
Then the two brothers sat down.
Ishtar went up on to the wall of Uruk the
   Sheepfold.
She was contorted with rage, she hurled down
   curses,
   "That man, Gilgamesh, who reviled me has
      killed the Bull of Heaven!"
Enkidu listened to Ishtar saying this,
And he pulled out the Bull of Heaven's shoulder
   and slapped it into her face:
   "If I could only get at you as that does,
   I would do the same to you myself,
   I would hand its intestines on your arms!"
. . .
Then daylight came. [And] Enkidu said to
   Gilgamesh,
   "O my brother, what a dream [I saw] last night!
   Anu, Elil, Ea, and heavenly Shamash [were in
      the assembly].
   And Anu said to Ellil, 'As they have slain the
      Bull of Heaven,
   So too they have slain Huwawa, who [guarded]
      the mountains pla[nted] with pines'."
And Anu said, "One of them [must die]."
Ellil replied: "Let Enkidu die, but let Gilgamesh
   not die."
Then heavenly Shamash said to valiant Ellil,
"Was it not according to your word that they slew
   the Bull of Heaven and Huwawa? Should now
   innocent Enkidu die?"

But Ellil turned in anger to heavenly Shamash
   saying,
   "(The fact is), you accompanied them daily, like
      one of their comrades."
Enkidu lay down before Gilgamesh, his tears
   flowing like streams.
   "O my brother, my brother is so dear to me.
   But they are taking me from my brother."
And: "I shall sit among the dead, I shall [] the
   threshold of the dead;
Never again [shall I see] my dear brother with my
   own eyes."
. . .
He decided to curse the harlot too.
   "Come, Shamhat, I shall fix a fate for you!
   [Curses(?)] shall not cease for ever and ever.
   I shall curse you with a great curse!
   Straight away my curses shall rise up against
      you!
   You shall never make your house voluptuous
      again,
   You shall not release [] of your young bulls,
   You shall not let them into the girls' rooms.
   Filth shall impregnate your lovely lap (?),
   The drunkard shall soak your party dress with
      vomit,
. . .
   You shall never obtain the best cosmetic [oil (?),]
   Bright silver, people's affluence, shall not
      accumulate in your house,
. . .
   The crossroads (?) shall be your only sitting
      place,
   Waste ground your only lying place, the shade
      of a city wall your only sitting place.
   Thorns and spikes shall skin your feet,
   The drunkard and the thirsty shall slap your
      cheek,
. . .
   Because you defiled me when I was pure,
   Because you seduced me in the open country
      when I was pure."
Shamash heard the utterance of his mouth.
Immediately a loud voice called down to him
   from the sky:
   "Enkidu, why are you cursing my harlot
      Shamhat,

Who fed you on food fit for gods,
Gave you ale to drink, fit for kings,
Clothed you with a great robe,
Then provided you with Gilgamesh for a fine
    partner?
And now Gilgamesh, the friend who is a
    brother to you
Will lay you to rest on a great bed
And lay you to resent on a bed of loving care,
And let you stay in a restful dwelling, the
    dwelling on the left.
Princes of the earth will kiss your feet.
He will make the people of Uruk weep for you,
    mourn for you,
Will fill the proud people with woe,
And he himself will neglect his appearance
    after you(r death).
Clothed only in a lionskin, he will roam the
    open country."
Enkidu listened to the speech of Shamash the
    warrior.
[His anger abated (?)]; his heart became quiet
    (*about 2 lines missing*)
"Come, Shamhat, I shall change your fate!
My utterance, which cursed you, shall bless
    you instead.
Governors and princes shall love you,
The single-league man shall smite his thigh
    (for you),
The double-league man shall shake out his
    locks (for you).
The herdsman shall not hold back for you, he
    shall undo his belt for you.
He shall give you ivory, lapis lazuli, and gold,
Rings (and) brooches (?) shall be presents for
    you.
    . . .
Gilgamesh mourned bitterly for Enkidu his
    friend,
And roamed open country.
"Shall I die too? Am I not like Enkidu?
Grief has entered my innermost being,
I am afraid of Death, and so I roam open
    country.
I shall take the road and go quickly
To see Ut-napishtim, son of Ubara-Tutu.
    . . .

[Gilgamesh spoke to her, to Siduri the alewife],
    "[How could my cheeks not be wasted, nor my
        face dejected],
    [Nor my heart wretched, nor my appearance
        worn out],
    [Nor my grief in my innermost being],
    [Nor my face like that of a long-distance
        traveller],
    [Nor my face weathered by cold and heat . . .],
    [Nor roaming open country, clad only in a
        lionskin?]
    [My friend whom I love so much, who
        experienced every hardship with me],
    [Enkidu, whom I love so much, who
        experienced every hardship with me—]
    [The fate of mortals conquered him!] Six days
        [and seven nights I wept over him],
    [I did not allow him to] be buried, [until a
        worm fell out of his nose].
    [I was frightened and].
    I am afraid of Death, [and so I roam open
        country].
    The words of my friend [weigh upon me].
    [I roam open country] for long distances; the
        words of my friend Enkidu weigh upon
        me.
    I roam open country on long journeys.
    [How, O how] could I stay silent, how, O how
        could I keep quiet []?
    My friend whom I love has turned to clay:
    Enkidu my friend whom I love [has turned to
        clay.]
    Am I not like him? Must I lie down too,
    Never to rise, ever again?"
Ut-napishtim spoke to him, to Gilgamesh, "Why
    do you prolong grief, Gilgamesh?
    Since [the gods made you] from the flesh of
        gods and mankind,
    Since [the gods] made you like your father and
        mother,
    [Death is inevitable (?)] at some time, both for
        Gilgamesh and for a fool,
    But a throne is set down [for you (?)] in the
        assembly [].
    . . .
    [Why (?)] have you exerted yourself? What
        have you achieved (?)?

You have made yourself weary for lack of sleep,
You only fill your flesh with grief,
You only bring the distant days (of reckoning)
    closer.
Mankind's fame is cut down like reeds in a
    reed-bed.

. . .

Nobody sees Death,
Nobody sees the face of Death,
Nobody hears the voice of Death.
Savage Death just cuts mankind down.
Sometimes we build a house, sometimes we
    make a nest,
But then brothers divide it upon inheritance.
Sometimes there is hostility in [the land],
But then the river rises and brings flood-water.
Dragonflies drift on the river,
Their faces look upon the face of the Sun.
(But then) suddenly there is nothing.
The sleeping (?) and the dead are just like each
    other,
Death's picture cannot be drawn.
The primitive man (is as any) young man (?).
When they blessed me,
The Anunnaki, the great gods, assembled;
Mammitum who creates fate decreed destinies
    with them.
They appointed death and life.
They did not mark out days for death,
But they did so for life."

. . .

Ut-napishtim spoke to him, to Gilgamesh,
"Let me reveal to you a closely guarded matter,
    Gilgamesh,
And let me tell you the secret of the gods.
Shuruppak is a city that you yourself know,
Situated [on the bank of] the Euphrates.
That city was already old when the gods
    within it
Decided that the great gods should make a flood.
There was Anu their father,
Warrior Ellil their counsellor,
Ninurta was their chamberlain,
Enuugi their canal-controller.
Far-sighted Ea swore the oath (of secrecy) with
    them,

So he repeated their speech to a reed hut,
"Reed hut, reed hut, brick wall, brick wall,
Listen, reed hut, and pay attention, brick wall:
(This is the message:)
'Man of Shuruppak, son of Ubara-Tutu,
Dismantle your house, build a boat.
Leave possessions, search out living things.
Reject chattels and save lives!
Put aboard the seed of all living things, into
    the boat.
The boat that you are to build
Shall have her dimensions in proportion,
Her width and length shall be in harmony,
Roof her like the Apsu.'
I realized and spoke to my master Ea,
'I have paid attention to the words that you
    spoke in this way,
My master, and I shall act upon them.
But how can I explain myself to the city, the
    men and the elders?'
Ea made his voice heard and spoke,
He said to me, his servant,
'You shall speak to them thus:
"I think that Ellil has rejected me,
And so I cannot stay in your city,
And I cannot set foot in Ellil's land again."'

. . .

When the first light of dawn appeared
The country gathered about me.
The carpenter brought his axe,
The reed-worker brought his stone,

. . .

On the fifth day I laid down her form.
One acre was her circumference, ten poles each
    the height of her walls,
Her top edge was likewise ten poles all
    round.
I laid down her structure, drew it out,
Gave her six decks,
Divided her into seven.
Her middle I divided into nine,
Drove the water pegs into her middle.
I saw to the paddles and put down what was
    needed:
Three *sar* of bitumen I poured into the kiln,
Three *sar* of pitch I poured into the inside.

Three *sar* of oil they fetched, the workmen who
carried the baskets.
Not counting the *sar* of oil which the dust (?)
soaked up,
The boatman stowed away two more *sar* of oil.
At the [] I slaughtered oxen.
I sacrificed sheep every day.
I gave the workmen ale and beer to drink,
Oil and wine as if they were river water
They made a feast, like the New Year's Day
festival.
When the sun [rose (?)] I provided hand oil.
[When] the sun went down the boat was
complete.
[The launching was (?)] very difficult;
Launching rollers had to be fetched (from)
above (to) below.
Two-thirds of it [stood clear of the water line
(?)].
I loaded her with everything there was,
Loaded her with all the silver,
Loaded her with all the gold
Loaded her with all the seed of living things,
all of them.
I put on board the boat all my kith and kin.
Put on board cattle from open country, wild
beasts from open country, all kinds of
craftsmen.

. . .

When the first light of dawn appeared,
A black cloud came up from the base of the sky.
Adad kept rumbling inside it.
Shullat and Hanish were marching ahead,
Marched as chamberlains (over) (?) mountain
and country.
Erakal pulled out the mooring (?) poles,
Ninurta marched on and made the weir(s)
overflow.
The Anunnaki had to carry torches,
They lit up the land with their brightness.
The calm before the Storm-god came over
the sky,
Everything light turned to darkness.
[]
On the first day the tempest [rose up],
Blew swiftly and [brought (?) the flood-weapon],

Like a battle force [the destructive *kašūšu*-weapon]
passed over [the people]
No man could see his fellow,
Now could people be distinguished from the sky.
Even the gods were afraid of the flood-weapon.
They withdrew; they went up to the heaven of
Anu.
The gods cowered, like dogs crouched by an
outside wall.
Ishtar screamed like a woman giving birth;
The Mistress of the Gods, sweet of voice, was
wailing,
"Has that time really returned to clay,
Because I spoke evil in the gods' assembly?
How could I have spoken such evil in the gods'
assembly?
I should have (?) ordered a battle to destroy my
people;
I myself gave birth (to them), they are my own
people,
Yet they fill the sea like fish spawn!"
The gods of Anunnaki were weeping with her.
The gods, humbled, sat there weeping.
Their lips were closed and covered with scab.
For six days and [seven (?)] nights
The wind blew, flood and tempest overwhelmed
the land;
When the seventh day arrived the tempest, flood
and onslaught
Which had struggled like a woman in labour,
blew themselves out (?).
The sea became calm, the *imhullu*-wind grew
quiet, the flood held back.
I looked at the weather; silence reigned,
For all mankind had returned to clay.
The flood-plain was flat as a roof.
I opened a porthole and light fell on my cheeks.
I bent down, then sat. I wept.
My tears ran down my cheeks.
I looked for banks, for limits to the sea.
Areas of land were emerging everywhere (?).
The boat had come to rest on Mount Nimush.

. . .

When the seventh day arrived,
I put out and released a dove.
The dove went; it came back,

For no perching place was visible to it, and it
  turned around.
I put out and released a swallow.
The swallow went; it came back,
For no perching place was visible to it, and it
  turned round.
I put out and released a raven.
The raven went, and saw the waters receding.
And it ate, preened (?), lifted its tail and did not
  turn round.
Then I put (everything?) out to the four winds,
  and I made a sacrifice,
Set out a *surqinnu*-offering upon the mountain
  peak,
Arranged the jars seven and seven;
Into the bottom of them I poured (essences of?)
  reeds, pine, and myrtle.
The gods smelt the fragrance,
The gods like flies gathered over the sacrifice.

. . .

As soon as Ellil arrived
He saw the boat. Ellil was furious,
Filled with anger at the Igigi gods.
"What sort of life survived? No man should have
  lived through the destruction!"
Ninurta made his voice heard and spoke,
He said to the warrior Ellil,
"Who other than Ea would have done such a
  thing?
For Ea can do everything?"
Ea made his voice heard and spoke,
He said to the warrior Ellil,
"You are the sage of the gods, warrior,
So how, O how, could you fail to consult, and
  impose the flood?
Punish the sinner for his sin, punish the criminal
  for his crime,
But ease off, let work not cease; be patient, let not
  []
Instead of your imposing a flood, let a lion come
  up and diminish the people.
Instead of your imposing a flood, let a wolf come
  up and diminish the people.
Instead of your imposing a flood, let famine be
  imposed and [lessen] the land.
Instead of your imposing a flood, let Erra rise up
  and savage the people.

I did not disclose the secret to the great gods,
I just showed Atrahasis a dream, and thus he
  heard the secret of the gods."
Now the advice (that prevailed) was his advice.
Ellil came up into the boat,
And seized my hand and led me up.
He led up my woman and made her kneel down
  at my side.
He touched our foreheads, stood between us,
  blessed us:
"Until now Ut-napishtim was mortal,
But henceforth Ut-napishtim and his woman
  shall be as we gods are.
Ut-napishtim shall dwell far off at the mouth of
  the rivers."

. . .

Ut-napishtim spoke to him, to Gilgamesh,
  "Gilgamesh, you came, weary, striving,
  What can I give you to take back to your
    country?
  Let me reveal a closely guarded matter,
    Gilgamesh,
  And let me tell you the secret of the gods.
  There is a plant whose root is like
    camel-thorn,
  Whose thorn, like a rose's, will spike [your
    hands].
  If you yourself can win that plant, you will find
    [rejuvenation (?)]."
When Gilgamesh heard this, he opened
  the pipe,
He tied heavy stone to his feet.
They dragged him down into the Apsu, and [he
  saw the plant].
He took the plant himself: it spiked [his hands].
He cut the heavy stones from his feet.
The sea threw him up on its shore.
Gilgamesh spoke to him, to Ur-shanabi the
  boatman,
  "Ur-shanabi, this plant is a plant to cure a
    crisis!
  With it a man may win the breath of life.
  I shall take it back to Uruk the Sheepfold; I
    shall give it to an elder to eat, and so try
    out the plant.
  Its name (shall be): "An old man grows into a
    young man.""

I too shall eat (it) and turn into the young
   man that I once was."
At twenty leagues they ate their ration.
At thirty leagues they stopped for the night.
Gilgamesh saw a pool whose water was cool,
And went down into the water and washed.
A snake smelt the fragrance of the plant.
It came up silently and carried off the plant.
As it took it away, it shed its scaly skin.
Thereupon Gilgamesh sat down and wept.
His tears flowed over his cheeks.
[He spoke to (?)] Ut-shanabi the boatman,
   "For what purpose (?), Ur-shanabi, have my
      arms grown weary?
   For what purpose (?) was the blood inside me
      so red (?)?
   I did not gain an advantage for myself,
. . .

And the spirit of Enkidu came out of the Earth
   like a gust of wind.
They hugged and kissed (?),
They discussed, they agonized.
   "Tell me, my friend, tell me, my friend,
   Tell me Earth's conditions that you found!"
   "I can't tell you, my friend, I can't tell you!
   If I tell you Earth's conditions that I found,
   You must sit (and) weep!
   I would sit and weep!
   [Your wife (?),] whom you touched, and your
      heart was glad,
   Vermin eat [like (?)] an old [garment].
   [Your son (?) whom] you touched, and your
      heart was glad,
   [Sits in a crevice (?)] full of dust.
   'Woe' she said, and groveled in the dust.
   'Woe' he said, and groveled in the dust."

STUDY QUESTIONS

1. What are the gods' reasons for their humbling of Gilgamesh?
2. Contrast the relationship between Enkidu and Gilgamesh with the relationships between Gilgamesh and female figures in the narrative. What does the document suggest about the superiority of same-sex friendship to heterosexual encounters?

1.5 FROM THE LAWS OF HAMMURABI, CA. 1772 BCE

This law code, assembled by King Hammurabi of Babylon, consists of almost three hundred laws and accompanying punishments. It is recorded in the Akkadian language in cuneiform on several tablets (one of which is on display at the Louvre Museum in Paris). Although the most famous of these laws—"An eye for an eye, a tooth for a tooth"—deals with responses to harmful acts, many of the laws deal with economic peace, such as proper payment of wages, or social peace, such as the framework for divorce.

From *The Code of Hammurabi, King of Babylon*, translated by Robert Francis Harper, 1904. Available online at: https://en.wikisource.org/wiki/The_Code_of_Hammurabi_(Harper_translation).

When the lofty Anu, king of the Anunnaki, and Bel, lord of heaven and earth, he who determines the destiny of the land, committed the rule of all mankind to Marduk, the chief son of Ea; when they made him great among the Igigi; when they pronounced the lofty name of Babylon; when they made it famous among the quarters of the world and in its midst established an everlasting kingdom whose foundations were firm as heaven and earth—at that time, Anu and Bel called me, Hammurabi, the exalted prince, the worshiper of the gods, to cause justice to prevail in the land, to destroy the wicked and the evil, to prevent the strong from oppressing the weak, to go forth like the Sun over the Black Head Race, to enlighten the land and to further the welfare of the people. Hammurabi, the governor named by Bel, am I, who brought about plenty and abundance; . . . obedient to the mighty Shamash; . . . who rebuilt E-babbara for Shamash, his helper; . . . the powerful king, the Sun of Babylon, who caused light to go forth over the lands of Sumer and Akkad; the king, who caused the four quarters of the world to render obedience; the favorite of Nana, am I. When Marduk sent me to rule the people and to bring help to the country, I established law and justice in the land and promoted the welfare of the people.

[ON JUSTICE]

1. If a man bring an accusation against a man, and charge him with a (capital) crime, but cannot prove it, he, the accuser, shall be put to death. . . .
3. If a man, in a case (pending judgment), bear false (threatening) witness, or do not establish the testimony that he has given, if that case be a case involving life, that man shall be put to death.
4. If a man (in a case) bear witness for grain or money (as a bribe), he shall himself bear the penalty imposed in that case.
5. If a judge pronounce a judgment, render a decision, deliver a verdict duly signed and sealed and afterward alter his judgment, they shall call that judge to account for the alteration of the judgment which he had pronounced, and he shall pay twelve-fold the penalty which was in said judgment; and, in the assembly, they shall expel him from his seat of judgment, and he shall not return, and with the judges in a case he shall not take his seat. . . .

[ON PROPERTY]

9. If a man, who has lost anything, find that which was lost in the possession of (another) man; and the man in whose possession the lost property is found say: "It was sold to me. I purchased it in the presence of witnesses;" and the owner of the lost property say: "I will bring witnesses to identify my lost property": if the purchaser produce the seller who has sold it to him and the witnesses in whose presence he purchased it, and the owner of the lost property produce witnesses to identify his lost property, the judges shall consider their evidence. The witnesses in whose presence the purchase was made and the witnesses to identify the lost property shall give their testimony in the presence of god. The seller shall be put to death as a thief; the owner of the lost property shall recover his loss; the purchaser shall recover from the estate of the seller the money which he paid out.
10. If the purchaser do not produce the seller who sold it to him, and the witnesses in whose presence he purchased it (and) if the owner of the lost property produce witnesses to identify his lost property, the purchaser shall be put to death as a thief; the owner of the lost property shall recover his loss.
11. If the owner (claimant) of the lost property do not produce witnesses to identify his lost property, he has attempted fraud (has lied), he has stirred up strife (calumny), he shall be put to death. . . .
22. If a man practice brigandage and be captured, that man shall be put to death.
23. If the brigand be not captured, the man who has been robbed, shall, in the presence of god, make an itemized statement of his loss, and . . . the governor, in whose province and jurisdiction the robbery was committed, shall compensate him for whatever was lost.
24. If it be a life (that is lost), the city and governor shall pay one mana of silver to his heirs. . . .

[ON IRRIGATION]

53. If a man neglect to strengthen his dyke and do not strengthen it, and a break be made in his dyke and the water carry away the farm-land, the man in whose dyke the break has been made shall restore the grain which he has damaged.

54. If he be not able to restore the grain, they shall sell him and his goods, and the farmer whose grain the water has carried away shall share (the results of the sale).

55. If a man open his canal for irrigation and neglect it and the water carry away an adjacent field, he shall measure out grain on the basis of the adjacent fields.

56. If a man open up the water and the water carry away the improvements of an adjacent field, he shall measure out ten GUR of grain per GAN. . . .

[ON TRADE]

104. If a merchant give to an agent grain, wool, oil or goods of any kind with which to trade, the agent shall write down the value and return (the money) to the merchant. The agent shall take a sealed receipt for the money which he gives to the merchant.

105. If the agent be careless and do not take a receipt for the money which he has given to the merchant, the money not receipted for shall not be placed to his account.

108. If a wine-seller do not receive grain as the price of drink, but if she receive money by the great stone, or make the measure for drink smaller than the measure for corn, they shall call that wine-seller to account, and they shall throw her into the water.

109. If outlaws collect in the house of a wine-seller, and she do not arrest those outlaws and bring them to the palace, that wine-seller shall be put to death.

110. If a priestess who is not living in a MAL.GE.A, open a wine-shop or enter a wine-shop for a drink, they shall burn that woman. . . .

[ON SLAVERY]

117. If a man be in debt and sell his wife, son or daughter, or bind them over to service, for three years they shall work in the house of their purchaser or master; in the fourth year they shall be given their freedom.

118. If he bind over to service a male or female slave, and if the merchant transfer or sell such slave, there is no cause for complaint. . . .

[ON MARRIAGE AND CHILDREN]

128. If a man take a wife and do not arrange with her the (proper) contracts, that woman is not a (legal) wife.

129. If the wife of a man be taken in lying with another man, they shall bind them and throw them into the water. If the husband of the woman would save his wife, or if the king would save his male servant (he may). . . .

131. If a man accuse his wife and she has not been taken in lying with another man, she shall take an oath in the name of god and she shall return to her house. . . .

136. If a man desert his city and flee and afterwards his wife enter into another house; if that man return and would take his wife, the wife of the fugitive shall not return to her husband because he hated his city and fled. . . .

138. If a man would put away his wife who has not borne him children, he shall give her money to the amount of her marriage settlement and he shall make good to her the dowry which she brought from her father's house and then he may put her away. . . .

141. If the wife of a man who is living in his house, set her face to go out and play the part of a fool, neglect her house, belittle her husband, they shall call her to account: if her husband say: "I have put her away," he shall let her go. On her departure nothing shall be given to her for her divorce. If her husband say: "I have not put her away," her husband may take another woman. The first woman shall dwell in the house of her husband as a maid servant.

142. If a woman hate her husband, and say: "thou shalt not have me," they shall inquire into her antecedents for her defects; and if she have been a careful mistress and been without reproach and her husband has been going about

and greatly belittling her, that woman has no blame. She shall receive her dowry and go to her father's house.

143. If she have not been a careful mistress, have gadded about, have neglected her house and have belittled her husband, they shall throw that woman into the water. . . .

145. If a man take a wife and she do not present him with children and he set his face to take a concubine, that man may take a concubine and bring her into his house. That concubine shall not rank with his wife.

146. If a man take a wife and she give a maid servant to her husband, and that maid servant bear children and afterwards would take rank with her mistress; because she has borne children, her mistress may not sell her for money, but she may reduce her to bondage and count her among the maid servants. . . .

150. If a man give to his wife field, garden, house or goods and he deliver to her a sealed deed, after (the death of) her husband, her children cannot make claim against her. The mother after her (death) may will to her child whom she loves, but to a brother she may not.

159. If a man, who has brought a present to the house of his father-in-law and has given the marriage settlement, look with longing upon another woman and say to his father-in-law, "I will not take thy daughter;" the father of the daughter shall take to himself whatever was brought to him.

160. If a man bring a present to the house of his father-in-law and give a marriage settlement and the father of the daughter say, "I will not give thee my daughter;" he (*i.e.*, the father-in-law) shall double the amount which was brought to him and return it. . . .

162. If a man take a wife and she bear him children and that woman die, her father may not lay claim to her dowry. Her dowry belongs to her children. . . .

165. If a man present field, garden or house to his favorite son and write for him a sealed deed; after the father dies, when the brothers divide, he shall take the present which the father gave him, and over and above they shall divide the goods of the father's house equally.

168. If a man set his face to disinherit his son and say to the judges: "I will disinherit my son," the judges shall inquire into his antecedents, and if the son have not committed a crime sufficiently grave to cut him off from sonship, the father may not cut off his son from sonship. . . .

170. If a man's wife bear him children and his maid servant bear him children, and the father during his lifetime say to the children which the maid servant bore him: "My children," and reckon them with the children of his wife, after the father dies the children of the wife and the children of the maid servant shall divide the goods of the father's house equally. The child of the wife shall have the right of choice at the division. . . .

185. If a man take in his name a young child as a son and rear him, one may not bring claim for that adopted son. . . .

191. If a man, who has taken a young child as a son and reared him, establish his own house and acquire children, and set his face to cut off the adopted son, that son shall not go his way. The father who reared him shall give to him of his goods one-third the portion of a son and he shall go. He shall not give to him of field, garden or house. . . .

[ON ASSAULT]

195. If a son strike his father, they shall cut off his fingers.

196. If a man destroy the eye of another man, they shall destroy his eye.

197. If one break a man's bone, they shall break his bone.

198. If one destroy the eye of a freeman or break the bone of a freeman he shall pay one mana of silver.

199. If one destroy the eye of a man's slave or break a bone of a man's slave he shall pay one-half his price. . . .

206. If a man strike another man in a quarrel and wound him, he shall swear: "I struck him without intent," and he shall be responsible for the physician.

207. If (he) die as a result of the stroke, he shall swear (as above), and if he be a man, he shall pay one-half mana of silver. . . .

[ON THE ECONOMICS OF MEDICAL TREATMENT]

215. If a physician operate on a man for a severe wound (or make a severe wound upon a man) with a bronze lancet and save the man's life; or if he open an abscess (in the eye) of a man with a bronze lancet and save that man's eye, he shall receive ten shekels of silver (as his fee).

216. If he be a freeman, he shall receive five shekels.

217. If it be a man's slave, the owner of the slave shall give two shekels of silver to the physician.

218. If a physician operate on a man for a severe wound with a bronze lancet and cause that man's death; or open an abscess (in the eye) of a man with a bronze lancet and destroy the man's eye, they shall cut off his fingers. . . .

221. If a physician set a broken bone for a man or cure his diseased bowels, the patient shall give five shekels of silver to the physician.

222. If he be a freeman, he shall give three shekels of silver.

223. If it be a man's slave, the owner of the slave shall give two shekels of silver to the physician. . . .

[ON CONSTRUCTION]

228. If a builder build a house for a man and complete it, (that man) shall give him two shekels of silver per SAR of house as his wage.

229. If a builder build a house for a man and do not make its construction firm, and the house which he has built collapse and cause the death of the owner of the house, that builder shall be put to death. . . .

233. If a builder build a house for a man and do not make its construction meet the requirements and a wall fall in, that builder shall strengthen that wall at his own expense. . . .

EPILOGUE

The righteous laws, which Hammurabi, the wise king, established and (by which) he gave the land stable support and pure government. Hammurabi, the perfect king, am I. I was not careless, nor was I neglectful of the Black-Head people, whose rule Bel presented and Marduk delivered to me. . . .

The great gods proclaimed me and I am the guardian governor, whose scepter is righteous and whose beneficent protection is spread over my city. In my bosom I carried the people of the land of Sumer and Akkad; under my protection I brought their brethren into security; in my wisdom I restrained (hid) them; that the strong might not oppose the weak, and that they should give justice to the orphan and the widow, in Babylon, the city whose turrets Anu and Bel raised; in Esagila, the temple whose foundations are firm as heaven and earth, for the pronouncing of judgments in the land, for the rendering of decisions for the land, and for the righting of wrong, my weighty words I have written upon my monument, and in the presence of my image as king of righteousness have I established.

The king, who is pre-eminent among city kings, am I. My words are precious, my wisdom is unrivaled. By the command of Shamash, the great judge of heaven and earth, may I make righteousness to shine forth on the land. By the order of Marduk, my lord, may no one efface my statutes, may my name be remembered with favor in Esagila forever. Let any oppressed man, who has a cause, come before my image as king of righteousness! Let him read the inscription on my monument! Let him give heed to my weighty words! And may my monument enlighten him as to his cause and may he understand his case! May he set his heart at ease! (and he will exclaim): "Hammurabi indeed is a ruler who is like a real father to his people; he has given reverence to the words of Marduk, his lord; he has obtained victory for Marduk in North and South; he has made glad the heart of Marduk, his lord; he has established prosperity for the people for all time and given a pure government to the land." . . .

In the days that are yet to come, for all future time, may the king who is in the land observe the words of righteousness which I have written upon my monument! May he not alter the judgments of the land which I have pronounced, or the decisions of the country which I have rendered! May he not efface my statues! If that man have wisdom, if he wish to give his land good government, let him give attention to the words which I have written upon my monument! And may this monument enlighten him as to procedure and administration, the judgments which I have pronounced, and the decisions which I have rendered for the land! And let him rightly rule his

Black-Head people; let him pronounce judgments for them and render for them decisions! Let him root out the wicked and evildoer from his land! Let him promote the welfare of his people!

Hammurabi, the king of righteousness, whom Shamash has endowed with justice, am I. My words are weighty; my deeds are unrivaled [. . .] and the bringing to honor.

STUDY QUESTIONS

1. How, specifically, is Hammurabi proclaiming himself an agent of divine power, especially at the document's beginning and conclusion?
2. What does the document suggest about the relative status of women in Babylonian society at this period?
3. When are financial and capital punishments applied in the code, and is there a consistent principle at work here?

1.6 "LOYALIST TEACHING," CA. 1550–1000 BCE

An Egyptian set of instructions, this text speaks as a father to his children. Two subjects are advised on: first, that loyalty and obedience to the pharaoh are absolutely necessary (because the pharaoh will protect his supporters), and second, that a member of society must also be respectful of his fellow citizens and participate in civic duty. Thus, all the teachings encourage order in the face of chaos. Although fragmented, these teachings exude the zeal and devotion of the "father" for a harmonious society.

Praise the king within your bodies! 2
Be close to his Majesty in your hearts!
Put terror of him throughout the day!
Create acclamation for him at every season!
He is the Perception which is in breasts: his eyes
   probe every body.
He is the Sungod under whose governance one
   lives:
the man under his shade will have great
   possessions.
He is the Sungod by whose rays one sees:
he illuminates the Two Lands more than the sun.
. . .

The king is Sustenance; his speech is Plenty. 5
The man he makes is someone who will always
   exist.
He is the heir of every god,
the protector of his creators.
They strike his opponents for him.
. . .

Fight for his name! Respect his oath! 6
Make no opposition against a reward of his giving.
Acclaim the Red-king! Worship the White Crown!
Pay homage to the uplifter of the Double Crown!
You should do these things, so that your limbs
   may prosper!

You will find this good for all time—
being on earth, without sorrow,
passing lifetime in peace!
Enter into the earth which the king gives!   7
Rest in the place of all time!
Join with the eternal cavern!—
with your children's homes full of love for you,
your heirs remaining in your positions.
Conform [to] my example! Do not neglect my
    words!
Make good the rule of my making!
May you speak to your children!   8
Speech has taught, since the time of the God.
I am a noble to be listened to,
whose understanding is recognized by his lord.
Do not overstep my example! Do not be
    indifferent to my pattern!
You should be free from disloyal action!
The son who hears will be a faultless man.
Can any plan of his not succeed?

       *

You will praise these things after years,   9
for this soundness gives landfall.
Another method for developing your hearts,
—which is even better—concerning your servants:
care for men, organize people,
that you may secure servants who are active!
It is mankind who create all that exists;
one lives on what comes from their hands.
They are lacking, and then poverty prevails.

The professions are what provide provisions.   10
A house is empty, with its foundations uprooted,
and the very sound of them re-establishes its walls!
The man who sleeps until dawn is a lord of many;
there will be no sleep for the solitary man.
No one sends a lion on a mission.
No herd can isolate himself from the walled
    enclosure;
its voice is like the thirsty creature's outside the well,
with [decay] around it, and the wailing of birds.

One must long for the Nileflood, then one
    profits by it;   11

no ploughed field exists of itself.
The cattle who belong to a cowherd are great:
it is the cattleherd who can drive the wild bull.
it is [the herdsman] who brings [the animals]
    across to land.
[The shepherd] will be a plentiful flock, without
    number!
To God, [these are] excellent professions.
Someone who is capable in them is a clever man.
Do not make a field-worker wretched with taxes—
let him be well off, and he will still be there for
    you the next year.
If he lives, you have his hands;
you ruin him, and then he plans to turn vagabond.
. . .
It is the evil man who destroys his own
    mound   13
a town is founded for the man who is loved.
Patience is a man's monument.
Quietness is excellent, [calmness] is good.
The man who foresees what will come [has never
    been thwarted];
the man with powerful authority prevails.
The merciful—the cow bears for him;
the bad herdsman—his herd is small.

Fight for men in every respect!   14
They are a flock, good for their lord.
Evidently by them alone one lives;
they are good also when joining the earth.
You should look to [your . . . who . . .]!
You should watch over your funerary priests:
the son is disloyal, but the priest remains!
It is a kind man who is named "heir."
Lay the noble dead to rest; make invocations in
    their name;
[honour] the blessed dead; bring food-offer[ings]!
[This is better for] the doer than for the man for
    whom it is done—
the beneficiary protects the man who is still on
    earth."

So it ends, from start to finish,
as found in writing.

STUDY QUESTIONS

1. Why should a man be loyal to the pharaoh, and what specific benefits can he expect to gain?
2. How does the document elevate seemingly ignoble professions and relate them to the king's job?

1.7 EGYPTIAN *BOOK OF THE DEAD*: "NEGATIVE CONFESSION," IN USE CA. 1550–50 BCE

Used in the Egyptian funeral rite for a millennium, the *Book of the Dead*—perhaps more properly translated as the *Book of Going Forth into Day*—corresponds to the various steps to the Egyptian afterlife. Most commonly written in hieroglyphics,[1] the *Book of the Dead* provides spells for the departed soul's journey. This selection, the "Negative Confession," represents the dead person's oath to the god Osiris that he had not committed any of the forty-two sins that would bar his way to the afterlife. The rational path of the *Book of the Dead* reflects the Egyptian concept that the gods are not merely capricious beings unconcerned with the well-being of humanity.

Homage to thee, O Great God, Lord of Maäti, I have come to thee, O my Lord, that I may behold thy beneficence. I know thee, and I know thy name, and the names of the Forty-Two who live with thee in the Hall of Maäti, who keep ward over sinners, and feed upon their blood on the day of estimating characters before Un-Nefer [. . .] Behold, I have come to thee, and I have brought *maät* (*i.e.*, truth, integrity) to thee. I have destroyed sin for thee.

I have not sinned against men.
I have not oppressed [my] kinsfolk.
I have done no wrong in the place of truth.
I have not known worthless folk.
I have not wrought evil.
I have not defrauded the oppressed one of his goods.

I have not done the things that the gods abominate.
I have not vilified a servant to his master.
I have not caused pain.
I have not let any man hunger.
I have made no one to weep.
I have not committed murder.
I have not commanded any to commit murder for me.
I have inflicted pain on no man. . . .
I have not committed fornication. . . .
I did not encroach on the fields [of others].
I have not added to the weights of the scales.
I have not misread the pointer of the scales.
I have not taken milk from the mouths of children.
I have not driven cattle from their pastures. . . .
I have not stopped water [when it should flow].
I have not cut the dam of a canal. . . .

[1] A language written using symbols (images) that each stand for meanings, sounds, or a combination.

I have not turned away the cattle [intended for] offerings.

I have not repulsed the god at his appearances.
I am pure. I am pure. I am pure. I am pure.

STUDY QUESTIONS

1. In what ways does this document lack "any positive sense of morality," addressing the nonperformance of evil rather than the active doing of good?
2. Should the pharaoh play an economic role, facilitating progress for his people in certain respects?

1.8 GREAT HYMN TO THE ATON, 1400–1300 BCE

This hybrid hymn and poem to the Egyptian sun-god Aton is attributed to the founder of Egyptian monotheism, King Akhenaten, whose name means "living spirit of Aton." Although this brand of monotheism did not persist, this poem expresses an appreciation of a world attuned to the rising and setting of the sun—the embodiment of Aton—and inhabited by a multitude of cultures united in their devotion to this single deity. Consider the individual elements that the author praises Aton for creating.

Thou appearest beautifully on the horizon of
heaven,
Thou living Aton, the beginning of life!
When thou art risen on the eastern horizon,
Thou hast filled every land with thy beauty.
Thou art gracious, great, glistening, and high over
every land;
Thy rays encompass the lands to the limit of all
that thou hast made:
As thou art Re, thou reachest to the end of them;
(Thou) subduest them (for) thy beloved son.
Though thou art far away, thy rays are on earth;
Though thou art in *their* faces, *no one knows thy
going.*
When thou settest in the western horizon,
The land is in darkness, in the manner of death.
They sleep in a room, with heads wrapped up,

Nor sees one eye the other.
All their goods which are under their heads might
be stolen,
(But) they would not perceive (it).
Every lion is come forth from his den;
All creeping things, they sting.
Darkness *is a shroud,* and the earth is in stillness,
For he who made them rests in his horizon.
At daybreak, when thou arisest on the horizon,
When thou shinest as the Aton by day,
Thou drivest away the darkness and givest thy rays.
The Two Lands are in festivity *every day,*
Awake and standing upon (their) feet,
For thou hast raised them up.
Washing their bodies, taking (their) clothing,
Their arms are (raised) in praise at thy
appearance.

From J. B. Pritchard, ed., *Ancient Near Eastern Texts Relating to the Old Testament*, 3rd ed. Princeton, NJ: Princeton University Press, 1969, pp. 369–71.

All the world, they do their work. . .
Creator of seed in women,
Thou who makest fluid into man,
Who maintainest the son in the womb of his
    mother,
Who soothest him with that which stills his
    weeping,
Thou nurse (even) in the womb,
Who givest breath to sustain all that he has made!
When he descends from the womb to *breathe*
On the day when he is born,
Thou openest his mouth completely,
Thou suppliest his necessities.
When the chick in the egg speaks within the shell,
Thou givest him breath within it to maintain him.
When thou hast made him his fulfillment within
    the egg, to break it,
He comes forth from the egg to speak at his
    completed (time);
He walks upon his legs when he comes forth
    from it.
How manifold it is, what thou hast made!
They are hidden from the face (of man).
O sole god, like whom there is no other!
Thou didst create the world according to thy desire,
Whilst thou wert alone:
All men, cattle, and wild beasts,
Whatever is on earth, going upon (its) feet,
And what is on high, flying with its wings.
The countries of Syria and Nubia, the *land* of Egypt,
Thou settest every man in his place,
Thou suppliest their necessities:
Everyone has his food, and his time of life is
    reckoned.
Their tongues are separate in speech,
And their natures as well;
Their skins are distinguished,
As thou distinguished the foreign peoples.
Thou makest a Nile in the underworld,
Thou bringest it forth as though desirest
To maintain the people (of Egypt)

According as thou madest them for thyself,
The lord of all of them, wearying (himself) with
    them,
The lord of every land, rising for them,
The Aton of the day, great of majesty.
All distant foreign countries, thou makest their
    life (also),
For thou hast set a Nile in heaven,
That it may descend for them and make waves
    upon the mountains,
Like the great green sea,
To water their fields in their towns.
How effective they are, thy plans, O lord of
    eternity!
The Nile in heaven, it is for the foreign peoples
And for the beasts of every desert that go upon
    (their) feet;
(While the true) Nile comes from the underworld
    for Egypt. . .
Thou are in my heart,
And there is no other that knows thee
Save thy son Nefer-kheperu-Re Wa-en-Re,
For thou hast made him well-versed in thy plans
    and in thy strength.
The world came into being by thy hand,
According as thou hast made them.
When thou hast risen they live,
When thou settest they die.
Thou art lifetime thy own self,
For one lives (only) through thee.
Eyes are (fixed) on beauty until thou settest.
All work is laid aside when thou settest in
    the west.
(But) when (thou) risest (again),
[Everything is] made to flourish for the king, . . .
Since thou didst found the earth
And raise them up for thy son,
Who came forth from thy body:
the King of Upper and Lower Egypt, . . . Akh-en-
    Aton, . . . and the Chief Wife of the King . . .
    Nefert-iti, living and youthful forever and ever.

STUDY QUESTIONS

1. How is Aton described?
2. Are Aton's qualities that of an impersonal god or of a god that enjoys intimate relations with human beings?

CHAPTER 2

THE MONOTHEISTS: JEWS AND PERSIANS

2.1 CREATING, DESTROYING, AND RENEWING THE WORLD: GENESIS CHAPTERS 1–8

The first book of the Bible combines ancient folklore, legend, traditional historical narrative, and literary invention to create a compelling narrative that stretches from God's creation of the world (in two different versions, in the first two chapters) through His wrathful destruction of it in a great flood and the subsequent renewal of life by Noah and his descendants. The middle third of Genesis describes the lives of the three great Hebrew patriarchs—Abraham, Isaac, Jacob—while the final section of the book tells the story of the children of Jacob, most notably Joseph. Joseph, it should be noted, is the first of the Hebrew heroic figures never to experience direct contact with God. Joseph's is the first life of pure faith—that is, of believing in and obeying God despite never seeing or hearing Him.

CHAPTER 1

[1]In the beginning God created the heaven and the earth. [2]Now the earth was unformed and void, and darkness was upon the face of the deep; and the spirit of God hovered over the face of the waters. [3]And God said: "Let there be light." And there was light. [4]And God saw the light, that it was good; and God divided the light from the darkness. [5]And God called the light Day, and the darkness He called Night. And there was evening and there was morning, one day.

[6]And God said: "Let there be a firmament in the midst of the waters, and let it divide the waters from the waters." [7]And God made the firmament, and divided the waters which were under the firmament from the waters which were above the firmament; and it was so. [8]And God called the firmament Heaven. And there was evening and there was morning, a second day.

[9]And God said: "Let the waters under the heaven be gathered together unto one place, and let the dry

The Holy Scriptures According to the Masoretic Text: A New Translation with the Aid of Previous Versions and with Constant Consultation of Jewish Authorities.—Excerpted from Jewish Publication Society of America Version on Wikipedia, the free encyclopedia.

land appear." And it was so. [10]And God called the dry land Earth, and the gathering together of the waters called the Seas; and God saw that it was good. [11]And God said: "Let the earth put forth grass, herb yielding seed, and fruit-tree bearing fruit after its kind, wherein is the seed thereof, upon the earth." And it was so. [12]And the earth brought forth grass, herb yielding seed after its kind, and tree bearing fruit, wherein is the seed thereof, after its kind; and God saw that it was good. [13]And there was evening and there was morning, a third day.

[14]And God said: "Let there be lights in the firmament of the heaven to divide the day from the night; and let them be for signs, and for seasons, and for days and years; [15]and let them be for lights in the firmament of the heaven to give light upon the earth." And it was so. [16]And God made the two great lights: the greater light to rule the day, and the lesser light to rule the night; and the stars. [17]And God set them in the firmament of the heaven to give light upon the earth, [18]and to rule over the day and over the night, and to divide the light from the darkness; and God saw that it was good. [19]And there was evening and there was morning, a fourth day.

[20]And God said: "Let the waters swarm with swarms of living creatures, and let fowl fly above the earth in the open firmament of heaven." [21]And God created the great sea-monsters, and every living creature that creepeth, wherewith the waters swarmed, after its kind, and every winged fowl after its kind; and God saw that it was good. [22]And God blessed them, saying: "Be fruitful, and multiply, and fill the waters in the seas, and let fowl multiply in the earth." [23]And there was evening and there was morning, a fifth day.

[24]And God said: "Let the earth bring forth the living creature after its kind, cattle, and creeping thing, and beast of the earth after its kind." And it was so. [25]And God made the beast of the earth after its kind, and the cattle after their kind, and every thing that creepeth upon the ground after its kind; and God saw that it was good. [26]And God said: "Let us make man in our image, after our likeness; and let them have dominion over the fish of the sea, and over the fowl of the air, and over the cattle, and over all the earth, and over every creeping thing that creepeth upon the earth." [27]And God created man in His own image, in the image of God created He him; male and female created He them. [28]And God blessed them; and God said unto them: "Be fruitful, and multiply, and replenish the earth, and subdue it; and have dominion over the fish of the sea, and over the fowl of the air, and over every living thing that creepeth upon the earth."

[29]And God said: "Behold, I have given you every herb yielding seed, which is upon the face of all the earth, and every tree, in which is the fruit of a tree yielding seed—to you it shall be for food; [30]and to every beast of the earth, and to every fowl of the air, and to every thing that creepeth upon the earth, wherein there is a living soul, [I have given] every green herb for food." And it was so. [31]And God saw every thing that He had made, and, behold, it was very good. And there was evening and there was morning, the sixth day.

CHAPTER 2

[1]And the heaven and the earth were finished, and all the host of them. [2]And on the seventh day God finished His work which He had made; and He rested on the seventh day from all His work which He had made. [3]And God blessed the seventh day, and hallowed it; because that in it He rested from all His work which God in creating had made. [4]These are the generations of the heaven and of the earth when they were created, in the day that the LORD God made earth and heaven.

[5]No shrub of the field was yet in the earth, and no herb of the field had yet sprung up; for the LORD God had not caused it to rain upon the earth, and there was not a man to till the ground; [6]but there went up a mist from the earth, and watered the whole face of the ground. [7]Then the LORD God formed man of the dust of the ground, and breathed into his nostrils the breath of life; and man became a living soul.

[8]And the LORD God planted a garden eastward, in Eden; and there He put the man whom He had formed. [9]And out of the ground made the LORD God to grow every tree that is pleasant to the sight, and good for food; the tree of life also in the midst of the garden, and the tree of the knowledge of good and evil.

[10]And a river went out of Eden to water the garden; and from thence it was parted, and became four heads. [11]The name of the first is Pishon; that is it which compasseth the whole land of Havilah, where there is gold; [12]and the gold of that land is good; there

is bdellium and the onyx stone. [13]And the name of the second river is Gihon; the same is it that compasseth the whole land of Cush. [14]And the name of the third river is Tigris; that is it which goeth toward the east of Asshur. And the fourth river is the Euphrates.

[15]And the LORD God took the man, and put him into the garden of Eden to dress it and to keep it. [16]And the LORD God commanded the man, saying: "Of every tree of the garden thou mayest freely eat; [17]but of the tree of the knowledge of good and evil, thou shalt not eat of it; for in the day that thou eatest thereof thou shalt surely die."

[18]And the LORD God said: "It is not good that the man should be alone; I will make him a help meet for him." [19]And out of the ground the LORD God formed every beast of the field, and every fowl of the air; and brought them unto the man to see what he would call them; and whatsoever the man would call every living creature, that was to be the name thereof. [20]And the man gave names to all cattle, and to the fowl of the air, and to every beast of the field; but for Adam there was not found a help meet for him. [21]And the LORD God caused a deep sleep to fall upon the man, and he slept; and He took one of his ribs, and closed up the place with flesh instead thereof. [22]And the rib, which the LORD God had taken from the man, made He a woman, and brought her unto the man. [23]And the man said: "This is now bone of my bones, and flesh of my flesh; she shall be called Woman, because she was taken out of Man." [24]Therefore shall a man leave his father and his mother, and shall cleave unto his wife, and they shall be one flesh.

[25]And they were both naked, the man and his wife, and were not ashamed.

CHAPTER 3

[1]Now the serpent was more subtle than any beast of the field which the LORD God had made. And he said unto the woman: "Yea, hath God said: Ye shall not eat of any tree of the garden?" [2]And the woman said unto the serpent: "Of the fruit of the trees of the garden we may eat; [3]but of the fruit of the tree which is in the midst of the garden, God hath said: Ye shall not eat of it, neither shall ye touch it, lest ye die." [4]And the serpent said unto the woman: "Ye shall not surely die; [5]for God doth know that in the day ye

eat thereof, then your eyes shall be opened, and ye shall be as God, knowing good and evil." [6]And when the woman saw that the tree was good for food, and that it was a delight to the eyes, and that the tree was to be desired to make one wise, she took of the fruit thereof, and did eat; and she gave also unto her husband with her, and he did eat. [7]And the eyes of them both were opened, and they knew that they were naked; and they sewed fig-leaves together, and made themselves girdles.

[8]And they heard the voice of the LORD God walking in the garden toward the cool of the day; and the man and his wife hid themselves from the presence of the LORD God amongst the trees of the garden. [9]And the LORD God called unto the man, and said unto him: "Where art thou?" [10]And he said: "I heard Thy voice in the garden, and I was afraid, because I was naked; and I hid myself." [11]And He said: "Who told thee that thou wast naked? Hast thou eaten of the tree, whereof I commanded thee that thou shouldest not eat?" [12]And the man said: "The woman whom Thou gavest to be with me, she gave me of the tree, and I did eat." [13]And the LORD God said unto the woman: "What is this thou hast done?" And the woman said: "The serpent beguiled me, and I did eat." [14]And the LORD God said unto the serpent: "Because thou hast done this, cursed art thou from among all cattle, and from among all beasts of the field; upon thy belly shalt thou go, and dust shalt thou eat all the days of thy life. [15]And I will put enmity between thee and the woman, and between thy seed and her seed; they shall bruise thy head, and thou shalt bruise their heel."

[16]Unto the woman He said: "I will greatly multiply thy pain and thy travail; in pain thou shalt bring forth children; and thy desire shall be to thy husband, and he shall rule over thee."

[17]And unto Adam He said: "Because thou hast hearkened unto the voice of thy wife, and hast eaten of the tree, of which I commanded thee, saying: Thou shalt not eat of it; cursed is the ground for thy sake; in toil shalt thou eat of it all the days of thy life. [18]Thorns also and thistles shall it bring forth to thee; and thou shalt eat the herb of the field. [19]In the sweat of thy face shalt thou eat bread, till thou return unto the ground; for out of it wast thou taken; for dust thou art, and unto dust shalt thou return."

[20]And the man called his wife's name Eve; because she was the mother of all living. [21]And the Lord God made for Adam and for his wife garments of skins, and clothed them.

[22]And the Lord God said: "Behold, the man is become as one of us, to know good and evil; and now, lest he put forth his hand, and take also of the tree of life, and eat, and live for ever." [23]Therefore the Lord God sent him forth from the garden of Eden, to till the ground from whence he was taken. [24]So He drove out the man; and He placed at the east of the garden of Eden the cherubim, and the flaming sword which turned every way, to keep the way to the tree of life.

CHAPTER 4

[1]And the man knew Eve his wife; and she conceived and bore Cain, and said: "I have gotten a man with the help of the Lord." [2]And again she bore his brother Abel. And Abel was a keeper of sheep, but Cain was a tiller of the ground. [3]And in process of time it came to pass, that Cain brought of the fruit of the ground an offering unto the Lord. [4]And Abel, he also brought of the firstlings of his flock and of the fat thereof. And the Lord had respect unto Abel and to his offering; [5]but unto Cain and to his offering He had not respect. And Cain was very wroth, and his countenance fell. [6]And the Lord said unto Cain: "Why art thou wroth? and why is thy countenance fallen? [7]If thou doest well, shall it not be lifted up? and if thou doest not well, sin coucheth at the door; and unto thee is its desire, but thou mayest rule over it." [8]And Cain spoke unto Abel his brother. And it came to pass, when they were in the field, that Cain rose up against Abel his brother, and slew him.

[9]And the Lord said unto Cain: "Where is Abel thy brother?" And he said: "I know not; am I my brother's keeper?" [10]And He said: "What hast thou done? the voice of thy brother's blood crieth unto Me from the ground. [11]And now cursed art thou from the ground, which hath opened her mouth to receive thy brother's blood from thy hand. [12]When thou tillest the ground, it shall not henceforth yield unto thee her strength; a fugitive and a wanderer shalt thou be in the earth."

[13]And Cain said unto the Lord: "My punishment is greater than I can bear. [14]Behold, Thou hast driven me out this day from the face of the land; and from Thy face shall I be hid; and I shall be a fugitive and a wanderer in the earth; and it will come to pass, that whosoever findeth me will slay me." [15]And the Lord said unto him: "Therefore whosoever slayeth Cain, vengeance shall be taken on him sevenfold." And the Lord set a sign for Cain, lest any finding him should smite him. [16]And Cain went out from the presence of the Lord, and dwelt in the land of Nod, on the east of Eden.

[17]And Cain knew his wife; and she conceived, and bore Enoch; and he builded a city, and called the name of the city after the name of his son Enoch. [18]And unto Enoch was born Irad; and Irad begot Mehujael; and Mehujael begot Methushael; and Methushael begot Lamech. [19]And Lamech took unto him two wives; the name of one was Adah, and the name of the other Zillah. [20]And Adah bore Jabal; he was the father of such as dwell in tents and have cattle. [21]And his brother's name was Jubal; he was the father of all such as handle the harp and pipe. [22]And Zillah, she also bore Tubal-cain, the forger of every cutting instrument of brass and iron; and the sister of Tubal-cain was Naamah. [23]And Lamech said unto his wives:

Adah and Zillah, hear my voice;
Ye wives of Lamech, hearken unto my speech;
For I have slain a man for wounding me,
And a young man for bruising me;
[24]If Cain shall be avenged sevenfold,
Truly Lamech seventy and sevenfold.

[25]And Adam knew his wife again; and she bore a son, and called his name Seth: "for God hath appointed me another seed instead of Abel; for Cain slew him." [26]And to Seth, to him also there was born a son; and he called his name Enosh; then began men to call upon the name of the Lord.

CHAPTER 5

[1]This is the book of the generations of Adam. In the day that God created man, in the likeness of God made He him; [2]male and female created He them, and blessed them, and called their name Adam, in the day when they were created. [3]And Adam lived a hundred and thirty years, and begot a son in his own likeness, after his image; and called his name Seth. [4]And the days of Adam after he begot Seth were eight hundred years; and he begot sons and daughters.

⁵And all the days that Adam lived were nine hundred and thirty years; and he died.

⁶And Seth lived a hundred and five years, and begot Enosh. ⁷And Seth lived after he begot Enosh eight hundred and seven years, and begot sons and daughters. ⁸And all the days of Seth were nine hundred and twelve years; and he died.

⁹And Enosh lived ninety years, and begot Kenan. ¹⁰And Enosh lived after he begot Kenan eight hundred and fifteen years, and begot sons and daughters. ¹¹And all the days of Enosh were nine hundred and five years; and he died.

¹²And Kenan lived seventy years, and begot Mahalalel. ¹³And Kenan lived after he begot Mahalalel eight hundred and forty years, and begot sons and daughters. ¹⁴And all the days of Kenan were nine hundred and ten years; and he died.

¹⁵And Mahalalel lived sixty and five years, and begot Jared. ¹⁶And Mahalalel lived after he begot Jared eight hundred and thirty years, and begot sons and daughters. ¹⁷And all the days of Mahalalel were eight hundred ninety and five years; and he died.

¹⁸And Jared lived a hundred sixty and two years, and begot Enoch. ¹⁹And Jared lived after he begot Enoch eight hundred years, and begot sons and daughters. ²⁰And all the days of Jared were nine hundred sixty and two years; and he died.

²¹And Enoch lived sixty and five years, and begot Methuselah. ²²And Enoch walked with God after he begot Methuselah three hundred years, and begot sons and daughters. ²³And all the days of Enoch were three hundred sixty and five years. ²⁴And Enoch walked with God, and he was not; for God took him.

²⁵And Methuselah lived a hundred eighty and seven years, and begot Lamech. ²⁶And Methuselah lived after he begot Lamech seven hundred eighty and two years, and begot sons and daughters. ²⁷And all the days of Methuselah were nine hundred sixty and nine years; and he died.

²⁸And Lamech lived a hundred eighty and two years, and begot a son. ²⁹And he called his name Noah, saying: "This same shall comfort us in our work and in the toil of our hands, which cometh from the ground which the Lᴏʀᴅ hath cursed." ³⁰And Lamech lived after he begot Noah five hundred ninety and five years, and begot sons and daughters. ³¹And all the days of Lamech were seven hundred seventy and seven years; and he died.

³²And Noah was five hundred years old; and Noah begot Shem, Ham, and Japheth.

CHAPTER 6

¹And it came to pass, when men began to multiply on the face of the earth, and daughters were born unto them, ²that the sons of God saw the daughters of men that they were fair; and they took them wives, whomsoever they chose. ³And the Lᴏʀᴅ said: "My spirit shall not abide in man for ever, for that he also is flesh; therefore shall his days be a hundred and twenty years." ⁴The Nephilim were in the earth in those days, and also after that, when the sons of God came in unto the daughters of men, and they bore children to them; the same were the mighty men that were of old, the men of renown.

⁵And the Lᴏʀᴅ saw that the wickedness of man was great in the earth, and that every imagination of the thoughts of his heart was only evil continually. ⁶And it repented the Lᴏʀᴅ that He had made man on the earth, and it grieved Him at His heart. ⁷And the Lᴏʀᴅ said: "I will blot out man whom I have created from the face of the earth; both man, and beast, and creeping thing, and fowl of the air; for it repenteth Me that I have made them." ⁸But Noah found grace in the eyes of the Lᴏʀᴅ. ⁹These are the generations of Noah. Noah was in his generations a man righteous and whole-hearted; Noah walked with God. ¹⁰And Noah begot three sons, Shem, Ham, and Japheth.

¹¹And the earth was corrupt before God, and the earth was filled with violence. ¹²And God saw the earth, and, behold, it was corrupt; for all flesh had corrupted their way upon the earth. ¹³And God said unto Noah: "The end of all flesh is come before Me; for the earth is filled with violence through them; and, behold, I will destroy them with the earth. ¹⁴Make thee an ark of gopher wood; with rooms shalt thou make the ark, and shalt pitch it within and without with pitch. ¹⁵And this is how thou shalt make it: the length of the ark three hundred cubits, the breadth of it fifty cubits, and the height of it thirty cubits. ¹⁶A light shalt thou make to the ark, and to a cubit shalt thou finish it upward; and the door of the ark shalt thou set in the side thereof; with lower, second, and third stories shalt thou make it.

¹⁷"And I, behold, I do bring the flood of waters upon the earth, to destroy all flesh, wherein is the breath of life, from under heaven; every thing that

is in the earth shall perish. [18]But I will establish My covenant with thee; and thou shalt come into the ark, thou, and thy sons, and thy wife, and thy sons' wives with thee. [19]And of every living thing of all flesh, two of every sort shalt thou bring into the ark, to keep them alive with thee; they shall be male and female. [20]Of the fowl after their kind, and of the cattle after their kind, of every creeping thing of the ground after its kind, two of every sort shall come unto thee, to keep them alive. [21]And take thou unto thee of all food that is eaten, and gather it to thee; and it shall be for food for thee, and for them." [22]Thus did Noah; according to all that God commanded him, so did he.

CHAPTER 7

[1]And the LORD said unto Noah: "Come thou and all thy house into the ark; for thee have I seen righteous before Me in this generation. [2]Of every clean beast thou shalt take to thee seven and seven, each with his mate; and of the beasts that are not clean two [and two], each with his mate; [3]of the fowl also of the air, seven and seven, male and female; to keep seed alive upon the face of all the earth. [4]For yet seven days, and I will cause it to rain upon the earth forty days and forty nights; and every living substance that I have made will I blot out from off the face of the earth." [5]And Noah did according unto all that the LORD commanded him.

[6]And Noah was six hundred years old when the flood of waters was upon the earth. [7]And Noah went in, and his sons, and his wife, and his sons' wives with him, into the ark, because of the waters of the flood. [8]Of clean beasts, and of beasts that are not clean, and of fowls, and of every thing that creepeth upon the ground, [9]there went in two and two unto Noah into the ark, male and female, as God commanded Noah. [10]And it came to pass after the seven days, that the waters of the flood were upon the earth.

[11]In the six hundredth year of Noah's life, in the second month, on the seventeenth day of the month, on the same day were all the fountains of the great deep broken up, and the windows of heaven were opened. [12]And the rain was upon the earth forty days and forty nights. [13]In the selfsame day entered Noah, and Shem, and Ham, and Japheth, the sons of Noah, and Noah's wife, and the three wives of his sons with them, into

the ark; [14]they, and every beast after its kind, and all the cattle after their kind, and every creeping thing that creepeth upon the earth after its kind, and every fowl after its kind, every bird of every sort. [15]And they went in unto Noah into the ark, two and two of all flesh wherein is the breath of life. [16]And they that went in, went in male and female of all flesh, as God commanded him; and the LORD shut him in.

[17]And the flood was forty days upon the earth; and the waters increased, and bore up the ark, and it was lifted up above the earth. [18]And the waters prevailed, and increased greatly upon the earth; and the ark went upon the face of the waters. [19]And the waters prevailed exceedingly upon the earth; and all the high mountains that were under the whole heaven were covered. [20]Fifteen cubits upward did the waters prevail; and the mountains were covered. [21]And all flesh perished that moved upon the earth, both fowl, and cattle, and beast, and every swarming thing that swarmeth upon the earth, and every man; [22]all in whose nostrils was the breath of the spirit of life, whatsoever was in the dry land, died. [23]And He blotted out every living substance which was upon the face of the ground, both man, and cattle, and creeping thing, and fowl of the heaven; and they were blotted out from the earth; and Noah only was left, and they that were with him in the ark.

[24]And the waters prevailed upon the earth a hundred and fifty days.

CHAPTER 8

[1]And God remembered Noah, and every living thing, and all the cattle that were with him in the ark; and God made a wind to pass over the earth, and the waters assuaged; [2]the fountains also of the deep and the windows of heaven were stopped, and the rain from heaven was restrained. [3]And the waters returned from off the earth continually; and after the end of a hundred and fifty days the waters decreased. [4]And the ark rested in the seventh month, on the seventeenth day of the month, upon the mountains of Ararat. [5]And the waters decreased continually until the tenth month; in the tenth month, on the first day of the month, were the tops of the mountains seen.

[6]And it came to pass at the end of forty days, that Noah opened the window of the ark which he had

made. [7]And he sent forth a raven, and it went forth to and fro, until the waters were dried up from off the earth. [8]And he sent forth a dove from him, to see if the waters were abated from off the face of the ground. [9]But the dove found no rest for the sole of her foot, and she returned unto him to the ark, for the waters were on the face of the whole earth; and he put forth his hand, and took her, and brought her in unto him into the ark. [10]And he stayed yet other seven days; and again he sent forth the dove out of the ark. [11]And the dove came in to him at eventide; and lo in her mouth an olive-leaf freshly plucked; so Noah knew that the waters were abated from off the earth. [12]And he stayed yet other seven days; and sent forth the dove; and she returned not again unto him any more.

[13]And it came to pass in the six hundred and first year, in the first month, the first day of the month, the waters were dried up from off the earth; and Noah removed the covering of the ark, and looked, and behold, the face of the ground was dried. [14]And in the second month, on the seven and twentieth day of the month, was the earth dry.

[15]And God spoke unto Noah, saying: [16]"Go forth from the ark, thou, and thy wife, and thy sons, and thy sons' wives with thee. [17]Bring forth with thee every living thing that is with thee of all flesh, both fowl, and cattle, and every creeping thing that creepeth upon the earth; that they may swarm in the earth, and be fruitful, and multiply upon the earth." [18]And Noah went forth, and his sons, and his wife, and his sons' wives with him; [19]every beast, every creeping thing, and every fowl, whatsoever moveth upon the earth, after their families; went forth out of the ark.

[20]And Noah builded an altar unto the LORD; and took of every clean beast, and of every clean fowl, and offered burnt-offerings on the altar. [21]And the LORD smelled the sweet savour; and the LORD said in His heart: "I will not again curse the ground any more for man's sake; for the imagination of man's heart is evil from his youth; neither will I again smite any more every thing living, as I have done. [22]While the earth remaineth, seedtime and harvest, and cold and heat, and summer and winter, and day and night shall not cease."

STUDY QUESTIONS

1. Compare the different readings. How are they similar? How are they different? What picture of humans' relationship with God emerges from these passages?
2. Do these passages support the hypothesis that the Bible is a patchwork of many different hands?

2.2 BOOK OF EXODUS: MOSES AND PHARAOH, CHAPTERS 7, 11–12, AND 14

The origins of the Bible remain subject to debate even after three thousand years of intense study. The first books to be composed, scholars agree, were the five books of Torah, which began to appear in various forms around 950 BCE and perhaps a bit later. What makes dating the texts so

The Holy Scriptures According to the Masoretic Text: A New Translation with the Aid of Previous Versions and with Constant Consultation of Jewish Authorities.—Excerpted from Jewish Publication Society of America Version on Wikipedia, the free encyclopedia.

challenging is that several authors and editors had a hand in the process. Most biblical scholars hold to the so-called Documentary Hypothesis, which postulates that the texts as they survive result from the intertwining of several writers' work, writers known by the initials J, E, D, and P. The readings below, from the Book of Exodus, include selections identified with the J author (known as the "Yahwist") and the P author (the "Priestly Author").

> **Note to Reader:**
>
> Normal type = J author. **Bold type = P author.**

CHAPTER 7

[1]And the Lord said unto Moses: "See, I have set thee in God's stead to Pharaoh; and Aaron thy brother shall be thy prophet. [2]Thou shalt speak all that I command thee; and Aaron thy brother shall speak unto Pharaoh, that he let the children of Israel go out of his land. [3]And I will harden Pharaoh's heart, and multiply My signs and My wonders in the land of Egypt. [4]But Pharaoh will not hearken unto you, and I will lay My hand upon Egypt, and bring forth My hosts, My people the children of Israel, out of the land of Egypt, by great judgments. [5]And the Egyptians shall know that I am the Lord, when I stretch forth My hand upon Egypt, and bring out the children of Israel from among them." [6]And Moses **and Aaron** did so; as the Lord commanded them, so did they. [7]And Moses was fourscore years old, **and Aaron fourscore and three years old,** when they spoke unto Pharaoh.

[8]**And the Lord spoke unto Moses and unto Aaron, saying:** [9]**"When Pharaoh shall speak unto you, saying: Show a wonder for you; then thou shalt say unto Aaron: Take thy rod, and cast it down before Pharaoh, that it become a serpent."** [10]**And Moses and Aaron went in unto Pharaoh, and they did so, as the Lord had commanded; and Aaron cast down his rod before Pharaoh and before his servants, and it became a serpent.** [11]Then Pharaoh also called for the wise men and the sorcerers; and they also, the magicians of Egypt, did in like manner with their secret arts. [12]**For they cast down every man his rod, and they became serpents; but** Aaron's rod swallowed up their rods. [13]**And Pharaoh's heart was hardened, and he hearkened not unto them; as the Lord had spoken.**

[14]And the Lord said unto Moses: "Pharaoh's heart is stubborn, he refuseth to let the people go. [15]Get thee unto Pharaoh in the morning; lo, he goeth out unto the water; and thou shalt stand by the river's brink to meet him; and the rod which was turned to a serpent shalt thou take in thy hand. [16]And thou shalt say unto him: The Lord, the God of the Hebrews, hath sent me unto thee, saying: Let My people go, that they may serve Me in the wilderness; and, behold, hitherto thou hast not hearkened; [17]thus saith the Lord: In this thou shalt know that I am the Lord—behold, I will smite with the rod that is in my hand upon the waters which are in the river, and they shall be turned to blood. [18]And the fish that are in the river shall die, and the river shall become foul; and the Egyptians shall loathe to drink water from the river.'

[19]**And the Lord said unto Moses: "Say unto Aaron: Take thy rod, and stretch out thy hand over the waters of Egypt, over their rivers, over their streams, and over their pools, and over all their ponds of water, that they may become blood; and there shall be blood throughout all the land of Egypt, both in vessels of wood and in vessels of stone."** [20]**And Moses and Aaron did so, as the Lord commanded;** and he lifted up the rod, and smote the waters that were in the river, in the sight of Pharaoh, and in the sight of his servants; and all the waters that were in the river were turned to blood. [21]And the fish that were in the river died; and the river became foul, and the Egyptians could not drink water from the river; **and the blood was throughout all the land of Egypt.** [22]**And the magicians of Egypt did in like manner with their secret arts; and Pharaoh's heart was hardened, and he**

hearkened not unto them; as the Lord had spoken. [23]And Pharaoh turned and went into his house, neither did he lay even this to heart. [24]And all the Egyptians digged round about the river for water to drink; for they could not drink of the water of the river.

[25]And seven days were fulfilled, after that the Lord had smitten the river. [26]And the Lord spoke unto Moses: "Go in unto Pharaoh, and say unto him: Thus saith the Lord: Let My people go, that they may serve Me. [27]And if thou refuse to let them go, behold, I will smite all thy borders with frogs. [28]And the river shall swarm with frogs, which shall go up and come into thy house, and into thy bed-chamber, and upon thy bed, and into the house of thy servants, and upon thy people, and into thine ovens, and into thy kneading-troughs. [29]And the frogs shall come up both upon thee, and upon thy people, and upon all thy servants."

. . .

CHAPTER 11

[1]And the Lord said unto Moses: "Yet one plague more will I bring upon Pharaoh, and upon Egypt; afterwards he will let you go hence; when he shall let you go, he shall surely thrust you out hence altogether. [2]Speak now in the ears of the people, and let them ask every man of his neighbour, and every woman of her neighbour, jewels of silver, and jewels of gold." [3]And the Lord gave the people favour in the sight of the Egyptians. Moreover the man Moses was very great in the land of Egypt, in the sight of Pharaoh's servants, and in the sight of the people.

[4]And Moses said: "Thus saith the Lord: About midnight will I go out into the midst of Egypt; [5]and all the first-born in the land of Egypt shall die, from the first-born of Pharaoh that sitteth upon his throne, even unto the first-born of the maid-servant that is behind the mill; and all the first-born of cattle. [6]And there shall be a great cry throughout all the land of Egypt, such as there hath been none like it, nor shall be like it any more. [7]But against any of the children of Israel shall not a dog whet his tongue, against man or beast; that ye may know how that the Lord doth put a difference between the Egyptians and Israel. [8]And

all these thy servants shall come down unto me, and bow down unto me, saying: Get thee out, and all the people that follow thee; and after that I will go out." And he went out from Pharaoh in hot anger.

[9]And the Lord said unto Moses: "Pharaoh will not hearken unto you; that My wonders may be multiplied in the land of Egypt." [10]And Moses and Aaron did all these wonders before Pharaoh; and the Lord hardened Pharaoh's heart, and he did not let the children of Israel go out of his land.

CHAPTER 12

[1]And the Lord spoke unto Moses and Aaron in the land of Egypt, saying: [2]"This month shall be unto you the beginning of months; it shall be the first month of the year to you. [3]Speak ye unto all the congregation of Israel, saying: In the tenth day of this month they shall take to them every man a lamb, according to their fathers' houses, a lamb for a household; [4]and if the household be too little for a lamb, then shall he and his neighbour next unto his house take one according to the number of the souls; according to every man's eating ye shall make your count for the lamb. [5]Your lamb shall be without blemish, a male of the first year; ye shall take it from the sheep, or from the goats; [6]and ye shall keep it unto the fourteenth day of the same month; and the whole assembly of the congregation of Israel shall kill it at dusk. [7]And they shall take of the blood, and put it on the two side-posts and on the lintel, upon the houses wherein they shall eat it. [8]And they shall eat the flesh in that night, roast with fire, and unleavened bread; with bitter herbs they shall eat it. [9]Eat not of it raw, nor sodden at all with water, but roast with fire; its head with its legs and with the inwards thereof. [10]And ye shall let nothing of it remain until the morning; but that which remaineth of it until the morning ye shall burn with fire.

[11]"And thus shall ye eat it: with your loins girded, your shoes on your feet, and your staff in your hand; and ye shall eat it in haste—it is the Lord's passover. [12]For I will go through the land of Egypt in that night, and will smite all the first-born in the land of Egypt, both man and beast; and against all the gods of Egypt I will execute judgments: I am the Lord.

[13]And the blood shall be to you for a token upon the houses where ye are; and when I see the blood, I will pass over you, and there shall no plague be upon you to destroy you, when I smite the land of Egypt.

[14]"And this day shall be unto you for a memorial, and ye shall keep it a feast to the LORD; throughout your generations ye shall keep it a feast by an ordinance for ever. [15]Seven days shall ye eat unleavened bread; howbeit the first day ye shall put away leaven out of your houses; for whosoever eateth leavened bread from the first day until the seventh day, that soul shall be cut off from Israel.

[16]"And in the first day there shall be to you a holy convocation, and in the seventh day a holy convocation; no manner of work shall be done in them, save that which every man must eat, that only may be done by you. [17]And ye shall observe the feast of unleavened bread; for in this selfsame day have I brought your hosts out of the land of Egypt; therefore shall ye observe this day throughout your generations by an ordinance for ever. [18]In the first month, on the fourteenth day of the month at even, ye shall eat unleavened bread, until the one and twentieth day of the month at even. [19]Seven days shall there be no leaven found in your houses; for whosoever eateth that which is leavened, that soul shall be cut off from the congregation of Israel, whether he be a sojourner, or one that is born in the land. [20]Ye shall eat nothing leavened; in all your habitations shall ye eat unleavened bread."

[21]Then Moses called for all the elders of Israel, and said unto them: "Draw out, and take you lambs according to your families, and kill the passover lamb. [22]And ye shall take a bunch of hyssop, and dip it in the blood that is in the basin, and strike the lintel and the two side-posts with the blood that is in the basin; and none of you shall go out of the door of his house until the morning. [23]For the LORD will pass through to smite the Egyptians; and when He seeth the blood upon the lintel, and on the two side-posts, the LORD will pass over the door, and will not suffer the destroyer to come in unto your houses to smite you.

[24]"And ye shall observe this thing for an ordinance to thee and to thy sons for ever. [25]And it shall come to pass, when ye be come to the land which the LORD will give you, according as He hath promised, that ye shall keep this service. [26]And it shall come to pass, when your children shall say unto you: What mean ye by this service? [27]that ye shall say: It is the sacrifice of the LORD's passover, for that He passed over the houses of the children of Israel in Egypt, when He smote the Egyptians, and delivered our houses."

And the people bowed the head and worshipped. [28]And the children of Israel went and did so; as the LORD had commanded Moses and Aaron, so did they.

[29]And it came to pass at midnight, that the LORD smote all the first-born in the land of Egypt, from the first-born of Pharaoh that sat on his throne unto the first-born of the captive that was in the dungeon; and all the first-born of cattle. [30]And Pharaoh rose up in the night, he, and all his servants, and all the Egyptians; and there was a great cry in Egypt; for there was not a house where there was not one dead. [31]And he called for Moses and Aaron by night and said: "Rise up, get you forth from among my people, both ye and the children of Israel; and go, serve the LORD, as ye have said. [32]Take both your flocks and your herds, as ye have said, and be gone; and bless me also." [33]And the Egyptians were urgent upon the people, to send them out of the land in haste; for they said: "We are all dead men." [34]And the people took their dough before it was leavened, their kneading-troughs being bound up in their clothes upon their shoulders. [35]And the children of Israel did according to the word of Moses; and they asked of the Egyptians jewels of silver, and jewels of gold, and raiment. [36]And the LORD gave the people favour in the sight of the Egyptians, so that they let them have what they asked. And they despoiled the Egyptians.

[37]And the children of Israel journeyed from Rameses to Succoth, about six hundred thousand men on foot, beside children. [38]And a mixed multitude went up also with them; and flocks, and herds, even very much cattle. [39]And they baked unleavened cakes of the dough which they brought forth out of Egypt, for it was not leavened; because they were thrust out of Egypt, and could not tarry, neither had they prepared for themselves any victual.

[40]Now the time that the children of Israel dwelt in Egypt was four hundred and thirty years. [41]And it came to pass at the end of four hundred and thirty

years, even the selfsame day it came to pass, that all the host of the LORD went out from the land of Egypt. ⁴²It was a night of watching unto the LORD for bringing them out from the land of Egypt; this same night is a night of watching unto the LORD for all the children of Israel throughout their generations.

⁴³And the LORD said unto Moses and Aaron: "This is the ordinance of the passover: there shall no alien eat thereof; ⁴⁴but every man's servant that is bought for money, when thou hast circumcised him, then shall he eat thereof. ⁴⁵A sojourner and a hired servant shall not eat thereof. ⁴⁶In one house shall it be eaten; thou shalt not carry forth aught of the flesh abroad out of the house; neither shall ye break a bone thereof. ⁴⁷All the congregation of Israel shall keep it. ⁴⁸And when a stranger shall sojourn with thee, and will keep the passover to the LORD, let all his males be circumcised, and then let him come near and keep it; and he shall be as one that is born in the land; but no uncircumcised person shall eat thereof. ⁴⁹One law shall be to him that is home-born, and unto the stranger that sojourneth among you."

⁵⁰Thus did all the children of Israel; as the LORD commanded Moses and Aaron, so did they.

⁵¹And it came to pass the selfsame day that the LORD did bring the children of Israel out of the land of Egypt by their hosts.

. . .

CHAPTER 14

¹And the LORD spoke unto Moses, saying: ² "Speak unto the children of Israel, that they turn back and encamp before Pi-hahiroth, between Migdol and the sea, before Baal-zephon, over against it shall ye encamp by the sea. ³And Pharaoh will say of the children of Israel: They are entangled in the land, the wilderness hath shut them in. ⁴And I will harden Pharaoh's heart, and he shall follow after them; and I will get Me honour upon Pharaoh, and upon all his host; and the Egyptians shall know that I am the LORD." And they did so.

⁵And it was told the king of Egypt that the people were fled; and the heart of Pharaoh and of his servants was turned towards the people, and they said:

'What is this we have done, that we have let Israel go from serving us? ⁶And he made ready his chariots, and took his people with him. ⁷And he took six hundred chosen chariots, and all the chariots of Egypt, and captains over all of them. ⁸And the LORD hardened the heart of Pharaoh king of Egypt, and he pursued after the children of Israel; for the children of Israel went out with a high hand. ⁹And the Egyptians pursued after them, all the horses and chariots of Pharaoh, and his horsemen, and his army, and overtook them encamping by the sea, beside Pi-hahiroth, in front of Baal-zephon.

¹⁰And when Pharaoh drew nigh, the children of Israel lifted up their eyes, and, behold, the Egyptians were marching after them; and they were sore afraid; and the children of Israel cried out unto the LORD. ¹¹And they said unto Moses: "Because there were no graves in Egypt, hast thou taken us away to die in the wilderness? wherefore hast thou dealt thus with us, to bring us forth out of Egypt? ¹²Is not this the word that we spoke unto thee in Egypt, saying: Let us alone, that we may serve the Egyptians? For it were better for us to serve the Egyptians, than that we should die in the wilderness."¹³And Moses said unto the people: "Fear ye not, stand still, and see the salvation of the LORD, which He will work for you to-day; for whereas ye have seen the Egyptians to-day, ye shall see them again no more for ever. ¹⁴The LORD will fight for you, and ye shall hold your peace."

¹⁵And the LORD said unto Moses: "Wherefore criest thou unto Me? speak unto the children of Israel, that they go forward. ¹⁶And lift thou up thy rod, and stretch out thy hand over the sea, and divide it; and the children of Israel shall go into the midst of the sea on dry ground. ¹⁷And I, behold, I will harden the hearts of the Egyptians, and they shall go in after them; and I will get Me honour upon Pharaoh, and upon all his host, upon his chariots, and upon his horsemen. ¹⁸And the Egyptians shall know that I am the LORD, when I have gotten Me honour upon Pharaoh, upon his chariots, and upon his horsemen."

¹⁹And the angel of God, who went before the camp of Israel, removed and went behind them; and the pillar of cloud removed from before them, and stood behind them; ²⁰and it came between the

camp of Egypt and the camp of Israel; and there was the cloud and the darkness here, yet gave it light by night there; and the one came not near the other all the night.

²¹And Moses stretched out his hand over the sea; and the LORD caused the sea to go back by a strong east wind all the night, and made the sea dry land, **and the waters were divided.** ²²And the children of Israel went into the midst of the sea upon the dry ground; and the waters were a wall unto them on their right hand, and on their left. ²³And the Egyptians pursued, and went in after them into the midst of the sea, all Pharaoh's horses, his chariots, and his horsemen. ²⁴And it came to pass in the morning watch, that the LORD looked forth upon the host of the Egyptians through the pillar of fire and of cloud, and discomfited the host of the Egyptians. ²⁵And He took off their chariot wheels, and made them to drive heavily; so that the Egyptians said: "Let us flee from the face of Israel; for the LORD fighteth for them against the Egyptians."

²⁶And the LORD said unto Moses: "Stretch out thy hand over the sea, that the waters may come back upon the Egyptians, upon their chariots, and upon their horsemen." ²⁷And Moses stretched forth his hand over the sea, and the sea returned to its strength when the morning appeared; and the Egyptians fled against it; and the LORD overthrew the Egyptians in the midst of the sea. ²⁸And the waters returned, and covered the chariots, and the horsemen, even all the host of Pharaoh that went in after them into the sea; there remained not so much as one of them. ²⁹But the children of Israel walked upon dry land in the midst of the sea; and the waters were a wall unto them on their right hand, and on their left.

³⁰Thus the LORD saved Israel that day out of the hand of the Egyptians; and Israel saw the Egyptians dead upon the sea-shore. ³¹And Israel saw the great work which the LORD did upon the Egyptians, and the people feared the LORD; and they believed in the LORD, and in His servant Moses.

STUDY QUESTIONS

1. Compare the different readings. How are they similar? How are they different? How do these passages provide evidence for the Hebrews' belief that they were the Chosen People?
2. In return for God's favor, what special moral and ethical obligations does God ask the Hebrews to follow?

2.3 BOOK OF JEREMIAH, PROPHECY TO ISRAEL, CHAPTERS 7 AND 8, WRITTEN CA. 600–500 BCE

Jeremiah (late seventh–early sixth century BCE) was a prophet in Jerusalem who warned the Israelites that their sinful behavior would bring God's punishment—an outcome embodied by the destruction of Jerusalem by the Babylonians (586 BCE). Recorded in a poetic style, the message

The Holy Scriptures According to the Masoretic Text: A New Translation with the Aid of Previous Versions and with Constant Consultation of Jewish Authorities.—Excerpted from Jewish Publication Society of America Version on Wikipedia, the free encyclopedia.

from God preached by Jeremiah threatens desolation for the land and tragedy for its people because they have been disobedient to God's law. In a time of perceived social breakdown, where God's people shed blood and abuse their neighbors, Jeremiah's voice is a reforming force intended to stave off God's punishment.

CHAPTER 7

¹The word that came to Jeremiah from the LORD, saying: ²Stand in the gate of the LORD's house, and proclaim there this word, and say: Hear the word of the LORD, all ye of Judah, that enter in at these gates to worship the LORD.

³Thus saith the LORD of hosts, the God of Israel: Amend your ways and your doings, and I will cause you to dwell in this place.

. . .

¹⁶Therefore pray not thou for this people, neither lift up cry nor prayer for them, neither make intercession to Me; for I will not hear thee. ¹⁷Seest thou not what they do in the cities of Judah and in the streets of Jerusalem? ¹⁸The children gather wood, and the fathers kindle the fire, and the women knead the dough, to make cakes to the queen of heaven, and to pour out drink-offerings unto other gods, that they may provoke Me. ¹⁹Do they provoke Me? saith the LORD; do they not provoke themselves, to the confusion of their own faces? ²⁰Therefore thus saith the LORD God: Behold, Mine anger and My fury shall be poured out upon this place, upon man, and upon beast, and upon the trees of the field, and upon the fruit of the land; and it shall burn, and shall not be quenched.

. . .

²⁷And thou shalt speak all these words unto them, but they will not hearken to thee; thou shalt also call unto them, but they will not answer thee. ²⁸Therefore thou shalt say unto them:

This is the nation that hath not hearkened
To the voice of the LORD their God,
Nor received correction;
Faithfulness is perished,
And is cut off from their mouth.

. . .

CHAPTER 8

⁴Moreover thou shalt say unto them: Thus saith the LORD:

Do men fall, and not rise up again?
Doth one turn away, and not return?
⁵Why then is this people of Jerusalem slidden
    back
By a perpetual backsliding?
They hold fast deceit,
They refuse to return.
⁶I attended and listened,
But they spoke not aright;
No man repenteth him of his wickedness,
Saying: "What have I done?"
Every one turneth away in his course,
As a horse that rusheth headlong in the battle.
⁷Yea, the stork in the heaven
Knoweth her appointed times;
And the turtle and the swallow and the crane
Observe the time of their coming;
But My people know not
The ordinance of the LORD.

. . .

For from the least even unto the greatest
Every one is greedy for gain,
From the prophet even unto the priest
Every one dealeth falsely.
¹¹And they have healed the hurt of the daughter of
    My people lightly,
Saying: "Peace, peace", when there is no peace.
¹²They shall be put to shame because they have
    committed abomination;
Yea, they are not at all ashamed,
Neither know they how to blush;
Therefore shall they fall among them that fall,
In the time of their visitation they shall stumble,
Saith the LORD.
¹³I will utterly consume them, saith the LORD;

There are no grapes on the vine,
Nor figs on the fig-tree,
And the leaf is faded;
And I gave them that which they transgress.
[14]Why do we sit still?
Assemble yourselves, and let us enter into the
     fortified cities,
And let us be cut off there;
For the LORD our God hath cut us off,
And given us water of gall to drink,
Because we have sinned against the LORD.
[15]We looked for peace, but no good came;
And for a time of healing, and behold terror!

[16]The snorting of his horses is heard from Dan;
At the sound of the neighing of his strong ones
The whole land trembleth;
For they are come, and have devoured the land
     and all that is in it,
The city and those that dwell therein.
[17]For, behold, I will send serpents, basilisks,
     among you,
Which will not be charmed;
And they shall bite you, saith the LORD.
[18]Though I would take comfort against
     sorrow,
My heart is faint within me.

STUDY QUESTIONS

1. What forms does disobedience to God take, in Jeremiah's estimation?
2. Remember that the document was read after the destruction of Jerusalem by the Babylonians. Could even more destruction be threatened as a result of future disobedience?

2.4 FIRST BOOK OF KINGS, KING SOLOMON AND THE TEMPLE, CHAPTERS 6–8, CA. 1000–900 BCE

The Book of Kings picks up the story of Israel at the death of King David (970 BCE) and describes the transgressions of his heirs over the course of the next four centuries—creating a justification for the Babylonian Empire's destruction of Israel and Judea in the sixth century BCE. This selection describes—in painstaking detail—the construction of the First Temple of Jerusalem, built by King Solomon (r. 970–931 BCE). After reading the lavish description of this holy site, consider the psychological effect of its complete destruction at the hands of the Babylonian invaders in 586 BCE.

CHAPTER 6

[1]And it came to pass in the four hundred and eightieth year after the children of Israel were come out of the land of Egypt, in the fourth year of Solomon's reign over Israel, in the month Ziv, which is the second month, that he began to build the house of the LORD. [2]And the house which king Solomon built for the LORD, the length thereof was threescore

The Holy Scriptures According to the Masoretic Text: A New Translation with the Aid of Previous Versions and with Constant Consultation of Jewish Authorities.—Excerpted from Jewish Publication Society of America Version on Wikipedia, the free encyclopedia.

cubits, and the breadth thereof twenty cubits, and the height thereof thirty cubits. ³And the porch before the temple of the house, twenty cubits was the length thereof, according to the breadth of the house; and ten cubits was the breadth thereof before the house. ⁴And for the house he made windows broad within, and narrow without. ⁵And against the wall of the house he built a side-structure round about, against the walls of the house round about, both of the temple and of the sanctuary; and he made side-chambers round about; ⁶the nethermost story of the side-structure was five cubits broad, and the middle was six cubits broad, and the third was seven cubits broad; for on the outside he made rebatements in the wall of the house round about, that the beams should not have hold in the walls of the house.

⁷For the house, when it was in building, was built of stone made ready at the quarry; and there was neither hammer nor axe nor any tool of iron heard in the house, while it was in building.

⁸The door for the lowest row of chambers was in the right side of the house and they went up by winding stairs into the middle row, and out of the middle into the third. ⁹So he built the house, and finished it; and he covered in the house with planks of cedar over beams. ¹⁰And he built the stories of the side-structure against all the house, each five cubits high; and they rested on the house with timber of cedar.

¹¹And the word of the LORD came to Solomon, saying: ¹²"As for this house which thou art building, if thou wilt walk in My statutes, and execute Mine ordinances, and keep all My commandments to walk in them; then will I establish My word with thee, which I spoke unto David thy father; ¹³in that I will dwell therein among the children of Israel, and will not forsake My people Israel."

¹⁴So Solomon built the house, and finished it. ¹⁵And he built the walls of the house within with boards of cedar;

. . .

¹⁹And he prepared the Sanctuary in the midst of the house within, to set there the ark of the covenant of the LORD. ²⁰And before the Sanctuary which was twenty cubits in length, and twenty cubits in breadth, and twenty cubits in the height thereof, overlaid with pure gold, he set an altar, which he covered with cedar. ²¹So Solomon overlaid the house within with pure gold; and he drew chains of gold across the wall before the Sanctuary; and he overlaid it with gold. ²²And the whole house he overlaid with gold, until all the house was finished; also the whole altar that belonged to the Sanctuary he overlaid with gold.

²³And in the Sanctuary he made two cherubim of olive-wood, each ten cubits high. ²⁴And five cubits was the one wing of the cherub, and five cubits the other wing of the cherub; from the uttermost part of the one wing unto the uttermost part of the other were ten cubits. ²⁵And the other cherub was ten cubits; both the cherubim were of one measure and one form. ²⁶The height of the one cherub was ten cubits, and so was it of the other cherub.

²⁷And he set the cherubim within the inner house; and the wings of the cherubim were stretched forth, so that the wing of the one touched the one wall, and the wing of the other cherub touched the other wall; and their wings touched one another in the midst of the house. ²⁸And he overlaid the cherubim with gold. ²⁹And he carved all the walls of the house round about with carved figures of cherubim and palm-trees and open flowers, within and without. ³⁰And the floor of the house he overlaid with gold, within and without.

³¹And for the entrance of the Sanctuary he made doors of olive-wood, the door-posts within the frame having five angles. ³²And as for the two doors of olive-wood, he carved upon them carvings of cherubim and palm-trees and open flowers, and overlaid them with gold; and he spread the gold upon the cherubim, and upon the palm-trees. ³³So also made he for the entrance of the temple door-posts of olive-wood, within a frame four-square; ³⁴and two doors of cypress-wood; the two leaves of the one door were folding, and the two leaves of the other door were folding. ³⁵And he carved thereon cherubim and palm-trees and open flowers; and he overlaid them with gold fitted upon the graven work. ³⁶And he built the inner court with three rows of hewn stone, and a row of cedar beams.

³⁷In the fourth year was the foundation of the house of the LORD laid, in the month Ziv. ³⁸And in the eleventh year, in the month Bul, which is the eighth month, was the house finished throughout all the

parts thereof, and according to all the fashion of it. So was he seven years in building it.

CHAPTER 7

. . .

[48]And Solomon made all the vessels that were in the house of the LORD: the golden altar, and the table whereupon the showbread was, of gold; [49]and the candlesticks, five on the right side, and five on the left, before the Sanctuary, of pure gold; and the flowers, and the lamps, and the tongs, of gold; [50]and the cups, and the snuffers, and the basins, and the pans, and the fire-pans, of pure gold; and the hinges, both for the doors of the inner house, the most holy place, and for the doors of the house, that is, of the temple, of gold.

[51]Thus all the work that king Solomon wrought in the house of the LORD was finished. And Solomon brought in the things which David his father had dedicated, the silver, and the gold, and the vessels, and put them in the treasuries of the house of the LORD.

CHAPTER 8

[1]Then Solomon assembled the elders of Israel, and all the heads of the tribes, the princes of the fathers' houses of the children of Israel, unto king Solomon in Jerusalem, to bring up the ark of the covenant of the LORD out of the city of David, which is Zion. [2]And all the men of Israel assembled themselves unto king Solomon at the feast, in the month Ethanim, which is the seventh month. [3]And all the elders of Israel came, and the priests took up the ark. [4]And they brought up the ark of the LORD, and the tent of meeting, and all the holy vessels that were in the Tent; even these did the priests and the Levites bring up. [5]And king Solomon and all the congregation of Israel, that were assembled unto him, were with him before the ark, sacrificing sheep and oxen, that could not be told nor numbered for multitude.

[6]And the priests brought in the ark of the covenant of the LORD unto its place, into the Sanctuary of the house, to the most holy place, even under the wings of the cherubim. [7]For the cherubim spread forth their wings over the place of the ark, and the cherubim covered the ark and the staves thereof above. [8]And the staves were so long that the ends of the staves were seen from the holy place, even before the Sanctuary; but they could not be seen without; and there they are unto this day. [9]There was nothing in the ark save the two tables of stone which Moses put there at Horeb, when the LORD made a covenant with the children of Israel when they came out of the land of Egypt.

[10]And it came to pass, when the priests were come out of the holy place, that the cloud filled the house of the LORD, [11]so that the priests could not stand to minister by reason of the cloud; for the glory of the LORD filled the house of the LORD.

[12]Then spoke Solomon:

The LORD hath said that He would dwell in the thick darkness.
[13]I have surely built Thee a house of habitation,
A place for Thee to dwell in for ever.

[14]And the king turned his face about, and blessed all the congregation of Israel; and all the congregation of Israel stood. [15]And he said:

"Blessed be the LORD, the God of Israel, who spoke with His mouth unto David my father, and hath with His hand fulfilled it, saying: [16]Since the day that I brought forth My people Israel out of Egypt, I chose no city out of all the tribes of Israel to build a house, that My name might be there; but I chose David to be over My people Israel.

[17]"Now it was in the heart of David my father to build a house for the name of the LORD, the God of Israel. [18]But the LORD said unto David my father: Whereas it was in thy heart to build a house for My name, thou didst well that it was in thy heart; [19]nevertheless thou shalt not build the house; but thy son that shall come forth out of thy loins, he shall build the house for My name. [20]And the LORD hath established His word that He spoke; for I am risen up in the room of David my father, and sit on the throne of Israel, as the LORD promised, and have built the house for the name of the LORD, the God of Israel. [21]And there have I set a place for the ark, wherein is

the covenant of the LORD, which He made with our fathers, when He brought them out of the land of Egypt."

²²And Solomon stood before the altar of the LORD in the presence of all the congregation of Israel, and spread forth his hands toward heaven; ²³and he said: "O LORD, the God of Israel, there is no God like Thee, in heaven above, or on earth beneath; who keepest covenant and mercy with Thy servants, that walk before Thee with all their heart; ²⁴who hast kept with Thy servant David my father that which Thou didst promise him; yea, Thou spokest with Thy mouth, and hast fulfilled it with Thy hand, as it is this day. ²⁵Now therefore, O LORD, the God of Israel, keep with Thy servant David my father that which Thou hast promised him saying: There shall not fail thee a man in My sight to sit on the throne of Israel, if only thy children take heed to their way, to walk before Me as thou hast walked before Me.²⁶Now therefore, O God of Israel, let Thy word, I pray Thee, be verified, which Thou didst speak unto Thy servant David my father.

²⁷"But will God in very truth dwell on the earth? behold, heaven and the heaven of heavens cannot contain Thee; how much less this house that I have builded! ²⁸Yet have Thou respect unto the prayer of Thy servant, and to his supplication, O LORD my God, to hearken unto the cry and to the prayer which Thy servant prayeth before Thee this day; ²⁹that Thine eyes may be open toward this house night and day, even toward the place whereof Thou hast said: My name shall be there; to hearken unto the prayer which Thy servant shall pray toward this place. ³⁰And hearken Thou to the supplication of Thy servant, and of Thy people Israel, when they shall pray toward this place; yea, hear Thou in heaven Thy dwelling-place; and when Thou hearest, forgive.

. . .

⁵⁴And it was so, that when Solomon had made an end of praying all this prayer and supplication unto the LORD, he arose from before the altar of the LORD, from kneeling on his knees with his hands spread forth toward heaven. ⁵⁵And he stood, and blessed all the congregation of Israel with a loud voice, saying:

⁵⁶"Blessed be the LORD, that hath given rest unto His people Israel, according to all that He promised; there hath not failed one word of all His good promise, which He promised by the hand of Moses His servant. ⁵⁷The LORD our God be with us, as He was with our fathers; let Him not leave us, nor forsake us; ⁵⁸that He may incline our hearts unto Him, to walk in all His ways, and to keep His commandments, and His statutes, and His ordinances, which He commanded our fathers. ⁵⁹And let these my words, wherewith I have made supplication before the LORD, be nigh unto the LORD our God day and night, that He maintain the cause of His servant, and the cause of His people Israel, as every day shall require; ⁶⁰that all the peoples of the earth may know that the LORD, He is God; there is none else. ⁶¹Let your heart therefore be whole with the LORD our God, to walk in His statutes, and to keep His commandments, as at this day."

⁶²And the king, and all Israel with him, offered sacrifice before the LORD. ⁶³And Solomon offered for the sacrifice of peace-offerings, which he offered unto the LORD, two and twenty thousand oxen, and a hundred and twenty thousand sheep. So the king and all the children of Israel dedicated the house of the LORD.

STUDY QUESTIONS

1. What are the terms of God's covenant with Israel, and is there an implied threat if the terms of the contract are broken?
2. Why are the people and their priests advised to worship God and follow his very specific directions?

2.5 THE BOOK OF JONAH: PROPHECY, PENANCE, AND RESISTANCE, CA. 400 BCE

Jonah is one of the Twelve, or the Lesser, Prophets—but lesser only in the sense that these books are considerably shorter than those of the great prophets like Isaiah, Jeremiah, and Ezechiel. Composed sometime around 400 BCE, the tale it tells is set in the reign of Jeroboam II (786–746 BCE), the time of the Assyrian Empire's conquest of Israel. In Jewish liturgy, Jonah is read on the afternoon of Yom Kippur, the Day of Atonement, the holiest day of the year.

CHAPTER 1

¹Now the word of the LORD came unto Jonah the son of Amittai, saying: ²"Arise, go to Nineveh, that great city, and proclaim against it; For their wickedness is come up before Me."

³But Jonah rose up to flee unto Tarshish from the presence of the LORD; and he went down to Joppa, and found a ship going to Tarshish; so he paid the fare thereof, and went down into it, to go with them unto Tarshish, from the presence of the LORD.

⁴But the LORD hurled a great wind into the sea, and there was a mighty tempest in the sea, so that the ship was like to be broken. ⁵And the mariners were afraid, and cried every man unto his god; and they cast forth the wares that were in the ship into the sea, to lighten it unto them. But Jonah was gone down into the innermost parts of the ship; and he lay, and was fast asleep. ⁶So the shipmaster came to him, and said unto him: "What meanest thou that thou sleepest? arise, call upon thy God, if so be that God will think upon us, that we perish not."

⁷And they said every one to his fellow: "Come, and let us cast lots, that we may know for whose cause this evil is upon us." So they cast lots, and the lot fell upon Jonah. ⁸Then said they unto him: "Tell us, we pray thee, for whose cause this evil is upon us: what is thine occupation? and whence comest thou? what is thy country? and of what people art thou?" ⁹And he said unto them: "I am a Hebrew; and I fear the LORD, the God of heaven, who hath made the sea and the dry land." ¹⁰Then were the men exceedingly afraid, and said unto him: "What is this that thou hast done?" For the men knew that he fled from the presence of the LORD, because he had told them. ¹¹Then said they unto him: "What shall we do unto thee, that the sea may be calm unto us?" for the sea grew more and more tempestuous. ¹²And he said unto them: "Take me up, and cast me forth into the sea; so shall the sea be calm unto you; for I know that for my sake this great tempest is upon you." ¹³Nevertheless the men rowed hard to bring it to the land; but they could not; for the sea grew more and more tempestuous against them. ¹⁴Wherefore they cried unto the LORD, and said: "We beseech Thee, O LORD, we beseech Thee, let us not perish for this man's life, and lay not upon us innocent blood; for Thou, O LORD, hast done as it pleased Thee." ¹⁵So they took up Jonah, and cast him forth into the sea; and the sea ceased from its raging.

¹⁶Then the men feared the LORD exceedingly; and they offered a sacrifice unto the LORD, and made vows.

The Holy Scriptures According to the Masoretic Text: A New Translation with the Aid of Previous Versions and with Constant Consultation of Jewish Authorities.—Excerpted from Jewish Publication Society of America Version on Wikipedia, the free encyclopedia.

CHAPTER 2

¹And the LORD prepared a great fish to swallow up Jonah; and Jonah was in the belly of the fish three days and three nights. ²Then Jonah prayed unto the LORD his God out of the fish's belly. ³And he said:

> I called out of mine affliction
> Unto the LORD, and He answered me;
> Out of the belly of the nether-world cried I,
> And Thou heardest my voice.
> ⁴For thou didst cast me into the depth,
> In the heart of the seas,
> And the flood was round about me;
> All Thy waves and Thy billows
> Passed over me.
> ⁵And I said: "I am cast out
> From before Thine eyes";
> Yet I will look again
> Toward Thy holy temple.
> ⁶The waters compassed me about, even to the
>   soul;
> The deep was round about me;
> The weeds were wrapped about my head.
> ⁷I went down to the bottoms of the mountains;
> The earth with her bars closed upon me for ever;
> Yet hast Thou brought up my life from the pit,
> O LORD my God.
> ⁸When my soul fainted within me,
> I remembered the LORD;
> And my prayer came in unto Thee,
> Into Thy holy temple.
> ⁹They that regard lying vanities
> Forsake their own mercy.
> ¹⁰But I will sacrifice unto Thee
> With the voice of thanksgiving;
> That which I have vowed I will pay.
> Salvation is of the LORD.

¹¹And the LORD spoke unto the fish, and it vomited out Jonah upon the dry land.

CHAPTER 3

¹And the word of the LORD came unto Jonah the second time, saying: ²'Arise, go unto Nineveh, that great city, and make unto it the proclamation that I

bid thee." ³So Jonah arose, and went unto Nineveh, according to the word of the LORD. Now Nineveh was an exceeding great city, of three days' journey. ⁴And Jonah began to enter into the city a day's journey, and he proclaimed, and said: "Yet forty days, and Nineveh shall be overthrown."

⁵And the people of Nineveh believed God; and they proclaimed a fast, and put on sackcloth, from the greatest of them even to the least of them. ⁶And the tidings reached the king of Nineveh, and he arose from his throne, and laid his robe from him, and covered him with sackcloth, and sat in ashes. ⁷And he caused it to be proclaimed and published through Nineveh by the decree of the king and his nobles, saying: "Let neither man nor beast, herd nor flock, taste any thing; let them not feed, nor drink water; ⁸but let them be covered with sackcloth, both man and beast, and let them cry mightily unto God; yea, let them turn every one from his evil way, and from the violence that is in their hands. ⁹Who knoweth whether God will not turn and repent, and turn away from His fierce anger, that we perish not?"

¹⁰And God saw their works, that they turned from their evil way; and God repented of the evil, which He said He would do unto them; and He did it not.

CHAPTER 4

¹But it displeased Jonah exceedingly, and he was angry. ²And he prayed unto the LORD, and said: "I pray Thee, O LORD, was not this my saying, when I was yet in mine own country? Therefore I fled beforehand unto Tarshish; for I knew that Thou art a gracious God, and compassionate, long-suffering, and abundant in mercy, and repentest Thee of the evil. ³Therefore now, O LORD, take, I beseech Thee, my life from me; for it is better for me to die than to live." ⁴And the LORD said: "Art thou greatly angry?"

⁵Then Jonah went out of the city, and sat on the east side of the city, and there made him a booth, and sat under it in the shadow, till he might see what would become of the city. ⁶And the LORD God prepared a gourd, and made it to come up over Jonah, that it might be a shadow over his head, to deliver him from his evil. So Jonah was exceeding glad because of the gourd. ⁷But God prepared a worm when

the morning rose the next day, and it smote the gourd, that it withered. ⁸And it came to pass, when the sun arose, that God prepared a vehement east wind; and the sun beat upon the head of Jonah, that he fainted, and requested for himself that he might die, and said: "It is better for me to die than to live." ⁹And God said to Jonah "Art thou greatly angry for the gourd?" And he said: "I am greatly angry, even unto death." ¹⁰And the LORD said: "Thou hast had pity on the gourd, for which thou hast not laboured, neither madest it grow, which came up in a night, and perished in a night; ¹¹and should not I have pity on Nineveh, that great city, wherein are more than sixscore thousand persons that cannot discern between their right hand and their left hand, and also much cattle?"

STUDY QUESTIONS

1. What do you think the huge fish represents? What is the significance of Jonah remaining inside its belly for three days and three nights?
2. What qualities of Jonah make him a prophet?

2.6 THE CYRUS CYLINDER, CA. 539 BCE

Founder of the Achaemenid Persian Empire, Cyrus (Kurosh) the Great rose to the throne of a small kingdom in 559 BCE; by the time of his death in 529, he had brought virtually the entire Near East under his control. In 539, he conquered Babylon and drove out Nabonidus, the last of the Neo-Babylonian kings. However, he was hailed as a liberator by the priests of the Babylonian god Marduk, and he issued a remarkable document, in which he praised himself for the restoration of all temples, priesthoods, and cults in his vast empire. The text, which was publicized in Akkadian, an ancient Mesopotamian language, is preserved on a clay cylinder, today called the Cyrus Cylinder and housed in the British Museum.

On account of their complaints, the lords of the gods became furiously angry and left their [the Babylonians'] land; the gods, who dwelt among them, left their homes. . . .. In all lands everywhere [the god Marduk] searched; he looked through them and sought a righteous prince after his own heart, whom he took by the hand. He called Cyrus, king of Anshan, by name; he appointed him to lordship over the whole world.

The land of Qutu, all the Umman-manda, he cast down at his feet. The black-headed people, whom he gave his hands to conquer, he took them in justice and righteousness. Marduk, the great lord, looked joyously on the caring for his people, on his pious works and his righteous heart. To his city, Babylon, he caused [Cyrus] to go; he made him take the road to Babylon, going as a friend and companion at his side. His numerous troops, in unknown numbers, like the waters of a river, marched armed at his side. Without battle and conflict, he permitted him to enter Babylon. He spared his city, Babylon, a calamity. Nabonidus, the king, who did not fear him, he delivered into his hand.

. . .

When I [Cyrus] made my triumphal entrance into Babylon, I took up my lordly residence in the royal palace with joy and rejoicing; Marduk, the great lord, moved the noble heart of the residents of Babylon to me, while I gave daily attention to his worship. My numerous troops marched peacefully into Babylon. In all Sumer and Akkad I permitted no enemy to enter.

The needs of Babylon and of all its cities I gladly attended to. The people of Babylon [and . . .], and the shameful yoke was removed from them. Their dwellings, which had fallen, I restored. I cleared out their ruins. Marduk, the great lord, rejoiced in my pious deeds, and graciously blessed me, Cyrus, the king who worships him, and Cambyses, my own son, and all my troops, while we, before him, joyously praised his exalted godhead.

. . .

And the gods of Sumer and Akkad—whom Nabonidus, to the anger of the lord of the gods, had brought into Babylon—by the command of Marduk, the great lord, I caused them to take up their dwelling in residences that gladdened the heart. May all the gods, whom I brought into their cities, pray daily before Bel and Nabu for long life for me, and may they speak a gracious word for me and say to Marduk, my lord, "May Cyrus, the king who worships you, and Cambyses his son, their [. . .] I permitted all to dwell in peace [. . .]."

STUDY QUESTIONS

1. How and why did Cyrus incorporate local deities into his public image after subjugating Babylon?
2. How does this document compare with other texts on peace and justice in Mesopotamia?

CHAPTER 3

THE ANCIENT GREEKS: FROM ARRIVAL TO GLORY

3.1 HESIOD, *WORKS AND DAYS*, CA. 735–700 BCE

A contemporary of Homer, the Greek author Hesiod produced his two major works, *Theogony* (a genealogical account of the gods) and *Works and Days*, around the last third of the eighth century BCE. *Works and Days* is part letter to his brother Perses, part advice column, and part abstract musing on human righteousness. According to Hesiod, the current Sixth Age of Man, the "race of iron," is consigned to labor; yet this labor is the key to success and happiness. Accordingly, Hesiod provides snippets of advice, from farming to the choice of a proper wife.

Now listen closely. If you wish, I will tell you
    another tale—
and tell it well—about how the gods and
    mankind share the same origin.
The race of men made by the Immortals on high
    Olympus
were made of gold. Kronos then ruled in heaven,
    and mankind lived
like gods themselves, free of worry, toil, and
    sorrow. The misery of age
did not afflict them; from head to foot they
    delighted in feasts,
knew no pains, and died simply by falling asleep.
    They lacked
for nothing. The fertile earth brought forth its
    fruits in plenty,

without any labor on their part; they had only the
    delight of harvesting
as they pleased, happy in their bounty. Since that
    time, when the Earth
closed over that race, they have lived on as spirits,
    by Zeus' design,
to watch over mortal men and bestow them with
    blessings.
Such has been Zeus' reward to them.
Next came the race of silver to live on high
    Olympus,
a lesser race, sharing neither shape nor spirit with
    those of before.
Their sons lived with their mothers for a hundred
    years, playing

Translation by Clifford Backman.

childish games; but when the years passed and they reached the age
of young manhood, then their lives were full of pain and were
cut short on account of their simple-mindedness. They could not
resist doing harm to one another; they refused to serve the Immortals
and to make sacrifice on the sacred altars of the gods (as is demanded of all peoples everywhere). So Zeus, the son of Kronos, in rage
over their refusal to honor the deities on Olympus, did away with them.
The earth closed over them, since which time they are called the
Mortal Blessed below. They have their honor, but are of second rank.
Then Father Zeus created a third race of men out of bronze
—nothing like the silver one—created them out of ash trees. Terrible
and savage, besotted with the baleful work of Ares, a violent race.
They did not till the land, their hearts being too stubborn. Ungainly giants
they were, great in strength with powerful arms reaching out
from mighty shoulders and torsos. They had bronze armor and bronze
houses. They worked all manner of things in bronze since they did not
know iron. Their own violent ways brought them down, and they
passed to cold Hades, leaving no good names behind them. Strong
as they were, black death got the better of them, and they
abandoned the light of the sun; over this race too the Earth closed.
Then Kronos' son, Zeus, placed a fourth race upon the vast and fertile Earth,
a dutiful and noble race of the divine heroes called demigods,
the predecessors of Man. Brutal war and strife brought them down,
some of them below the seven gates of Thebes, in Cadmea,

as they contended for Oedipus' inheritance; others sailed over the deep sea
to Troy, in the war for fair-haired Helen. There some were swallowed by Death,
but Father Zeus, Kronos' son, spared others and set them at far reaches
of the Earth, well away from men, where they live in bliss
in the Isles of the Blessed near deep-currented Oceanus:
especially blessed are these heroes, for the fertile land they inhabit
brings forth its bounty three times a year.
How much better it would be to have died before the fifth race
of men, or to be born after their passing! Ours is an age of iron,
filled with toil and misery that never cease, day or night. Truly the gods
give our race endless suffering and hardship, even as they sometimes mix
some joy into our sorrow. Father Zeus will bring an end to our race too;
the signs will be when we are born with gray hairs, when fathers and
children have nothing in common, when neither hosts nor guests will be
hospitable, and friendship between brothers will cease. Respect for parents
shall end, despite all the warnings of the gods, and the young will rail harshly
at their elders and fail to support them in their age. They will rule by force,
attacking each other's cities. They will have no respect for truthful men,
or the righteous and upright. Evil-doers and criminals they shall lift up
instead, and might shall make right. Villains will lie and deceive,
defrauding their betters and breaking sacred oaths. In their misery
all people will be beset by Envy, the bringer of misfortune and the shaper
of hate-filled faces. At that time, truly, Decency and Moral Judgment
will quit the Earth, hiding their faces in white robes, and return to

High Olympus, abandoning mankind forever and taking refuge
with the Immortals. Black suffering shall be mankind's fate, with
nothing to help them against evil.

. . .

If your heart desires wealth, do as I say and work. Work! And work!
"When the daughters of Atlas, the Seven Sisters, rise in the morning sky
begin the harvest, but plow the fields again before they set."
They remain hidden for forty days and forty nights, and with the
turning of the year they reappear, at the time for the sharpening of iron.
This is the law of the land, for both those who dwell near the sea
and those glens and meadows far from it: if you would have a fertile land
you must be naked when you drive the oxen, naked when you sow,
and naked when you reap—or else Demeter's gifts will fail to come
in due season and you will know hunger. You will beg for your bread

and earn nothing—just as you have now come to me. But I will give
you nothing more. Work, Perses, you fool! Do the work laid out for you
and for all by the gods. If not, your fate will be suffering—Yes, and for your
wife and children too!—for your neighbors will hear your pleas and turn away

. . .

It is wiser to marry a girl who lives near you, and to choose her carefully,
or else your neighbors will surely laugh at your foolishness. For there
is no blessing greater to a man than a good wife, and no curse worse
than a bad one, a scold who needs no hot iron in order to brand her man;
be he ever so strong, she will wear him down before his time. . . .
Now do as I say: do all that you can to avoid becoming the subject of rumor,
for a rumor is a terrible burden—easy to pick up, but hard to bear, and nearly impossible
to set down. No rumor ever dies, if enough people hear it. In this way, indeed,
a rumor is immortal.

STUDY QUESTIONS

1. What are the causes of toil and misery for people in Hesiod's time?
2. How is work a function of a man's overall reputation in the community?

3.2 HOMER, *THE ILIAD*, 800–700 BCE

This epic poem retells the ten-year-long siege of the city of "Ilium," or Troy (in modern-day Turkey), by the mighty forces of the Greek brothers Agamemnon and Menelaus. The war, sparked by the abduction of Menelaus's wife Helen by the Trojan prince Alexander (or Paris), quickly

Translation by Clifford Backman.

became a battleground for the gods themselves. The first two selections provide a portrait of the militant posturing and tenuous hierarchy in the Greek camp, after Agamemnon threatens to seize invincible Achilles's slave-girl. The third selection describes the wretched death of Hector, Alexander's brother, at the hands of his mortal foe, Achilles. Homer's use of epithets (concise descriptions designed to remind the audience of character traits while fitting into the poem's meter), like "gleaming-helmeted Hector," bring vibrancy to the elegant poetry.

Agamemnon refuses to release his slave-girl. Apollo's wrath. **(Book I, ll. 1–52.)**

Anger, O Goddess! Let the dreadful anger of
    Achilles, the son of Peleus,
be your song—an anger that brought countless
    sufferings on the Achaeans,
sent many brave souls to Hades, and left the
    remains of heroes unnumbered
as prey for dogs and vultures. Thus was the will of
    great Zeus carried out.
Start from the moment when [King Agamemnon],
the son of Atreus, and god-like Achilles fell out
    with one another.
Which of the gods brought them to quarrel? The
    son of Zeus and Leto—Apollo.
For he was angry at Agamemnon and so sent a
    plague upon the Greeks' camp,
Decimating the people there in return for the
    dishonor the son of Atreus
had done to Chryses—Apollo's own priest.
    Chryses had come
to the Achaeans' ships bearing a great ransom
    with which to free
his daughter Briseis. He carried in his hand the
    golden scepter of Apollo,
wreathed in bands, and begged of all the
    Achaeans—but especially of
Agamemnon [and Menelaus], the two sons of
    Atreus, who commanded them all.
"Sons of Atreus!" he cried, "and all you well-
    armored Achaeans!
May the gods who dwell on Olympus grant that
    you sack Priam's city,
and may they give you a fair wind home!
But release my daughter in return for this ransom,
    out of reverence for Apollo,

the son of Zeus!"
At this, the Achaeans were of a single mind to pay
    due respect to the priest
and accept the ransom he offered, but
    Agamemnon, son of Atreus,
refused outright. He berated the priest, instead,
    and angrily dismissed him.
"Never let me catch you, old man, loitering about
    our ships
or trying to approach me again! If I do catch you,
    your scepter and priestly bands
will do you no good. I will not release your
    daughter! No! She will instead
grow old in Argos, far from her native home,
    working at the loom and in my bed!
Now go, and pester me no more, while you're still
    in one piece!"
Thus he spoke, and the frightened old man
    obeyed. He walked away in silence,
but when he got to the shore of the booming sea
    he prayed to Lord Apollo,
whom beautiful Leto bore:
"Hear me, O Master of the Silver Bow!" he cried,
    "Protector of Cilla
and mighty Ruler of Tenedos! O Sminthian! If
    ever I have pleased you
by building shrines in your honor or burning the
    fat thighbones of cattle
or goats upon your altars—grant this prayer of
    mine:
Let loose your arrows on the Danaans! Avenge my
    tears!"
Thus he prayed, and Phoebus Apollo heard him.
    With his heart full of anger
the god swooped down from Olympus, bearing
    his bow and quiver.

The arrows on his back rattled from the rage he
felt as he descended.
His face dark as night, Apollo settled at a distance
from the Greek ships.
His bow sounded like rolling thunder as he
rained arrows on the Achaeans.
First he shot their mules and dogs, then quickly
turned upon the soldiers themselves. Funeral
pyres burned night and day.
For nine days his arrows fell on the Greeks—
and on the tenth day, at last, Achilles call the men
to assembly.

After being criticized by Achilles, Agamemnon rises in anger to denounce him. (Book I, ll. 101–20)

And then Agamemnon, the son of Atreus, ruler of
the plain, rose in wrath.
His heart filled with fury, and his eyes blazed like
flames.
Glaring first at Calchas he uttered the threat:
"You prophet of doom! Not once have you ever
prophesied
anything good on my behalf! Catastrophe is what
you live for—never anything good!
Not a single good word has passed your lips, nor
a good action follow!
Now you stand among all the Greeks and
pronounce that the god who afflicts them
does so on account of me, because I refused the
ransom for Chryses' daughter
so that I could keep her as my own, in my home. I
admit it! I prefer her
to my own wife Clytemnestra. She loses nothing
in comparison—
not in beauty or stature, mind or skill.
Yet still . . . I am willing to give her back, if it is
better that way.
For I want this army to survive, not perish. In
return, however,
I demand another prize of honor be given me at
once. For I, alone of all the Argives,
will not go wanting. That would not be proper.
Every man here can see that my due reward is
going elsewhere."

When Agamemnon threatens to take Achilles' slave-girl, Briseis, to compensate for the loss of Chryses' daughter, Achilles lashes out in fury. (Book I, ll. 148–71)

With glowering eyes swift-footed Achilles frowned
at Agamemnon and said:
"You shameless, greedy, selfish man! Who among
the Greeks can ever
obey your commands after this, either on march
or in battle?
I did not come here out of my own quarrel with
the Trojan spearmen;
they have done no wrong to me. They have stolen
no cattle or horses of mine,
nor destroyed any of my crops in the rich soil of
Phthia.
Miles and miles of shadowy mountains and
roaring seas separate us.
No! It was for you—you cur!—for you that we all
came, fighting to avenge you
And your brother Menelaus upon the Trojans! But
you've forgotten this, you dog!
And now you threaten to strip me of my own
prize-girl,
one for whom I fought hard, and whom all the
Greeks awarded me.
Not once have I done as well as you,
when the soldiers apportion the plunder from
any Trojan fortress.
Time and again I have fought more, hand-to-
hand, than ever you did.
But whenever the time comes for splitting
the booty, the greater share is always
yours,
while I, worn out with fighting, take my smaller
reward back to my ships.
But this time I shall sail for Phthia!
It would be better for me to return home in my
curved ships.
I will not stay here, dishonored, to keep piling up
riches for you!"

Achilles is persuaded not to set sail, but remains stubbornly in his tent and refuses to fight.

Without him, the Greeks lose battle after battle against the Trojans. Eventually the common soldiers begin to grumble. One of them, named Thersites, complains to Agamemnon on their behalf. (Book II, ll. 211–77)

Gradually, the men sat back down. But one of
   them would not stop.
This fellow, talkative Thersites, whose mind was a
   treasure-chest of trouble,
kept flinging abusive words at Agamemnon and
   the other commanders,
just to entertain the troops. The most intemperate
   man who went to Troy,
he was bow-legged and lame in one foot,
   round-shouldered
and always slumping over his chest. His skull was
   misshapen and
covered with mangy stubble. How much
   Achilles and Odysseus, his two favorite
   targets,
hated him! This time, however, it was
   Agamemnon at whom he hurled abuse,
the son of Atreus with whom the men were
   already furious.
"What have you got to complain about,
   Agamemnon? What more do you covet?
Your tents are bulging with bronze and beauties—
   after all, we hand over
the best of both to you first of all, whenever we've
   finished taking a stronghold.
Perhaps it's more gold you're after? No doubt
   someone from among the Trojans
will bring you piles of it as ransom for his son—a
   son, by the way, whom
one of us foot-soldiers actually captured.
Or maybe you need a new girl for your bed, one
   kept apart for your sole use?
It is a poor commander who sends common men
   to death for so little."
Thus spoke Thersites, railing at Agamemnon,
   leader of men. But then Odysseus,
glaring at the fellow beneath his deep brow,
   snarled angrily at him:
"Shut up, you loud-mouth! You bag of hot air!

How dare you speak thus to your commander!
   I swear that of all the soldiers
who followed the sons of Atreus to Troy, there is
   no wretch worse than you.
You've no right to daydream about going
   home,
or to criticize or protest against kings.
None of us knows how this war will end—
whether we'll sail home in victory or defeat. But
   you blather on and on,
whining about Atreus' son Agamemnon—our
   leader—because our own men
have rewarded him richly. I am telling you now—
   and may these words come to pass:
If I hear your whining voice one more time, may
   my own head
be knocked from my shoulders and may I never
   again be called
the father of Telemachus, if I don't seize you, strip
   off your raiment
and drive you naked through the camp, beating
   you all the way!"
After saying this, Odysseus smacked Thersites
   mightily on his back and
shoulders with his staff. A bloody welt crawled up
   the soldier's back where
the gold-studded staff had landed. A tear welled
   in Thersites' eye,
which he quickly wiped away as he collapsed in
   shame. As for the other soldiers,
angry as they were they could not help laughing,
   and whispered to one another:
"Did you see that? Odysseus has done a thousand
   great feats in this war,
both in council and on the field—but nothing to
   top this! He shut that fool up,
and it'll be a long time, I wager, before that no-
   good braggart dares
to criticize a king again!"

Achilles, rejoining the war after the death of his best friend Patroclus, finally corners the Trojan hero Hector, who had killed him.
   Their confrontation provides the climactic scene of the poem. Achilles has chased Hector

***three times around the city walls; at last,
ashamed of his fear, Hector turns and faces his
certain death. (Book 22, ll. 247–65, 292–372,
395–408.)***

When the two men finally squared off and faced
    one another,
Hector was the first to speak, declaring:
"Three times you have chased me around Priam's
    city, but
I will run from you no longer, Achilles, son of
    Peleus.
I was afraid, but now my soul commands me to
    stand and face you,
whether this results in my own death or in yours.
    Come!
Let us call upon the gods—the best guarantors of
    all covenants—
to bear witness to a solemn pact between us.
    I vow
that if Zeus grants me the victory I will do no
    dishonor
to your body, and once I have stripped you of
    your great armor
I will hand your body over to the Greeks. Will you
    grant me the same?"
But swift-footed Achilles glowered at him and
    replied:
"You're mad if you think I'll make a similar
    promise!
There are no 'solemn oaths' between lions and
    their mortal prey,
or between wolves and the lambs they seek—only
    evil thoughts
without end. There is no friendship
    between us,
no polite truces—only violence until one of us
    lies dead
and the war-god Ares is glutted with
    his blood."

. . .

Hector saw that the end was near . . . and drew
    the sharp sword that hung
On his left flank—great and mighty it was—and
    gathered his will.
Like an eagle who swoops from on high through
    dark clouds to seize

a young lamb or cowering hare, so did Hector
    swoop down on Achilles,
brandishing his sword.
With wild fury in his heart Achilles drew in to his
    chest
the beautiful shield Hephaisteus had made for
    him, and lowered his
bright four-horned helmet. . . .
Like the evening star that shines first and fairest in
    the heavens
with the fall of night, so shone the glint of
    sunlight off the keen spear
lying poised in Achilles' right hand, as he plotted
    how to do the
most harm to goodly Hector. He surveyed him
    coldly, looking for
the best place to land a blow. But Hector was
    well-armored,
his flesh covered in the bronze gear he had
    stripped from Patroclus
after slaying him. A small opening showed,
    however, where
his collar-bone divided the neck from his
    shoulders—the bare gullet
where the destruction of life comes quickest.
Rushing forward, Achilles drove his spear-point
    into the spot,
clear through Hector's neck. The heavy spear did
    not cut
Hector's windpipe, however, leaving him a chance
    to speak
as he fell to the dust at exulting Achilles' feet.
"Hector!" cried Achilles, "did you really think you
    could kill
Patroclus, steal his armor, and be safe from me?
    Fool!
Though left far behind, by the hollow ships, I still
    remained—
a greater foe in arms than even he—and it is I
    who have brought
you to your knees. Know this for certain: while
    the Greeks
give Patroclus an honorable burial, your corpse
    will lie
as carrion for dogs and vultures!"
Fading fast, gleaming-helmeted Hector spoke:

"I beg you, Achilles, on your soul and those of
your parents—
do not let me be devoured by the dogs in your
camp!
Take all the bronze and gold my father and good
mother will offer
in ransom. And let them have my body, so that
our Trojan
men and women may build me a proper funeral
pyre!"
Swift-footed Achilles shot him an angry glance
and shouted:
"No begging nonsense, you whiney little dog!
No 'By your soul!' and 'The honor of your parents!'
I wish I had it in me to cut you up and eat you raw,
so great is the hurt you caused me! There is no
man alive
who can save you from the carrion pack—not even
if ten or twenty times a ransom was laid out
before me,
with promises of even more to follow!
Not even if Priam offered me your own weight in
gold.
No, your mother will make no pyre for you, nor
offer
any funeral-lament for the son she bore. No!
The dogs and vultures will have every scrap of you!"
Then Hector spoke his last:
"Now, at last, I see you clearly, and know what
must be.
Your heart is made of iron, and there's no
persuading you.
But consider this: my end may bring the gods'
wrath upon you,
great as you are, after Paris and Phoebus Apollo
destroy you at the city-gates."
As he spoke, Death enfolded him. Hector's soul
left his body and flew to Hades, bewailing the fate
that
had ended his life in the world as a young man.
Achilles watched him die, and finally said:
"Go ahead and die! I accept my own fate
whenever Zeus and the other gods will it."
As he spoke, Achilles pulled his spear from
Hector's neck,
laid it aside, and stripped the blood-stained
armor from
Hector's shoulders. And as he did so, other Greeks
came
running up to see Hector's noble body and
handsome face—
and each one, as he drew near, gave him another
blow.

. . .

Achilles had in mind all manner of foul
treatments for noble
Hector's body. He pierced the tendons behind his
feet, from heel
to ankle, and threaded ox-hide cords through
each hole and tied them
to his chariot, letting Hector's head trail in
the dust.
Then he mounted his chariot, raised high the
stripped armor
he had won, and with a flick of the reins drove his
eager team of horses on.
They sped forward and a cloud of dust was kicked
up by
Hector's dragging corpse, his dark hair flowing.
The head that
was once so fair became covered with dirt. Thus
did Zeus
deliver him to his enemy, to be defiled in his own
land.

STUDY QUESTIONS

1. How is the theme of "anger," displayed by both men and gods, developed throughout the epic?
2. How are the reasons for the Trojan War bound up in Agamemnon's need to maintain command of his troops?

3.3 THE BEGINNING OF HISTORICAL WRITING: HERODOTUS AND THUCYDIDES

HERODOTUS, *THE PERSIAN WARS*

Herodotus (484–423 BCE) is commonly regarded as the first historian in the Western tradition, in the sense that he did not simply compile lists of deeds performed by people but created an interpretive prose narrative that pointed to causes and consequences. To write his history of the wars between the Greeks and Persians, he traveled throughout Greece, Asia Minor, the Holy Land, and Egypt, interviewing people as he went and examining cultural norms and both geographical and economic conditions. It is not too much to call him an ethnographer as well as a historian. Below is the opening of his work.

I, Herodotus of Halicarnassus, here present my researches so that the great deeds of mankind will not be forgotten. May such wonderful and glorious deeds—some performed by the Greeks, others by the barbarians—not go unsung, and neither the various causes that led them to make war upon each other.

Persian chroniclers insist that it was the Phoenicians who caused their strife, for when those Phoenicians moved from their home near the Red Sea and settled in the lands they currently inhabit, they immediately began to undertake long voyages carrying cargo from Egypt and Assyria and bringing it to other places, including our own Argos.

At that time, Argos surpassed in every way every other town in the land we call Greece, and when the Phoenicians arrived there they put all their cargo up for sale. Only five or six days later they had sold almost everything they had brought with them. But at that point the king's daughter came down to the coast, accompanied by many other women. Her name was Io (it is the same in both the Greek and Persian traditions) and she was the daughter of Inachus. The Argive women were standing by the stern of the ship, eyeing what was left for sale and choosing the things they liked the most, when the Phoenician sailors let out an excited shout and rushed at them. Most of the women managed to escape, but Io and some others were captured, forced on board the vessel, and carried off to Egypt.

According to the Persians, this is how Io came to Egypt. Her abduction thus began the conflict (but the Greeks tell a different story). Soon thereafter, the Persians continue, several Greeks whom they cannot name but who must have been from the island of Crete, sailed to the port of Tyre in Phoenicia and abducted that king's daughter, named Europa, thus making matters even.

But then the Greeks committed a new injustice by sailing a warship to Asia in the territory of Colchis and venturing into the river Phasis, where they pursued a particular mission and after completing it they likewise abducted the daughter of that territory's king. Her name was Medea. The king of Colchis sent a messenger to Greece in order to demand Medea's return plus compensation for her abduction, but the Greeks replied (all this is still according to the Persian version of events) that since they had received no compensation for Io's abduction by the Persians they would pay none to the Colchians.

Translation by Clifford Backman.

A generation later, apparently, King Priam of Troy's son, Alexander, heard these stories and decided that he wanted to abduct a wife from Greece for himself, assuming that he would not have to pay compensation for his crime since the Greeks had paid none for theirs. And so, he abducted Helen. The Greeks responded by demanding Helen's return and a compensatory payment, but when their messengers had stated their case they were themselves blamed for stealing Medea. How could they demand satisfaction and compensation for their loss when they had offered none for the abductions that they had committed?

Up to this point the abductions on each side had cancelled each other out, but the Persians insist that the Greeks are the ones to blame for all that came next, for they invaded Asia when the Persians had not yet taken up any arms against Europe. Their argument goes as follows: "Men who abduct women are unjust, but men who see such abductions as a cause for revenge are fools. Wise men pay no attention to such things for it is obvious that the only women abducted are those who do not resist being taken." The Persians say that they never made an issue of the women carted off from Asia, but the Greeks mustered an entire army to invade Asia on account of a single Greek woman and destroyed the kingdom of Priam. It was for that reason, they conclude, that the Persians regarded the Greeks as enemies—for the whole of Asia they regard as their own, together with all the peoples in it, but Greece and Europe they hold as entirely separate.

So much for the Persian point of view. In summary: the fall of Troy to the Greeks was the start of Persia's enmity towards them. The Phoenicians, it should be noted, disagree with the Persians regarding Princess Io. They claim that they brought her to Egypt but she came with them willingly. Moreover, they say that she slept with their own captain while they were in port at Argos, and it was her sense of shame when she discovered she was pregnant by him that she made up her mind to leave, for she did not wish to embarrass her parents.

So say the Persians and the Phoenicians. For my own part, I will not take one side or the other. I will, however, single out the one man whom I directly know committed injustice against the Greeks. Once I have done so, I will continue with my story from that point, discussing in turn the events that transpired in cities great and small. For many cities that were formerly great have since been brought low, and many of those that are great now were in earlier times low indeed. Human fates play themselves out in diverse venues, I have learned, and so I will pay attention wherever it is due.

THUCYDIDES, *THE PELOPONNESIAN WAR*

Thucydides (460–400 BCE) is the second great name in historical writing. He tells us that he recognized the importance of the Peloponnesian War as soon as the conflict began and spent twenty years conducting interviews and poring through documentary records to analyze what happened and why. His gifts of critical analysis are considerable, and he is widely considered a more incisive writer than Herodotus. His prose style is complex, highly allusive, and sometimes downright labyrinthine. Moreover, he frequently interrupts his narrative by inserting scenes entirely of his own creation—the most famous of these being Pericles's Funeral Oration, the Melian Dialogue, and the Mytilenian Debate—where he invents conversations that illustrate the attitudes that governed Athenian actions, but do not purport to reflect what was actually said at the time. The opening of his *History* is below.

Translation by Clifford Backman.

Thucydides the Athenian wrote this history of the war between the Spartans and the Athenians, and he began to work on it as soon as the war itself began, since he was convinced the war would be of more importance and of greater consequence than any conflict that came before it. This belief was well-founded. The build-up to war was thorough and extensive on both sides, and it was also clear that most of the Hellenic peoples were queueing up on one side or the other, and that those which had not yet done so were busy contemplating it. This was the greatest movement of peoples ever—not only among the Greeks but of the barbarians as well, and in fact one could even say of all human history. While one cannot speak with complete certainty about events in the deep past, nor even of those that preceded this particular war even by a little bit, for such is the nature of time, nevertheless all the evidence found in the research that it was possible to make in this case leads to the confident conclusion that nothing had ever happened on a scale that compared to this, whether one is talking about warfare or any other matter.

For it appears that the land of Greece had no settled population in ancient times. Migrations were the norm, with tribes constantly abandoning their homes in the face of other tribes who came in greater numbers. Lacking any commerce or freedom of communication by land or by sea, cultivating only as much of the land as provided bare subsistence, having no capital, never bringing their fields under the plow (since they could never be confident that some invader would come by and steal everything they had), and believing that the needs of daily life could be as easily found elsewhere, they cared little about having to move about, and as a result they built many cities or fortifications. The most fertile lands were subject to the most frequent changes of inhabitants; specifically, the regions now called Thessaly, Boeotia, the Peloponnese (most of it anyways, excepting Arcadia), and several other sites across Greece. The fertility of these places favored the concentration of wealth among only a small number of people, which in turn led to factionalism (the cause of much ruin) and further invasions. This is why the region called Attica never experienced a change of inhabitants: the poor quality of its soil meant that from earliest times it was free from factionalism. This is the proof for my claim that constant migration was the principal cause of the lack of development throughout the other regions: namely, that the strongest refugees from war or factionalism throughout Greece took refuge with the Athenians from very early times. The already large population of the city thus grew to such an extent that Attica could not hold them all, and thus they sent out colonies to Ionia.

Another point in favor of my assertion that ancient times were a period of great weakness is the fact that there is no sign of any common action among all the peoples of Greece prior to the Trojan War. Indeed, there was not even a common name for the land until the time of Hellenos, the son of Deucalion. Prior to this, the land simply went by the names of the various tribes, especially of the Pelasgians. It was not until Hellenos and his sons came to power in Phthiotis and were welcomed as allies in other sites that the peoples gradually took on the common name of Hellenes. Even so, it took a long time for the name to be adopted by all. Homer, who was born long after the Trojan War, bears witness to this, for he never refers to the whole mass of Greek soldiers as Hellenes. Indeed, he reserves the word for the troops under the command of Achilles, from Phthiotis—the original Hellenes. Throughout his poems he identifies the whole Greek side as *Danaans*, *Argives*, and *Achaeans*; nor does he ever use the term *barbarian*. (This is probably because the peoples had not yet been thought of by others as a distinctive whole.) Thus it was that, prior to the Trojan War, the Hellenic peoples—not only those who first adopted the name, one after another, but also those who came to it later—were too weak and too disparate to undertake any action in common.

It was not until they had acquired familiarity with the sea that they could have undertaken a joint expedition like the War. The first person we know to have possessed a fleet, according to tradition, was Minos. He ruled over the Hellenic Sea, including the Cyclades, where he expelled the Carians, established the first colonies, and set up his sons as governors. He did all he could to put down the piracy rampant in those waters—something he had to do in order to secure revenues for himself.

From earliest times both the Hellenes and the barbarians living along the coast or on the islands were drawn to piracy, the more so as maritime trade increased. Under strong leaders, and motivated as much by greed as a desire to help the needy, they would attack unfortified towns, some of which were mere villages, and plunder them. For many, this became their principal livelihood and a cause for renown, since there was no disgrace associated with it. One sees this even now, in the honor that some people pay to successful pirates. Our ancient poets frequently depict people openly inquiring whether certain voyagers might be pirates—as if no one would ever be insulted by such a question or reproach the questioners for asking it. The same sort of marauding took place on land, too. Many people in Greece carry on the tradition even today—the Ozolian Locrians, for example, and the Aetolians and Acarnanans. People in those parts still follow the custom of always carrying arms, a holdover from piratical habits.

At one time, all the Hellenes carried arms since their homes were unprotected and their contacts with outsiders unsafe. Indeed, carrying a weapon was as much an aspect of everyday life for them as it was for the barbarians. The fact that people in some parts of Greece still follow the ancient customs bears witness to the idea that at one time this way of life was common to all.

Now the Athenians were the first to set aside their weapons and to pursue a more peaceful and pleasurable way of life. Until fairly recently, the elderly rich among them still wore linen tunics and bound their coiled hair with golden pins in the shape of grasshoppers. This fashion, in fact, spread to their kindred in Ionia and long prevailed among the elderly there, too. In contrast, a modest style of dress that is more to the taste of today appeared first among the Spartans, among whom the wealthy tried to adopt the ways of the common people. The Spartans were also the ones who began the practice of wrestling and performing gymnastics with naked, oiled bodies. In the past, athletes wore belted codpieces, even in the Olympic Games, but the practice has since died out. It continues among some of the barbarians, though, especially in Asia, at their boxing and wrestling matches. There are many other commonalities between the customs of the ancient Hellenes and the barbarians of today.

STUDY QUESTIONS

1. What is similar and what is dissimilar in the way Herodotus and Thucydides approach historical writing? Which style has greater appeal for you? Why?
2. If Herodotus and Thucydides were alive, how would they respond to the way historians write today? How would they critique *The Cultures of the West*?

3.4 HERODOTUS ON THE EGYPTIANS, FROM *HISTORIES*, ca. 450–420 BCE

The Greek writer Herodotus (ca. 484–425 BCE) is known as the Father of History. His nine-volume account of four Persian kings is the first major extant work to display a critical use of varied sources, categorized information, and a narrative that supports his historical argument even as it spins off into digressions. Herodotus's major claim is that the Persian method of expansion and conquest ultimately spelled its end in Greece, following the Greek and Persian wars (499–449 BCE). In this passage from Book Two of his *Histories*, Herodotus illustrates his method of ethnographic research. He uses the oral testimony of Egyptian scholars he has met, together with etymological evidence, to posit the ancient origins of groups like the Hebrews.

I am convinced that the names of almost all the Greek gods come from Egypt, for my investigations clearly show that the names are foreign and almost certainly from Egypt because the Egyptians have had gods with the same names ever since their country began. There are exceptions: Poseidon and Dioscuroi, for example, whom I discussed earlier, also Hera, Hestia, the Charites and the Nereïds. I report only what the Egyptians themselves think. As for our gods whose names they do not know, I believe these came from the Pelasgian—again with the exception of Poseidon, about whom the Greeks learned from the Libyans. Only the Libyans have known the name Poseidon and have paid it due honor from the start of their history. It is worth mentioning that the Egyptians do not share our custom of worshipping heroes.

So there are religious customs (plus some other matters that I will get to) that the Greeks certainly adopted from the Egyptians; but other rites have come to us not from the Egyptians but from the Pelasgians—such as making images of Hermes with a phallus. The Athenians were the first Greeks to pick up this custom and they spread it to the rest. Just when the Athenians took a leading role among all the Greeks, the Pelasgians began to dwell in their land; in fact, this is how the Pelasgians came to be regarded as Greeks themselves. Any man who has been initiated in the sacred mysteries of the Cabeiroi—which the people of Samothrace perform, having learned the rites from the Pelasgians—knows what I mean, for the same Pelasgians who lived among the Athenians had previously lived in Samothrace. The Samothracians learned the rites from them. Thus the Athenians were the first Greeks to make images of Hermes with a phallus: they learned it from the Pelasgians, who embellished the practice with a sacred legend that was itself adopted into the sacred rites in Samothrace.

According to what I heard at Dodona, these Pelasgians originally would offer prayers and sacrifices to all their deities without distinguishing between them either by name or title, on the assumption that they had all played a role in creation and all shared in the offerings presented to them. Much later, however, they learned the names of all the gods from the Egyptians. All the gods, that is, except Dionysius, whose name they never heard until much later. At some point they consulted the oracle at Dodona about the names of the gods (Dodona being the most ancient of all Greek oracles and at that time the only one), and they asked whether or not they should adopt the names they had learned from

Translation by Clifford Backman.

non-Greeks. The oracle replied that they should do so, and from that time on the Pelasgians performed all their sacrifices using the names, which is how the Greeks came to know them.

About other matters, though—such as how the various gods and goddesses were born, or whether they were all in existence from the very beginning, and what each of them looked like—the Greeks knew nothing until quite recently. It seems to have been, in fact, only since yesterday or the day before, for the poets Hesiod and Homer, who lived no more than four hundred years before my time, were the ones who described the gods' births, gave them titles, associated each with specific qualities and arts, and described their appearance. Other poets [who described such things] who are said to have lived before Hesiod and Homer actually came after them, in my opinion. The priestesses at Dodona passed on all the knowledge I alluded to first, but the ideas about Hesiod and Homer are my own.

In Egypt I heard the following account of the Greek and Libyan oracles. Several priests of the temple to Zeus at Thebes reported that two of their priestesses had been captured and carried off by some Phoenicians, and they had heard that one was sold as a slave in Libya, the other as a slave to some Greeks. These were reportedly the very women who established the oracles I referred to above. When I asked how the Egyptians had learned all of this, they answered that the Theban priests had searched far and wide for the two women, but to no avail. Soon afterward, however, the Egyptians began to hear stories of the two oracles.

I first heard from the priests at Thebes, and the priestesses at Dodona confirmed it, that two black doves flew from Thebes to Egypt; one landed ultimately in Libya but the other returned to Thebes, where it landed in an oak tree and began to speak in human language. It said that a temple to Zeus was to be built on the site, and the people of Thebes reckoned that it was the gods speaking through the bird, and so they built the temple. The dove that flew to Libya, they say, told the Libyans to build a temple to Ammon, which is also Zeus' temple. Three priestesses of Dodona told me all of this: Promeneia was the eldest, Timarete came next, and the youngest being Nicandra. But several others who worked at the temple confirmed their account.

I have an opinion of my own, however. If the Phoenicians did actually abduct the priestesses and sold them, as the story goes, one in Libya and the other in Greece (which in earlier times was called Pelasgia) must have been sold to the group known as the Thesprotians. Enslaved among that group, she must then have built a temple to Zeus under an actual oak tree. It would only be natural for her, a priestess of Zeus' temple at Thebes, to have brought the cult of Zeus to this new place. Later, once she had learned to speak Greek, she established an oracle, I am guessing, and spread the tale of her sister's enslavement in Libya by the same Phoenicians who had sold her.

More than that, I suspect the people of Dodona called these women "doves" because they were non-Greeks and therefore their speech sounded to them like birdsong. "After some time they spoke with human speech," they said; what else could this mean but that they learned to speak the language the others could understand? A non-Greek tongue sounded to them like birdsong—for really, who ever heard of a bird with human speech? And when they say that the doves were black, they mean only that the women were Egyptian. It is simply a coincidence that the way that oracles speak in Thebes, in Egypt, and at Dodona are similar—same thing for the method of divination.

It is also true that the Egyptians were the first people to establish solemn gatherings who would then process in order and approach their temples. The Greeks learned the practice from them. My evidence: the simple fact that the Egyptians have done this forever, whereas we Greeks have only just begun the practice.

The Egyptians hold solemn assemblies frequently—not just once a year. The assemblies with the greatest energy and excitement are those at the city of Bubastis, for the goddess Artemis, and at Busiris, for Isis. In Busiris, in fact, there stands an enormous temple to Isis. Busiris is in the middle of the Egyptian Delta, and "Isis" is the same as the Greek "Demeter." They also hold a sacred assembly at Saïs for the goddess Athena; another at Heliopolis for Helios, the Sun; yet another at Buto in honor of Leto; and still another at Papremis in honor of Ares.

STUDY QUESTIONS

1. How is Herodotus applying a rational framework to the various stories he has heard?
2. In his opening paragraph Herodotus claims that he is writing history to preserve the "great deeds/wonders (ta thaumata, in Greek)" displayed by "both the Hellenes and the barbarians." Does his analysis primarily display Greek cultural curiosity or cultural chauvinism?

3.5 THUCYDIDES, *PELOPONNESIAN WAR,* CA. 500–450 BCE

Thucydides (ca. 460–395 BCE) has been credited with holding Greek historical work to a more scientific standard—divorcing it further from myth as a historical source and retaining a strictly chronological arrangement. His great eight-volume work details the war (431–404 BCE) between Sparta, the polis of military rigor, and Athens, the polis of democracy and philosophy, as well as their allied coalitions. This selection recounts the speech made by the Athenian general Pericles (ca. 495–429 BCE) in honor of the dead from the first year of the Peloponnesian War. Consider how Pericles attempts to renew the spirits of those who mourn fallen Greeks.

During that same winter, and following long-established custom, the people of Athens held a public funeral for the first men to die in the war. This is how the ceremony goes.

Several days before the service they put up a tent in which they lay out the bones of the fallen. This way anyone can bring whatever offerings they like to their own dead. On the day of the funeral they bring in, on wagons, coffins made of cypress (there is a separate coffin for each tribe); then they place the bones in their respective coffins. A single empty bier, suitably adorned, represents all the dead whose bodies have not been found or recovered. Any one who wishes to join the procession may do so, whether foreigner or native, and the women of the dead men's families also attend the funerals and mourn at the gravesites. The burials take place in the public cemetery, which is located in the most beautiful suburbs of the city, where they always bury their war-dead. The only exceptions are those who died in the battle of Marathon, whose extraordinary bravery was thought to deserve burial on the field where they fell.

When the coffins have been laid in the earth, a man chosen by the city for his discernment and high reputation delivers a fitting eulogy, and afterwards everyone departs. This, in sum, is how they performed their funerals, and the custom was followed whenever possible throughout the war.

[Editor's note: Pericles was chosen to deliver the eulogy at the first state funeral after the start of the war with Sparta.]

"Before I speak in praise of the dead, let me recount the basic principles by which our community lives and which have made us what we are; and

Translation by Clifford Backman.

recount also the institutions and qualities that have raised us to greatness. For I think the subject is fitting on the present occasion; moreover, this entire assembly, both foreigners and natives, may gain some benefit from the telling.

"Our ways are not like those of our neighbors. We don't copy others, but are an example to them. Our form of government is called a democracy, for we serve the interest of the many, not the few. While our laws give equal rights to all in private disputes, public preferment recognizes individual distinction. Pride of place in public service thus depends on merit rather than rotation. As for poverty—it is no bar to office. Any man who has the ability, no matter how lowly his rank, can do the city some good. We conduct our public affairs freely and in the open, and we do not judge one another in our private lives. We are not angered when a neighbor pursues his private pleasures, nor do we glare in disapproval (which is a harmless thing, perhaps, but a painful one in its own way). We are obliging in our private doings and we obey the law in our public ones, since fear of offending either our authorities or our laws keeps us from doing wrong. We especially respect the laws that protect the injured, as well as those unspoken laws the breaking of which brings disgrace. . . .

"We value beauty without extravagance, and intellect without loss of manly vigor. We value wealth for the uses to which it can be put, not for show or boasting. We find no disgrace in poverty, only in the failure to avoid it. Our political leaders manage state business as well as their domestic affairs, and even those who are kept busy making a living know something about politics. If a man has no interest at all in public affairs, we alone call his life not quiet but useless. If we are not all involved in creating policy, we are at least good judges of it. We believe action is not hampered by discussion itself but by the failure to discuss policies thoroughly before any action is taken. We differ from other people by our combination of deliberation and action; to others, their blindness results from their ignorance, and they regard discussion as hesitation. True strength of spirit resides in those who have the clearest understanding of life's joys and sorrows, and do not on that account shrink from any danger. . . .

"To sum up, I say that our city, taken all in all, is the teacher of all Greece. Every last one of us seems capable of combining the self-reliance necessary to enjoy life and the ability to adapt with grace and ease to every challenge life presents to us. This is not empty boasting but a verifiable fact, proven by the power our city has won by our character. Athens, alone among today's states, is greater than its reputation; only her enemies, and no one else's, are not ashamed to have suffered defeat at her hands. None of her subjects can complain of being ruled by an undeserving master. Our greatness does not lack for witnesses—there are countless monuments to our power that will make us the wonder of current and future generations. We need no Homer to sing our praises, nor any poet whose fine words will please for a while, only later to fall victim to historical truth. The simple fact is that we have forced open every sea-lane and every nation to our daring and have planted everywhere permanent memorials to our triumphs and failures.

"This, then, is the city for which these men fought and died in their noble determination not to lose. All we who survive should gladly suffer likewise in her service. . . .

"When you consider her greatness, bear in mind that it was the handiwork of valiant men who knew their duty and took pride in doing it, men who, if they ever failed in some enterprise refused to burden the city with a share of their ill-fortune and instead offered up their courage as the best gift they could present her with. All of them alike gave their lives for her and were rewarded with praises that never grow old and with the most worthy of all tombs—not the dust where their bodies lie, but our hearts where the memory of them lives forever and their glory is recalled on every suitable occasion. The whole earth is a tomb for famous men, whose record consists not only of words inscribed on tombstones in their native land but of the unwritten words that live in men's hearts even in foreign lands—the living memory of their spirit rather than their deeds. Strive to emulate these men, understanding full well that happiness is freedom—and that freedom results from courage. You need not fear the dangers of war. . . .

"To the surviving parents of those who lie before us I offer consolation rather than sympathy. For you know that ours is a world of constant and unpredictable change, in which the best fate that can befall us is to attain honor. We commemorate the honorable deaths of our fallen and we commend the honorable grief you now suffer—for it is a blessing indeed to enjoy a life in which honor is attained in the living of it and in the departure from it."

STUDY QUESTIONS

1. In what specific ways does Pericles see Athens as "the school for Hellas"?
2. How does Pericles argue that Athens's cultural achievements result from its democratic political system?

CHAPTER 4

THE CLASSICAL AND HELLENISTIC AGES

4.1 AESCHYLUS, *PROMETHEUS BOUND,* UNDATED; 500–400 BCE

This drama is attributed to Aeschylus (ca. 525–456 BCE), often called the Father of Tragedy. It lyricizes the plight of Prometheus, a Titan, who has been chained to a rock face above the sea, exposed to the elements. Zeus punishes Prometheus for the crime of stealing firebrands from the gods to bring fire—and with it, industry, skill, and enlightenment—to humankind. Prometheus's monologue glorifies and, in a way, justifies his actions. It also enables us to understand what the gods had to fear from Prometheus's disobedience and why the character of "Fire-Bearer" intrigues us to this day.

[PROMETHEUS SPEAKS]

Don't think my silence is the result of pride or a
  stand-offish nature!
My heart is brokenly bitter at the outrageous
  treatment I have received.
As for these new gods and their attributes—who
  gave them to them, if not I?
But I'll hold my tongue; no point in my saying
  what you already know.
Listen instead to what I have to say about human
  suffering.
They were mere children before I gave them
Minds of their own and the ability to think! I say
  this now

Not in order to reproach them but to explain
  what led me
To gift them so.
When they first looked around, they looked in
  vain;
When listening, they did not truly hear.
  They were
Like figures in a dream and lived out their lives
Comprehending nothing. They did not know
How to raise brick-walled houses to protect
  themselves
Against the sun, or how to build with wood.
They just scurried about, in dark and dreary caves,
Living underground like ants.

Translation by Clifford Backman.

They could not grasp the concepts of winter, or of
Springtime in full flower, or of fruitful summer.
No—they just labored on, without a clue,
Until I showed them the risings and the settings
Of the far-off stars.
There's more: that greatest of tools—writing!—
I gave to them. Writing! The boon to memory and
The mother of all arts. And it was I who
Domesticated wild animals for them, taming the
    beasts
To accept harness and saddle, to slave in packs,
    and relieve
Humans of their heaviest labors.
It was I who tamed horses to pull chariots—one
    of the Delights of prosperity—and none other
    than I
Who discovered how men might be sailors,
    roaming
Over the seas with wings of linen.
But now I am wretched—I, who invented such
    devices
For mankind, am helpless to get myself out of this
Miserable state I'm in.
Chorus: Your punishment is indeed shameful.
    Thus driven mad,
You're like a poorly skilled doctor who has fallen
    sick—
Despairing and unable to know the medicine that
    will cure you.
Prometheus: When you hear the rest you'll be
    even more amazed
At the clever skills and arts I contrived.
Greatest of all: if someone great fell ill and there
    was
No remedy that could be eaten or drunk, or
    applied as an ointment,

And because of this the victim wasted away—I
    showed men
How to blend soothing remedies that protect
    them
Against all diseases.
I determined how to prophesy, how to interpret
One's dreams after waking, how to read omens in
    off-hand
Comments and in things briefly glimpsed.
I taught them how to read signs in the
    flock-flights
Of taloned birds—which patterns are auspicious,
    and which ones
Foretell of bad news. I taught them too what these
    portents meant
For the various aspects of their lives—their loves
    and hatreds,
And their matings.
I taught them how to read the entrails [of
    sacrificed animals]—
The smoothness and color a gall-bladder must
    have in order
To satisfy the gods, or the required shape of a
    liver, or how
To roast bones with the thighs wrapped in fat.
Thus I taught them divination, the difficult art
Of augury by fire, which had been kept from
    them for so long.
All these things and more I gave, including
Iron, bronze, gold, and silver—all the buried
    blessings of mankind.
Who, other than I, can claim to have bestowed all
    of these?
No one except a lying braggart.
Here is my whole tale in a single phrase:
Prometheus founded all the arts of humankind.

STUDY QUESTIONS

1. In what specific and general ways does Prometheus claim to have benefited humankind?
2. Why was he punished for this assistance by the other gods?

4.2 PLATO, *SYMPOSIUM*, 385–380 BCE

Plato (ca. 424–ca. 348 BCE), a student of the famed dialectician Socrates and teacher of Aristotle, is a crucial link in the development of the Western intellectual chain—redefining philosophy, rhetoric, logic, ethics, and other disciplines according to his idea that the material world is a mere copy of a perfect spiritual world. This text consists of the dialogue that occurred at a drinking party where each character must deliver a speech in praise of Love. Alcibiades—who drunkenly appears mid-text—delivers a speech on his lover Socrates, who is present at the party. Alcibiades draws a distinction between the value of a gorgeous exterior (such as his own) and that of inner brilliance (as that of Socrates).

Suddenly there was a large noise: a large group of people, all of them drunk, jostled the outer door; in the background was a flute-girl they had brought with them. Agathon then shouted to his servants, "Go see who it is. If it's any friends of ours, show them in; if not, tell them the party's over and we're going to bed."

A moment later the voice of Alcibiades—very drunk, very loud—could be heard in the courtyard, wanting to know where Agathon was and demanding to be brought to him. He was half-carried into the house by the flute-girl and some others, but once they got him to the doorway he managed to stand by himself, crowned with an impressive wreath made of ivy and violets from which several ribbons hung down around his head. Alcibiades called out, "Good evening, gentlemen! I'm plastered, but may I join your party? If you say No, then I'll just place my wreath on young Agathon here and leave. That's all I came here to do, anyway. I couldn't make it to the celebration yesterday, but now I'm here to remove this wreath from my own head and put it on Agathon's—such a cute and clever little guy! Oh! You laugh at me because I'm drunk? That's OK, go ahead. But you know I'm right! So tell me, now that you know why I'm here, can I stay? Have a little drink with me?"

Everyone called out and begged him to come in and join us. Agathon asked him to sit right next to him, and so, with a little help from his friends, Alcibiades joined Agathon. He tried to take off his wreath and give it to Agathon but the ribbons were caught in his hair and the whole thing covered his eyes, so he couldn't see that Socrates had made room for him as soon as he had entered. So Alcibiades ended up sitting between Socrates and Agathon. As soon as he was settled, he threw his arms around Agathon, kissed him, and managed to get the wreath on his head.

Agathon ordered his servants to take off Alcibiades' sandals. "Put your feet up! There's room for three on my couch."

"Wonderful idea," replied Alcibiades, "but who's the third?" And turning around as he spoke, he saw Socrates. "Good Lord!" he cried, jumping to his feet. "Socrates! You cornered me again! Always when I least expect it. So, what do you want now, Socrates? How did you just happen to be on this couch, eh? Why aren't you with Aristophanes or someone else we could tease you about? How did you just happen to end up next to the cutest guy in the room?"

"Agathon, protect me!" called Socrates. "You've no idea what it's like to be in love with this man. I fell for him the first time I laid eyes on him—and now he won't let me have two words with another man! And not even two words! If I even look at an attractive

Translation by Clifford Backman.

man he goes crazy with jealousy. He screams and shouts and seems like he's ready to slap me around. Please get him under control and tell him to forgive me [for lying next to Agathon]. You'll have to rescue me, if he gets violent. Really, his passion for me is terrifying!"

"I swear I'll never forgive you," cried Alcibiades, "You'll pay for this!" Then he turned to Agathon and said, "But just for now let me have a few of these ribbons, and I'll make a wreath for him too since he has such a lovely old head. Otherwise he'll make a scene and bitch that I made a crown for you, Agathon, for your first victory, but never made one for him despite the fact that he's never lost an argument in his life."

Alcibiades then took a few ribbons and draped them over Socrates' head, then lay back on the couch. Then he suddenly leapt back up again. "Come, come, everyone—you all look entirely too sober, and I won't stand for it. Everyone have a drink! Now, do you remember our agreement? We must have a Master of Ceremonies! But who should that be, I wonder? Until one of you is drunk enough for the job, I appoint myself. Agathon, I want the biggest drinking cup you've got. No, never mind that—tell your servant to bring *that* over here."

He had seen the cooling jar, which he reckoned could hold more than two quarts. He had the servants fill it to the brim with wine, and he drank it all right down. Then he told them to fill it again, but this time for Socrates.

"Not that it'll do any good," said Alcibiades. "We all know, friends, that Socrates will drink anything set in front of him, but none of us has ever seen him drunk."

The servant filled the jar for Socrates, and as he was drinking it Eryximachus called to Alcibiades, "This isn't right! We're not here simply to pour the wine down our throats in silence! Let's have some conversation, or some singing! What you're doing isn't acceptable."

"Ah, Eryximachus," answered Alcibiades, "best of sons of the best and soberest of fathers! How are you?"

"I'm well, thank you," Eryximachus said. "Now, how shall we entertain ourselves?"

"However you like!" said Alcibiades, "I'm yours to command. 'One physician is worth a million men.'[1] Prescribe for us what you think is best."

"Listen to this, then," said Eryximachus. "Earlier we decided to spend the evening with each of us, going from left to right, giving the best speech he could in praise of Love. Now, we've all had our say, so you should go next. You certainly have had your share to drink; now that your cup's empty, it's your turn. Once you finish, then you're free to choose a new topic for Socrates, on your right, and when he's done we'll all go round the circle again."

"A splendid idea, Eryximachus! But is it fair to compare the speech of a drunkard with the speeches of men who are still sober? Besides, my friend, you don't really believe a word of what Socrates said just now? The opposite is true! If I ever dare to praise another man—even a god!—in front of him, Socrates lights into me."

"Hold your tongue," warned Socrates.

"Oh, don't try to deny it," shouted Alcibiades. "No! I refuse to speak in praise of anyone in front of Socrates *except* Socrates."

"Well then, go ahead. Do as you wish, and give us a speech in praise of Socrates," said Eryximachus.

"Do you really think I should? Really? Should I just let loose and give him his just desserts in front of everyone?"

"Now wait one minute," interrupted Socrates. "What are you thinking of doing? Mock me with your 'song of praise'?"

"I promise to say nothing but the truth. Is that OK?"

"I'm all in favor of hearing the truth, even from you. Go right ahead," said Socrates.

"All right, I will," said Alcibiades. "But here's what you can do: If I say anything that's not true, stop me and call me a liar. I may make mistakes, but I won't intentionally lie. But don't get upset if I get confused and put things in the wrong order; I shall say things as they come to me. But be patient—even someone who wasn't drunk would find it difficult to describe your extraordinary self.

---

[1] *Iliad* 11.514.

"Friends, I speak in praise of Socrates! But I find I must use images to do so. You and he may think I am doing this to make fun of him, but that isn't so. I am merely aiming at truth.

"Look, doesn't he resemble one of those statues of Silenus you find in so many shops? The kind where he's sitting and holding his pipe or flute, but he's hollow—and when you open him up he's filled with tiny little statues of various gods.

"Look again, doesn't he resemble Marsyas the satyr? Now hold on, Socrates! Even you can't deny that you look just like them. In outer appearance, at least. But you resemble them in other ways too, as you're about to hear.

"For starters, you're a vile, impudent bully. Don't deny it—I'll bring in witnesses if need be. And although you don't play the flute you're quite the player, greater even than Marsyas, who needed an instrument in order to cast spells on others. (So too do any others who play his tunes. Even Olympus played Marsyas' tunes—he learned them directly from him.) No matter who plays his music, from the greatest musician to the simplest flute-girl, his melodies are divine and have the power to cast a spell over men and prepare them to encounter the god and his mysteries. And Socrates, the only difference between you and Marsyas is that you don't need instruments, but can cast your spells by using words alone. Most people hardly ever pay real attention to a speech-giver, even to the greatest orators, but let anyone—man, woman, or child—listen to you speak, or even to a second-hand account of what you've said, and he is both enchanted and possessed.

"If I were to describe the effect his words always have on me, you'd think I'm drunk! I can feel his power even now, even though I'm the one speaking. But I swear to you, whenever he starts to speak my heart races in my chest, tears stream down my cheeks, and I'm a goner. Even the crazy Corybantes seem sane, compared to me, and I'm not the only one.[2] I've listened admiringly to many great orators, including Pericles, but none of them has ever had this effect on me; none has ever touched me so deeply that I began to wonder if my life was any better than that of a wretched slave. Yet that's exactly how this 'Marsyas' here to my right makes me feel all the time—like my life isn't worth living. No, you can't say this isn't true, Socrates! I have no doubt you could have that exact effect on me at this moment, if I gave you the chance. He traps me into thinking that my life in politics is a waste of time, and that the only things that matter are the things I care least about: namely, my faults, which he says need immediate attention. So I refuse to listen to him. He is like a Siren whose call could hold me captive forever.

"He is the only man in the world who makes me feel ashamed of myself. Surprised to hear I'm capable of that? It's true. I know I'm powerless to prove him wrong, whenever he tells me how I ought to live; but as soon as I'm on my own again, I go right back to my vices. That's why my life has become one long struggle to get away and keep away from him! When I run into him again, I instantly feel ashamed of myself again, for I know I've done nothing to better myself even though I promised him I would. Sometimes I think I'd be happier if he were dead. It's true! But I know that if he were to die I would feel even worse. So you see, I can't live with him or without him. What's left to do, therefore?

"That is the effect his satyr's music has on me, and not only on me. Lots of others. So he is like a satyr, and in all kinds of ways. Let me tell you about his powers because they are truly extraordinary. I assure you, none of you understands the truth about him the way I do.

"Since I've started on the topic, let me tell you the truth about him. First of all, he's crazy for pretty boys and stalks them relentlessly, like he's in a trance. Second, he's always saying that he's an ignoramus, one who knows absolutely nothing. Just like Silenus, right? And this is just scratching the surface! Fellow drinkers, I wonder if you have any idea how sober and cautious a man he is on the inside? It turns out, he really doesn't care whether or not a boy is pretty. He doesn't care a bit whether someone is rich, or beautiful, or famous, or any of the things that most people admire. In truth, he regards all these things as beneath contempt, and I'm telling you he feels the same

---

[2] The Corybantes were fanatical worshippers in the cult of Cybele, known for dancing and chanting themselves into a frenzy.

way about us. His whole public life is a sham, one big game of pretending. I doubt if anyone here has ever seen him when he's really serious. One time, though, let me tell you, I caught him when he was opened up like one of those Silenus statues and I saw the small godlike treasures he keeps hidden inside. They were so beautiful, so precious, so amazing, that I lost my will entirely and had to do whatever he asked of me.

"At the time I thought what he wanted most of all was me. What an opportunity! Because I was so confident in my good looks, I really believed that if I simply let him have his way with me, he would teach me everything he knew. He and I had never been alone together, at that point, since I always had one or two of my attendants with me. So I dismissed my attendant and went to meet Socrates alone.

"Now everyone pay close attention, because I want only to say what's true. So if I make a mistake, Socrates, please correct me.

"There I was, at last, alone with him. I assumed that he would start by saying to me whatever words lovers use when they find themselves alone together, and I was enjoying the moment—but then, nothing. Nothing happened at all. Socrates just started talking to me the way he always had done, and at the end of the day he left.

"My next idea was to invite him to come with me to the gymnasium. We exercised together for a while—and I was certain that that would lead to something, especially when no one was around—but he just wrestled with me a few times, nothing more. What else can I say? Nothing happened.

"When I finally admitted to myself that my little plan had failed, I decided on a full-frontal assault. No way was I going to withdraw from a battle that I had begun myself! I needed to know just what was going on between us, and so I invited him to dinner—switching roles, as though I was the pursuer and he was the pursued. Now, it took some time before he accepted my invitation, but one day he finally came. He left soon after eating, that first time, and I was too timid to try to stop him, but on our second time I introduced a new conversation topic just as we were finishing our meal—and that kept him talking well into the night. At a certain point he said he needed to get going, but I, using the lateness of the hour as

an excuse, persuaded him to spend the night at my house. He laid back down on the couch he had used for eating, the one right next to mine. We were alone.

"So far, you must admit, my story has been rather proper, one I could tell in any company. Were it not for the truth of an old adage, however—'There is truth in wine, once the servants leave'—you would never have heard the rest of the tale, as I'm about to tell you right now. After all, it wouldn't be fair to Socrates if in offering him a 'song of praise' I failed to mention one of his proudest achievements. Well, then. Have you heard the old saying about snakebites—that once you've received one you'll only talk about it with someone else who's received one, for no one else could understand the pain and how you reacted to it? Let me tell you, what happened to me next hurt more than if a snake has bitten me in my most sensitive organ: my heart! Or maybe my soul, or whatever you call it. Anyway, it was struck and bitten by philosophy. Philosophy, whose grip on the young is as relentless and vicious as a viper's, and makes them do the most remarkable things. Everyone here—you Phaedrus, you Agathon, Eryximachus, Pausanias, Aristodemus, and Aristophanes (I don't need to mention Socrates himself)—all of you have experienced the Bacchic madness of philosophy, and that's why you're entitled to hear the rest of my tale. I know all of you will understand and forgive me for what I did then, and admit now. As for you servants, and for anyone else who overhears me: shut your ears! This tale is not for you!

"So there we were. The lights were put out, the servants had gone. It was the perfect moment, I thought, to speak out and tell him openly what I had in mind. So I shook him, and whispered, 'Socrates, are you asleep?'

"'Not in the least,' he answered.

"'Do you know what I'm thinking?'

"'No, not really.'

"I said, 'You're the only deserving lover I've ever had, but you're so shy! Now here's what I think. I'd be a fool not to give you anything you wanted. You can have me. You can have all that I own. You can even have whatever my friends own! For nothing is so important to me as becoming the best man I can possibly be, and no one can help me achieve that better than you. Given who and what you are—why, I'd be more embarrassed by what some smart people would say if I *didn't* take you as my lover than I would be by what some idiots would say if I *did*.'

"Socrates listened carefully, then replied in that unmistakably ironic tone of his. 'My dear Alcibiades,' he said, 'if everything you say about me is true, then you've already achieved more than you realize. For if it's true that I really could make you a better man, then you must see in me a beauty that is beyond words, one that makes your own handsomeness pale in comparison. So, tell me. Is this really a fair trade you're proposing? You desire more of me than it seems you're entitled to; for you are offering me the mere appearance of beauty in return for the real thing, "like trading gold for bronze."[3] You should think again, my dear boy, for you may be wrong. I might be of no use to you whatsoever. The mind sees most sharply only after our eyes have grown weak with age—and you have a long way to go before you reach that age.'

"When I heard him say all of this, I replied, 'There's nothing more I can say. I've told you exactly what I think. Now it's up to you to say what you think is best, in our mutual interest.'

"'You're right,' Socrates said, 'From this moment on, let's always think as a team. That way we'll always do what is best for both of us.'

"And so, thinking that my words had hit their target and that Socrates was struck by my arrows, I didn't want to give him another chance to start talking, so I jumped to my feet and spread my blanket over him. (It was the middle of winter—but still that's all the clothing he wore!) Then I slipped under the covers and put my arms around this amazing one-of-a-kind man, and spent the night next to him. Socrates, you can't deny a word of this! Despite all my efforts, this fellow turned me down. The arrogant bastard! What a rude thing to do! He rejected my beauty, of which I am so proud! So now, gentlemen of the jury (for that's what you are in this case) you may pass judgment on Socrates' arrogant and outrageous behavior. I swear by all the gods and goddesses, my

---

[3] *Iliad* 6.232–236.

night with him was as uneventful as if I had spent it with my own father or older brother. And how do you think I felt the next morning? Humiliated, of course! But even so I couldn't help but admire his character, his self-control, his resolve. Here was a man whose strength and wisdom were beyond anything I had ever imagined. How could I possibly hate him? I couldn't bear the thought of losing his friendship, but saw no way to persuade him. I knew as well as anyone that he cares even less for money than Ajax cared about what weapons his foes carried, and now the only plan I had been able to hatch to get him had failed. I didn't know what to do and saw no purpose in living any longer. This was true slavery of a kind that no other men were aware.

"Now all of this happened before Athens invaded Potidaea, where we served together in our units and shared the same tents. At first Socrates put up with the hardships of the campaign better than me, and better in fact than any soldier in our army. When our supply lines had been cut, as often happens in war, no one dealt with the lack of food better than he did—even though he is the person who most enjoys a good feast. He accepted the lack of drink too, even though whenever he wants to he can drink anyone under the table. No one in our unit, in fact, ever saw him drunk! (I'll say a bit more about this in a minute.)

. . .

"Would you like to hear what he was like in battle? He really deserves having this story told. Now, you all know that I was decorated for bravery in that battle; but did you know that in that same battle Socrates saved my life? Yes, he did! I was wounded, and he refused to leave me behind, and he rescued me and all my armor! Socrates, you know for a fact that I told the generals right there on the spot that you were the one who deserved a medal. There's no fault in what I said then or in what I say now. The generals, though, cared more about my social standing and so they gave the medal to me, but you know that you were even more excited than they were, for me to get it.

"You ought to have seen him during our miserable retreat from Delium. I rode with the cavalry, while Socrates was with the infantry. The army was scattered everywhere. Socrates was retreating with our friend Laches. By luck I saw them and shouted some words of encouragement. 'I'll never leave you behind!' and that sort of thing. Since I was on horseback I wasn't in any real danger, so I seized the opportunity to watch Socrates—something I hadn't been able to do at Potidaea. The most obvious thing of all was how calm he was, especially compared to Laches. In fact, Aristophanes, some words of yours came to my mind; you see, he was simply meandering along just like he was taking a stroll through the city—even though he was on a battlefield: 'with a conceited gait and a wandering eye.[4] There he was, observing everything, keeping his eyes out for friends and foes alike. Even at a distance I could see how brave he was and how he would put up a fight against anyone who came at him. That's what saved them both, in fact. For most people put as much distance as possible between themselves and someone like him, on a battlefield. If you want to survive, you chase the ones who run away.

. . .

"Here's something I should have mentioned earlier: Socrates' ideas and arguments, too, are just like those statues of Silenus. When you listen to him argue, everything he says strikes you as ridiculous because he uses words coarser than the hides worn by a satyr. He's always talking about pack mules or blacksmiths, cobblers or tanners; he's always pressing the same old points in the same old ways. If you are an idiot, or maybe just inexperienced, it's impossible to listen to him without laughing. But if we are then when those arguments open up like one of the statues—if you see what's behind their surface—you see right away that nothing else could possibly be true. These are ideas worthy of the gods, filled with little gems of virtue on the inside. They are of great—in fact, the greatest—value to anyone who wishes to become the best man he can be.

"So here ends my song to Socrates. I haven't avoided criticizing him too. I've told you how miserably he treated me. (And he's done the same thing to others: Charmides and Euthydemus, for starters!) He has deceived us all. First he approaches you with an interest, and before you know it you're the one who's in love with him! I'm warning you, Agathon, don't let him trick you! Remember the agony we all have experienced. Be careful. And don't be slow—like the fool in the proverb—to learn from your own mistakes."

Alcibiades' frank speech had made us all laugh like crazy, especially since it was so obvious how much he was still in love with Socrates. Socrates then replied, "Why, you're perfectly sober after all! You must be, or else you wouldn't have been able to conceal your true motive so well; but you let it slip, Alcibiades, at the very end of your speech. Your real motive all along has been to cause trouble between Agathon and me! You want me to love you and you alone—so that you and you alone can then be in love with Agathon. Well, we're not tricked; we see through your little satyr-play. Dear Agathon, let's not let him get away with it. Let no one ever come between us!"

Then Agathon said to Socrates, "You know, you're right! The proof of it is in the fact that he literally came between us here on our couch. Why would he have done that, if not to separate us? But he won't get away with it. I'm coming over to lie next to you right now."

"That's it," said Socrates, "come here and lie on this other side of me."

Alcibiades then shouted, "Dear God! You see how he makes me suffer? He kicks me when I'm down, and never relents. Come, Socrates, don't be so selfish. Let's share him. Have Agathon lie down between us."

"That can't be done," answered Socrates. "You've already delivered your 'song of praise,' so now it's my turn to praise whoever is on my right. But if Agathon were next to you, then he would give a 'song of praise' in my honor again—when in fact I want to now sing a praise to him. Come, come! Don't be so jealous! Let me sing the boy's praises."

"Oh, wonderful!" cried Agathon. "Nothing will make me stay next to you now, Alcibiades. I'm moving, and that's that. I simply have to hear what Socrates has to say about me!"

"There we go again, the same old story," said Alcibiades. "No one can get close to a really good-looking boy whenever Socrates is around! Did you notice how smoothly, how gracefully he got Agathon to lie down next to him?"

---

[4] Aristophanes, *Clouds*, line 362.

At that moment, as Agathon was changing places, a large party of drunks charged into the room and joined our party. The front gate had been left open when someone was leaving. There was noise everywhere, and everyone was drinking, but in no particular order. According to Aristodemus, a bunch of the original guests made their excuses and left: Eryximachus, Phaedrus, and a few others. Aristodemus himself fell asleep and stayed that way for a long time. (It was winter, the nights were long.) He awoke just as dawn began to break. He could hear roosters crowing, and when he looked around he saw that many others had also fallen asleep, or had simply left.

Only Agathon, Aristophanes, and Socrates were still awake, and they were still drinking out of a large cup they shared, passing it from left to right. Socrates was talking. Aristodemus couldn't remember exactly what they were discussing—he was still half-asleep and had missed the first part of the conversation anyway—but he caught on that Socrates was trying to prove to them that authors should be able to handle tragedy and comedy equally; any tragedian worth his salt should also be a comic poet. Socrates was close to finishing his argument, but in plain fact the others could hardly follow a word he was saying. They were sleepy. Aristophanes in fact had fallen asleep in the middle of Socrates' talk; and it wasn't long before Agathon too drifted off, just as day was breaking.

Once they were asleep, Socrates got up and left, with Aristodemus close behind as usual. He says that Socrates walked straight to the Lyceum, washed, and spent the entire day going about his normal business. Only when the following evening fell did he finally go home to rest.

STUDY QUESTIONS

1. How does the dialogue underscore the importance of self-control, in terms of both drink and sex?
2. Is Socrates attracted to Alcibiades's way of life? Is Alcibiades attracted to Socrates's approach?

4.3 ARISTOTLE, "ON THE ELEMENTS OF TRAGEDY" (*POETICS*, BOOK VI), CA. 335 BCE

Aristotle (384–322 BCE), student of Plato and tutor to Alexander the Great, reshaped Western philosophy by envisioning a unity among logic, physics, morality, politics, and other studies. This portion from his literary theory text *Poetics* exhibits Aristotle's classic method of deconstructing a concept into its logical, definable, building-block parts.

We will speak later of hexameter-poetry and comedy, so let us turn now to the subject of tragedy. First we must recollect all we have said earlier about it and fashion a formal definition. Tragedy is the representation of an action that is serious and of sufficient magnitude as to be complete in itself; its

From Aristotle, *Poetics*, Chapters 6 and 7. Translation by Clifford Backman.

language consists of every type of literary technique—with each technique being displayed in a discrete part of the play; its form is dramatic, not narrative; and it culminates in an emotional catharsis that transcends pity and fear. Its language incorporates rhythm, harmony, and song—and when I say its techniques are displayed in discrete parts of the play, I mean that some parts are worked out through verse alone, and other parts through song alone.

Since "the representation of tragedy" implies persons acting on a stage, two things obviously follow: first, that elements of spectacle must be part of tragedy; and second, that song and diction must be part of it as well. By "diction" I mean simply the metrical arrangement of the words. "Song," of course, is a term everyone understands.

Tragedy, to repeat, is the representation of action. But action implies agents who possess distinctive qualities of character and thought, for it is from these that we ascribe certain qualities to their actions. Character and thought are the natural causes from which all actions spring, and the success or failure of a tragedy depends on those very actions. The "plot" of a tragedy consists of the arrangement of incidents in the representation of its action. "Character," on the other hand, consists of whatever leads us to ascribe certain qualities to the play's various agents. An agent's "thought" is shown in whatever he says in proving a certain point or expressing a particular truth. Tragedy, therefore, has six distinct parts that determine its quality: plot, character, language, thought, spectacle, and song. Two of these make up the medium of the representation; one comprises the manner of representation; and the other three constitute the objects of the representation. These six elements complete the list. All six, we may confidently state, have been used by every one of our great poets. Every play, in fact, contained the elements of spectacle, character, plot, language, song, and thought.

The most important of the six elements is the arrangement of the incidents that make up the story, for tragedy is more a representation of actions and life than a representation of persons. Life consists of actions, and life's end consists of the nature of the actions we take rather than our qualities. Our character determines our qualities, but it is our actions that

make our lives happy—or the opposite. In a tragedy, therefore, people do not act in order to portray characters; they portray the characters in order to present the action. The actions that make up the plot are the whole point of tragedy, and the whole point of anything is to be what it truly is. A tragedy cannot exist without action, but it may exist without character. The tragedies of most of our [contemporary] poets are character-less; the same can be said of poets in general. The same is true in painting—just compare [the works of] Zeuxis and Polygnotus. Polygnotus depicts character very well, but the paintings of Zeuxis are devoid of it. Again: if you string together a series of speeches that depict character, no matter how much skill there is in their style and diction the series will fail to produce the true tragic effect, whereas a play that is lacking in style and diction but has a plot made of well-constructed incidents will have much more success. And by far the most powerful elements of emotional engagement in any tragedy—namely the *peripeteia* [Reversal of Fortune] and the discovery-scene—are essential elements of the plot. A further proof is the fact that novice tragedians master diction and character before they learn to construct an artful plot. This is true of almost all the early dramatists.

We insist, therefore, that plot is the first principle of a tragedy—its heart and soul, one might say. The characters come second. It is the same thing as in painting: for even the most beautiful colors, if laid out without any order or design, will not give the same pleasure as a simple black-and-white sketch of a portrait. Tragedy is the representation of action; it portrays characters only for the sake of advancing the action. Third in order is thought—the power to say whatever can be said, or whatever is appropriate to say, in a situation. In a tragedy's speeches, this is the function of politics and rhetoric. Our older dramatists made their characters speak like statesmen, while our present ones make their characters speak like rhetoricians. Character, in tragedy, is the quality that reveals a person's moral purpose—how he decides upon the things he chooses or avoids. There is no room for character, therefore, in a speech that discusses a subject to which the person is indifferent. Thought, however, is shown in everything one says in arguing for or against something, or in presenting a universal maxim. Fourth among the literary elements of tragedy is diction, by which I mean (as I explained earlier) the expression of individuals' thoughts in words. This is equally true in verse and in prose. In regard to the two remaining elements: song takes precedence over spectacle. Spectacle has undeniable emotional power but it is the least artistic of all the elements, the least poetic. The power of tragedy, after all, can be felt even apart from performance and actors; and besides, the staging of spectacle is more a matter for the set-designer than for the poet.

Now that we have defined the constituent elements of tragedy, let us turn to the proper construction of the plot—the first and most important step. We established that tragedy is a representation of an action that is complete and whole, and of a certain magnitude; whole things exist, after all, that have no magnitude at all. An action that is whole and complete has a beginning, a middle, and an end. A beginning is something that does not necessarily follow from some earlier cause, but which does have something that comes of necessity after it. An end, on the other hand, is something that necessarily follows some earlier thing but has nothing necessarily following after it. A middle, of course, is something that follows some earlier and which leads to something that comes afterward. Any well-constructed tragedy must observe these principles and cannot either begin or end haphazardly. Any beautiful thing, whether it be a living creature or an object made up of various parts, must have an order in the arrangement of its parts, and its must have a certain magnitude. Beauty is a function of order and magnitude. A tiny animal organism cannot be beautiful [to us] since our perception of it cannot help but be limited to an almost imperceptible fraction of time. An immense creature—one that is, say, a thousand miles long—also cannot be beautiful [to us] since we cannot take it all in and therefore lose any sense of its unity and wholeness. In just the same way, then, as living organisms must have a certain degree of magnitude (namely, one that permits us to see its order and wholeness), so too must a plot in a tragedy be of a certain length, one that can be held in the memory. As far as the time-limit of a play goes, that is of no concern to dramatic theory; it is just an issue for the stagers of public performances and for the spectators. At one time it was the rule that plays were timed by a water-clock, but that was because they needed to fit one hundred tragedies [into a single festival]. As far as poetic theory is concerned: the longer the drama the more beautiful it will be, provided it does not violate the perspective of magnitude. As a rule of thumb, a play that allows the tragic hero to pass through a variety of probable or necessary stages, whether from bad fortune to good or from good fortune to bad, will suffice to meet the demand for magnitude.

STUDY QUESTIONS

1. How does Aristotle approach poetic theory? How does he analyze the genre of tragedy?
2. Why, for Aristotle, is plot the most important element of a play?
3. Does Aristotle provide a reasonable explanation of the effects of watching tragedy, in your estimation?
4. How is the audience invited to identify with the tragic hero? Can you think of tragic characters, whether from ancient or more modern plays, that support Aristotle's arguments?

4.4 DIOGENES LAËRTIUS, "LIFE OF ZENO OF CITIUM," *THE LIVES AND OPINIONS OF EMINENT PHILOSOPHERS*, CA. 300–250 BCE

A biographer of the Greek philosophers, Diogenes Laërtius (third century CE) has preserved personal information about philosophers whose entire body of work has been lost. Zeno of Citium (ca. 334–ca. 262 BCE), from whose writings only disconnected fragments remain, is known as the Father of Stoicism; most of what we know about his life comes from Laërtius's account. Although his facts are occasionally unreliable, Laërtius jumps energetically from Zeno's appearance to his temper to his writings, embedding excerpts from other writers in his own account. Consider how Laërtius displays Zeno's full expression of the Stoic convictions throughout his daily life— actually living the philosophy.

Zeno was a citizen of Citium on the island of Cyprus. It was a Greek city [at that time] but had been settled originally by the Phoenicians. . . . He studied with Crates, although some sources (like Timocrates in his work *Dion*) assert that he studied also with Stilpo and Xenocrates and also with Polemo. Hecaton says (and in this he is supported by Apollonius of Tyre, in Book One of his work *On Zeno*) that Zeno, when young, consulted an oracle to find out how he could live the best sort of life, and that the divine spirit said he should join his flesh with that of the dead. Grasping the meaning of this right away, Zeno went off to read the works of the ancient writers.

This is how he met Crates. Aboard a merchant vessel sailing from Phoenicia (it had a cargo of purple dye), he was shipwrecked near Piraeus. He travelled then to Athens and sat down next to a bookseller's stall. Zeno was about thirty, at that time. He saw that the bookseller was reading Book Two of Xenophon's *Memorabilia*, a work that Zeno knew and enjoyed. He asked the bookseller where he might find people like [Socrates], and as if by fate at that very moment Crates came walking by. The bookseller pointed and said, "Follow him." From that very day Zeno studies with Crates. . . .

He use to lay out his arguments while strolling back and forth in the Stoa named after Peisanax but more commonly known as the Painted Stoa—on account of the painting made within it by Polygnotus.[1] Zeno always insisted that the space be cleared of bystanders, for during the rule of the Thirty Tyrants some 1,400 Athenians were massacred there. Nevertheless, people always came to hear him lecture there, and that is how they began to be called Stoics. . . .

Zeno always maintained that opinion was the enemy of knowledge, and that the one thing we need the most is more time. Someone once asked him to define what a friend is. His reply: "Another me." They also say that he once was beating a slave for stealing something, and when the slave cried out "But I was fated to steal!" Zeno answered "Then you were also fated to be beaten!"

---

[1] A stoa was a covered portico, usually surrounding a garden.

From Diogenes Laertius, *Lives of the Stoics*, Book 7. Translation by Clifford Backman.

STUDY QUESTIONS

1. In what ways does Zeno always appear open to new ideas?
2. Is this form of teaching, from examples and the emulation of great men, an effective one?

4.5 BOOK OF EZRA, REBUILDING THE TEMPLE, CHAPTERS 1–3 AND 5–6, WRITTEN CA. 480–420 BCE

The Book of Ezra picks up the story of the Israelites after the Babylonian Captivity (ca. 586–538 BCE), which ends when the Persian king Cyrus defeats the Babylonians and restores the Israelites to their homeland with permission to rebuild the Temple in Jerusalem. Ezra, in whose name this book is written, was a priest who has been credited with restoring the Torah and its laws to Jerusalem. This selection records King Cyrus's decree; it describes the rebuilding of the Second Temple in Jerusalem, a central spot of worship and symbol of Jewish identity that stood until its destruction by the Romans during the Jewish Revolt in 70 CE.

CHAPTER 1

¹Now in the first year of Cyrus king of Persia, that the word of the LORD by the mouth of Jeremiah might be accomplished, the LORD stirred up the spirit of Cyrus king of Persia, that he made a proclamation throughout all his kingdom, and put it also in writing, saying: ²"Thus saith Cyrus king of Persia: All the kingdoms of the earth hath the LORD, the God of heaven, given me; and He hath charged me to build Him a house in Jerusalem, which is in Judah. ³Whosoever there is among you of all His people—his God be with him—let him go up to Jerusalem, which is in Judah, and build the house of the LORD, the God of Israel, He is the God who is in Jerusalem. ⁴And whosoever is left, in any place where he sojourneth, let the men of his place help him with silver, and with gold, and with goods, and with beasts, beside the freewill-offering for the house of God which is in Jerusalem."

⁵Then rose up the heads of fathers' houses of Judah and Benjamin, and the priests, and the Levites, even all whose spirit God had stirred to go up to build the house of the LORD which is in Jerusalem. ⁶And all they that were round about them strengthened their hands with vessels of silver, with gold, with goods, and with beasts, and with precious things, beside all that was willingly offered. ⁷Also Cyrus the king brought forth the vessels of the house of the LORD, which Nebuchadnezzar had brought forth out of Jerusalem, and had put them in the house of his gods; ⁸even those did Cyrus king of Persia bring forth by

The Holy Scriptures According to the Masoretic Text: A New Translation with the Aid of Previous Versions and with Constant Consultation of Jewish Authorities.—Excerpted from Jewish Publication Society of America Version on Wikipedia, the free encyclopedia.

the hand of Mithredath the treasurer, and numbered them unto Sheshbazzar, the prince of Judah. ⁹And this is the number of them: thirty basins of gold, a thousand basins of silver, nine and twenty knives; ¹⁰thirty bowls of gold, silver bowls of a second sort four hundred and ten, and other vessels a thousand. ¹¹All the vessels of gold and of silver were five thousand and four hundred. All these did Sheshbazzar bring up, when they of the captivity were brought up from Babylon unto Jerusalem.

CHAPTER 2

. . .

⁶⁴The whole congregation together was forty and two thousand three hundred and threescore, ⁶⁵beside their men-servants and their maid-servants, of whom there were seven thousand three hundred thirty and seven; and they had two hundred singing men and singing women. ⁶⁶Their horses were seven hundred thirty and six; their mules, two hundred forty and five; ⁶⁷their camels, four hundred thirty and five; their asses, six thousand seven hundred and twenty.

⁶⁸And some of the heads of fathers' houses, when they came to the house of the LORD which is in Jerusalem, offered willingly for the house of God to set it up in its place; ⁶⁹they gave after their ability into the treasury of the work threescore and one thousand darics of gold, and five thousand pounds of silver, and one hundred priests' tunics.

⁷⁰So the priests, and the Levites, and some of the people, and the singers, and the porters, and the Nethinim, dwelt in their cities, and all Israel in their cities.

CHAPTER 3

¹And when the seventh month was come, and the children of Israel were in the cities, the people gathered themselves together as one man to Jerusalem. ²Then stood up Jeshua the son of Jozadak, and his brethren the priests, and Zerubbabel the son of Shealtiel, and his brethren, and builded the altar of the God of Israel, to offer burnt-offerings thereon, as it is written in the Law of Moses the man of God. ³And they set the altar upon its bases; for fear was upon them because of the people of the countries, and they

offered burnt-offerings thereon unto the LORD, even burnt-offerings morning and evening. ⁴And they kept the feast of tabernacles, as it is written, and offered the daily burnt-offerings by number, according to the ordinance, as the duty of every day required; ⁵and afterward the continual burnt-offering, and the offerings of the new moons, and of all the appointed seasons of the LORD that were hallowed, and of every one that willingly offered a freewill-offering unto the LORD. ⁶From the first day of the seventh month began they to offer burnt-offerings unto the LORD; but the foundation of the temple of the LORD was not yet laid. ⁷They gave money also unto the hewers, and to the carpenters; and food, and drink, and oil, unto them of Zidon, and to them of Tyre, to bring cedar-trees from Lebanon to the sea, unto Joppa, according to the grant that they had of Cyrus king of Persia.

⁸Now in the second year of their coming unto the house of God at Jerusalem, in the second month, began Zerubbabel the son of Shealtiel, and Jeshua the son of Jozadak, and the rest of their brethren the priests and the Levites, and all they that were come out of the captivity unto Jerusalem; and appointed the Levites, from twenty years old and upward, to have the oversight of the work of the house of the LORD. ⁹Then stood Jeshua with his sons and his brethren, and Kadmiel and his sons, the sons of Judah, together, to have the oversight of the workmen in the house of God; the sons of Henadad also, with their sons and their brethren the Levites.

¹⁰And when the builders laid the foundation of the temple of the LORD, they set the priests in their apparel with trumpets, and the Levites the sons of Asaph with cymbals, to praise the LORD, according to the direction of David king of Israel. ¹¹And they sang one to another in praising and giving thanks unto the LORD: "for He is good, for His mercy endureth for ever toward Israel." And all the people shouted with a great shout, when they praised the LORD, because the foundation of the house of the LORD was laid. ¹²But many of the priests and Levites and heads of fathers' houses, the old men that had seen the first house standing on its foundation, wept with a loud voice, when this house was before their eyes; and many shouted aloud for joy; ¹³so that the people could not discern the noise of the shout of joy from the noise

of the weeping of the people; for the people shouted with a loud shout, and the noise was heard afar off.

. . .

CHAPTER 5

. . .

³At the same time came to them Tattenai, the governor beyond the River, and Shethar-bozenai, and their companions, and said thus unto them: 'Who gave you a decree to build this house, and to finish this structure?' ⁴'Then spoke we unto them after this manner [, wrote they]: What are the names of the men that build this building?' ⁵But the eye of their God was upon the elders of the Jews, and they did not make them cease, till the matter should come to Darius, and then answer should be returned by letter concerning it.

. . .

CHAPTER 6

¹Then Darius the king made a decree, and search was made in the house of the archives, where the treasures were laid up, in Babylon. ²And there was found at Ahmetha, in the palace that is in the province of Media, a roll, and therein was thus written: "A record. ³In the first year of Cyrus the king, Cyrus the king made a decree: Concerning the house of God at Jerusalem, let the house be builded, the place where they offer sacrifices, and let the foundations thereof be strongly laid; the height thereof threescore cubits, and the breadth thereof threescore cubits; ⁴with three rows of great stones, and a row of new timber, and let the expenses be given out of the king's house; ⁵and also let the gold and silver vessels of the house of God, which Nebuchadnezzar took forth out of the temple which is at Jerusalem, and brought unto Babylon, be restored, and brought back unto the temple which is at Jerusalem, every one to its place, and thou shalt put them in the house of God."

⁶"Now therefore, Tattenai, governor beyond the River, Shethar-bozenai, and your companions the Apharesachites, who are beyond the River, be ye far from thence; ⁷let the work of this house of God alone; let the governor of the Jews and the elders of the Jews build this house of God in its place. ⁸Moreover I make a decree concerning what ye shall do to these elders of the Jews for the building of this house of God; that of the king's goods, even of the tribute beyond the River, expenses be given with all diligence unto these men, that they be not hindered. ⁹And that which they have need of, both young bullocks, and rams, and lambs, for burnt-offerings to the God of heaven, wheat, salt, wine, and oil, according to the word of the priests that are at Jerusalem, let it be given them day by day without fail; ¹⁰that they may offer sacrifices of sweet savour unto the God of heaven, and pray for the life of the king, and of his sons. ¹¹Also I have made a decree, that whosoever shall alter this word, let a beam be pulled out from his house, and let him be lifted up and fastened thereon; and let his house be made a dunghill for this; ¹²and may the God that hath caused His name to dwell there overthrow all kings and peoples, that shall put forth their hand to alter the same, to destroy this house of God which is at Jerusalem. I Darius have made a decree; let it be done with all diligence."

¹³Then Tattenai, the governor beyond the River, Shethar-bozenai, and their companions, because that Darius the king had thus sent, acted with all diligence. ¹⁴And the elders of the Jews builded and prospered, through the prophesying of Haggai the prophet and Zechariah the son of Iddo. And they builded and finished it, according to the commandment of the God of Israel, and according to the decree of Cyrus, and Darius, and Artaxerxes king of Persia. ¹⁵And this house was finished on the third day of the month Adar, which was in the sixth year of the reign of Darius the king. ¹⁶And the children of Israel, the priests and the Levites, and the rest of the children of the captivity, kept the dedication of this house of God with joy. ¹⁷And they offered at the dedication of this house of God a hundred bullocks, two hundred rams, four hundred lambs; and for a sin-offering for all Israel, twelve he-goats, according to the number of the tribes of Israel. ¹⁸And they set the priests in their divisions, and the Levites in their courses, for the service of God, which is at Jerusalem; as it is written in the book of Moses.

¹⁹And the children of the captivity kept the passover upon the fourteenth day of the first month. ²⁰For the priests and the Levites had purified themselves

together; all of them were pure; and they killed the passover lamb for all the children of the captivity, and for their brethren the priests, and for themselves. [21]And the children of Israel, that were come back out of the captivity, and all such as had separated themselves unto them from the filthiness of the nations of the land, to seek the LORD, the God of Israel, did eat, [22]and kept the feast of unleavened bread seven days with joy; for the LORD had made them joyful, and had turned the heart of the king of Assyria unto them, to strengthen their hands in the work of the house of God, the God of Israel.

STUDY QUESTIONS

1. How does the Persian Cyrus come to be enlisted as an agent of the Hebrews' God?
2. What motivates the renewal of the Jews' contract with God after their return from exile?

4.6 LYSIAS, "AGAINST ERATOSTHENES,"
CA. 400 BCE

Lysias (ca. 445–380 BCE) is numbered among the great orators of classical Greece. Thirty-four of his speeches survive in their entirety; fragments of nearly 150 others have been identified. A once wealthy man who had lost his money in the harsh years after Athens's defeat in the Peloponnesian War, Lysias earned his living as a speechwriter for politicians and trial lawyers. In the speech that follows, Lysias lays out the case against the crimes committed by all the Thirty Tyrants, but especially against one of them, Eratosthenes, who was accused of murdering Lysias's brother, Polemarchus, in a political purge. Eratosthenes was one of the group that briefly ruled in Athens immediately after the war; Polemarchus was a philosopher whose house provides the setting for Plato's dialogue *The Republic*. Lysias argues that Eratosthenes and all the Thirty Tyrants should be condemned as criminals for murdering their political opponents, despoiling what was left of Athenian democracy, and stealing or extorting money from the citizens.

Gentlemen of the jury, the challenge I face is not in knowing how to begin my remarks but in how and when to end them. The acts committed [by the defendant] are so many and so heinous that I could not even invent greater monstrosities than those he has committed, nor could I even describe the whole truth of his crimes no matter how much I wanted to. I would either run out of the time permitted me or collapse in exhaustion. Moreover, it seems to me that I must do the opposite of what has been done usually in the past when an accuser explained his hostility towards the defendant. This case calls instead for explaining the

Translation by Clifford Backman.

defendant's hatred of our city, as shown by the multitude of offenses he has committed against her. Let me be clear: I speak not without personal enmity and suffering; yet I speak primarily for the reasons we all have, in anger, and in the interest of the public. I have never been personally engaged in a court case before, neither on my own account nor on behalf of someone else, but this man's actions compel me to speak out in accusation even though I dread that my inexperience will cause me to be unworthy of the task of speaking on my brother's behalf. I will try to state the case before you, from beginning to end, as briefly as I can.

Pericles himself urged our father Cephalus to settle in this city. Over the next thirty years none of our family appeared in any law-case as either prosecutor or defendant; we lived, in those democratic times, in such a way as to avoid offending anyone or suffering any wrong from anyone. When the Thirty [Tyrants] came in control of our government—which they did through corruption and evil-doing—they determined to purge Athens not only of criminals but of innocent citizens devoted only to virtue and justice. . . . They easily persuaded bloodthirsty mobs who wanted revenge [for Athens's defeat], but in reality they only wanted to confiscate money. They made sure to include two poor men out of every ten whom they arrested in order to save themselves from the charge they were motivated by money and were simply taking sensible actions on behalf of the state. . . .

[After I myself managed to escape to Megara] Eratosthenes arrested my brother Polemarchus and the other Tyrants sentenced him to death by hemlock without so much as making a formal charge against him and giving him a chance to defend himself at trial. . . . They seized seven hundred shields, all inlaid with gold, silver, and copper; they stole jewelry, furniture, and more women's clothing than they were expecting to find; they confiscated a hundred and twenty slaves, kept the best of them and handed the rest over to the Treasury. Their greed was so great that one of them—Melobius—even snatched the twisted gold earrings from Polemarchus' wife's ears. . . . They sent many citizens into exile in foreign lands; put many more to death and then deprived them of burial; denied citizenship to others who had earned

it and forbade their daughters to marry. And now they have the audacity to come before you and defend their actions, saying they are not guilty of these vile, shameful acts. . . .

So I now proceed to my questioning. Gentlemen of the jury, bring him forth to the stage. . . .

L: Did you arrest Polemarchus, or not?

E: I dreaded doing it, but I was ordered to do so by the government.

L: Were you in the Council when the charges were made against us?

E: Yes.

L: Did you vote in favor of the death penalty or against it?

E: Against it.

L: You opposed our death sentences?

E: I did.

L: Why? Was the sentence just or unjust?

E: Unjust.

L: Oh, you poor lost soul! So you testified in our favor, in order to save our lives, but you assisted in the arrest that would lead to our deaths! And when our lives were in the hands of the Council's majority-vote, you insist that you argued against our executions, but you alone arrested Polemarchus and imprisoned him – you, the one person who might have saved him! . . .

Now suppose he is telling the truth in saying he opposed the arrest and death-sentence. Even so, why should we believe his claim that acted under orders? . . . Who in that situation would be least likely to be given orders for the arrest—the man who spoke most passionately against them? . . .

Eratosthenes, if you had wanted to play the part of a just citizen, you would have warned the men fated to an evil death rather than have laid hands on them so that they could be killed. Your deeds reveal the man you are. You did not regret what you did; you took pleasure in it, and this court should decide this case on the basis of your actions instead of your words. . . .

I ask the court: If this Eratosthenes were your own brother or son, what would you do—acquit him? He has to prove one of two things—either that he did not arrest Polemarchus at all, or that he did so according to the law of justice. But he has already admitted that he took Polemarchus into custody unjustly [by stating that he had argued against doing so], and has therefore made your verdict an easy one. . . . I could almost stop here, for I hold that an accuser needs say no more once he has shown that a defendant has committed acts worthy of the death-penalty, the most severe penalty our state can impose. There is no need to draw out more accusations against men like these, for even if they were killed twice for each of their crimes they still would not get what they deserve on account of their crimes. Notice that this fellow does even resort to the common stratagem of speaking not to the specific charges but assuring you instead that they have been good soldiers who have seized many enemy ships while in positions of command, and have turned many enemy cities into allies. All you would have to do is to ask them where they have killed as many of our enemies as they have of our own citizens, or to name the city they won for us that can compare to our own city which they have enslaved! . . .

Such is my accusation against Eratosthenes and his complicit friends—those friends on whom he bases his defense. The contest between him and our city is not an equal one, for whereas he once both accused and stood in judgment over the citizens brought before him, today we are the prosecutors. This man and his colleagues, who executed without trial men guilty of no wrong-doing, you ought now to judge according to the law. What punishment—even an unlawful one—can make up for the injuries they have committed against our city? What penalty could be commensurate with their evils? If you put them and their children to death, would that punishment requite the murders of our persecuted fathers, sons and brothers? If you confiscate their wealth and property, would that adequately compensate the city or our fellow citizens for what they pillaged from us? And if there is no sentence you can order that would punish them enough, would it not be shameful to impose anything less than what their victims would have desired?

I do not doubt that this Eratosthenes is brazen enough to attempt to defend his actions before you judges who are his actual victims and witnesses to his evil. That is the both the measure either of his contempt for you and of his confidence in those who will speak on his behalf. . . . You may wonder whether those [who plead his case] will pretend to be honorable men, as though their virtue outweighs the defendant's villainy. I only wish they had been as energetic on our city's behalf as Eratosthenes was in trying to destroy us. . . . If these defendants are acquitted they will be free once more to destroy our city; their dead victims, though, will have no recourse to justice. . . .

Some say that Eratosthenes was the least evil of the Thirty and that we therefore ought to let him go free; but can it be possible that his offenses do not deserve the death penalty? You need to act in accordance with his deeds. If you convict him, you will be showing your indignation at what he did. If you acquit him, you will be seen as people who aspire to similar evils yourselves—but without the supposed excuse of merely "carrying out the orders" of the Thirty. . . . Don't condemn yourselves by acquitting them, and remember that your vote is not in secret: everyone in the city will know what each of you decides. . . . I have made no secret of my zeal to defend our temples, which these have either sold or desecrated; to defend our city, which they have despoiled; our arsenal, which they have demolished; and our dead, whom you were unable to protect in life and must therefore now vindicate in death.

STUDY QUESTIONS

1. How does Lysias argue that Eratosthenes and all the Thirty Tyrants should be condemned as criminals for murdering their political opponents?
2. According to Lysias, how have Eratosthenes and the Thirty Tyrants undermined Athenian democracy?

CHAPTER 5

ROMANS AND REPUBLICANS

5.1 THE BATTLE OF CANNAE, 216 BCE, FROM LIVY, *FROM THE FOUNDING OF THE CITY*, BOOK 22, CHAPTERS 34–57

The Battle of Cannae in 216 BCE was Rome's defining moment in the Punic Wars. After the Romans had lost fifty thousand soldiers in the first two years of the war, at Cannae Hannibal's smaller army surrounded the much larger Roman one and completely destroyed it. The Romans lost another fifty thousand men; only ten thousand escaped to tell the tale. It appeared that the Romans were about to lose the war. But not only did they continue the fight, they also expanded the theaters of operation. The following account of the battle begins with the contentiousness that arose over the consular elections for 216 BCE, where two bitterly opposed consuls were elected, Gaius Terentius Varro, an inexperienced, rabble-rousing plebeian whose emotional appeals to the plebs opposed the delaying tactics of the dictator Quintus Fabius Maximus and rashly promised a quick end to the war with Hannibal, and Lucius Aemilius Paullus, a distinguished, experienced, and cautious patrician implacably opposed to Varro and the plebeians. The two were at odds throughout the campaign, with disastrous results. The Roman historian Livy (ca. 60 BCE–17 CE), in his work *From the Founding of the City*, described the events leading up to the battle and the battle itself in great detail.

The elections[1] were held amid a bitter struggle between the patricians and the plebs. C. Terentius Varro,[2] a member of their own order, had ingratiated himself with the plebs by his attacks upon the leading men in the state and by all the tricks known to the demagogue. His success in shaking the influence of Fabius[3] and weakening the authority of the Dictator had invested him with a certain glory in the eyes

---

Canon Roberts, trans., *Titus Livius. The History of Rome*, vol. 3. London: Dent, 1905.

[1] For the year 216 BCE.

[2] Varro was a complete outsider, a "New Man"—that is, a person none of whose ancestors had held the office of Consul.

[3] Quintus Fabius Maximus, who had been appointed Dictator after the disastrous Roman defeat at the Battle of Lake Trasimene in 217 BCE. By implementing his "Fabian Strategy" of restricting military operations to raids and guerilla warfare but not engaging Hannibal's main army, Fabius got the nickname Cunctator, "The Delayer."

of the mob, and they did their utmost to raise him to the consulship. The patricians opposed him with their utmost strength, dreading lest it should become a common practice for men to attack them as a means of rising to an equality with them. Q. Baebius Herennius, a relation of Varro, strengthened the feeling in favor of his own candidate. "It was by the nobility," he declared, "who had for many years been trying to get up a war, that Hannibal was brought into Italy, and when the war might have been brought to a close, it was they who were unscrupulously protracting it. We shall never see the end of the war until we have elected as our Consul a man who is really a plebeian, that is, one from the ranks. The plebeian nobility[4] have all been initiated into the same mysteries; when they are no longer looked down upon by the patricians they at once begin to look down upon the plebs. One consulship at all events belongs to the Roman plebs; the people will freely dispose of it and give it to the man who prefers an early victory to prolonged command."

Harangues like these kindled intense excitement among the plebs. There also were three patrician candidates in the field, P. Cornelius Merenda, L. Manlius Vulso, and M. Aemilius Lepidus, and two plebeians who now were ennobled, C. Atilius Serranus and Q. Aelius Paetus. But the only one elected was C. Terentius Varro, so that the elections for appointing his colleague were in his hands. The nobility compelled L. Aemilius Paullus to come forward. On the next election day, after all Varro's opponents had retired, Paullus was given to him not so much to be his colleague as to oppose him on equal terms.

The armies were increased, but as to what additions were made to the infantry and cavalry, the authorities vary so much, both as to the numbers and nature of the forces, that I should hardly venture to assert anything as positively certain. Some say that 10,000 recruits were called out to make up the losses; others, that four new legions were enrolled so that they might carry on the war with eight legions. Some authorities record that both horse and foot in the legions

were made stronger by the addition of 1000 infantry and 100 cavalry to each, so that they contained 5000 infantry and 300 cavalry, whereas the allies[5] furnished double the number of cavalry and an equal number of infantry. Thus, according to these writers, there were 87,200 men in the Roman camp when the Battle of Cannae[6] was fought. One thing is quite certain; the struggle was resumed with greater vigor and energy than in former years, because the Dictator had given them reason to hope that the enemy might be conquered.[7] But before the newly raised legions left the city the Decemvirs[8] were ordered to consult the Sibylline Books[9] owing to the general alarm that had been created by fresh portents. It was reported that showers of stones had fallen simultaneously on the Aventine in Rome and at Aricia; that the statues of the gods among the Sabines had sweated blood, and cold water had flowed from the hot springs. This latter portent created more terror, because it had happened several times. In the colonnade near the Campus Martius[10] several men had been killed by lightning. The proper expiation of these portents was ascertained from the Sibylline Books.

After completing the enrolment the Consuls waited a few days for the contingents furnished by the Latins and the allies to come in. Then a new departure was made; the soldiers were sworn in by the Military Tribunes.[11] Up to that day there had only

---

[4] Plebeians who, unlike Varro, did have a Consul in their family background. The consulate had been open to plebeians since 367 BCE.

[5] The "socii," or Italian allies, defeated peoples and cities of Italy not governed by Rome but expected to contribute troops for Rome's wars.

[6] In Apulia in far southeastern Italy, the site of one of Rome's most disastrous military defeats.

[7] By his policy of harassing but not directly confronting Hannibal.

[8] The "Ten Men in Charge of Carrying out Sacrificial Duties," five patricians and five plebeians. They were in charge of consulting the Sibylline Books.

[9] Books believed to have been purchased from a Sibyl (a prophetess) by King Tarquin the Proud. They were consulted in times of emergencies to find the proper expiatory rites needed to regain the favor of the gods.

[10] The "Field of Mars," where, in earlier Roman history, the army was accustomed to assemble.

[11] Each legion had six Military Tribunes, chosen by the Senate and by vote of the people.

been the military oath binding the men to assemble at the bidding of the Consuls and not to disband until they received orders to do so. It had also been the custom among the soldiers, when the infantry were formed into companies of 100, and the cavalry into troops of 10, for all the men in each company or troop to take a voluntary oath to each other that they would not leave their comrades for fear or for flight, and that they would not quit the ranks save to fetch or pick up a weapon, to strike an enemy, or to save a comrade. This voluntary covenant was now changed into a formal oath taken before the Tribunes.

Before they marched out of the city, Varro delivered several violent harangues, in which he declared that the war had been brought into Italy by the nobles, and would continue to feed on the vitals of the Republic if there were more generals like Fabius; he, Varro, would finish off the war the very day he caught sight of the enemy. His colleague, Paullus, made only one speech, in which there was much more truth than the people cared to hear. He passed no strictures on Varro, but he did express surprise that any general, while still in the city before he had taken up his command, or become acquainted with either his own army or that of the enemy, or gained any information as to the lie of the country and the nature of the ground, should know in what way he should conduct the campaign and be able to foretell the day on which he would fight a decisive battle with the enemy.

As for himself, Paullus said that he would not anticipate events by disclosing his measures, for, after all, circumstances determined measures for men much more than men made circumstances subservient to measures. He hoped and prayed that such measures as were taken with due caution and foresight might turn out successful; so far rashness, besides being foolish, had proved disastrous. He made it quite clear that he would prefer safe to hasty counsels, and in order to strengthen him in this resolve Fabius is said to have addressed him on his departure in the following terms:

"You are mistaken, Lucius Paullus, if you imagine that you will have less difficulty with Gaius Terentius than with Hannibal. I rather think the former will prove a more dangerous enemy than the latter. With

the one you will only have to contend in the field, the opposition of the other you will have to meet everywhere and always. Against Hannibal and his legions you will have your cavalry and infantry, when Varro is in command he will use your own men against you. If he carries out his threat and brings on an action at once, some place or other will be rendered more notorious by our defeat than even Trasimene.[12] The only rational method of carrying on war against Hannibal is the one that I have followed. We are carrying on war in Italy, in our own country on our own soil, everywhere round us are citizens and allies, and time and circumstance are making us more efficient, more circumspect, more self-reliant. Hannibal, on the other hand, is in a foreign and hostile land, far from his home and country, confronted everywhere by opposition and danger; nowhere by land or sea can he find peace; nowhere does he see anything that he can call his own, he has to live on each day's pillage. He has hardly a third of the army with which he crossed the Ebro.[13] He has lost more by famine than by the sword, and even the few he has cannot get enough to support life. Do you doubt then, that if we sit still we shall get the better of a man who is growing weaker day by day, who has neither supplies nor reinforcements nor money? Varro, although he is a Roman Consul, will desire just what Hannibal the Carthaginian commander desires. Hannibal will only feel contempt for a man who runs all risks; he will be afraid of one who never takes a rash step."

The Consul's reply was far from being a cheerful one, for he admitted that the advice given was true, but not easy to put into practice. What power or authority would a Consul have against a violent and headstrong colleague? With these words Paullus, it is said, set forward, escorted by the foremost men among the patricians; the plebeian Consul was

---

[12] The Roman defeat at the Battle of Lake Trasimene the year before, where incompetent Roman generals had allowed the Roman army to be trapped between a mountain and a lake.

[13] The Spanish river that marked the northern boundary of Carthaginian territory. It was Rome's violation of the Ebro Treaty of 226 that had led to the Second Punic War.

attended by his plebeian friends, more conspicuous for their numbers than for the quality of the men who composed the crowd. When they came into camp the recruits and the old soldiers were formed into one army, and two separate camps were formed, the new camp, which was the smaller one, being nearer to Hannibal, while in the old camp the larger part of the army and the best troops were stationed.

An incident occurred that still further encouraged Varro's impetuous and headstrong temperament. Parties were sent to drive off the foragers; a confused fight ensued owing to the soldiers rushing forward without any preconcerted plan or orders from their commanders, and the contest went heavily against the Carthaginians. As many as 1700 of them were killed, the loss of the Romans and the allies did not amount to more than 100. The Consuls commanded on alternate days, and that day happened to be Paullus' turn. He checked the victors who were pursuing the enemy in great disorder, for he feared an ambuscade. Varro was furious, and loudly exclaimed that the enemy had been allowed to slip out of their hands, and if the pursuit had not been stopped the war could have been brought to a close. Hannibal did not very much regret his losses. On the contrary, he believed that they would serve as a bait to the impetuosity of the Consul and his newly-raised troops, and that he would be more headstrong than ever. What was going on in the enemy's camp was quite as well known to him as what was going on in his own; he was fully aware that there were differences and quarrels between the commanders, and that two-thirds of the army consisted of new recruits.

Owing to the want of grain, Hannibal decided to move into the warmer parts of Apulia, where the harvest was earlier and where, owing to the greater distance from the enemy, desertion would be rendered more difficult for the fickle-minded part of his force. He ordered campfires to be lighted, and a few tents left where they could be easily seen, in order that the Romans, remembering a similar stratagem,[14] might be afraid to move. Statilius, however, was sent to reconnoiter with his Lucanians.[15] He reported that he had caught a distant view of the enemy in line of march, and the question of pursuit was discussed. As usual, the views of the two Consuls were opposed, but almost all present supported Varro, not a single voice was given in favor of Paullus, except that of Servilius, Consul in the preceding year. The opinion of the majority of the council prevailed, and so, driven by destiny, they went forward to render Cannae famous in the annals of Roman defeats. It was in the neighborhood of this village that Hannibal had fixed his camp with his back to the sirocco that blows from Mount Vulture[16] and fills the arid plains with clouds of dust. This arrangement was a very convenient one for his camp, and it proved to be extremely advantageous afterward, when he was forming his order of battle, for his own men, with the wind behind them, blowing only on their backs, would fight with an enemy who was blinded by volumes of dust.

The Consuls followed the Carthaginians, and when they reached Cannae and had the enemy in view they formed two entrenched camps. Hannibal now saw his hopes fulfilled, that the Consuls would give him an opportunity of fighting on ground naturally adapted for the movements of cavalry, the arm in which he had so far been invincible, and accordingly he placed his army in order of battle, and tried to provoke his foe to action by repeated charges of his Numidians.[17] The Roman camp was again disturbed by a mutinous soldiery and Consuls at variance, Paullus bringing up against Varro the fatal rashness of Sempronius and Flaminius,[18] Varro retorting by pointing to Fabius as the favorite model of cowardly and inert commanders, and calling gods and men to witness that it was through no fault of his that Hannibal had acquired, so to speak, a prescriptive right to Italy; he had had his hands tied by his colleague; his

---

[14] A stratagem previously used by the Dictator Fabius Maximus to escape from Hannibal.

[15] An Italic people of southern Italy.

[16] An extinct volcano in Lucania in southern Italy.

[17] A native North African people known for its excellent cavalry.

[18] Sempronius had lost the Battle of the Trebia River in 218 BCE and Flaminius had lost the Battle of Lake Trasimene in 217.

soldiers, furious and eager for fight, had had their swords and arms taken away from them. Paullus, on the other hand, declared that if anything happened to the legions flung recklessly and betrayed into an ill-considered and imprudent action, he was free from all responsibility for it, although he would have to share in all the consequences. "See to it," he said to Varro, "that those who are so free and ready with their tongues are equally so with their hands in the day of battle." While time was thus being wasted in disputes instead of deliberation, Hannibal withdrew the bulk of his army, who had been standing most of the day in order of battle, into camp. He sent his Numidians, however, across the river[19] to attack the parties who were getting water for the smaller camp. They had hardly gained the opposite bank when with their shouting and uproar they sent the crowd flying in wild disorder, and galloping on as far as the outpost in front of the rampart, they nearly reached the gates of the camp. It was looked upon as such an insult for a Roman camp to be actually terrorized by irregular auxiliaries that one thing, and one thing alone, held back the Romans from instantly crossing the river and forming their battle line—the supreme command that day rested with Paullus. The following day Varro, whose turn it now was, without any consultation with his colleague, exhibited the signal for battle and led his forces drawn up for action across the river. Paullus followed, for although he disapproved of the measure, he was bound to support it. After crossing, they strengthened their line with the force in the smaller camp and completed their formation. On the right, which was nearest to the river, the Roman cavalry were posted, then came the infantry; on the extreme left were the cavalry of the allies, their infantry were between them and the Roman legions. The javelin men with the rest of the light-armed auxiliaries formed the front line. The Consuls took their stations on the wings, Terentius Varro on the left, Aemilius Paullus on the right.

As soon as it grew light Hannibal sent forward the Balearics[20] and the other light infantry. He then crossed the river in person and as each division was brought across he assigned it its place in the line. The Gallic and Spanish horse he posted near the bank on the left wing in front of the Roman cavalry; the right wing was assigned to the Numidian troopers. The center consisted of a strong force of infantry, the Gauls and Spaniards in the middle, the Africans at either end of them. You might fancy that the Africans were for the most part a body of Romans from the way they were armed, they were so completely equipped with the arms, some of which they had taken at the Trebia, but the most part at Trasimene. The Gauls and Spaniards had shields almost of the same shape but their swords were totally different, those of the Gauls being very long and without a point, the Spaniard, accustomed to thrust more than to cut, had a short handy sword, pointed like a dagger. These nations, more than any other, inspired terror by the vastness of their stature and their frightful appearance: the Gauls were naked above the waist, the Spaniards had taken up their position wearing white tunics embroidered with purple, of dazzling brilliancy. The total number of infantry in the field was 40,000, and there were 10,000 cavalry. Hasdrubal was in command of the left wing, Maharbal of the right; Hannibal himself with his brother Mago commanded the center. It was a great convenience to both armies that the sun shone obliquely on them, whether it was that they had purposely so placed themselves, or whether it happened by accident, because the Romans faced the north, the Carthaginians the south. The wind, called by the inhabitants the Vulturnus,[21] was against the Romans, and blew great clouds of dust into their faces, making it impossible for them to see in front of them.

When the battle shout was raised the auxiliaries ran forward, and the battle began with the light infantry. Then the Gauls and Spaniards on the left engaged the Roman cavalry on the right; the battle was not at all like a cavalry fight, for there was no room for maneuvering, the river on the one side and the infantry on the other hemming them in, compelled them to fight face to face. Each side tried to force their

---

[19] The Aufidus River, just south of the battle site.

[20] From the Balearic Islands in the Mediterranean Sea east of Spain; known for their skill as slingers.

[21] The Roman god of the east wind.

way straight forward, until at last the horses were standing in a closely pressed mass, and the riders seized their opponents and tried to drag them from their horses. It had become mainly a struggle of infantry, fierce but short, and the Roman cavalry was repulsed and fled. Just as this battle of the cavalry was finished, the infantry became engaged, and as long as the Gauls and Spaniards kept their ranks unbroken, both sides were equally matched in strength and courage. At length after long and repeated efforts the Romans closed up their ranks, echeloned their front,[22] and by the sheer weight of their deep column bore down the division of the enemy that was stationed in front of Hannibal's line and was too thin and weak to resist the pressure. Without a moment's pause they followed up their broken and hastily retreating foe until they took to headlong flight. Cutting their way through the mass of fugitives, who offered no resistance, they penetrated as far as the Africans who were stationed on both wings, somewhat further back than the Gauls and Spaniards who had formed the advanced center. As the latter fell back the whole front became level, and as they continued to give ground it became concave and crescent-shaped, the Africans at either end forming the horns. As the Romans rushed on incautiously between them, they were enfiladed[23] by the two wings, which extended and closed round them in the rear. On this, the Romans, who had fought one battle to no purpose, left the Gauls and Spaniards, whose rear they had been slaughtering, and commenced a fresh struggle with the Africans. The contest was a very one-sided one, for not only were they hemmed in on all sides, but wearied with the previous fighting they were meeting fresh and vigorous opponents.

By this time the Roman left wing, where the allied cavalry were fronting the Numidians, had become engaged, but the fighting was slack at first owing to a Carthaginian stratagem. About 500 Numidians, carrying, besides their usual arms and missiles, swords concealed

under their coats of mail, rode out from their own line with their shields slung behind their backs as though they were deserters, and suddenly leaped from their horses and flung their shields and javelins at the feet of their enemy. They were received into their ranks, conducted to the rear, and ordered to remain quiet. While the battle was spreading to the various parts of the field they remained quiet, but when the eyes and minds of all were wholly taken up with the fighting they seized the large Roman shields that were lying everywhere among the heaps of slain and commenced a furious attack upon the rear of the Roman line. Slashing away at backs and hips, they made a great slaughter and a still greater panic and confusion. Amid the rout and panic in one part of the field and the obstinate but hopeless struggle in the other, Hasdrubal, who was in command of that arm, withdrew some Numidians from the center of the right wing, where the fighting was feebly kept up, and sent them in pursuit of the fugitives, and at the same time sent the Spanish and Gallic horse to the aid of the Africans, who were by this time more wearied by slaughter than by fighting.

Paullus was on the other side of the field. In spite of his having been seriously wounded at the commencement of the action by a bullet from a sling, he frequently encountered Hannibal with a compact body of troops, and in several places restored the battle. The Roman cavalry formed a bodyguard round him, but at last, as he became too weak to manage his horse, they all dismounted. It is stated that when someone reported to Hannibal that the Consul had ordered his men to fight on foot, he remarked, "I would rather he handed them over to me bound hand and foot." Now that the victory of the enemy was no longer doubtful this struggle of the dismounted cavalry was such as might be expected when men preferred to die where they stood rather than flee, and the victors, furious at them for delaying the victory, butchered without mercy those whom they could not dislodge. They did, however, repulse a few survivors exhausted with their exertions and their wounds.

All were at last scattered, and those who could regained their horses for flight. Cn. Lentulus, a Military Tribune, saw, as he rode by, the Consul covered with blood sitting on a boulder. "Lucius Aemilius," he said, "the one man whom the gods must hold guiltless of

---

[22] By advancing in misaligned columns, a tactic made famous by the Theban general Epaminondas in the 370s and 360s BCE.

[23] Surrounded.

this day's disaster, take this horse while you have still some strength left." The Consul replied: "Cornelius, do not waste in useless pity the few moments left in which to escape from the hands of the enemy. Go, announce publicly to the Senate that they must fortify Rome before the victorious enemy approaches, and tell Q. Fabius privately that I have ever remembered his precepts in life and in death. Suffer me to breathe my last among my slaughtered soldiers." Lentulus escaped on horseback in the rush. The other Consul escaped with about fifty cavalry to Venusia. 45,500 infantry, 2700 cavalry, almost an equal proportion of Romans and allies, are said to have been killed.

Such was the battle of Cannae, a battle as famous as the disastrous one at the Allia River[24]; not so serious in its results, owing to the inaction of the enemy, but more serious and more horrible in view of the slaughter of the army. For the flight at the Allia saved the army although it lost the city, whereas at Cannae hardly fifty men shared the Consul's flight, nearly the whole army met their death in company with the other Consul.

Hannibal's officers all surrounded him and congratulated him on his victory, and urged that after such a magnificent success he should allow himself and his exhausted men to rest. Maharbal, however, the commandant of the cavalry, thought that they ought not to lose a moment. "That you may know," he said to Hannibal, "what has been gained by this battle I prophesy that in five days you will be feasting as victor in the Capitol. Follow me; I will go in advance with the cavalry; they will know that you are come before they know that you are coming." Hannibal told Maharbal that he commended his zeal, but he needed time to think out his plans. Maharbal replied, "You know how to win victory, Hannibal, but you do not how to use it."[25] That delay is believed to have saved the city and the nation.

The reports that reached Rome left no room for hope that even these remnants of citizens and allies were still surviving; it was asserted that the army with its two Consuls had been annihilated and the whole of the forces wiped out. Never before, while the city itself was still safe, had there been such excitement and panic within its walls. Over and above these serious disasters, considerable alarm was created by portents that occurred. Two Vestal virgins, Opimia and Floronia, were found guilty of unchastity. One was buried alive, as is the custom, at the Colline Gate,[26] the other committed suicide. L. Cantilius, one of the pontifical secretaries, now called "Minor Pontiffs," who had been guilty with Floronia, was whipped in the Comitium by the *Pontifex Maximus* so severely that he died under it. This act of wickedness, coming as it did among so many calamities, was regarded as a portent, and the Decemvirs were ordered to consult the Sibylline Books. Q. Fabius Pictor[27] was sent to consult the Oracle of Delphi as to what forms of prayer and supplication they were to use to propitiate the gods, and what was to be the end of all these terrible disasters. Meanwhile, in obedience to the Sibylline Books, some strange and unusual sacrifices were made, human sacrifices among them. A Gallic man and a Gallic woman and a Greek man and a Greek woman were buried alive under the Forum Boarium.[28] They were lowered into a stone vault, which had on a previous occasion also been polluted by human victims, a practice most repulsive to Roman feelings.

Yet, in spite of all their disasters, no one anywhere in Rome mentioned the word "Peace," either before the Consul's return or after his arrival. Such a lofty spirit did the citizens exhibit in those days that although the Consul[29] was coming back from a terrible defeat for which they knew he was mainly responsible, he was met by a vast concourse drawn from every class of society, and thanks were formally voted to him because he "had not despaired of the Republic." Had he been commander-in-chief of the Carthaginians there was no torture to which he would not have been subjected.[30]

---

[24] Where the Romans were defeated by the Gauls in 390 BCE.

[25] One of the most famous quotations of antiquity.

[26] One of the gates of Rome.

[27] The first Roman writer of history, who wrote in Greek ca. 200 BCE.

[28] The "Cattle Forum" in Rome.

[29] Varro.

[30] The Carthaginians executed defeated generals.

STUDY QUESTIONS

1. What were the main reasons for the Roman army's crushing defeat? What were the principal reasons for Hannibal's success?
2. Livy reports that when news of the defeat reached Rome, "never before . . . had there been such excitement or panic within its walls." Which members of Roman society were singled out for punishment as a result of the defeat?

5.2 THE LAND LAW OF TIBERIUS GRACCHUS, 133 BCE

In 133 BCE, Tiberius Gracchus was a decorated war hero with impeccable family credentials: he was the maternal grandson of Scipio Africanus, who had defeated Hannibal in 202 BCE, and his sister was married to Scipio Aemilianus, who had destroyed Carthage in 146 BCE. If he had worked within the system, he could have expected to have a stellar political career, but instead he chose to become a reformer. Realizing that it was becoming more and more difficult to find recruits for the Roman army who met the requirement for property ownership, as tribune of the Plebs he proposed legislation to distribute public land (land owned by the government) to landless plebeians and thus make them eligible for military service. The introduction of this law brought a resurgence of the same class conflicts as had been manifested between the consuls Paullus and Varro before the Battle of Cannae in 216 CE. The law was opposed vigorously by senators who had been renting the land and looked on it as their own. Tiberius therefore ignored tradition and took his law directly to the Council of the Plebs without consulting the senate. The law passed. Soon thereafter, Tiberius again violated tradition for running for tribune of the Plebs a second time in a row. This was too much for the senators, who instigated a riot and clubbed Tiberius to death. This was the first use of violence in Roman politics; it would not be the last. These reforms of Tiberius and the subsequent reforms of his brother, Gaius Gracchus (123–121 BCE), marked the beginning of the end of the Roman Republic. Senators on both sides of the issues were no longer able to reach behind-the-scenes compromises as they had in the past and were increasingly willing to put their own personal ideas about what was good for Rome ahead of the best interests of the state as a whole. As a result, the hard-won unity within the senate that had allowed the senate to govern effectively began to break down, and other groups, such as the equestrians, the Italian allies, and the plebs, assumed greater roles in politics. The pursuit of senatorial self-interest would culminate with generals who were willing to use their armies to seize control of the government. Tiberius's career is fulsomely discussed by the second-century CE Greek biographer Plutarch.

John Dryden, *The Lives of the Noble Greeks and Romans, Vol. 2.* Revised by A. H. Clough. Boston: Little, Brown, 1910.

Tiberius and Gaius were sons of Tiberius Gracchus, who, although he had been Censor[1] at Rome, twice Consul, and had celebrated two triumphs, derived his more illustrious dignity from his virtue. Therefore, after the death of the Scipio who conquered Hannibal, he was judged worthy to take Scipio's daughter Cornelia in marriage. A short time afterward he died, leaving Cornelia with twelve children by him. Cornelia took charge of the children and of the estate, and showed herself so discreet, so good a mother, and so magnanimous, that Tiberius was thought to have made no bad decision when he elected to die. For when Ptolemy the king offered to share his crown with her and sought her hand in marriage, she refused him, and remained a widow. In this state she lost most of her children, but three survived; one daughter, who married Scipio the Younger,[2] and two sons, Tiberius and Gaius, whose lives I now relate. These sons Cornelia reared with such scrupulous care that although confessedly no other Romans were so well endowed by nature, they were thought to owe their virtues more to education than to nature. The younger Tiberius, accordingly, serving in Africa under the younger Scipio, who had married his sister, and sharing his commander's tent, soon learned to understand that commander's nature and led all the young men in discipline and bravery; yes, he was first to scale the enemy wall.[3]

While he remained with the army Tiberius was the object of much good will, and on leaving it he was greatly missed. Tiberius then began to agitate his agrarian laws. The occasion of this was as follows. Of the territory that the Romans won in war from their neighbors, a part they sold, and part they made public land, and assigned it for occupation to the poor and indigent among the citizens on payment of a small rent into the public treasury. And when the rich began to offer larger rents and drove out the poor, a law was enacted forbidding the holding by one person of more than five hundred acres of land. For a short time this enactment gave a check to the rapacity of the rich, and was of assistance to the poor, who remained in their places on the land that they had rented and occupied the allotment that each had held from the outset. But later on the neighboring rich men, by means of fictitious personages, transferred these rentals to themselves and finally held most of the land openly in their own names. Then the poor, who had been ejected from their land, no longer showed themselves eager for military service and neglected the bringing up of children. Soon all Italy was conscious of a dearth of freemen and was filled with gangs of foreign slaves, by whose aid the rich cultivated their estates, from which they had driven away the free citizens. An attempt was therefore made to rectify this evil by Gaius Laelius the comrade of Scipio,[4] but the men of influence opposed his measures, and he, fearing the disturbance that might ensue, desisted, and received the surname of "The Wise" (for the Latin word "sapiens" has that meaning). Tiberius, however, on being elected Tribune of the Plebs, took the matter directly in hand. His brother Gaius, in a certain pamphlet, wrote that as Tiberius was passing through Tuscany[5] on his way to Numantia,[6] and observed the dearth of inhabitants in the country and that those who tilled its soil or tended its flocks there were barbarian slaves, he then first conceived the public policy that was the cause of countless ills to the two brothers. The energy and ambition of Tiberius, however, were most of all kindled by the people themselves, who posted writings on porticoes, house-walls, and monuments calling upon him to recover for the poor the public land.

He did not, however, draw up his law by himself, but took counsel with the citizens who were foremost in virtue and reputation, among whom were Crassus the *Pontifex Maximus*, Mucius Scaevola the jurist,[7]

---

[1] Two Censors were appointed every five years to take the census (a survey of property ownership), oversee the membership list of the Senate, and let out contracts for construction work.

[2] Cornelia's daughter Sempronia married her cousin, Scipio Aemilianus, grandson of Scipio Africanus.

[3] The first soldier to scale the wall of an enemy city received the "corona muralis," or "mural crown," one of the highest Roman military decorations.

---

[4] That is, Scipio Africanus.

[5] In northwestern Italy, homeland of the Etruscans.

[6] The final stronghold of rebels in Spain.

[7] A legal expert.

who then was Consul, and Appius Claudius,[8] his father-in-law. And it is thought that a law dealing with such great injustice and rapacity never was drawn up in milder and gentler terms. For men who ought to have been punished for their disobedience and to have surrendered with payment of a fine the land that they were illegally enjoying, these men it merely ordered to abandon their unjust acquisitions upon being paid the value and to admit into ownership of them such citizens as needed assistance. But although the rectification of the wrong was so considerate, the people were satisfied to let bygones be bygones if they could be secure from such wrong in the future. The men of wealth and substance, however, were led by their greed to hate the law, and by their wrath and contentiousness to hate the law-giver, and tried to dissuade the people by alleging that Tiberius was introducing a re-distribution of land for the confusion of the body politic and was stirring up a general revolution.

But they accomplished nothing, for Tiberius, striving to support a measure that was honorable and just with an eloquence that would have adorned even a meaner cause, was formidable and invincible whenever, with the people crowding around the rostra,[9] he took his stand there and pleaded for the poor. "The wild beasts that roam over Italy," he would say, "have every one of them a cave or lair to lurk in, but the men who fight and die for Italy enjoy the common air and light, indeed, but nothing else. Houseless and homeless they wander about with their wives and children. And it is with lying lips that their Imperators[10] exhort the soldiers in their battles to defend tombs and shrines from the enemy, for not a man of them has a hereditary altar, not one of all these many Romans an ancestral tomb, but they fight and die to support others in wealth and luxury, and although they are styled masters of the world they have not a single clod of earth that is their own."

Such words as these, the product of a lofty spirit and genuine feeling, and falling upon the ears of a people profoundly moved and fully aroused to the speaker's support, no adversary of Tiberius could successfully withstand. Abandoning therefore all counter-pleading, they addressed themselves to Marcus Octavius,[11] another one of the Tribunes of the Plebs, a young man of sober character, discreet, and an intimate companion of Tiberius. On this account Octavius at first tried to hold himself aloof, out of regard for Tiberius, but he was forced from his position, as it were, by the prayers and supplications of many influential men, so he set himself in opposition to Tiberius and staved off the passage of the law. Now, the decisive power is in the hands of any Tribune who interposes his veto, for the wishes of the majority avail not if one Tribune is in opposition. Incensed at this procedure, Tiberius withdrew his considerate law, and introduced this time one that was more agreeable to the multitude and more severe against the wrongdoers, because it simply ordered them to vacate without compensation the land that they had acquired in violation of the earlier laws.

When the appointed day was come and Tiberius was summoning the people to the vote, the voting urns were stolen away by the party of the rich, and great confusion arose. The supporters of Tiberius, however, were numerous enough to force the issue, and were banding together for this purpose, when Manlius and Fulvius, men of consular dignity, fell down before Tiberius, clasped his hands, and with tears besought him to desist. Tiberius, conscious that the future was now all but desperate, and moved by respect for the men, asked them what they would have him do. They replied that they were not competent to advise in so grave a crisis, and urged him with entreaties to submit the case to the Senate. To this Tiberius consented.

But the Senate in its session accomplished nothing, owing to the prevailing influence of the wealthy class in it, and therefore Tiberius resorted to a measure that was illegal and unseemly, the ejection of Octavius from his office, for he was unable in any other

---

[8] Appius Claudius Pulcher, Consul in 143 BCE and later a Censor.

[9] The speaker's platform in the Roman Forum.

[10] Victorious army generals.

---

[11] An ancestor of Augustus, the first Roman emperor.

way to bring his law to the vote. In the first place, however, he begged Octavius in public, addressing him with kindly words and clasping his hands, to give in and gratify the people, who demanded only their just rights, and would receive only a trifling return for great toils and perils. But Octavius rejected the petition, and therefore Tiberius, after premising that, because they were colleagues in office with equal powers and differed on weighty measures, it was impossible for them to complete their term of office without open war, said he saw only one remedy for this, and that was for one or the other of them to give up his office. Indeed, he urged Octavius to put to the people a vote on his own case first, promising to retire at once to private life if this should be the will of the citizens. But Octavius was unwilling, and therefore Tiberius declared that he would put the case of Octavius unless Octavius should change his mind upon reflection.

With this understanding, he dissolved the assembly for that day, but on the following day, after the people had come together, he mounted the rostra and once more attempted to persuade Octavius. When, however, Octavius was not to be persuaded, Tiberius introduced a law depriving him of his tribuneship, and summoned the citizens to cast their votes upon it at once. Now, there were five and thirty tribes,[12] and when seventeen of them had cast their votes, and the addition of one more would make it necessary for Octavius to become a private citizen, Tiberius called a halt in the voting, and again entreated Octavius, embracing him and kissing him in the sight of the people and fervently begging him not to allow himself to be dishonored, and not to attach to a friend responsibility for a measure so grievous and severe.

On hearing these entreaties, we are told, Octavius was not altogether untouched or unmoved; his eyes filled with tears and he stood silent for a long time. But when he turned his gaze toward the men of wealth and substance who were standing in a body together, his awe of them, as it would seem, and his fear of ill repute among them, led him to take every risk with boldness and bid Tiberius do what he pleased. And so the law was passed, and Tiberius ordered one of his freedmen to drag Octavius from the rostra, for Tiberius used his freedmen as officers, and this made the sight of Octavius insultingly dragged along a more pitiful one. Moreover, people made a rush at him, and although the men of wealth ran in a body to his assistance and spread out their hands against the crowd, it was with difficulty that Octavius was snatched away and safely rescued from the crowd; and a trusty servant of his who stood in front of his master and protected him, had his eyes torn out, against the protest of Tiberius, who, when he perceived what had been going on, ran down with great haste to appease the tumult.

After this the agrarian law was passed, and three men were chosen for the survey and distribution of the public land, Tiberius himself, Appius Claudius his father-in-law, and Gaius Gracchus his brother, who was not at Rome, but was serving under Scipio[13] in the expedition against Numantia. These measures were carried out by Tiberius quietly and without opposition. The aristocrats,[14] however, who were vexed at these proceedings and feared the growing power of Tiberius, heaped insult upon him in the Senate. When he asked for the customary tent at public expense for his use when dividing up the public land, they would not give it, although other men often had obtained one for less important purposes, and they fixed his daily allowance for expenses at nine obols.[15] These things were done on motion of Publius Nasica,[16] who surrendered completely to his hatred of Tiberius. For he was a very large holder of public land, and bitterly resented his being forced to give it up.

---

[12] Originally, Roman citizens were distributed among three tribes (from Latin *tribus*, "one third") based on family descent; subsequently thirty-five geographic tribes, based on place of residence, were used for political voting purposes.

[13] Scipio Aemilianus, who had been appointed when the Roman offensive against the Spaniards bogged down.

[14] The senators who opposed Tiberius.

[15] A small Greek silver coin; this was an insultingly small sum.

[16] Publius Scipio Nasica, a cousin of Scipio Aemilianus and Consul in 138 BCE

And now Attalus Philometor[17] died, and Eudemus of Pergamum brought to Rome the king's last will and testament, by which the Roman people was made his heir. At once Tiberius courted popular favor by bringing in a bill that provided that the money of King Attalus, when brought to Rome, should be given to the citizens who received a parcel of the public land, to aid them in stocking and tilling their farms. And as regarded the cities that were included in the kingdom of Attalus, he said it did not belong to the Senate to deliberate about them, but he himself would submit a pertinent resolution to the people. By this proceeding he gave more offense than ever to the Senate, and Pompeius,[18] rising to speak there, said that he was a neighbor of Tiberius, and therefore knew that Eudemus of Pergamum had presented Tiberius with a royal diadem and purple robe, believing that he was going to be king in Rome.[19]

And now Tiberius' friends, observing the threats and the hostile combination against him, thought that he ought to be made Tribune again for the following year. Once more, therefore, Tiberius sought to win the favor of the multitude by fresh laws, reducing the time of military service, granting appeal to the people from the verdicts of the judges, adding to the judges, who at that time were composed of senators only, an equal number from the equestrian order, and in every way at length trying to maim the power of the Senate from motives of anger and contentiousness rather than from calculations of justice and the public good. And when, as the voting was going on, the friends of Tiberius perceived that their opponents were getting the better of the contest, because all the people were not present, and in the first place resorted to abuse of his fellow Tribunes, and so protracted the time. Next, they dismissed the assembly, and ordered that it should convene on the following day. Then Tiberius, going down into the Forum, at

first supplicated the citizens in a humble manner and with tears in his eyes. Next, he declared he was afraid that his enemies would break into his house by night and kill him, and thereby so wrought upon his hearers that great numbers of them took up their station about his house and spent the night there on guard.

At break of day there came to the house the man who brought the birds with which auspices are taken, and he threw food before them. But the birds would not come out of the cage, with the exception of one, although the keeper shook the cage right hard and even the one that came out would not touch the food, but raised its left wing, stretched out its leg, and then ran back into the cage.[20] At the same time also many of his friends on the Capitol came running to Tiberius with urgent appeals to hasten thither, because matters there were going well. And in fact things turned out splendidly for Tiberius at first, as soon as he came into view the crowd raised a friendly shout, and as he came up the hill they gave him a cordial welcome and ranged themselves about him, that no stranger might approach.

But after Mucius[21] began once more to summon the tribes to the vote, none of the customary forms could be observed because of the disturbance that arose on the outskirt of the throng, where there was crowding back and forth between the friends of Tiberius and their opponents, who were striving to force their way in and mingle with the rest. Moreover, at this juncture Fulvius Flaccus, a senator, posted himself in a conspicuous place and because it was impossible to make his voice heard so far, indicated with his hand that he wished to tell Tiberius something meant for his ear alone. Tiberius ordered the crowd to part for Flavius, who made his way up to him with difficulty, and told him that at a session of the Senate the party of the rich, because they could not prevail upon the Consul to do so, were purposing to kill Tiberius themselves, and for this purpose had under arms a multitude of their friends and slaves.

---

[17] Attalus III (138–133 BCE), king of Pergamum in western Anatolia.

[18] Elected Tribune of the Plebs in the next year, 132 BCE, he continued to oppose the Gracchi brothers.

[19] Claiming that a politician wanted to become "king" was the worst accusation that could be made.

---

[20] This was a very bad omen.

[21] Publius Mucius Scaevola, one of the two Consuls and a legal expert.

Tiberius, accordingly, reported this to those who stood about him, and they at once girded up their togas, and breaking in pieces the spear-shafts with which the officers keep back the crowd, distributed the fragments among themselves, that they might defend themselves against their assailants. Those who were farther off, however, wondered at what was going on and asked what it meant. Whereupon Tiberius put his hand to his head, making this visible sign that his life was in danger, because the questioners could not hear his voice. But his opponents, on seeing this, ran to the Senate and told that body that Tiberius was asking for a crown; and that his putting his hand to his head was a sign having that meaning. All the senators, of course, were greatly disturbed, and Nasica demanded that the Consul should come to the rescue of the state and put down the tyrant. The Consul replied with mildness that he would resort to no violence and would put no citizen to death without a trial; if, however, the people, under persuasion or compulsion from Tiberius, should vote anything that was unlawful, he would not regard this vote as binding. Thereupon Nasica sprang to his feet and said: "Because, then, the chief magistrate[22] betrays the state, all you who wish to preserve the laws, follow me!" With these words he covered his head with the skirt of his toga and set out for the Capitol. All the senators who followed him wrapped their togas about their left arms[23] and pushed aside those who stood in their path, no man opposing them, in view of their dignity, but all taking to flight and trampling upon one another.

Now, the attendants of the senators carried clubs and staves that they had brought from home, and the senators themselves seized the fragments and legs of the benches that were shattered by the crowd in its flight, and went up against Tiberius, at the same time smiting those who were drawn up to protect him. Of these there was a rout and a slaughter, and as Tiberius himself turned to flee, someone laid hold of his garments. So he let his toga go and fled in his tunic. But he stumbled and fell to the ground among some bodies that lay in front of him. As he strove to rise to his feet, he received his first blow, as everybody admits, from Publius Satyreius, one of his colleagues,[24] who smote him on the head with the leg of a bench. And of the rest more than three hundred were slain by blows from sticks and stones, but not one by the sword.

This is said to have been the first sedition at Rome, since the abolition of royal power, to end in bloodshed and the death of citizens; the rest although neither trifling nor raised for trifling objects, were settled by mutual concessions, the nobles yielding from fear of the multitude, and the people out of respect for the Senate. And it was thought that even on this occasion Tiberius would have given way without difficulty had persuasion been brought to bear upon him, and would have yielded still more easily if his assailants had not resorted to wounds and bloodshed, for his adherents numbered not more than three thousand. But the combination against him would seem to have arisen from the hatred and anger of the rich rather than from the pretexts that they alleged, and there is strong proof of this in their lawless and savage treatment of his dead body. For they would not listen to his brother's request that he might take up the body and bury it by night, but threw it into the river along with the other dead. Nor was this all; they banished some of his friends without a trial and others they arrested and put to death.

But the Senate, trying to conciliate the people now that matters had gone too far, no longer opposed the distribution of the public land, and proposed that the people should elect a commissioner in place of Tiberius. So they took a ballot and elected Publius Crassus, who was a relative of Gracchus. Moreover, because the people felt bitterly over the death of Tiberius and were clearly awaiting an opportunity for revenge, and because Nasica was already threatened with prosecutions, the Senate, fearing for his safety, voted to send him to Asia. For when people met Nasica they did not try to hide their hatred of

---

[22] The Consul Mucius.

[23] To give themselves more room to maneuver because the toga was a very confining garment.

---

[24] Another one of the Tribunes of the Plebs.

him, but grew savage and cried out upon him wherever he chanced to be, calling him an accursed man and a tyrant, who had defiled with the murder of an inviolable and sacred person the holiest and most awe-inspiring of the city's sanctuaries. And so Nasica stealthily left Italy. He roamed and wandered about in foreign lands ignominiously, and after a short time ended his life at Pergamum.

STUDY QUESTIONS

1. Why did plebeians support Tiberius Gracchus's land law? Why did patricians oppose it?
2. Why are the reforms sponsored by Tiberius and his brother Gaius considered the beginning of the end of the Roman Republic?

5.3 VIRGIL, *THE AENEID*, BETWEEN 29 AND 19 BCE

Publius Vergilius Maro (70–19 BCE) is the author of three major Latin poems, the most famous of which was his commissioned epic, *The Aeneid*, which recounts the tribulations of the pious hero Aeneas, who fled the Trojan War and wandered the known world until he settled in Italy, symbolic of the founding of Roman civilization. Because Aeneas is the son of the goddess Venus, Virgil also thus creates a divine genealogy for Aeneas's purported descendent: the Roman emperor Augustus (63 BCE–14 CE). In this way, the enchanting poetry of the epic plays a political role as well. This opening scene begins in medias res and recounts the queen goddess Juno's destruction of the Trojan fleet, showcasing Aeneas's leadership qualities.

I sing of arms and a man—the man driven by fate, the man who
first came from the shoals of Troy to Italy, and to the Lavinian shore,
buffeted cruelly across land and sea by the will of the gods,
by fierce Juno's remorseless rage, and long enduring the wreck of war,
until he founded a city and brought his gods to Latium,
whence rose the Latin people, the lords of Alba Longa,
and the walls of noble Rome. Tell me, Muse, what caused it—
Juno's rage—how the queen of heaven was so galled
that she drove a man so renowned for virtue to endure
such dangers and face so many trials. Can such anger
exist in the minds of gods?

From Virgil, *Aeneid*, Book 1. Translation by Clifford Backman.

There was an ancient city, Carthage, held by Tyrian
    settlers,
opposite Italy and the distant mouth of the Tiber, a
    city
rich in wealth and the savage arts of war. Juno, they
    say,
loved this one city above all others, more than even
    Samos.
Here she kept her weaponry and her chariot, and
    hoped and strove
that, Fate permitting, the city would gain supremacy
over all the world. But she had long ago heard
that descendants of Trojan blood would one day
    overthrow
her Tyrian stronghold, and that from them a nation
    would arise
that was wide-ruling and proud in war, and bring
    about

Libya's ruin. The Fates had decreed it. Fearing this, and
bearing in mind the long-ago war she had fought at
    Troy
for her dear Argos' sake—
—and the seed of that anger and its bitter sorrow
still had not left the depths of her heart: the judg-
    ment of Paris,
the injury to her slighted beauty, the people she
    hated,
the honors given to abducted Ganymede—
Juno, the daughter of Saturn, driven farther into
    anger by this,
hurled into the sea those Trojans whom the Greeks
    and pitiless
Achilles had spared, keeping them far from Latium.
Driven by Fate from one sea to another, they wan-
    dered for years:
So hard a task it was, to found the Roman people.

STUDY QUESTIONS

1. Why and how are the opening lines of the *Iliad* invoked here?
2. How is Virgil grafting Roman history onto the story of the Trojan War and why?

5.4 EULOGY FOR A WIFE: "IN PRAISE OF TURIA," 100–1 BCE

Of the many hundreds of inscriptions that survive from ancient Rome, one of the longest and most interesting is the so-called *Laudatio Turiae*. This inscription, which dates to the first century BCE, records an elderly Roman widower's eulogy for his recently deceased wife of forty years. The woman's name, like her husband's, does not survive; a somewhat doubtful tradition suggests that her name was Turia. The couple were evidently of high economic and social status—the husband was a political figure and a veteran of the civil war of 49–45 BCE—and thus can hardly be taken as representative of all of Roman society. The *Laudatio* nevertheless offers a unique view into family life and gender roles. The stone bearing the inscription—now, regrettably, broken and with several pieces missing—is in the Museo Nazionale Romano in Rome. The text appears in *Corpus inscriptionum latinarum*, vol. 6, no. 31670.

Translation by Clifford Backman.

You were orphaned unexpectedly just before the day of our wedding, when your parents were murdered as they strolled alone in the countryside—and the responsibility to avenge their deaths fell to you, since I had already left for Macedonia and your sister's husband Cluvius had gone to the province of Africa. You did your duty to your family so honorably by making persistent demands in the pursuit of justice that we could not have done any better even if we had been present. You had much in common with your sister, a virtuous lady indeed. Once you had completed your task and secured the punishment of the guilty ones, you preserved your modesty by leaving your own home [the one we shared] and moving into the household of my mother until the day of my return. There my family tried to persuade you that your father's will, which had recognized you and I as his heirs, was actually invalid because my own father's marriage to my mother had been a *coemptio* [NB. A type of marriage contract, with unique inheritance stipulations]. Had the law decided that this actually was the case, all of your father's property—including your very self— would have fallen into my family's hands, and your sister too would have inherited nothing since she was under the legal authority of Cluvius.

How well do I recall how you reacted to this news, even though I was then far off! You resisted with determination, arguing our common cause that your father's will was not invalid and that his property had become ours together rather than yours alone. Your resolve to defend your father's will was so great, in fact, that you declared that you were determined to share your half of the estate with your sister regardless of the court's judgment and never to submit to my family's guardianship since their legal claim to it was baseless on account of the fact that there was no evidence that your family was part of my family's clan and hence was not subject to their jurisdiction. Even if your father's will had been declared null and void, you insisted, my family had no legal standing to prosecute since the families are not part of the same clan. Your firm resolve forced them to yield, and they dropped the law suit entirely—and in this way you completely succeeded in your self-appointed mission to fulfill your obligations to your father, your duty to your sister, and your loyalty to me.

Marriages like ours that end with death instead of divorce are rare. We were lucky enough to enjoy forty years together without friction, and I only wish that our marriage's end had come about through my own passing rather than through yours. It is more just for the older partner to submit to fate first.

Shall I describe your domestic virtues—your loyalty, obedience, kind-heartedness, even temper? Your love of spinning and weaving? Your religious observance without naïveté? Your modesty in dress and adornment? Shall I describe your love of your friends and your devotion to family? You took care of my mother as well as you did your own parents and toiled to provide her with as comfortable a life as you did for them. Innumerable are the fine qualities you shared with every married woman of good repute, but my desire is to focus on your own unique virtues, for truly few women have had to face and endure the hardships that confronted you in life and compelled you to action. It is thanks to Providence that such trials are rare for women.

We worked together to preserve intact all the property we received from your parents. You had no interest in keeping for yourself what you had completely entrusted to me. We divided our duties in such a way that I watched over your property while you watched over mine. I will pass silently over the details of this aspect of our life together, for fear of inadvertently claiming for myself credit that rightfully is yours. May the words I have already recorded bear witness to the truth of your character.

You extended your generosity to countless friends as well as to your beloved family. One could name many women worthy of this praise, but the only one who equaled you in kindness was your sister. Together, the two of you raised in your own homes numerous nieces and other relations worthy of the attention, and you provided them with dowries sufficient for them to obtain worthy marriages. Every time the two of you made such choices, Cluvius and I willingly joined you in assuming responsibility for them. Admiring your generosity, we added properties and estates of our own and transferred them into your patrimony lest your holdings should suffer diminishment. I say this not to congratulate Cluvius and myself but in order to make known that our admiration of your generosity was so great that we thought it an honor to support you in your gifts by enabling you to make even more.

I likewise will pass over without mentioning a number of your other kindnesses. . . .

[*Several lines missing.*]

You provided amply for all my needs when I was in exile and even made it possible for me to live in some comfort, by sending me all of your gold and jewelry and by keeping me well-supplied with slaves, money, and provisions, which you ingeniously snuck past the spies set by our enemies. You pleaded for my very life throughout my time abroad, and because of your courageous entreaties the men with power over me became convinced that they should spare me. Their mercy saved me, but it was your courage that inspired their mercy.

And in the midst of all this, you successfully defended one of our homes, the one I had purchased from [T. Annius] Milo when he was in exile, when some of his men seized the opportunity offered by the civil war and tried to break into the house and pillage it. But you fought them off and defended what was ours. . . .

[*Several lines missing.*]

. . . for had it not been for your efforts in keeping me alive, there would have been no one (namely, me) for him [G. Julius Caesar] to rescue, and thus I owe my life and my return to my country to you as well as to Caesar.

Why now publicize our secret, personal plans and private conversations like this? Why describe how, when warned by urgent reports about the imminent dangers that threatened me, I was saved by your advice? Why proclaim how you counselled me not to tempt fate by rash action and instead prepared a safe hiding space for me—employing Cluvius and your sister as accomplices in the deed, thus having the entire family share in my danger? If I tried to tell the whole tale, no end of time would pass. It is enough to say that the only thing that mattered to us was my safe hiding.

Still, I must admit that the most bitter and painful experience of my life was to learn what happened to you. When, thanks to Caesar's kindness and good judgment I was called back from exile and restored to citizenship, his colleague Marcus Lepidus, who was then in Rome (and while Caesar himself was temporarily absent), grew angry with your protestations regarding my recall. You had fallen at his feet and begged, but he ordered his men to grab you and half-drag half-carry you away like a slave. But although your body was covered in bruises your spirit was unbroken and you repeatedly reminded him of Caesar's edict and his pleasure in my reinstatement. You received a barrage of blows and curses, but you nevertheless recited the words of Caesar's edict aloud, so that everyone would know that it was on account of Lepidus that I was still facing danger. In the end, he paid a price for his behavior.

What could be worthier of praise than this bravery of yours? Because of your fortitude you gave Caesar an opportunity to show his mercy—thus saving my life— and to denounce Lepidus for his insolent cruelty.

But why say more? Let me be brief, for a speech in praise of your noble deeds should be brief lest it run the risk of describing them unworthily. Instead, let me simply declare to the world that your great actions saved my life.

When peace was restored and the government settled, we finally enjoyed happy and quiet times. We dreamed of having children, but Fate denied us that pleasure. What would we have lacked in life, had Fate, which had long favored us in so many ways, allowed that to happen? But She chose a different course for us, and killed our hopes. The many things you did in response to this adversity, and the countless others you attempted to do, would be remarkable and praiseworthy in other women, but they are hardly worth mentioning when set aside your other virtues, and so I will pass over them.

Despairing of your barrenness and saddened that I was without children, you feared that by staying in our marriage I might glumly abandon all hope of having a family, and so you proposed a divorce so that I could be free to live in our house and enjoy another woman's fertility. You intended, based on our well-known like-mindedness, to find and secure a wife who was worthy of me and suitable to my character; and you insisted that you would consider any future children as communal and would treat them as your own.

You swore that you would not divide up our inheritance—hitherto held in common by us—but would leave it under my control but, if I so wished, under your management. You would keep nothing for your own, not a single remnant, and would gladly assume the role and duties of a sister or mother-in-law.

I admit that this idea so angered me that I nearly went out of my mind. It horrified me so much that I barely kept my senses. How could a divorce even be contemplated before Fate had rendered Her final decree? How could you even imagine ceasing to be my wife while I was still alive, when you had remained so faithful to me when I had been nearly exiled from life itself? What desire or need for children could have been so great as to make me cast aside loyalty and trade the certain for the uncertain? Let me say no more! You remained with me as my wife. I could not have agreed with your suggestion without dishonoring my name and making both of us miserable.

Still, what could be more praiseworthy and deserving of commemoration than your devotion to me? When I could not have children by you, you took it upon yourself to at least offer me the chance of having them through another wife.

If only the years had allowed us to remain married until I, the older partner, had been carried to the grave first. That would have been more just, for then you could have paid your last respects to me. Then I could have died while you still lived on, standing in for the daughter I never had. But you were fated to go before me, and now you leave me filled with the sorrow of missing you and miserable at being denied the comfort of children.

For my part, I will continue on, bending my thoughts to your judgments and guided by your counsel. But all your wise precepts and instructions should give way to the praises you have so deservedly won. These praises will be my consolation and I will thereby not miss what I hereby consecrate to immortality, to be remembered forever.

The blessings that came from your life will not desert me. The thought of your good fame brings me strength of mind, and I learn from the example of your deeds enough that I shall resist Fortune—for She has not robbed me of everything since She has allowed the memory of you to grow great with praise. But in losing you I have lost all tranquility. When I recall how you could foresee and protect me against the many dangers that surrounded me, I break down under the misery and cannot keep my promise. Natural grief tears away my power of self-control and I am overwhelmed by sorrow. Grief and fear torment me, and I am defenseless against them. When my mind looks back over the dangers I faced in years past and contemplates what the future has in store for me, I collapse in weakness. Deprived of your wonderful help, I cannot bear my sorrow and I feel as though I live merely to grieve and mourn.

Let me end by saying that you were worthy of every good thing, but it was not in my power to give you them all. I have hereby followed your last wishes as though they were law. Anything more that I can do, I will do.

I pray that your watchful gods grant you rest and protection.

STUDY QUESTIONS

1. How does the *Laudatio Turiae* offer insight into gender and family roles in Roman society? What virtues does Turia's husband extol the most?
2. What larger political events serve as a backdrop to the eulogy? How do they put the *Laudatio Turiae* into historical context?
3. How does this text illustrate inheritance practices and property rights in Roman society?

CHAPTER 6

ROME'S EMPIRE

6.1 EPICTETUS, *ENCHIRIDION*, I, V, XIV, RECORDED 100–150 CE

The Greek philosopher Epictetus (55–135 CE) expounded on how Stoic philosophy must be more than an intellectual pursuit—it must direct one's way of life. One must stop struggling against inevitable Fate and accept events with discipline rather than emotion. In the early second century, some of his dictates were recorded by his disciple Arrian in the *Enchiridion*, or "Handbook." These selections illustrate Epictetus's commitment to the daily application of Stoic values, such as self-control and acceptance of death, to achieve worth and find peace.

Some things we can control, others we cannot. We can control things like our opinions, our interests, our goals, our worries—in a word, our own actions. What we cannot control consists of things like our bodies, our properties, our reputation, our social position—in a word, whatever is not our own doing. . . . Strive to be able to say to any unfortunate occurrence, "You are just an image [of suffering], not the thing [Suffering] itself," and then think about it with the principles we have taught—and this one most of all: whether the [unfortunate occurrence] pertains to one of the things we can control or to one of the things we cannot control. If the latter, then you should say that the whole matter means nothing to you. . . .

Worry only about those things that you can control. . . . If you worry about sickness, death, or poverty you will always be miserable. Stop worrying about

what you cannot control, and worry about what you can control. Try to suppress your desires, for if you desire what is not in your control, you will live in constant disappointment. . . .

People do not fear specific things but the ideas and notions they associate with those things. For example, death itself is not frightening, or else it would have appeared so to Socrates. The real terror of death is the frightful notions we have about it. So, whenever we are scared, worried, or upset about something, let us not attribute it to the thing that scares, worries, or upsets us—but rather to our ideas about it. It is an ignorant person who blames his unhappiness on something outside of himself; a half-educated person will blame himself; but someone fully knowledgeable will blame neither any thing nor himself. . . .

Translation by Clifford Backman.

Do not ask for things to happen as you want them to; instead, desire that things happen as they in fact do—that's the way to live. . . .

You are a fool if you wish your wife, children, and friends to live forever, because that is wanting to control what you cannot control, or wanting to possess a power that belongs to another [i.e. God]. Similarly, you are a fool if you want your servant to be not so dishonest, for that is desiring his vice to be not vicious but good. But you can control your longing to have your desires fulfilled. Focus on what you are in fact able to do. . . .

You should live your life as though you are a guest at a dinner-party. Has someone passed a serving platter to you? Then reach out and take a modest portion. If the platter passes you by, don't reach out to stop it. Has the platter not yet come to you? Don't reach for it, but wait for it to come your way. This is how you should act in regard to your children, your wife, public honors, and wealth, and if you do, then you will have earned a place at the feast of the gods. . . .

Remember always that you are an actor in a drama, in the role chosen for you by the Author. Maybe a short role, and maybe a long one. In whatever role He has cast you—a pauper or a cripple, a statesman, or a common person—play it naturally. Your duty is to play the role, not to assign it. . . .

If you wish to be a philosopher, prepare to be laughed at. The crowd will sneer at you and cry out, "Oh, look who's a philosopher all of a sudden!" or "And where does that patronizing look come from, eh?" Be careful not to wear a patronizing look, and keep your mind focused on the matters that God (who made you for philosophy) intends. Remember: if you stay true to your calling, the people who laugh at you now will later admire you. But if you give in to their taunts, you will be doubly a failure. . . .

Keep silence, for the most part, and when you must speak use few words. To engage in a long conversation is certainly allowable, but only when the occasion is appropriate and the conversation has nothing to do with base topics like gladiators, horse races, sports heroes, or feasts. Neither should you care about specific people, whether to blame, praise, or compare them to others. Whenever you can, steer a conversation away from such topics and toward worthy ones. Among strangers, it is best to keep silent. Do not laugh too easily, too frequently, or excessively. Avoid swearing altogether, if you can; if you can't, do it as little as possible. Avoid vulgar public entertainments. . . . Provide for your body's needs, but do not indulge it in the delights of meat, drink, clothing, housing, or even family. Get rid of everything showy and refined. Before you marry, abstain as much as you can from [sexual] contact with women. If you must give in to lust, do it lawfully. But do not sit in judgment and disapproval of those who give themselves sexual liberties—and do not boast of your own abstinence.

When someone tells you that another person has been gossiping about a mistake you have made, do not make excuses for your behavior but simply reply, "He must not know all my other faults, or else he would not have mentioned only that one." . . .

When engaging anyone in conversation, but especially someone of superior station, ask yourself first how Socrates or Zeno would behave in your situation. Then you cannot fail to behave properly. . . .

Men make mistresses of girls as young as fourteen, and these, perceiving that they are valued only for the pleasure they give to men, begin to give themselves over solely to adornment. Instead, we should strive to help them understand that their real value resides in their decency, modesty, and good behavior. . . .

Whatever moral principles you devise for yourself, obey them as though they were divine commands and that you would be guilty of the worst impiety by violating any of them. Pay no attention to what others say of you, for that is no concern of yours. . . . You are no longer a boy, but a grown man . . . so think yourself worthy of living a mature life. Let whatever is the best thing you can do in any situation be your guiding principle. . . .

Finally, keep these three maxims always in mind:

> Guide me, Oh Jupiter, and you, Oh Destiny,
> to whichever place you have chosen for me.
> [Cleanthes]

I follow gladly. If I were wicked and wretched and did not wish to follow, I still would have to.
The man who accepts his fate is deemed wise among men,

and knows the laws of heaven. [Euripides]
Crito, if my death pleases the gods, then let it come.
Anytus and Melitus can kill me, but they cannot hurt me. [Plato]

STUDY QUESTIONS

1. How should the example of Socrates inform the behavior of a wise person?
2. What specific instances does Epictetus give concerning the virtues of moderation?

6.2 TACITUS, *HISTORIES*, BEFORE 117 CE

Gaius Cornelius Tacitus (56–after 117 CE) is perhaps the most renowned Latin historian. As an active statesman, including holding the posts of consul and later governor of Asia, Tacitus had access to the inner workings of imperial Rome under Nero and his successors—which provides the cogent factual and analytical basis of this text. In his other major work, *The Annals*, Tacitus provides one of the earliest non-biblical references (15.44) to the historical Jesus. The introduction to *Histories* describes Tacitus's view of the state of affairs in his day; his selection on Jewish practices, although he misunderstands them, nonetheless provides some insight into how the Romans viewed this ancient monotheistic religion and culture.

I begin these *Histories* with the year [69 CE] when Servius Galba held the consulship for the second time and Titus Vinius was his partner. Many authors have written of the preceding 820 years, reckoning from the founding of our city, and in describing all the doings of the Roman people they wrote with equal parts of eloquence and liberality. After the battle at Actium, when the only way to preserve peace was for all power to be held by a single man, those great writers passed away. The truthfulness of history took a blow, too, first through men's acquired ignorance of public matters (since they no longer played a role in them), and second through the passion to flatter their new masters

even though they hated them. Between the people's servile nature, on the one hand, and their hatred, on the other, all regard for posterity disappeared. We instinctively recoil from any writer's use of an adulating tone, but we pay rapt attention when he makes snide and spiteful remarks, because a fawning tone implies a dishonorable servility but bitchiness comes across (though falsely) as bold honesty. . . .

I am beginning the history of an era filled with disasters, frightful wars, and bitter civil strife. Even the period's peaceful times had their horrors. Four emperors died by the sword; there were three civil wars and even more foreign ones, and some of the conflicts

Translation by Clifford Backman.

had both qualities at once. Successes in the east were matched with losses in the west. There was trouble in Illyricum. Gaul's loyalty was never certain. Britain was crushed, but then abandoned. The Suevi and Sarmatiae joined forces to repel us. The Dacians scored a renowned victory over us, then suffered a renowned defeat. And the Parthians were spurred to action by the deceits committed by that fraud, Nero. Italy herself was struck by disasters, some entirely unexpected and others the result of a long build-up. The cities of rich Campania were swallowed whole and buried. Rome itself was beset with riots that consumed some of its most venerable temples; citizens set fire even to the Capitol itself. People profaned our sacred rites; our greatest nobles gave themselves to corruption; the sea was clogged with refugees, its rocks bloodied by violence. Even worse horrors took place in the capital city. Nobility and wealth became causes for political accusations, as did either accepting or declining public office. If one maintained a life of virtue, one was done for. The rewards gained by rumor-mongers were more disgusting than their crimes, for while some snatched up consulships and priestly offices as booty, others grabbed procuratorships and positions of a more personal nature. But they all stole and pillaged in every direction, paying no heed to the hatred and terror they aroused in people. Slaves were bribed to betray their masters, and freedmen to inform on their patrons. Even those without any enemies were brought down—by their own friends.

Bad as it was, the age wasn't so utterly bereft of good qualities that it did not exhibit a few examples of virtuous action. Mothers followed their sons into exile, as wives did for their husbands. Some kinsmen were brave, and some sons-in-law were loyal. Some slaves remained true to their masters even when subjected to torture. Some men of virtue were driven to the ultimate sacrifice [i.e. suicide] and faced it with courage, and their last moments resembled the most fabled deaths of antiquity. Despite the reckless chaos of men's actions, there were divine prodigies to be seen in the skies and on the earth: cautioning rumbles of thunder, for instance, and other signs of things to come, both auspicious and gloomy, doubtful and certain. In sum, at no other time did so many terrible disasters strike the Roman people, nor was

there clearer proof that the gods care nothing for our happiness—only for our punishment.

* * * * *

(5.1–9)

Since I am about to describe the last days of a great and renowned city, it is fitting that I first describe its origins. According to some authorities, the Jews began as exiles from the island of Crete who settled on the northern coast of Africa about the time when Jupiter overthrew Saturn from his throne. The evidence for this resides in their name, since the Idaei were the people who lived by the famous mountain on Crete called Mount Ida, and these Idaei became gradually known as the Judaei by the lengthening of their name in the vernacular. Others maintain the Jews originated in Egypt in the time of Isis, when excess population flowed into neighboring lands under the guidance of the figures Hierosolymus and Judas. Many others claim the Jews began as a race from Ethiopia who were driven out by the loathing of their neighbors to find a new homeland during the time of King Cepheus. A few insist they are Assyrians, a rabble who failed to find land to settle in Mesopotamia and so seized a part of Egypt, but not before establishing a number of cities in what is called Judaea, along the border with Syria. Lastly, some writers hold that the Jews sprang from quite a distinguished root, being none other than the Solymi people celebrated by Homer, who named their most famous city after themselves: Hierosolyma.

Almost all writers, however, agree that at some point in the past a terrible disfiguring disease struck Egypt, for which King Bocchoris turned to the oracle of Hammon to discover the cure. Hammon instructed the king to purify his realm by driving out of the land this detestable race of Jews. The Jews were diligently rounded up and sent into the desert, where they remained, miserable, idle, and forsaken, until one of them, Moyses by name, convinced them to expect no rescue from God or man. They should rely only on themselves, and take for their leader whoever might guide them out of their present misery. . . .

Wanting to secure his own position of authority, Moyses gave the Jews a unique form of worship, one that runs counter to everything practiced by all other nations. What is sacred to us is worthless to them, and they allow themselves what is forbidden to us. In their temple they have consecrated an image of the animal who guided them during their long, parched wandering. They slay rams, in derision of Hammon, and sacrifice oxen, to mock the Egyptian worship of Apis. They refuse to eat pork, which they associate in memory with leprosy. (Swine are vulnerable to the disease.) They commemorate the long hunger of their wanderings by performing regular fasts, eating only an unleavened bread in honor of what they had grabbed, in their haste, when entering exile. . . .

Among themselves the Jews are unfailingly honest and compassionate, but they regard all other nations as their hated enemies. They sit apart from other peoples at meals and will not sleep under the roof of a non-Jew. As a race they are almost uniquely prone to lust, yet they will not couple with foreign women. . . . They practice circumcision as a way to distinguish themselves from others; anyone who joins their religion must submit to the custom. They despise all the gods of other nations. . . . The Jews have only a mental image of their God as a single essence, and regard representations of God in human form, made out of perishable materials, as profanations.

They believe only the essence of things to be supreme and eternal. . . . and do not allow any images to be put up in their cities—not even to flatter their own kings or to pay respect to our emperor. . . .

Their country is bounded by Arabia to the east, Egypt to the south, Phoenicia and the Mediterranean to the west. To the north it commands a sweeping view of Syria. As a people the Jews are healthy and do not tire easily. Rain is uncommon in Judaea but the soil there is fertile. . . . Judaea consists largely of scattered villages but it does have some cities. Jerusalem is the capital where once stood a temple of immense grandeur. . . . Only a Jew was allowed to approach its gates, and only their priests were permitted to cross the threshold. . . .

Pompey was the first Roman to subdue the Jews, and availing himself of the right of conquest he entered their temple. That is how it became known that it was empty, with no image of their God inside and their shrine possessing no secret knowledge. The walls of Jerusalem were subsequently destroyed, but the temple was left standing. . . . Under the emperor Tiberius everything remained quiet. When Caligula, however, ordered his own statue to be set up in the temple, the Jews opted for war.

STUDY QUESTIONS

1. What was the effect, in Tacitus's opinion, of one-man rule on the entire state's moral character?
2. How does Tacitus relate the exclusivity of Jewish culture to the resentment of Jews by others?

6.3 FROM SUETONIUS, *LIVES OF THE TWELVE CAESARS: CALIGULA; CLAUDIUS*, CA. 119 CE

A friend of Pliny the Younger, Suetonius (69–122 CE) also kept company with the Roman emperors Trajan and Hadrian, whose secretary he became. Although his *Lives of the Caesars* (from Julius Caesar to Domitian) has often been accused of being gossipy and melodramatic, Suetonius made

Translation by Clifford Backman.

use of the senatorial archives that he accessed as an imperial secretary to bolster his accounts with documentary evidence. Suetonius's lives of Caligula and Claudius display different reigns by these arguably brilliant leaders—the first driven by megalomania and the second by scholarly interests.

[Caligula]

So much for Caligula the emperor; now we speak of Caligula the monster. . . . Almost as though he wore a royal diadem, he turned the image of the Principate into that of an absolute monarchy. Since his lackeys told him he surpassed all other princes and kings, he started to claim divine power for himself, even to the point of sending to Greece for the most beautiful and sacred of all its statues of the gods (even those of Jupiter on Mount Olympus), and ordered their heads to be removed and replaced with likenesses of his own. . . . He put up a special shrine to himself as a god, complete with a staff of priests, the finest animals for sacrifices, and a life-sized statue of himself made of gold, which was dressed each day in clothes identical to whatever he was wearing that day. . . .

He ordered his own brother Tiberius Gemellus to be killed by a military tribune without warning, and he likewise forced his father-in-law Silanus to slash his own throat with a razor. . . . He spared his uncle Claudius simply so that he could make fun of him. . . . He made a habit of fornicating regularly with all three of his sisters, seating them just below him at banquets while his wife lay just above. It is widely reported that he took Drusilla's virginity when she was still a child; his grandmother Antonia, it is said, caught them in bed together. . . . When Drusilla died [38 CE] he proclaimed a period of public mourning; during this time he regarded it a capital crime if anyone laughed, bathed, or dined with their families. . . .

His gift for cruelty is shown by the following episodes. When the price of beef, for feeding the wild beasts that fought in his gladiatorial shows, was deemed too high, he ordered criminals to be fed to them instead. He looked out at a group of elderly convicts from a colonnade, and without bothering to read out the charges against them simply ordered them all to be led away, "one bald head after another." He condemned a number of men of high rank to be branded like cattle with a hot iron and sent to work in the mines or at road-building; others were caged like animals or thrown to the wild beasts. A few had their bodies sawn through.

[Claudius]

. . . Claudius became emperor at the age of fifty [41 CE]. . . . He was a modest, unpretentious man who refused to take the title of imperator. . . . He always sought the Senate's approval before recalling anyone from exile, and asked that the commander of the Praetorian Guard and military tribunes might accompany him to his house as a gracious favor of the Senate. He also made sure to seek the permission of the consuls before scheduling any fairs to be held on his private estates. . . . As a consequence, it took no time at all for his behavior to win him the respect and devotion of the people. So great was their affection for him that when a rumor spread that he had been attacked and killed on a visit to Ostia, the people were horrified. Crowds quickly surrounded soldiers and senators everywhere, calling them traitors and assassins, and did not relent until several magistrates brought forth a number of witnesses to swear that Claudius was in fact quite safe and making his way peaceably back to the capital.

STUDY QUESTIONS

1. How might Caligula's cruelty have resulted from his unrivaled control of Rome?
2. Was Claudius's seeming respect for the Senate merely a fraud?

6.4A. MARCUS AURELIUS, *MEDITATIONS*, CA. 170–180 CE

Written while Marcus Aurelius (121–180 CE) was on campaign in land that includes modern-day Hungary and Austria, these compiled thoughts (written in Greek) reveal the Roman emperor's Stoic beliefs. Intended as a type of personal guide or reflective exercise, the *Meditations* touch on mortality, morality, social cares, and self-control, among other themes. Consider the Roman emperor's elegant tone as well as his modest views of the transience of life, which contrast with his supreme political status.

Begin every morning by saying to yourself, "Today I will encounter meddling, ingratitude, arrogance, deceit, envy, and selfishness, and all of these things will be due to their offenders' ignorance of the difference between Good and Evil. But I myself have long recognized the nature and magnificence of the Good, and the nature and meanness of Evil; the nature, too, of the one who does wrong, for he is my brother (not in the physical sense of blood and seed, but as a fellow-creature endowed with intellect and a share of the divine). Therefore none of those things can harm me, for no one can implicate me with what is base. Neither can I be angry with my brother, nor hate him, for we were created to work together, like a man's two feet or hands, two eyelids, or two rows of teeth, upper and lower. To oppose each other, therefore, is against Nature. Anger and aversion are obstructions."

* * * * *

Bear in mind always that as a Roman and a man you should perform your duties well and with dignity and in a spirit of kindness, liberality, and justice. In so doing you free yourself of the burden of all cares; and you will be successful in this so long as you approach every deed as if it were the last action of your life, setting aside inattentiveness and the desire to avoid the dictates of reason, hypocrisy, self-regard, and complaint about what life has doled out to you. You can see how little a man needs in order to lead a quiet life—which is a divine life. The gods themselves will require nothing more from a man who lives this way.

* * * * *

Even if he were to live for three thousand years or as many as ten thousand, every man has but one life to live and to lose—this one, and no other. Remember this, for all lives, the longest and the shortest, come to the same end. The present moment is the same to everyone, although that which perishes [at any moment] is not the same; that is why that which is lost appears to be only a mere moment. A man, after all, cannot lose either the past or the future, for how can anyone take from him what he does not possess? So remember these two things: first, that all eternal things are similar and come round in a circle, and it makes no difference at all whether one sees the same things for a hundred years or two hundred or for however so great a time; second, the man who lives the longest and the one who lives the briefest life both lose the same thing. The present moment is the only thing that one can lose, for it is all that one possesses—and you can only lose what you possess.

* * * * *

A man's soul does violence to itself when it turns into a canker or tumor upon the universe, to the extent that that is possible. To be irritated at anything that

From Marcus Aurelius, *Meditations* 6.1. Translation by Clifford Backman.

happens is to cut oneself off from Nature, since Nature consists of the natures of all things combined. The soul also does violence to itself when it turns away from any person or advances upon any with the intent to harm—such are the souls of the wrathful. The soul does a third kind of violence to itself when it surrenders itself to pleasure or pain, a fourth kind when it dissembles and does or says something insincerely or falsely. And a fifth kind of violence when it allows itself any act or movement that is without purpose or does anything thoughtlessly and without a care to its correctness. For it is right that even the smallest actions be done for a reason. The whole point of being a rational creature, after all, is to follow the dictates of reason and the law of the most ancient city and state.

The span of a human life is a mere point, its substance is in constant flux, its perception ever dim, the makeup of the body given to decay, its soul is a whirl, its destiny hard to determine, and its fame a matter without any meaning. In a word, everything that makes up a human body is a moving stream, what makes up the soul is a dream and vapor; life is a battle, a journey by a stranger, and what comes afterward is oblivion. What, then, is the one sure guide for a man in life? Philosophy. But Philosophy requires that a man keep his spirit free from violence and harm, above all pains and pleasures; that he does nothing without a purpose nor anything falsely and hypocritically; that he act without feeling that a duty should be left to another man's care; and that he accept everything that happens, everything that is fated—for everything comes from the place from which he himself comes. Finally, he accepts death with a calm mind, since death is nothing more than the dissolving of the particles of which every living being is made. If no harm comes to the elements themselves as they continually rearrange themselves in new being, why should a man fear the change the dissolving represents? For it is part of Nature, and nothing in Nature is evil.

STUDY QUESTIONS

1. How is Marcus Aurelius emulating the advice of Epictetus (Document 6.1), and would this have been more difficult for an emperor to follow?
2. Why would accepting the transience of life lead to calmness in the face of death?

6.4B. THE THIRD-CENTURY IMPERIAL-SUCCESSION CRISIS

The massive and chaotic mess of Rome's civil war is made clear by this simple list of the individuals who held, however briefly, the imperial title in the third century. Almost all were generals. As you can see, only five died of natural causes.

Emperor	Reign	Manner of death
Commodus	180–192	Murdered
Pertinax	193	Murdered
Didius Julianus	193	Murdered
Pescennius Niger	193–194	Killed in battle
Clodius Albinus	193–197	Killed in battle
Septimus Severus	193–211	Natural death (!)
Caracalla	211–217	Murdered
Geta	211	Murdered
Macrinus	217–218	Murdered
Diadumenianus	218	Murdered
Elagabalus	218–222	Murdered
Seleucus	218–222	Probably murdered
Uranius	218–222	Probably murdered
Gellius Maximus	218–222	Murdered
Verus	218–222	Murdered
Severus Alexander	222–235	Murdered
Sallustius	225–227	Murdered
Taurinus	225–227	Suicide
Maximinus Thrax	235–238	Murdered
Magnus	235–238	Killed in battle
Quartinus	235–238	Killed in battle
Gordian I	238	Suicide
Gordian II	238	Killed in battle
Pupienus	238	Murdered
Balbinus	238	Murdered
Gordian III	238–244	Killed in battle
Sabinianus	240	Killed in battle
Philippus Arabus	244–249	Killed in battle
Pacatianus	248	Murdered
Iotapianus	248	Murdered
Silbannacus	249	Killed in battle
Sponsianus	249	Killed in battle
Philippus Iunior	249	Murdered
Decius	249–251	Killed in battle
Priscus	250	Murdered
Licinianus	250	Murdered
Henerrius	251	Killed in battle
Hostilian	251	Plague
Trebonianus Gallus	251–253	Murdered
Volusianus	251–253	Murdered
Aemilianus	253	Murdered
Valerian	253–260	Murdered
Mareades	259	Murdered
Gallienus	253–268	Murdered
Ingenuus	260	Suicide
Regalianus	260	Murdered

Emperor	Reign	Manner of death
Macrianus I	260–261	Natural death (!)
Macrianus II	260–261	Murdered
Quietus	260–261	Murdered
Postumus	260–269	Murdered
Piso	261	Murdered
Valens	261	Murdered
Ballista	261	Murdered
Mussius Aemilianus	261	Murdered
Memor	261	Murdered
Aureolus	262	Murdered
Celsus	267	Murdered
Saturninus	267	Murdered
Claudius II	268–270	Plague
Censorinus	268–270	Murdered
Laelianus	269	Murdered
Marius	269	Murdered
Victorinus	269–270	Murdered
Quintilius	270	Suicide
Aurelian	270–275	Murdered
Domitianus	271–272	Murdered
Urbanus	271–272	Murdered
Septimius	271–272	Murdered
Tetricus I	271–274	Natural death (!)
Tetricus II	273–274	Natural death (!)
Firmus	273	Killed in battle
Felicissimus	271	Killed in battle
Faustinus	274	Probably murdered
Tacitus	275–276	Murdered
Florianus	276	Murdered
Probus	276–282	Murdered
Bonosus	280	Suicide
Proculus	280–281	Murdered
Saturninus	281	Murdered
Carus	282–283	Struck by lightning
Numerian	283–284	Murdered
Carinus	283–285	Murdered
Diocletian	288–305	Natural death (!)

6.5 SULPICIA SEVERA, SIX POEMS

Sulpicia Severa (born around 40 BCE) is one of the very few women from ancient Rome whose poems have survived and been identified. She came from a prominent family—her father was a noted jurist who had studied law and oratory under Cicero, and her uncle Messalla (mentioned in the second poem below) was a famous general—but little else is known about her. Only six brief poems survive, having been included in a popular anthology of love poems called the *Corpus Tibullianum*, and they record the emotional tumult felt by a young woman in love with a man named Cerinthus. While the couple have enjoyed some erotic play, Cerinthus longs for more and apparently turns to a prostitute when Sulpicia refuses the sexual completion that they both desire. It is unclear if this episode actually occurred since this type of lovers' conflict was a fairly common trope in the romantic poetry of the Augustan era. The poems appear here in the order they appear in the *Corpus Tibullianum*, but they could be re-ordered in a number of ways, and would tell a different story each time.

1.

Love has come to me at last, a love so great
That hiding it is more shameful than revealing it.
The Muses, Camena and Cytherea, heard my prayer
And brought him here into my arms.
Venus has kept her promises. Let others talk: they
Have never known the joys I now possess.
I wish I could send my love-notes unsealed,
Not caring who might read them before my beloved.
I rejoice in our sin, and to feign otherwise would be a shame
Since I am worthy of being with so worthy a man.

Tandem venit amor, qualem texisse pudori
quam nudasse alicui sit mihi fama magis.
Exorata meis illum Cytherea Camenis
attulit in nostrum deposuitque sinum.
Exsolvit promissa Venus: mea gaudia narret,
dicetur si quis non habuisse sua.
Non ego signatis quicquam mandare tabellis,
ne legat id nemo quam meus ante, velim.
Sed peccasse iuvat, vultus componere famae

taedet: cum digno digna fuisse ferar.

2.

It's my stupid birthday and I have to spend it
in the boring farm-world without my Cerinthus.
What can compare to the City? Some country house
in the cold Aretian fields, is that a place for a girl?
Stop trying so hard to please me, Messalla,
This isn't the right time for a trip: it's cruel!
Since you will not let me do as I choose, my body
Is your prisoner but my heart and soul are free.

Invisus natalis adest, qui rure molesto
Et sine Cerintho tristis agendus erit.
Dulcius urbe quid est? an villa sit apta puellae
atque Arretino frigidus amnis agro?
Iam nimium Messalla mei studiose, quiescas,
non tempestivae, saeve propinque, viae!
Hic animum sensusque meos abducta relinquo
arbitrio quamvis non sinis esse meo.

Translation by Clifford Backman.

3.

You know what? Your girl's sad spirit is uplifted
Since we're spending my birthday after all here in
Rome!
Let's all spend the whole day together—
A bit of good luck you weren't expecting!

Scis iter ex animo sublatum trite puellae?
natali Romae iam licet esse suo.

Omnibus ille dies nobis natalis agatur,
qui nec opinanti nunc tibi forte venit.

4.

It is a good thing you've shown me the man you are
Before I fell too quickly, like a fool, into your bed.
Go enjoy your whore, instead of Sulpicia Servius!
Watch out for your clothes, and be sure to fill her
purse!
There are others who care for me, whom it would
pain
If I lost you to the bed of a Nobody.

Gratum est, securus multum quod iam tibi de me
permittis, subito ne male inepta cadam.
Sit tibi cura togae potior pressumque quasillo
scortum quam Servi filia Sulpicia:

Solliciti sunt pro nobis, quibus illa dolori est,

ne cedam ignoto, maxima causa, toro.

5.

Are you properly worried for your girl, Cerinthus,
Now that fever torments my whole wearied body?
I would not wish to survive this sad state
Unless I knew that that is what you want too.
What good would it do me to get over this illness
If you can bear my sorrow with so calm a heart?

Estne tibi, Cerinthe, tuae pia cura puellae,
quod mea nunc vexat corpora fessa calor?
A! ego non aliter tristes evincere morbos
optarim, quam te si quoque velle putem.
At mihi quid prosit morbos evincere, si tu
nostra potes lento pectore ferre mala?

6.

I may not seem to you, My Light, to have the same
passion
That I seemed to have had a few days ago
If I, being young, did something so stupid
(a thing I regret more than anything I've ever done):
When I left you alone last night
Because I feared showing you how much I desire
you.

Ne tibi sim, mea lux, aeque iam fervida cura

ac videor paucos ante fuisse dies,
si quicquam tota commisi stulta juventa,
cuius me fatear paenituisse magis,
hesterna quam te solum quod nocte reliqui,
ardorem cupiens dissimulare meum.

STUDY QUESTIONS

1. How would you describe the love Sulpicia feels for Cerinthus?
2. Sulpicia lived over two thousand years ago. Would you say her sentiments are fresh and vital for persons alive today? Why or why not?

CHAPTER 7

THE RISE OF CHRISTIANITY IN A ROMAN WORLD

7.1 JOSEPHUS, *THE JEWISH WAR*, CA. 75 CE

Titus Flavius Josephus (37–ca. 100) was a Roman citizen and Jewish historian. His contemporary work (written in Greek) chronicles the Jewish War (66–70 CE)—a bitter revolt against the Roman occupation of Judea, which resulted in the destruction of the Second Temple in 70 CE. This selection details the Roman invasion of Jerusalem and its gruesome aftermath. In writing about the Jewish religion in the first century, Josephus also provides a window into burgeoning Christianity—including references to the historical Jesus and John the Baptist.

CHAPTER 1

The suffering in Jerusalem grew worse every day, and the leaders of the rebellion, who were themselves already in agony, were made even more miserable by the effects of the famine on the general populace. The number of corpses that lay in piles everywhere was indeed a horrible sight, and produced such a noxious stench that it hindered the movement of those who attempted to march forth from the city to fight the Romans. Even so, once the soldiers were suited up and in formation they marched without fear even though they sometimes had to step on the bodies. They did not consider this an offense to the dead or any sort of ill-omen for themselves, for they already bore the guilty stain of killing ten thousand of their own people, and as they moved against the Romans they acted as though they reproached God Himself—for being too slow in punishing them. They continued fighting, but without any hope of victory. . . .

When the Romans finished building their ramparts, the battlements struck fear in the Romans and the Jews alike. The Jews saw that their city would certainly fall if they could not destroy the ramparts by fire, and the Romans feared that they would not be able to replace them, if the Jews managed to burn them down, since the surrounding area was then so deforested and their men so exhausted by labor. . . . What discouraged the Romans the most was the fact that the Jews' courage was stronger than the sufferings they had had to endure. . . .

Translation by Clifford Backman.

CHAPTERS 3–4

The rebels in the temple struggled every day to drive the Roman soldiers from their battlements. One day—it was the twenty-seventh day of Tamuz—they devised a plan. They stuffed the entire western portico with dry materials, bitumen, and pitch, all the way to the beams that supported the roof, and then made a show of sloughing off in a state of exhaustion. This inspired the most rash of the Romans to get excited and attempt to pursue them. They set the ladders against the portico and climbed atop it. That was when the more prudent Romans understood what was happening and stopped their climb. But by this time the roof was full of soldiers—and the Jews immediately set the whole trap on fire. Flames flew everywhere in an instant. The Romans who had halted their climb were anguished by the fate of their fellows, who cried out in distress. Seeing themselves surrounded by flames, they threw themselves headlong from the roof, some into the city streets and some into the temple courtyard itself, right in the midst of their enemies. . . . Among the Romans was a young man named Longus, who deserves to be remembered—so let him serve as a monument to all those who were slain. The Jews admired this Longus very much on account of his courage, and very much wanted him dead. They promised him no harm, if he would surrender himself to them. His brother Cornelius, however, told him not to hand himself over, since to do so would tarnish his honor and that of the whole Roman army. And so Longus lifted his sword and killed himself. . . .

The number of Jews who died of famine in the city was prodigious, their sufferings unspeakable. If so little as a morsel of any kind of food was found, violence broke out and even best friends would take arms against each other in order to get it. . . . People ran about in a daze, stumbling and staggering like mad dogs, reeling against doors like drunkards. . . . Their hunger was so great that they put anything at all into their mouths, even things that the vilest animals would not touch: belts and sandals, the leather that they stripped from their shields, husks of straw. . . . But why should I go on listing the shameful level that famine drove people

to? Especially when I have a story to tell unlike any story in any book of history. . . .

There was a woman named Mary, the daughter of Eleazar, who came from the village of Bethezob (which means "house of hyssop" in Hebrew) beyond the Jordan River. Of good family and wealth, she had fled to Jerusalem like everyone else and was there when the Roman siege began. Everything she possessed that she had brought with her had been snatched away, including whatever food she had managed to save, by the rapacious guardsmen who burst into her house every day in search of something to eat. This drove her half-crazed and prompted her to hurl abuse and threats at the rebels, who, though they grew very angry at her, refrained from ending her misery by killing her. . . . When the famine grew so bad that it pierced her very bowels, she was driven to a point of madness . . . and snatching up her infant son, she said to him, "Poor child! How can I save you from this war, this famine, these rebels? As for the Romans, if we survive the war they will make us slaves. The famine will kill us, though, before our enslavement begins. And these rebels are a worse scourge than the other two. So come, dear child. Be my food, be a curse upon the rebels, and a warning to the whole world. Your death completes the sufferings of the Jews." Having said these words, she killed her son and roasted him. After she had eaten half of his body, she took the other half and put it away, and at this very moment the rebels returned to her home. Despite the horrible scent they warned her that they would cut her throat on the spot if she did not hand over whatever she had been cooking. Mary then replied that she had a nice portion for each of them and took the covering off what was left of her son. The men were filled with horror and revulsion as they looked at the sight. "Come and eat!" she said. "This is my son. I did this myself. Eat, here's food for you; I've already had some. No? Don't pretend that you're more delicate than a woman, or that you have more compassion for him than I do. But if you're going to be so fussy, and reject my sacrificial offering, leave the second half for me too." Hearing this, the men withdrew with a shudder. Nothing had ever shaken them so, yet they found it difficult to leave the boy's remains with the mother. Soon the whole city had learned of this dreadful occurrence and everyone shuddered to picture the scene to themselves. Fearing that they too could be driven to such an extreme, many prayed for death and regarded those who had already perished as fortunate not to have survived to hear of such wretchedness. . . .

When two of the legions had finished building their ramparts, on the eighth day of the month of Ab, Titus ordered his battering rams to be brought forward and set against the western wall of the inner temple. Prior to this, a variety of smaller siege engines had blasted the wall non-stop for six days without making a crack in it. . . . But by this time some soldiers had already set fire to the gates, the silver-plating on which failed to stop the flames from reaching the wood underneath. The fire spread quickly then, and in no time reached the cloisters. When the Jews saw the flames engulfing more and more of the temple their spirits broke and they collapsed to the ground so horrorstruck that hardly any of them ran to quench the fire or to flee; instead they watched in stunned silence. . . .

Titus sought his commanders' opinions about what should be done about the temple. Some of them advocated following the rules of warfare and demolishing it, since the Jews would never cease their rebellions against Rome so long as the temple stood. Others recommended that Titus save the building for the Jews on condition that they abandon it, remove all their weaponry from it, and surrender—but if the Jews refused, they urged, then Titus should let the flames consume it, since in that case the building could be regarded as more of a military base than a sacred dwelling. In such a case, they urged, the impiety of burning a sacred site would belong not with the Romans but with the rebels whose actions had led to this result. . . . [In the end] Titus ordered a company of volunteers to make their way through the ruins and put out the fire. . . . But when Titus retired for the night several Jews who had been lying in wait leapt out at the Romans once more, attacking those who were attempting to quench the fire in the inner temple. The Romans drove off their attackers and proceeded all the way to the innermost sanctum of the temple, whereupon one of the soldiers, unbidden and unconcerned for the consequences of his rash

act, snatched a burning timber and set fire to a gilt-edged window, through which ran a passageway that extended to all the rooms on the north side of the temple. The flames quickly spread even further, and the Jews let out a great cry . . . for it was then certain that their entire holy house would perish.

CHAPTERS 8–10

Then one of the temple priests—Jesus, the son of Thebuthus—came forward, having received Caesar's grant of safe-passage, bringing various treasures that had been deposited in the temple. He handed over to Caesar a treasure of candlesticks, tables, cisterns and vials, all made of solid gold and very heavy. He surrendered a number of veils and garments too, each studded with precious stones, and a great number of other precious vessels that they had used in their worship. Phineas, the temple's treasurer, also brought forth a wealth of purple and scarlet cloaks and priestly vestments, such as were worn in the Holy of Holies, along with vast quantities of cinnamon, cassia, and other sweet spices which they regularly used to mix together and offer as incense to God. . . .

Caesar, seeing so great a multitude of Jews in the city, but aware that his own men were exhausted from killing, ordered that no more Jews should be killed except those who had taken arms against Rome; all the rest were to be taken alive. . . . The number of captives was ninety-seven thousand, and the number of the dead was one million and one hundred thousand—the majority of whom were Jews who did not live in Jerusalem itself but had come up to the city for the feast of unleavened bread. . . . The number of those who perished exceeded those ever destroyed before by man or God, anywhere in the world. To consider only the publicly-known accounts, the Romans killed some, carried over others as captives, and even searched underground for more. Finding many of these latter ones, the Romans broke open the ground and killed everyone they found. They also found some two thousand Jews who had already killed themselves underground, and some who had died of famine. The stench of these corpses was so great that most of the Romans had to withdraw. Some others, though, were greedy, climbed over and picked through the heaps of dead bodies. The Jews had hidden much treasure in these caverns, enough to make many Romans think any way of acquiring it was unlawful. . . .

Thus was Jerusalem taken, in the second year of the reign of Vespasian, on the eighth day of the month of Elul. . . . From the time of King David, the first Jew to rule from there, to that of Titus'

destruction of the temple were one thousand, one hundred, and seventy-nine years. But from the building of the city to its end were two thousand, one hundred, and seventy-seven years. Neither its antiquity, nor its riches, neither the spread of its people over all the earth, nor the extraordinary veneration given to it as a holy site, could save it from destruction. Thus ended the siege of Jerusalem.

STUDY QUESTIONS

1. What were, according to Josephus, the Romans' reasons for burning down the temple?
2. How did the Romans display humane qualities in the midst of the siege and sack of Jerusalem? Could these descriptions have resulted from Josephus's overall motives in writing?

7.2 PLINY THE YOUNGER, LETTERS, 97–112 CE

The nephew of the naturalist Pliny the Elder, Gaius Plinius Caecilius Secundus, called Pliny the Younger (61–112), passed through the *cursus honorum* under the emperors Domitian and Trajan. A friend of Tacitus (author of Document 6.2) and employer of Suetonius (author of Document 6.3), Pliny the Younger also wove his personal experiences of imperial Rome into his works. In his "Letter to Tacitus," Pliny poignantly describes his uncle's death in the eruption of Mount Vesuvius (79); in his "Letter to Trajan," he recounts his understanding of early Christianity in the Roman Empire.

To Tacitus

You asked me to send you an account of my uncle's death, so that you may describe it accurately in your writings. I am honored by your request—for if this disaster is recorded by you, I am sure that it will live forever in memory. . . .

On the 24th of August, in early afternoon, my mother asked my uncle to take a look at a cloud of

unusual size and shape. . . . He rose from his books and mounted a small hill nearby, from which he could get a better view of the uncommon sight. It was not clear at first which mountain the cloud was surrounding, but we later learned, of course, that it was Mount Vesuvius. The cloud, as it rose up from the mountain, was shaped rather like a pine tree and shot up to a tremendous height. . . . It appeared bright

Translation by Clifford Backman.

in some places, and dark and mottled in others, because of the dirt and ashes cast up in it. . . . My uncle ordered his small boat to be readied, and climbed on board. . . . He steered his course directly at the danger, the better to see what was happening and to dictate his observations of the whole dreadful scene [to his secretary]. . . . He got so close to the mountain that cinders, pumice-stones, and blackened bits of burning rock were falling into his boat, getting thicker and hotter the closer he drew. . . . Wide tongues of flame burst from the sides of Vesuvius, showing bright and clear. . . .

[After landing and advancing to the villages and towns under the mountain] he witnessed houses rocking from side to side as though shaken from their foundations by repeated blows. In the open fields burning rocks and cinders fell in profusion . . . forcing them to tie pillows to their heads with table napkins as their only defense against the storm of stones . . . They thought it best to return to the shore and see if they could embark, but the waves were extremely high and roiling. My uncle lay down on a sail-cloth that his servants had spread out for him, and called twice for some water to drink. He drank, but as he did so a wall of sulphurous flames came so close that they had to rise and leave. Helped by two servants, my uncle stood—and instantly fell over, dead. I suppose he suffocated on the noxious fumes.

To Trajan

I always turn to you, my lord, when in doubt—for there is no one I trust better to guide me when I am uncertain and to teach me when I am ignorant of any matter. I have never had anything to do with a trial of Christians, and don't know what charges are made against them, or how they are investigated, and what degree of bother to go through in the effort. I am more than a little uncertain about whether to treat them all the same or to make concessions to the young and the aged among them. Are they to be pardoned if they express contrition? If a man used to be a Christian but has since ceased to be one, is he to be free of punishment? If one is a Christian but has otherwise committed no offense, should he be charged [with a crime]? Or do we prosecute only those Christians who commit additional offenses?

In dealing with the Christians who have been brought before me, I have done as follows. First, I questioned them as to whether or not they were Christians. Those who acknowledged it I then questioned a second and third time, threatening them with punishment. Those who persisted in their ways, I had executed. Whatever the nature of their beliefs, I decided, they deserved punishment simply for being so stubborn and obstinate. There were some among them who were Roman citizens, and I signed orders for them to be transferred to Rome.

Accusations against others then spread, as so often happens, and several things followed. An anonymous affidavit was published that listed the names of many people who were believed to be Christians. Those who denied that they were or had ever been Christians I put to the test; I had them invoke the Roman gods, offer prayer and incense and wine to your image (which I had ordered to be brought together for this specific purpose—along with statues of the gods), and curse Christ. It is said that no true Christian can be forced to do any one of these things—and so those who passed the test I ordered to be released. Others named by the anonymous tipster swore oaths that they were Christians—but then they denied it, saying that they used to be Christians but had long since ceased to be, anywhere from three to twenty-five years ago. These too all worshiped your image, sacrificed to the statues of the gods, and cursed Christ.

They testified, though, that the extent of their former error had been limited to meeting with other Christians on a fixed day, before dawn, and singing responsively a hymn to Christ as their god, and that they swore simply not to commit fraud, theft, or adultery, not to bear false witness, and not to refuse to return anything that had been entrusted to them. Having done this, they said, they usually separated but reassembled later [and somewhere else] in order to share a meal. A simple, regular meal, I should add. But they insisted that they had ceased even this limited participation after, in accordance with your instruction, I had released an edict forbidding political associations. Naturally, I thought it prudent to find out if this was really true by torturing two slave-women whom the Christians call "deaconesses." All that I learned from this, though, was disgusting and gross superstition.

That is when I stopped my investigation and hurried to consult you. The matter strikes me as warranting this appeal because of the number of people involved. There are many lives at stake—of every age and rank, and both sexes. This superstition is spreading like a contagion and is now to be found not only in the cities but also in villages and on farms; nevertheless, it is possible to stop it and cure it. It is abundantly clear that our temples, which for a time had been almost deserted, have once again begun to be frequented; that the established rites, so long neglected, are being resumed; and that sacrificial animals are coming in from everywhere—animals for which not too long ago hardly a single purchaser could be found. This is why I think it easy to imagine multitudes of people returning [to Roman ways] if an opportunity for amnesty is offered.

[Trajan responded to Pliny with a brief letter of his own.]

You did well, Pliny, in sifting through the cases of the people charged with being Christians. It is not possible to lay down a single rule to serve as a fixed guide. Christians should not be sought out, but if any are accused and brought before you, and if you find them guilty, they should be punished. There is one exception to this rule. Anyone who denies being a Christian and proves it by worshipping our gods should be granted amnesty even if he was under suspicion in the past. Anonymous public accusations should have no place in our justice—for it would establish a dangerous precedent to accept such accusations, and it would be against the spirit of our age.

STUDY QUESTIONS

1. How did Pliny the Elder's scientific curiosity lead to his death in 79 CE?
2. Were Pliny's goals and methods in dealing with the Christians brought before him reasonable? Were the Christians merely stubborn?

7.3 CELSUS/ORIGEN, *CONTRA CELSUS*, BOOK I, CHAPTERS 6 AND 28; BOOK III, CHAPTER 62; BOOK IV, CHAPTER 73; BOOK VIII, CHAPTERS 41, 49, AND 55, CA. 177 CE

The Greek philosopher Celsus (second century) wrote a treatise against early Christians entitled *On the True Doctrine*. Although this work has not survived on its own, it was incorporated into the treatise *Against Celsus* by Origen (ca. 184–ca. 253), a theologian and church father who quoted many passages and then responded to Celsus's accusations, claim by claim. In this way, scholars

http://web.archive.org/web/20060201230403/http://duke.usask.ca/~niallm/252/Celstop.htm/.
Translation by Clifford Backman.

can recreate much of Celsus's original text. The portions included here reveal Celsus's accusations of doctrine (such as the virgin birth), historical points (Jesus's affiliation with the lowest classes), and the relationship between Christians and their God.

Note to Reader:

Celsus's words appear in regular type; Origen's interpolations are in italics.

It is by invoking the names of demons and reciting incantations that the Christians seem to possess [miraculous] power. That was how [Jesus] accomplished his marvels—by sorcery—and since he understood that others would eventually learn the same skills and do the same things as he, and that they would boast of doing them "by the power of the Lord," he therefore denied them admittance to his kingdom. But if he excludes sorcerers for doing the same things he had done, then he is wicked. And if he is not wicked for what he did, then neither are those who do the same. . . . [1.6]

Celsus describes the case of the Jew who disputed with Jesus and defeated Him (or so he thought) on a variety of points. In the first place, he accuses Christ of having invented the story of His virgin birth, and reproaches Him for having been born in a Jewish village to a poor rustic who made her living by spinning and was denounced by her carpenter-husband because of her adultery. Rejected by her husband, she wandered aimlessly for a while until, in her shame, she gave birth to the bastard Jesus. This Jesus, being poor, eventually found work as a servant in Egypt—where he learned some of the magical powers that the Egyptians pride themselves on knowing. It was then that he returned to his homeland, full of himself because of his new knowledge, and by means of these powers proclaimed himself a God. . . . [1.28]

I charge the Christians with nothing more than the truth, as you can see by the following. In other cults, anyone who wishes to invite [an outsider] to participate in its mysteries always says, "Anyone with clean hands and a pure tongue, [enter]," or "Whoever is without pollution, whose spirit knows no evil, and who has lived a just and upright life, [enter]." These are the invitations used by those who promise to purify people of sin. But who do these Christians invite? Every sinner! Everyone devoid of understanding! Whoever is a child! In a word, any miserable person at all! That's who they say will be received in the kingdom of God. But is a thief not a sinner? A cad? A burglar? A poisoner? One guilty of sacrilege? A grave-robber? Who wouldn't a man invite [into a cult], if he would invite such criminals as these? . . . [3.59]

The Christians say that it was specifically to sinners that God was sent. But why was he not sent to those who were without sin? What is wrong with not being sinful? It seems that God will welcome the unrighteous man who repents his wickedness but not the righteous man who approaches God with virtue from the very beginning! . . . [3.62]

Isn't it ridiculous to think that the same God who, in his righteous fury, threatened the Jews, then killed them all (including their infants), and destroyed their city by fire, would send his own son among them, to endure the sufferings this Jesus endured? . . . [4.73]

You may mock and scorn the statues of our divinities—but if you were to insult Bacchus or Hercules face-to-face you would feel the consequence of it. But those who crucified your God when He was living among you suffered nothing, neither then nor later. And what has happened since his death to make anyone believe that he wasn't a fake, this "Son of God"? So: the God who sent his own son to earth with teachings meant for all mankind let his son be treated abominably, and let his teachings vanish—and all without showing a single sign of concern? What father was ever so cruel? Now, you can say that he suffered so much because he wanted to, that it was his desire to endure all that came at him. But then you have to allow that the same could be true of those [pagan] gods you revile and reject—that they too want to be reviled, and that they are therefore now bearing it all patiently. You have to play fair on both sides. But [watch out]: our gods always punish those who scorn them. Get ready to run and hide, or be caught and perish! . . . [8.41]

Do you not see the absurd contradiction in making so much of the human body as you do—to look expectantly for it to rise from the dead—as if it were the single most precious part of us, and yet, on the other hand, to treat it with such scorn that you willingly expose it to torture? Any person who values the body yet can think such things, is someone who doesn't deserve to be reasoned with. Instead, he exposes himself as a gross being, polluted, and determined to reject common sense for no reason at all. I wish to converse with people who hope to enjoy eternal life with God by means of their spirit or mind—whether they want to call it a "spiritual substance," or a "spirit of holy and blessed intelligence," or a "living soul," or a "heavenly and eternal offspring of a divine spiritual nature," or any other name they wish. For these are the people who are right—the ones who understand that those

who live upright lives shall be blessed, and those who are unjust shall receive eternal torment—and who never waver from this truth. . . . [8.49]

[The Christians] have to make a choice. If they want to refuse to render due service to the [pagan] gods and respect to those men who preside over their cults, then let them not grow to manhood, take wives, or have children; let them take no part in the business of life; and let them leave this world with all possible speed and leave no one behind them, so that their whole hateful race may disappear from the face of the earth. On the other hand, though, if they wish to marry and raise children, to taste the fruits of the earth and to partake of all of life's blessings and its appointed sorrows (for Nature has decreed a portion of sorrows to all men, since sorrows must exist—and earth is the only place for them), then they must accept the duties of life until they are released from its bonds, and they must pay the honor due to those gods who control the affairs of this life—unless, that is, they want to appear ungrateful. But it would be gross injustice, if they wish to receive the blessings that the gods bestow, but pay them nothing in return. [8.55]

STUDY QUESTIONS

1. Could Celsus's criticisms be used to recreate Christian beliefs, even central ones, in the period he was writing (late second century)?
2. In what ways are the charges of injustice and immorality applied to Christians, and were such charges deserved?

7.4A. THE NICENE CREED, TWO VERSIONS

This creed was recorded at the Council of Nicaea (325 CE) to clarify early Christian beliefs as they were confronted with Arian heresy. The heretic Arius (ca. 250–336) held that although Jesus was the divine Son of God, he was also created, meaning that he was not eternal alongside God the Father. This posed problems for the orthodox Christian belief in a Trinity that was made of three

Translation by Clifford Backman.

distinct persons (Father, Son, and Holy Spirit) who were also one being—thus, threatening the Son's eternal nature also threatened this unity. These versions of the Nicene Creed reveal how doctrine changed over time to accommodate and clarify changing Christian realities.

THE FIRST VERSION OF THE NICENE CREED

We believe in one God, the Father Almighty,
  Maker of all things seen and unseen.
We believe in one Lord, Jesus Christ, the Son of
  God,
The only-begotten of the Father, God of God,
  Light of Light,
true God of true God, begotten—not made—
one in substance with the Father.
Through Him all things were made, both those in
  heaven and those on earth.
For us men and for our salvation He came down
  from Heaven, was incarnate, and was made
  man.
He suffered [death] and rose again on the third
  day. He ascended into Heaven and He shall
  come again to judge the quick and the dead.
  We believe in the Holy Spirit.

And anyone who says that there was a time when
  the Son of God was not, or that before He was
  begotten He was not, or that He was made of
  things that were not, or that He is of different
  substance or essence [from the Father], or
  that He is created, subject to change, or to
  conversion—the Catholic and Apostolic
  Church anathematizes him.

THE FINAL VERSION OF THE NICENE CREED

We believe in one God, the Father Almighty,
  maker of heaven and earth, and of all that is,
  seen and unseen.

We believe in one Lord, Jesus Christ, the only

Son of God.
  eternally begotten of the Father, God
  from God, Light from Light,
  true God from true God, begotten—not
  made—
  one in Being with the Father.
  Through Him all things were made.
  For us men and for our salvation He
  came down from heaven; by
  the power of the Holy Spirit he
  was born of the Virgin Mary,
  and became man.
  For our sake He was crucified under
  Pontius Pilate; He suffered,
  died, and was buried. On the
  third day He rose again in
  accordance with the Scriptures;
  He ascended into Heaven and
  is seated at the right hand of
  the Father. He will come again
  in glory to judge the living and
  the dead, and His kingdom will
  have no end.

We believe in the Holy Spirit, the Lord, the giver
  of life, who proceeds from the Father and
  the Son. With the Father and the Son he is
  worshipped and glorified. He has spoken
  through the prophets.

We believe in one holy Catholic and apostolic
  Church. We acknowledge one baptism for
  the forgiveness of sins. We look for the
  resurrection of the dead and the life of the
  world to come. Amen.

STUDY QUESTIONS

1. What caused a need for a document of this type, and how was it designed to be used?
2. How do both versions of the creed deal with the specific, if thorny, issue of the Christian Trinity?

7.4B. MINUCIUS FELIX, *OCTAVIUS*, CHAPTER 30, "RITUAL CANNIBALISM CHARGE AGAINST CHRISTIANS," 200–300 CE

Although little is known of Minucius Felix's personal information, his work *Octavius* provides many telling details about early understandings of the Christian faith. *Octavius* is staged as a discussion between a pagan, Caecilius Natalis, and a Christian, Octavius Januarius, where Minucius Felix plays the peacekeeper. In this way, the author is able to correct misunderstandings and assumptions about Christian faith and practice.

I would like to meet the man who thinks or says that we engage in the blood-sacrifice of babies! Who can possibly believe anyone could injure an infant, so small, so tender, to draw blood from it and drain its life away before it even has a chance to live? The only person capable of doing such a thing is the one capable of thinking such a thing! Romans, I have seen you abandon your children to wild beasts and birds of prey! I have seen you crush them and strangle them! O, what miserable deaths. You have women who drink potent potions to end the lives that have begun in their wombs—murder before birth. And all these things you have learned from your gods. Saturn not only exposed his children—he devoured them. Parents in parts of Africa have been known to kiss and caress their bawling babies, soothing them so that Saturn not be given a sacrifice who was in tears. Both the Tauri of Pontus and the Busiri of Egypt immolate their own house-guests as a sacred rite. The Gauls inhumanely offer human sacrifices to Mercury. Roman priests have been known to bury Greek men and women alive—yes, and Gallic ones too! To this very day you worship Jupiter Latiaris with murder—a suitable sacrifice, actually, for a son of Saturn, gorged as he is with the blood of evil criminals. I believe it was Saturn himself taught Catiline how to swear a blood-oath to a political conspiracy; who taught Bellona to bathe her sacred rites in human gore; and who taught men to treat epilepsy by drinking human blood—a "cure" worse than the disease itself. Good followers of Saturn are those who eat the wild beasts in the arena, wet and dripping with the blood of their victims, and fattened with the flesh and entrails of men. No! To we Christians it is unlawful to see or permit murder. And not only do we shrink from human blood, we won't even use the blood of animals in our food.

Our devilish attackers have spread another lie about us too—namely, that we engage in incestuous orgies; our detractors' goal is to stoke popular loathing against us, staining the glory of our modesty with an outrageous charge, so that people will hate us before they even have a chance to learn the truth. That is what your hatchet-man Fronto did. He levied a charge at us but offered no evidence, only some random rhetorical accusations. Other peoples, however, are the founders of this vile horror. Among the Persians son and mother are permitted promiscuous relations. Men marry their own sisters in Egypt as well as in Greece. Your legends and stage-tragedies—which you both read and hear with such pleasure—are filled with tales of incest. You worship incestuous gods who have intercourse with their own mothers, sisters, and daughters. Is it any wonder that you permit and indulge in incest yourselves? Wretches!

Translation by Clifford Backman.

You probably even engage in it without knowing it, gratifying your lust, as you do, constantly, and fathering children everywhere. But in your wanderings you expose your children at home to the lusts of others. Is it any wonder, then, that all of you eventually return to your own seed? Thus you continue the stain of incest without knowing it.

We [Christians], however, preserve our modesty—not only in our appearance but in our hearts, living as we do, gladly, within the bonds of faithful marriage. We each approach our one and only wife, if we desire to procreate, or we approach no one at all. At our banquets the only thing we share is our food, and our banquets are modest and sober. We do not indulge in entertainments and long bouts of drinking. We temper our joy with gravity and chaste conversation. Our bodies too are chaste—and more than chaste, since many of us choose lives of sworn celibacy; we delight in our chastity but make no boast of it. So far are we, in fact, from incestuous indulgence that many of us cannot even hear of normal sexual relations between men and women without blushing.

STUDY QUESTIONS

1. From what specific practices of the Christians did the charges of incest and cannibalism ultimately, if mistakenly, derive?
2. How does Octavius turn these charges against non-Christians?

7.5 THE GOSPEL OF THOMAS, CA. 300–400 CE

Discovered in 1945, the Gospel of Thomas numbers among the fifty-two writings preserved in a cave in Egypt. Written in Coptic, the Gospel of Thomas—the disciple of Jesus—is an extra-biblical text read by Gnostics. Although it was never accepted in the canonical Bible, the Gospel of Thomas was popular in certain geographical regions like Syria, where Thomas converted Christians after Jesus's death. The 114 sayings in this "Gospel" partly reflect the familiar sayings from the four synoptic Gospels and partly emerge from Gnostic understandings of early Christian tenets.

Jesus said, "If you do not abstain from the world, you will not find the kingdom of God. And if you do not keep the Sabbath, you will not see the Father." [1.4–11]

Jesus also said, "I stood amidst the world and appeared to the people in the flesh. I found everyone satiated, and no one thirsty. My heart worries about the children of man because they are blind in their hearts and they do not see." [1.11–21]

Jesus also said, "Wherever there are three, they are without God; but where there is only one, I say

From the *Oxyrhynchus Papyri*, no. 1, 654, and 655. Translation by Clifford Backman.

that I am with him. Lift the stone and there you will find me. Split the wood, and I am there." [1.23–30]

And Jesus said, "A prophet is not accepted in his own land, nor does a physician heal those who know him." [1.30–5]

Jesus also said, "A city set on the summit of a high mountain can neither fall nor be hidden." [1.36–41]

These are the hidden sayings that Jesus spoke when alive and that Judas, also called Thomas, wrote down. And he said, "Whoever understands how to interpret these sayings will not taste death." [654.1–5]

"Let the seeker not stop seeking until he finds [what he seeks]; and when he finds it, he will marvel. When he marvels, he will have authority; and when he has authority, he will know peace." [654.5–9]

Jesus also said, "If those leading you say 'The kingdom [of God] is in the sky,' then the birds of the sky will guide you. If they say 'The kingdom is below ground,' then the fish of the sea will lead you. The kingdom of God is within you, and without

you. Whoever knows himself will find this out. And when you know yourself, you will know that you are the children of the living Father. But if you do not know yourself, you live in poverty and you are poor." [654.9–21]

Jesus also said, "A person old in years will not hesitate to ask a child—even if he is only seven days old—about his place in life . . . For many who are first will be last, and many who are last will be first."[654.21–7]

Jesus also said, "Know what is in front of your face, and that which is hidden from you will be revealed. For there is nothing hidden that will not be made clear, and nothing buried that will not be raised again." [654.27–31]

His disciples said to Jesus, "When will we be visible? When will we be able to see you?" And Jesus answered, "When you are naked and not ashamed." [655i.17–23]

STUDY QUESTIONS

1. Is a collection of sayings like this one more useful than the narrative basis of the canonical Gospels (Matthew, Mark, Luke, and John)?
2. How does the document reveal the effect of "secret" knowledge imparted among Gnostic Christians?

7.6 AUGUSTINE OF HIPPO, SEVENTH DISCOURSE ON THE GOSPEL OF JOHN

The bishop of Hippo (in modern Algeria), Saint Augustine (354–430) shaped the theology and philosophy of Christianity on the brink of the end of the Roman Empire. Originally a heretical Manichean, Augustine experienced a personal conversion and entered into study with Saint Ambrose (ca. 330–397). Augustine's major works include *City of God*, a treatise on the eternal world

Translation by Clifford Backman.

beyond earth, and the autobiographical *Confessions*. Although he wrote many memorable texts on large, definitive issues—from the doctrine of original sin to just war theory—Augustine also devoted himself to pastoral care. This sermon, preached to his congregation while a pagan festival temptingly occurred outside the church, reveals a more personal side of Augustine's understanding of man's relationship to God.

No one has ever seen God. Yet, if we love one another, God remains in us, and his love is brought to perfection in us. This is how we know that we remain in him and he in us, that he has given us of his Spirit. Moreover, we have seen and testify that the Father sent his Son as savior of the world. Whoever acknowledges that Jesus is the Son of God, God remains in him and he in God. We have come to know and to believe in the love God has for us. God is love, and whoever remains in love remains in God and God in him.

Love is a sweet word, but sweeter still is the deed. We cannot be always speaking of it, for we have so many things to do and our daily business pulls us in different directions. It's not that we don't have nothing better to talk about—we just don't have the time to sit around and talk about love. But although we cannot be always talking about it, we may always be loving. Just as with the "Alleluia" that we sing daily this time of year—are we in fact always singing it? Of course not. We don't sing "Alleluia" for an hour, by which I mean not only that we don't sing it for an entire hour but that we don't even sing it for a single minute out of every hour. We're too busy with other things.

"Alleluia," as you know, means "Praise the Lord." The person who praises God aloud cannot always be doing it, but the one who praises God by the way he lives his life, can do so always. Acts of mercy and love, the holiness of piety, chastity, and sobriety—all these are things we can practice all the time, in public or at home, with others or alone in our rooms, while conversing or keeping quiet, when busy or at leisure. And we should practice them always, because all of these are internal virtues. . . .

Dear brothers, you heard earlier in the Gospel reading (at least if you were listening not only with your ears but with your heart), "Take care not to perform righteous deeds in order that people may see them." [Matt 6.1] Now, did Jesus mean by this, that we should hide from the eyes of others the good things we do, out of fear of being seen? But if we fear spectators, then we will never have imitators—and so we ought to be seen doing good, but we should not do good in order to be seen doing it. . . . Do good not to win praise for yourself but for the God who has given you the ability to do good. . . . I tell you, my brothers, and in fact I would not let this go unsaid: Take up good works whenever you can, regardless of the season, the day, and the hour. . . . What you can, when you can. . . . Let your charity never cease or be interrupted. Love always, in every season. As it is written, "Let mutual love continue." [Heb 13.1]

Some of you have probably been wondering, while I've been talking about this epistle of St. John, why it is "brotherly" love he emphasizes so much. . . . He speaks over and over again of this love—and yet he seldom mentions the love we should have for God. (He does mention love for God, of course.) Similarly, he says hardly a word about loving our enemies. He extols and preaches charity with the greatest energy, but tells us only to love one another rather than to love our enemies. But we just heard, in our Gospel reading, "For if you love those who love you, what recompense will you have? Do not the tax collectors do the same?" [Matt 5.46]. . . . Love is like fire: it touches first what is nearest before extending to what is further away. A beloved person is closer to you than a stranger, and a benign stranger is closer to you than a sworn enemy. So give your love to those who are closest to you . . . then extend it to strangers who have done you no ill, and then extend it again to your enemies. This is what the Lord requires of us—and it explains why John here says nothing about loving an enemy. . . .

All love—both common human love (for which we use the word *amor*) and spiritual love (the love we have for what we aspire to, and for which we use the word *dilectio*)—involves desiring the well-being of the one loved. Whether we mean *dilectio* or *amor* (the latter being the word Christ used when He asked, "Peter, do you love me?" [John 21.17]), we do not mean that we love others in the way, say, that a glutton loves fowl—for he loves fowl in order to kill them and eat them; his love desires the end of their existence. We love food in order to consume it and be strengthened by it—but that is not how we love people. That love is benevolent and springs from a desire to do good for others. If there is no good we can do for someone, the desire for it alone suffices to prove our love. We certainly don't wish someone to be wretched, so that we can extend mercy to him! Feed the hungry, certainly; but how much better it would be if no one knew hunger and we had no one to give bread to. Clothe the naked, but oh, that all were clothed and need did not exist! We bury the dead, but how we look forward to the time when life is eternal and no one dies! We reconcile those who are in disagreement, yet how much we hope for the eternal peace of Jerusalem, where everyone shall live in harmony! . . .

Dear brothers, I've spoken at some length here, because the importance of the love we give to others requires it. If there be no love in us, then my words are useless; but if we have that love, then my words will be like oil cast upon a flame. To one without a feeling of love, perhaps my words may kindle it; to one with flame already lit, perhaps my words will fuel it. . . . "If we love one another, God remains in us, and his love is brought to perfection in us." [1 John 4.12] Begin to love, and be perfected—for God has thereby begun to dwell within you, and his in-dwelling will make you perfect. "This is how we know that we remain in him and he in us, that he has given us of his Spirit." [1 John 4.13] Thanks be to God! . . .

So much do I love to speak about love that I almost wish this epistle had no end. No other text is so impassioned in calling us to love; there is no sweeter message that can be preached to us, nor more healthful for us to imbibe—but only if we acknowledge God's gift by living in love. Let us not forget to be thankful for such a great and gracious gift. God had only one Son, but desires that He be not an only child. He wishes us to be His brothers, adopted by Him into eternal life.

STUDY QUESTIONS

1. How does Augustine describe the feeling of "love" in terms of actual deeds?
2. What is the style of this sermon, and how might it have appealed to an audience?

CHAPTER 8

THE EARLY MIDDLE AGES

8.1 PROCOPIUS, TWO VIEWS OF THE EMPEROR JUSTINIAN, FROM *THE SECRET HISTORY*, CA. 554 CE

Procopius (d. 565), as the emperor Justinian's official biographer, worked close to the emperor and accompanied his general, Belisarius, on his campaigns to restore imperial authority over Italy and North Africa. His two authorized works—*The Wars of Justinian* and *The Buildings of Justinian*—are seldom read by anyone but specialists. His unauthorized and anonymous *Secret History*, however, has become famous. In it, Procopius unleashes a stream of pent-up hostility towards Justinian, his wife Theodora, the general Belisarius, and his wife Antonina. His claims about Theodora's sexual adventures are exaggerated and perhaps entirely fictional. The whole tenor of the *Secret History* is one of a perverse fantasia.

Such is how things stood in Constantinople and everywhere else, for as is the case with any disease, the evil that started there in the capital quickly spread throughout the entire empire. But the emperor [Justinian] hardly noticed anything wrong at all, for he was incapable of seeing even what was happening in front of his own eyes in the Hippodrome. He was, in fact, a cretin, with no more sense than an ass that follows, with a twitch of its ears, anyone who pulls on its reins.

Behaving this way, he made a mess of everything. No sooner had he taken over the government from his uncle than he began to squander the public's money wildly, once he got his hands on it. He wasted a lot of it on the Huns, time and again, for supposedly serving the empire, which resulted, predictably, in our provinces being constantly attacked—for once the savages had tasted imperial wealth, they were forever on the road to the capital. He was as quick to throw money into the sea, by erecting at vast expense a series of breakwaters to hold back the surging waves. These stretched far out into the sea, as though he believed he could rival the roaring strength of the ocean with the power of cash.

He confiscated for himself the private estates of many Roman citizens throughout the land, either by accusing them of some crime they had never

Translation by Clifford Backman.

committed or by flattering them into thinking they were giving him a gift. Others, who actually had committed murders and other felonies, made over their estates to him and thus escaped prosecution; while still others, who were engaged in fraudulent suits to gain control of their neighbors' lands, when they realized they couldn't win in the courts, simply transferred their claim to Justinian and left the whole matter. In this way, by means of empty gestures, they won the emperor's favor and gained access to him by handing over property they had no legal claim to— all at their victims' expense.

This seems a fitting time to describe Justinian's personal appearance. In body he was neither tall nor short, just average; not thin (in fact, slightly fat). He had a round and not-unpleasant face. Even after a two-day fast he had good color. To sum up his appearance quickly, he bore a strong resemblance to [the emperor] Domitian, the son of Vespasian, whose behavior so outraged the Romans that they were not satisfied even with hacking him to pieces, but appeased their wrath by a Senate decree that his name should be obliterated from all inscriptions, and that no statue or portrait of him should be allowed to survive. Thus his name was chiseled out of every inscription in the empire and everywhere else it appeared, leaving the rest intact; that is why no likeness of him exists anywhere, except for a single bronze statue, which survived in the following way.

Domitian's wife was a respectable woman of good birth who had never done the slightest wrong to anyone and never assented to any of her husband's evil doing. Being held in such affectionate regard, she was sent for by the Senate, who invited her to ask any favor of it at all—to which she replied only that she would like to bury his body and put up a bronze statue of him somewhere. The Senate agreed, and the widow, whose secret desire was to create a memorial of the savagery of those who had butchered her husband, devised a plan. Collecting the pieces of Domitian's corpse, she fitted them together and stitched the body up, then took it to the sculptors and ordered them to reproduce in bronze the form of the wretch. The artists quickly produced the statue, which she subsequently took and set up in the street that leads to the Capitol, on the right-hand side as you approach from the Forum. It stands there to this day, a reminder to all both of Domitian himself and his tragic death.

One can see clearly in this statue the very likeness of Justinian—his build, expression, and general appearance.

So much for his outward appearance, but it is beyond my ability to describe his inner character, for he was both a villain and a dupe. In plain language, an asshole. He was deceitful, never speaking a word of truth to anyone, but fell for any lie that anyone wanted to tell him. His character was an unnatural mixture of stupidity and wickedness—an example of a saying by one of the ancient Peripatetic philosophers, that sometimes opposite qualities can combine in a man's character, like the blending of colors. But I will try to describe him as accurately and truly as I can, based on the facts.

Well, then. He was a fraud and a cheat. Hypocritical, cruelly two-faced, secretive; a practiced con artist who never showed any genuine emotion but could shed tears either of joy or sorrow, depending on the situation, whenever he perceived the need. A liar in every word—and not just in a haphazard way, but with real determination, affirming his schemes in writing and with the most solemn oaths, even in dealings with the public. But he regularly broke every agreement and pledge he ever made, like a contemptible slave who stands by his lies until only the threat of torture can drive him to confess the truth. A faithless friend and a treacherous enemy, with a crazed lust for murder and plunder; quarrelsome, extremely unruly, easily led to anything evil but stubbornly refusing any suggestion to do good. Quick to plot mischief and carry it out, but averse even to hearing a word of any noble action.

How could anyone describe his character in words? He had all the vices described above, and more, to an inhuman degree, as though Nature herself had withheld every inclination to evil from the rest of mankind, solely for the purpose of implanting them in the soul of this one man. On top of everything else, he was overeager to hear accusations against anyone, and overeager to inflict punishment, for he never bothered to listen to the facts of any case and simply issued his verdict as soon as he had heard the accuser's side of any story. He gave orders to seize towns, pillage cities, and enslave entire countries without a moment's hesitation, without any provocation at all. If one wanted to tally up all the calamities that have befallen Rome from the very beginning of history, and compare them with this man's crimes, I am confident that Justinian would be reckoned to have murdered more people than anyone, ever.

As for other people's money, he had no scruples at all and never even bothered to offer an excuse, justifiable or not, for confiscating what was not his. But once money was in his hands he was more than ready to squander it in wasteful expenditure or by throwing unnecessary bribes at the barbarians. In short, he saved none and allowed no one else to save any either, apparently driven not by avarice but simple envy of anyone who had money. Thus he drove all wealth from the Roman realm and became the cause of near-universal poverty.

Such, then, was the outline of Justinian's character, so far as I am able to describe it.

He married a woman who nearly destroyed Roman society from top to bottom, and whose character and upbringing I must now try to explain.

There was a fellow here in Constantinople named Acacius; he was a member of the Green faction and worked as a keeper of the Circus animals, specifically he was the bear-warden. He became ill and died during Anastasius' reign, leaving behind three daughters named Comito, Theodora, and Anastasia. (Comito was the eldest, being just shy of seven years old.) His widow remarried and hoped her new husband would share in the job of managing her family and the Circus animals—but an official in the Green party, a dance-instructor named Asterius, was bribed to remove the newlyweds from their position. He was able to do so because the dancing-masters had authority over such offices; and he used his power to install his own chief accountant in the job. One day, when the Circus was packed with people, the wife placed wreaths on her daughters' heads and bands on their arms, and made a show of them in public as beggars. The Greens would not lift a finger for them, but the Blues, whose own bear-warden had recently died, awarded their open position to the family.

As soon as each girl had grown to a suitable age and seemed mature enough, their mother put her on the stage, since they were all attractive girls. In no time at all Comito, the eldest, was one of the most popular whores in the city. Theodora, the second-born, went about dressed like a slave-girl, in a short tunic with long sleeves, and acted as her sister's servant, following her everywhere and carrying a small bench on which she sat whenever appearing in public. Theodora was at that time not quite ready to give anyone a true woman's fuck, and so she offered instead the vile service rendered by male prostitutes. She was not choosy and made herself available to the lowest sort of customer, even to slaves, who, after accompanying their masters to the theater, rushed to her in order to divert themselves in this revolting way. She worked in a brothel for quite some time and specialized in this unnatural type of sex. Once she had grown and developed a woman's body, however, she joined the other whores on stage and quickly became known as the type of slut our ancestors used to call "soldiers' slop." She had no musical talent for either the flute or the harp, and was not even skilled enough to join a company of dancers; her only attraction was her body, every part of which she placed at any customer's disposal. . . . Being a tease, Theodora loved to keep her customers waiting, but by constantly finding new ways to fuck she always kept horny men coming to her. She also never waited to be solicited, and used lewd talk and gestures to entice men, especially teens, to come to her, and so it seemed that she was more wholeheartedly devoted to lust than anyone yet born. Sometimes she would attend "potluck dinner parties" with no fewer than ten young studs in tow, all at the peak of their powers and with no other thought in their minds than fucking, and she would spend the entire night screwing every single one of them; and even after she had exhausted every one of them, she would then turn her attention to the servants—as many as thirty of them!—and screw them all. But even then she was not satisfied. . . .

Justinian was mad with passion for her. At first he kept her merely as a mistress, although he promoted her to patrician status, which opened the door to her acquiring influence and a large fortune. Now as it often happens to men who are sexually enslaved to a particular woman, Justinian had no greater delight than in showering Theodora with every favor and treasure at his disposal—and he had the entire Empire at his disposal. With Theodora's help, he impoverished the people more than ever before, not only in the capital but throughout the realm. . . .

And that is how Theodora, reared and "educated" as she was, against all the odds ascended to the imperial throne. It never even occurred to Justinian that his choice was a shocking one. Given his position, he had the pick of every high-born noble woman in the world, of the most impeccable character and the most unimpeachable reputation for modesty. . . . But no, he had to select the lowest woman in the world! Ignoring everything known about her, as recorded here, he preferred to marry a diseased whore who was guilty, through abortion, of countless child-murders!

STUDY QUESTIONS

1. How does Procopius describe Justinian and Theodora?
2. How truthful is Procopius's biographical sketch? What motives could have influenced the way he describes Justinian and Theodora?

8.2 GILDAS, *ON THE RUIN AND CONQUEST OF BRITAIN*, CA. 525–540 CE

Gildas (500–570) was a British cleric living when the last of Roman rule in Britain was snuffed out by Germanic invaders (the era that gave birth to the Arthurian legends). As the primary contemporary account of British events in the sixth century, Gildas' three-part sermon offers his explanation of why the situation had become so dire: because of the sins and corruption of the British kings, people, and clergy. The work is modeled on the biblical prophets who decry the state of the world and warn society that it must change before it is too late.

[1.3–4] The island of Britain sits almost at the edge of the world, off to the west and northwest, where it plays its part in what is called the divine balance that sustains the entire world. From its southwestern tip it stretches some eight hundred miles to the north and another two hundred across, not counting several promontories that reach out from curved bays. It is protected by broad, impassable seas on all sides except for the straits on the southern coast, where ships cross to Belgian Gaul. It benefits from the estuaries of two great rivers—the Thames and the Severn—along which valuable goods from other lands came via ships. There are also many smaller streams, twenty-eight cities, numerous strongholds, and some other major, if unremarkable, monuments—walls, fortified towers, gates, and houses whose roofs are firmly built even though they appear dangerously high. Britain is rich with widespread plains, well-situated hills that are amenable to

Translation by Clifford Backman.

cultivation, and mountains that provide convenient pasturage for cattle. Colorful flowers line the paths along these highlands, giving them a beautiful appearance like that of a bride adorned with bright jewels. The land is fed by many clear springs, whose flowing waters bring a cascade of snow-white gravel; by many bright rivers that move with a gentle murmur, offering to those relaxing on their banks a promise of sweet sleep; and by many lakes that over-flow with cool streams of living water.

The history of this island, so proud and resilient from its origins, is one of ungrateful rebellion—rebellion against God, against its fellow men, and sometimes against distant kings and their peoples. Of all that reckless men are capable of doing, what vileness and unrighteousness can be worse than to deny God the fear that is owed Him, to deny charity to one's fellow man, and to deny honor to those in positions of authority over them? What can do greater harm to our faith than to violate heavenly and human desires, or, having already violated these, to give oneself over to lusts and selfishness?

I pass over in silence the ancient sins by which the whole human race was held in bondage before the coming of Christ; neither will I bother to narrate the most hellish horrors (surpassing in number even those of the Egyptians) of my native land. True, some of these exist even today, to disfigure our land everywhere according to their savage custom. . . . The only evils I wish to publicize are those our island has suffered, and has at times inflicted on others, since the time of the Roman emperors. I will do this to the best of my ability. No native writings or records can assist me, since these (if they even existed!) have been destroyed by fires or carted off in ships carrying our exiled leaders. Instead, I have to rely on foreign writers whose accounts are far from clear, since they contain so many gaps.

[1.23–26] In stout ships of war under full sail came the cries of a brood of fierce cubs born of a savage lioness—the Saxons—whose cries came to us as omens and auguries. A prophecy had foretold that they would occupy for three hundred years the country towards which they directed their prows, half of that time (that is, 150 years) spent in ravaging the land. They sailed under the command of

their brutish leader and sank their deadly talons in the eastern shore of our island, and their homeland, seeing the success of this first contingent, sent out another ship, and another, to join their bastard companions. Thus were the seed of iniquity and the root of bitterness planted in our soil, until the poisonous plant grew and developed strong branches and full foliage. Having gained a foothold, the Saxons negotiated to have us supply them with provisions, as though they were our defenders preparing to endure great hardship on our account. For a time our provisions closed the dog's maw, to use an expression; but soon enough they complained that our monthly offerings were insufficient and declared that if we did not increase their volume they would break our treaty with them and lay waste the whole island. They did not wait long to turn their threats into deeds.

Because of our earlier sins, the fire of divine vengeance blazed across our land from coast to coast, stoked continually by the wretches from the east. This fire devoured all the scattered settlements and lands, and did not stop until it had consumed nearly the entire island, licking the western ocean with its red and savage tongue. The catastrophe bears comparison with that of the Assyrians upon Judaea, for there was fulfilled among us, as among the Jews, the prophet's lament, "They have set your sanctuary on fire, profaned your name's abode by razing it to the ground," [Ps 74.7] and again, "O God, the nations have invaded your inheritance; they have defiled your holy temple." [Ps 79.1] All our settlements were brought low with the repeated blows of battering rams. Our people were cut down everywhere by gleaming swords and raging fires, including the priests and bishops. Sadly, the streets of our villages are filled with the ruins of once-high towers that have been pulled to the ground, with stones pried from fences or left over from the smashing of sacred altars, with dismembered pieces of human bodies that are so covered with lurid clots of blood that they look as though the people had been run through a wine-press, and whose only chance for any kind of burial is to rot in the ruins of collapsed homes; all the rest will simply fill the stomachs of ravenous beasts and birds. . . .

Some surviving wretches were apprehended in the mountains and killed in heaps; others were so overcome by hunger that they surrendered themselves to their enemies, to be enslaved forever. . . . Eventually the barbaric raiders returned to their homeland, and what was left of our people came together from all around, as bees rush to their hive when a storm is brewing, and prayed as one to God with their whole hearts. As the phrase goes, "burdening the air with unnumbered prayers" they begged not to be destroyed. Rather, they took up arms and elected to challenge their conquerors in battle under the leadership of Ambrosius Aurelianus, a man of modest character. Alone of all the Romans, he had managed to survive the tumultuous times (his parents, being clothed in imperial purple, had been killed), and his descendants in my own time are fallen far from his ancient nobility. Nevertheless, these people gained a victory, with God's help.

Since that time, our people won some more victories and so did our enemy. Indeed, the Lord is testing our nation—the Israel of today—and the depth of its love for Him. The struggle continued up to the time of the battle of Badon Hill, the last great slaughter inflicted upon us. This was in the year of my birth, one month less than forty-four years ago, and to this very day not one of our villages is what it used to be. Instead, all lie desolate, routed, and ruined. . . .

Britain has kings, but they are nothing but tyrants. Britain has judges, but they are wicked men who engage in non-stop plunder and pillage of helpless commoners, to the delight and benefit of criminals and thieves everywhere. [Our rulers] have innumerable wives—harlots and adulteresses all. They swear oaths only to perjure themselves and to lie every time they make a vow. They fight wars, but evil ones against their own subjects. And while they pursue simple thieves relentlessly throughout the entire country, the robbers who sit with them at their noble tables are not only esteemed but rewarded. . . .

[108] But why mince words? . . . I will say what I mean. . . . You are not priests of God but enemies to Him, not bishops but practiced sinners! Not ministers of Christ, but traitors to the holy apostles whom you supposedly succeed! You may have heard the words of the apostle Paul but you have not absorbed them and you do not feel their weight. Like stone idols which can neither see nor hear, you stood at the altar while his words came pouring down like thunder at you! "Brethren," he said, "this saying is trustworthy and deserves full acceptance." [1 Tim 1.15] He spoke of trustworthiness and deserving. "Whoever aspires to the office of bishop desires a noble task." [1 Tim 3.1] But you seek the bishops' offices out of covetousness, without even pretending it involves spiritual worthiness; you certainly put no store in good works. "Therefore a bishop must be irreproachable, married only once, temperate, self-controlled, decent, hospitable, able to teach, not a drunkard, not aggressive, but gentle, not contentious, not a lover of money." [1 Tim 3.2–3] This calls for tears, not more words. . . . How horribly things have changed, to see the commands of heaven crushed under foot. The lot of you arm yourselves with deeds and words in order to attack these teachings, to destroy them. Teachings that one ought to suffer for and lay down one's life for!

[110] Priests! Not a single one of you should flatter yourself on the purity of your body. The souls of your flock . . . will be asked on the Day of Judgment, and they will denounce you as murderers of souls! . . .

May Almighty God, the God of all consolation and mercy, preserve His very few good priests from all evil, and make them citizens of His city the Heavenly Jerusalem, where is the assembly of all saints. In the name of the Father, Son, and Holy Spirit, to whom be honor and glory for ever and ever. Amen.

STUDY QUESTIONS

1. How is the idea of a contract between the Britons and God introduced here, and what hope is there that God will protect against the invaders?
2. What considerations might have prompted the Romans to withdraw from Britain in the fifth century?

8.3 GREGORY OF TOURS, *HISTORY OF THE FRANKS*

Gregory served as bishop of Tours from 573 until his death in 594. He wrote many hagiographies, which he collected into three volumes: the *Lives of the Fathers*, the *Glory of the Confessors*, and the *Glory of the Martyrs*. He is best remembered, however, for his lengthy and rambling *History of the Franks*, which covers the period from St. Martin of Tours (d. 397) to the year 591. Switching back and forth between the family of Clovis and the various bishops of northern France, he tries to present the Merovingian era as a chapter in God's plan for Christianizing western Europe. In the two passages below, he describes the last four years of Clovis's life (r. 481–511) (Bk. II, ch. 35–42) and Gregory's own encounter with a Jew in the court of King Chilperic (r. 561–584) (Bk. VI, ch. 5).

CLOVIS' LAST YEARS (BOOK II, CH. 35–42)

[II, 35] King Alaric II of the Visigoths, seeing that Clovis was overrunning one nation after another, sent ambassadors to him, saying, "Dear brother, it would be wise for us to meet—if you are interested, and God willing." Clovis agreed and rode to meet Alaric. They convened just outside the village of Amboise, which is on an island in the Loire river, in the diocese of Tours. They negotiated and settled upon a treaty of eternal friendship, which they celebrated with a shared feast, after which they both rode home in peace. At that time there were countless people in Gaul eager for Frankish rule.

[36] One consequence of this treaty, however, was that Bishop Quintinianus of Rodez fell from favor and was driven out by the people of his own city, who had long criticized him, saying, "If it were up to you, the Franks would be our lords!" It did not take long for their resentment to burst into open quarrel with the bishop, for the Visigoths who lived in the city were suspicious of Quintinianus' loyalties, and the rest of the townsmen went so far as to accuse him publicly of wanting to hand the city over to the Franks. And so a plot was hatched to assassinate him. Quintinianus found out about it and fled one night, together with

his most trusted attendants, to Clermont, where he was kindly received by St. Eufrasius, the bishop who had succeeded Aprunculus. Eufrasius was a native of Dijon. He gave Quintinianus fine lodgings amid fields and vineyards, insisting that "This diocese has ample resources to support us both—for the charity preached by the blessed Apostle [St. Martin] must be carried on by all of God's ministers." The bishop of Lyons also gave Quintinianus some property that he administered in Clermont. For more details regarding St. Quintinianus, the wrongs done to him, and the miracles performed by God through him, see the pertinent chapter in my *Lives of the Fathers*.

[37] "I cannot bear seeing Arians living in Gaul," Clovis announced one day to his ministers. "We're going to attack them, and with God's help we'll crush them and take over all their land." Everyone agreed with this idea, and so Clovis assembled his army and marched on Poitiers. Along the way, some of his troops passed through the diocese of Tours, so Clovis gave an order that, out of respect for St. Martin, none of his men should requisition anything in the region except fodder and water. It happened that one soldier came upon some hay belonging to an elderly, poor farmer, and the soldier said to him, "The king says we

Translation by Clifford Backman.

cannot take anything but fodder, right? Well, this hay is fodder; we won't be going against orders if we take it." Then he knocked the old man down and took his hay. When this was reported to Clovis, he pulled out his sword and executed the soldier on the spot. "We can give up any hope of winning this campaign if we offend St. Martin!" he declared. Thus he made his point, and the rest of the army took nothing in the region after that. Then Clovis sent messengers loaded with gifts to the church of St. Martin, saying, "Go, and bring me back good tidings from God's house." And then he prayed, "O Lord, if you are on my side and wish to deliver into my hands the wretched [Arian] heretics who have shown themselves so hostile to you, then give us a sign as these messengers enter St. Martin's church, a sign that shows clearly your support for me, your servant Clovis."

The messengers set out, and as they had been commanded they soon arrived at Tours; they entered the church exactly when the choir's soloist was singing the antiphon:

> You girded me with valor for war,
>   subjugated my opponents beneath me.
> You made my foes expose their necks to me;
>   those who hated me I silenced. [Ps. 18.39–40]

When the messengers heard this, they gave thanks to God, made their vows to St. Martin, and returned gladly to report to the king.

When Clovis and his army reached Vienne, they could find no way to cross the river since it was swollen from heavy rains, and so he prayed that night that God would show him a way across. The next morning, as it happened, a large doe appeared and entered the river. Everyone recognized that this was a heavenly sign, and that they could follow the doe across the river. Once on the other side, Clovis marched toward Poitiers. They made camp one evening and saw a pillar of fire rise from the local church of St. Hilary and advance toward them. To everyone this appeared a clear sign that that blessed saint was adding his support to Clovis' campaign to rout the heretics, against whom St. Hilary had himself done battle in defense of the faith. Clovis instantly gave orders forbidding

any looting by his men as they passed through the region—and indeed no one took from anyone.

On the outskirts of Poitiers at that time there lived a saintly and God-fearing man named Maxentius, who, although the abbot, lived in seclusion from the rest of his monastery. It would be pointless to mention the name of the monastery at that time, for it is now known only as the Cell of St. Maxentius. When the monks there saw the approach of some Frankish soldiers they hurried to their abbot and begged him to come out and bless them. He took such a long time in coming out of his cell that the monks grew frightened and forced his door open; then they pushed him out into the open. Maxentius walked fearlessly up to the troops, presumably to ask them not to harm the monastery, when all of a sudden a soldier drew his sword and swung it at Maxentius' head—but his arm froze in mid-air, right by the abbot's ear, and the sword clattered to the ground. The soldier instantly threw himself at the saint's feet and begged forgiveness. His companions, seeing all of this, raced back to the main army filled with dread that they would have to pay with their lives for such an offense. The saint, meanwhile, rubbed the soldier's arm with holy oil and made the sign of the Cross over him, and instantly the man recovered. Thus, thanks to Maxentius, the monastery escaped unharmed. Maxentius performed many more miracles in his lifetime, as any reader who is interested may find in my *Life of Maxentius*. But this particular event occurred in the fifteenth year of Clovis' reign.

Soon thereafter, Clovis met King Alaric [II] and his army of Visigoths on the battlefield at Vouillé, about ten miles from Poitiers. After several volleys of javelins, the soldiers fought hand to hand; in the end the Visigoths fled (as they so often did), giving the victory to Clovis, who had God on his side. (One of Clovis' allies in this fight was Chloderic, the son of Sigibert the Lame. Sigibert had been lame ever since being wounded in the knee in a battle against the Alamanni at their fortress at Zülpich.) Clovis killed Alaric. Just as the Goths were fleeing, however, two of them turned and rushed suddenly at Clovis, one on each side, and struck him with their spears. Fortunately, thanks to his stout leather corselet and his speedy horse, Clovis escaped—but he very nearly died.

A large contingent from Auvergne, under the jurisdiction of Apollinaris, took part in this battle but their commanders (all of senatorial rank) were all killed. Alaric's son, Amalaric, escaped and made it all the way to Spain, where he ruled wisely for many years. Clovis, meanwhile, sent his own son, Theuderic, to Clermont, passing through Albi and Rodez on the way. Theuderic brought every place he passed by under his father's rule, and thus all the lands between the Visigoths and the Burgundians came to belong to Clovis. Alaric II had been king for twelve years. Clovis spent the winter in Bordeaux, seized all of Alaric's treasure at Toulouse, and then advanced to Angoulême—where God showed him such favor that the city's walls collapsed of their own weight when Clovis merely looked at them. Clovis drove the Visigoths from the city and took command. This was the culmination of his victorious campaign, and afterward he returned to Tours where he bestowed countless gifts upon the church of St. Martin.

[38] One day some letters arrived for Clovis from the [Byzantine] emperor Anastasius I [r. 491–518], conferring the title of consul on him. There was a ceremony in St. Martin's, where Clovis stood and assumed a purple tunic and the military robes [of the empire], and crowned himself with a diadem. Then he mounted his horse and rode among the people, showering them with gold and silver coins, as he progressed from the doorway of St. Martin's to the cathedral at Tours. From that day forward he was addressed either as "consul" or "augustus." After Tours he went on to Paris, which he made the seat of his government. His son Theuderic accompanied him.

[39] After Bishop Eustochius of Tours died, Licinius was ordained his successor—the eighth bishop after St. Martin himself. The war I described just above took place during Licinius' episcopacy, and it was in his time too that Clovis came to Tours. Licinius is reported to have spent time in the east and even to have visited the Holy Land; some say he went all the way to Jerusalem and saw the very site of Our Lord's death and resurrection, about which we have read in the gospels.

[40] While living in Paris Clovis sent a secret message to Sigibert's son, Chloderic. He wrote, "Your father is old and lame in one leg. When he dies his kingdom will pass, rightfully, to you—and my alliance will come with it." Chloderic was thus tempted by a lust for power and began to plot his own father's death.

One day Sigibert exited the city of Cologne and crossed the Rhine river, since he wanted to walk in the forest at Buchau. In the middle of the day he took a nap in his tent, which is when Chloderic loosed assassins on him. Having murdered his father, Chloderic then took possession of the realm. But by God's judgment, Sigibert's killer fell into the very trap he had laid for his father. He dispatched messengers to Clovis to announce Sigibert's death—"My father is dead," he wrote, "and I have seized both his kingdom and his treasure. Send messengers of your own to me, and I will gladly bestow upon you anything you desire from this treasure." To this Clovis replied, "Thank you for your good will. Please do show your treasure to my messengers—but you may keep it all."

When the messengers arrived, they examined all the treasure that Chloderic was eager to show them. "This was the chest in which my father kept all his gold coins," boasted Chloderic.

Clovis' men replied, "Plunge your hand down to the bottom of the chest, so we can see how much is there." And as soon as Chloderic leaned forward to do so, one of the Frankish envoys raised his double-sided axe and split his skull with it. Thus did the wretch Chloderic share his father's fate.

After Clovis heard that both Sigibert and Chloderic were dead he traveled to Cologne himself and ordered all the town's inhabitants to assemble. "While I was boating down the Scheldt river, Chloderic, the son of your king, conspired against his own father and spread a rumor that I was the one who wanted him dead. Sigibert fled through the forest at Buchau, but Chloderic's assassins caught up with him and killed him. Then when Chloderic was showing off his father's treasure, he too was murdered—by whom, I don't know. I am not responsible in any way. I have no interest to murder any of my fellow kings, for regicide is a terrible crime. But things have happened in this way, I advise you to make the best of the situation by turning to me and putting yourself freely under my authority."

The people, hearing him, pounded their shields and roared their approval, then they raised Clovis up on a shield and acclaimed him their king. This is how he acquired Sigibert's kingship, treasure, and people. With every passing day God inspired more and more people to submit themselves to Clovis, who consequently grew enormously in power—for he always walked before God with an upright heart and did whatever was pleasing in His sight.

[41] Clovis' next victim was Chararic. This fellow had been asked to help Clovis during his struggles with Syagrius, but he had remained neutral. He gave aid to neither side, preferring to wait to see who would win before declaring allegiance, and this is why Clovis now moved against him. He cleverly trapped Chararic and threw him in prison. He ordered both Chararic and his son to be tied up, then had their hair cut off, with the subsequent order that they be ordained as priest and deacon, accordingly. At this, Chararic burst into tears and cried out, "All you have done is cut leaves from a tree that is still green and thriving; they'll soon grow back, larger than ever! Death to the man who has done this to me!" Clovis heard about this, and so he had their heads cut off too, and after they were both dead he seized their kingdom, treasure, and people too.

[42] The king at Cambrai at that time was Ragnachar, a man so lost to lechery that he could not even leave the women of his own family alone. He had a counselor named Farro who defiled himself with the same filthy habit. It was said of this man that whenever Ragnachar had anything—whether food, gift, or anything else—placed before him, he would proclaim "It's good enough for me and Farro!" This put all the Franks in their retinue in a great rage. And so Clovis bribed Ragnachar's bodyguards with armbands and sword-belts that looked like gold but were really just cleverly gilded bronze, and with these he hoped to turn Ragnachar's men against him. Clovis then sent his army against Ragnachar; and when Ragnachar dispatched spies to bring back information on the invaders and asked them upon their return, how strong the attackers were, they replied: "They're good

enough for you and Farro!" Clovis himself finally arrived and arranged his soldiers for battle. Ragnachar watched as his army was crushed and tried to sneak away, but his own soldiers captured him, tied his hands behind his back, and brought him—together with Ragnachar's brother, Ricchar—before Clovis.

"Why have you disgraced our Frankish people by allowing yourself to be tied up?" asked Clovis. "It would have been better for you if you had died in battle." And with that, he lifted his axe and split Ragnachar's skull. Then he turned to his brother Ricchar and said, "And as for you, if you had stood by your brother's side he would not have been bound in this way." And he struck Ricchar with another blow of his axe and killed him. When these two were dead, the bodyguards who had betrayed them discovered that the golden gifts they had received from Clovis were fake. It is said that when they complained of this to Clovis he answered, "That is all the gold a man should expect when he willingly lures his own ruler to death," adding that they should be grateful for escaping with their lives instead of being tortured to death for having betrayed their masters. Hearing this, the men begged for mercy, asking only for their lives.

Now both of these kings, Ragnachar and Ricchar, were relatives of Clovis; so was their brother Rignomer, whom Clovis had put to death at Le Mans. Then, having killed all three, Clovis took over their kingdoms and their treasuries. He carried out the killing of many other kings and blood-relations in the same way—of anyone, really, whom he suspected of plotting against his realm—and in so doing he gradually extended his control over the whole of Gaul. One day he summoned an assembly of all his subjects, at which he is reported to have remarked about all the relatives he had destroyed, "How sad it is for me to live as a stranger among strangers, without any of my family here to help me when disaster happens!" But he said this not out of any genuine grief for their deaths, but only because he hoped somehow to flush out another relative whom he could kill.

GREGORY AND THE JEW (BOOK VI, CH. 5)

King Chilperic, who was then still at Nogent-sur-Marne, sent his baggage train ahead while he made the rest of his plans to travel to Paris. I had gone to pay my respects before he left, and while I was visiting him a Jew named Priscus came in. This fellow was on familiar terms with the king, having been an agent on his behalf in some commercial ventures. Chilperic placed his hand on the Jew's head, in a gentle manner, and said to me, "Come, bishop! You lay your hand on him too!" Instantly the Jew pulled away. "'O faithless and perverse generation!'" the king quoted [Matthew 17.17], "why can't you accept what was promised to you by your own prophets? Can't you see that the mysteries of the Church were foretold by the sacrifices of your own people?"

The Jew answered, "God has no need of a son! He never had a son, and He does not have any partner in His kingdom! Indeed, He Himself said, through Moses, 'See now that I, I alone, am he, and there is no god besides me. It is I who bring both death and life, I who inflict wounds and heal them.'" [Deut. 32.39]

The king responded, "But God brought forth, by His Spirit, His own eternal Son from a womb—a Son no younger than Himself in time, and no lesser than Himself in power. For God said, 'From the womb of the morning-star have I begotten you' [Psalm 110.3]. This Son, born at the beginning of time, He later sent to heal the world. Your own prophet has declared, 'He sent His word and healed them.' And as for your other claim, that God never had a Son, listen to another of your prophets, who put these words in His mouth: 'Shall I bring a mother to the point of birth, and yet not let her child be born?' He said this in regard to the people born in Him by faith."

The Jew answered, "How is it possible that God should be made man, or be born of a woman, or submit to lashing, or be condemned to death?"

At this point the king grew silent, so I took up the debate myself. "God's becoming man, as the Son of God," I said, "was the result of our needs, not His—for if He had not become man, then He could not have saved us from the prison of sin and servitude to the Devil. And now, as in the story we've both read of David slaying Goliath, I'll run you through with your own sword, pulling my proof not from the Gospels or the writings of any apostle (none of which you would accept) but from your own Scriptures. Listen to this, one of your own prophets prophesying:

He is both God and man, and who has known him?
"And also by the same:
Such is our God;
and no other is to be compared to him
He has uncovered the whole way of
    understanding,
and has given her to Jacob, his servant,
to Israel, His beloved.
Afterwards did He show Himself upon earth,
And conversed with mortals. [Baruch 3.37–38]
"And here is proof that He was born of a Virgin,
    from another of your prophets:
    Behold, a virgin shall conceive and bear a son,
    And shall call him Emmanuel, "God is with
        us." [Isaiah 7.14]
"Still another prophet showed beyond doubt that
    He would submit to being lashed:
    They pierced my hands and feet, and divided
        my garments among them. [Psalms 22.17]
"In another place this same prophet says:
    They gave me poison for my food;
    And for my thirst they gave me vinegar to drink.
    [Psalms 69.22]
"And finally, to show that it would be through
    the Cross that He would restore the world
    (long lost to Satan) to His Kingdom, the same
    prophet David says:
The Lord reigns from a tree. [Psalms 96.10]

"But this doesn't mean that He did not reign before [the Crucifixion], together with the Father. Instead it means that He accepted a new and unprecedented dominion over the people whom He delivered from slavery to Satan."

The Jew then replied, "But why would God need to suffer these things?"

"I have already answered you," I said. "Mankind was innocent at Creation, but was tricked by the Serpent's guile and led to break God's commandment. Thus, he was cast out of Paradise and condemned to suffer on the earth. It was only by the death of Christ, God's True and Only Son, that man was reconciled to God."

The Jew asked, "But couldn't God have sent more prophets or messengers to call mankind back to the path of salvation? Why did He Himself have to be humbled in the flesh?"

I retorted, "Mankind was inclined to sin from the very beginning of time. The Great Flood, the destruction of Sodom, the plagues on Egypt, the miracle of the parting of the sea and the river Jordan—none of these were enough to frighten mankind into obedience. He kept on resisting God's word and refusing to believe the prophets. More than that, he even killed the prophets who were preaching repentance! No, if God Himself had not come down from heaven, man's salvation would never have happened. We were reborn by Christ's baptism, cured by His wounds, raised up by His Resurrection, and glorified by His Ascension. Your own prophet declares the necessity of God's coming to heal us:

> He bore the punishment that makes us whole,
>   and by his wounds we were healed. [Isaiah 54.5]
"and he continues:
> He bore the sins of many and interceded for
>   the transgressors. [Isaiah 53.12]
"and:
> Like a lamb led to slaughter,
>   Or a sheep silent before shearers
>   He did not open his mouth.
> Seized and condemned, he was taken away.
> Who would have thought any more of his
>   destiny?
"and:
> The Lord of Hosts is his name. [Isaiah 54.5]

"This is the One of Whom Jacob speaks—the very Jacob whom you proudly claim as your ancestor—when he blesses his son, Judah; for in addressing Judah it is as though he is addressing Christ, the Son of God, in person:

> You, Judah, shall your brothers praise
> —your hand on the neck of your enemies;
> the sons of your father shall bow down to you.
> Judah is a lion's cub,
> You have grown up on prey, my son.
> He crouches, lies down like a lion,
> Like a lioness—who would dare rouse him? . . .
> His eyes are darker than wine,
> And his teeth are whiter than milk. [Genesis
>   49.8–9, 12]

"And even though Christ Himself said, 'No one takes [My life] from me, but I lay it down on my own,' the apostle Paul wrote, 'If you confess with your mouth that Jesus is Lord and believe in your heart that God raised him from the dead, you will be saved.'"

In spite of all my proofs, this wretched Jew was unyielding and showed no sign at all of believing me; instead, he just stood there in silence. King Chilperic recognized that he would never be made to feel remorse, no matter what we said, and so he turned to me and said that he had to leave but wanted my blessing first. "Bishop," he said, "I will say to you the words Jacob said to the angel: 'I will not let you go unless you bless me.'" [Genesis 32.26] And as he said this he ordered water to be brought to him. We both washed our hands, and I said a prayer. Then I took some bread, gave thanks to God for it, and received it along with the king. We drank some wine, and wished each other Farewell as we departed. Chilperic mounted his horse and set off for Paris, together with his wife, children, and all the members of his household.[1]

----

[1] Compare the biblical passages as translated by the Jewish Publication Society, noting first that the book of Baruch is not accepted in the Jewish canon.

Isaiah 7.14: "Assuredly, my Lord will give you a sign of His own accord! Look, the young woman is with child and about to give birth to a son. Let her name him 'Immanuel.'"

Psalm 22.17: "Dogs surround me; a pack of evil ones closes in on me, like lions [they maul] my hands and feet."

Psalm 69.22: "They give me gall for food, vinegar to quench my thirst."

Psalm 96.10: "Declare among the nations, 'The Lord is king!' The world stands firm; it cannot be shaken; He judges the people with equity." Isaiah 54.5: "For He who made you will espouse you—His name is 'Lord of Hosts.' The Holy One of Israel will redeem you—He is called 'God of all the Earth.'"

Isaiah 53.12: "Whereas he bore the guilt of many and made intercession for sinners."

Genesis 49.8–9, 12: "You, O Judah, your brothers shall praise; Your hand shall be on the nape of your foes; Your father's sons shall bow low to you. Judah is a lion's whelp; On prey, my son, have you grown. He crouches, lies down like a lion, Like the king of beasts—who dare rouse him? . . . His eyes are darker than wine; His teeth are whiter than milk."

STUDY QUESTIONS

1. Gregory of Tours was an accomplished hagiographer, a person who wrote biographies of saints, martyrs, and other holy people. What elements from this excerpt of his life of Clovis resemble a hagiography? How does Gregory portray Clovis?
2. In the High and Later Middle Ages, disputations were formal debates between Christian and Jewish theologians. Although Gregory's encounter with a Jew in the court of King Chilperic occurs centuries before the first recorded disputations, how is it a type of disputation? How is the Jew portrayed? Who wins the debate?

8.4 GREGORY THE GREAT, "LIFE OF ST. BENEDICT," 593 CE

As a revered pope and saint, Gregory (540–604) is best known for his reforms of Christian life, from revising the liturgy to his "Rule for Pastors" for improving care of Christians. This selection is taken from Gregory's "Life of St. Benedict," an account of St. Benedict of Nursia (ca. 480–563), father of Western monasticism and founder of the Benedictine Order. Although St. Benedict's organization of a monastic community was highly practical, Gregory depicts him here predominantly as a miracle-worker and visionary, thus highlighting his mystical side.

[1] There once was a man who led a most venerable life, blessed by grace and in name, for he was called Benedict. Even as a youth he possessed the mind of a mature man. He was always younger in years than he was in virtue, and although he lived in the world and had opportunity to enjoy all the delights it has to offer, he always despised vain pleasure. The world's vanities he regarded as worthless nothings. Born to noble parents in the district of Nursia, Benedict was raised in Rome where he had the opportunity to study the human arts, but since he saw so many people, similarly situated, fall into dissolute and base ways, he stepped back from the world he knew. He feared becoming too well acquainted with lewdness, which would end only in a headlong fall into a dangerous and godless existence. Therefore, he gave up his studies and renounced his claim to his father's house and wealth, and wanting nothing more than to serve God, he went out in search of a place where he could pursue his longing for a holy purpose in life. He went forth, armed with a simple wisdom that took the place of his learned but ignorant scholarship.

I was unable to unearth all the marvelous things he did in his life, but I did manage to learn any number of things about him (which I know record) from four of his disciples: Constantinus, an exceptional and pious man who succeeded Benedict as abbot; Valentinianus, who was in charge of the Lateran Abbey for many years; Simplicius, the third minister-general of Benedict's order; and Honoratus,

Translation by Clifford Backman.

who is currently the abbot of the monastery where Benedict began his sanctified life.

[2] One day when Benedict was alone, temptation came to him in the form of a blackbird that flew so closely about his face that, if he could, the holy man might have grabbed it with his hand. Instead, he simply blessed himself by making the sign of the cross—and the bird flew away. He was beset, however, by a terrible bout of temptation of the flesh such as he had never experienced before.

He had once happened to see a particular woman, and the spirit of temptation burned her memory into his mind, and the image of her now inflamed him with lust so powerfully that for a moment the servant of God nearly was overcome with it. The thought of abandoning his wilderness life came upon him, but with God's grace he came to his senses. Seeing a thick patch of briar- and nettle-bushes growing nearby, Benedict threw off his clothing and leapt headlong into them, rolling back and forth so long that by the time he stood up his flesh was covered with the most pitiful lacerations. The wounds to his body cured the wounds to his soul by turning its pleasure into pain, and by the searing hurt to his outer form, he quenched the raging fire of lustful thought within his soul. One fire replaced another, and he overcame his sin.

He would often tell his disciples in later years that this episode so reduced any temptation of the flesh in him that he scarcely ever felt it anymore. Many people soon began to abandon the world too, in the hope of becoming one of his disciples—for having freed himself from temptation he turned himself into a man of masterful virtue. In the book of Exodus, recall, Moses commands the Levites that while men may serve as priests from the age of twenty-five, only those aged fifty and above may be ordained as keepers of the holy vessels. [Num 8.24–6]

[11] Another time a group of monks were working on an extension to a certain wall when the Old Enemy [Satan] appeared to Benedict, that man of God, as he was praying in his cell, and jeered at him, saying that he was going to cause trouble with the monks. Benedict's spirit then rushed to the monks' aid, telling them to be careful for the devil was at hand. No sooner had Benedict's voice spoken than the Evil Spirit knocked down the wall on which the monks had been working, and killed a young monk—a boy,

really, the son of a certain nobleman. This pitiful occurrence drove everyone into a profound grief, not for the wall but for the death of their little brother. The monks wasted no time in bringing the sad news to Benedict, who quickly ordered them to bring him the lad's body. Being so mangled and maimed, the body had to be delivered in a sack since the stones of the wall had not only broken the boy's limbs but had crushed his very bones.

Benedict had the monks lay the boy on the floor in his cell, on the precise spot where he always knelt when in prayer. Then he sent the monks away, closed his cell door, and immediately began to pray. What a marvel then occurred! Within the space of an hour Benedict's prayers had healed the boy, who stood up as lively as ever and returned to his work, helping the monks repair the wall. The Old Serpent had thought he could insult Benedict, but Benedict emerged triumphant.

[38] The cave [at Subiaco] where Benedict first took up his solitary vigil even to this day continues to work miracles, if those who pray there are in need of them. What I am about to tell you happened only recently. A certain woman had so lost the use of reason that she became insane and spent days and night on end walking up and down and back and forth, in mountains, in valleys, through woods and fields, and rested only when she collapsed from exhaustion, wherever that happened to occur. It happened one day that, wandering again at random, she chanced to arrive at Blessed Benedict's cave. Not knowing anything about the site, she entered the cave and spent the night. The following morning she awoke fully healed, her mind and wits as sound as they had ever been, and to the day she died she lived a healthy existence, as though her madness had never happened. . . .

There can be no doubt that the saints perform countless miracles at the spot where they lie buried. . . . Since simple-minded people might doubt whether or not a particular saint is actually present to hear their prayers, he or she works an even greater miracle at the site [than elsewhere] to compensate for the weakness of the visitors' souls. But he whose mind is firmly fixed on God has a stronger faith, and he knows that the saint is there in spirit to hear his prayer even though he may not be there in body. For as Our Savior himself said, "If I do not go, the Advocate will not come to you." [John 16.7]

STUDY QUESTIONS

1. What specific forms did Benedict's renunciation of the world take?
2. How does Benedict's goal of a solitary life relate to those of the "desert fathers" of the church?

8.5 BEDE, *ECCLESIASTICAL HISTORY OF ENGLISH PEOPLE*, COMPLETED CA. 731 CE

The Venerable Bede (ca. 673–735), as he is known, is also called the Father of English History not only because of the wide scope of his account, but also because he applied historical inquiry to his work—interviewing living witnesses to events, interpreting, and moving beyond the hagiographies used by his fellow writers. As the title indicates, Bede is a source for the particular development of the "insular" church—that is, of the British Isles—in contrast with the church of continental Europe. The first portion of this selection recounts the arrival of St. Augustine of Canterbury, who was sent by Pope Gregory the Great to establish an English church and convert the pagan locals; the second portion memorializes Pope Gregory.

[1.25] Encouraged by the kind words of the blessed father Gregory, Augustine and his fellow-servants of Christ resumed their work in God's name and soon arrived in Britain. The most powerful of the kings at that time was Ethelbert of Kent, whose realm extended northward to the river Humber, which marks the boundary of the northern and southern Angles. To the east lay the island of Thanet, which the English reckon as six hundred hides from end to end. A waterway of roughly three furlongs, called the Wantsum, separates Thanet from the mainland and can be crossed at only two places. This is where Augustine and his companions—reported to have numbered forty—landed. Following Pope Gregory's instructions, the missionaries had brought Frankish interpreters with them, and they sent them to Ethelbert to deliver the news that they had come from Rome and that anyone who heard their message would undoubtedly receive the joy of eternal life in the kingdom of heaven with the one, true and living God. Ethelbert listened to what the interpreters had to say, and sent back the message that Augustine and his companions were to stay on the island; the king would provide for them all until he had decided what course of action to take. He was already familiar with Christianity, since his wife Bertha—a member of the Frankish royal house—was a Christian. Indeed, her family had consented to the marriage only on the condition that she should remain free to hold and practice her faith without any hindrance, and to this end they had assigned a bishop, Liuthard, to accompany her as a spiritual guide.

Translation by Clifford Backman.

Several days later King Ethelbert came to Thanet and summoned Augustine and his companions to an open-air audience. He was careful not to meet them inside any house, for he maintained the ancient English superstition about practicers of magic, that they work their spells of deception and control best when indoors. The monks, though, were empowered by God, not the Devil, and they duly approached Ethelbert while carrying a silver cross as a standard and a wooden placard on which they had painted a likeness of Our Lord and Savior. They began by singing a litany for their own eternal salvation and for those on whose account they had come this far. The king then commanded them to sit and bade them to preach the "Word of Life" to him and his court. When they had done so, Ethelbert replied, "Fair words and fair promises. But their content is new to us, and seems doubtful. I cannot accept them, if that means abandoning the ancient beliefs by which I and the whole English nation have lived. But you have travelled far, and I can see the honest sincerity of your desire to share with us what you find to be true and worthy. We will not harm you, but instead extend our hospitality to you. We do not forbid you to preach to our people and to convert however many you can; in fact, we will provide you with all the supplies you need."

The king awarded them a residence in the city of Canterbury, which was his capital, and remained true to his word, granting the missionaries full provisions and not restricting their freedom to preach. According to tradition, the monks approached the city while carrying aloft the holy cross and the painted likeness of Our Lord and King Jesus Christ, and, as was their custom, singing aloud, "We pray to you, O Lord, in all your mercy, that although we are all sinners, you turn your wrath away from this city and from your holy house. Amen."

[1.26] As soon as they had settled into the house given them by the king, the missionaries started to emulate the life of the apostles and the early Church: constant prayer; fasting and keeping vigils; and preaching the Word of Life to any who would listen. Material things meant little to them, and they would accept gifts of food and other necessities only from those to whom they preached. They gladly endured any hardship, even death, for the sake of the truth they proclaimed, and as a consequence, after a brief time, a number of the heathens, who admired the simplicity of their holy lives and the promise of their heavenly message, converted and were baptized. On the eastern side of the city there stood an old church consecrated to Saint Martin that had been built during Roman times; this was where the Christian queen mentioned above came to pray. The missionaries and their converts congregated there to sing psalms, pray, celebrate Mass, preach, and baptize, until King Ethelbert's own conversion gave them even more freedom to preach and to build or restore churches throughout the realm.

Eventually the king and others [in his court], guided by the holy example of the missionaries' lives and moved by their promises of salvation (the truth of which was confirmed by many miracles that they performed), also converted and were baptized. From that point on, large crowds gathered daily to hear God's Holy Word, and they too abandoned their pagan rites and entered the unity of Christ's Holy Church as full-fledged believers. Ethelbert was pleased by their conversions and faithfulness, but he still refused to compel anyone to accept Christianity, for he had learned well from his teachers and spiritual guides that service to Christ must be freely undertaken and never the result of force. Before long he gave his teachers at Canterbury another residence, one appropriate to their station, and a variety of landholdings to provide for their needs.

[2.1] Gregory was born a Roman, the son of Gordian and a descendant of many noble and devout ancestors, among whom was Felix, the former bishop of that see [of Rome] and a man of great distinction in Christ's Church, and Gregory dutifully maintained the family tradition by the nobility and devotion of his own religious life. With God's help he took his natural gifts for worldly success and dedicated them entirely to attaining heavenly glory—for he withdrew from secular life and sought admission to monastic life. There he lived a life of such perfection in grace that in later years he would weep at the memory of how firmly his mind was then set on high things, soaring above everything transient, and how completely he dedicated himself to thoughts of heaven. It was as though, while rooted in his body, he could transcend its bounds in contemplation. He even looked forward to death—something most men regard as a punishment—as the entry to a new life and the reward for all his labors. Whenever he mentioned this, he did so not to call attention to his superior virtue then, but to lament what he regarded as the decline in his virtue as a result of his pastoral work. Once, conversing intimately with his deacon Peter about his earlier life in the spirit, Gregory said sadly, "Pastoral work requires me to deal with worldly men. And compared to the cloudless beauty of my former life, my spirit now feels polluted with the muck and mire of worldly affairs. After being wasted in attending to the mundane matters of countless people, my soul tries to meditate on purely spiritual matters, but can't help but do so with diminished energy. Comparing what I have to put up with now, with what I have lost, I can't help feeling that the burden is great—greater than ever. . . ."

From the day he was called from his monastic life, was ordained to priestly life, and was sent to Constantinople as the representative of the Holy See, Gregory never gave up his spiritual exercises, even amid the maelstrom of earthly politics. Some of his fellow monks had accompanied him to the imperial city, out of devotion to him, and he always maintained a regular religious observance with them. This served as an anchor for him, holding him fast to the peaceful shore of prayer-life even while his daily life tossed on the endless waves of worldly affairs; studying with them always refreshed his mind after it was worn down by mundane things. . . .

Here I must stop to tell a story handed down by our forebears that explains the origins of Gregory's deep desire for the salvation of our [English] nation. The story goes, that one day some merchants, recently arrived in Rome, put their goods on display in the market-square when Gregory happened to be among the crowd who gathered around. His eye fell upon some boy-slaves who were for sale—fair-skinned, fine-cut features, and with beautiful hair. Intrigued by them, he asked where in the world they had come from.

"They are from Britain," he was told; "everyone there looks like this."

He asked next if the Britons were Christians or still ignorant heathens.

"They are pagans," came the answer.

"Oh, how sad!" Gregory sighed, "How sad that such bright-faced people are still in the clutches of the Author of Darkness, and that such graceful features conceal minds ignorant of God's grace! Tell me, what is the name of these people?"

"They're called 'Angles,'" someone said.

"The name suits them," Gregory replied, "for their faces are angelic. It would be a good thing if they shared in the inheritance of the angels in heaven. Tell me, what is the name of the province they come from?"

"Deira," came the answer.

"That's good," said Gregory. "They will one day be rescued from the wrath [*de ira*] of God and called to the mercy of Christ. And what is the name of their king?"

"Aelle," he was told.

To which Gregory replied one last time, making a play on the king's name, "Then it is fitting that their land shall one day echo with the praise of God, our Creator, with the 'Alleluia.'"

STUDY QUESTIONS

1. Why does the king endorse the Christian mission in his territories, even before he himself converts?
2. How are the needs of the spirit and the body contrasted throughout Gregory's life?

8.6 DHUODA, *HANDBOOK FOR WILLIAM*, 841–843 CE

A strikingly rare example of a well-versed female author in the Carolingian period, the noble-woman Dhuoda (ca. 803–ca. 843) recorded a list of courtly guidelines for her son William, who was retained as a hostage by King Charles the Bald to ensure the loyalty of Dhuoda's husband. In a world of belligerent conflict between the heirs of Charlemagne, Dhuoda, right before her death, instructs William in how to become a loyal vassal, a useful member of court, and, above all, a good Christian. In the genre of a "mirror" or "handbook," this work expresses a mother's sense of loss blended with pride and hope for her distant son.

In the name of the Holy Trinity, here begins the handbook which Dhuoda, his mother, sent to her son William.

I know very well how most women rejoice to be with their children in this world, but I, Dhuoda, live far away from you, William, am anxious and want to do something special for you—so I am sending you this little book of mine, written down [by a scribe] in my name. Read it and learn from it, keeping it as a mirror, so to speak. I rejoice in the hope that it may remind you, when you are reading it, of how you should behave—for my sake.

[Pr 1.1] For we humans, attaining perfection requires great and persistent effort. We combat evil things by applying the medicines that counteract them. We must struggle not only against worldly people who burn in the maw of Envy but also, as the Apostle [Paul] says, we must combat "the evil spirits in the heavens." [Eph 6.12] Why? Because there are people who, despite their worldly success and material wealth and out of some secret malice, still are jealous of others and plot against them as much as they can, even while feigning friendship.

[Pr 1.4] You have many books at hand—and you will receive more—in which to read and excite your curiosity, to ponder and scrutinize, and to contemplate; you also have (and will receive more) learned men who can teach you and by whose example you can most easily learn how to behave in both aspects of your life. Consider how it is with doves—who keep watch for herons and falcons, their predators, even when drinking clear-flowing waters, lest they be captured—they fly away, laughing, and escape to wherever their pleasure takes them. You will do likewise if you, in your reading, look to the words of the orthodox saints and those Fathers who went before us, and if you observe how the greatest magnates and court figures faithfully obey the commands of God and their earthly lords. Follow their examples, if you can, and you will not only avoid the hidden snares set by those of evil spirit, but you will also elude the clutches of those who are your open enemies. Then you will increase in spiritual and physical strength and, with Christ's help, succeed. Read and consider closely what is written in Solomon's book, "I will now praise the godly, our ancestors, in their own time." [Sira 44.1]

[Pr 1.5] Although we are merely unimportant exiles who do not number among the great magnates, yet we bear within ourselves the faults of this world and are thus always pulled downward rather than lifted up toward heaven. But according to the warning given in the Old Testament, we ought to bear the names of the twelve patriarchs on our foreheads, just as the Holy Scripture commands us, according to the

Translation by Clifford Backman.

vision granted to Ezechiel, to take as our examples the creatures with six wings and eyes in both the front and the back of their heads. And so I offer this to you as a guiding principle: detest the wicked, flee from the immoral, the sluggish, and the proud; and in all that you do, avoid those who are sick in their souls. Why? Because they lay snares, like mousetraps, to deceive people. They never give up paving the way to scandal and wickedness—even if they themselves tumble in order to bring others down with them. This has happened in the past; I exhort you to avoid it in the present and future. May God permit that your fate be in no way joined to theirs.

[Pr 1.6] Inquire into, hold close, and observe faithfully the examples of those men of great worth in the past, present, and future who have proven their faithfulness to God and have persevered in this world. That is the meaning of the Scripture verse that commands us to hold the written names of the twelve patriarchs in our hands and to wear them on our foreheads, and to keep our eyes looking both forward and behind. These are virtues! When these twelve men were in this world they were constantly aiming toward heaven, growing and flourishing toward God. Wise in faith and soul, theirs was a happy path as they set themselves to worthy ends in thought and deed, and they left behind for us an example, so that in seeking that same path, we may do as they did. . . .

[Pr 6.1] If by chance your heart suffers harm, perhaps at the instigation of the devil, by the temptation to fornicate, or any other goading of the flesh, resist it with chastity, and keep in mind the purity of the blessed patriarch Joseph, and of Daniel, and of those others who maintained the purity of their bodies and souls by faith as regarded their masters and neighbors. They deserved to be saved and given high honor, and to be gathered up by the Lord among the number of His saints. For as the Apostle says, "God will judge the immoral and adulterers;" [Heb 13.4] and the Psalmist relates that those who fornicate will perish far from you. And the Apostle likewise says,

among other things, "Every other sin a person commits is outside the body, but the immoral person sins against his own body." [1 Cor 6.18]

[Pr 6.2] Therefore, son, avoid fornication and keep your mind turned away from prostitutes. It is written, "Do not let your passions be your guide, but keep your desires in check." [Sira 18.30] Do not let your soul fly away in pursuit of evil desires. For if you do risk giving in to one of these ills, then certainly they will make you fall upon your sword or into the hands of your enemies. They will say with the prophet [Isaiah], "Bow down, that we may walk over you." [Isa 51.23] May this never happen to you! . . . By seeking God's help, you may escape the thrill of such embraces and such tempestuous turmoil. It is indeed the eyes in your head that ignite the flesh to carnal desire, yet the struggle against these evils is an interior one. . . . "Death has come up through our windows," [Jer 9.20] and "Everyone who looks at a woman with lust has already committed adultery with her in his heart." [Matt 5.28]

[Pr 6.3] But for those who maintain continence and suppress all carnal desires, you will find it written, "The lamp of the body is the eye. If your eye is sound, your whole body will be filled with light." [Matt 6.22] . . . Learned teachers do not deny sanctified marriage to the union of flesh, but they do strive to root out filthy and wrongful fornication. Enoch was chaste, along with Noah, Abraham, Isaac, Jacob, Joseph, and Moses, and all those others who struggled to keep their hearts pure in Christ through the institution of marriage. What more can I say?

[Pr 6.4] And so, my son, whether you keep your body in the splendid gift of virginity, or in the chastity of the marriage-union, you will be free from starting this great sin. Your mind will rest secure and be in that peace that comes through the eight beatitudes. And there will be fulfilled in you, along with other worthies, as it is written, the worthy praise offered by many: "Blessed are the clean of heart, for they will see God." [Matt 5.8]

STUDY QUESTIONS

1. Why does Dhuoda see sexuality as a particular temptation to young men?
2. What is suggested by Dhuoda's frequent allusions to the Bible in her arguments?

8.7 *THE CORPUS OF ROMAN LAW*

The *Corpus iuris civilis* ("Body of Roman Law") was compiled by a team of legal scholars at the court of the Byzantine emperor Justinian in the sixth century. The work is divided into three parts: the *Codex* brings together, in an organized fashion, all the laws issued by the central Roman government up through the reign of Hadrian; the *Digest* (also called the *Pandects*) gathers the laws issued since Hadrian and adds the legal opinions of Rome's leadings jurists; the *Institutes*, from which the passage below is drawn, is a summary and abridgement of the first two and served as an introductory textbook for those wanting to study Roman law. The passages quoted below outline the legal definitions of some individuals in the empire.

I, 3. THE LAW REGARDING PERSONS

All Roman law pertains either to persons, things, or actions. We shall speak first of persons, since there is little point in knowing the law if one does not know the persons regarding whom it was made. The fundamental distinction is between the rights of free persons and those of slaves.

1. Freedom—the quality which makes men free—is the ability to do what one pleases unless prevented by force or prohibited by law.
2. Slavery is an institution in the laws of many nations by which one man is defined as the property of another, contrary to natural right.
3. The word designating slaves is *servi* because the generals who spare their lives by selling them do not put them to death. Another term for slaves is *mancipia* owing to the fact that these persons are taken from the enemy by the force of a strong hand.
4. Some slaves are born into their position, others acquire it. Those born of a slave-mother are themselves slaves; those others become slaves by the law of nations (that is, when captured in battle) or by the civil law (as when a freeman over the age of twenty allows himself to be sold in order to pay off a debt).

5. There is no distinction before the law in the condition of slaves. Among freemen, however, many distinctions apply since some are born free and others have been set free.

I, 4. THE FREE-BORN

An *ingenuus* is someone who is free from birth, having been born to married parents, themselves both free, whether born free or made free, or one of whom was born free while the other was made free. When the mother is free and the father is a slave, the child is born free; the same applies when a mother is free and the father is unknown, since no legal father can be said to exist. Whether or not a mother is free at the time she gives birth is determinative, not whether or not she was a slave when she conceived; but if she is a freewoman at the point she conceives yet a slave when she gives birth, the child is defined as born free since the mother's misfortune ought not to prejudice her unborn child. The next question that arises is: If a pregnant slave woman is made free but is enslaved a second time before her child is born, is the child born free or as a slave? According to Marcellus, the child is born free since the mother's attainment of free status, however brief, suffices to benefit the child—and this seems right.

Translation by Clifford Backman.

When a man has been born free he does not cease to be an *ingenuus* if he happens later to be enslaved and loses his franchise. It has frequently been asserted in law that enfranchisement does not determine the rights of birth.

I, 5. THOSE MADE FREE

Freedmen are those individuals who have been freed from legal servitude. *Manumission* is the term for making free, since it means "freeing from the hand." Whenever anyone is enslaved, he or she is "under the hand" or authority of someone else, and manumission frees one from this authority. The practice arose from the law of nations, for by that law all people were born free and since slavery was not yet known, neither was manumission; but when slavery became part of the law of nations, the practice of manumission soon followed. This is how the law of nations came to recognize the three distinctions or the free, the enslaved, and the freed.

1. Manumission is performed in various ways: in front of a church; according to the imperial laws or edicts; or in the presence of friends by letter, will, or any other expression of a freeman's last wishes. A slave can also be freed in the other ways specified by the decrees of the current emperor and his predecessors.
2. A master can manumit a slave of his at any time, even when a magistrate (e.g. a praetor, *praesens*, or proconsul) happens to pass by, is one his way to the baths, or going to a theater.
3. Freedmen used to be divided into three categories. Some who were manumitted obtained complete liberty and became Roman citizens; a second group received a less complete form of liberty and became *Latini* under the *lex Iulia Norbana*; and a third group held a still lesser form of liberty and were called *dediti* by the *lex Aelia Sentia*. This lowest class, the *dediti*, has long ceased to be recognized in law and even the *Latini* have become relatively rare. Out of imperial benevolence . . . we have made all freedmen whatsoever full Roman citizens regardless of the [former] slaves' ages, the concerns of the manumittors, or the method of manumission, while also introducing other procedures by which slaves may become full Roman citizens—which is henceforth the only kind of liberty under the law.

I, 8. SLAVES

We turn now to a discussion of the laws regarding the next two class of persons – those who are free and those who exist under the legal authority of others. Of these latter, some are under the authority of parents, others under that of masters. We shall treat first of those subservient to others, for once we have defined who these people are we will better understand those who are free.

First, those subject to masters.

1. All slaves are subject to their masters whose power derives from the law of nations, which asserts that all masters have the power and life and death over their slaves, and that everything belonging to a slave belongs to his master.
2. In our time it is established that no citizens may use this measure of violence against a slave except for a cause recognized by imperial law, as stated in a decree by the emperor Antoninus Pius, which asserts that anyone who kills his own slave without such a just cause is subject to the same penalty as one who kills a slave belonging to another. A second decree by the same ruler forbids the use of excessive brutality by masters. This law was enacted after hearing reports from various provincial governors about slaves who seek sanctuary [from cruel treatment] in temples or at the feet of statues of the emperor; whereupon the emperor decreed that a master whose treatment of his slave is egregious might be persuaded instead to sell that slave for a fair price and thus suffer no financial loss. This was indeed a wise decision, one that supports the common principle that no one should misuse his property. . . .

I, 9. PATERNAL AUTHORITY

All the children begotten in lawful marriage are under the authority of their fathers.

1. Marriage is the union of a man and a woman in an insoluble bond.

2. Paternal power over children is a unique trait of Roman citizens, since no other people have the degree of power over their children that we do.

3. Any child born to a man and his wife in under paternal power, as is the child born to your son and his wife whether grandson or granddaughter, along with your great-grandchildren and all other descendants. A child born to your daughter, however, is under the father's paternal power, not your own.

I, 10. MARRIAGE

Citizens are bound together in marriage when they have been united according to the law, that is, a male when he is a legal adult or a son who has at least reached puberty, and the female likewise attains marriageable age. The female must first obtain consent from her father, under whose parental power she lives, since this is demanded by common sense as much as by law and must in fact precede the marriage. It has been asked: Can the [minor] son or daughter of a madman marry? Opinions on this have been divided, and therefore we declare that both may marry without their mad father's consent, as detailed in our recent law.

1. Not every man and woman can marry; for many, marriage is forbidden. For example, no man can marry his own daughter or granddaughter, and no woman can marry her son or grandson. If such marriages occur, both parties are guilty of the crime of incest; this is the case even if the son or daughter in question is adopted, and even if the adoption is dissolved for any reason. No one can marry an adopted child or grandchild even if the child has been emancipated [from the adoption].

2. Restrictions less severe perhaps but still operative exist on marriages between collateral relatives: a brother and sister, for example, cannot marry whether they share both a father and mother or only one of the two. No one may marry an adopted sibling either, although the law permits such a marriage if the adoption has been vitiated. If a man wishes to adopt his son-in-law he must first legally emancipate his own daughter; conversely, if he wishes to adopt his daughter-in-law he must emancipate his son.

3. No man may marry the daughter or granddaughter of either his brother or sister. If a man is prohibited from marrying any particular woman, he is also prohibited from marrying any daughter or niece of that woman. The law sees no impediment, however, to a man marrying the daughter of a woman whom his father has adopted, since that daughter bears no natural or legal relation to him.

4. The children of two brothers or sisters, or of a brother and sister [that is, cousins], may marry.

5. No man may marry his paternal or maternal aunt, nor his paternal or maternal great-aunt, even if she is his aunt only by adoption, since they are viewed by the law as sharing ancestors.

6. Other restrictions on marriage remain. For example, no man may marry his wife's daughter or his son's wife, for the law considers both step-daughters and daughters-in-law to be a man's daughters. . . .

7. A man may not marry his wife's mother or his father's wife, since the law holds them both to be his own mothers. Even if those women are unmarried [that is, widowed or divorced], they are still legally the man's mother-in-law or step-mother. . . .

8. The son of a man by his first marriage may marry the daughter of the man's [second] wife from her first marriage may marry; also the daughter of a man by his first marriage and the son of a man's [second] wife by her first marriage. This is true even if the man and his second wife have produced children of their own.

9. If a man divorces his wife and she later has a daughter from her second marriage, that daughter is not the first husband's step-daughter; this law contradicts the earlier law of the emperor Julian, who forbade marriage between them. A woman who is betrothed to a man's son is not legally that man's daughter-in-law, neither is a man's betrothed wife the step-mother of a man's son, until the marriages occur.[1]

---

[1] Thus a man could marry his son's fiancée, or a son his father's fiancée, if those first-planned marriages did not take place.

10. Slaves who are related either as father and daughter or as brother and sister may not marry.

11. Still other types of marriages are prohibited by long-standing laws as enumerated in the books of the *Digest* (or *Pandects*).

12. If any persons unite themselves in contravention of these rules, they are not married; they are not husband and wife; no dowry or inheritance exists; and no children produced by such a relation are under the man's paternal power. Such offspring are regarded as the children conceived in prostitution and have no legal father; they are called *spurii*—from the Greek *sporados,* meaning "of unknown parentage"—or *sine patre,* "fatherless." When such an illegal relation is broken, no legal claim can be made for a dowry, and the persons who contracted such a union are subject to all the penalties set forth in other imperial laws.

13. It occasionally happens that children are born who are not immediately under their fathers' paternal power but come under it afterwards; examples of this would be a son born out of wedlock whom a court later recognizes as being under the man's paternal power, or a child born of a free and marriageable though unmarried woman with whom a man cohabited. In either case the child would come under the man's paternal power after legal instruments of dowry are issued in accordance with the laws. These laws confer the same legal rights to any children subsequently born of that union once the man and woman are legally married.

STUDY QUESTIONS

1. How do these laws define an individual? What distinguishes a free person from an enslaved person?

2. What duties do sons owe their fathers? What obligations do husbands owe their wives? How do these codes compare to legal precepts today?

CHAPTER 9

THE EXPANSIVE REALM OF ISLAM

9.1 EXCERPTS FROM THE QUR'AN, 600–700 CE

The Holy Qur'an was revealed to Prophet Muhammad over the course of twenty-two years, from 610 to 632. The *surat* ("chapter") that follows came early, while Muhammad was still living in Mecca. It describes the ranks of the good and the evil, from the angels in heaven to the earthly prophets (and those who rejected them). It is interesting to compare these verses with the corresponding passages in the Hebrew Bible. Note, for instance, that here Abraham offers his son Ismail (born of his servant-woman Hagar), rather than Isaac (born of his wife Sarah), as a sacrifice to God. Words and phrases in square brackets are added to complete the sense of the sentence and do not appear in the Arabic.

SURAT 37. AS-SAFFAT: THOSE RANGED IN RANKS

In the name of Allah, Most Gracious, Most Merciful.

[vv. 1–21]

> By those who range themselves in ranks,
> those who so are strong in repelling [evil],
> those who thus proclaim the Message [of Allah]!
> Verily, verily, your God is One!
> Lord of the heavens and of the earth,
> and all between them, and Lord of every point at
> the rising of the sun!
> We have indeed decked the lower heaven with
> beauty
> [in] the stars,—

> [for beauty] and for guard against all obstinate
> rebellious Satans.
> [So] they should not listen their ears in the
> direction
> of the Exalted Assembly and they are cast away
> from every side,
> repulsed. And for them is a perpetual
> chastisement,
> except such as snatch away something by stealth,
> and they
> are pursued by a flaming fire, of piercing
> brightness.
> Just ask their opinion: Are they the more difficult
> To create, or the [other] beings We have
> created?
> Them have We created out of a sticky clay!

Truly dost thou marvel while they ridicule,
And when they are admonished, pay no heed,—
And, when they see a Sign, turn it to mockery,
And say, "This is nothing but evident sorcery!
What! When we die, and become dust and bones,
Shall we [then] be raised up [again]?
And also our fathers of old?"
Say thou: "Yea, and ye shall then be humiliated
[on account of your evil],
then it will be a single [compelling] cry;
and behold, they will begin to see!
They will say, 'Ah! Woe to us! This is the Day of
Judgment!'
[A voice will say,] 'This is the Day
of sorting out, whose truth ye [once] denied!'"

[vv. 22–74]

"Bring ye up," it shall be said, "the wrong-doers
and their wives, and the things they worshipped—
besides Allah, and lead them to the Way, to the
[Fierce] Fire!
But stop them, for they must be asked:
'What is the matter with you, that ye help not
each other?'"
Nay, but that day they shall submit [to Judgment],
And they will turn to one another,
And question one another.
They will say: "It was ye who used to come to us
From the right hand."
They will reply: "Nay, ye yourselves had no faith!
Nor had we any authority over you. Nay, it was
ye who were a people in obstinate rebellion!"
"So now has been proved true, against us, the
Word
of our Lord that we shall indeed [have to] taste
[the punishment for our sins]:
We led you astray: for truly we were ourselves
astray."
Truly, that Day, they will [all] share in the
Chastisement.
Verily, that is how We shall deal with Sinners.
For they, when they were told that there is
no god except Allah, would puff themselves up
with Pride,
and say: "What! Shall we give up our gods
For the sake of a Poet possessed?"

Nay! He has come with the [very] Truth,
And he confirms [the Message of] the messengers
[before him].
Ye shall indeed taste of the Grievous
Chastisement;—
And you are requited naught save what ye did.
But the chosen servants of Allah,—
For them is a Sustenance determined,
Fruits; and they [shall enjoy] honour and dignity,
In Gardens of delight.
Facing each other on raised couches,
Round will be passed to them a Cup
From a clear-flowing fountain,
Crystal-white, of a taste
Delicious to those who drink [thereof],
Free from headiness;
Nor will they suffer intoxication therefrom.
And besides them will be chaste women;
restraining
Their glances, with big eyes [of wonder and
beauty].
As if they were [delicate] eggs closely guarded.
Then they will turn to one another and question
one another.
One of them will say:
"I had an intimate companion [on the earth],
who used to say, 'Do you really believe?
When we die and become dust and bones, shall we
Indeed receive rewards and punishments?'"
He said: "Would you like to look down?"
He looked down and saw him in the midst
of the Fire.
He said: "By Allah! Thou wast little short
Of bringing me to perdition!
Had it not been for the Grace of my Lord,
I should certainly have been among those
brought [there]!
Is it [the case] that we shall not die,
Except our first death, and that we shall not be
punished?"
Verily this is the supreme triumph,
For the like of this let all strive, who wish to strive.
Is that the better entertainment or the Tree of
Zaqqum?
For We have truly made it [as] a trial
For the wrong-doers.

For it is a tree that springs out of the bottom of
    Hell-fire:
The shoots of its fruit-stalks
Are like the heads of devils:
Truly they will eat thereof and fill their bellies
    therewith.
Then on top of that they will be given
A mixture made of boiling water.
Then shall their return be to the [Blazing] Fire.
Truly they found their fathers on the wrong Path;
So they [too] were rushed down on their
    footsteps!
And truly before them, many of the ancients went
    astray;—
But We sent aforetime among them, warners.
Then see what was the End of those who were
    warned
Except the chosen servants of Allah.

[vv. 75 –113]

[In the days of old] Noah cried to Us,
and We are the Best to hear prayer.
And We delivered him and his people from the
    great Calamity,
and made his progeny to endure [on this earth];
and we left [this blessing] for him among
    generations
to come in later times:
"Peace and salutation to Noah among the
    nations!"
Thus indeed do We reward those who do right.
For he was one of Our believing Servants.
Then the rest We overwhelmed in the Flood.
Verily from his party was Abraham.
Behold, he approached his Lord with a sound
    heart.
Behold, he said to his father and to his people,
"What
is that which ye worship?
Is it a Falsehood—gods other than Allah that ye
    desire?
Then what is your idea about the Lord of the
    Worlds?"
Then did he cast a glance at the Stars,
and he said: "I am indeed sick [at heart]!"
So they turned away from him, and departed.

Then did he turn to their gods and said,
"Will ye not eat [of the offerings before you]?
What is the matter with you that ye speak not?"
Then did he turn upon them, striking [them] with
    the right hand.
Then came [the worshippers] with hurried steps
    to him.
He said: "Worship ye that which ye have
    [yourselves] carved?
But Allah has created you and your handiwork!"
They said: "Build him a furnace, and throw him
    into the blazing fire!"
[This failing], they then plotted against him,
but We made them the ones most humiliated!
He said: "I will go to my Lord! He will surely
    guide me!
O my Lord! Grant me a righteous [son]!"
So We gave him the good news of a
    forbearing son.
Then, when [the son] reached [the age of
serious] work with him, he said: "O my son!
I have seen in a dream that I offer thee in sacrifice.
Now I see what is thy view!" The son said:
"O my father! Do as thou art commanded:
Thou will find me, if Allah so wills one of the
    steadfast."
So when they had both submitted [to Allah],
and he had laid him prostrate on his forehead
    [for sacrifice],
We called out to him, "O Abraham!
Thou hast already fulfilled the dream!"—thus
    indeed
do We reward those who do right.
For this was a clear trial—
and We ransomed him with a monstrous sacrifice:
And We left for him among generations [to come]
    in later times:
"Peace and salutation to Abraham!"
This indeed do We reward those who do right
for he was one of Our believing Servants.
And We gave him the good news
of Isaac—a prophet—one of the Righteous.
We blessed him and Isaac: but of their progeny
are [some] that do right, and [some] that
    obviously
do wrong, to themselves.

[vv. 114 –138]

Again, [of old] We bestowed Our favour on Moses
and Aaron,

and We delivered them and their people from
[their] Great distress,

and We helped them, so they were victorious;

and We gave them the Book which helps to make
things clear;

and We guided them to the Straight Way.

And We left for them among generations [to
come] in later times:

"Peace and salutation to Moses and Aaron!"

Thus indeed do We reward those who do right.

For they were two of Our believing Servants.

So also was Elias among those sent [by Us].

Behold, he said to his people,

"Will ye not fear [Allah]? Will ye call upon Baal

and forsake the Best of Creators,—

Allah, your Lord and Cherisher,

and the Lord and Cherisher of your fathers of
old?"

But they rejected him, and they will certainly
be called up [for punishment],

except the chosen Servants of Allah [among
them].

And We left for him among generations
[to come] in later times:

"Peace and salutation to such as Elias!"

Thus indeed do We reward those who do right.

For he was one of Our believing Servants.

So also was Lüt among those sent [by Us].

Behold, We delivered him and his adherents, all

except an old woman who was among those who
lagged behind:

Then We destroyed the rest.

Verily, ye pass by their [sites] by day—

and by night: Will ye not understand?

[vv. 139–182]

So also was Jonah among those sent [by Us].

When he ran away [like a slave from captivity]

to the ship [fully] laden,

he [agreed to] cast lots, and he was of the
rebutted:

Then the big Fish did swallow him,

and when he had done acts worthy of blame.

Had it not been that he [repented and] glorified
Allah,

he would certainly have remained inside the Fish

till the Day of Resurrection.

But We cast him forth on the naked shore in a
state of sickness,

and We caused to grow, over him, a spreading
plant

of the Gourd kind.

And We sent him [on a mission]

to a hundred thousand [men] or more.

And they believed; so We permitted them

to enjoy [their life] for a while.

Now ask them their opinion: Is it that thy Lord

has [only] daughters, and they have sons?—

Or that We created the angels female, and they

are witnesses [thereto]?

Behold, they say, out of their own invention,

"Allah has begotten children"? But they are liars!

Did He [then] choose daughters rather than sons?

What is the matter with you? How judge ye?

Will ye not then receive admonition?

Or have ye an authority manifest?

Then bring ye your Book [of authority] if ye be
Truthful!

And they have invented a kinship

between Him and the Jinns: But the Jinns know

[quite well] that they will be brought before Him.

Glory to Allah! [He is free] from the things they
ascribe [to Him]!

Not [so do] the Servants of Allah, the chosen ones.

For, verily, neither ye nor those ye worship

can lead [any] into temptation concerning Allah,

except such as are [themselves] going to the
blazing Fire!

[The angels] "Not one of us but has a place
appointed;

And we are verily ranged in ranks [for service],

and we are verily those who declare [Allah's] glory!"

And there were those who said,

"If only we had had before us a Message

from those of old,

we should certainly have been Servants of Allah,

sincere [and devoted]!"

But [now that the Qur'an has come], they reject it:

But soon will they know!
Already has Our Word been passed before [this]
to Our Servants sent [by Us],
that they would certainly be assisted,
and that Our forces,—they surely must conquer.
So turn thou away from them for a little while,
and watch them [how they fare], and they soon
shall see [how thou farest]!
Do they wish [indeed] to hurry on our
Punishment?
But when it descends upon their courtyards

before them, Evil will be the morning for those who
were warned [and heeded not]!
So turn thou away from them for a little while,
and watch [how they fare] and they shall soon see
[how thou farest]!
Glory to thy Lord, the Lord of Honour
and Power! [He is free] from what they ascribe
[to Him]!
And Peace on the messengers!
And Praise to Allah, the Lord and Cherisher
of the Worlds.

STUDY QUESTIONS

1. How do these verses from the Qur'an compare with corresponding passages in the Hebrew Bible?
2. Culturally, what is the significance of the Qur'an's depiction of Abraham offering his son Ishmail as a sacrifice rather than Isaac? How would this important difference shape Arab and Muslim identity?

9.2 IBN ISHAQ, *THE LIFE OF MUHAMMAD*

Ibn Ishaq (704–770) is one of the earliest of the Prophet's biographers. The original text of his biography does not survive; it was edited, separately, by two of his pupils, and only one of those recensions (made by Ibn Hisham) survives. Below are two passages—one depicting the famous "night journey" of the Prophet's spirit to Jerusalem and its vision of paradise and the other a narrative of the fate of the Jewish community at Medina, the Banu Qurayza. Some scholars reject this (long) section of Ibn Ishaq's work, arguing that it cannot be trusted since it derives only from the recollections of Jewish converts to Islam.

THE NIGHT JOURNEY

I have heard the traditions that were passed on by Abdullah b. Mas'ud, Abu Sa'id al-Khudri, the Prophet's wife Aisha, Mu'awiya b. Abu Sufyan, al-Hasan b. Abu'l-Hasan al-Basri, Ibn Shihab al-Zuhri, Qatada, and Umm Hani d. Abu Talib. Each person passed on what he or she was told about what happened when the Prophet went on his Night Journey, and I have

---

Translation by Clifford Backman.

placed their information together in what follows. The question of the *masra* of the Journey, and the details surrounding it, is so complicated that only the power and authority of Allah Himself can understand it—a lesson for us all who would learn, and a blessing and mercy for all who believe. But surely it was by the will of Allah that He took the Prophet by night and showed him all that He wished him to see, proving to the Prophet the mighty authority and power by which Allah accomplishes whatever He wants.

The traditions I have heard assert that Abdullah b. Mas'd reported that al-Buraq—the winged animal whose stride reached as far as a man can see, and on whom all earlier prophets rode—was brought to Muhammad, who mounted it. The Prophet's Companion [Gabriel] flew with him, and together they saw all the wonders of heaven and earth before landing, at last, at the temple in Jerusalem. There they saw the friends of God—Abraham, Moses, and Jesus— standing with a group of prophets. The Apostle prayed with them, after which someone brought him three jars, one of milk, one of wine, one of water. The Apostle [later] said, "When these jars were brought forward I heard a voice, saying 'If he chooses the water, he and his people will drown; if he chooses the wine, he and his people will lose their way; but if he chooses the milk, he and his people will be rightly guided.' I chose the one with milk, and drank it, and then Gabriel said to me, 'You and your people will be rightly guided, O Muhammad.'"

* * * * *

A member of Abu Bakr's family told me that the Prophet's wife Aisha used to say, "The Apostle remained with me, but Allah took his spirit, that night."

Ya'qub b. Utba b. al-Mughira b. al-Akhnas reported to me what Mu'awiya b. Abu Sufyan replied, when someone asked him about the Night Journey of the Prophet: "It was truly a vision from Allah." This report does not disagree with the report of al-Hasan, since it was Allah Himself who said, "I have shown you this vision as a test for mankind." Neither does it disagree with Allah's word in the story of Abraham and his son, when Abraham said, "O son! I have seen in a dream that I am to make a sacrifice of you," and then acted upon it. In my opinion, Allah's revelation

comes to His prophets whether they are awake or asleep.

I have heard, too, that the Apostle used to say, "My eyes may sleep, but my heart stays awake." Allah alone knows the truth of revelation, and how it was that Muhammad saw his vision. Asleep or awake, it all truly happened.

Now al-Zuhri claimed to have heard from Sa'id b. al-Musayyab that the Prophet once described Abraham, Moses, and Jesus to some of his companions, in talking about that night, and supposedly said, "I never saw a man who resembled me as much as Abraham did. Moses had a red face, was tall and thin, had curly hair and a hooked nose, like a member of the Shanu'a tribe. Jesus, the son of Mary, was of medium height, and he also had ruddy skin, but he had many freckles on his face and had long straight hair, like one who has just emerged from a bath. It is possible that his hair was dripping with water, but there was no water visible on it. The one among you who looks most like Jesus is Urwa b. Mas'ud al-Thaqafi."

* * * * *

One in whom I trust reported to me, on the authority of Abu Sa'id al-Khudri: "I once heard Allah's Apostle say, 'When I was finished in Jerusalem, a ladder appeared before me—the finest I have ever seen. It was the ladder that all men see, when Death approaches them. My companion [Gabriel] climbed it with me. When we reached the Gate of the Watchers we beheld an angel, Isma'il, who was its guard. He had twelve thousand angels under his authority, each one of whom had another twelve thousand under its command.' Whenever the Apostle told this story, he always added, *No one but Allah knows the strength of His army.* [Sura 74.31] When Gabriel brought me forward, Isma'il asked me who I was, and when I told him that I was Muhammad he asked me if I had been entrusted with a mission. When I replied that I had, he wished me well."

Another witness, one who heard it from someone who had heard it directly from Allah's Apostle, reported that Muhammad said: "When I entered the lowest heaven, all the angels smiled and welcomed me, and they all wished me well—except for one. This one spoke along with the others but he did not smile or show any joy. I asked Gabriel the reason for that one's behavior, and he answered that [that angel] has never smiled and never will—but if by chance he ever were to smile, he would smile at me; and the reason he never smiles is because he is Malik, the Keeper of Hell. I said to Gabriel. . . . 'Would you tell him to show me Hell?' 'Certainly,' answered Gabriel, adding, 'O Malik, show Muhammad Hell.' Then Malik raised the lid that covers Hell. Flames shot so high into the sky that I feared they would devour everything, and so I begged Gabriel to order Malik to send the flames back to where they had come from—which he did. The feeling of [the flames'] return to Hell was like the descent of a shadow. Once the flames were back in place, Malik replaced the lid."

Abu Sa'id al-Khudri relates that the Apostle said: "When I entered the lowest heaven I saw a man sitting in judgment of the spirits who passed before him. To some he would say, 'A good soul in a good body!' while to others he would frown and say, 'An evil spirit in an evil body!' I asked Gabriel who this was, and he replied that it was our ancestor Adam, reviewing all the souls of his descendants. The souls of all believers gave him great delight, but the souls of unbelievers filled him with disgust, as I described.

"Then I saw some men with distended lips, like those of a camel; they held in their hands flaming coals. They would thrust these down their throats, and the burning coals would then emerge from their anus. Gabriel told me these were the damned who [in life] had stolen and consumed the wealth belonging to orphans.

"Then I saw some other men, suffering like the family of Pharaoh. They had enormous bellies, so large that they trampled over their own stomachs like a herd of camels maddened by thirst. Having been cast into Hell, they constantly tramped themselves ever deeper, unable to get out of their own way. These were those guilty of usury.

"Then I saw sitting men sitting at a table, with piles of good fat meat in from of them, but also piles of stringy, stinking meat. They were eating only the rancid meat. These were the damned who forsook the women whom Allah had permitted to them [i.e., their wives] and pursued only the women denied them [i.e., mistresses].

"Then I saw women hanging from their breasts. These were the women who had given their husbands bastard children."

I heard from Ja'far b. 'Amr, who heard it from al-Qasim b. Muhammad, that the Apostle said: "Allah's wrath is great against any woman who brings a bastard into her family. Bastards deprive legitimate sons of their inheritance-portion, and learn private things they have no right to know."

As related by Sa'id al-Khudri, "the Messenger of God said: 'Next I was lifted up to the second heaven, where I encountered the cousins Jesus, the son of Mary, and John, the son of Zakariah. In the third heaven there was a man with a face like a full moon—Joseph, the son of Jacob. In the fourth heaven I saw a man named Idris—and We raised him to a lofty station [Sura 19.57]. In the fifth heaven I saw a man with long white hair and beard, more handsome than any man I have ever met. This was Aaron, son of Imran, beloved by his people. In the sixth heaven I saw a man with dark skin and a hooked nose, like those of the Shanu'a tribe. This was my brother Moses, son of Imran. Then in the seventh heaven I saw a man sitting on a throne, beside the gate that led to the immortal abode [i.e., Paradise]. Every day seventy thousand angels went in, never to emerge until the Day of Resurrection. I have never seen a man more like me—this was Abraham, my father. Abraham himself took me, then, into Paradise, where I saw a woman with ruby-red lips. I asked her whose woman she was, for she was very pleasing to me. She answered, "Zayd b. Haritha." Later, the Apostle of Allah told this story to Zayd, and made him very happy."[1]

THE MASSACRE OF THE BANU QURAYZA

Muhammad issued an order that no one was to perform the afternoon prayer until after he had reached Banu Qurayza, and he sent Ali ahead of him, bearing the Apostle's banner. The soldiers rallied when they saw it, and Ali advanced as far as the town's fortifications. While camped outside the town, Ali heard

---

[1] Zayd was the adopted son of Muhammad and his first wife Khadija.

some Jews say insulting things about Muhammad, which prompted him to turn quickly and rush to meet the Apostle on the road. He told him that he did not need to come any closer or deal with the miserable Jews.

"Why not?" Muhammad asked. "Did you hear them slandering me?" And after Ali replied that he had done exactly that, the Prophet went on, "Once they see me they will stop."

Then the Apostle approached the Jews' fortifications and cried out, "Listen, you animals! God has rejected you and brings His vengeance upon you!" . . .

The Prophet stopped by one of the Jews' wells near Banu Qurayza, at a place called the Well of Ana. His men joined him. Some of them arrived after the evening prayer, but they had skipped the afternoon prayer because of what the Prophet had said about not praying the afternoon prayer until he had arrived at Banu Qurayza. These men had kept busy instead with a multitude of preparations for battle, in the time for afternoon prayer, and they prayed the afternoon prayer after the evening prayer, as the Prophet had instructed them. Allah did not blame them in His Book, and neither did the Prophet reproach them. . . .

[The Muslim army besieged Banu Qurayza for 25 days. Finally the Jews asked the Prophet to send an emissary with whom they could discuss the terms of surrender.]

Then the Jews sent a message to the Apostle, saying, "Send us Abu Lubaba . . . so that we may negotiate." Muhammad agreed and sent him. The Jews rose to meet him, and suddenly the [Jewish] women and children raced up to him with tears in their eyes, crying "O, Abu Lubaba! What should we do? Should we surrender to Muhammad?"

"Yes," replied Abu Lubaba, and as he spoke he drew his finger across his throat, indicating that otherwise they would be slaughtered. He felt sorry for them; nevertheless, he afterwards reported, "I knew before I had taken a single step that I had been disloyal to Allah and His Messenger [in warning the Jews of their fate]." He left Banu Qurayza—only he did not return to Muhammad. Instead he shackled himself to a column in the [nearby]

mosque and vowed, "I will not leave this place until Allah forgives me for what I have done!" He further swore that he would not return to Banu Qurayza nor allow himself to be seen anywhere in the town where he had been disloyal to Allah and His Apostle.

Muhammad, meanwhile, waited a long time for Abu Lubaba to return, and when he heard what his emissary had done, he said, "If Abu Lubaba had come to me, I would have asked Allah to forgive him. But since he has sworn his oath I will not let him leave the mosque until Allah forgives him."

I later heard from Yazid b. Abdullah b. Qusayt how the Apostle of God learned of Allah's forgiveness of Abu Lubaba. It happened one morning while the Prophet was at home with Umm Salama. She said to me, "One morning at sunrise I heard the Apostle laugh. 'Why are you laughing?' I asked him. He answered, 'Because Abu Lubaba has been forgiven.' 'May I tell him?' I asked. When the Messenger agreed, Yazid hurried to the mosque and stood in the doorway of the women's quarter—this was before the wearing of veils was required of women—and announced, 'Rejoice, Abu Lubaba! Allah has forgiven you!' Several men then rushed forward to release him from his shackles, but he said, 'No! Not until the Prophet himself frees me by his own hand!' Soon the Apostle himself came by as he was going to morning prayer, and he set Abu Lubaba free."

[After the Jews surrendered, Muhammad decided their fate.]

And so the Jews surrendered. Muhammad confined them in Medina in the vicinity of d. al-Harith, a woman of al-Najjar, and walked to the marketplace (which is the site of today's market, still, in Medina) and had several trenches dug. Afterwards he gave orders for the Jews to be brought to him in small groups, and he cut off their heads. Two whom he singled out were Huyayy b. Akhtab (that enemy of Allah!) and the Jewish leader, Ka'b b. Asad. Altogether he killed between six hundred and seven hundred of them, although some sources claim a number as high as eight hundred or even nine hundred. All of them, as they were brought forward to Muhammad, asked Ka'b what was going to happen to them. He replied, "Death, by God! What do you expect? Can't you see that he [Muhammad] never stops summoning, and that no one ever returns?"

It went on like this until the Apostle had put an end to all of them. At the last, Huyayy b. Akhtab himself was brought forward. He wore an elaborate robe in which he had torn countless holes, by sticking his fingers through the fabric, in order to ruin its value as booty. His hands were tied with a rope that hung around his neck. When he saw the Apostle of Allah he declared, "I swear by our God that I do not regret opposing you! Anyone who forsakes God will be forsaken!" And then he turned to his men and said, "God's command is just—for He has called in His Book for a massacre of the sons of Israel." Then he sat down and his head was cut off. . . .

I learned from Muhammad b. Ja'far b. al-Zubayr (who had heard it from Urwa b. al-Zubayr) that the Prophet's wife Aisha once said, "Only one Jewish woman was killed. She had been standing with me and talking. All of a sudden she started to laugh loudly; this is when the Apostle of Allah was beheading her [peoples'] men in the marketplace. A voice came out of nowhere and called her name. 'By heaven, what is happening?' I asked. 'I am to be killed,' was her reply. 'But why?' I asked. 'Because of something I once did,' she answered. Then she was taken away and beheaded." Afterwards Aisha used to say sometimes, "I will always marvel at her good spirit and her laughter when she knew she was going to die."

. . . Then the Apostle divided the spoils of Banu Qurayza—the property, the women, and the children—among the Muslims after taking out a one-fifth portion. He decreed the amount of shares to each person: each horseman received three shares (two for the horse, one for its rider); each foot-soldier received one share. On the day of the battle against Banu Qurayza, there were thirty-six horsemen. It was the first time that booty was distributed, after taking out a one-fifth portion, and it was the precedent used by the Prophet for dividing the spoils from all future raids.

After this the Messenger of Allah sent Sa'id b. Zayd al-Ansari (the brother of b. Abdul-Ashhal) with a number of the Jewish women of Banu Qurayza to Najd, where he sold them for weapons and horses.

The Apostle had chosen one of the Jewish women for himself. She was Rayhana d. Amr b. Khunafa, a woman of the Banu Amr b. Qurayza. She remained with him until she died. The Apostle proposed to marry her and place the veil on her, but she said, "No. Keep me for yourself, if you will, but do not marry me. That will be better for both of us." So the Apostle left her and put her away in anger at the fact that she had shown disdain for Islam, once she was captured, and clung to her Judaism. But one day the Prophet was sitting with his companions when he heard the approach of sandaled feet behind him. He announced, "I hear Tha'laba b. Sa'ya coming! She is bringing good news: Rayhana has accepted Islam!" This gave him great pleasure.

STUDY QUESTIONS

1. Ibn Ishaq's biography of the Prophet Muhammad is an important document for understanding the history of the early Muslim community. Reading this excerpt from the "night journey," what impact do you think the Prophet's vision of paradise would have on believers?

2. A very different side of the Prophet Muhammad is portrayed in the narrative of the massacre at Banu Qurayza. What are the historical consequences of the Prophet Muhammad serving as both a military and a spiritual leader of the Muslim community? Compare the depiction of the Jews of Banu Qurayza with Gregory of Tours's depiction of the Jew in the court of King Chilperic. What are the similarities? What are the differences?

9.3 AL-GHAZALI, *THE DELIVERER FROM ERROR*

Abu Hamid al-Ghazali (1058–1111) is widely regarded as medieval Islam's greatest thinker, a Muslim counterpart to Christianity's St. Augustine. Born in the Khurasan province in today's Iran, he was a precocious youth who quickly showed extraordinary intellectual ability. He studied Islamic law, *kalam* (a kind of elementary theology), philosophy, and the sciences, excelling in all. At the early age of thirty-four he was appointed professor of Islamic sciences at the Nizamiyah *madrasa* in Baghdad, perhaps the most prestigious academic position in the caliphate. A few years later, however, he went through a spiritual crisis that resulted in his loss of belief in religious rationalism and his embrace of the mystical Sufi tradition. He spent several years in travel and meditation and then reemerged in public life and devoted his last years to teaching Sufism. His memoir *al-Munqidh min al-dalal* (*The Deliverer from Error*) describes his spiritual journey. Below is a passage recounting his discovery of Sufism.

Having had my fill of these types of teachings, I turned my mind instead to the Way of the Sufis, which I understood as a discovery that can be made not by the intellect but by action. Sufi wisdom consists of a kind of carving away, ridding oneself of bad habits and vicious sentiments—for these are spiritual stumbling blocks—in order to empty one's heart of everything except the thought and remembrance of Allah. I soon found that the theory was easier than the practice. I began studying Sufi teachings by reading their books . . . until I had learned all that I could, of their teachings. Gradually, however, it became clear to me that the essence of their wisdom cannot be acquired through study; it can only be attained by tasting it, by ecstatic release, by transformative experience. Consider how great is the difference between knowing the definitions, causes, and symptoms of health and stability, and actually being healthy and stable. . . . In a similar way, there is a difference between knowing the definition, causes, and symptoms of mystical rapture and actually experiencing it—and consequently longing to rid oneself of the things of this world. . . .

I had already clearly learned that my only hope of achieving eternal blessedness lay in pious living and denying my heart its passions, and that the necessary way to begin was to detach my heart from the world, to withdraw utterly from this place of illusion, and to devote myself solely to Allah, the Most High, and His eternal realm. I understood that I could achieve this only by turning my back on fame and fortune, and to flee from all my activities and relationships. I focused on the reality of my existence and beheld the extent to which I was consumed on all sides. My daily actions—even the most noble of them, being engaged in public and private teaching—were devoted to sciences that mattered nothing to my journey to the realm of paradise. My public teaching was not intended, as it should have been, to glorify Allah but was geared and driven by my desire for fame and honor. I saw that I was standing on the edge of a cliff that was giving way, about to fall into the Endless Fire, unless I changed my ways.

I meditated endlessly on this, wanting to do something about my life while I still had the ability.

Translation by Clifford Backman.

One day I would be determined to quit Baghdad and cut myself off from all responsibilities—but then the next day I would change my mind. One step forward, then one step back. In the morning I might long only for the things of the afterlife, but by evening my baser desires would come to the fore. Earthly concerns held me in chains, while spiritual longing cried out, "Get away! Get away! A long journey awaits you, and time is running out. All the [intellectual] trappings that engulf you are nothing but trickery and nonsense. When will you prepare for the afterlife, if not now? If you will not cut yourself away from earthly concerns now, when will you ever?" Then my spirit would revive and I would be determined, absolutely determined, to take off and flee; but Satan was quick to respond. . . .

When I realized how powerless I was to make up my mind, how totally paralyzed I was, how lost I was with no idea how to proceed, I turned to Allah the Most High, and He "Who listens to the distressed when he calls on Him" [Qur'an 27.62] answered me. He guided my heart away from fame and fortune, away from family, children, and friends. I announced publicly my decision to leave for Mecca, even though I secretly intended to go instead to Syria, since I feared the caliph and my colleagues learning of my plan to reside in Damascus. I was crafty and careful in my arrangement about leaving Baghdad, just as I was rock-steady in my resolve never to return. All the religious leaders in Iraq talked about me incessantly, since none of them could imagine that my departure had a spiritual motive. My position among them, after all, they regarded as the pinnacle of status. "That is their attainment of knowledge." [Qur'an 53.30] . . .

I left Baghdad after distributing whatever wealth I had accumulated, setting aside only as much as I needed to survive and to support my children. I explained to everyone that my Iraqi fortune was intended to support the people, being my pious alms [zakat]. Truly this is the best of all possible arrangements available to a scholar, to support his family. Then I went to Damascus, where I lived for two years. I devoted myself entirely to ascetic withdrawal, solitude, and spiritual disciple, in order to purify my soul, to increase in virtue, and to clean my heart and keep it focused always on Allah the Most High—all

as I had been taught by the writings of the Sufi masters. I often prayed all day in the mosque, all alone, isolated high up in the minaret. I went from Damascus to Jerusalem, shutting myself daily in the Dome of the Rock. Eventually I felt called to make the *hajj*, to receive the blessings of Mecca and Medina, and to visit the tomb of the Prophet of Allah (May Allah's peace and blessing be upon him!), after first visiting the tomb of Ibrahim the Friend of Allah (May Allah's peace and blessing be upon him!). So I set out for the Hijaz.

Just then, however, certain problems and pleas from my children drew me back to Baghdad, even though I had been utterly resolved never to return there. But even while back in Baghdad I chose to live apart, desiring not to disturb the purification of my heart or my constant mindfulness of Allah. Local events, family issues, and the daily need for sustenance pressed in upon me, however, and marred my peaceful solitude. The state of spiritual ecstasy came to me only seldom, although I never stopped pursuing it. Obstacles always appeared in my way, but I never gave up the pursuit.

I lived this way for ten years. It is impossible to describe in detail the things that were revealed to me in those ecstasies that did come, but I can say this much—in the hope that it may be of some use: The Sufis are without a doubt the ones who most perfectly follow the ways of Allah the Most High, who live the best of all lives, the most holy, and the most pure. Not even if one combined all the knowledge of the scholars, all the wisdom of the sages, and all the teachings of the theologians, the total still would not equal even a single aspect of Sufi conduct and belief—for everything a Sufi does and meditates upon, whether in public or in private, is inspired by the light of prophecy, and no light on earth shines brighter than the light of prophecy.

How else to describe it? The first requirement of Sufism is purity, the total purification of the heart from everything other than Allah the Most High. It is the complete absorption of the heart by mindfulness of Allah, reminiscent of the prayer *Allahu al-akhbar*. The goal is to dissolve oneself into Allah. . . .

As soon as one sets upon the Sufi path, visions reveal themselves. Even when wide awake, a Sufi may see angels or the spirits of the prophets, and may hear their voices teaching him. One's spirit can ascend beyond seeing visions of forms and likenesses, to reach a stage that is beyond words. To even attempt to describe this stage is to commit an error that one must be careful to avoid. In only a most general way, the ascent is a closeness to Allah that some call absorption, or identification, or union—all these words fail.

STUDY QUESTIONS

1. How is Al-Ghazali's story of how he embraced Sufism similar to other stories of religious conversion and spiritual awakening?
2. Comparing Al-Ghazali with Ibn Rushd, how is Sufism a different form of Islam? How are they compatible?

9.4 ONE THOUSAND AND ONE NIGHTS, 1100–1200 CE

Also known as *The Arabian Nights*, the multiauthored, massive work *One Thousand and One Nights* brings together tales and legends from Persian, Arabic, Indian, and Mesopotamian traditions. The first Arabic version dates to twelfth-century Cairo, Egypt. This composite work is held together by the story of Scheherazade, a Persian queen who stays the moment of her execution by engaging Shahryar, a king who beheaded each of his virginal wives the day after their marriage, in intriguing cliffhanger stories. The most famous selections from this work are the tales of Aladdin and Sinbad; this selection below reveals a comical, irreverent side of Scheherazade's voice and hints at mutual views of contemporary Muslims, Jews, and Christians sharing a common public space.

"This tale, however, is not more wonderful than the story of what happened in the case of the tailor, the hunchback, the Jew, the inspector and the Christian." "What was that?" asked the king, AND SHAHRAZAD EXPLAINED:

I have heard, O fortunate king, that once upon a time, in the old days, in the city of China there lived a tailor, an open-handed man with a liking for pleasure and entertainment. He used to go out with his wife from time to time to see the sights. One afternoon, the two of them went early and came back home towards the evening. On their way home, they found a hunchback whose strange appearance would raise a laugh even from a man who had been cheated in a bargain and which would dispel the grief of the sad. The tailor and his wife went over to look at him, and they invited him to come home with them to keep them company that night. He agreed and accompanied them.

Night had now fallen and the tailor went off to the market, where he bought a fried fish, together with bread, lemons and a milky dessert. On returning, he set the fish before the hunchback and they ate. His wife then took a large bit of fish and crammed it into her guest's mouth, which she covered with her hand, telling him that he had to swallow it in one gulp. "And I shall not allow you to chew it." The hunchback did swallow it, but it contained a solid bone which stuck in his throat and, his allotted span having come to an end, he died.

Morning now dawned and Shahrazad broke off from what she had been allowed to say. Then, when it was the twenty-fifth night, SHE CONTINUED:

I have heard, O auspicious king, that when the tailor's wife gave the hunchback a mouthful of fish to eat, as his allotted span had ended, he died instantly. "There is no might and no power except with God," exclaimed the tailor. "Poor man, that he should die like this at our hands!" "Why are you wasting time?" said his wife. "Haven't you heard what the poet says:

Why do I try to console myself with the
    impossible,
When I have never met a friend who bears my
    sorrows?
How can one sit on a fire before it is put out?
To sit on fire brings harm."

"What am I to do?" asked her husband. "Get up," she said. "Carry the man in your arms and spread a silk covering over him. We must do this tonight, and I shall go in front, with you following behind. You are to say: 'This is my son and this is his mother, and we are taking him to see the doctor.'" On hearing this, the tailor got up and carried the hunchback in his arms, while his wife kept saying: "My son, may you recover; what is paining you and where are the symptoms of smallpox showing?" Everyone who saw them said: "These people have a child with smallpox." They continued on their way, asking for the doctor's house, until they were directed to the house of a Jewish physician. They knocked on the door and down came a black slave girl, who opened it. When she saw a man carrying a child and accompanied by a woman, she asked: "What's the matter?" The tailor's wife replied: "We have a child with us and we would like the doctor to have a look at him. Take this quarter dinar, give it to your master, and let him come down to see my sick son." The girl went up and the tailor's wife came through the door and said to her husband: "Leave the hunchback here and then let's make our escape." The tailor agreed, and propping the hunchback against the wall, he and his wife made off.

The slave girl went to the Jew and told him: "There is someone at the door with a sick person. His wife is with him and he has handed me a quarter dinar for you to go down to look at him and to prescribe something suitable." The Jew, delighted to see the money, got up quickly and went off in the dark, but as soon as he put his foot down, he stumbled over the corpse. "O Ezra!" he cried. "O Moses and the Ten Commandments! O Aaron and Joshua, son of Nun! I seem to have stumbled over this sick man and he has fallen down the stairs and died. How can I get the corpse out of my house?" He carried it inside and told his wife what had happened. She said: "Why are you sitting there? If you wait until daybreak, then both you and I will lose our lives. We have to take him up to the roof and drop him onto the house of our neighbor, the Muslim. As he is an inspector in charge of the king's kitchens, if he is left there overnight, the dogs will come down from the roofs and drag it off, for they do a great deal of damage to all the stuff that he brings home."

So the Jew and his wife went up to their roof, carrying the hunchback, and they lowered him to the ground by his arms and legs, leaving him by the wall, before going off. No sooner had they done this than the inspector came home, opened the door and went up, carrying a lighted candle. He noticed a man standing in the corner under the ventilation shaft. "By God!" he exclaimed. "This is a fine thing! It must have been a man who has been stealing my stores!" Turning to the corpse, he said: "It was you who has been stealing the meat and the fat, when I thought it was the cats and dogs of the neighbourhood. I have put myself in the wrong by killing them, when all the time it was you, coming down from the roof." He took up a large hammer and, brandishing it, he went up to the corpse and struck it on the breast. When he found that the man was dead, he was moved with grief, and, fearing for his own life, he exclaimed: "There is no might and no power except with God Almighty! May God curse the fat and the sheep's tail!" He then added: "How was it that I brought this man's life to an end with my own hand?" The inspector looked at his victim and found that he was a hunchback. "Wasn't it enough for you to be a hunchback," he asked, "that you had to become a thief and steal meat and fat? O God, the Shelterer, cloak me with Your gracious covering." He then hoisted the corpse on to his shoulders as the night was ending and took it out of his house. He continued to carry it until he reached the edge of the market, where he propped it up at the side of a shop at the head of an alley. He then left the corpse and made off.

A Christian, the king's broker, was the next to appear on the scene. He was drunk and had come out to go to the baths, realizing in his drunkenness, that is was nearly time for matins. He went on, staggering as he walked, until, when he was near the corpse, he squatted down to urinate. Then, casting a sideways glance, he saw someone standing there. As it happened, at the beginning of that night his turban had been stolen and when he saw the hunchback leaning against the wall, he imagined the man meant to steal the one that he now had on. So he balled his fist and struck the hunchback on the neck, felling him to the ground. He called to the market watchman, and then, in the excess of his drunkenness, he set about belabouring the corpse and trying to strangle it. The watchman came up and found the Christian kneeling on the Muslim and hitting him. "What has he done?" he asked. The Christian said: "He wanted to steal my turban." "Get away from him," ordered the watchman, and when the Christian had got up, he went to the hunchback and found him dead. "By God," he said, "this is a fine thing—a Christian killing a Muslim," and after having tied the Christian's hands, he took him to the house of the *wali*. All the while the Christian was saying to himself: "O Messiah, O Holy Virgin, how could I have killed this man and how quickly he died from a single blow!" Drunkenness vanished, to be replaced by care, and the Christian together with the hunchback spent the rest of the night until morning in the *wali*'s house.

In the morning, the *wali* sentenced "the killer" to be hanged. The executioner was ordered to proclaim his crime; a gallows was set up under which the Christian was made to stand, and the executioner came and put a rope around his neck. He was on the point of hanging him when the inspector made his way through the crowd. When he saw the Christian about to be hanged, he cleared a way for himself and then said: "Don't do it; it was I who killed him." "Why did you do that?" asked the *wali*. "I came home last night," he said, "and found that he had come down through the ventilation shaft and had stolen my goods, so I struck him on the chest with a hammer and he died. I carried him off to the market and propped him up in a lane nearby." He added: "It is not enough for me to have killed a Muslim that I should kill a Christian as well? I am the one to be hanged." On hearing this, the *wali* freed the Christian and told the executioner to hang the inspector on his own confession. The executioner took the rope from the neck of the king's broker and put it round that of the inspector, who was made to stand under the gallows.

He was about to be hanged when, all of a sudden, the Jewish doctor came through the crowd, shouting to them and to the executioner: "Don't do it! It was I and I alone who killed him. I was at home last night when a man and a woman knocked at my door bringing with them this hunchback, who was sick. They gave my servant girl a quarter of a dinar. She told me about them and handed me the money, but it turned out that the pair had brought the hunchback into the house, left him on the stairs and gone off. I came down to look at him, but in the darkness I tripped over him and he fell down to the bottom of the stairs, killing himself on the spot. My wife and I carried him up to the roof and lowered him into the ventilation shaft of this inspector, who lives next door to us. The man was dead, but when the inspector came and found him in his house, he took him for a thief and struck him with a hammer so that he fell to the ground, leaving the inspector to think he had killed him. Isn't it enough for me to have unknowingly killed one Muslim that I should knowingly be responsible for the death of another?"

When the *wali* heard this, he told the executioner to release the inspector and to hang the Jew. The executioner took him and put the rope round his neck, but at that the tailor came through the crowd and told him to stop: "It was I and I alone who killed the man. Yesterday I went out to see the sights, and in the evening I met this hunchback, drunk and singing at the top of his voice to his tambourine. I invited him home and bought a fish, which we sat down to eat. My wife took a piece of it and making it into a mouthful, she crammed it into his gullet where a bit of it stuck, killing him instantly. Then my wife and I took him to the Jew's house. The servant girl came down and opened the door for us, and I told her to tell her master that a woman and a man were at the door with a sick person and to ask him to come and look at him. I gave her a quarter of a dinar and while she went up to her master, I carried the hunchback to the head of the stairs and propped him up there, after which my wife and I went away. The Jew came down and tripped over the hunchback and thought that he had killed him. Is that right?" he asked the Jew. "Yes," said the Jew, at which the tailor turned to the *wali* and said: "Release the Jew and hang me."

When the *wali* heard what he had to say, he was astonished by the whole affair, which he said should be recorded in books. Then he told the executioner to release the Jew and to hang the tailor on his own confession. "I'm tired of this," complained the executioner. "I bring one man forward and put another one back and no one gets hanged." Then he put the rope round the tailor's neck.

So much for these people, but as for the hunchback, the story goes that he was the king's fool and that the king could not bear to be parted from him. After getting drunk, he had left the king and had been away all night. As he was still not back by midday the next day, the king asked some of his courtiers about him, and they replied: "Master, his dead body was brought to the *wali*, who ordered his killer to be hanged. Then a second and third person arrived, each of them claiming to have killed him and each telling the *wali* the reason for it." When the king heard this, he called to his chamberlain, telling him to go to the *wali* and to fetch him all those concerned.

When the chamberlain went there, he found the executioner about to hang the tailor. "Don't do it!" he shouted, and he told the *wali* what the king had said. He then brought everyone, the *wali*, the tailor, the Jew, and the Christian and the inspector, and had the corpse of the hunchback carried along with them. When the *wali* stood before the king, he kissed the ground and told him what had happened to each of them—but there is nothing to be gained from repetition. The king himself was filled with amazement and delight at the story, and gave orders that it should be recorded in letters of gold. He then asked those present whether they had ever heard anything more astonishing than the story of that hunchback.

At that, the Christian came forward and said: "Your majesty, if you give me leave, I will tell you of something that happened to me which was more remarkable, stranger and more entertaining than the story of the hunchback." When the king told him to produce his story, HE SAID: . . .

STUDY QUESTIONS

1. How does the story particularly satirize Jews and Christians living among Muslims?
2. How does the story suggest that it is human nature to cover up one's mistakes and come to erroneous conclusions?

9.5 MAIMONIDES, *LETTER TO YEMEN*, 1172 CE

R. Moshe b. Maimon (1135–1204) was the greatest Jewish scholar of the Middle Ages. Born in Cordoba, during the regime of the Almoravids, he studied Torah and Talmud with his father, who was also a rabbi, and read Greek philosophy in the Arabic translations then circulating in Spain. He became a physician, which is how he supported his family after they (along with many other Jews) went into exile after the brutal Almohad regime replaced the relatively benign Almoravids in 1148. Maimonides lived in Morocco for many years before settling in Fustat, Egypt. An extraordinarily prolific writer, Maimonides composed his *Letter to Yemen* in 1172, in response to a request for guidance from the Jewish community there, which was experiencing persecution from two sources—the harsh local Islamic ruler, and a Jewish reformer who had declared himself the Messiah and announced the approaching End of Days.

Remember always that ours is the true, divine, authentic religion, as revealed to us by Moses, who is preeminent among all the prophets from beginning to end. It is through this faith that the Holy One has set us apart from the rest of mankind. The Holy Scripture says: "Yet it was to your fathers that the Lord was drawn in His love for them, so that He chose you, their lineal descendants, from among all peoples—as is now the case" [Deut. 10.15]. This is not owing to our merits, though. It was the will of the Holy One, because our forefathers knew Him and submitted to Him. We read: "It is not because you are the most numerous of peoples that the Lord set His heart on you and chose you—indeed, you are the smallest of peoples; but it was because the Lord favored you and kept the oath He made to your fathers that the Lord freed you with a mighty hand and rescued you from the house of bondage, from the power of Pharaoh king of Egypt" [Deut. 7.7–8]. The Holy One has set us apart with His laws and teachings, and our unique status is the consequence of those commandments and statutes. The Scripture says of His mercies to us: "What great nation has laws and rules as perfect as all this Teaching that I set before you this day?" [Deut. 4.8]. This is why all the nations on the earth rise up against us, out of their envy and malice. This is why all the kings of the earth persecute us, out of their hatred and injustice. All have wanted to impede the Lord, but in vain. From tyrant to slave, everyone who has ever lived since the time of the Covenant and has sought dominion on earth, if he was violent and crude, has tried from start to finish to destroy our Law and obliterate our religion. Whether by sword, murder, or riot, all have done so—Amalek, Sisera, Sennacherib, Nebuchadnezzar, Titus, Hadrian, and others. May their bones be ground into dust! And they are only the first of two types of men who have tried to impede the Lord's will.

The second type consists of the most civilized and sophisticated of peoples—the Syrians, the Persians, and the Greeks. These too have tried to destroy our Law and obliterate our religion, but they have done so with crafty arguments and the controversies their thinking has stirred up. They try to undermine the Law with their argumentative writings, to obliterate it with words just as the tyrants attempt to do with swords. Neither of them, however, will ever succeed, for we possess the Holy One's promise, through Isaiah, that He will destroy all who seek to weaken the Law or demolish it with armies. The Holy One

Translation by Clifford Backman.

will destroy them—but this must be understood as a metaphor only, a way of saying that any enemy's attempts will be wholly frustrated. . . .

And after [the Syrians, Persians, and Greeks] there came a new sect that combined their methods into one, both conquest and controversy, thinking thus they could wipe out the entire Jewish nation and religion. This sect claimed the power of prophecy and established a new religion, contrary to our own. They claimed an equally divine revelation, in the hope of raising doubt and creating confusion. . . . The first to do so was Jesus the Nazarene. May his bones be ground into dust! He was a Jew, having a Jewish mother, but his father was a Gentile, for our Law states that a child born of a Jewish mother and Gentile father (or, of course, of a Jewish mother and a slave) is a true Jew. Thus one can only call Jesus a non-Jew in an indirect manner of speaking, for he led his followers to believe he was a prophet sent by the Lord to explain the Law, and to believe that he was the Messiah anticipated by all. But his teaching of the Law was faulty and opened the way to its total annulment, the undoing of its commandments, and the breaking of its prohibitions. Our sages of blessed memory rendered a fitting punishment on him, after learning of his reputation and teachings. . . .

Another sect arose not long afterwards, a sect based on Jesus and taught by one whose lineage was of Esau. He [Paul] did not set out to create an entirely new religion. He was not an offense to Israel, and he stirred up no antagonism [toward the Jews] among his followers. The faults of his teachings, however, were obvious to everyone, and his activity ceased when we caught him. His fate is well known.

After [Paul] came the Madman [Muhammad], who followed the path laid out for him by his predecessor. The Madman, however, had ambition to rule others and subject them to his power, and so he invented his well-known religion [Islam].

All of these men presumed to compare their ravings with our divine religion, but only an idiot would set human inventions alongside divine revelations. Our religion differs from theirs as much as a living person differs from a statue of marble, wood, bronze, or silver, no matter how elegantly carved. . . .

Only someone who knows nothing at all about the Holy Scriptures' hidden meanings and the Law's deeper truths could possibly think our religion has anything

in common with any other he compares it to. Only such an imbecile would equate the fact that our Law contains commandments and prohibitions, and that other religions also detail permitted and not-permitted actions; or that both contain systems of required rituals, positive and negative commands, and apportion rewards and punishments thereby. Only if one grasps the inner meanings of the Law can one appreciate the fact that the essence of our true religion rests on the deep, hidden meanings of its commandments and prohibitions—every single one of which will benefit anyone straining after perfection, by removing every impediment that stands between him and his goal. . . . The teachings of those religions that outwardly resemble our own, however, have no deeper meaning. They are mere imitations of ours. Their supporters have copied our faith in order to give themselves honor by pretending to be like us. Their fakery is obvious to those who know, which makes them laughingstocks and fools; one laughs at them just as one laughs when seeing apes imitate the actions of men.

This foolishness was prophesied by Daniel, when he predicted that arrival of someone who would proclaim a religion supposedly like ours, with its own Scriptures and oral traditions, and would be arrogant enough to proclaim a special revelation from the Lord and to have spoken with Him, among other extraordinary things. Here we see Daniel prophesying the rise of the Arabs after the destruction of Rome, with his declaration of the appearance of the Madman who would destroy Rome, Persia, and Byzantium. . . . Bear in mind that the Holy One told Daniel that He would destroy the Madman despite his successes and endurance, and destroy also the followers of his predecessors [Jesus and Paul]. All those who have persecuted us will perish in the end—those who sought to destroy us with the sword, those who used argument, and those who now mimic us. . . .

You write that there is a man in one of your cities who claims to be the Messiah. I am not surprised, neither at him nor his followers. No doubt the man is mad, and as a sick person he is not to be condemned or rebuked; an illness is not the fault of the sufferer. As for his followers, I suspect they fell under his sway because of the wretchedness of their lives and their failure to understand the true meaning and importance of the Messiah. They probably are confusing the

Messiah for the son of their anticipated Mahdi. But I am surprised that you, an enlightened man who has read the teachings of the rabbis, are tempted to believe in him. Don't you know, my brother, that the Messiah will be a prophet more luminous than any who has come in Moses' wake, and that a willfully false prophet deserves capital punishment. . . .

Remember, the Christians falsely attribute prophetic power to Jesus the Nazarene—may his bones be ground into dust!—and believe he rose from the dead and performed other miracles. Even if (just for the sake of argument) these claims were true, there still would be no reason to believe Jesus is the Messiah. I could show you a thousand proofs from the Holy Scriptures to contradict their claim.

In the end, who would ever claim Messiahship except one who wishes to make a public fool of himself? If this man you mention acts out of pride or spite, I would say he deserves death, but it appears to me instead that he has a melancholy and confused mind, and so I advise you—for your own good as well as for his—to put him in chains and detain him until the Gentiles learn that he is insane. Once you have broadcast loudly the news of this man and his illness, you can then release him without putting him at risk. If the Gentiles learn of him after you have incarcerated him, they will examine him and declare him mad, and you will be left unmolested. But if you do nothing about him until after the Gentiles have learned of him, then you will incur their wrath.

Remember, my brother: the Holy One has thrown us among the Arabs who now persecute us so severely. The Scriptures warned us of the unfair laws they would raise against us: "Our enemies themselves shall judge us" [Deut. 32.31] Never did any nation abuse, belittle, demean and hate us, the way they do.

STUDY QUESTIONS

1. How does Maimonides describe the defects of both Christianity and Islam?
2. Maimonides lived in Cordoba, Spain, at the same time as Ibn Rushd. What does this say about Spanish culture during the Middle Ages?

9.6 USAMAH IBN MUNQIDH, *MEMOIRS*, 1183 CE

A Muslim knight, diplomat, and poet, Usamah ibn Munqidh (1095–1188) provides a distinctive account of living on the receiving end of the Latin Crusades. Usamah served the Muslim leaders Zengi, Nur al-Din, and finally Saladin—to whom he dedicated his work—but had Crusader friends, too. Written in Arabic, Usamah's *Memoirs* are a string of anecdotes and morality tales that reveal how the Muslims and Christians managed to live side by side in Syria. Interspersed among the hostilities are genuine moments of entertainment and camaraderie, such as the section reprinted here in which the Templars defend Usamah at prayer, or his exaggerated disbelief that a woman would cast aside a Muslim nobleman in favor of a Frankish shoemaker.

From Philip Hitti, *An Arab-Syrian Gentleman and Warrior in the Period of the Crusades: Memoirs of Usāmah Ibn-Munqidh*. Princeton, NJ: Princeton University Press. Licensed through Copyright Clearance Center.

A leopard jumps from a church window and kills a Frank.—In the church of Hunak was a window forty cubits high. Every day at noontime at leopard would come and jump to the window, where it would sleep until the end of the day, at which time it would jump down and go away. At that time, Hunak was held as a fief by a Frankish knight named Sir Adam, one of the devils of the Franks. Sir Adam was told the story of the leopard and he said, "As soon as ye see it, let me know." The leopard came as it was wont to do and jumped into the window. One of the peasants came and told Sir Adam about it. The latter put on his coat of mail, mounted his horse, took his shield and lance and came to the church, which was all in ruins with the exception of one wall which was standing and in which the window was. As soon as the leopard saw him, it jumped from the window upon him while he was on his horse, broke his back and killed him. It then went away. The peasants of Hunak used to call that leopard, "the leopard that takes part in the holy war" [al-namir al-mujāhid].

One of the characteristics of the leopard is that in case it wounds a man and a mouse urinates on the wound, the man dies. It is very difficult to keep the mouse away from one wounded by a leopard. In fact, they sometimes go so far as to fix a bed for him in the midst of water and tie cats all around him for fear of the mice.

. . .

Prefers to be a Frankish shoemaker's wife to life in a Moslem castle.—A number of maids taken captive from the Franks were brought into the home of my father (may Allah's mercy rest upon his soul!). The Franks (may Allah's curse be upon them!) are an accursed race, the members of which do not assimilate except with their own kin. My father saw among them a pretty maid who was in the prime of youth, and said to his housekeeper, "Introduce this woman into the bath, repair her clothing and prepare her for a journey." This she did. He then delivered the maid to a servant of his and sent her to al-Amir Shihab-al-Din Malik ibn-Salim, the lord of the Castle of Ja'bar, who was a friend of his. He also wrote him a letter saying, "We have won some booty from the Franks, from which I am sending thee a share." The maid suited Shihab-al-Din, and he was pleased with her. He took her to himself

and she bore him a boy, whom he called Badran. [80] Badran's father named him his heir apparent, and he became of age. On his father's death, Badran became the governor of the town and its people, his mother being the real power. She entered into conspiracy with a band of men and let herself down from the castle by a rope. The band took her to Saruj, which belonged at that time to the Franks. There she married a Frankish shoemaker, while her son was the lord of the Castle of Ja'bar.

. . .

Newly arrived Franks are especially rough: One insists that Usāmah should pray eastward.—Everyone who is a fresh emigrant from the Frankish lands is ruder in character than those who have become acclimatized and have held long association with the Moslems. Here is an illustration of their rude character.

Whenever I visited Jerusalem I always entered the Aqsa Mosque, beside which stood a small mosque which the Franks had converted into a church. When I sued to enter the Aqsa Mosque, which was occupied by the Templars [al-dāwiyyah], who were my friends, the Templars would evacuate the little adjoining mosque so that I might pray in it. One day I entered this mosque, repeated the first formula, "Allah is great," and stood up in the act of praying, upon which one of the Franks rushed on me, got hold of me and turned my face eastward saying, "This is the way thou shouldest pray!" A group of Templars hastened to him, seized him and repelled him from me. I resumed my prayer. The same man, while the others were otherwise busy, rushed once more on me and turned my face eastward, saying, "This is the way thou shouldest pray!" The Templars again came in to him and expelled him. They apologized to me, saying, "This is a stranger who has only recently arrived from the land of the Franks and has never before seen anyone praying except eastward." Thereupon I said to myself, "I have had enough prayer." So I went out and have been surprised at the conduct of this devil of a man, at the change in the color of his face, his trembling and his sentiment at the sight of one praying toward the *qiblah*.

. . .

Their judicial trials.—I attended one day a duel in Nablus between two Franks. The reason for this was that certain Moslem thieves took by surprise one of the villages of Nablus. One of the peasants of that village was charged with having acted as a guide for the thieves when they fell upon the village. So he fled away. The king sent and arrested his children. The peasant thereupon came back to the king and said, "Let justice be done in my case. I challenge to a duel the man who claimed that I guided the thieves to the village." The king then said to the tenant who held the village in the fief, "Bring forth someone to fight the duel with him." The tenant went to his village, where a blacksmith lived, took hold of him and ordered him to fight the duel. The tenant became thus sure of the safety of his own peasants, none of whom would be killed and his estate ruined.

I saw the blacksmith. He was a physically strong young man, but his heart failed him. He would walk a few steps and then sit down and ask for a drink. The one who had made the challenge was an old man, but he was strong in spirit and he would rub the nail of his thumb against that of the forefinger in defiance, as if he was not worrying over the duel. Then came the viscount [al-bishkund], i.e., the seignior of the town, and gave each one of the two contestants a cudgel and a shield and arranged the people in a circle around them.

The two met. The old man would press the blacksmith backward until he would get him as far as the circle, then he would come back to the middle of the arena. They went on exchanging blows until they looked like pillars smeared with blood. The contest was prolonged and the viscount began to urge them to hurry, saying, "Hurry on." The fact that the smith was given to the use of the hammer proved now a great advantage to him. The old man was worn out and the smith gave him a blow which made him fall. His cudgel fell under his back. The smith knelt down over him and tried to stick his fingers into the eyes of the adversary, but could not do it because of the great quantity of blood flowing out. Then he rose up and hit his head with the cudgel until he killed him. They then fastened a rope around the neck of the dead person, dragged him away and hanged him. The lord who brought the smith now came, gave the smith his own mantle, made him mount the horse behind him and rode off with him. This case illustrates the kind of jurisprudence [85] and legal decisions the Franks have—may Allah's curse be upon them!

. . .

Reflections of Usāmah on old age.—Little did I realize at that time that the disease of senility is universal, infecting everyone whom death has neglected. But now that I have climbed to the summit of my ninetieth year, worn out by the succession of days and years, I have become myself like Jawad, the fodder dealer, and not like the generous man [al-jāwad] who can dissipate his money. Feebleness has bent me down to the ground, and old age has made one part of my body enter through another, so much so that I can now hardly recognize myself; and I continually bemoan my past. Here is what I have said in describing my own condition:

> When I attained in life a high stage
> For which I had always yearned, I wished for
>   death.
> Longevity has left me no energy
> By which I could meet the vicissitudes of time
>   when hostile to me.
> [98] My strength has been rendered weakness,
>   and my two confidants,
> My sight and my hearing, have betrayed me, since
>   I attained this height.
> When I rise, I feel as if laden
> With a mountain; and when I walk, as though I
>   were bound with chains.
> I creep with a cane in my hand which is wont
> To carry in warfare a lance and a sword.
> My nights I spend in my soft bed, unable to sleep
> And wide awake as though I lay on solid rock.
> Man is reversed in life: the moment
> He attains perfection and completion, then he
>   reverts to the condition from which he started.

STUDY QUESTIONS

1. What proof does Usāmah offer of the uncivilized nature of the French invaders of the Middle East?
2. How does he demonstrate Islamic cultural, if not always military, superiority in his account?

9.7 IBN RUSHD, *ON THE HARMONY OF RELIGIOUS LAW AND PHILOSOPHY*

Ibn Rushd (full name: Abu al-Walid Muhammad b. Ahmad b. Muhammad b. Rushd) was born in Cordoba, the grand capital city of Islamic Spain, in 1126. His family was a prominent one, made up of distinguished religious jurists and physicians, and he received a sound classical Islamic education. He later served as a *qadi* and physician, but his greatest intellectual love was for philosophy. His most important works, apart from his commentaries of Aristotle, were *On the Harmony of Religious Law and Philosophy*, *The Methods of Proof in Regard to Religious Doctrine*, and *The Incoherence of the Incoherence*. The last book was a response to *The Incoherence of the Philosophers* by al-Ghazali—hence the odd title. Translated below is an abridged version of the third chapter of *On the Harmony of Religious Law and Philosophy*; it treats the issues of fate and predestination. Ibn Rushd died in Marrakesh, Morocco, in 1198.

The question of fate and predestination is one of the most complicated questions in all religion, because the traditional teachings on this problem, when closely viewed, are seen to be contradictory. But this is also true of rational efforts to address it. The first contradictions appear in the Qur'an and the hadith. Many verses in the Qur'an proclaim as universal truth that all things are predestined, and that man is fated to do all that he does; but many other verses say, to the contrary, that man's actions are freely chosen and not fated at all.

These are some verses that say everything is determined and inevitable (many others could be cited as well):

"Say: 'Yes, those of old and those of later times, all will certainly be gathered together for the meeting appointed for a Day Well-Known." [Qur'an 56.49]

"Allah doth know what every female [womb] doth bear, but how much the wombs fall short [of their time or number] or do exceed. Every single thing is with Him in [due] proportion. He knoweth the Unseen and that which is open: He is the Great, the Most High." [Qur'an 13.8–9]

"No misfortune can happen on earth or in your souls but is recorded in a Book before We bring it into existence: That is truly easy for Allah." [Qur'an 57.22]

As for verses that state that man's actions are the result of his free will, or that proclaimed things are possibly and not necessarily going to happen:

"Whatever misfortune happens to you, is because of the things your hands have wrought, and for many [a sin] He grants forgiveness." [Qur'an 42.31]

"But those who have earned evil will have a reward of like evil." [Qur'an 10.27]

"Those who believe, and do deeds of righteousness, and establish regular prayers and give zakat, will have their reward with their Lord: on them shall be no fear, nor shall they grieve." [Qur'an 2.277]

Sometimes contrary statements even appear within a single passage:

"It is part of the Mercy of Allah that thou dost deal gently with them. Wert thou severe or harsh hearted they would have broken away from about thee: so pass over [their faults], and ask for [Allah's] forgiveness for them; and consult them in affairs [of moment]. Then, when thou hast taken a decision, put thy trust in Allah. For Allah loves those who put their trust [in Him]. If Allah helps you, none can overcome you.

Translation by Clifford Backman.

If He forsakes you, who is there, after that, that can help you? In Allah, then, let believers put their trust." [Qur'an 3.159–160]

or

"Whatever good, [O man!] happens to thee, is from Allah; but whatever evil happens to thee, is from thyself and We have sent thee as a Messenger to [instruct] mankind. And enough is Allah for a witness. He who obeys the Messenger, obeys Allah: but if any turn away, We have not sent thee to watch over them." [Qur'an 4.80–81]

We can see this also in the Prophet's *hadith*. On one occasion he said, "Every child is born in the true religion [Islam]. It is his parents who later turn him into a Jew or a Christian." But on another occasion he said, "Some people were created for Hell and live lives fit for it; others were created for Heaven and live lives fit for it." Clearly the first teaching states that the situation one is born into is the cause of disbelief, since true belief is natural to all, but the second teaching says that evil and disbelief are set by Allah and man is fated to follow them.

Because of this, Muslims have split into two factions. The first are the Mutazilites, who believe that one's goodness or wickedness result from one's own action—and that one will be rewarded or punished accordingly. The Jabarites hold the opposite view, asserting that one is fated to do whatever one does in life.

The Asharites are a group that has tried to follow a compromise between these two extremes. They maintain that one chooses one's actions, but the power to perform the actions is the creation of Allah—and only in this sense one can say that Allah creates the actions themselves. This, however, makes no sense, for if an action and the power to perform it are both created by Allah, then the man is logically compelled to perform it. This is only one reason for the confused split over this problem. . . .

It may be asked, therefore, how is the contradiction between tradition and reason to be reconciled—which surely is the role of religion, not to keep divided what ought to be reconciled by pursuing a middle course? It is clear, first of all, that Allah created the power we possess to perform deeds that are contradictory. But our actions are not brought to fulfillment except from outside of us, by Allah's intention for us, which removes the obstacles to our doing them; therefore, our actions

are only effected when our will and ability are in alignment with Allah's intent. In this way our completed actions result from our own will and from the fitness of our will with Allah's design for us, from the outside, and this alignment is what we call predestination. Allah's design therefore neither impels our actions nor hinders them, but it is the cause of our willing the actions. Our intentions are produced either by our imagination or by our desire to effect something that is not in our power but is in the power of something outside of us. For example: if we see something good, we admire it and desire to acquire it even though it is not in our power to achieve. Similarly, if we see something bad, we turn from it instinctively. Our intention, our will, depends on causes outside ourselves. . . .

To understand causes is to understand the secret knowledge of the essence of a thing before it comes into existence. But since it is the arrangement of causes that brings something into existence at a particular time, the knowledge of a thing must exist prior to the thing itself. To understand all causation, therefore, is to know what exists and what does not exist at any given moment. Praised be Allah, Who has complete understanding of all creation and all causation! This is what the words "Keys of the secret" mean in the verse "With Him are the keys of the Unseen, the treasures that none knoweth but He. He knoweth whatever there is on the earth and in the sea. Not a leaf doth fall but with His knowledge: There is not a grain in the darkness [or depths] of the earth, nor anything fresh or dry [green or withered], but is [inscribed] in a Record Clear [to those who can read]." [Qur'an 6.59]

If this argument is true, then it should now be clear how we freely choose our own actions even while they are predetermined by fate. This reconciliation is the true purpose of religion, and of those Qur'anic verses and *hadith* that appeared contradictory. In defining those passages' universal nature in this way, all contradictions disappear—and so do all doubts raised by the apparent contradictions. Everything that comes into existence by means of our will is brought to fulfillment by the combination of our will and the causes that lie outside us. Doubts arise when we take in account only one aspect of agency. . . .

[Al-Ghazali] writes that a man who asserts any cause to be co-existent with Allah is like a man who equates the role of a pen, in writing, with the work of the scribe who uses it. In other words, the pen and the man are both to be called scribes, because the word *writing* can be applied to both. That word, however, is the only thing they share; apart from it, they have nothing in common. Such is the case with the word *creator*, when we apply it to Allah and to causation. But I argue back that his example is faulty, because Allah is the creator of the essences of everything that affects causation, whereas in al-Ghazali's example the scribe is not the creator of the essence of the pen, and of the act of writing, and of the words written. This is why I say that there is no creator but Allah—a statement that harmonizes our perceptions, our reason, and our religion. . . .

So praises to "the Wise, the All-Knowing!" [Qur'an 67.14] Allah has shown us the truth in His Book, "And what will explain to thee what is the Day of Sorting Out?" [Qur'an 77.14] And again, "He has made subject to you the Night and the Day; the Sun and the Moon; and the Stars are in subjection by His command: verily in this are Signs for men who are wise." [Qur'an 16.12] And again, "And He is Allah: there is no god but He. To Him be praise, at the first and at the last." [Qur'an 28.70] He also says, "This is [true] guidance: And for those who reject the Signs of their Lord is a grievous chastisement of abomination." [Qur'an 45.11] There are many other verses that I could cite on this matter. If there were no wisdom in the messages with which Allah has favored us, we would not possess the blessings that we have and for which we are ever grateful to Him.

STUDY QUESTIONS

1. How does Ibn Rushd present the contradictions in the Qur'an and in traditional teaching concerning predestination and free will? What arguments does Ibn Rushd put forward to reconcile the seemingly irreconcilable contradictions between faith and reason?
2. Compare Ibn Rushd's approach to Islamic doctrine with that of Al-Ghazali's in *The Deliverer from Error*. How are they different? How are they similar?

9.8 MAIMONIDES, *GUIDE FOR THE PERPLEXED*, 1100–1200 CE

The famed rabbi Moses Maimonides (1135–1204) lived a wandering life as a philosopher and physician in North Africa, since he left Spain in exile after the harsh Almohad invasion of the Iberian Peninsula (1148). Fascinated with Greek philosophy and Islamic scientific knowledge, Maimonides traveled to Morocco, the Holy Land, and Egypt. He consolidated Jewish law from the Torah in his great fourteen-volume work, the Mishneh Torah (completed ca. 1180), which lays out all rules of Jewish observance. The *Guide for the Perplexed*, written in the form of a letter to a questioning student, reveals Maimonides's philosophical contributions rather than his thoughts on Jewish theology and law.

Moses Maimonides, *Guide for the Perplexed*. Translated by M. Friedländer, 1904.

CHAPTER V

When the chief of philosophers (Aristotle) was about to inquire into some very profound subjects, and to establish his theory by proofs, he commenced his treatise with an apology, and requested the reader to attribute the author's inquiries not to presumption, vanity, egotism, or arrogance, as though he were interfering with things of which he had no knowledge, but rather to his zeal and his desire to discover and establish true doctrines, as far as lay in human power. We take the same position, and think that a man, when he commences to speculate, ought not to embark at once on a subject so vast and important; he should previously adapt himself to the study of the several branches of science and knowledge, should most thoroughly refine his moral character and subdue his passions and desires, the offspring of his imagination; when, in addition, he has obtained a knowledge of the true fundamental propositions, a comprehension of the several methods of inference and proof, and the capacity of guarding against fallacies, then he may approach the investigation of this subject. He must, however, not decide any question by the first idea that suggests itself to his mind, or at once direct his thoughts and force them to obtain a knowledge of the Creator, but he must wait modestly and patiently, and advance step by step.

In this sense we must understand the words "And Moses hid his face, for he was afraid to look upon God" (Exod. iii. 6), though retaining also the literal meaning of the passage, that Moses was afraid to gaze at the light which appeared to his eye; but it must on no account be assumed that the Being which is exalted far above every imperfection can be perceived by the eye. This act of Moses was highly commended by God, who bestowed on him a well deserved portion of His goodness, as it is said: "And the similitude of the Lord shall he behold" (Num. xii. 8). This, say our Sages, was the reward for having previously hidden his face, lest he should gaze at the Eternal. (*Talm. B. Berakot Fa.*)

But "the nobles of the Children of Israel" were impetuous, and allowed their thoughts to go unrestrained: what they perceived was but imperfect. Therefore, it is said of them, "And they saw the God of Israel, and there was under his feet," etc. (Exod. xxiv. 10); and not merely, "and they saw the God of Israel"; the purpose of the whole passage is to criticize their act

of seeing and not to describe it. They are blamed for the nature of their perception, which was to a certain extent corporeal—a result which necessarily followed, from the fact that they ventured too far before being perfectly prepared. They deserved to perish, but at the intercession of Moses this fate was averted by God for the time. They were afterwards burnt at Taberah, except Nadab and Abihu, who were burnt in the Tabernacle of the congregation, according to what is stated by authentic tradition. (*Midr. Rabba ad locum.*)

If such was the case with them, how much more is it incumbent on us who are inferior, and on those who are below us, to persevere in perfecting our knowledge of the elements, and in rightly understanding the preliminaries which purify the mind from the defilement of error: then we may enter the holy and divine camp in order to gaze: as the Bible says, "And let the priests also, which come near to the Lord, sanctify themselves, lest the Lord break forth upon them" (Exod. xix. 22). Solomon, also, has cautioned all who endeavour to attain this high degree of knowledge in the following figurative terms, "Keep thy foot when thou goest to the house of God" (Eccles. iv. 17).

I will now return to complete what I commenced to explain. The nobles of the Children of Israel, besides erring in their perception, were, through this cause, also misled in their actions: for in consequence of their confused perception, they gave way to bodily cravings. This is meant by the words, "Also they saw God and did eat and drink" (Exod. xxiv. 11). The principal part of that passage, viz., "And there was under his feet as it were a paved work of a sapphire stone" (Exod. xxiv. 10), will be further explained in the course of the present treatise. All we here intend to say is, that wherever in a similar connection any one of the three verbs mentioned above occurs, it has reference to intellectual perception, not to the sensation of sight by the eye: for God is not a being to be perceived by the eye.

It will do no harm, however, if those who are unable to comprehend what we here endeavour to explain should refer all the words in question to sensuous perception, to seeing lights created [for the purpose], angels, or similar beings.

CHAPTER VI

The two Hebrew nouns *ish* and *ishshah* were originally employed to designate the "male and female" of human beings, but were afterwards applied to the "male and female" of the other species of the animal creation. For instance, we read, "Of every clean beast thou shalt take to thee by sevens," *ish ve-ishto* (Gen. Vii. 2), in the same sense as *ish ve-ishshah*, "male and female." The term *zakar u-nekebah* was afterwards applied to anything designed and prepared for union with another object. Thus we read, "The five curtains shall be coupled together, one (*ishshah*) to the other" (*ah. otah*) (Exod. xxvi. 3).

It will easily be seen that the Hebrew equivalents for "brother and sister" are likewise treated as homonyms, and used, in a figurative sense, like *ish* and *ishshah*.

CHAPTER VII

It is well known that the verb *yalad* means "to bear," "they have born (*ve-yaledu*) him children" (Deut. xxi. 15). The word was next used in a figurative sense with reference to various objects in nature, meaning, "to create," e.g., "before the mountains were created" (*yulladu*) (Ps. xc. 2); also, "to produce," in reference to that which the earth causes to come forth as if by birth, e.g., "He will cause her to bear (*holidah*) and bring forth" (Isa. lv. 10). The verb further denotes, "to bring forth," said of changes in the process of time, as though they were things which were born, e.g., "for thou knowest not what a day may bring forth" (*yeled*) (Prov. xxvii. 1). Another figurative use of the word is its application to the formation of thoughts and ideas, or of opinions resulting from them: comp. "and brought forth (*veyalad*) falsehood" (Ps. vii. 14); also, "and they please themselves in the children (*yalde*) of strangers" (Isa. ii. 6), i.e., "they delight in the opinions of strangers." Jonathan the son of Uzziel paraphrases this passage, "they walk in the customs of other nations."

A man who has instructed another in any subject, and has improved his knowledge, may in like manner be regarded as the parent of the person taught, because he is the author of that knowledge: and thus the pupils of the prophets are called "sons of the prophets," as I shall explain when treating of the homonymity of *ben* (son). In this figurative sense, the verb *yalad* (to bear) is employed when it is said of Adam, "And Adam lived a hundred and thirty years,

and begat (*va-yoled*) a son in his own likeness, in his form" (Gen. V. 3). As regards the words, "the form of Adam, and his likeness," we have already stated their meaning. Those sons of Adam who were born before that time were not human in the true sense of the word, they had not "the form of man." With reference to Seth who had been instructed, enlightened and brought to human perfection, it could rightly be said, "he (Adam) begat a son in his likeness, in his form." It is acknowledged that a man who does not possess this "form" (the nature of which has just been explained) is not human, but a mere animal in human shape and form. Yet such a creature has the power of causing harm and injury, a power which does not belong to other creatures. For those gifts of intelligence and judgment with which he has been endowed for the purpose of acquiring perfection, but which he has failed to apply to their proper aim, are used by him for wicked and mischievous ends; he begets evil things, as though he merely resembled man, or simulated his outward appearance. Such was the condition of those sons of Adam who preceded Seth. In reference to this subject the Midrash says: "During the 130 years when Adam was under rebuke he begat spirits," i.e., demons; when, however, he was again restored to divine favour "he begat in his likeness, in his form." This is the sense of the passage, "Adam lived one hundred and thirty years, and he begat in his likeness, in his form" (Gen. v. 3).

CHAPTER VIII

Originally the Hebrew term *makom* (place) applied both to a particular spot and to space in general; subsequently it received a wider signification and denoted "position," or "degree," as regards the perfection of man in certain things. We say, e.g., this man occupies a certain place in such and such a subject. In this sense this term, as is well known, is frequently used by authors, e.g., "He fills his ancestors' place (*makom*) in point of wisdom and piety"; "the dispute still remains in its place" (*makom*), i.e., *in statu quo* [*ante*]. In the verse, "Blessed be the glory of the Lord from His place" (*mekomo*) (Ezek. iii. 12), *makom* has this figurative meaning, and the verse may be paraphrased "Blessed be the Lord according to the exalted nature of His existence," and wherever *makom* is applied to God, it expresses the same idea, namely, the distinguished position of His existence, to which nothing is equal or comparable, as will be shown below (Ch. LVI).

It should be observed that when we treat in this work of any homonym, we do not desire you to confine yourself to that which is stated in that particular chapter; but we open for you a portal and direct your attention to those significations of the word which are suited to our purpose, though they may not be complete from a philological point of view. You should examine the prophetical books and other works composed by men of science, notice the meaning of every word which occurs in them, and take homonyms in that sense which is in harmony with the context. What I say in a particular passage is a key for the comprehension of all similar passages. For example, we have explained here *makom* in the sentence "Blessed be the glory of the Lord from His place" (*mekomo*); but you must understand that the word makom has the same signification in the passage "Behold, a place (*makom*) is with me" (Exod. xxxiii. 26), viz., a certain degree of contemplation and intellectual intuition (not of ocular inspection), in addition to its literal meaning "a place," viz., the mountain which was pointed out to Moses for seclusion and for the attainment of perfection.

CHAPTER IX

The original meaning of the word *kisse*, "throne," requires no comment. Since men of greatness and authority, as, e.g., kings, use the throne as a seat, and "the throne" thus indicates the rank, dignity, and position of the person for whom it is made, the Sanctuary has been styled "the throne," inasmuch as it likewise indicates the superiority of Him who manifests Himself, and causes His light and glory to dwell therein.

Compare "A glorious throne on high from the beginning is the place of our sanctuary" (Jer. xvii. 12). For the same reason the heavens are called "throne," for to the mind of him who observes them with intelligence they suggest the Omnipotence of the Being which has called them into existence, regulates their motions, and governs the sublunary world by their beneficial influence: as we read, "Thus saith the Lord, The heavens are my throne and the earth my footstool" (Isa. lxvi. 1); i.e., they testify to my Existence, my Essence, and my Omnipotence, as the throne testifies to the greatness of him who is worthy to occupy it.

This is the idea which true believers should entertain; not, however, that the Omnipotent, Supreme God is supported by any material object; for God is incorporeal, as we shall prove further on; how, then, can He be said to occupy any space, or rest on a body? The fact which I wish to point out is this: every place distinguished by the Almighty, and chosen to receive His light and splendour, as, for instance, the Sanctuary or the Heavens, is termed "throne"; and, taken in a wider sense, as in the passage "For my hand is upon the throne of God" (Exod. xvii. 16), "the throne" denotes here the Essence and Greatness of God. These, however (the Essence and Greatness of God) need not be considered as something separate from the God Himself or as part of the Creation, so that God would appear to have existed both without the throne, and with the throne: such a belief would be undoubtedly heretical. It is distinctly stated, "Thou, O Lord, remainest for ever; Thy throne from generation to generation" (Lam. v. 19). By "Thy throne" we must, therefore, understand something inseparable from God. On that account, both here and in all similar passages, the word "throne" denotes God's Greatness and Essence, which are inseparable from His Being.

Our opinion will be further elucidated in the course of this Treatise.

STUDY QUESTIONS

1. Does Maimonides's *Guide* suggest that there are potential dangers in inquiring too closely into philosophical matters?
2. Is there a contradiction between his characterization of Aristotle as "chief of philosophers" and his close reading of Hebrew scripture?

CHAPTER 10

REFORM AND RENEWAL IN THE GREATER WEST

10.1 EINHARD, *LIFE OF CHARLEMAGNE*, WRITTEN CA. 817–833

Einhard (ca. 775–840) was a longtime scholar and companion in the Carolingian court during the reigns of Charlemagne and his son, Louis the Pious. In a short, charming work perhaps modeled on Suetonius's *Lives of the Twelve Caesars* (Document 6.3), Einhard provides a glimpse into the daily life of Charlemagne—his likes and dislikes, his accomplishments and shortcomings. Although history remembers Charlemagne as a man of insatiable ambition and tireless political work, Einhard tempers this protodivine view with the reminder that Charlemagne, for all his imperial titles, also loved the company of his family and friends.

X. Charles also subdued the Bretons, who live on the sea coast, in the extreme western part of Gaul. When they refused to obey him, he sent an army against them, and compelled them to give hostages, and to promise to do his bidding. He afterwards entered Italy in person with his army, and passed through Rome to Capua, a city in Campania, where he pitched his camp and threatened the Beneventans with hostilities unless they should submit themselves to him. Their duke, Aragis, escaped the danger by sending his two sons, Rumold and Grimold, with a great sum of money to meet the King, begging him to accept them as hostages, and promising for himself and his people compliance with all the King's commands, on the single condition that his personal attendance should not be required. The King took the welfare of the people into account rather than the stubborn disposition of the Duke, accepted the proffered hostages, and released him from the obligation to appear before him in consideration of his handsome gift. He retained the younger son only as a hostage, and sent the elder back to his father, and returned to Rome, leaving commissioners with Aragis to exact the oath of allegiance, and administer it to the Beneventans.

From Einhard, *The Life of Charlemagne*. Translated by David Ganz. Ann Arbor: University of Michigan Press, 1961, pp. 34–7, 39–43. Einhard. *The Life of Charlemagne*. University of Michigan Press, © 1960.

He stayed in Rome several days in order to pay his devotions at the holy places, and then came back to Gaul.

XI. At this time, on a sudden, the Bavarian war broke out, but came to a speedy end. It was due to the arrogance and folly of Duke Tassilo. His wife, a daughter of King Desiderius, was desirous of avenging her father's banishment through the agency of her husband, and accordingly induced him to make a treaty with the Huns, the neighbors of the Bavarians on the east, and not only to leave the King's commands unfulfilled, but to challenge him to war. Charles' high spirit could not brook Tassilo's insubordination, for it seemed to him to pass all bounds; accordingly he straightaway summoned his troops from all sides for a campaign against Bavaria, and appeared in person with a great army on the river Lech, which forms the boundary between the Bavarians and the Alemanni. After pitching his camp upon its banks, he determined to put the Duke's disposition to the test by an embassy before entering the province. Tassilo did not think it was for his own or his people's good to persist, so he surrendered himself to the King, gave them the hostages demanded, among them his own son Theodo, and promised by oath not to give ear to any one who should attempt to turn him from his allegiance; so this war, which bade fair to be very grievous, came very quickly to an end. Tassilo, however, was afterward summoned to the King's presence, and not suffered to depart, and the government of the province that he had had in charge was no longer entrusted to a duke, but to counts.

XII. After these uprisings had been thus quelled, war was declared against the Slavs who are commonly known among us as Wilzi, but properly, that is to say in their own tongue, are called Welatabians. The Saxons served in this campaign as auxilliaries among the tribes that followed the King's standard at his summons, but their obedience lacked sincerity and devotion. War was declared because the Slavs kept harassing the Adodriti, old allies of the Franks, by continual raids, in spite of all commands to the contrary. A gulf of unknown length, but nowhere more than a hundred miles wide, and in many parts narrower, stretches off towards the east from the Western Ocean. Many tribes have settlements on its shores; the Danes and Swedes, whom we call Northmen, on the northern shore and all the adjacent islands; but the southern shore is inhabited by the Slavs and Aïsti, and various other tribes. The Welatabians, against whom the King now made war, were the chief of these; but in a single campaign, which he conducted in person, he so crushed and subdued them that they did not think it advisable thereafter to refuse obedience to his commands.

. . .

XIV. The Saxon War next came to an end as successful as the struggle had been long. The Bohemian and Livonian wars that next broke out could not last long; both were quickly carried out under the leadership of the younger Charles. The last of these wars was the one declared against the Northmen called Danes. They began their career as pirates, but afterward took to laying waste the coasts of Gaul and Germany with their large fleet. Their King Godfred was so puffed with vain aspirations that he counted on gaining empire over all Germany, and looked upon Saxony and Frisia as his provinces. He had already subdued his neighbors the Adodriti, and made them tributary, and boasted that he would shortly appear with a great army before Aixla-Chapelle, where the King held his court. Some faith was put in his words, empty as they sound, and it is supposed that he would have attempted something of the sort if he had not been prevented by a premature death. He was murdered by one of his own bodyguard, and so ended at once his life and the war that he had begun.

XV. Such are the wars, most skillfully planned and successfully fought, which this most powerful king waged during the forty-seven years of his reign. He so largely increased the Frank kingdom, which was already great and strong when he received it at his father's hands, that more than double its former territory was added to it. The authority of the Franks was formerly confined to that part of Gaul included between the Rhine and the Loire, the Ocean and the Balearic Sea; to the part of Germany which is inhabited by the so-called Eastern Franks, and is bounded by Saxony and the Danube, the Rhine and the Saale—this stream separates the Thuringians from the Sorabians; and to the country of the Alemanni and Bavarians. By the wars above mentioned he first made tributary Aquitania, Gascony, and the whole of the region of the Pyrenees as far as the River Ebro, which rises in the land of the Navarrese, flows through the most fertile districts of Spain, and empties into the Balearic Sea, beneath the walls of the city of Tortosa. He next reduced and made tributary all Italy from Aosta to Lower Calabria, where the boundary line runs between the Beneventans and the Greeks, a territory more than a thousand miles long; then Saxony, which constitutes no small part of Germany, and is reckoned to be twice as wide as the country inhabited by the Franks, while about equal to it in length; in addition, both Pannonias, Dacia beyond the Danube, and Istria, Liburnia, and Dalmatia, except the cities on the coast, which he left to the Greek Emperor for friendship's sake, and because of the treaty that he had made with him. In fine, he vanquished and made tributary all the wild and barbarous tribes dwelling in Germany between the Rhine and the Vistula, the Ocean and the Danube, all of which speak very much the same language, but differ widely from one another in customs and dress. The chief among them are the Welatabians, the Sorabians, the Abodriti, and the Bohemians, and he had to make war upon these; but the rest, by far the larger number, submitted to him of their own accord.

XVI. He added to the glory of his reign by gaining the good will of several kings and nations; so close, indeed, was the alliance that he contracted with Alfonso, King of Galicia and Asturias, that the latter, when sending letters of ambassadors to Charles, invariably styled himself his man. His munificence won the kings of the Scots also to pay such deference to his wishes that they never gave him any other title than lord, or themselves than subjects and slaves: there are letters from them extant in which these feelings in his regard are expressed. His relations with Aaron, King of the Persians, who rules over almost the whole of the East, India excepted, were so friendly that this prince preferred his favor to that of all the kings and potentates of the earth, and considered that to him alone marks of honor and munificence were due. Accordingly, when the ambassadors sent by Charles to visit the most holy sepulcher and place of resurrection of our Lord and Savior presented themselves before him with gifts, and made known their master's wishes, he not only granted what was asked, but gave possession of that holy and blessed spot. When they returned, he dispatched his ambassadors with them, and sent magnificent gifts, besides, stuffs, perfumes, and other rich products of the Eastern lands. A few years before this, Charles had asked him for an elephant, and he sent the only one that he had. The Emperors of Constantinople, Nicephorus, Michael, and Leo, made advances to Charles, and sought friendship and alliance with him by several embassies; and even when the Greeks suspected him of designing to wrest the empire from them, because of his assumption of the title Emperor, they made a close alliance with him, that he might have no cause of offense. In fact, the power of the Franks was always viewed by the Greeks and Romans with a jealous eye, whence the Greek proverb "Have the Frank for your friend, but not for your neighbor."

STUDY QUESTIONS

1. How does the document reinforce Charlemagne's status as a Christian warrior, particularly in his use of oaths and relics?
2. What does the exchange of gifts reveal about the scope and purpose of international relations in the period?

10.2 POPE GREGORY VII, *LETTERS*

Gregory VII (r. 1073–85) was the most zealous and radical of the reforming popes—so much so that the Church Reform is widely named after him. Although he certainly was a forceful figure, it would be a mistake to consider him only as a Machiavellian pursuer of power for its own sake. The following sampler from his collected letters shows his personality from a variety of angles.

LETTER TO THE BISHOP OF LINCOLN, REGARDING A PRIEST SENT TO ROME TO CONFESS HIS GUILT IN KILLING A MAN (1073)

Bishop Gregory, servant of the servants of God, to Bishop Remedius of Lincoln, in England, sends greetings and apostolic blessing.

The bearer of this letter—the priest whom you charged, in your letter to me, with the crime of murder—cannot ever be permitted to serve the sacred altar in future, by any sanction of the holy fathers. Neither can I consent to his restitution [to holy orders], for that (Heaven forbid!) would go against canon law.

However, if you, in your compassion, find that he displays before God sufficient penance for the crime he committed, then as an act of charity you should see to it that he is granted some means of support from the Church, lest he be crushed by poverty and led to ungodly living. While he may never, under any condition, merit a return to priestly life, he may justifiably receive some provision from the Apostolic See.

On the other matter for which you wrote—namely, your request that I absolve you of your own sins by the authority of the chief Apostles, Sts. Peter and Paul, in whose place I, however unworthy, serve—I hereby do so, so long as you do all you can to preserve the purity of your body as a temple before God.

And as for your final request, that I command your best services on my behalf, I hereby issue this particular demand—that you strengthen me with your prayers, so that we may together be worthy of eternal joy.

LETTER TO THE BISHOP OF CHALON-SUR-SAÔNE, REGARDING REPORTS OF SIMONY AND OTHER ABUSES COMMITTED BY KING PHILIP I OF FRANCE (1073)

I have learned from several trusted sources that among the rulers of our time who have brought ruin to God's Church by greedily putting it up for sale. . . . King Philip of France so greatly oppresses the French churches that he seems to have become the epitome of this hateful sin. His actions are even more offensive since they occur in a realm widely known for its good judgment, piety, strength, and its steadfast devotion to the Roman Church. I am particularly outraged (that is, not simply as a matter of fulfilling my duties as pope) by his actual destruction of churches. We need to condemn much more severely such audacious attacks on our very religion. Through his chamberlain Alberic, the king gave us every assurance that he would respect our position, reform his personal life, and set the churches of France in good order.

For these reasons I wish now to test the value of his promise in regard to the church of Mâcon, which has long lacked a bishop and has been reduced

Translation by Clifford Backman.

practically to rubble, and therefore it is my desire that he permit the archdeacon of Autun, unanimously elected by the clergy and people there and (I am told) approved by the king, to be installed as the new bishop of Mâcon—and that this installation take place, as of course it ought, without any payment of money. If Philip refuses, let him know without any doubt that I will not permit such ruination of the Church, but will attack his stubborn persistence in disobedience with all the canonical severity I possess, by the authority of the Blessed Apostles Sts. Peter and Paul. Either the king will abandon his evil commerce in the heresy of simony and freely allow worthy people to be installed in the leadership of the Church, or the people of France will be cut down by the sword of a general anathema. Unless they intend to reject the Christian faith altogether, the people will refuse to obey him in future.

I go to the trouble of entrusting this letter to you, my ever-watchful and loving brother [in Christ], so that you will convey it to King Philip and make every possible effort—in writing, speech, or action—to persuade him to allow the church of Mâcon, and every French church, to be provided with pastors according to canon law. I have laid this duty upon you because I know you to be of sound judgment and to be close to the king. If I have overlooked anything, please supply it by your own keen intelligence. May you carry out this purpose in such a way that you win God's favor and my good will.

AN EARLY CALL TO CRUSADE (1074)

Bishop Gregory, servant of the servants of God, to all who are willing to defend the Christian faith, sends greetings and apostolic blessing.

You should know that the person bearing this letter, having returned from across the sea, came to Rome and met with me, in which meeting he repeated the news we have already heard from so many others—namely, that a pagan people have vanquished the Christians [in the East] and with unimaginable cruelty have laid waste to all the lands almost to the very walls of Constantinople; that these conquered territories they are now ruling with tyrannical violence; and that they have slain untold thousands of Christians as though they were so many sheep. Out of our love for God and our wish to be recognized as Christians, we ought to be overwhelmed with grief at the wound done to this great [Byzantine] empire and the murder of so many faithful Christians, and yet we are called to more than grief alone. The example of Our Redeemer and the bonds of brotherly love summon us to offer our lives in order to liberate them: "Because He has laid down His life for us, and we ought to lay down our lives for our brothers" [1 John 3.16].

You should therefore know that, trusting in God's mercy and the power of His might, we are now doing all that we can to prepare to bring aid to the Christian [Byzantine] Empire as soon as possible, and therefore we beseech and admonish you, by the faith in which you are united through Christ in caring for all the sons of God, and by the authority of St. Peter, the Prince of the Apostles, to feel compassion for the wounds and blood of your brethren and the threat now confronting the aforesaid empire. For the sake of Christ we beg you to join in the difficult task of bringing aid to our brothers. Send us your messengers at once, informing us of what God inspires you to do in this matter.

LETTER TO THE DIOCESE OF CONSTANCE (1075)

Gregory, bishop and servant of the servants of God, to all the clergy and laity, both great and small, in the diocese of Constance who love Christian law, greetings and an apostolic blessing.

We sent to our brother Otto, your bishop, a most earnest letter in which (as our office requires) we ordered him, by our apostolic authority, to root out the heresy of Simony from his church and to uphold by zealous preaching the requirement of chastity among the clergy, and to enforce its steadfast maintenance by episcopal visitation. The words of the Gospels and the letters of the apostles, not to mention the decrees of authoritative council and the teachings of our most honored doctors have all commended it, and so we cannot disregard the issue or neglect it without risking great injury to our soul and the souls of all the people of Christ. Your bishop, however, has been inspired neither by reverence for St. Peter's command nor by the duty of his office—for we have discovered that he has not made any efforts to carry out our fatherly instructions. Instead, we have heard that he has openly permitted his clergy to act in ways repugnant to our (indeed, St. Peter's) command—which turns his guilt of disobedience into one of rebellion. For he has not only allowed clergy who already had women to keep them, but has even permitted those who did not have women the unlawful shamelessness of taking them!

Having learned of this, we were deeply angered and sent him a second letter that made the depth of our indignation quite clear and enjoined him even more sharply to obey our command. At the same time we summoned him to appear at the Roman Synod called for the first week of the next season of Lent, to give an account of himself and to explain to the entire assembly the reasons (if there can possibly be any) for his disobedience.

Dearest sons, we bring all of this to your attention in order to help save your souls. For if he remains determined to be openly hostile and belligerent to St. Peter and the Holy and Apostolic See, then it is clearly shown that a man who does not honor his mother and father has no right to expect or ask their faithful children to give obedience to him. It is unseemly for a man who submits to no master to lord it over disciples of his own. Therefore, by our apostolic authority, as already stated, we charge all of you, both great and small, who stand on the side of God and St. Peter to show [Bishop Otto] neither respect nor obedience while he continues in his determined obstinacy; you need not fear endangering your souls on this account. For if he remains determined to resist our commands, as we have already stated, then by the authority of St. Peter we absolve all of you from every necessity to obey him; even if you are bound to him by a sacred oath, as long as he is a rebel against God and the Apostolic See you shall owe him no loyalty at all—for a man should obey no one before his Creator, Who has pride of place over all others. We are obliged to resist anyone who is self-proud against God, so that he may, in the face of this resistance, learn to turn back to the path of righteousness.

What a dangerous thing it is, and how far removed from Christian law, to refuse to be obedient, especially to the Holy See—as you can learn from the words of the blessed prophet Samuel (the very words that Pope Gregory [I] took care to expound in the last book of his *Moralia*). We set them in writing now, so that we may keep them before us; in this way you will know beyond doubt that this is no new teaching we are speaking of. We are merely rehearsing the ancient teaching of the holy fathers: "But Samuel said, 'Obedience is better than sacrifice, to listen, better than the fat of rams. For a sin of divination is rebellion, and arrogance, the crime of idolatry'" [1 Sam 15.22–23]. It is right that obedience be valued more than sacrifices, because in sacrifice we kill flesh that is not our own, but in obedience we kill our own will. How much more readily a man pleases God to the extent he overcomes his own willful pride and sacrifices himself before God's eyes by the sword of His command! Disobedience, though, is likened to the sin of witchcraft in order to show by contrast how great is the virtue of obedience; the contrast makes it clear how much we should praise the latter. For if rebellion is like the sin of witchcraft, and stubbornness like the crime of idolatry, then only obedience brings the reward of faith—for without obedience a man can appear to be faithful while actually being the opposite.

TO THE ALMORAVID RULER OF MAURETANIA, THANKING HIM FOR HIS RECENT GIFTS AND THE RELEASE OF SOME PRISONERS (1076)

God, Who created the universe and without Whom we can neither do nor even think anything good, has inspired you, in your heart, to this act of kindness; and as He enlightens all who come into this world, He has enlightened your mind to this end. The Almighty God, Who desires that all people be saved and none perish, mercifully urges us, above all, that apart from loving Him we love one another, desiring to do nothing to another that we would not want done to ourselves. For this reason, we—that is, you and I—are especially obliged to show to the nations an example of this loving kindness, for we believe and confess the same One God, although in different ways, and we praise and worship Him daily as the Creator of all things and the Ruler of this world. As the Apostle [Paul] says: "He is our peace, Who has made us both one." [Eph. 2.14] Many of our leading figures here in Rome, when I informed them of your gracious act in the name of God, expressed admiration and approval of your good will and virtue. . . .

The Lord knows that we extend to you our love, for His honor, and that we hope for your salvation and glory, both in this life and in the next; and we pray in our heart and with our lips that God will lead you to the Abode of Happiness, the bosom of the holy patriarch Abraham, after many years of life here on earth.

TO ABBOT PETER OF FUCECCHIO AND PRIOR RUDOLF OF CAMALDOLI (1081?)

Gregory, bishop and servant of the servants of God, to Abbot Peter of Fucecchio and Prior Rudolf of Camaldoli, greetings and an apostolic blessing.

You requested that I absolve Ughiccio the son of Bulgarelli even though he has neither confessed his sin nor repented of it. As you know, before he sinned so grievously I held him dear and loved him more than any of his fellow-princes in Tuscany, because, like his father before him, he worked diligently to defend the good and to establish true religion in his lands. That is why, if it were at all possible to agree to your request, I would gladly grant him absolution on account of his own former goodness and his wife's current prayers, along with your own request. But neither reason nor the custom of the Holy Church permits this; neither does the example of the Holy

Fathers offer a precedent for absolving someone who has been properly and canonically excommunicated, refuses to admit his fault, and does not seek forgiveness with his whole heart. Unless a man repents with his whole heart and confesses his sin, any absolution offered him would be without effect and could only be regarded as a lie.

But since Count Ughiccio continues to defend his wickedness by insisting his excommunication was unjust and done in order to win political points elsewhere, he should himself investigate and ponder the writings of the Holy Fathers on such matters. He should remember that he took part in a sacrilegious conspiracy by the citizens of Lucca and not make matters worse for himself by defending his actions. On top of this, he brought down the sword of anathema on himself for a second and no less serious failing: he allowed, and even encouraged, the lawfully and canonically installed bishop of Lucca to be driven from his church.

In all honesty, I would not wish to excommunicate anyone against the dictates of justice, not even if I knew that I myself would have to suffer going into exile or risk injury on that account; for every person, even the most insignificant, is someone for whom Christ shed His blood. But in order to persuade Count Ughiccio to repent his crime in a fitting, Christian way, I would gladly risk any harm or danger that might come to me, and therefore I urge you and plead with you to remember him in your daily prayers, imploring God's mercy to visit, soften, and turn to penitence Ughiccio's heart and mind—so that through sincere penance, tears, and pleas for forgiveness for his sins Ughiccio may some day be counted again, by his performance of good works, among the members of the Holy Church.

STUDY QUESTIONS

1. What sort of pope emerges from the letters of Gregory VII? How would you describe his political outlook?
2. What picture of the second half of the eleventh century emerges from Gregory's correspondence? Is it a connected world?

10.3 GUIBERT DE NOGENT, *GESTA DEI*, 1107–1108

The French monk Guibert of Nogent (ca. 1055–1124) entered the church at around the age of twelve, but his firsthand knowledge of knights and, most important, crusaders gives his *God's Deeds* through the Franks a particularly personalized account of the curiosities of the First Crusade (1096–1099). Guibert also wrote a protoautobiography—the first major example since Augustine's *Confessions* in the fifth century—that reveals his interior mode of thought. These selections from *God's Deeds* vividly describe crusader events: a battle between the Turks and the crusaders, a false miracle, the experience of viewing the city of Antioch for the first time, and the difficulties and curiosities of war.

BOOK IV

After the count of Saint-Gilles heard that the Turks, who usually supplied the garrison for the city of Antioch, had left the stronghold, he sent part of his army ahead to take possession of the city and to maintain control of it. He chose four men from among the leaders of his army, of whom three had the same name, that is, Peter, and the fourth was called William of Montpellier, a man well known among us for his feats of arms, and he gave them 500 knights to lead. And so, not far from the above-mentioned city, they entered a valley and in that valley found a fort, and there they heard that the Turks, with a large army, were in control of the city of Antioch, and in addition they learned that the Turks were making great preparations of men and arms, to defend themselves against the French, in case they attacked. Therefore, one of those Peters we named above, whose surname had been derived from a place called Roaix, separating himself from his companions, entered a valley of a town named Rugia, [151] where he found Turks and Saracens, with whom he fought. After killing many of them, he pursued the others. The Armenians took notice of this and, pleased with the man's bravery, and impressed by his unusual boldness against the Turks, surrendered voluntarily to

his command. Quickly thereafter he was given control of a city named Rusa [152] when its inhabitants capitulated, and several other forts surrendered to him. The rest of the army departed from Coxon, the city we mentioned, and marched through high mountains along incredibly rocky paths so narrow that no one could pass the man in front of him, but each man had to proceed one step at a time, stepping carefully, in single file. A deep gulley lay beneath the narrow, rough path, so that if a horse happened to push up against another horse, he would fall to instant death. There you would have seen armed men, who, having just been converted by the hardship and starvation of the journey from knights into foot-soldiers, were suffering wretchedly, smashing their fists, tearing their hair, begging for the relief of death, selling their shields, helmets, and all of their arms, regardless of their true worth, for three or four, perhaps five cents. When they could find no buyer, they threw their shields and other fine equipment into the gulley, to disencumber their weakened, endangered bodies. When they finally emerged from these rocks and precipices, after unbearable suffering, they entered a town called Marasim, [153] whose inhabitants came forth joyfully to meet them, bringing abundant supplies to sell to the soldiers.

The rich earth replenished the exhausted men, until the presence of their leader Bohemund, who was following those who were waiting for him there, was restored to them.

Finally, they arrived in the plains where the renowned city of Antioch was situated, whose particular glories, beyond those by means of which she flourished in this world, are those which grew out of her Christian fame. Pharphar was the name of the river on which she was located. When our men had reached a place near the bridge over that river, some of them, who had been assigned the task of forming the vanguard of the army, met up with a large force of Turks, who were well supplied with provisions, and were hurrying to bring aid to the besieged. When our men saw them, they charged with Frankish ferocity, and almost instantly defeated them and scattered them in all directions. Like charging rams, they tore them to pieces, and the Turks threw away the arms that only moments before had been able to inspire terror. The mass of foot-soldiers fled through their own lines, in their haste and confusion wounding and crushing their own allies. The madness of pride now felt humiliation, and the man who anticipated taking pleasure in heaping up destruction upon us was now happy if he could get himself out alive, even though dishonored. Those who had come to bring aid to the besieged were turned into instant, filthy piles of cadavers. The Almighty mercifully converted what they had brought to aid the besieged into gifts for the besiegers. Thus after they had been destroyed, like grain crushed by hail, great quantities of grain and wine fell into our hands, and the foot-soldiers acquired the valuable horses, camels, mules, and asses that remained. And so our men built camps on the shore of the above-mentioned river. Bohemund, together with 4000 of his best men, undertook blockade of the city's gate, and remained on guard all that night to prevent anyone from getting in or out. The next day, the twelfth calends of November, [154] the fourth day of the week, in the middle of the day, the army arrived, set up camp, and began a blockade of three of the city's gates; the fourth gate was left free, since it was inaccessible to the besiegers because of the great height of the surrounding mountains, and the narrowness of its paths. However, not only the inhabitants, but the Turks themselves who were inside the city were so frightened by us that none of them came out to fight us. No one put up any resistance, but instead they behaved as though we had come to the market, and this pretense of peace continued, as though a truce had been declared, for fifteen days. The city was surrounded by signs that augured well for beginning this siege; fresh abundance of everything necessary to sustain life was vividly present; I am surprised that at that time the crusaders found abundant grapes hanging on the vines everywhere, wheat shut up not in granaries, but in ditches and underground pits. The trees had plenty of apples, and whatever made their lives more comfortable was supplied by an extremely fertile soil. The Armenians and the Syrians, who formed the entire population of the city (except for the Turks, who, as I mentioned earlier, were not permanent residents), since they inhabited the city itself, and were titular Christians, visited us in great numbers, and told them whatever they had learned among us. They enticed the Franks with their deceptive, repeated lies, and, whispering in their ears, using the most flattering terms, they claimed that they shunned the Turks, although they did not allow their own wives to go beyond the city limits; when they left the Franks, and were back in the city, they reported to the Turks whatever news they had been able to gather about the weaknesses of the Christian side. Thus, informed by the Syrians about our plans, the Turks from time to time rushed out from the city to sneak up upon our men and attack them as they were searching for food, and they covered over the most used paths and made unexpected attacks upon them as they sought the mountains and the sea, never permitting them to rest from ambush or open attack. Not far off was a fort named Harenc [155] in which they had placed a garrison of the fiercest Turkish warriors, who made frequent raids upon the Franks when they were unprepared. Our leaders, unwilling to suffer such affronts, sent a large force of cavalry and infantry to find out where those who were doing so much harm to their men were concealing themselves. When they found their hiding place, they at first attacked them, but then, cleverly simulating flight, they permitted themselves to be brought to a position where they knew that Bohemund was waiting in ambush. At that point, two of our men died in pursuit of the Turks. Coming out of his hiding-place, Bohemund fell upon the enemy, leading the group who appeared to have turned their backs, delivering the punishment they deserved by attacking the Turks with all his forces. He killed many of them, made others prisoners, and brought those he had captured back to the gate of the city, where, to terrify the citizens who were watching, he ordered that they be decapitated. Some of the citizens, however, climbed to the top of this gate and wore out our men by discharging so many arrows that a cloud of missiles flowed in the midst of Bohemund's camp, and one woman died when struck by one of the arrows. Finally, the leaders consulted with each other, and decided to set up a fort at the top of a mountain which they called Malregard, and which, as a formidable stronghold, might serve to drive away the Turks. Thus the fort was being constructed, and there you would have seen the greatest princes laboring at carrying rocks. There no poor man might complain that he had to endure hardships inflicted upon him by the power of great men, since those who were in charge would permit themselves no rest in bringing the work to completion. For they knew by the instinct of pious nature, even if they had not read it, what Marius, according to Sallust, said, "If you behave gently, but rule the army firmly, you will be a master, not a general." [156] And when the fort was built, the leaders took turns guarding it. Christmas was near, and the grain and other food for the body began to diminish severely, and throughout the army everything that was for sale was expensive. There was no energy to go even a moderate distance to seek food; within the territory held by those who called themselves Christians almost nothing to eat could be found; no one could go into the Saracen region without large military force. Therefore, compelled by hunger, the leaders held a meeting to discuss how to deal with the danger of such a large group of men starving unless something were done for them. Finally, they decided to send part of the army to search everywhere for supplies, while the others maintained the siege they had undertaken. Bohemund then said, "If, O powerful soldiers, it seems prudent to you, I, with the support of the army of the count of Flanders,

shall devote myself to the effort of procuring food." The offer was accepted gratefully by the younger men, since they were worn out by greater thirst and more urgent need for food. The day after the Lord's Nativity, which was the second day of the week, had been celebrated, with what emotion and energy they could muster, the two princes just mentioned, together with 20,000 foot-soldiers and cavalry, set out as swiftly and as energetically as they could to attack the Saracen provinces. Meanwhile the Turks, Arabs, Saracens, and other Gentiles, who had assembled from Jerusalem, Damascus, Aleph, [157] and other places, with one purpose in mind, to bring aid, hastened to Antioch in large numbers. They had heard that the Christians were coming into their own lands, to gather food and other supplies; as dusk fell, they moved in formation towards the place where they had learned our men were, with an eagerness that would soon be turned to grief. They divided themselves into two lines of battle, setting the first in front of us, and moving to position the other behind us. But the count of Flanders, trusting in divine power, with the sign of the Cross fixed to his heart and body, relying confidently on the excellent count Bohemund, attacked the enemy with the courage to be expected of such men. The battle began, but from the first moment of contact, the enemy turned in flight. The battle turned into victory, and many a sharp spear shattered in the bodies of those who had turned their backs to flee. The enemy's shields were battered by long ashwood lances that were struck with such force that they dwindled into slivers. No helmet prevented a head struck by the edges of the Crusaders' swords from being wounded; and they found the stitching of their so-called impenetrable cuirasses too fragile. Armor protected no part of the body; whatever the barbarians thought firm was weak; whatever the Franks touched shattered. The field was covered with innumerable corpses, and the thick pile of dead men disturbed the evenness of the grassy field. Everywhere the earth, sprinkled with the hateful blood of Gentiles, grew dark. Those who survived the carnage we inflicted saved their lives by their speed afoot, and were pleased to unburden themselves of their spoils, not out of generosity towards us, but to increase their speed. Our state of mind changed utterly: fear changed into courage, battle into victory, mourning into joy, hunger into plenty. He who was naked now had clothing, those who were on foot now had chariots, the poor man had money, the man who had been cast out now danced with gratitude and joy. While these things were going on, the fact that Bohemund and the count of Flanders were not present at the siege was not hidden from the Turks who were in control of Antioch. Made more confident by their absence, they came out, though cautiously, to challenge us in battle more often, trying to find out where the besiegers were weakest. Finally, seeing day, the third day of the week, that seemed apt for trying their courage, they made a sudden assault, and killed many of our foot-soldiers and knights, who were caught unaware. The magnificent bishop of Puy lost a mainstay of his court, the man who was his standard-bearer, who was among those who perished. Had not the river upon whose banks their camp was pitched separated them, the carnage among the Christians would have been very great. Meanwhile, Bohemund was on his way back, having pillaged the Saracen provinces; he was traveling through the mountainous area in which Tancred was staying, thinking that there he might be able to find something to help the men besieging Antioch. Although some of our men had carried off whatever they could see, many found nothing at all, and returned empty-handed, that is, without anything that could be eaten. Bohemund, however, never without a plan, when he saw them wandering about unsuccessfully, spoke these words, "If you are looking for material with which to sustain life, if you want to provide adequately for the bodily needs dictated by hunger,

then while you search for food do not risk your lives. Stop scurrying through the pathless mountains, since you know that your enemies are preparing hidden traps for you in these horrible, desolate places. Let the army move forward united, for each is made stronger by the presence of the other, so that if one part is attacked violently, the other may offer assistance. For even as a sheep, if it escapes from the shepherd's grasp, is exposed to the wolf's jaws, so the knight, if he wanders forth alone from the tents of his companions, invariably becomes a plaything for plunderers. Therefore, remain together with each other and with your men, and rather eat very little food than feed upon rare delicacies in permanent captivity. To go out and come back together, to take pleasure in being together, to do nothing rash, these are the things that sensible men do; anyone who wanders away wishes to die." He spoke, and returned to his companions, without enriching the besiegers in no way by his return. But the clever Armenians and Syrians, when they saw that the army's food was running out, and there was nothing left to buy, traveled about among all the places that they knew, bought grain, and brought it back to the army that was suffering from a lack of supplies. They sold the grain at inordinate prices, so that the amount of grain a single ass could carry brought eight of their besants, which they called "purpled," approximately 120 sous. Clearly those who could not possibly pay such a price were in great danger of succumbing to a terrible crisis of hunger. And if the leaders were already becoming hard pressed to pay such price, what could he do who, for all his previous wealth, was now all but a pauper?

STUDY QUESTIONS

1. What is the role of the Christian God in this battle?
2. What does the document reveal about Western Christians' prejudices against non-Catholic Christians in the Greater West?

10.4 PETER ABELARD, *SIC ET NON*

Peter Abelard (1079–1142) was an early proponent of the new learning of the twelfth-century Renaissance. A rascally student and later a brilliant teacher, he made a name for himself with his first important book, *Sic et Non* (*Yes and No*), which was a compilation of contradictory passages from patristic sources and church councils. Abelard's purpose was to highlight the fact that ecclesiastical tradition alone is insufficient to lead the faithful to truth. A critical intelligence and the application of logic were required—precisely the tools offered by the new learning. The preface to the book is printed below. The ellipses [. . .] consist mostly of examples he quotes to illustrate his points.

If some of the writings of the saints not only differ from one another but actually contradict each other, we ought not to rush to judgment (given the sheer multitude of their written words) about those great figures by whom the world itself is to be judged—for as the Scriptures say, "The saints shall judge the nations" [Wisdom 3.7–8], and also, "You will also sit as a judge" [Matthew 19.28]. So let us not presume to dismiss as liars, or condemn as mistaken, those men of whom the Lord Himself said, "Whoever listens to you, listens to Me; and whoever rejects you, rejects Me" [Luke 10.16]. Remembering our own weakness of mind, let us be more sure of our lack of understanding than of their inability to write, for they are the ones of whom He Who is Truth Itself once said, "For it is not you who are speaking, but the Spirit of your Father Who speaks through you" [Matthew 10.20]. Is it any wonder, then, since we lack the Spirit through Which these things were written, spoken, and revealed to the saints, that we should also lack the means to understand their teachings? Especially given the fact that each of those writers is as overflowing in wisdom as in words. As Cicero pointed out, sameness in everything destroys the appetite and causes one to feel queasy; and so it is fitting that the writings of our forefathers vary on issue after issue and that they are not cheapened by the use of low, common language. As St. Augustine observed, ideas should not be reviled simply because they are obscure; indeed, they should be more highly valued, the more difficult they are to investigate and understand. Considering the great diversity of the people we are talking about, it is to be expected that their writings are an assortment. The precise meaning of any of their words might be unknown or unfamiliar to many readers. And if we are going to use these texts for considering matters of doctrine, we ought to pay more attention to how they have been understood [down the centuries] than how their specific wording functions, as no less an expert on language than the great grammarian Priscian has taught us. . . .

Whenever we confront writings of the saints that appear to contradict truth, we ought to be especially careful not to be misled by false attributions of authorship or corruptions in the text, for there are many apocryphal works in circulation that have saints' names attached to them in order to give them greater authority, and even the texts of the Holy Scriptures are sometimes corrupted by scribal errors. This is what St. Jerome, the most trustworthy author and reliable translator of all, warned of in his letter to Laeta, concerning her daughter's education: "Let her be wary of all apocryphal writings. Even if she wants to read them not for their dogmatic truth but only to enjoy their miracle stories, she should know that they were not written by the men listed as their authors. It takes a great deal of discernment

Translation by Clifford Backman.

to find any gold hidden in such mud." . . . [Jerome also found scribal errors in the Holy Gospels:] "We find another instance in the gospel of Matthew, where it says 'then he gave back the thirty pieces of silver, as it is written in the book of the prophet Jeremiah' [Matthew 27.9]. Only we do not find this phrase in Jeremiah; it is in Zechariah [Zachariah 11.13]. Behold—an error, just like any other." Is it any wonder, then, since scribes in their ignorance have even introduced errors into the gospels, if we see mistakes creeping into the writings of the later Church Fathers, which are far less authoritative? Therefore, when we encounter anything in the books of the saints that seems to be contradictory to truth, the pious, humble, and charitable thing to do . . . is to assume that at that specific point the text may have been corrupted or incorrectly translated, or else to acknowledge that we do not understand it.

No less important is it to consider whether such passages come from writings by the saints that they themselves later retracted or corrected once they had discovered the truth. St. Augustine did this many times. Or perhaps they were writing to cite the opinion of someone else rather to express than their own view—as Ecclesiastes often did, introducing many unsound statements into the Scriptures. He wanted to be understood, not to stir up confusion. . . .

It is an element of everyday speech to describe the existence of things according to the perceptions of our senses. For example, we know that no truly empty space exists anywhere in the world—that is, a space that utterly lacks air or any other type of matter—and yet we straightforwardly call a box or chest "empty" because that is how our sense of sight perceives it. We judge things by the evidence of our eyes: thus, sometimes we speak of the starry heavens, and sometimes not; sometimes we say the sun is hot, and other times not; sometimes we say the moon is more or less bright, and sometimes not so much. Similarly, we sometimes say that things will remain the same forever, when it is clear to us that they will not. Why is it so surprising, therefore, if we occasionally find ideas expressed by the Holy Fathers in their writings that are their own opinions rather than the actual truth? Whenever contradictory things are said

about a single issue, we must be careful to distinguish statements offered with the force of a command, from those offered with a measure of indulgence, and from those offered as exhortations to perfection. Only by considering the intentions behind such passages, can we hope to find a remedy for statements that oppose one another.

If a statement is a direct command, we must decide if it is general or specific—that is, one applicable to everyone in general, or to certain individuals alone. We need to take into account when certain statements were made, or the reasons for their being made, because it often happens that what one time-period permitted, another one forbade, and what is often commanded with great insistence is sometimes tempered with flexibility. It is especially necessary to make these distinctions when dealing with the Church's decrees and canons. It will be easy to resolve many controversies if we can be on our guard for different authors using the same words but for different purposes.

Any reader who cares to resolve conflicts in the writings of the saints will pay attention to all these matters. If a conflict is so great that it cannot be resolved by reasoning, then the authorities must be weighed against one another, and whichever side has stronger evidence and more likelihood [of being correct] should be retained above all. Thus did St. Isidore say to the bishop of Massio: "To close this letter of mine, let me add that whenever opposing opinions are found in the acts of Church council, more weight should be given to the view that is of greater and more ancient authority."

Indeed, it has happened that various prophets have lacked, at times, the grace of prophecy, but being in the habit of prophesying have offered false statements of their own making, believing as they made them that the spirit of prophesy was truly upon them. God allowed the errors to occur as a means of keeping the prophets humble—that they might recognize more clearly what things come from the Spirit of God, and what comes from their own spirits; and know that when they possess the spirit of prophecy they have it as a gift from the Holy Spirit, Who can neither lie nor be mistaken. For when this Spirit is upon one, just as it does not bestow all its gifts on one person, so does it not enlighten the mind of the prophet regarding everything; instead, it reveals a bit here, and a bit there, and whenever it clarifies one thing it conceals another. St. Gregory said as much in his first homily on Ezechiel, using clear examples. And even St. Peter, the prince of the apostles, shimmering with miracles and the gifts of divine grace after the extraordinary pouring out of the Holy Spirit, promised by God, and who taught his disciples nothing but the truth, was not ashamed to abandon a pernicious untruth [he had asserted] about the practice of circumcision and various other ancient rites, after he was publicly and soundly corrected (although in a friendly way) by the Apostle Paul.

When it becomes clear that even the prophets and apostles were no strangers to error, what is the surprise in finding some mistakes in the numerous writings of the holy fathers, or in their scribal transmission? Just as these saints should not be accused of lying, if at one time or another they have said something contrary to the truth, for they were acting out of simple ignorance rather than duplicity—so too, and in the same way, one ought not impute to presumption or sinfulness something that someone says out of love and in order to teach. For as all know, God distinguishes between actions on the basis of the intentions that lay behind them, as it says in Matthew, "If your eye is sound, your whole body will be full of light" [Matthew 6.22]. And in the treatise *On Ecclesiastical Discipline* by St. Augustine: "Have charity, and do what you can." . . . For it is one thing to lie, quite another to make an error when speaking—so long as one falls away from the truth by mistake rather than out of malice. If God allows this to happen even to His holy saints, as we have pointed out, in situations where no harm is done to the faith, then it does not fail to bear fruit for those very saints, who undertake all things for the sake of the good. Even the Doctors of the Church—who are so diligently attentive—believe that there exist errors in their writings that need correction; this is why they grant to posterity the license to emend those texts or simply not to

follow them, if they themselves did not have the time to retract or correct their works. . . .

One ought to read literature not with the requirement of believing it but with the freedom to judge it. And in order that the room for this freedom be not lost, and that the healthy work of treating difficult questions and translating their language and style is not denied to later authors, the excellence of the canonical authority of the Old and New Testaments has been set apart from the books of later authors. If anything there strikes the reader as absurd, he cannot say that the author of this or that book did not possess the truth. Either the manuscript is corrupt, or the translator made a mistake, or the reader has failed to understand. . . .

[St. Augustine] calls the canonical writings of the Old and New Testaments texts about which it is heresy to say that something in them contradicts truth. In this regard he wrote, in his fourth letter to St. Jerome: "In commenting on the Letter of Paul to the Galatians I came across something that distressed me terribly. But if something in the Holy Scriptures is, or can be shown to be, a lie (even a "white lie") then what authority will the text have thereafter? How can anyone pass judgment on the Scriptures? Who is so shameless as to crush them under the heavy weight of falsehood?" And in another letter on the same issues: "It seems to me to be an exceedingly dangerous thing to regard anything in holy books as a lie—that is, to think that the men through whom the Scriptures were written and passed on to us would have lied about anything in their books. For if a single lie, even the smallest one, is acknowledged to exist in so lofty an authority, then not a single particle of the books will remain, which someone will not explain away as the invention or imagining of the author's mind, using this incredibly dangerous excuse whenever someone comes across something difficult to practice or hard to believe." . . .

With these points now made, may it please you that I have here endeavored to gather various passages from the holy fathers that stand out in my memory on account of their apparently differing opinions on various issues. May these passages inspire young readers to strenuous exercise in seeking out the truth, and may the search make them sharper readers in the end. The first key to wisdom is defined, of course, as determined and frequent questioning. Aristotle, the most insightful philosopher of them all, urged his students to embrace the act of questioning with their whole hearts; in his preface "Ad aliquid" he wrote: "Perhaps it is difficult to declare confidently on matters of this sort, unless one does it often and in great detail; but it would not be useless to doubt a number of specific points." For indeed, by doubting we come to questioning, and by questioning we discover the truth. "Seek, and you will find," said the One Who is Truth Itself; "knock, and the door will be opened for you." He taught us with His own moral example. Sitting at age twelve amidst His teachers and inquiring into those things He wanted to discover, He showed us by His questions the way to be a student rather than the way to be a teacher by exposition, even though the full and complete wisdom of God was present in Him. Therefore, when certain passages of Scripture are laid before us, the authority of those very Scriptures is commended the more they excite the reader and spur him to seek out their truth.

For this reason it pleased me, in this current book, to compile into a single volume numerous passages from the writings of the saints, following the decree of Pope Gelasius regarding the books that are held to be authentic. Thus it is assured that I have introduced nothing from apocryphal writings. I have appended excerpts from the *Retractations* of St. Augustine, from which it will be clear that I have quoted nothing that he himself later retracted or corrected.

STUDY QUESTIONS

1. How does Abelard construct his argument that ecclesiastical tradition alone is insufficient to lead the faithful to truth? What evidence does he provide to support his case?
2. What are the characteristics of Abelard's argument that make it representative of the new rational approach to understanding that emerged in the twelfth century?

10.5 OTTO OF FREISING, *THE TWO CITIES*

Bishop Otto of Freising (1115–1158) is one of our best sources for the German empire from the tenth to twelfth centuries. His book *The Two Cities* is an example of a "universal history": in eight books it proceeds from the creation of the world and the story of Adam and Eve to Otto's own time. The goal of "universal history" was to view contemporary events in the broadest possible context in the effort to see God's hand at work in the world. In this passage from Book Six (Ch. 27–33), Otto relates the German leaders' role in spreading Latin Christianity into eastern Europe, among the Poles and Hungarians.

Translation by Clifford Backman.

[27] In the year 1001 from the Incarnation of Our Lord, the emperor Otto [III] died without an heir, and Duke Henry of Bavaria, the son of Hezilo, was elected to succeed him by all the nobles. He was the eighty-seventh ruler in line from Augustus. Henry waged many wars—bravely, successfully—throughout Germany, Bohemia, Italy, and Apulia until God finally granted him his rest, and being so devout in his Christian faith, he established the renowned bishopric of Bamberg and endowed it with the many lands and honors we see in our own lifetime. Moreover, he gave his sister Gisela in marriage to Stephen, the king of the Hungarians, in return for having Stephen and all his people convert to the true faith. The Hungarians, to this day a most pious Christian people, regard Stephen as the founder of their faith and even revere him as a saint. But the pious emperor Henry departed from the world in his twenty-fourth year as duke (the eleventh of his years as emperor) and was buried in the cathedral church at Bamberg, where, as is well known, his tomb is today renowned for the miracles performed at it.

[28] In the year 1025 from the Incarnation of Our Lord, Conrad, a Frank, was unanimously elected to succeed Henry, who had died without an heir and had personally recommended Conrad, even though Conrad had not been a royal favorite during Henry's time on the throne. Conrad thus became the eighty-eighth in line from Augustus. On his father's side, Conrad was descended from Duke Conrad of Worms, who had died in Otto [III's] wars against the Hungarians; on his mother's side, his ancestors included the most illustrious princes of Gaul, descended from the ancient race of Trojans, and baptized in the faith by the Blessed Remigius. Conrad's wife was also named Gisela, who sprang from the ancient and glorious blood of the Carolingians. As one writer put it:

> When one adds four generations to the ten
>   already shown,
> From Charlemagne's line comes Gisela, for her
>   wisdom renowned.

She had previously been married to Duke Ernest of Swabia, the brother of Margrave Albert of Upper Pannonia, and have given him two children, Ernest and

Herman; it was after her husband's death that she married the Conrad we are discussing.

As king, Conrad was energetic in war, wise in counsel, tactful, sagacious, utterly devoted to the Christian faith, and was filled with the humility that is so becoming in a king. Early in his reign, Duke Boleslaw, the Polish noble recently defeated in battle by Conrad's predecessor Henry, plotted to break away from the empire and establish a kingdom of his own, but he died unexpectedly and was succeeded by his son Mieszko. This Mieszko planned to follow his father's intentions, and towards that end he drove his own brother Otto from his principality, and so King Conrad led his army into Poland in order to restore Otto to his rightful place and punish Mieszko for the harm he had caused. Mieszko proved unable to repulse the king's attack, and so, having taken a few shards of Germany, he fled to Duke Udalrich of Bohemia, who had already set himself up as an enemy of the kingdom.

Udalrich, however, hoped to get back into Conrad's good graces by handing Mieszko over to him, only to find that Conrad, being so chivalrous by nature, refused to receive an enemy from the hands of a traitor. Meanwhile Otto had taken possession of the Polish duchy and sent to Conrad the crown that his and Mieszko's father had unlawfully and disgracefully fashioned for himself. Otto made a further point of subjecting himself to Conrad in all things. Not long after this, Otto died at the hands of a treacherous armorer, and Mieszko—now an exile instead of a king—went to Conrad to beg forgiveness. Thanks to the intercession of Queen Gisela, Conrad restored to Mieszko a one-third part of what he had previously held entire, and it is well known that that smaller province has remained subject to the German kings ever since and has paid tribute to them.

Around the same time two kinsmen of Conrad's—the duke of Worms, also named Conrad, and Ernest, the duke of Swabia and the Alemanni (who was also King Conrad's stepson)—rose up in rebellion, just when the king had departed for Italy, first naming his infant son Henry as his successor. Queen Gisela, Duke Ernest's mother, advised him quickly to travel to Italy to reconcile with the king and offer him aid. Conrad's military train celebrated the start of Easter at Vercelli, where he met with Margrave Rainier and the citizens of Lucca; once these had submitted to him, he marched on to Rome.

[29] In the year 1027 from the Incarnation of the Lord, Conrad was crowned in Rome by Pope John on the very day of the Easter Festival. He entered the coronation ceremony walking in the position of honor between King Canute of England and Duke Rudolph of Burgundy—Queen Gisela's uncle; and from the people of Rome he received the titles *emperor* and *augustus*. At some point during the week a riot broke out between the local citizens and the emperor's troops, and a terrible battle ensued, in which many Romans fell or fled and the emperor emerged victorious. He promptly made peace with the citizens, however, and withdrew his troops from the city. He also captured a notorious local bandit named Tahselgart and hanged him. But as he was returning to France by way of the Pyrenees, Conrad learned that his stepson, Duke Ernest, had once again rebelled against him, having been so advised by Count Werner [of Kiburg]. Conrad then rendered a most solemn judgment against him, and by the authority of his royal majesty he banned Ernest from land and sea, compelling him to go into exile in the forest—where he was subsequently killed by some of the king's loyal followers. Ernest's brother, Herman, succeeded to the dukedom.

[30] Around the same time King Rudolph of Burgundy (also known as Gallia Lugdunensis) died. In his will he bequeathed his crown to his nephew Henry, who was Conrad's son. . . .

[31] When Rudolph made this bequest, Count Odo of Gallia Celtica (the son of Rudolph's sister) advanced the unreasonable claim that the kingdom belonged by right to him instead of Henry, and he led his army into it just when the emperor Conrad was busy subjecting the Poles, as mentioned earlier. When the emperor heard of Odo's action, he marshaled his own army to invade Burgundy. This was around Christmas-time, however, and so it was too cold for his men to march all the way there, and so they waited until the following summer. In three weeks they had reduced all of Odo's land to dust and ashes, forcing him to plead for mercy, and only after Odo gave assurance under a solemn vow that he would not further trouble Burgundy did Conrad return home.

The next year Conrad ventured into Burgundy once more and accepted the submission of all the princes there, including the Metropolitan of Lyons; taking several of them as hostages-to-the-court he returned to Germany in peace. Not too much later he ventured into Italy to squash a rebellion by a rabble of insolent commoners who had nearly unseated their noble masters. He celebrated Christmas at Verona, then traveled by way of Brescia and Cremona to Milan, where he arrested the bishop for having joined a conspiracy against him, and handed him over to the Poppo, the Patriarch of Aquileia. The bishop eventually escaped, unnoticed, and fled, which prompted Conrad, after celebrating Easter Day at Ravenna that spring, to lay waste to the district surrounding Milan, conquering and demolishing many strongholds while receiving the submission of many others. Then he marched on to Cremona, where he met with the pope, whom he received most graciously and treated with the utmost respect. After he sent the pope on his way [back to Rome], Conrad journeyed to the mountain districts [to the north] in order to avoid the summertime heat.

But while these events were taking place in Italy, Count Odo once again broke his vow and rose up against Conrad one more time, in Gaul. He died in disgrace, however, for when he was besieging a certain stronghold called Bar-le-Duc, he was killed by Duke Gozelo of Lorraine and some other troops loyal to the king, who then sent his standard to Italy as a token of their victory that was sure to please the emperor. Also at that time the bishops of Piacenza, Vercelli, and Cremona were convicted of treason and sent into exile, although this was and still is a controversial matter. Soon thereafter the emperor was celebrating Christmas at Parma when a riot broke out in which Conrad's chamberlain was killed. The emperor was enraged by this and attacked the city most bitterly. The citizens defended themselves bravely, but in the end too many of them fell to ward off Conrad's attack. The city was put to the torch.

Around this time the pope in Rome excommunicated the archbishop of Milan, who had also rebelled against Conrad. The emperor was then on the other side of the Apennines, having brought all of the eastern portion of Italy under his control, and was entering

Apulia. (Queen Gisela, in the meantime, had gone on pilgrimage to Rome and would rejoin him later.) He passed through Capua, Benevento, and a great many other cities of that region, and planned to return home by way of the Adriatic coastline, but the district was suffering from a contagion that made the air unhealthy to breathe, and many of his leading nobles and other soldiers died, including Duke Hermann, the son of Queen Gunnhild (who was, in her turn, the bride of Conrad's son), and Duke Conrad of Franconia. These catastrophic losses inspired a poet to compose some verses on the fragility of human life; their style is simple but tragically expressive. They begin with the lines:

> Let him with a voice both clear and strong
> Gather all around him to hear this song.

Not much later, but after he had returned from Italy, the emperor took ill in the middle of the Feast of Pentecost, which he was celebrating in Frisia, in the city of Utrecht, and died. It was the seventeenth year of his reign as duke and the fourteenth of his reign as emperor. They buried his heart and other vital organs there in Utrecht and transported the rest of his body to Speyer, where it was laid to rest in the Marienkirche.

[32] In the year 1040 from the Incarnation of Our Lord, Henry III, the son of the aforesaid Queen Gisela, began his sole reign as the eighty-ninth emperor in line from Augustus—having already started to govern while his father was still alive. With Henry the imperial title finally returned to someone born of the ancient and noble stock of Charlemagne. Henry equaled his father in all respects and even surpassed him in the best qualities. He governed with moderation, although he made a rash mistake at the very start of his reign when he launched a campaign against the Bohemians, who were opposed to his rule, and lost many men in the dense forests there. These losses fueled his righteous indignation, however, and prompted him to inflict far greater damages on the people of Bohemia until their duke finally submitted to him. He also made frequent war on the Hungarians. When, instigated by the rebel leader Obo, they treacherously drove their own king, Peter, into exile, however, Henry gave him refuge. At the urging

of Margrave Albert (whose brother-in-law he was), Henry marched into Pannonia with an army that, though small in number, won a great victory against a large Hungarian force; thus did Henry restore Peter to his throne—a victory that inspired Herman the Lame to compose the poem that begins:

> This voice of mine must sing a lay.

Henry married Agnes, the daughter of the most illustrious nobleman in Gaul, Duke William of Poitou and Aquitaine. At the wedding celebration, which was held, according to custom, at Ingelheim, he gave to all the poor in the region the money that would otherwise have gone to the jesters and actors (those limbs of Satan!) who attended but went away empty-handed. Sadness accompanied the celebrations, though, since young Leopold, the most illustrious son of Margrave Albert, was carried off by an early death. Mourned by all, he was buried in the city of Trèves by his uncle Poppo, who was archbishop there. This was the Leopold who, together with his father, seized the Eastern March from the Hungarians and defeated, against tremendous odds, the huge army led by the traitor Obo, who was harassing his border. It was a dangerous undertaking, even for one as brave as Leopold.

About the same time a shameful state of confusion beset the Church in Rome, for three men (one of whom was called Benedict) usurped the papal throne all at once, dividing between them the office and its revenues. One sat in St. Peter's Cathedral, the second in the church of Santa Maria Maggiore, and the third (Benedict) in the Lateran Palace. I have heard from eyewitnesses that all three lived a dissolute life. A certain priest named Gratian, a devout man filled with compassion for Mother Church on account of the wretched state She had fallen into, approached the three usurpers and by the zeal of his piety persuaded them, with money, to vacate their seats. Benedict, the most stubborn person of the group, insisted on keeping the revenues from England. The people of Rome proclaimed this priest as the great liberator of the Church and chose him to be the new pope, Gregory VII. When King Henry heard about this he summoned his army and marched into Italy. Gratian met him at Sutri and reportedly offered the king a precious crown, to assuage his anger. Henry initially received him with fitting honors but later assembled a synod of bishops, who, together with the king, persuaded him to withdraw from the papacy because he had disgraced himself with simony; in Gratian's place they appointed Bishop Suitger of Bamberg, who took the name Clement, and the whole Church consented to his appointment. According to tradition, Hildebrand had followed Gratian across the Alps and into Italy, and later, when he himself was made pope, he took the name Gregory out of love for him. Gratian's name has since been removed from the list of popes. As Lucan once wrote:

> The gods upheld the victorious cause, Cato the defeated one.

And this is true of Hildebrand, who was much the most zealous and unyielding supporter of the Church, and the most vigorous opponent of the opinions of the emperor and the German bishops [regarding lay investiture] that ultimately carried the day.

The Roman Church, in our opinion, has been so weakened in the canonical election of popes that Clement and the four men who succeeded him, were included in the list of popes only because the emperor decided to place their names on it. I shall describe later how the Church regained Her freedom, through the tireless exertions of Hildebrand, then Leo, and then Alexander—all of which I learned from the testimony of men I trust.[1]

[33] In the year 1047 from the Incarnation of Our Lord, the victorious King Henry III was crowned emperor and *augustus* at Rome by Pope Clement on Christmas Day, the ninetieth ruler in line from Augustus. Upon leaving Rome Henry led his army through Apulia before returning home to Germany. In the same year Suitger—that is, Pope Clement—died and was succeeded by Poppo, the patriarch of Aquileia [who took the name Damasus II].[2] A short time later King Peter of Hungary lost his eyesight and his kingship at the hands of a courtier named Andrew. When Poppo/Damasus died, Bishop Bruno of Toul succeeded him as head of the Church and took the name Leo IX. He came from a noble Frankish family and was King Henry's own choice to succeed to the throne of St. Peter. According to one report Henry was traveling through Gaul shortly after becoming emperor and visited the monastery of Cluny—where the aforementioned Hildebrand happened to hold the office of prior. Hildebrand [accompanied Henry to Rome and] boldly rebuked Leo for having risen to the papacy with the aid of a layman, saying with pious zeal that it was an unlawful seizure by force of the government of the Church. Hildebrand then urged Leo to trust him, promising that he could manipulate things in such a way that the Church's liberty to hold a free election would be restored, and that King Henry would not be roused to anger. Leo agreed, took off his papal robe, and put on again a pilgrim's garb. Then Leo and Hildebrand set off together for Rome, where, with Hildebrand's help, Leo was elected as supreme pontiff by the clergy and people of the city. Thus did the Church regain the right to free election.

Henry, in the meantime, invaded Lorraine and forced Duke Godfrey and Duke Baldwin to capitulate. After this, a synod was held at Mainz in the presence of Pope Leo and Henry. The king once again invaded Pannonia to put down Lord Andrew, who had arrogantly deposed King Peter and usurped the Hungarian throne. The Hungarians, though, fled from the German army and either hid or destroyed the stocks of food they had; with no way to keep his soldiers fed or supplied, Henry therefore laid waste the whole countryside, and then returned home. The next year he invaded Pannonia yet again, taking Pope Leo with him.

---

[1] Otto should not have been quite so trusting of his interviewees, since the account he gives in Ch. 32 is filled with errors. The priest Gratian was actually one of the three usurper-popes, under the name Gregory VI. His meeting with Henry III took place at Piacenza, not Sutri. Henry's synod did take place at Sutri (December 1046), but it ousted only Gratian/Gregory and the second pope, Sylvester III; the third pope, Benedict IX, had remained in Rome and refused to recognize the synod. His pseudo-pontificate ended only with his death in 1048.

---

[2] Another mistake—Damasus II was not Poppo of Aquileia, but Poppo, bishop of Brixen, another German. He died within a year.

Then the Normans—a restless people—invaded Apulia. Led by Duke Robert Guiscard, a man of common birth but uncommon energy, they inflicted every type of misery on the people there, using guile and violence in equal measure. Pope Leo, after returning to Rome with an army, wanted to bring the Normans to heel, making them subject to the Church and the German Empire. He marched against the Normans, and a great battle ensued. Many died, and Leo was forced to flee to Benevento. So many died, in fact, that to this day the people of Benevento point to a hill that they insist is made of the piled-up bones of all those killed that day. Leo died one year later and is buried in St. Peter's in Rome; his tomb is renowned for the miracles it performs. Gebhardt of Eichstätt succeeded him, taking the name Victor, and then another German succeeded him, taking the name of Stephen.

The next time Henry went to Italy he returned to Germany with his kinswoman Beatrice, the mother of Mathilda. Beatrice's husband, Margrave Boniface, had just died. Henry himself took ill not long afterwards at a place called Bodfeld, which is on the border of Saxony and Thuringia. He performed a public confession of his sins, and died. It was the seventeenth year of his reign as duke and the eleventh of his reign as emperor. He is buried next to his father. Herman the Lame has thoroughly described his deeds and virtues, as well as those of his father, in a short book.

STUDY QUESTIONS

1. What about Otto's history makes it a "universal history"? How is time viewed in Otto's history of the Holy Roman Empire? Why does Otto infuse his account with references from classical antiquity?
2. How does Otto characterize the popes?

10.6 FROM *THE SONG OF ROLAND,* CA. 1140–1170

This *chanson de geste* was passed down orally for several generations and recorded between 1140 and 1170. The oldest existing work of vernacular French literature, it recounts the story of the brave count Roland, a kinsman of the emperor Charlemagne, who led the rear guard of the Frankish army into Spain on a mission to liberate Christian cities from Saracen, or Muslim, rule. Historically, the devastating battle described in this story occurs in 778 in a mountain pass in the Pyrenees, called Roncevaux (or Roncevalles, on the Spanish side of the mountains)—but between the Frankish forces and local Basque tribes, not Muslims as depicted in this story. A troubadour would have sung this tale; allegedly, it was performed for the army of William the Conqueror while waiting on the Norman beach to cross the English Channel. Consider how this tale might have appealed to aristocratic, warrior audiences.

91

Roland has made his way to the Spanish pass,
Riding Veillantif, his good, swift horse.
The arms he bears become him well.

. . .

But he brandishes his spear, 1155
And turn its point towards the sky,
A pure white pennon fixed upon its tip,
And its golden streamers fluttering down upon
    his hands.
His body is noble, his face fair and smiling;
His companion follows closely behind 1160
And the Franks hail him as their protector.
Towards the Saracens he looks fiercely
And humbly and tenderly towards the Franks.
And he addressed them in a courtly fashion:
"My lord barons, gently, not too fast! 1165
These pagans are heading for great slaughter;
Today our spoils will be fine and noble.
No king of France has ever had such wealth."
At these words the armies come together.

. . .

111

The battle is awesome and intense.
Oliver and Roland strike mighty blows;
The archbishop deals more than a thousand.
The twelve peers do not hold back 1415
And the Franks strike in unison.
The pagans die in their hundreds and thousands;
Those who do not flee have no escape from death.
Whether they like it or not, they meet their end.
The Franks lose their best defenders; 1420
They will not see their fathers and kinsmen again,
Nor Charlemagne who awaits them in the pass.
In France there is a most terrible storm,
A tempest with thunder and strong winds,
Rain and hail in great quantity.
Lightning strikes again and again
And the whole earth, in truth, begins to quake.
From Saint Michel del Peril to Seinz,
From Besançon to the port of Wissant,
There is no house whose walls do not
    collapse. 1430
At high noon a great darkness gathers;
There is light only when the sky is rent.
No one could see it without a feeling of dread.

Many say: "It is all over with us;
The end of the world is upon us." 1435
They do not know it, but their words are wrong;
It is the great sorrow for the death of Roland.

. . .

115

The archbishop is first to start the battle.
He sits astride the horse he took from Grossaille,
A king whom he killed in Denmark.
The horse is mettlesome and fleet of foot;
Its hooves are hollowed out and its legs flat.
It is short in the haunches and broad in the
    crupper,
Long in the flank and high along its back;
Its tail is white and its mane yellow,
Its ears small and its head tawny. 1495
There is no beast which can match it for pace.
The archbishop spurs on with great valour;
He will not miss this chance to attack Abisme.
He goes to deal him a prodigious blow to the
    shield
With its precious stones, amethyst
    and topaz, 1500
Esterminals and blazing carbuncles.
A devil gave this shield to him in Val Metas
And it was presented to him by the emir Galafres.
Turpin strikes it and in no way spares it;
After his blow it is not, I think, worth a penny
    piece. 1505
He slices him through from one side to the other,
Flinging him dead in an empty spot.
The Franks say: "This is an act of great valour;
In the archbishop's hands the crozier is truly
    safe."

. . .

134

Count Roland with pain and distress
Sounds his Oliphant in great agony.
The clear blood gushes forth from his mouth
And in his skull the temple bursts.
The sound of the horn which he holds
    carries far; 1765
Charles hears it, as he makes his way through the
    pass.
Duke Naimes heard it and the Franks listen to it.
The king said: "I can hear Roland's horn;

He would never have blown it, if he were not in
a fight."
Ganelon replies: "There is no battle;   1770
You are old, hoary and white-haired.
Such words make you seem like a child;
You are well aware of Roland's great pride.
It is a wonder that God has stood for it so long.

. . .

171

Roland feels that he has lost his sight;
He rises to his feet, exerting all his strength.
All the colour has drained from his face.
Before him lies a dark-hued stone;   2300
On it he strikes ten blows in sorrow and
bitterness.
The steel grates, but does not break or become
notched;
"O, Holy Mary," said the count, "help me!
O, my good sword Durendal, what a fate you
have suffered!
Now that I am dying, I have no more need
of you;   2305
With you I have won so many battles in the field
And conquered so many vast lands,
Which Charles with the hoary-white beard now
holds.
May you never be owned by a man who flees in
battle!
A very fine vassal has held you for so long   2310
There will never be such a man in blessed France."

172

Roland struck the sardonyx stone;
The steel grates, but does not shatter or become
notched.
When he saw that he could not break it,
He begins to lament over it to himself: 2315
"O, Durendal, how fair and clear and white you
are!
How you shimmer and sparkle in the sun!
Charles was in the Sales of Maurienne,
When through his angel God on high told him
To give you a captain to count.   2320
Then the noble and mighty king girded it on me.
With it I conquered Anjou and Brittany
And with it I conquered Poitou and Maine;
With it I conquered Normandy the free

And with it I conquered Provence and
Aquitaine   2325
And Lombardy and all Romagna.
With it I conquered Bavaria and all Flanders
And Burgundy and all Apulia.
And Constantinople, which rendered homage to
him.
In Saxony his commands are obeyed.   2330
With it I conquered Scotland and Ireland
And England, which became his domain;
With it I have conquered so many lands and
countries
Which Charles with the white beard now holds.
For this sword I grieve and sorrow;   2335
I should rather die than leave it in pagan hands.
God, our Father, spare France this disgrace!"

173

Roland struck upon the dark-hued stone;
He hacks away more of it than I can tell.
The sword grates, but neither breaks
nor shatters;   2340
It rebounds towards heaven.
When the count sees that he cannot break it,
He lamented over it to himself very softly:
"O, Durendal, how fair and sacred you are!
In the golden hilt there are many relics: 2345
Saint Peter's tooth and some of Saint Basil's
blood;
Some hair from the head of my lord Saint Denis
And part of the raiment of the Blessed Virgin.
It is not right for pagans to possess you;
You must be wielded by Christians.   2350
May no coward ever have you!
With you I have conquered vast lands.
Charles with the hoary-white beard now holds
them;
They have made the emperor mighty and rich.

. . .

176

Count Roland lay down beneath a
pine tree;   2375
He has turned his face towards Spain.
Many things began to pass through his mind:
All the lands which he conquered as a warrior,
The fair land of France, the men of his lineage,
Charlemagne, his lord, who raised him.   2380

He cannot help weeping and heaving great sighs;
But he does not wish to be unmindful of himself.
He confesses his sins and prays for the grace of God:
"True Father, who has never lied,
You who brought back Lazarus from
    the dead   2385
And rescued Daniel from the lions,
Protect my soul from every peril
And from the sins which I have committed in my
    life."
He proffered his right glove to God;
Saint Gabriel took it from his hand.   2390
Roland laid his head down over his arm;
With his hands joined he went to his end.
God sent down his angel Cherubin
And with him Saint Michael of the Peril.
With them both came Saint Gabriel.   2395
They bear the count's soul to paradise.

177

Roland is dead, God has his soul in heaven.
The emperor arrives at Rencesvals;

There is no road or path there,
No open space, no yard or foot,   2400
Not covered with either Franks or pagans.
Charles cries out: "Where are you, fair
    nephew?
Where is the archbishop and Count Oliver?
Where is Gerin and his companion Gerer?
Where is Oton and Count Berenger,   2405
Yvon and Yvoire, whom I loved so dearly?
What has become of the Gascon Engeler,
Duke Samson and Anseis the brave?
Where is Gerard of Roussillon, the old,
And the twelve peers whom I had
    left behind?"   2410
To what avail, when no one could reply?
"O God," said the king, "what great sorrow
That I was not here when battle commenced."
He tugs at his beard like a man beset
    with grief;
His brave knights shed tears.   2415
Twenty thousand fall to the ground in a faint.

STUDY QUESTIONS

1. What does the document reveal about codes of "courtesy" in feudal culture?
2. How is Christianity offered as a justification for violence against the enemy, in the warriors' words and actions?

10.7 TROTULA OF SALERNO, *HANDBOOK ON THE MALADIES OF WOMEN*, CA. 1200

Originally associated with a female physician named Trotula of Salerno (eleventh–twelfth century), this compendium of medical care for women deals with infertility, childbirth, and birth control methods, as well as cosmetics, beautification techniques, and dietary advice. These selections pinpoint a handful of concerns that medieval women had, from family planning to aesthetics.

Translation by Clifford Backman

Here begins the *Book on the Maladies of Women* according to Trotula.

When God, the Creator of the universe, first established the world, He distinguished between the individual natures of things—each according to its kind—and He endowed human nature with a single dignity above all other things: He gave humans freedom of reason and intellect. This gift set mankind above the condition of all animals. And God, in wanting to sustain human generation in perpetuity, carefully and providentially created males and females, thus establishing the foundation for the production of offspring. And He created them in such a way, to ensure the arrival of fertile offspring, that their natures formed a pleasing interlocking mixture; for the males He constitutes a hot and dry nature, to which He opposed the cool and wet nature of the females. Thus, should a man overflow with an excess of one of his qualities, the woman could contain it. In this way the stronger qualities of heat and dryness dominate the man, who is the stronger and worthier of the sexes, while the weaker qualities of coolness and wetness dominate the woman, who is the weaker and less worthy sex. God did this so that the male, in his strength, might pour out his essence into the woman just as seed is sown in a field, and that the female, in her weakness a natural subject to the man, might receive the seed provided by Nature.

But because women are weaker than men and frequently experience childbirth, maladies often abound in them, especially in the organs dedicated to Nature's work; and whether because of their fragile nature, shame, or embarrassment, they seldom reveal their sufferings and illnesses (which occur in such a private area) to any physician. Their general misfortune is pitiable, and this fact, together with the prompting of a certain specific woman stirring my heart, has led me to give clear explanations about their maladies and how to restore them to health. With God's help I have worked diligently to collect passages from the better parts of the works of Galen and Hippocrates, to the end that I might discuss and explain the causes, symptoms, and cures of women's diseases.

[74] Some women are incapable of conception, either because they are too skinny and lean, or because they are too fat and the flesh of the womb-orifice shuts out the man's seed and does not let it enter. Other women's wombs are smooth and slick, which means that the man's seed, once received, cannot be kept inside. This also happens sometimes because the man's seed is too watery; once it enters the womb, its excessive fluidity causes it to flow outside. Some men, too, have very cold and dry testicles, and they rarely generate, if ever, because their seed is incapable of the task.

[75] Treatment. If a woman is barren either on account of her own difficulty or her man's, let the following treatment be attempted. Take two pots and place some wheat bran in each one; add some of the man's urine to one of the pots, and add some of the woman's urine to the other. Let the pots sit for nine or ten days. If the barrenness is the woman's fault, you will find many worms in her pot and the bran will stink; you will find the same thing in the man's pot if the barrenness is his fault. If you find this in neither of the pots, then neither of them is at fault and they should be able to conceive if aided by certain medicines.

[83] If a woman chooses not to conceive, she should wear against her naked flesh the uterus of a goat that has never had offspring.

[86] Another method would be to take a weasel and remove its testicles without killing it. The woman should then wrap them in the skin of a goose or of some other animal, and wear them against her naked bosom. Then she will not conceive.

[87] If a woman has previously been badly torn in childbirth and fears ever getting pregnant again, she should put into her afterbirth as many grains of barley or spurge as the number of years she wishes to remain barren. If she wishes to remain barren forever, she should put in a whole handful.

[126] A wet nurse should be young and have good coloring—a woman who mixes a little red with white, who is neither too close to, nor too far removed from, her last birth, who is unblemished, whose breasts are not too flabby nor too swollen but who has a healthy, ample chest, and who is moderately fat.

[127] Diet. A wet nurse should avoid eating salty, spicy, and acidic foods, and anything in which the heat is strong; also, astringent foods like leeks and onions;

and any of those spices that are added to give food more flavor, such as pepper, garlic, or rocket—but especially garlic. She should avoid stress and be careful not to induce her menses. If her milk runs low, she should eat porridge made of bean-flour or rice; she should also have wheat bread mixed with milk, sugar, and perhaps some fennel—for these things increase the milk supply. If her milk becomes too thick, let her nourishment be cut back, and compel her to work. One could also give her a vinegary syrup or light wine. If her milk becomes too thin, on the other hand, her foods should be thick and strong, and she should get extra sleep. If the child's bowels are loose, the wet nurse should eat whatever makes her constipated.

[245] There is an ointment used by noble women that removes hairs, refines the skin, and removes blemishes. Take the juice from the moist leaves of a cucumber and mix them with almond milk in a bowl. Add quicklime and orpiment; then add some gum resin that has been beaten together with a little wine. Let the mixture rest for a day and a night. Then cook. Once it has been well cooked, remove the gum resin and add a little oil or wine, plus some quicksilver. Remove the concoction from the heat, and add a powder made of the following herbs: mastic, frankincense, cinnamon, nutmeg, and clove, all in equal amounts. The ointment thus produced has a sweet smell and gently softens the skin. Noblewomen in Salerno regularly use this as a depilatory.

[246] Once a woman has rubbed herself all over with this ointment, she should sit in very hot steam—but she should not further massage her skin or else it will become chapped. Once in the steam, she should simply pull out her pubic hairs.

If they do not come out easily, she should pour hot water over herself and wash herself thoroughly, though drawing her hand gently over her skin. If she scrubs too vigorously when her skin is tender, she will be quickly excoriated by the ointment. Having done all this, let her enter a lukewarm bath and be washed well. She should then exit the bath, take a paste made of bran and hot water, strained, and pour it over her body, for this cleanses and smooths the skin. Then she should wash again in warm water, and stand to let her skin dry a little. Then she should take a mixture of henna and egg whites, and rub this all over her body. This too smooths the flesh, and removes any inflammation that may have resulted from the depilatory. Let her remain thus anointed for a while, then rinse herself with warm water, wrap herself in a very white linen cloth, and go to bed.

[250] If a woman desires long black hair, she should take a green lizard, remove its head and tail, and cook it in regular cooking oil. Then rub the oil into her hair. It will make the hair long and black.

[251] A method acquired from the Saracens. Take the rind of an extremely sweet pomegranate and grind it, then boil it in vinegar or water, and strain it. Add to the residue a large amount of powder made from apples or alum, until it reaches the texture of a poultice. Wrap this, like dough, around the entire head. Afterward, mix some bran with oil in a pot and heat it until the bran is burnt. Then sprinkle the bran-ash on the head. She should then wet her hair thoroughly, then wrap her head a second time in the method described. Leave it on overnight, for best results. Then wash the hair, and it will be completely black.

STUDY QUESTIONS

1. How are male and female bodies distinguished in "scientific" terms, especially in respect to degree of heat and moisture?
2. Was it dangerous for Trotula to include information drawn from "pagan" and Muslim sources (and perhaps from direct observation by women such as midwives)?

10.8 A MUSLIM TRAVELER DESCRIBES THE RUS: EXCERPT FROM IBN FADLAN'S *RISALA*, CA. 921

We know little about Ibn Fadlan; even his ethnicity is uncertain. He was an expert in Islamic religious law (a *faqih*), and in 921 the Abbasid caliph al-Muqtadir (r. 908–32) dispatched him as a member of an embassy to the Muslim client-state of Bulgars who lived near the confluence of the Volga and Kama Rivers. His travelogue (*Risala*, or "Journeys") provides the first detailed description of the Vikings who settled in Russia and established what would become the kingdom of Kievan Rus. In this passage he describes the Viking custom of burying the dead.

I saw some Rus people when they were camped along the river Volga while on one of their trade journeys. They were the best representatives of their people I ever saw: as tall as date-palms, with yellow hair and reddish skin. The Rus wear neither tunics nor robes; their men wear a cloak that covers one side of their bodies while leaving their opposite hand free. Each man carries an axe, a sword, and a knife—and is never without them all. Their swords are broad-bladed and grooved, like those of the Franks. All the men are tattooed from the tips of their fingers to their necks with images of green trees and other such things.

Their women wear boxes on their breasts, one on each. Some boxes are made of iron, others of copper, silver, or gold; the costliness of the boxes indicates the wealth of each woman's husband. Wives also wear gold and silver necklaces; each necklace represents ten thousand dirhams of her husband's wealth, and some of the women have many. Their most valued ornaments, though, are beads made of green glass. These resemble, in manufacture, some of the ceramic items I saw on their ships. The women trade these beads with one another, or else buy them from one another—sometimes at the exorbitant price of a dirham for a single bead! The beads are then strung as necklaces.

The Rus are the dirtiest creatures God ever made. They defecate and urinate anywhere, without shame. Like beasts, they do not wash their privates after sex and do not wash their hands after eating. After their travels they drop anchor (or, as with the ones I saw, tie up their ships along the shore of a river like the great Volga) and build large wooden huts for themselves on the shore. Each hut can hold between ten and twenty people. Inside, each man rests on a couch. They have lovely slave girls with them, whom they will sell to slave-merchants eventually, and each man has sexual intercourse with a slave girl whenever he wishes, even in front of his companions. Sometimes the whole company gets involved, each with his own girl, all in each other's presence. If a merchant happens along who wants to buy a girl, he simply looks on and waits for the man to be finished.

They wash their faces and heads every day, but they do it in the foulest and most disgusting way imaginable. Every morning a servant-girl carries in a tub of water, which she presents to her master. He washes his hands, face, and hair in it, then combs out his hair, blows his nose, and spits—all right into the tub. The servant then brings the tub to the next person, who does the same, and to the next, until everyone in the entire household has washed their face and hair, blown their nose, and spat into the water.

* * *

Once I had heard a bit of the various actions they perform when one of their great leaders dies, including cremation, I was eager to learn more. One day, finally, I learned all about the death of one of their great men. First, they placed him in a grave—which had a kind of roof on it—for a period of ten days, during which time they had several garments cut and sewn for him. (Now, if a poor man dies they simply make a little boat, lay him in it, and set it alight. But when a rich man dies they gather all his goods and divide them into thirds—one third for his family, another to pay for his funeral garb, and the last portion to provide the liquor that everyone will drink until the day when the dead man's slave-girl will offer herself to be killed and cremated with her master. Indeed, they drink non-stop, night and day, until they stupefy themselves. Some of them even die with their drinking cups still in their hands.)

Now, when the man I first mentioned died, his slave-girls were asked, "Which one of you wants to die with him?" one of them answered, "I will." She was then handed over to two young women whose job it was to watch over her. They accompanied her everywhere and even washed her feet with their own hands. Meanwhile, the dead man's funeral garments were prepared and everything was made ready for the funeral. The slave-girl busied herself throughout this time with drinking, singing, and indulging in every pleasure.

When the day of the cremation finally arrived, I went to the river to see the burial ship. It had been drawn up onto the shore [. . .] and was being guarded. A kind of dome or pavilion had been constructed in the middle of the ship and was covered with cloth; then they brought a couch with a mattress, decorated in the Greek style, and set them on the boat. An old woman, whom they called the Angel of Death, then came forward and made up the couch, mattress, and furnishings. She is the person in charge of preparing all the clothes, arranging all the funeral settings, and actually killing the slave-girl. She was a large woman, fat and grim.

The men then moved to the grave, removed the earth from the wooden roof over the dead man, pulled off the roof itself, then lifted out the dead body that was still wrapped in its funeral garb. The corpse had turned black, because of how cold that country is. They removed the liquor, fruits, and musical instruments that had been buried with him. The corpse did not yet reek, because of the cold, but had only changed color. The people then dressed him in new trousers, stockings, boots, tunic, a fine cloak with gold buttons, and a fur-trimmed hat. They

carried him onto the ship and into the pavilion, and set him on the mattress, propped up with pillows, before bringing gifts of liquor, fruits, and flowers, followed by bread, meat, and onions. Everything was set before the dead man. At this point they carried in a dog, which they promptly cut in half and set inside the ship, along with the man's weapons, which were placed at his side. They then took two horses and made them gallop until they were sweating; they then cut the horses into pieces with their swords and placed the pieces in the boat too. They likewise killed a rooster and a hen and threw those in also. At this point the slave-girl who had asked to be killed went throughout the entire camp, into every hut, and the master of each hut had sexual intercourse with her. "Tell your master that I did this out of love for him," each said to the girl afterwards.

On Friday afternoon the men led the slave-girl to a construction that resembled the frame of a door and lifted her high by the feet so that she stood overlooking this object. She spoke some words, after which they lowered her; then they lifted her up a second time and she said something more, then was lowered again. This was all repeated a third time. The crowd then brought the girl a young hen. She cut off its head, which she tossed aside, and threw the hen's body into the burial ship. When I asked my interpreter to explain, he said that the first time the men had lifted her she had called out, "I can see my mother and my father!" The second time she had said, "I see all my relatives who have died, all seated together!" The third time, she had called out, "I see my master in paradise—how beautiful and green it is! He is surrounded by servants, young and old! He is calling me—quick, take me to him!" So, then the men led her to the burial-ship. She removed two bracelets she was wearing and handed them to the old woman whose job it was to kill her, the one called the Angel of Death. Next, she took off two rings that she had on her fingers and handed these to the Angel of Death's two daughters, who were in attendance. The crowd then raised her onto the burial-ship, but she halted before entering the pavilion.

The men approached her, carrying shields and staves. Given a cup of liquor, she sang briefly and drank; my guide explained that she was bidding farewell to her slave-girl companions. Given another cup of it, she sang a longer song while the Angel of Death urged her to drink and enter the pavilion where her master lay. It was clear to me that the girl was hesitant. She tried to enter but could only poke her head inside. The Angel of Death, however, quickly seized her by the nape of her neck and guided her in. Instantly the men began to beat their shields with their staves so the girl's cries could not be heard, lest the other slave-girls grew too afraid ever to perform the same task for their masters. Six men then entered the pavilion and one by one they all had sexual relations with the girl, after which they left her laying at her master's side. Two men then held her feet and two others gripped her hands. The Angel of Death then re-entered the pavilion, wound a rope around the girl's neck and placed the ends of the rope in the hands of the last two men. She then drew out a large dagger, which she repeatedly plunged into the girl's chest while the men strangled her with the rope until she was dead.

After the girl was dead and had been laid out next to her master, one of the dead man's family members took a lit piece of wood from a fire and walked naked toward the boat, so that he might set it aflame. He walked backwards, however, keeping his face turned toward the crowd. One hand held the burning torch, while the other covered his exposed backside.

The crowd then came forward, each carrying a piece of tinder or larger firewood, which the kinsman lit with his torch before it was added to the boat. The flames quickly engulfed the piled-up wood, then the boat, the pavilion, the [dead] man and slave-girl, and everything that was on the ship. A strong wind blew and whipped up the flames so they became fiercer and hotter.

One of the Rus men stood beside me, and I overheard him say something to my interpreter. When I asked what he had said, my guide answered, "He says that you Arabs are fools, because you take your most dear and beloved fellows and bury them in the ground where they are eaten by insects and worms, whereas when we burn our beloved ones, they enter paradise immediately." Then he started to laugh loudly. When I asked him to explain, he answered, "Our companion's god loved him so much he sent the wind to carry him away in only an hour." In truth, only an hour had indeed passed before the ship, the wood, the slave-girl and her master were nothing but ashes and cinders.

Then they piled up a mound in the place where the ship had lain after they had pulled it from the river, and in the middle of this mound they erected a tall wooden post on which they carved the man's name and the name of the Rus king at that time. Then they all departed.

STUDY QUESTIONS

1. What type of society emerges from Ibn Fadlan's portrait of the burial customs of the Rus?
2. Shortly after Ibn Fadlan wrote his travelogue, the Rus converted to Christianity. What effect do you think this had on their burial customs?

CHAPTER 11

WORLDS BROUGHT DOWN

11.1 DANTE ALIGHIERI, THREE SPEECHES FROM *THE DIVINE COMEDY*, CA. 1308–1321

Translated below are three famous speeches from Dante's (ca. 1265–1321) *The Divine Comedy,* one each from the *Inferno,* the *Purgatorio,* and the *Paradiso.* In the first, Dante encounters Odysseus, who suffers in the eighth circle of Hell and relates how he arrived there. In the second passage, Dante's guide, the Roman poet Virgil, bids Dante goodbye after leading him through Hell and Purgatory; as a non-Christian, he can ascend no higher. The third speech consists of the hymn to the Virgin Mary that Dante here places in St. Bernard of Clairvaux's mouth, as he begs her assistance in leading Dante to the great climax of the epic: the vision of God. All of the music of Dante's language is lost in translation, but here are my best efforts.

INFERNO 26.90–142

When I finally left Circe, who had held me,
    beguiled,
for more than a year near Gaeta (before it was
    styled
as such by Aeneas), neither love for my child,
nor pity for my father—then bent with age—
nor my love for Penelope—the source of her
    joy—
could overcome my longing for another stage

where I could experience the richness of life
and learn all I could of a world that was rife
with the vices and virtues of men.

That is why I set out for the open sea
with only one ship and a small company
of those by whom I never deserted would be.

From one shore to the next, I went as far as
    España,
and the land of Morocco, and the isle of Sardinia,
and all the other islands that are bathed by the
    sea.

I and my comrades had already grown
old and slow when we finally reached the place
where Hercules set up his guard of stone
to block anyone from venturing beyond.

Translation by Clifford Backman.

On our right was Seville, on our left was Ceuta,
but I sailed on. "O brothers!" I shouted,
"You have seen already many dangers,
a hundred thousand of them, so you're no
strangers
to risk as you've come here, the far west.

You must not now deny yourselves the challenge
of going yet further west, and range
beyond the sun, and explore the unpeopled world.

Remember your lineage, the seed that gave you
birth!
You were not made to live here on Earth
like brutes. You must pursue knowledge and true
worth!"

I so inspired my comrades with this little speech
to continue our journey, they pushed forward
with a screech
and it took all my strength to hold them back,
within reach.

So, turning our ship, with the stern towards
morning,
we pulled on our oars; it was as though they were
wings
and we flew, always somewhat to the left
inclining.

In the sky at night I beheld the strange stars
of the South Pole. The familiar stars, the ones that
were ours,
had fallen from the sky and lay below the
horizon.

Five times did the light from the moon come
down,
and brighten, and fail, after we had left familiar
ground
and to that hard passage we ourselves had bound,

when suddenly a mountain, distant and dark,
rose before us, high over our barque—
the highest mountain I'd ever seen, grim and
stark.

We were glad at first, but our joy turned to sorrow
when from that place a fierce whirlwind did blow
that hammered at our ship and crushed the prow.

Three times the whirlwind whipped us around,
and then a fourth time the cyclone wound
and flipped us, stern skyward, our prow pointing
down.

And as though Someone desired it: the ship sank,
and we drowned.

PURGATORIO 27.115–142

"Today your hungering will be put
to peaceful rest through the sweet fruit
that all mortals seek among life's branches."

Thus did Virgil speak, and to his solemn words
nothing ever spoken to me before
could compare, for the delight they offered.

Urge upon urge to climb ever higher
came upon me, and with every new step
I felt the strength of wings lifting me up.

When the whole staircase lay beneath us
and we stood at last on the highest step,
Virgil fixed his eyes on me, and said:

"My son, you have now seen the passing
and the eternal fires, and have reached the place
beyond which I cannot go.

I have brought you to this point through wit and art;
but now let joyfulness be your guide.
You have passed steeps and narrows. Now, the
other side!

Behold the sun that shines upon your brow!
See there! Grasses and flowers and shrubs
that the Earth produces, all on its own.

You can rest here now, or stroll a while
until you behold the glad and lovely eyes
that once, full of tears, sent me to your side.

Expect no other word or signal from me.
Your will is now strong and healthy and free;
to act against it would be a mistake.

I crown and miter you, lord of yourself."

PARADISO 3 3.1–21

O Virgin Mother, daughter of your own son,
most humble and exalted of all creatures,
fixed goal of all in God's eternal plan,

it was you who so ennobled human nature
so greatly that He Who created us did not disdain
to make Himself man, one with His creation.

Within your womb was rekindled the love
that provided the warmth needed for this flower
to come to bloom within this everlasting peace.

For all here in Paradise you are the noon-time torch
of charity—and down on earth, for mortal men,
you are the living spring of hope.

Lady, you are so great and so powerful,
that anyone who seeks grace without turning to
    you
is like one wishing to fly without wings.

Not only does your loving kindness race
to anyone who asks for it, but it often times
flows freely even before the asking.

In you is compassion, in you is pity,
in you generosity—in you is brought together
everything that is good in creation.

Here is a man, who from the lowest depth
of the universe up to this high place
has witnessed, one by one, the lives of souls;

he begs you to grant him through your grace
the power to lift his vision higher still,
to witness the goal of salvation.

And I, who never burned for my own vision
more than I burn for his, offer you all my
    prayers—
and I pray they are enough—

that you, through your own prayers,
    may disperse
the cloud of his mortality, that he might have
the Sum of All Joy revealed to his eyes.

I pray you also, O Queen who can achieve
whatever you wish, keep his affections sound
once he has had his vision, and returns.

May you protect him from the stirrings of the
    flesh.
Behold!—Beatrice, with all the saints,
clasp their hands in prayer, to win your
    assent!"

STUDY QUESTIONS

1. What vision of the cosmos is conveyed by these three speeches?
2. Why is Odysseus condemned to the inferno? What does Virgil represent? Why can he not ascend any higher than Purgatory? How is Bernard of Clairvaux's hymn to the Virgin representative of the cult of Mary?

11.2 DANTE ALIGHIERI, *THE DIVINE COMEDY*, "PAOLO AND FRANCESCO IN HELL," CA. 1308–1321

Dante's great epic tells of his journey through Hell, Purgatory, and Heaven, guided at first by the Roman poet Virgil and then by his beloved Beatrice. Hell consists of a deep, terraced pit, each level representing a different sin, where the souls of the lost receive their fitting punishments. After passing through Limbo (where dwell the souls of the virtuous non-Christians—Homer, Plato, Aristotle, Caesar, Cicero, Averroës, Avicenna, and Saladin among them), they enter the circle of the Lustful. Dante sees many famous lovers, but spends most of his time visiting with two contemporaries of his, Francesca da Rimini and her lover Paolo Malatesta, who was also her brother-in-law.

After I heard my Master recite the names
  Of all these lovers—knights and dames—
I was dazed with pity, confused, and ashamed.
I said, "With all my heart, dear Poet, I wish to speak
  With those two there, who move with such mystique,
  Gliding lightly on the winds, both strong and weak."
And he said, "You will see, when they draw near,
  That if you ask them, in the name of their love so dear,
  To tell their tale, they will comply. Soon you will hear."
Then a gusty blast drove the pair beside us
  And I called over the wind, "If it not be denied us,
  O battered souls, come and tell us your tale. Oblige us."
Like doves who, driven by desire and will,
  Stretch out their wings and soar high until
  They reach their nest, ready to take their fill
Of their love, so did these two fly from the throng there

That surrounded Dido, toward us, through the malignant air,
  So strongly did my tender call affect the pair.
"O gracious creature, O one so good,
  Who through even this foul atmosphere would
  Come visit us, who stained the world with blood!
Were it in our power to be friends with the Universal King
  We would ask Him to grant you peace, for you bring
  A spirit of generous pity for the pain we're suffering.
Whatever you wish to say, to ask, or to know,
  Is our pleasure to help your understanding to grow,
  Especially here where the mighty wind has ceased to blow.
The land where I was born lies on the shore
  Where the Po River and the waters that feed it, both great and poor,
  Flow to where they flow no more.
Love, which quickly can seize the most gentle heart,

Translation by Clifford Backman.

Gripped this man here—he lusted for my
body's art
In a way that still tears my soul apart.
Then Love, which spares no beloved from love's
ration,
Gripped me as well with such a lusty passion
That, as you see, it binds us still, in a fashion.
And Love then caused us both to die;
Cain's Hell awaits our killer!—That is our cry!"
Such were the words the air carried, like a sigh.
When those guilty souls had finished their tale
I bowed my head in sadness at their betrayal.
My Poet asked, "What do you think of
suffering on that scale?"
At length I spoke: "Master, I cannot explain:
All those sweet thoughts of love, and desire's
strain,
Brought these two lovers so much pain!"
Then I turned to the pair and tried to speak.
"Francesca," I began, "the torment you suffer
is so bleak
That my eyes fill with tears that roll down my
cheek.
But please, I beg you: In your blissful hours—
How, by what signs, did Love's great powers
Allow the two of you to know each other's
desires?"
"There is no pain that is greater," she began, "(if
I may),
Than to remember, here, on this grim-bleak
day,

The happiness we had then. Your Guide
knows, and can say
As much! But if you truly wish to know
How such a love as ours did grow,
I'll tell you—my words and tears both shall
flow.
One day we sat reading, to pass the time,
Of Sir Lancelot's [and Guinevere's] passionate
crime.
We were alone, and innocent, and in our
prime.
Over and over again, as we read, our eyes
Met, and our faces flushed, and with tender
sighs
We yielded—at the moment when with
passionate cries
Those two lovers brought together their trembling
lips.
Imagining that he was, like Lancelot, in the
grips
Of like love, this one here, who forever trips
By my side, gently kissed me. I doubt not
whether
It was that book which brought us together;
And yet all that day we read no further."
As she spoke these lines, poor Guido wept
So fully and movingly that pity swept
Over me. Dazed and swooning, I then
stepped
To one side, and fell near-dead to Hell's stony
floor.

STUDY QUESTIONS

1. How do Francesca and Paolo embody the code of chivalry? How do they transgress the code?
   What is the meaning of the reference to Lancelot?
2. What attitude does Dante take toward Paolo and Francesca?

11.3 GIOVANNI BOCCACCIO, "THE GREAT PLAGUE," 1353

The Decameron is Giovanni Boccaccio's (1313–1375) literary masterpiece, a tapestry of one hundred short stories told by a group of friends who fled Florence at the outbreak of the Black Death; to amuse themselves, each tells a story—one each day for ten days. Boccaccio prefaced the collection with a famous prologue that sets the scene; it is one of the most powerful surviving contemporary descriptions of the plague that hit Europe at the very end of 1347. Boccaccio lost his father to the plague, a fact that probably inspired the somber description he offers below.

I tell you, then, that in the 1348th year from the Blessed Incarnation of the Son of God there appeared in Florence, the fairest of all Italian cities, the deadly plague. Whether it was spread by the influence of the celestial bodies, or came upon us men through the just wrath of the Lord as punishment for our sins, it had originated many years earlier in the East, where it annihilated innumerable people, propagating itself relentlessly from place to place until it came at last, calamitously, to the West.

In Florence, in the early spring of the aforesaid year, the wretched effects of the disease appeared for the first time, with symptoms that were beyond belief—and despite all that human ingenuity and care could think of to avert it: the whole city cleansed of pollutants by officials appointed especially for the purpose, the refusal to admit entry into the town by anyone appearing ill, and the adoption of countless other precautions to maintain good health. Despite too all the humble prayers addressed to God, and chanted repeatedly in public processions, by the devout.

The symptoms of the sick differed from those in the East, where a nosebleed was the first visible hint of the inevitable approach of death. Among the men and women in Florence alike, the first sign of the pestilence was the appearance of certain tumors in the groin or the armpits. These swellings usually grew to the size of an apple or of an egg; sometimes, larger, sometimes smaller. The common folk called these tumors *gavoccioli*. From the groins and armpits these *gavoccioli* spread quickly and randomly in every direction. Once the spreading had begun, a second symptom appeared: livid black spots along the arms and thighs. Sometimes these spots were few in number but large in size; sometimes they were just the opposite—many but small. The spots were as certain a sign of the victim's approaching death as were the *gavoccioli*. Every effort by physicians, whether in technique or medicine, proved no match for either the symptoms or the sickness itself. Whether because the plague was fundamentally untreatable or because our physicians were simply not up to the challenge, hardly anyone contracted the disease and recovered; instead, most victims were dead within three days of the first visible symptom and usually without showing a fever or any other accompanying symptom. Apart from the actual physicians, a horde of men and women without the least bit of medical knowledge tried to care for the sick, but in their ignorance they applied all the wrong remedies.

The viciousness of the plague was made even worse by every type of human contact, which passed the disease from one person to another just as a raging fire devours every flammable thing brought in contact with it. But this proved even worse, for a

Translation by Clifford Backman.

person did not need to touch or converse with an inflicted sufferer in order to place himself in immediate and deadly peril; anyone who even touched the clothes of the sick, or anything else that the sufferer had used or touched, was apt to contract the disease.

What I am about to say seems unbelievable, and if many so people—myself included—had not witnessed it directly, I would hardly dare to write it down; a single witness would never suffice.

So virulent and unstoppable was the pestilence that it was propagated not only from person to person but, even more startling, it was observed many times to spread from objects belonging to one of the sick or newly dead to some animal (that is, not a human being at all) and to cause not merely the animal's sickening but its almost instantaneous death. Let me describe for you something I once saw with my own eyes. The rags of a poor beggar who had succumbed to the plague were left lying it a street; two hogs approached and rooted their snouts around in them and then, taking them in their teeth, slapped the rags back and forth with shakes of their heads, and then all of a sudden they convulsed once or twice and dropped to the ground dead, as though poisoned. They fell on the very rags they had been unlucky enough to disturb.

These happenings, plus countless others that were similar in nature or even worse, caused a host of fears and wild beliefs to take root among those who survived, with the result that they settled on a single and cruel precaution—namely, they all sought to preserve their own health by avoiding or running away from anyone who was sick and from anything that belonged to them. . . .

In the face of so much suffering and misery, all respect for law—whether divine or human—broke down and virtually disappeared, because the administrators and executors of the laws were, like everyone else, either dead or ill, and they had too few subordinate officials available to carry out any of their duties. The result? Everyone was free to do whatever they wanted. Most people steered a middle course between the extremes of either fasting obsessively (like some did) or indulging themselves in drinking and wantonness (as many others did). Instead, they simply took care to meet their needs and satisfy their appetites. Instead of locking themselves away, they walked about freely—although usually with a posy of flowers in their hands, or a bundle of fragrant herbs or a packet of different spices, which they continually pressed to their noses, thinking to comfort their brains against the stench of corpses, sick bodies, and medicine that filled the air. Others pursued the more selfish but probably safer alternative of simply running away, believing that the best and most effective measure against the disease was distance. Convinced of this, and caring for no one but themselves, vast numbers of men and women abandoned the city, their homes, their relatives, their estates and belongings altogether and fled to the countryside or even further, as if God in His wrath would use this plague to punish mankind for its sins on the basis of where they happened to be, and attack only those who happened to be within city walls. Perhaps they thought that the entire urban population would be annihilated, that the city's last hour had finally arrived.

Not all the people in any particular group died; nor did all the people in any particular group survive. To the contrary, many fell ill in each and every camp. But having established themselves as examples to the healthy, those who survived languished away with virtually no one to care for them, abandoned by everyone. Not only did one town-dweller avoid another, neighbor avoid neighbor, or relative avoid relative, everyone communicating only at great distance, but the plague had so struck people's hearts that brothers abandoned brothers, uncles their nephews, sisters their brothers, and even wives their husbands. Worst of all, and almost beyond belief, mothers and fathers deserted their own children and refused to care for them, abandoning them like strangers. . . .

Many people died, therefore, who might have survived if they had received any help. That is why, apart from the natural virulence of the plague itself, the number of deaths reported day and night was so enormous that it dumbfounded everyone who heard it, to say nothing of the people who witnessed it directly. And that is why a number of new customs arose among those who survived, customs altogether contrary to established ways of doing things. . . .

Among the city's common folk, the burghers for the most part, a pathetic spectacle appeared.

Whether immobilized by hopelessness or unable to leave because of concern for their property, they remained in the city and so fell ill by the thousands every day, and lacking anyone to care for them or help them, they almost inevitably died without exception. Many dropped dead right in the streets, day and night; others, who died in their homes, were only discovered when the stench of their rotting corpses caught their neighbors' attention. As a result, dead bodies lay everywhere. People soon fell into a regular routine, more out of fear of contamination by the corpses than out of respect or affection for the dead: acting alone or with the help of others, they would take the bodies of the newly deceased out of their homes and leave them lying outside their front doors. Anyone who came down the street, especially early in the morning, thus saw countless corpses every day. Funeral biers were then sent for, and if there were none of these available, workers carrying mere planks of wood would cart the bodies away. It was not uncommon to see a single bier that had two or even three corpses on it—a husband and wife, perhaps, or a group of siblings, or a father and his son, or some other clutch of relatives. It would be impossible to count the number of times when two priests, carrying a cross in front of a bier on the way to a burial, would suddenly have three or four other biers fall in line behind them; thinking themselves on their way to conduct a single burial, they would find by the time they reached the churchyard that they were six, seven, or eight more to perform. Even so, no tears or candles or mourners were involved, to honor the dead. Conditions were so bad that most people showed no more care for the human dead than nowadays they show for a dead goat, for it was quite clear that death—the one thing that, in normal times, no wise man ever accepted with patience (even though it happened relatively rarely and unobtrusively)—had been brought home to even the most feeble-minded; the problem was that the catastrophe was so unimaginably great that no one was really able to care. There were so many corpses arriving at all the churches every day, and almost by the hour, that in no time at all they ran out of consecrated ground, especially if, as by ancient custom, they were to grant a separate burial plot for each person. So when all the graves were filled up, they dug huge pits in the churchyard, into which they placed newly arrived corpses by the hundreds, piling them atop each other like ship's cargo with only a thin layer of dirt over each, until each pit was filled.

In addition to all the calamities we suffered in the city, I ought to make clear for you that the dreadful things happening in the city were suffered in the countryside as well. In all the fortified towns the situation was just as in Florence, although on a smaller scale, but in the rural villages and the countryside proper the poor miserable peasants and their families, having no physicians or servants to help them in any way, collapsed in the dirt lanes, in their fields and cottages at all hours of day and night, dying more like animals than human beings. Like the townspeople, they paid no attention to their duties or possessions, believing each day might be their last, and so they did not bother to till the fields or tend to their animals or do anything to prepare for a future. Instead they just abandoned what they had, with the result that their oxen, asses, sheep, goats, pigs, chickens—even their faithful dogs—were driven away and allowed to roam at will through the fields, where the unreaped and ungathered crops were simply neglected. . . .

What more can be said, except that the cruelty of heaven (and possibly, to some degree, the cruelty of mankind) was so terrible that between March and June of that year, by the fierceness of the plague and the fact that so many of the sick were poorly cared for or flat-out abandoned at their neediest moment because the healthy were too frightened to approach them, more than one hundred thousand people died within the walls of Florence.

STUDY QUESTIONS

1. What makes Boccaccio's description of the plague "modern"?
2. What effects does the plague have on Florentine society?

11.4 JULIAN OF NORWICH, *REVELATIONS OF DIVINE LOVE*, AFTER 1373

Julian of Norwich (1342–ca. 1416) was an English anchoress who, near the age of thirty, received mystical visions of Jesus during a near-death experience. She recorded these visions in an English text that brought the message of God's unlimited love during a time of plague, war, and suffering. The main message of Julian's work is the unity of love from God—a notion often meditated on by Christian mystics, which floods the soul with light and warmth. Though she was never canonized, Julian remains a model of mystical devotion, particularly for those who suffer.

2

And when I was thirty and a half years old, God sent me a bodily sickness in which I lay for three days and three nights; and on the fourth night I received all the rites of the Holy Church and did not believe that I would live until morning. And after this I lingered on for two days and two nights. And on the third night I often thought that I was dying, and so did those who were with me. But at this time I was very sorry and reluctant to die, not because there was anything on earth that I wanted to live for, nor because I feared anything, for I trusted in God, but because I wanted to live so as to love God better and for longer, so that through the grace of longer life I might know and love God better in the bliss of heaven. For it seemed to me that all the short time I could live here was as nothing compared with that heavenly bliss. So I thought, "My good Lord, may my ceasing to live be to your glory!" And I was answered in my reason, and by the pains I felt, that I was dying. And I fully accepted the will of God with all the will of my heart.

So I endured till day, and by then my body was dead to all sensation from the waist down. Then I felt I wanted to be in a sitting position, leaning with my head back against the bedding, so that my heart could be more freely at God's disposition, and so that I could think of God while I was still alive; and those who were with me sent for the parson, my parish priest, to be present at my death. He came,

and a boy with him, and brought a cross, and by the time he came my eyes were fixed and I could not speak. The parson set the cross before my face and said, "Daughter, I have brought you the image of your Saviour. Look upon it and be comforted, in reverence to Him that died for you and me." It seemed to me that I was well as I was, for my eyes were looking fixedly upwards into heaven, where I trusted that I was going. But nevertheless, I consented to fix my eyes on the face of the crucifix if I could, so as to be able to do so for longer until the moment of my death; because I thought that I might be able to bear looking straight ahead for longer than I could manage to look upwards. After this my sight began to fail and the room was dim all around me, as dark as if it had been night, except that in the image of the cross an ordinary, household light remained— I could not understand how. Everything except the cross was ugly to me, as if crowded with fiends. After this I felt as if the upper part of my body was beginning to die. My hands fell down on either side, and my head settled down sideways for weakness. The greatest pain that I felt was shortness of breath and failing of life. Then I truly believed that I was at the point of death. And at this moment all my suffering suddenly left me, and I was as completely well, especially the upper part of my body, as I ever was before or after. I marveled at this change, for it seemed to me a mysterious work of God, not a natural one. And yet, although I felt comfortable, I still did not expect to live, nor did feeling more comfortable comfort me entirely, for I felt that I would rather have been released from this world, for in my heart I was willing to die.

3

And it suddenly occurred to me that I should entreat our Lord graciously to give me the second wound, so that He would fill my whole body with remembrance of the feeling of His blessed Passion, as I had prayed before; for I wanted His pains to be my pains, with compassion, and then longing for God. Yet in this I never asked for a bodily sight or any kind of showing of God, but for fellow-suffering, such as it seemed to me a naturally kind soul might feel for our Lord Jesus, Who was willing to become a moral man for love. I wanted to suffer with Him, while living in my mortal body, as God would give me grace.

And I suddenly saw the red blood trickling down from under the crown of thorns, all hot, freshly, plentifully and vividly, just as I imagined it was at the moment when the crown of thorns was thrust on to His blessed head—He who was both God and man, the same who suffered for me. I believed truly and strongly that it was He Himself who showed me this, without any intermediary, and then I said, *"Benedicite dominus!"* Because I meant this with such deep veneration, I said it in a very loud voice; and I was astounded, feeling wonder and admiration that He was willing to be so familiar with a sinful being living in this wretched flesh. I supposed at the time that our Lord Jesus of His courteous love would show me comfort before the time of my temptation. For I thought it might well be, by God's permission and under his protection, that I would be tempted by fiends before I died. With this sight of the blessed Passion, along with the Godhead that I saw in my mind, I saw that I, yes, and every creature living that would be saved, could have strength to resist all the fiends of hell and all spiritual enemies.

4

And at the same time that I saw this bodily sight, our Lord showed me a spiritual vision of Gis familiar love. I saw that for us He is everything that is good and comforting and helpful. He is our clothing, wrapping

and enveloping us for love, embracing us and guiding us in all things, handing about us in tender love, so that He can never leave us. And so, in this vision, as I understand it, I saw truly that He is everything that is good for us.

And in this vision He showed me a little thing, the size of a hazel-nut, lying in the palm of my hand, and to my mind's eye it was as round as any ball. I looked at it and thought, "What can this be?" And the answer came to me, "It is all that is made," I wondered how it could last, for it was so small I thought it might suddenly disappear. And the answer in my mind was, "It lasts and will last forever because God loves it; and in the same way everything exists through the love of God." In this little thing I saw three attributes: the first is that God made it, the second is that He loves it, the third is that God cares for it. But what does that mean to me? Truly, the maker, the lover, the carer; for until I become one substance with Him, I can never have love, rest or true bliss; that is to say, until I am so bound to Him that there may be no created thing between my God and me. And who shall do this deed? Truly, Himself, by His mercy and His grave, for He has made me and blessedly restored me to that end.

Then God brought our Lady into my mind. I saw her spiritually in bodily likeness, a meek and simple maid, young of age, in the same bodily form as when she conceived. God also showed me part of the wisdom and truth of her soul so that I understood with what reverence she beheld her God Who is her maker, and how reverently she marveled that He chose to be born of her, a simple creature of His own making. For what made her marvel was that He Who was her Maker chose to be born of the creature He had made. And the wisdom of her faithfulness, and knowledge of the greatness of her Maker and the littleness of her who was made, moved her to say very humbly to the angel Gabriel, "Behold, the handmaid of the Lord." With this sight I really understood that she is greater in worthiness and fullness of grace than all that God made below her; for nothing that is made is above her except the blessed Manhood of Christ. This little thing that is made that is below our Lady Saint Mary, God showed it to me as small as if it had been a hazel-nut. It was so small I thought it might have disappeared.

In this blessed revelation God showed me three nothings. Of these nothings this was the first I was shown, and all men and women who wish to lead the contemplative life need to have knowledge of it: they should choose to set at nothing everything that is made so as to have the love of God Who is unmade. This is why those who choose to occupy themselves with earthly business and are always pursuing worldly success have nothing here of

God in their hearts and souls: because they love and seek their rest in this little thing where there is no rest, and know nothing of God, Who is almighty, all wise and all good, for He is true rest. God wishes to be known, and is pleased that we should rest in Him; for all that is below Him does nothing to satisfy us. And this is why, until all that is made seems as nothing, no soul can be at rest. When a soul sets all at nothing for love, to have Him Who is everything that is good, then it is able to receive spiritual rest.

STUDY QUESTIONS

1. In what specific ways does Julian "experience" the suffering of Jesus in his Passion?
2. Does her vision of the Virgin Mary underscore the different experiences of a *female* mystic?

11.5 FROM FROISSART, "ON FLAGELLANTS," 1369–1400

A contemporary chronicler, Jean Froissart (ca. 1337–ca. 1405) offers a glimpse of the horrific world of the Black Death, which ravaged Europe in a virulent first bout in 1348–50, killing perhaps as much as 40 percent of the population. The Flagellants (from the Latin "to whip") were a penitential group that traveled in procession from city to city—unwittingly spreading the very disease they hoped to alleviate. Froissart's account reveals the panic that beset people in the face of chronic and inexplicable death and helps us understand how rational fourteenth-century citizens could turn to such drastic actions.

In the year of grace 1349 of Our Lord a group of penitents appeared, coming initially from Germany— wild people who performed their penance in public by scourging their backs with whips studded with

small iron points. With these whips they lashed themselves mercilessly between their shoulders. Some few of them were women who dressed in bloodstained rags; they feared for their souls and despaired of what

Translation by Clifford Backman.

the world might come to in the absence of a miracle. In doing their penance they chanted the most pitiable dirges about the birth and holy suffering of Our Lord, and implored God to end the plague. For it was a time of death, suffering, and plague, with people dropping dead all of a sudden throughout the whole world—at least a third of the human population.

The penitents I just mentioned travelled in companies from village to village, city to city, wearing hoods made of felt. Each company had its own color. By custom, law, and ordinance they could stay in each village only a single night and were pledged to proceed on their pilgrimage for thirty-three and a half days—one day for each year of Jesus Christ's earthly life, as the Holy Scriptures testify. Each company, therefore, processed for the prescribed thirty-three and a half days, after which it returned again to whatever village, city, or castle from which it had originally set out. They lacked for nothing throughout their pilgrimages, for the good people of each village and town they passed through provided them with food and refreshment. They never lodged in these places, though, out of fear that doing so might spread the malady even faster. Instead, whenever they entered anyone's home for food or refreshment they first kneeled as a group, out of humility, and recited three Our Fathers and three Hail Marys, and they always repeated the gesture when they took their leave.

They resolved countless conflicts and established fair peace continuously, these penitents and the good people who supported them; wherever there were people of differing opinions who could come to no agreement, they found compromise after the penitents intervened.

Included in their ordinances were many intelligent and useful things, and it was either these sound ideas or simple human nature that inclined these companies' members to go on these penitential processions. Whatever the case, they did not enter the kingdom of France, for Pope Innocent, who was then in office and living in Avignon, and his cardinals had given these companies some thought and had come to a firm decision about the penitents. They declared that public penance, and public support for it, was neither permissible nor acceptable; in fact, they declared that it was forbidden. Henceforth any clergy who was among them or was a member of their company or who served them as a curate, canon, or chaplain, or who shared their opinions was to be deprived of his benefice—and if he desired absolution, he would have to request it directly from Avignon. If one contrasts this decree with all that is generally known, one can see that the popes and the kings of France regarded them as enemies and rebels, and would not suffer another Hainault. For if the penitents were to make it to Cambrai or Saint-Quentin they would be able to reach the coast. If it should happen that the penitents got that far, and if any new people joined them, the Jews [in those cities] might fear for their lives and flee, being gone for more than two hundred years. For they have a saying:

> And there will come knights carrying iron mallets who will be terribly cruel, but lacking a leader they will not be able to exert their might or perform deeds outside the German empire. Nevertheless, when they come, we will all be killed.

So they'll flee, and truly at that time countless Jews will be slaughtered in land after land until at last the popes and the kings of Spain, Aragon, and Navarre, with great effort, will re-establish peace for them.

STUDY QUESTIONS

1. What did the Flagellants see as the primary cause of the Black Death?
2. How and why did they encounter opposition from church authorities?

11.6 JAKOB TWINGER, *CHRONICLE*, ca. 1382–1420

Jakob Twinger (1346–1420) was born at Königshofen, a small village near the city of Strasbourg. Ordained a priest in 1382, he began to write his *Chronicle* in the same year of his ordination and continued to add to it until his death, by which time he had brought the narrative forward to 1415. In 1395 he was appointed a canon of the Church of St. Thomas in Strasbourg and placed in charge of maintaining its archives—a source from which he regularly drew for his history. The passage below recounts the massacres visited on the Jews of Strasbourg in the wake of the Black Death.

In the year of Our Lord 1349 the most terrible pestilence in history occurred, spreading death from one end of the Earth to the other. Rampaging both on this side and the far side of the sea—it was in fact even deadlier among the Muslims than among the Christians—it killed so many people that in some places hardly a single person was left alive. Ships floated adrift on the sea, their holds bulging with goods, but with the entire crew dead and no one left to steer the ship. In Marseilles, the bishop and all the priests and monks died, taking more than half the city's population with them. In other cities and districts so many people perished that the desolation can hardly be described. The pope in Avignon cancelled the entire court's activities and locked himself in his chamber; no one was granted admission to him at all, and he kept a fire roaring in his room day and night. What had caused the epidemic? Even the wisest scholars and physicians could say only that it had to be the will of God. The effect of the plague here in Strasbourg was the same as elsewhere, and it lasted more than an entire year. Arriving in the summer of 1349, it killed approximately sixteen thousand people.

Everywhere throughout the world blame for the plague fell upon the Jews, who were loathed for supposedly causing the pestilence by poisoning the water-wells, and so they were thrown to the flames everywhere from the Mediterranean to Germany (except for in the city of Avignon, where the pope protected them). In the Swiss towns of Berne and Zofingen a number of Jews admitted, after being tortured, to poisoning the wells—and the poison was even found, so the townsmen burned the Jews throughout the region and wrote of their actions to the people in Strasbourg, Freiburg, and Basel, so that they might do the same.

Officials in the first two cities refused to take similar action—although in Basel the populace marched on the city hall and forced the town council to swear that they would in fact burn the Jews living there and never allow another Jew into the city for two hundred years; all the Jews of Basel were therefore arrested, and a hearing was scheduled to meet at Benfeld. The bishop of Strasbourg, all the nobility of Alsace, and representatives of the townsmen of Strasbourg, Freiburg, and Basel were in attendance, and they asked the Strasbourg officials what they intended to do with the arrested Jews. The officials replied that they had no cause to take action against the Jews, and demanded to know why the citizens of the city had closed up the wells and put away all the buckets. A huge, indignant roar rose

Translation by Clifford Backman.

from the crowd, and in the end it was the bishop and nobles of Strasbourg, and the people of the imperial cities, who decided to do away with the Jews— and as a result of their resolve, Jews throughout the region were fed to the flames. Jews who were merely expelled from their towns were invariably captured by the nearby peasant and were either cut down or drowned. . . .

[In Strasbourg, the officials who had refused to punish the Jews were deposed and replaced by a new council that gave in to the demands of the mob.]

On St. Valentine's Day, a Saturday, the new council had the Jews burned to death atop a wooden platform that they had ordered built in the Jews' cemetery; there were about two thousand of them, and they were all put to death, except for the few who declared themselves willing to receive baptism. Some children were pulled from the flames at the last moment and were forcibly baptized, against the will of their fathers and mothers who looked on. All debts to the Jews were cancelled, first, so the Jews were forced to surrender all pledges and bonds that they had taken as collateral. The town council seized all the Jews' cash, and divided it among the commoners. The money, of course, was the Jews' downfall. If they had been poor, and if the nobles had not been in debt to them, they would never have been killed. Once their money was distributed to the citizens, some of them gave a share of it to the local cathedral or some other church, on the advice of their confessors.

That is how the Jews of Strasbourg came to be burned. Much the same thing happened to the Jews in all the Rhineland cities, whether Free or Imperial or belonging to the nobles. Some places gave the Jews a trial, first; others, not. And in some places the Jews set fire to their own homes and cremated themselves. Afterwards, officials in Strasbourg decided that no Jew should be allowed to enter the city for a hundred years, but less than twenty years later a new council voted to permit Jews back. Thus did Jews return to Strasbourg in the year 1368 after the Incarnation of Our Lord.

STUDY QUESTIONS

1. According to Twinger, how are the Jews to blame for the plague?
2. Compare Twinger's account of the plague with Boccaccio's (Document 11.3). How are they different?

CHAPTER 12

RENAISSANCES AND REFORMATIONS

12.1 FRANCESCO PETRARCA, "LETTER TO POSTERITY"

This letter, which Francesco Petrarca (1304–1374) never finished, represents something of an autobiographical obituary. In it, he offers a summary of his life and achievements, which, interestingly, does not include his vernacular love poetry. He wanted above all to be remembered as a scholar, a lover of classical antiquity, and a Latin poet—especially as the author of the (paralyzingly dull) epic poem *Africa*, about the Roman general Scipio Africanus. Petrarca carries his life story as far forward as 1341; he left no notes about what he intended to include in the presumed second half of the letter.

It is possible that you may have heard of me, but I doubt it; a name as obscure and insignificant as mine cannot have travelled far in either time or space. But if you have heard of me, it may interest you to know the kind of man I was, or the results of my long labors—especially those you may have heard of, or, at any rate, those whose titles may have reached you.

To begin with myself, then, I should warn you that the things men say about me will differ considerably, since men are usually more influenced by whim than by truth whenever they are passing judgment on another; there is no limit to either praise or blame. The truth is that I was one of you, a poor mortal, of no exalted origin but neither of terribly lowly birth. I simply belonged, as Augustus Caesar once said of himself, to an ancient family. In disposition, I was not naturally perverse, nor was I wanting in modesty except as the contagion of custom may have corrupted me. My youth was gone before I realized it, and young manhood carried me away. Maturity eventually brought me to my senses and taught me, through experience, the truth I had long before read in books—namely, that youth and pleasure are vain. . . . In my prime I was blessed with an agile and active, though not particularly strong, body, and although I cannot boast of having been terribly handsome, I was good-looking enough in those days. I had a clear complexion, somewhere between light and dark, and I had lively eyes. For many years I enjoyed keen vision, but it deserted me all of a sudden around my

Translation by Clifford Backman.

sixtieth birthday and forced me, reluctantly, to wear glasses. I had always been perfectly healthy, but old age brought its usual array of complaints.

My parents were good people, Florentines both, and not very well off. I may as well admit it: they were in fact on the verge of poverty. They had been expelled from their native city, which is why I was born in exile at Arezzo, in 1304. . . . I have always been contemptuous of wealth; but it is not that I would not have liked to be rich—I simply hate the work and worry that seem always to accompany wealth. I never cared to give great banquets and have led a much happier life with a plain diet and ordinary foods. . . . On the other hand, the pleasure of dining with friends is great, and nothing gives me more delight than the unexpected arrival of a friend. Nothing irks me more than ostentation, for not only is it bad in itself, being opposed to humility, but it is distracting and annoying.

In my younger years I struggled constantly with an all-consuming but pure love affair, my only one, and I would have struggled with it even longer had not my love's premature death (bitter, but in the end, salutary for me) extinguished the last flames. I wish I could say that I have been free of the lusts of the flesh, but I would be lying if I did. I can at least say this, though: even while I was occasionally swept away by the ardor of my youth and temperament, I always detested such sins from the very depths of my soul. . . .

I have taken pride in others, though never in myself, and even as insignificant as I have been, I have also thought myself even more so. In anger I have often injured myself but never another. I have always had the greatest desire for honorable friendships, and have cherished them faithfully. I can make the following boast without fear, for I know I am speaking sincerely: while I am prone to taking offense, I am quick to forget—and I never fail to remember acts of generosity. I have had the good fortune to associate with kings and princes, and to enjoy the friendship of nobles, to such a point as to excite envy. But it is the cruel fate of aging that eventually we weep for friends who have passed away. Some of the greatest kings of this age have courted and cherished my friendship. They may know why. I certainly do not. With some of them I was on such terms that they seemed, in some

way, to be my guests, rather than I theirs. Their eminence in no way discomforted me; in fact, it brought me many advantages. I kept well away from many others of whom I was quite fond, for my innate longing for freedom was so strong that I carefully avoided those whose eminence seemed to threaten the liberty I loved so much.

I had more of a well-balanced mind than a keen one, one suited to many kinds of good and wholesome study but especially inclined to moral philosophy and poetry. Over time I paid less and less attention to the latter and found delight in sacred literature, discovering in it a hidden sweetness that I had earlier failed to appreciate. I came to regard works of poetry as mere amenities. I found many subjects interesting, yet focused especially on the study of antiquity, for I have always disliked our own age so much that, were it not for the love of those dearest to me, I would have preferred to live in any other period than our own. To forget the world in which we live, I have always striven to place my mind in other ages—and thus I came to love history. The conflicting opinions of people about the past have never offended me. When in doubt, I have made it a point to accept what seems to me the most probable explanation, or simply to yield to the authority of the historian I was reading. . . .

Along the breezy banks of the Rhône river I spent my boyhood, under the care of my parents, and then I spent my adolescence under the guidance of my own vanities. There were some long intervals spent abroad, though. I spent four years in the little town of Carpentras, which lies a little to the east of Avignon. In these two places I learned all that I could, considering my age, of grammar, logic, and rhetoric; or rather, I learned as much as is usually taught in school—and you, dear reader, will know how little that is. I then moved on to Montpellier for four years, to study law, and then to Bologna for three years more. . . . I was twenty-two when I finally returned home. Since habit has nearly the force of nature to it, I call Avignon—my place of exile—home. I was already beginning to make a name for myself there, and my friendship was sought by a number of prominent people. Why? I do not really know. I confess that it is now a source of surprise to me, although it seemed a natural enough thing then, when I was at the age when we are used to thinking ourselves deserving of the highest respect. I was courted first and foremost by the eminent and noble Colonna family, which then adorned the Roman Curia with their presence. . . . I spent many years in the house of Cardinal Giovanni Colonna, the brother of Giacomo, living not like a servant to Giovanni's lord but as if he were my father, or even better, my loving brother. It felt like living in my very own home. In time, though, youthful curiosity drove me to visit France and Germany. I invented a number of reasons to justify the journey to my elders, but the real impulse was simply my burning desire to see new sights. I went first to Paris, since I wanted to learn what was true in what I had heard about the city, and what was nonsense. Returning from this journey I went straightaway to Rome, which I had wanted to see ever since I was a child. There I soon came to revere Stefano Colonna, the great family's noble patriarch, an ancient hero who welcomed me in every possible way, as though I were his own son. The love and good will with which this marvelous man treated me lasted until the end of his life, and it lives on in my heart, where it will never fade until I myself cease to be.

Upon returning, I instantly felt the revulsion I have always had for city life, especially for the disgusting city of Avignon, which I truly abhorred. Seeking some means of escape, I was lucky enough to discover, about fifteen miles away, a delightful valley, narrow and secluded, called Vaucluse, where the Sorgue river (that prince of streams!) has its source. The charm of the site captivated me, and so I moved there together with all my books. If I were to tell you all that I did during my many years there, it would be a long story indeed. Almost every bit of writing I produced [in those years] was either done or begun there, or was at least conceived there; and those writings have been so numerous that even today they keep me busy and weary. My mind is like my body—more agile than strong; and while it was quite easy for me to think up new projects, I dropped many when they proved too difficult to carry out.

Inspired by the beauty of my surroundings, I undertook to write a pastoral or bucolic song: my *Bucolicum Carmen*. I also wrote *The Life of Solitude* (*De vita solitaria*), in two books, which I dedicated to the great man who is now Cardinal-Bishop Philip of Sabina, although at that time he was still the humble bishop of Cavaillon. He is the only one of my old friends who is still alive, and he has always loved me and treated me not as a bishop (as Ambrose did to Augustine) but as a brother. One Friday during Holy Week as I was hiking through those mountains I developed a powerful urge to write an epic poem, one based on Scipio Africanus the Great, who had been a favorite of mine since childhood. I began the project in a rush of enthusiasm, but because of a number of distractions I was forced to put it aside. The poem was called *Africa*, after its hero, and by some fate—my own or the poem's?—it did not fail to rouse the interest of many readers even before I published it. . . .

[In a long passage, omitted here, he describes how he was summoned to Rome by the members of the Senate, to receive the laurel crown—the highest honor for a poet in Roman tradition.]

I was very much pre-occupied with the honor I had just received, worried and fretful that I was unworthy of it, and as a result, when I was hiking through the hills again one day, I happened to cross the river Enza, in the area of Reggio Selvapiana and all of a sudden the beauty of the spot inspired me to finish writing my incomplete *Africa*. My enthusiasm for the project revived as from the dead and I wrote a number of lines that very day. More lines followed every day until I made it all the way to Parma, where I found a quiet, secluded house—which I later bought, and still own—and devoted myself to the poem with such energy that I completed it in no time at all, a fact that still amazes me to this day.

I was thirty-four years old. I returned to my home at the source of the Sorgue, to my beloved trans-Alpine solitude, after that long stay in Parma and Verona, where everyone I met, I am thankful to say, welcomed me with much greater honor that I deserved. Not long afterward, however, my reputation attracted the attention of Giacomo the Younger, of Carrara, an extraordinary man whose equal I doubt could be found even among the rulers of the age. He sent a constant stream of messengers and letters to me for years, no matter if I was in Italy or on the other side of the Alps, begging me to accept his friendship until at last, expecting little good to come of it, I decided to visit him and see what this persistence on the part of so eminent a man, a stranger to me, was all about. So I made my way to Parma, where I was received by him, who is now so dear to my memory, not as a mere mortal might be received but as the saints are received in Heaven—with so much joy and astonishing affection and respect that I cannot put it into words. Therefore, let me be silent. Among the many honors he gave me, he made me a canon of the cathedral of Padua (after he learned that I had been a cleric from boyhood) in order to strengthen my connection to him and his city. To put it bluntly, if he had not died so soon he would have put an end to all my wanderings.

But alas, nothing mortal lasts forever, and everything that is sweet eventually turns bitter. Giacomo had scarcely given two years to me, to his city, and to the entire world when God, Who had given him to us, took him away. It is not out of blind love for him that I believe neither I, the city, nor the world were worthy of him. Giacomo's son and successor, a man of genuine sensibility and distinction, was likewise very friendly and respectful to me, but I could not remain with him after the death of one to whom I was so intimately connected. We were even of the same age. I returned to France, not because I was wanting to see again the old familiar place but because I wanted to get free of my misery, like a sick man wants, by a change of scene.

STUDY QUESTIONS

1. How does Petrarca come to love the past? What are the reasons he gives for his desire to "place my mind in other ages"?
2. What role do important men like Stefano Colonna and Giaccomo the Younger of Carrara play in Petrarca's life? What does this say about the role of friendship in his scholarly career?

12.2 FROM ARIOSTO, *ORLANDO FURIOSO (MAD ORLANDO)*, 1516

Ludovico Ariosto (1474–1533) reprises the familiar characters from the "Song of Roland" (Document 10.6) in his epic romance, *Orlando Furioso*, itself a continuation of another poem (*Orlando Innamorato*). Occurring in a dreamy Renaissance version of the medieval world—including trips to Japan and the moon!—the plot centers on Orlando (a new Roland), who embodies the conflict between Muslims and Charlemagne's army by helplessly loving a pagan princess, Angelica. When Orlando discovers that Angelica has fallen in love with a Saracen named Medoro, he tips headfirst into a mania that leaves a trail of destruction across Europe. He can be saved only by his friends who bring him a flask with his "wits" inside—when he breathes it, he simultaneously falls out of love and regains his sanity.

Rudolf Gottfried, *Ariosto's Orlando Furioso.* Bloomington: Indiana University Press, 1964, pp. 184–6, 190–1, 343–7. Ariosto's Orlando Furioso, Rudolf Gottfried, © 1964. Reprinted with permission of Indiana University Press.

The day, the night to him were both alike;
Abroad upon the cold bare earth he lies;
No sleep, no food he takes, nor none would seek;
All sustenance he to himself denies.
Thus he began and ended half the week,
And he himself doth marvel whence his eyes
Are fed so long with such a spring of water,
And to himself thus reasons on the matter:

"No, no, these be no tears that now I shed;
These be no tears, nor can tears run so rife;
But fire of frenzy draw'th up to my head
My vital humor that should keep my life;
This stream will never cease till I be dead.
Then welcome, death, and end my fatal strife;
No comfort in this life my woe can minish
But thou, who canst both life and sorrow finish.

"These are not sighs, for sighs some respite have;
My gripes, my pangs no respite do permit;
The blindfold boy made me a seeing slave
When from her eyes my heart he first did hit.
Now all inflamed, I burn, I rage and rave
And in the midst of flame consume no whit:
Love sitting in my heart, a master cruel,
Blows with his wings, feeds with his will the fuel.

"I am not I, the man that erst I was;
Orlando, he is burièd and dead;
His most ungrateful love (ah, foolish lass)
Hath killed Orlando and cut off his head;
I am his ghost that up and down must pass
In this tormenting hell forever led,
To be a fearful sample and a just
To all such fools as put in love their trust."

Straightways he draweth forth his fatal blade
And hews the stones; to heav'n the shivers flee;
Accursèd was that fountain, cave, and shade,
The arbor and the flowers and every tree;
Orlando of all places havoc made
Where he those names together joined may see;
Yea, to the spring he did perpetual hurt
By filling it with leaves, boughs, stones, and dirt.

And having done this foolish, frantic feat,
He lays him down all weary on the ground,
Distempered in his body with much heat,
In mind with pains that no tongue can expound;
Three days he doth not sleep nor drink nor eat,
But lay with open eyes as in a sound;
The fourth, with rage and not with reason wakèd,
He rents his clothes and runs about stark naked.

His helmet here he flings, his pouldrons there;
He casts away his curats and his shield;
His sword he throws away, he cares not where;
He scatters all his armor in the field;
No rag about his body he doth bear
As might from cold or might from shame him
    shield;
And save he left behind this fatal blade,
No doubt he had therewith great havoc made.

But his surpassing force did so exceed
All common men that neither sword nor bill
Nor any other weapon he did need;
Mere strength sufficed him to do what he will.
He roots up trees as one would root a weed;
And e'en as birders laying nets with skill
Pare slender thorns away with easy strokes,
So he did play with ashes, elms, and oaks.
    . . .

Away they fled, but he pursued so fast
That some he caught, and some surprised with
    fear
Stood still, as oft it happens, all aghast,
Not knowing how to hide themselves nor where;
Some other ploughmen, seeing what had passed,
Thought it but little wit to tarry there,
But climbed, for fear, their houses and their
    churches,
Not trusting strength of elms, of beech and
    birches.

Among the rest he takes one by his heel
And with his head knocks out another's brain,
Which causèd both of them such pain to feel

As till Doomsday they never shall complain;
Another with his fist he made to reel
Till pain itself made him past sense of pain;
And when the men fled all away afeard,
Then with like rage he set upon their herd.
. . .
And finding no man there, nor small nor great,
For all were fled away from thence for awe,
As famine forced him, he sought out some
    meat;
And were it fine or coarse, the first he saw
In greedy sort he doth devour and eat,
Not caring if it roasted were or raw;
And when thus homely he had ta'en repast,
About the country bedlamlike he passed.

Then kneeling down as if he asked some boon
Of God or some great saint, that pot he brought
Which he had carried from beyond the moon,
The jar in which Orlando's wit was caught,
And closed it to his nostrils; and eftsoon
He drawing breath, this miracle was wrought:
The jar was void and emptied every whit,
And he restored unto his perfect wit.

As one that in some dream or fearful vision
Hath dreamt of monstrous beasts and ugly fiends
Is troubled, when he wakes, with superstition
And feareth what such ugly sight intends
And lying wake thinks of that apparition
And long time after in that fancy spends:

So now Orlando lay, not little musing
At this his present state and uncouth using.

He holds his peace, but lifting up his eyes
He sees his ancient friends King Brandimart
And Oliver and him that made him wise,
All whom he knew and lovèd from his heart;
He thinks, but cannot with himself devise
How he should come to play so mad a part;
He wonders he is nak'd and that he feels
Such store of cords about his hands and heels.

At last he said, as erst Sileno said
To those that took him napping in the cave,
"Release me!" with countenance so staid
And with a sheer so sober and so grave
That they unloosèd him as he them prayed
And suffered him his liberty to have
And clothèd him and comforted his sadness
That he conceivèd of his former madness.

Thus being to his former wits restored,
He was likewise delivered clean from love;
The lady whom he erst so much adored
And did esteem all earthly joys above
Now he despised, yea rather quite
    abhorred;
Now only he applies his wits to prove
That fame and former glory to recover
Which he had not lost the while he was
    a lover.

STUDY QUESTIONS

1. In what specific respects does Orlando's passion appear as madness?
2. Is Orlando still the ideal type of a Christian knight, even before he is released from his enchantment?

12.3 MACHIAVELLI, *DISCOURSES ON LIVY,*
CA. 1517

The humanist and statesman Niccolò Machiavelli (1469–1527) is best known for his Italian treatise *The Prince* on Renaissance city-state rulers—but his *Discourses on Livy* better clarify his republican ideals. In this response to Roman historian Livy, Machiavelli traces the origins of "good" republics. He comments on the maintenance of liberties, the role of religion, and the danger of societal fragmentation through conspiracy.

CHAPTER 5

WHETHER THE GUARDIANSHIP OF LIBERTY
MAY BE MORE SECURELY LODGED IN THE
PEOPLE OR IN THE UPPER CLASSES; AND
WHO HAS MORE REASON TO CREATE AN
UPRISING, HE WHO WISHES TO ACQUIRE OR
HE WHO WISHES TO MAINTAIN

Among the most necessary things established by those who have founded a republic in a prudent fashion is a safeguard for liberty, and according to whether it is well established or not, that free way of life is more or less enduring. Because in every republic there are men of prominence and men of the people, some doubt has arisen over whose hands into which this guardianship would best be placed. Among the Spartans and, in our own times, among the Venetians, it was placed in the hands of the nobles, but among the Romans it was placed in the hands of the plebeians.

For this reason, it is necessary to examine which of these republics made the best choice. If we were to explore the reasons, something could be said for both sides, but if we examine the results, we would choose the side of the nobles, since the liberty of Sparta and Venice endured longer than that of Rome. Turning to the causes, let me say, while first taking the side of the Romans, that the guardianship must be given to those who have less of an appetite to usurp it. No doubt, if we consider the goal of the nobles and that of the common people, we shall see in the former a strong desire to dominate and in the latter only the desire not to be dominated, and, as a consequence, a stronger will to live in liberty, since they have less hope of usurping it than men of prominence; just so, since the common people are set up as guardians of this liberty, it is reasonable to think that they will take better care of it, and, being incapable of appropriating it for themselves, they will not permit others to do so. On the other hand, those who defend the organization of Sparta and Venice declare that those who place the guardianship in the hands of the powerful accomplish two good things: first they better satisfy their ambition, and since they have a larger part to play in the republic with this club in their hands, they have more reason to be content; second they remove a kind of authority from the restless minds of the plebeians that is the cause of countless conflicts and disagreements in any republic and is likely to drive the nobility to despair, which, in the passing of time, will produce harmful consequences.

Discourses on Livy. Translated by Julia Conway Bondanella and Peter Bondanella. Oxford: Oxford University Press, 2010, 1666w from pp. 31–2, 53–6, 256–8, 275. By permission of Oxford University Press. License granted through PLS Clear.

As an example, they offer Rome itself, where, once the tribunes of the people had this authority in their hands, they did not consider it sufficient to have one plebeian consul and wanted two of them. After this, they wanted the censorship, the praetorship, and all the other positions of power in the city; nor did this suffice, for led by this same consuming desire, they then began in time to idolize those men they saw capable of beating down the nobility; and from this arose the power of Marius and the ruin of Rome. Truly, anyone who properly considers one side or the other could remain in doubt about which of the two should be chosen as the guardian of such liberty, not knowing which human disposition is more harmful in a republic: either that which wishes to preserve honour already acquired, or that which wishes to acquire honour yet to be possessed.

. . .

CHAPTER 12

HOW IMPORTANT IT IS TO TAKE ACCOUNT OF RELIGION, AND HOW ITALY, LACKING IN RELIGION THANKS TO THE ROMAN CHURCH, HAS BEEN RUINED

Those princes or republics that wish to maintain their integrity must, above all else, maintain the integrity of their religious ceremonies, and must always hold them in veneration, because there can be no greater indication of the ruin of a state than to see a disregard for its divine worship. This is easy to understand if one knows how the religion in the place where a man is born has been founded, because the life of every religion has its foundations in one of its principal institutions. The existence of the pagan religion was founded upon the responses of the oracles and the sect of diviners and soothsayers; all the other ceremonies, sacrifices, and rites depended upon them, because they simply believed that the god who could predict your future good or evil could also grant it to you.

. . .

Since many are of the opinion that the well-being of the Italian cities arises from the Roman church,

I want to discuss the arguments that occur to me against this opinion, and I shall cite as evidence two very powerful ones which, in my view, cannot be refuted. The first is that because of the evil examples set by this court, this land has lost all piety and religion; this brings with it countless disadvantages and countless disorders, because just as we take for granted every good thing where religion exists, so, where it is lacking, we take for granted the contrary. We Italians have, therefore, this initial debt to the church and to the priests, that we have become irreligious and wicked, but we have an even greater debt to them, which is the second cause of our ruin: that is, the church has kept and still keeps this land divided, and truly, no land is ever united or happy unless it comes completely under the obedience of a single republic or a single prince, as has occurred in France and Spain. The reason why Italy is not in the same condition and why it, too, does not have either a single republic or a single prince to govern it lies solely with the church, because although the church has its place of residence in Italy and has held temporal power there, it has not been so powerful nor has it possessed enough skill to be able to occupy the remaining parts of Italy and make itself ruler of this country, and, on the other hand, it has not been so weak that, for fear of losing control over its temporal affairs, it has been unable to bring in someone powerful to defend it against anyone in Italy who had become too powerful: this is seen to have happened in ancient times through a number of examples, as when with Charlemagne's assistance, the Lombards, already kings of almost all of Italy, were driven out, and when in our own times the church took power away from the Venetians with the aid of France and then chased out the French with the aid of the Swiss. Since it has not, therefore, been powerful enough to take possession of all of Italy, nor has it permitted anyone else to do so, the church has been the reason why Italy has been unable to unite under a single leader and has remained under a number of princes and lords, who have produced so much disunity and weakness that it has come to be easy prey not only to powerful barbarians but to anyone who might attack it. For this we Italians are indebted to the church and to no one else. Anyone who might wish to see this truth more clearly through actual experience needs to possess sufficient power to send the Roman court, with all the authority it possesses in Italy, to live in the lands of the Swiss, who are today the only people who live, with respect to religion and military institutions, as the ancients did, and he would observe that in a brief time the wicked customs of that court would create more disorder in that land than any other event that could at any time take place there.

. . .

CHAPTER 6

ON CONSPIRACIES

I did not think I should omit an analysis of conspiracies, since they represent a grave danger for princes and for private citizens. It is evident that many more princes have lost their lives and their states through conspiracies than through open warfare, because being able to wage open war against a prince is within the reach of very few, while the possibility of conspiring against him is open to everyone. . . . Truly golden is that maxim of Tacitus, which declares that men must honour past affairs and endure present ones, and that they should desire good princes, but regardless of what they are like, should tolerate them. And truly, anyone who does otherwise most often ruins himself and his native land.

. . .

Injuries must either be against property, lifeblood, or honour. To threaten someone's lifeblood is more dangerous than to execute him; or rather, making threats is extremely dangerous, while ordering executions involves no danger whatsoever, because a dead man cannot think about a vendetta, while those who remain alive most often leave the thinking to the dead. But anyone who is threatened and forced by necessity either to act or to suffer will become a very dangerous man to the prince, as we shall discuss in detail in the proper place. Besides this kind of necessity, injuries to property and honour are the two things that offend men more than any other kind of attack, and the prince must protect himself against them, because he can never strip a man of so much that he will not have a knife left with which to take his revenge; nor can he ever dishonour a man so much that he does not retain a heart and mind stubbornly intent on revenge.

. . .

Princes, therefore, have no greater enemy than a conspiracy, because if a conspiracy is organized against them, it either kills them or disgraces them; if it succeeds, they die, and if it is discovered and they kill the conspirators, people always believe that the conspiracy was an invention of the prince to give vent to his avarice and cruelty against their lives and property of those whom he has killed.

STUDY QUESTIONS

1. Does Machiavelli employ examples from the pre-Christian and his contemporary world equally?
2. Why does he see the church as an "impediment" to the political ambitions of Italians?

12.4 ERASMUS, "LETTER TO A FRIEND," "JULIUS EXCLUDED FROM HEAVEN," AND *INTRODUCTION TO THE GOSPELS*, FIRST PUBLISHED 1522

Desiderius Erasmus (ca. 1466–1536) was a Catholic priest who has also been called the Prince of the Humanists for his application of humanist principles to the religious disruption of the Reformation—he created new editions of the New Testament and wrote a handful of satires and other texts on Christian life. Although Erasmus was appalled by the abuses of the Catholic Church, he chose to try to address them while remaining a staunch Catholic. In 1512, Erasmus began work on a fresh Greek edition of the New Testament (with the Latin in parallel columns) that would share a beautified, holistic, and purified Word of God with Catholics in a time of religious turmoil. Interestingly, this would be the version used by Luther to make his own German translation (Document 12.6).

LETTER TO A FRIEND ON PRESENT CONDITIONS

It is no part of my nature, most learned Wolfgang, to be excessively fond of life; whether it is, that I have, to my own mind, lived nearly long enough, having entered my fifty-first year, or that I see nothing in this life so splendid or delightful, that it should be desired by one who is convinced by the Christian faith, that a happier life awaits those who in this world earnestly attach themselves to piety. But at the present moment I could almost wish to be young again, for no other reason but this, that I anticipate the near approach of a golden age; so clearly do we see the minds of princes, as if changed by inspiration, devoting all their energies to the pursuit of peace. The chief movers in this matter are Pope Leo, and Francis, King of France.

There is nothing this king does not do or does not suffer, in his desire to avert war and consolidate peace; submitting, of his own accord, to conditions which might be deemed unfair, if he preferred to have regard to his own greatness and dignity, rather than to the general advantage of the world; and exhibiting in this, as in everything else, a magnanimous and truly royal character. Therefore, when I see that the highest sovereigns of Europe, Francis of France, Charles the Catholic King, Henry of England and the Emperor Maximillian have set all their warlike preparations aside, and established peace upon solid, and as I trust adamantine foundations, I am led to a confident hope, that not only morality and Christian piety, but also a genuine and purer literature may come to renewed life or greater splendor; especially as this object is pursued with equal zeal in various regions of the world,—at Rome by Pope Leo, in Spain by the Cardinal of Toledo, in England by Henry, eighth of the name, himself not unskilled in Letters, and among ourselves by our young

From W. K. Fergison, ed., *Erasmi Opuscula*. Translated by M. P. Gilmore. The Hague: Martinus Nijhoff, 1933, pp. 65–8; From "De Libero Arbitrio" (1524). In *Desiderii Erasmi Roterodami Opera Omnia*. Edited by J. Clericus, translated by Brice M. Clagett. Lugduni Batavorum: Petri Vander Aa, 1703–1706, IX, 1240, 1244, 1248; From "De Libero Arbitrio" (1524). In *Desiderii Erasmi Roterodami Opera Omnia*. Edited by J. Clericus, translated by Brice M. Clagett. Lugduni Batavorum: Petri Vander Aa, 1703–1706, IX, 1215, 1219–20.

king Charles. In France King Francis, who seems as it were born for this object, invites and entices from all countries men that excel in merit or in learning. Among the Germans the same object is pursued by many of their excellent princes and bishops, and especially by Maximillian Caesar, whose old age, weary of so many wars, has determined to seek rest in the employments of peace, a resolution more becoming to his own years, while it is fortunate for the Christian world. To the piety of these princes it is due, that we see everywhere, as if upon a given signal, men of genius are arising and conspiring together to restore the best literature.

Polite letters, which were almost extinct, are now cultivated and embraced by Scots, by Danes and by Irishmen. Medicine has a host of champions; at Rome Nicolas of Leonice; at Venice Ambrosius Leo of Nola, in France William Cop, and John Ruelle, and in England Thomas Linacre. The Imperial Law is restored at Paris by William Budé, in Germany by Udalris Zasy; and Mathematics at Basel by Henry of Glaris. In the theological sphere there was no little to be done, because this science has been hitherto mainly professed by those who are most pertinacious in the abhorrence of the better literature, and are the more successful in defending their own ignorance as they do it under pretext of piety, the unlearned vulgar being induced to believe, that violence is offered to Religion, if any one begins an assault upon their barbarism. For in the presence of an ignorant mob they are always ready to scream and excite their followers to stone-throwing, if they see any risk of not being thought omniscient. But even here I am confident of success, if the knowledge of the three languages continues to be received in schools, as it has now begun. For the most learned and least churlish men of the profession do in some measure assist and favour the new system; and in this matter we are especially indebted to the vigorous exertions of James Lefèvrew of Étaples, whom you resemble not only in name, but in a number of accomplishments.

The humblest part of the work has naturally fallen to my lot. Whether my contribution has been worth anything, I cannot say; at any rate those who object to the world regaining its senses, are as angry with me, as if my small industry had had some influence, although the work was not undertaken by me with any confidence that I could myself teach anything magnificent; but I wanted to construct a road for other persons of higher aims, so that they might be less impeded by pools and stumbling-blocks in carrying home those fair and glorious treasures.

* * * * *

JULIUS II EXCLUDED FROM HEAVEN: JULIUS, HIS TUTELARY SPIRIT, AND SAINT PETER

JULIUS: What's the trouble here? Won't the doors open? The lock must have been changed or at least tampered with.

SPIRIT: Perhaps you haven't brought the right key, for this door will never be opened by the same key as you use for your money-box. So why haven't you brought both keys here, for this one that you have is the key of power not of knowledge?

JULIUS: This is the only one I ever had and I see no need of another as long as I have this.

SPIRIT: Nor indeed do I except that in the meantime we are shut out.

JULIUS: I am getting very angry. I will beat down these gates. Hey, someone in there, open this door at once! What is the matter? Will no one come? Why does the porter dally like this? No doubt he's snoring and probably drunk.

SPIRIT: (As always, he judges everyone else by himself!)

SAINT PETER: It's a good thing we have adamantine doors here; otherwise this man would have broken in. He must be some giant or satrap, a conqueror of cities. But, O immortal God, what stench! I will not open the door at once, but by looking out this little barred window find out what kind of a monster this may be. Who are you and what do you want?

JULIUS: Open as quickly as you can. If you had done your duty, you ought to have come out and meet me with all the pomp due an emperor.

SAINT PETER: Spoken imperiously enough. But first explain to me who you are.

JULIUS: As if you could not see for yourself!

SAINT PETER: See? Indeed I see a strange and hitherto unknown, not to say monstrous, spectacle.

JULIUS: Unless you are wholly blind, you must recognize this key even if you don't know the golden oak. And you see the triple crown and the pallium gleaming with gems and with gold.

SAINT PETER: Indeed I see a key silvered all over although it is only one and very different from those keys which Christ as the true pastor of the Church once gave over to me. And how should I recognize this proud crown? No barbarian tyrant ever wore such a one still less anyone who demanded to be admitted here. Nor does this pallium in the least move me who have always scorned and despised gold and gems as rubbish. But what is this? I see everywhere on key and crown and pallium the signs of that most wicked rogue and impostor Simon [Magus] who shares my name but not my way of life, and whom I long ago turned out of the temple of Christ.

JULIUS: If you are wise you will put aside this joking, for, in case you don't know, I am Julius the Ligurian and you will surely recognize the two letters P. M. if you learned to read at all.

SAINT PETER: I believe they stand for "Pestis Maxima" [Supreme Plague].

SPIRIT: Ha ha ha! How this soothsayer has hit the nail on the head!

JULIUS: No, "Pontifex Maximus" [Supreme Pontiff].

SAINT PETER: If you were three times "Maximus" and more even than Mercury Trismegistus, you would not come in here unless you were also "optimus," that is holy [*sanctus*].

JULIUS: If in fact it matters at all to be called "sanctus," you who are delaying the opening the doors for me have passed the bounds of imprudence since you during so many centuries have been called only "sanctus," while no one has ever called me anything but "sanctissimus." And there are six thousand bulls . . . in which I am not only named "most sacred lord" but am described by the very name of holiness itself, not *sanctus*, so that I did whatever I pleased.

SPIRIT: Even indulging in drunkenness.

JULIUS: They said that that made the sanctity of the most sacred lord Julius.

SAINT PETER: Then ask admission of those flatterers who made you most sacred and let them give you happiness who gave you sanctity. Although you think this is a question of no concern, will you be called "sanctus" whether you are or not?

JULIUS: I am exasperated. If I were only permitted to live, I should envy you neither that sanctity nor that felicity.

SAINT PETER: O what a revelation of a "most sacred mind"! Although I have now for some time been inspecting you from all sides, I notice in you many signs of impiety and none of holiness: And what does this strange crowd so very unpontifical want for itself? You bring some twenty thousand with you nor do I see anyone in such a great mob who has the countenance of a Christian. I see the loathsome dregs of men, smelling of nothing but brothels, drink-shops and gunpowder: It seems to me that hired robbers or rather infernal skeletons have rushed hither from hell to make war on heaven. Also the more I contemplate you yourself, the less do I see any vestige of an apostle. In the first place what kind of monster are you who, although you wear outside the garments of a priest, underneath bristle and clink with a covering of bloody armor? In addition to this how savage are your eyes, how stubborn your mouth, how threatening your brow and how haughty and arrogant your glance! It is shameful to have to say and at the same time disgusting to see that no part of your body is not defiled by the signs of your unrestrained and abominable lust: Not to speak of the fact that you always belch and smell of inebriation and drunkenness and indeed seem to me to have just vomited. This is so truly the condition of your whole body that you seem withered, wasted, and broken not so much by age and disease as by drunkenness.

SPIRIT: How graphically he has depicted him in all his colors.

SAINT PETER: Although I see that you have long been threatening me with your look, yet I cannot keep back what I feel. I suspect that you are that most pestilential heathen Julius returned from hell to make sport of me.

* * * * *

PARACLESIS: INTRODUCTION TO THE GOSPELS

I strongly dissent from those who are unwilling to have the Scriptures translated into the vernacular and read by the ignorant, as if Christ taught so complicated a doctrine that it can hardly be understood even by a handful of theologians or as if the arcanum of the Christian religion consisted in its not being known. It is perhaps reasonable to conceal the mysteries of kings but Christ seeks to divulge his mysteries as much as possible. I should like to have even the most humble women read the Evangel and the Epistles of St. Paul. And these ought also to be translated into all languages so that they might be read and known not only by Scots and Irishmen but also by Turks and Saracens. The first step is certainly to know the Scriptures in whatever manner. Although many will mock at them some will be captivated. Would that the ploughboy recited something from them at his ploughshare, that the weaver sang from them at his shuttle and that the traveler whiled away the tedium of his journey with their tales, indeed would that the converse of Christian men were drawn from them, for we are on the whole what our daily discourse reveals us to be. Let each attain what he can and express what he can. Let him who is behind not envy him who is ahead and let the leader encourage the follower without making him despair. Why should we restrict to a few a profession which is common to all? For since baptism in which the first profession of the philosophy of Christ is made is equally common to all Christians, since they share alike the other sacraments and finally the supreme reward of immortality, it is not fitting that the possession of dogma be relegated to those few whom we call theologians or monks. Although these latter constitute only a minute proportion of the Christian people nevertheless I could wish that they confirm more closely to what they head. For I fear lest there be found among the theologians those who are far from deserving this title, who discourse of earthly not of divine things and among the monks who profess poverty and contempt for the world you may find instead even more of the world. To me he is truly a theologian who teaches not with syllogisms and contorted arguments but with compassion in his eyes and his whole countenance, who teaches indeed by the example of his own life that riches are to be despised, that the Christian man must not put his faith in the defenses of this world but depend entirely on heaven, that he is not to return an injury for an injury, that he is to pray well for those who pray badly and do his best for those who deserve ill, that all good men ought to love and cherish each other as members of the same body and evil men tolerated if they cannot be corrected. Those who lose their goods, who are deposited of their possessions, who mourn—these are not to be pitied for they are the blessed and death is even to be desired by the pious for it is the passage to immortality. If anyone inspired by the spirit of Christ preaches things of this kind, if he inculcates, urges, invites, encourages, then he is a true theologian even if he should be a ditch digger or a weaver.

. . . For that which is especially according to nature easily comes into the minds of all. And what else is the philosophy of Christ which he himself calls a rebirth (*renascentia*) but a restoration of a nature which was originally created good?

* * * * *

ERASMUS ATTACKS LUTHER (1524)

What shall I say of the prodigal son? How could he have wasted his share of the inheritance had it not been his to do with as he pleased? But what he had, he held of his father; and we, too, remember that all our natural qualities are so many gifts of God. Besides, he enjoyed his share even when it was in his father's possession, and then it was in safer hands. What does it mean, then—his departure from his father after suddenly having demanded his share? Quite simply, to give oneself credit for one's natural qualities, and to use them, not in obeying the commandments of God, but in satisfying carnal lusts. And what means the hunger of the prodigal son? It is the sickness by which God directs the mind of the sinner towards self-knowledge, self-hatred, and regret for having left his Father. What is the meaning of the son's inner questioning, when he envisions confession and return? It is the human will adapting itself to the motivating grace that is also called, as we have said, "prevenient" grace. What about this Father who goes before his son on the way? It is the grace of God, which allows our will do to the good when we have determined to do it.

Besides, I ask, what merit could a man claim for himself who is indebted to Him from whom he received natural intelligence and free will for all he can do with these faculties? And yet God considers it meritorious in us not to turn our soul from His grace, and to enlist our talents in His service. That is enough to show that we make no mistake in attributing something to man, although we refer all his works to God as to their author: it is from Him, in fact, that man derives the power of making his strivings one with the operations of divine grace. . . . [The divine wisdom assists man] as guide and advisor, just as an architect directs his workman, draws his plans for him, explains the reason for them, corrects his faulty beginnings, and bolsters him if he loses courage: the work is attributed to the architect, without whose aid nothing would have been created, but no one pretends that the worker and pupil were worthless. What the architect is to his pupil, grace is to our will. That is why Paul writes to the Romans (8.26): "Even so His Spirit cometh to aid our weakness." Now no one calls a person who does nothing weak; that term, rather, is applied to him who lacks strength sufficient to accomplish what he undertakes; in the same sense, you do not say that some one helps you when he does everything. Now Scripture continually speaks of aid, support, succor, shelter. In order for there to be aid, the person aided has to do something. You would not say that the potter helps the clay to become a pot, or that the carpenter aids the axe in making a stool.

That is why, when our opponents declare that man can do nothing without the grace of God, therefore there are no good works by men, we confront them with this proof, which I believe more probable, that men can do everything with the aid of grace, therefore all human works can be good. As many passages as there are in Holy Scripture which mention succor, there are an equal number to establish free will, and they are countless; and I shall carry the day without any possible disagreement if the matter is judged by the number of proofs. . . .

In my opinion, similarly, free will could be preserved while completely avoiding this flagrant confidence in our own merits and the other dangers seen by Luther, without even considering those which we have cited above, and while retaining the main advantages of Lutheran teaching. This is what the doctrine means to me which attributes to grace all the first inspiration which enflames the soul, but which leaves to the human will, when it is not devoid of divine grace, a certain place in the unfolding of the drama. Now since this drama has three parts, the beginning, the development, and the fulfillment, we give the two extremities to grace and let free will enter only into the development. Thus two causes collaborate in the same given action, divine grace and the human will; but grace is the principal cause, the will a secondary one which could do nothing without the first, while grace is sufficient in itself—thus fire burns by its natural virtue, although God is the essential cause which sustains its action, without which the fire would lose all its power, if God happened to withdraw his support. . . .

But why, we are asked, leave a place for free will? In order to have something with which justly to accuse the impious who by their own decision stand outside divine grace; to acquit God of false charges of cruelty or injustice; to drive despair or arrogance far from us; to inspire us to effort. These are the reasons which have led almost all writers to admit free will; but it would remain ineffective without the perpetual aid of the grace of God, which justly prevents us from pride. But still it will be said: what good, then, is free will, if it can do nothing by itself? I shall only reply, "And what would be the use of man himself and all his faculties, if God acted on him as the potter on the clay, or even as He might act on a pebble?"

* * * * *

I take so little pleasure in dogmatizing that I should rather rank myself with the sceptics, whenever I am justified in so doing by the inviolable authority of Holy Scripture and by the decisions of the Church, to which I always submit my judgment quite willingly, whether or not I understand the reasons for what she decrees. And this temper of mind appears to me preferable to that of certain others, who, narrowly attached to their own views, never let any one deviate from them in anything, and who violently twist all the texts of Scripture in support of the position they have embraced once and for all. . . .

Here it will be objected: "Why the need of interpretation, when Scripture itself is perfectly clear?" But if it is as clear as all that, why, over the centuries, have such eminent men been blind on so important a point, as our opponents contend? If Scripture is without obscurity, why was there need for prophecies in apostolic times? That, I shall be told, was a gift of the Holy Spirit. But I should like to know whether, just as the gift of healing and the gift of tongues have ceased, this divine gift has not ceased also. And if it has not ceased, we must seek to learn to whom it could have passed. If it has passed to merely anyone at all, then every interpretation will be uncertain; if it has been received by no one, since today so many obscurities still torment the learned, no interpretation will be more certain. If I maintain that it resides in the successors of the apostles, it will be objected that over the centuries many men have succeeded the apostles who nevertheless had none of the apostolic spirit. And yet, everything else being equal, it will be sought in them, for it is more probably that God has infused His Spirit in those to whom He has given holy orders; just as we believe that grace is more clearly given to the baptized than to the unbaptized.

But, as we must, we shall admit no less than the possibility that the Spirit may actually reveal to some humble and illiterate person truths withheld from a host of learned men, as when Christ thanked His Father for the things He made known to the simple, to those whom the world thought mad—things he had hidden from the wise and the judicious, from the knowledge of scribes, Pharisees, and philosophers. And perhaps Dominic, perhaps Francis [the thirteenth century saints], were the kind of madmen who are allowed to follow their inspirations. But if Paul, in the day when this gift of the Spirit was in its full vigor, already warns men to check on whether these inspirations really come from God, what must we do in our worldly age? By what standard shall we judge opinions? By learning? But there are none but master scholars in both parties. By conduct? On

both sides, likewise, there are only sinners. But we find the chorus of saints all on the same side, defending free will. I am told, it is true, "They were nothing but men." But I only meant to compare men with one another, never with God. I am asked, what does the majority prove, with regard to spiritual insight? I answer, what does the minority prove? I am asked, how can a bishop's mitre be of use in understanding Holy Scripture? I answer, what good is a mantle or cowl? Again, how can philosophical studies make it easier to understand Holy Writ? And I reply, what use is ignorance? And again, how is the comprehension of texts connected with the meeting of a council, where it might be that no member had received the Spirit of God? I answer, what then is the value of private pseudo-councils of a few individuals, where there is only too clearly no possessor of the Spirit?

Do we remember this plea of Paul's, "Don't ask for proof that Christ lives in me"? Then the apostles were only believed to the extent to which their miracles confirmed their teaching. These days, on the contrary, anyone at all demands credence just because he declares he is filled with the spirit of the Gospel. Because the apostles drove out serpents, cured the sick, brought the dead to life, and gave the gift of tongues by the laying on of hands, men decided to believe, and not without difficulty, the paradoxes they taught. And today, when we see new teachers declaring things that common sense cannot even class as paradoxes, we have not yet seen one of them capable of curing a lame horse. And would to Heaven that, if they cannot work miracles, some of them would at least show the purity and simplicity of apostolic life, which to us, poor late-comers, would be miraculous enough!

I am not speaking specifically of Luther, whom I have never met and whose works give me a confused impression, but of certain others whom I have known more closely. It is they who in biblical controversies reject the interpretation of the Fathers which we suggest to them, they who cry unrestrainedly, "The Fathers were only men!" If they are asked what criterion can be used to establish the true interpretation of Scripture, since there are only men on both sides, they rely on the revelations of the Spirit. But if they are asked why the Spirit should favor them rather than those whose miracles have shone forth throughout the world, they answer if the Gospel had disappeared from the earth thirteen centuries ago. If you insist that their life be worthy of the Spirit, they retort that they are justified by faith, not by works. If you require miracles, they tell you that the time for them has long passed, and that there is no longer any need for them, now that the Scriptures are fully clarified. And then if you doubt that Scripture is clear precisely on the point where so many great minds have erred, you fall back into the same vicious circle.

Besides if we admit that he who possesses the Spirit is sure of understanding the Scriptures, how shall I be certain of what he has seen only partially? What shall I do when several learned men bring me different interpretations, each one swearing all the time that he has the Spirit? Especially, if we add that the Spirit does not reveal all truth to them fully, even he who has the Spirit can go wrong, and err on some point.

These are my objections to those who so easily reject the traditional interpretation of the Holy Books, and who propose their own as if it had plummeted from Heaven. Finally, assuming that the Spirit of Christ could have left His people in error on some secondary point without immediate repercussions on human salvation, how can we admit that for thirteen hundred years He abandoned His Church to error, and that in all the host of holy people not one could reveal to the Church that truth which, our recent arrivals pretend, constitutes the heart of all the Gospel teaching?

But to finish this matter: whatever others may arrogate to themselves is their own affair; as for me, I claim for myself neither wisdom nor sanctity, and I take no pride in my intellect, but I shall simply and carefully set forth the views which capture my allegiance. If any one wishes to teach me, I shall not meet the truth with a closed mind.

STUDY QUESTIONS

1. What lessons, particularly concerning warfare, does Erasmus hope that the kings of Europe will draw from reading his edition of the Gospels?
2. Did the behavior of the "Warrior Pope" Julius II warrant his being "excluded" from Heaven?
3. How did Erasmus reconcile the reading of Scripture and its interpretation in the correct, Christian spirit? Can every Christian interpret what he or she reads correctly?

12.5 MARTIN LUTHER, *ON THE FREEDOM OF A CHRISTIAN*, DEDICATORY LETTER TO POPE LEO X, 1520

Martin Luther (1483–1546) wrote his great work, *On the Freedom of a Christian*, in late 1520, after his contentious meetings (described briefly here) by the papal nuncios Cardinal Cajetan, Johann Eck, Andreas von Miltitz. It is the text in which he most fully worked out his doctrine that

Translation by Clifford Backman.

salvation is the free gift offered to us by a loving God in Christ, a gift that we need not earn or deserve but simply need to be willing to accept. To this notion of *sola fide* ("by our faith alone" we are saved) he adds that of *sola Scriptura* ("by the Scriptures alone" are we authoritatively taught), emphasizing that every Christian has the right to interpret the Scriptures for himself. His dedicatory letter to Leo X follows.

For the last three years I have been waging war against the monstrous evils of our time, and more than once I have been compelled to turn my mind to you, most blessed father Leo, since everyone thinks that you are the sole cause of my struggle and that therefore I must always have you on my mind. While it is true that the pointless wrath directed at me by the evil flatterers who surround you has led me to appeal to you to call a Church Council. . . . I have never been so estranged from Your Blessedness that I have not sought, in constant and tearful prayers to the Lord, for every good thing for you. I confess that I have begun to despise, and hope to silence, those people who are trying to terrify me by invoking the majesty of your name and office. The reason I am writing to you now, blessed Leo, is that those same people are accusing me of directing my energies at you personally out of a desire to offend you.

To speak plain truth: I cannot think of anything I have said about you that was not honorable and good. . . . I am not so foolish as to attack someone whom everyone praises; and indeed, it has been my aim, and always will be, to avoid all personal attacks—even on those individuals whose personal reputations are disgraceful. I take no delight in anyone's faults since I am only too aware of the beam in my own eye. I can never be the first to cast a stone at any sinner. And while it is true that I have sharply criticized impious doctrines and have never hesitated to condemn my adversaries, I have attacked only their impiety, not their personal morals. I make no apology for this. . . .

For these reasons, dear Leo, I beg you to receive this letter in my defense and to believe that I have never thought anything wicked towards your person. I desire that every eternal blessing may befall you, and please know that I have no dispute with anyone alive regarding personal morals. My only concern is the Word of Truth. On anything else I will yield to anyone, but I cannot and will not forsake or deny the Word. If anyone thinks otherwise of me or interprets my words in any other sense, he is mistaken and does not understand me.

Neither you nor anyone can deny, however, that Your See—the Roman Curia—is more corrupt than any kingdom of Babylon or city of Sodom, lost, desperate, and hopelessly impious. Against it I have railed, and I am outraged that the people of Christ are being cheated in your name and that of the Church of Rome. I have condemned it and will keep doing so as long as a faithful spirit lives in me. . . . For many years now, as you well know, nothing has flowed from Rome into the world except the wastage of goods, bodies, and souls, the foulest of all foul things. It is as clear as day to everyone alive that the Church of Rome, once the most holy of all churches, has become the most lawless den of thieves, the most shameless of brothels, and the very realm of sin, death, and hell. If Antichrist himself were to appear on earth, he could not conjure any way to add to its wickedness.

You, dear Leo, are a lamb in the midst of wolves. Like Daniel, you are surrounded by lions; like Ezekiel, you dwell among scorpions. . . . I grieve that you, who deserve to have lived in a better age, were made Pontiff in this one, for the Curia is not worthy of you or anyone like you. It deserves a Satan—and Satan is indeed more the ruler in that wicked Babylon than you are. . . . There is nothing under the vast heavens more corrupt, diseased, and loathsome than the Curia. It surpasses even the wickedness of the Turks. Once the gateway to Heaven, it is now the opened mouth of Hell. . . .

As I was moving ahead with my studies of the Holy Scriptures, Satan opened his eyes and goaded his servant Johann Eck (that notorious enemy of Christ!), in his limitless lust for fame, to pull me into open debate, where he tripped me up on a single comment that I made in passing in regard to the primacy of the Church. In his proud insolence, foaming at the mouth and gnashing his teeth, he boasted that he would risk anything for the glory of God and the honor of the Holy See. . . . but in truth he sought to promote not the primacy of St. Peter but his own prominence among the theologians of our time. . . .

Most excellent Leo, I pray you will allow me to plead my own cause and point blame at your true enemies. I believe you have heard by now how Cardinal Cajetan acted towards me—Cajetan, that rash, miserable, and traitorous legate of yours! When, out of reverence for you, I had placed myself and all my works in his hands, he could have made peace with me by one simple word, for I had vowed to remain silent and make an end of my case if he agreed simply to order my adversaries to do the same. But he was too proud to agree to this and instead defended my adversaries. He gave them free license to speak against me, and ordered me to recant (even though this was absolutely not part of his commission). This is how our dispute turned worse just when it was in the best position to be resolved. His tyranny vexed me and continues to do so, which is why everything that has occurred since then is entirely his fault, not mine. I had begged with all my might to be allowed to remain silent and let our conflict end. What more could I have done?

Next came Karl von Miltitz, another nuncio of yours, who exerted himself in every way imaginable, trying to resolve the conflict that proud Cajetan had so boldly made even worse. But even though he was aided by the illustrious Prince-Elector Friedrich, he could accomplish nothing more than arrange a single face-to-face meeting with me. At this meeting I again yielded to your great name and offered to keep silent and to accept as my judge either the archbishop of Trier or the bishop of Naumburg. Miltitz agreed, and the matter was settled. But even as we were coming to terms, Eck (your main enemy, Leo!) rushed in, carrying his *Leipzig Disputation*—the text he had used in his debate with Andreas Karlstadt—and, taking aim against me in an unexpected way, raised a new issue in regard to papal supremacy. Our plans for peace were crushed. Miltitz stood frozen while Eck argued with me and chose different judges [than those I had agreed to]. But nothing came of all this, for Eck's lies, pretenses, and trickery had brought matters to so confused, messy, and painful a state that no matter in which direction we proceeded, a greater conflagration was sure to arise. Eck's goal, after all, was not to

seek truth but his own renown. In this case too, I did nothing except what was fitting.

I must confess that on this particular occasion no small amount of the corruption in the Roman Curia came to light—but the offense was Eck's. His ambition and lust for fame revealed Rome's disgrace to the whole world. . . . Eck is your true enemy, Leo, and the enemy of your Curia. He is living proof that there is worse enemy than a flatterer, for what has been the result of his flattery but evil? Evil to the Church that is greater than any king could wreak upon it, for today the very name *Roman Curia* stinks in the nostrils of the world. . . .

Thus, I turn to you, blessed Father, and humbly beg you to stretch out your hand and silence, if possible, those flatterers who, despite their protestations, are the enemies of peace. No one should ever try to persuade you, Holy Father, that I am willing to recant—in so doing he will only make difficult matters worse. I reject all rules for how to interpret the Word of God for the simple reason that the Word, which teaches liberty in all matters, cannot be bound by rules. With the exception of these two statements, there is nothing I am not eagerly willing to do or to suffer in order to end this contention. I detest conflict, and I will challenge no one who does not challenge me. But if I am challenged, I refuse to remain silent in defense of my Lord Christ. You, blessed Leo, can put an end to all of this misery with a single word, a simple command to impose silence and peace on both sides. How I long to hear you give that command!

Beware of listening to the Sirens, dear Leo. They make you out to be more than a mere man, but partly a God who can order whatever you want in this world. It will not happen like that, not ever. You are the servant of servants, and are now in perhaps the most lamentable and dangerous position ever. Do not listen to the flatterers who say that you are the Lord of the world, that no one can be considered a Christian without your say-so, and that you have power over Heaven, Hell, and Purgatory. Such men are your enemies and a seeking to destroy your soul, as Isaiah says, "Those who led this people led them astray." They are wrong, those men who place you above Councils and the universal Church, and who claim that you alone have the right to interpret Scripture. Such men are filling the Church with their own impieties, and are doing so in your name! Satan has grown strong through such men, up to the time of your pontificate. . . .

It may seem presumptuous of me to deign to teach you; indeed, all men ought to be taught by you (especially those diseased souls who proclaim you the chief of all judges), but I am simply following in the tradition of St. Bernard [of Clairvaux], who addressed his book *Considerations* to Pope Eugenius [III]—a book, indeed, that every pope should know by heart. It is not from a desire to teach you [that I send you this book] but from that sense of duty and love that teaches us to care for our neighbors' well-being, casting aside all notions of worthiness and unworthiness, and concerned only for the dangers that threaten. I am aware how turbulently the storm-waves in Rome are tossing you about, threatening to subsume you in the infinite depths of the angry sea. So miserable is the condition in which you are now

living that any help at all, even from the lowest of those who love you, is not out of place. I set aside the majesty of your office and simply offer my loving care to your person. I will not flatter one in so perilous a situation as you are in now, and if this fact alone does not convince you that I am your friend and loyal subject, I will leave it to the Lord to see and to judge.

Lest I approach you empty-handed, dear Father, I bring you this treatise, published under your name, as a token of peace and good hope; it will show you the ways in which I would prefer to occupy myself, if only your wicked flatterers would leave me be. It is a small book in size, but one whose message, I believe, encapsulates all of Christian life, if you understand it right. Being poor, I have no other gift to offer; but you need no riches, only the gifts of the spirit. I commend myself to you, dear Blessed Father, and may the Lord Jesus preserve you forever. Amen.

Wittenberg; 6th September, 1520.

STUDY QUESTIONS

1. How does Luther outline the doctrine that salvation is the free gift offered to us by a loving God in Christ?
2. How does Luther argue that salvation is a gift that we need not earn or deserve but simply be willing to accept?

12.6 MARTIN LUTHER, "PREFACE TO THE NEW TESTAMENT," FIRST PUBLISHED 1522

Martin Luther (1483–1546), known for his unplanned split from the Catholic Church, was a theologian and monk. Among other major points, Luther condemned the Catholic notion that priests enjoyed special spiritual status over other Christians that enabled them to intercede

From Preserved Smith, *Luther's Correspondence*. Philadelphia: Lutheran Publishing Co., 1913, I, pp. 91–3; (A) From Luther, *The Bondage of Will* (1525). Translated by Henry Cole. Grand Rapids, Mich.: W. B. Eerdmans Publishing Co., 1931, pp. 74, 231, 384–5, 391. Original in WA, XVIII, 551 ff.; From Luther, *To the Christian Nobility of the German Nation* (1520). In *Luther's Primary Works*. Edited by Henry Wace and C. A. Buchheim. London: Hodder and Stoughton, 1896, pp. 162–75, passim.

for ordinary sinners; he rejected the use of *indulgences* to purchase forgiveness for sins; and he claimed that only God's grace, and not something a Christian could "earn," would bring him salvation. He translated the Bible into German to make it accessible to his literate compatriots. For these actions, he was excommunicated and threatened with death, and he ultimately became the unwitting founder of the first Protestant sect, Lutheranism. In this introduction to his German translation, Luther guides his readers through Jesus's teachings so that they may come to experience them on their own.

D. PREFACE TO LUTHER'S COLLECTED WORKS, 1545

[While working on the Psalms] I was absorbed by a passionate desire to understand Paul in his Epistle to the Romans. Nothing stood in my way but that one expression, "The justice of God is revealed in the Gospel" (Romans 1:17). For I hated these words, "the justice of God," because I had been taught to understand them in the scholastic sense as the formal or active justice whereby God, who is righteous, punishes unrighteous sinners. I was in the frame of mind of feeling that although I was living a blameless life as a monk, I was still a sinner with a troubled conscience before God, and I had no confidence that I could appease Him by my efforts. I did not love—nay, I hated the righteous God who punishes sinners, and I murmured with unbridled resentment, if not with unspoken blasphemy, against Him, saying, "As if it were not enough for miserable sinners who are eternally lost through original sin to be afflicted with every kind of calamity through the law of the Ten Commandments, without God's adding woe to woe through the Gospel and even threatening us with His justice and wrath in the Gospel." Thus I raged, my conscience wild and disturbed. Still I kept hammering away at those words of Paul, wishing passionately to know what he meant.

After I had pondered the problem for days and nights, God took pity on me and I saw the inner connection between the two phrases, "The justice of God is revealed in the Gospel" and "The just shall live by faith." Then I began to understand that this "justice of God" is the righteousness by which the just man lives through the free gift of God, that is to say "by faith"; and that the justice "revealed in the Gospel" is

the passive justice of God by which He takes pity on us and justifies us by our faith, as it is written, "The just shall live by faith." Thereupon I felt as if I had been born again and had entered Paradise through wide-open gates. Immediately the whole of Scripture took on a new meaning for me. I raced through the Scriptures, so far as my memory went, and found analogies in other expressions: "the work of God," i.e., what God works in us; "the strength of God," by which He gives us strength; "the wisdom of God," by which He makes us wise; "the power of God," "the blessing of God," "the glory of God."

Whereas the expression "justice of God" had filled me with hate before, I now exalted it as the sweetest of phrases with all the more love. And so this verse of Paul's became in truth the gate to Paradise for me.

* * * * *

G. LETTER TO STAUPITZ, MAY 30, 1518

I remember, reverend Father, among those happy and wholesome stories of yours, by which the Lord used wonderfully to console me, that you often mentioned the word *poenitentia*, whereupon, distressed by our consciences and by those torturers who with endless and intolerable precept taught nothing but what they called a method of confession, we received you as a messenger from Heaven, for penitence is not genuine save when it begins from the love of justice and of God, and this which they consider the end and consummation of repentance is rather its commencement.

Your words on this subject pierced me like the sharp arrows of the mighty, so that I began to see what the Scriptures had to say about penitence, and behold the happy result: the texts all supported and favored your doctrine, in so much that, while there had formerly been no word in almost all the Bible more bitter to me than *poenitentia* (although I zealously simulated it before God and tried to express an assumed and forced love), now no word sounds sweeter or more pleasant to me than that. For thus do the commands of God become sweet when we understand that they are not to be read in books only, but in the wounds of the sweetest Saviour.

After this it happened by the favor of the learned men who taught me Hebrew and Greek that I learned [from Erasmus' edition of the New Testament in Greek, note on Matthew 3:2] that the Greek word is *metanoia* from *meta* and *noun*, i.e., from "afterwards" and "mind," so that penitence or *metanoia* is "coming to one's right mind, afterwards," that is, comprehension of your own evil, after you had accepted loss and found out your error. This is impossible without a change in your affections. All this agrees so well with Paul's theology, that, in my opinion, at least, nothing is more characteristically Pauline.

Then I progressed and saw that *metanoia* meant not only "afterwards" and "mind," but also "change" and "mind," so that *metanoia* means change of mind and affection. . . .

Sticking fast to this conclusion, I dared to think that they were wrong who attributed so much to works of repentance that they have left us nothing of it but formal penances and elaborate confession. They were seduced by the Latin, for *poenitentiam agere* means rather a work than a change of affection and in no wise agrees with the Greek.

When I was glowing with this thought, behold indulgences and remissions of sins began to be trumpeted abroad with tremendous clangor, but their trumpets animated no one to real struggle. In short, the doctrine of true repentance was neglected, and only the cheapest part of it, that called penance, was magnified. . . . As I was not able to oppose the fury of these preachers, I determined modestly to take issue with them and to call their theories in doubt, relying as I did on the opinion of all the doctors and of the whole Church, who all say that it is better to perform the penance than to buy it, that is an indulgence. . . . This is the reason why I, reverend Father, who always love retirement, have unhappily been forced into the public view.

* * * * *

B. LUTHER REPLIES TO ERASMUS (1525)

You [Erasmus] alone in pre-eminent distinction from all others, have entered upon the thing itself; that is, the grand turning point of the cause; and have not wearied me with those irrelevant points about popery, purgatory, indulgences, and other like baubles, rather than causes, with which all have hitherto tried to hunt me down,—though in vain! You, and you alone, saw what was the grand hinge upon which the whole turned, and therefore you attacked the vital part at once; for which, from my heart, I thank you. . . .

The human will is, as it were, a beast between [God and Satan]. If God sit thereon, it wills and goes where God will; as the Psalm saith, "I am become as it were a beast before thee, and I am continually with thee." (Ps. 73:22–23.) If Satan sit thereon, it wills and goes as Satan will. Nor is it in the power of its own will to choose, to which rider it will run, nor which it will seek; but the riders themselves contend, which shall have and hold it. . . .

God is that Being, for whose will no cause or reason is to be assigned, as a rule or standard by which it acts; seeing that, nothing is superior or equal to it, but it is itself the rule of all things. For if it acted by any rule or standard, or from any cause or reason, it would be no longer the will of God. Wherefore, what God wills is not therefore right, because He ought or ever was bound so to will; but on the contrary, what takes place is therefore right, because He so wills. A cause and reason are assigned for the will of the creature, but not for the will of the Creator; unless you set up, over Him, another Creator. . . .

As to myself, I openly confess, that I should not wish "free-will" to be granted me, even if it could be so, nor anything else to be left in my own hands, whereby I might endeavor something towards my own salvation. And that, not merely because in so many opposing dangers, and so many assaulting devils, I could not stand and hold it fast (in which state no man could be saved, seeing that one devil is stronger than all men); but because, even though there were no dangers, no conflicts, no devils, I should be compelled to labour under a continual uncertainty, and to beat the air only. Nor would my conscience, even if I should live and work to all eternity, ever come to a settled certainty, how much it ought to do in order to satisfy God. For whatever work should be done, there would still remain a scrupling, whether or not it pleased God, or whether He required any thing more; as I proved in the experience of all those who believe in words, and as I myself learned to my bitter cost, through so many years of my own experience.

But now, since God has put my salvation out of the way of *my* will, and has taken it under *His own*, and has promised to save me, not according to my working or manner of life, but according to His own grace and mercy, I rest fully assured and persuaded that He is faithful, and will not lie, and moreover great and powerful, so that no devils, no adversaries can destroy Him or pluck me out of His hand. "No one (saith He) shall pluck them out of My hand, because My Father which gave them Me is greater than all" (John, 10:27–8). Hence it is certain, that in this way, if all are not saved, yet some, yea, many shall be saved; whereas by the power of "free-will" no one whatever could be saved, but all must perish together. And moreover, we are certain and persuaded, that in this way, we please God, not from the merit of our own works, but from the favour of His mercy promised unto us; and that, if we work less, or work badly, He does not impute it unto us, but, as a Father, pardons us and makes us better.

* * * * *

A. LUTHER CHALLENGES THE AUTHORITY OF THE ROMAN CHURCH (1520–1521)

The Romanists have, with great adroitness, drawn three walls round themselves, with which they have hitherto protected themselves, so that no one could reform them, whereby all Christendom has fallen terribly.

Firstly, if pressed by the temporal power, they have affirmed and maintained that the temporal power has no jurisdiction over them, but, on the contrary, that the spiritual power is above the temporal.

Secondly, if it were proposed to admonish them with the Scriptures, they objected that no one may interpret the Scriptures but the Pope.

Thirdly, if they are threatened with a council, they pretend that no one may call a council but the Pope.

Thus they have secretly stolen our three rods, so that they may be unpunished, and intrenched themselves behind these three walls, to act with all the wickedness and malice, which we now witness. . . .

Let us, in the first place, attack the first wall: [that the temporal power has no jurisdiction over the spiritual].

It has been devised that the Pope, bishops, priests, and monks are called the *spiritual estate*; princes, lords, artificers, and peasants are the *temporal estate*. This is an artful lie and hypocritical device, but let no one be made afraid by it, and that for this reason: that all Christians are truly of the spiritual estate, and there is no difference among them, save of office alone. As St. Paul says (I Cor. 12), we are all one body, though each member does its own work, to serve the others. This is because we have one baptism, one Gospel, one faith, and are all Christians alike; for baptism, Gospel, and faith, these alone make spiritual and Christian people.

As for the unction by a Pope or a bishop, tonsure, ordination, consecration, and clothes differing from those of laymen—all this may make a hypocrite or an anointed puppet, but never a Christian or a spiritual man. Thus we are all consecrated as priests by baptism. . . .

Therefore a priest should be nothing in Christendom but a functionary; as long as he holds his office, he has precedence of others; if he is deprived of it, he is a peasant or a citizen like the rest. Therefore, a priest is verily no longer a priest after deposition. But now they have invented *characteres indelibiles*, and pretend that a priest after deprivation still differs from a simple layman. They even imagine that a priest can never be anything but a priest—that is, that he can never become a layman. All this is nothing but mere talk and ordinance of human invention.

It follows, then, that between laymen and priests, princes and bishops, or, as they call it, between spiritual and temporal persons, the only real difference is one of office and function, and not of estate. . . .

Now see what a Christian doctrine is this: that the temporal authority is not above the clergy, and may not punish it. This is as if one were to say the hand may not help, though the eye is in grievous suffering. It is not unnatural, not to say unchristian, that one member may not help another, or guard it against harm? Nay, the nobler the member, the more the rest are bound to help it. Therefore I say, Forasmuch as the temporal power has been ordained by God for the punishment of the bad and the protection of the good, therefore we must let it do its duty throughout the whole Christian body, without respect of persons, whether it strike Popes, bishops, priests, monks, nuns, or whoever it may be. . . .

The second wall is even more tottering and weak: that they alone pretend to be considered masters of the Scriptures; although they learn nothing of them all their life. They assume authority, and juggle before us with impudent words, saying that the Pope cannot err in matters of faith, whether he be evil or good, albeit they cannot prove it by a single letter. That is why the canon law contains so many heretical and unchristian, nay unnatural laws; but of these we need not speak now. For whereas they imagine the Holy Ghost never leaves them, however unlearned and wicked they may be, they grow bold enough to decree whatever they like. But were this true, where were the need and use of the Holy Scriptures? Let us burn them, and content ourselves with the unlearned gentlemen at Rome, in whom the Holy Ghost dwells, who, however, can dwell in pious souls only. If I had not read it, I could never have believed that the devil should have put forth such follies at Rome and find a following. . . .

Therefore, it is a wickedly devised fable—and they cannot quote a single letter to confirm it—that it is for the Pope alone to interpret the Scriptures or to confirm the interpretation of them. They have assumed the authority of their own selves. And though they say that this authority was given to St. Peter when the keys were given to him, it is plain enough that the keys were not given to St. Peter alone, but to the whole community. Besides, the keys were not ordained for doctrine or authority, but for sin, to bind of loose; and what they claim besides this from the keys is mere invention. . . .

Only consider the matter. They must needs acknowledge that there are pious Christians among us that have the true faith, spirit, understanding, word, and mind of Christ; why then should we reject their word and understanding and follow a pope who has neither understanding nor spirit? Surely this were to deny our whole faith and the Christian Church. Moreover, if the article of our faith is right, "I believe in the holy Christian Church," the Pope cannot alone be right; else we must say, "I believe in the Pope of Rome," and reduce the Christian Church to one man, which is a devilish and damnable heresy. Besides that, we are all priests, as I have said, and have all one faith, one Gospel, one Sacrament; how then should we not have the power of discerning and judging what is right or wrong in matters of faith? . . . Balaam's ass was wiser than the prophet. If God spoke by an ass against a prophet, why should He not speak by a pious man against the Pope?

The third wall falls of itself, as soon as the first two have fallen. . . .

When need requires, and the pope is a cause of offence to Christendom, in these cases whoever can best do so, as a faithful member of the whole body, must do what he can to produce a true free council. This no one can do so well as the temporal authorities, especially since they are fellow-Christians, fellow-priests, sharing one spirit and one power in all things, and since they should exercise the office that they have received from God without hinderance, whenever it is necessary and useful that is should be exercised. . . .

As for their boasts of their authority, that no one must oppose it, this is idle talk. No one in Christendom has any authority to do harm, or to forbid others to prevent harm being done. There is no authority in the Church but for reformation. Therefore if the Pope wished to use his power to prevent the reformation of the Church, we must not respect him or his power; and if he should begin to excommunicate and fulminate, we must despise this as the doings of a madman, and, trusting in God excommunicate and repel him as best we may. . . .

And now I hope the false, lying spectre will be laid with which the Romanists have long terrified and stupefied our consciences. And it will be seen that, like all the rest of us, they are subject to the temporal sword; that they have no authority to interpret the Scriptures by force without skill; and that they have no power to prevent a council, or to pledge it in accordance with their pleasure, or to bind it beforehand, and deprive it of its freedom; and that if they do this, they are verily of the fellowship of antichrist and the devil, and have nothing of Christ but the name.

STUDY QUESTIONS

1. How did Luther find release from his torments by reading, closely, the book of Romans?
2. How did Luther recall developing his ideas concerning the doctrine of salvation by faith?
3. Is Luther's tone in writing excessively violent? Could his words be used to endorse actual violence?

12.7 FRANCESCO GUICCIARDINI, FLORENCE UNDER LORENZO DE' MEDICI

Francesco Guicciardini (1483–1540) was a wealthy lawyer with good political connections. Like many such figures in the Renaissance, he also had cultural and intellectual ambitions. In his later years he wrote a brilliant *History of Italy* that was one of the first works of history to combine the use of extensive archival records and a critical attitude toward political motivations and intentions. His *History of Florence*, however, is the work of a young man trying to feel his way in an unfamiliar discipline. Its most incisive passage is translated below and provides a closely observed portrait of Lorenzo de' Medici (1449–92), who ruled Florence from 1469 until his death. (Guicciardini, of course, did not know Lorenzo personally, being only nine years old when the ruler died.)

Lorenzo de' Medici was only forty-three years old when he died, after having ruled Florence for twenty-three years. He was only twenty when his father Piero died in 1469 and was still being advised by Messer Tommasso Soderini and some other elder politicians, but it took only a short time for him to come into his full strength and stature, such that he was able to govern the city just as he saw fit. . . .

Until he died in 1492 Lorenzo controlled and ran Florence as completely as if he were a Greek *tyrannos*. His renown was as widespread before his death as it has become after it. His greatness was so remarkable, and indeed without parallel in all of Florence's history, in fact, that I think it is not a mistake—and in fact may prove quite useful—if I describe his manner and character in some detail. I do not speak from my own experience, for I was still a mere boy when he died, but my information comes from reliable and trustworthy sources. Unless I have been lied to, what I am about to say is completely true.

Translation by Clifford Backman.

Lorenzo had many extraordinary virtues and a fair share of vices; some of the latter came to him naturally, while some others arose from necessity. His authority in the city was so complete that it is fair to say that Florence was not free in his time, but it enjoyed as many blessings and as much happiness as there could be in any other city that we call "free" but which is in fact under a *tyrannos*. Although not everything he did was admirable, most of his actions were so tremendous and noble that the more one studies them the more impressive they appear. Glory in arms and feats of military achievement do not figure among his successes, as they do among the great figures of antiquity, but that was more the circumstance of the times in which he lived than of his own failure. You will not read here of any brave defense of the city, a celebrated capture of a fortress, a brilliant strategy on the field of battle, or a glorious upset over enemies; Lorenzo's claim to fame includes no such military splendor. What one does find in his record is every possible sign of the virtues of civic life—no one, not even his enemies and rivals, would deny his brilliance in that regard. Who could? The simple fact that he ruled Florence for twenty-three years, always increasing its power and glory, proves the point. Bear in mind that Florence is an opinionated place, full of calculating and ambitious people, and since the city is small and cannot provide for everyone, to benefit some means to skip over others. Finally, the roster of great Italian and foreign princes who counted themselves as his friend attests to his reputation. . . .

He was generally of sound judgment and wise, but his intellect transcended politics. He committed a number of ill-considered actions, such as his war against Volterra in 1473, when he conspired to get the people of that town to rebel against him so that he could have an excuse to seize their alum mines; in so doing he ignited a fire that could have engulfed all of Italy, although things turned out well in the end. And he could have avoided the civil war of 1478 if he had handled relations with the pope [Sixtus IV, r. 1471–1484] and the king [Ferrante of Naples, r. 1458–1494] more skillfully, instead of playing the role of the aggrieved innocent for all it was worth and thereby causing the war and nearly costing himself and the city their lives. His subsequent trip to Naples, also, was too rash and hurried a decision, one that placed him directly in the hands of his enemy, an untrustworthy and traitorous king. The desperate need for peace partially excuses him, but many still live who think he could have achieved it much more safely and no less effectively had he negotiated from Florence.

He dreamed of glory and renown, and indeed he desired these more than anyone else of his time. His desire for them influenced his actions even in the most minor matters—for which he may justly be criticized. Whether he was penning verses, playing a game, or doing any little thing at all, he became enraged if someone else matched or bettered him. Even in matters of real importance his lust for glory influenced him excessively. He conspired and struggled against every prince in Italy, to the great displeasure of Duke Ludovico [Sforza of Milan, r. 1489–1500]. On the whole, his ambitions were admirable and in the end they did bring him fame and renown, both within Italy and elsewhere. He worked diligently to make Florence pre-eminent in all the arts. He founded the University of Pisa as a center for the humanities. When his advisors argued that the university would never have as many students as the universities in Padua or Pavia, he replied that he would be satisfied to have more professors than they, and indeed all the most famous and brilliant scholars in Italy taught there for a time. Lorenzo spared no expense or effort to hire them, and consequently they received extraordinarily high salaries. The humanities flourished in Florence under the tutelage of Messer Agnolo Poliziano; the study of Greek advanced under Messer Demetrios [Chalcondylas] and [Konstantinos] Lascaris; philosophy and art were the domain of Marsilio Ficino, Giorgio Benigno, Count [Giovanni] Pico della Mirandola, and other notable men. He was equally generous to the fields of vernacular poetry, music, architecture, painting, sculpture, and all other arts and disciplines. The city overflowed with superior talent, and all because Lorenzo, a universal man, was such an excellent judge of skilled men—all of whom competed with one another for his favor. In his infinite generosity, he lavished them with salaries and everything they needed for their work. For example, when he decided to establish a Greek library, he sent the learned Lascaris back to Greece to search for books of antiquity.

He employed the same liberality with princes everywhere in order to further his reputation; no expense, however great, was too much to pay if it helped him to keep the friendship of powerful people. Consequently, in places like Lyons, Milan, and Bruges, where he had business interests, his habit of spreading money everywhere made his expenses rise and his profits fall; the real fault, though, lay with some of his underlings, who did not have his talent. . . .

Lorenzo had a haughty personality. He disliked it when anyone contradicted him, and he spoke in few words, even in matters of importance, because he expected people to understand him intuitively. In casual conversation, though, he could be quite pleasant if somewhat facetious. His private home life was simple, not luxurious at all except for the banquets he threw, in which he lavished hospitality on his noble guests who visited Florence. He was lusty in his carnal appetites, and engaged in love affairs with real abandon. Some of these relationships lasted for years. So persistent was he in his conquests that many people think his extreme carnality weakened his body and brought on his early death. . . .

Many people thought him cruel and vindictive by nature, citing especially the case of the Pazzi Rebellion [of 1478], in which, after the shedding of so much blood he threw many innocents into prison and forbade the girls [of the Pazzi family] ever to marry, but one must remember how bitterly he resented the family's attempt to overthrow him, and so such harshness can hardly be surprising. Besides, he did eventually allow the Pazzi girls to marry, and freed the Pazzi boys on condition they left Florence forever. In other instances too we can see that he was not truly cruel or bloodthirsty, but simply had the flaw of excessive suspicion of others.

This troublesome suspiciousness arose not from his intrinsic nature but from the fact that he had a city-state to keep under control and had to do it by means of magistrates and laws in order to maintain the appearance that Florence was a free republic. . . .

His constant distrust of others forced him not to allow powerful families to form marriage alliances. He aimed always at pairing people off in a way that did not pose any threat to his power. Sometimes he did this by forcing some young man of standing to marry a woman who was not really acceptable. In fact, the truth is that soon enough hardly any marriages took place among the important classes without his direct permission. The same suspiciousness inspired him to appoint permanent chancellors at the courts in Rome, Naples, and Milan, in order to keep an eye on the ambassadors he sent to those places. These well-paid chancellors were present to lend assistance to the various ambassadors but their real purpose was to keep Lorenzo informed of their actions.

It is true that he kept himself constantly surrounded by a large number of armed guards, who were well rewarded for their service (in fact, he even bestowed a number of hospitals and holy shrines upon some of them). He did this not out of intrinsic distrust of people, however; the truth is that the Pazzi conspiracy was to blame. Even so, it was hardly the sort of thing proper to a republic and to a private citizen; it smacked more of a tyrant ruling his subjects. In the end, one has to conclude that although Florence under Lorenzo was not a free city, it was a city that could hardly have wished for a better and more pleasing tyrant. His good qualities and virtues produced an infinity of blessings, and while the nature of his tyranny occasioned some ill-doings, these were relatively minor and never worse than they needed to be.

STUDY QUESTIONS

1. According to Guicciardini, what were the virtues of Lorenzo de' Medici? Were his virtues confined to politics? What picture of court patronage and the arts emerges from Guicciardini's portrait of Lorenzo?

2. Based on this description, would you say that Guicciardini preferred strong leaders like Lorenzo over popularly elected governments? Why?

12.8 BENVENUTO CELLINI, *MY LIFE*, 1558–1563

Benvenuto Cellini (1500–1571) was an Italian goldsmith and sculptor—and part-time soldier—who inhabited the thrilling art world dominated by masters like Michelangelo and Da Vinci. A member of the Mannerist school, Cellini was patronized by dukes, popes, and the French king; his "artistic temperament" meant that he was often in trouble with his fellow artists—he was accused of four homicides over the course of his life. This selection from his autobiography illustrates the way in which his artistic excellence framed his every experience and relationship, both personal and professional.

15. Continuing to work with Master Pagolo Arsago, I earned a great deal of money, always sending the largest part of it to my good father. By the end of two years, following my father's entreaties, I returned to Florence, and once again I went to work with Francesco Salinbene, with whom I earned a good deal and worked very hard at learning. I started going around with Francesco di Filippo again, given that I was intent upon the pursuit of some pleasure, thanks to practicing that damned music, and I always saved certain hours of the day or night which I gave over to my studies. In that period I created a silver "heart-key," which is what these objects were called at that time. This was a belt three fingers in width that new bridges were in the custom of wearing, and it was made in low relief with some little figures in the round among the others. I made it for a man who was called Raffaello Lapaccini. Although I was very poorly paid, I gained so much honour from it that it was worth much more than the recompense I justly earned. During this period I had worked with many different people in Florence, where I had made the acquaintance of some very worthy men among the goldsmiths, such as that Marcone who was my first master, as well as others who had very good reputations but who did me down in my work and blatantly robbed me whenever they could. Once I saw this, I kept away from them and considered them wicked men and thieves.

. . .

16. One day it happened that as I was leaning against the shop of one of these goldsmiths he called out to me, partly reproaching and partly threatening me; to his remarks I responded that if they had done their duty towards me, I would have said of them what one says about honest and worthy men. But, since they had done the contrary they should complain about themselves and not about me. While I was standing there talking, one of them, their cousin, who was called Gherardo Guasconti, perhaps compelled by all of them together, waited until a pack-animal with a load passed by. This was a load of bricks. When the load was near me, this Gherardo pushed it against me so forcefully that he hurt me very badly. I immediately turned on him, and when I saw that he was laughing I gave him such a hard blow with my fist on his temple that he fell down unconscious, like a dead man; then I turned to his cousins and announced: "This is how to treat thieving cowards like you!" And because they were about to make some move, since there were several of them, incensed, I put my hand on a small knife that I had

Benvenuto Cellini, *My Life*. Translated by Julia Conway Bondanella and Peter Bondanella. Oxford: Oxford University Press, 2010, 1968w from pp. 24–9, 66–9, 124–5. By permission of Oxford University Press. License granted through PLS Clear.

and said: "Whichever one of you leaves his shop, the other will go fetch his confessor, because there'll be no use for a doctor." These words so terrified them that no one went to the assistance of his cousin. Immediately after I had left, their fathers and children ran to the Eight and claimed that I had assaulted them with a weapon in their own shops, something which was unheard of in Florence. The Eight had me summoned before them, whereupon I appeared; they gave me a severe reprimand and scolding, since they saw me dressed in a cloak, while the Guascontis wore the mantle and hood of well-bred people, but they did so also because while my adversaries had gone to speak with all these magistrates at their homes in private, I, lacking experience, had not spoken to any of them, since I relied upon being entirely in the right.

. . .

I felt as if I had been totally discredited, and it was not long before I sent for my cousin, who was called Master Annibale the surgeon, the father of Messer Librodoro Librodori, wanting him to serve as my guarantee. Annibale refused to come: for this reason, I became very indignant and, puffing myself up like an asp, decided to do something desperate. In all of this it is obvious how much the stars not so much influence us as force us into certain courses of action. Knowing how much this Annibale owed my family, my anger became so great that it turned toward a harmful course of action—being also somewhat hot-blooded by nature—and I stood waiting until the members of the Eight had gone out to dinner, then, while I remained there alone, seeing that the guards of the Eight were no longer keeping an eye on me, and inflamed with anger, I left the Palazzo, ran to my workshop, where I seized a large dagger, and bounded into the home of my adversaries, which served as both home and workplace. I found them at table, and that young Gherardo, who had been the main cause of my interrogation, threw himself upon me: I responded by stabbing him in the chest, piercing his tunic and vest through to the shirt without touching his flesh or doing him even the slightest harm. I thought, by the way in which my hand entered his garments and by the sound his clothes made, that I had hurt him very seriously, and when he fell terrified onto the floor, I shouted: "You traitor,

today is the day I kill you all." Believing that the Day of Judgment had arrived, his father, mother, and sisters threw themselves down on their knees, and at the top of their lungs they called out for mercy; once I saw that they had no defence against me and that Gherardo was stretched out on the floor like a dead man, I thought it too cowardly an act to attack them, but still furious, I ran down the stairs, and when I reached the street I came upon the rest of the clan, more than twelve of them: one of them held an iron shovel, another a huge iron pipe, while others carried hammers, anvils, and cudgels. I attacked them, like an enraged bull, throwing four or five to the ground, and I fell along with them, always striking out with my dagger, now at one, now at another. Those who had remained standing hastened as best they could to deal me some blows with both hands, with their hammers, cudgels, and anvils, and because God in His mercy sometimes intervenes in such matters, He kept us from doing each other any harm whatsoever. All I left there was my hat, captured by my adversaries although previously they had fled from it, which each one struck with his weapon; then they looked around them for their dead and wounded, but nobody had been harmed.

. . .

38. Skipping over a few things, I shall describe how Pope Clement, in order to save the papal tiaras, with all of the numerous large jewels belonging to the Apostolic Chamber, had me summoned, and he shut himself up alone in a room with me and Cavalierino. This Cavalierino had once worked in the stable of Filippo Strozzi: he was a Frenchman, a person of very humble origins, and since he was a very faithful servant, Pope Clement had made him an extremely rich man and trusted him as he did himself. This, with the Pope, Cavalierino, and me locked inside this room, they placed me before the tiaras with that large number of jewels belonging to the Apostolic Chamber, and I was given the commission of extracting them all from the gold in which they were set. And I did so: then I wrapped each of them up in small pieces of paper and sewed them up in the linings of some garments worn by the Pope and this Cavalierino. Then they gave me all the gold, which was around two hundred pounds, and

they told me to melt it down in as much secrecy as I could. I went to the Angel where my own room was located, and where I could lock the door so that no one would disturb me, and once I had built a small brick blast-furnace in the bottom of which I set a fairly large ash-tray shaped like a dish, I tossed the gold on the charcoal, which little by little dripped down into the dish. While this furnace was in operation, I constantly studied on how I could do our enemies harm, and since we had the enemy's trenches beneath us less than stone's throw away, I did them a great deal of damage in those trenches using some bits of old scrap, of which there were several piles, formerly used in the Castello as ammunition. Taking a saker and a falconet, both of which were broken a bit at the muzzle, I filled them with this scrap metal, and then as I opened fire with these weapons my shots flew down like mad, causing many unexpected injuries in the trenches. And so, keeping these weapons constantly loaded while I melted down that gold, a short time before the hour of vespers I saw a man mounted on a mule riding on the edge of the trench. This mule was moving along very swiftly, and the man was speaking to the men in the trenches. I stood ready to fire my artillery before he arrived in front of me. So, with good judgment, I commenced firing and hit him, knocking him directly in the face with one of those scraps of metal, while the rest hit the mule which fell down dead; I heard a tremendous uproar from the trench, and I fired another piece, not without doing them great damage. This man was the Prince of Orange, who was carried along the trenches to a certain inn nearby, where all the noblemen in the army quickly gathered. When Pope Clement learned what

I had done, he immediately sent for me and asked about the affair, and I explained everything to him and, moreover, I told him that he must have been a man of very great importance, since all the leaders of the army, as far as one could determine, immediately gathered at the inn to which they had carried him.

. . .

After I returned to Cornaro's home, a few days later Cardinal Farnese was elected Pope, and after immediately settling matters of the greatest importance, the Pope next asked me, saying that he did not want anyone else to make his coins. Hearing these words, a certain gentleman named Messer Latino Iuvinale, who was on intimate terms with the Pope, stated that I was a fugitive from a homicide I had committed on the person of a Milanese named Pompeo, and he put all my motives in the most favourable light. At those words, the Pope said: "I didn't know about the death of Pompeo, but I knew of Benvenuto's motives perfectly well, so write him out an order of safe conduct immediately, with which he will be completely secure." There was present a great friend of that Pompeo and close confidant of the Pope named Messer Ambruogio, a Milanese, and he said: "During the first days of your papacy, it would not be good to grant pardons of this sort." Turning toward him, the Pope said: "You don't understand the matter as well as I do. You should know that men like Benvenuto, unique in their profession, need not be subject to the law: especially not Benvenuto, since I know what good reasons he had." And after my safe-conduct was made out, I immediately began to serve the new Pope and was treated with the greatest favour.

STUDY QUESTIONS

1. How does Benvenuto use violence to reinforce his sense of honor?
2. Are the endorsements of Cellini offered by the popes surprising?

12.9 VASARI, *LIVES OF ARTISTS*, FIRST PUBLISHED IN 1550, REVISED AND ADDED TO UNTIL 1568

An architect and fresco painter in his own right—and even an apprentice to Michelangelo in his youth—Giorgio Vasari (1511–1574) is most fondly remembered for his personal accounts of roughly two hundred celebrated artists of Renaissance Italy. Using art historical analysis, Vasari talks capably about the production and technical elements of paintings, ambitious architectural projects, metalworking, and sculpture. Charming anecdotes about the greats—Giotto, Michelangelo, Botticelli, etc.—bring to life the world inhabited by these incredibly talented individuals. *The Life of Donatello* (1386–1466) provides glimpses into the artistic temperament exemplified by Cellini (Document 12.8), and the preface to Part III provides an overview of artistic development throughout the Renaissance.

THE LIFE OF DONATELLO, FLORENTINE SCULPTOR [1386–1466]

Donato, who was called Donatello by his relatives and thus signed some of his works this way, was born in Florence in the year 1303. And devoting himself to the art of design, he became not only an unusually fine sculptor and a marvellous statue-maker, but also grew experienced in stucco, quite skilled in perspective, and highly esteemed in architecture. His works possessed so much grace and excellence and such a fine sense of design that they were considered to be more like the distinguished works of the ancient Greeks and Romans than those of any other artist who has ever existed, and he is therefore quite rightly recognized as the first artisan who properly used the device of scenes in bas-relief. He worked out these scenes with such careful thought, true facility, and expert skill that it was obvious he possessed a true understanding of them and executed them with extraordinary beauty. Thus, no other artisan surpassed him in this field, and even in our own times, there is no one who is his equal.

Donatello was raised from childhood in the home of Ruberto Martelli, and with his fine qualities and the diligence with which he refined his skill, he not only earned Martelli's affection but that of this entire noble family. In his youth, he worked upon so many things that they were not very highly regarded because there were so many of them. But the thing which earned him a name and brought him recognition was an Annunciation in blue-grey stone which was placed in the church of Santa Croce in Florence at the altar in the chapel of the Cavalcanti family, for which he made a decoration in the grotesque style. Its base was varied and twisted, completed by a quarter-circle to which were added six putti carrying several garlands who seem to be steadying themselves by embracing each other as if they were afraid of the height. But Donatello demonstrated above all his great ingenuity and artistry in the figure of the Virgin, who, frightened by the sudden appearance of the angel, timidly but gently moves Her body in a very chaste bow, turning towards the angel greeting Her with the most beautiful grace, so that Her face reflects the humility and gratitude one owes to the giver of an unexpected gift, and even more so when the gift is so great. Besides this, Donatello proved his ability to carve masterful folds and turns in the robes

Giorgio Vasari, *Lives of the Artists*. Translated by Julia Conway Bondanella and Peter Bondanella. Oxford: Oxford University Press, 2009, 2731w from pp. 147–9, 153–4, 159–60, 277–9, 281–3. By permission of Oxford University Press. License granted through PLS Clear.

of this Madonna and the angel, and in suggesting the nude forms of his figures, he showed just how he was attempting to rediscover the beauty of the ancients which had already remained hidden for so many years. And he exhibited so much facility and skill in this work that no one could really expect more from him in design and judgement, or from the way he carved and executed the work.

In the same church below the choir screen beside the scenes frescoed by Taddeo Gaddi, Donatello took extraordinary pains in carving a wooden crucifix which, upon completing it and believing that he had produced a very rare object, he showed to Filippo di Ser Brunellesco, his very dear friend, in order to have his opinion of it. Filippo, who expected to see something much better from Donatello's description of it, smiled a bit when he saw it. When Donatello saw this, he begged Filippo for the sake of their friendship to give him his honest opinion of it, and so, Filippo, who was very candid, replied that it seemed to him as if Donatello had placed a peasant upon the cross and not a body like that of Jesus Christ, which was most delicate and represented, in all its parts, the most perfect human being born. Hearing himself criticized—and even more sharply than he had imagined—rather than receiving the praise he had hoped for, Donatello answered: "If it were as simple to create something as to criticize, my Christ would look like Christ to you and not like a peasant; take some wood and try to make one yourself." Without saying another word, Filippo returned home, and without anyone knowing, he set his hand to making a crucifix, seeking to surpass Donatello in order to vindicate his own judgement, and after many months he brought it to the highest degree of perfection. And once this was finished, he invited Donatello one morning to have lunch with him, and Donatello accepted the invitation. And so, they went together towards Filippo's home, and when they reached the Old Market, Filippo bought a few things and gave them to Donatello, saying: "Go on home with these things and wait for me there, and I'll be along shortly." Donatello therefore entered the house and, on the ground-floor, saw Filippo's crucifix in a perfect light, and stopping to examine it, he found it so perfectly finished that, realizing Filippo had

outdone him, and completely stupefied, as if he had lost his wits, he relaxing his grip on his apron; whereupon, the eggs, the cheese, and everything else fell out, breaking into pieces and spilling all over, and as he stood there stunned and amazed, Filippo caught up with him, and said with a laugh: "What's your plan, Donatello? How can we have lunch if you have spilled everything?" Donatello replied: "Personally, I've had enough for this morning, but if you want your share, take it. But no more, thank you: it's for you to make Christs and for me to make peasants."

. . .

It was said that a Genoese merchant had Donatello execute a very handsome life-size bronze head which was thin and light so that it could be carried over a long distance, and it was through Cosimo that Donatello received the commission for such a work. When it was finished and the merchant wanted to pay Donatello, he thought that the sculptor was asking too high a price. So the deal was referred to Cosimo, who had the bust carried to a courtyard above his palace and had it placed between the battlements overlooking the street so that it could be better seen. Wishing to settle the matter, Cosimo, who found the merchant far from the price asked by Donatello, turned to the merchant and declared that Donatello's price was too low. At this, the merchant, who thought it too high, declared that Donatello had worked upon it for only a month or a little more, and that this added up to more than half a florin per day. Donatello then turned angrily away, thinking himself too greatly offended, and told the merchant that in one hundredth of an hour he could spoil the labour and value of an entire year, and he gave the bust a shove, immediately breaking it upon the street below into many pieces and telling the merchant he proved himself more accustomed to bargaining for beans than for statues. The merchant regretted what he had done and wanted to give Donatello more than double his price if he would only recast the bust, but neither the merchant's promises nor Cosimo's entreaties could ever convince Donatello to redo it.

. . .

It is said that when Cosimo was about to die, he commended Donatello to the care of his son Piero who, as a most conscientious executor of his father's will, gave Donatello a farm in Cafaggiulo with enough income for him to live comfortably. Donatello was delighted by this, for he felt that with this more than secure income he would not risk dying from hunger. But he had only held it for a year when he returned to Piero and gave it back to him by means of a written contract, declaring that he did not wish to lose his peace of mind having to dwell upon domestic concerns or the troubles of his peasant tenant, who was underfoot every third day—first, because the wind blew the roof off his doves' hitch; next, because the Commune seized his livestock for taxes; and then, because the storm deprived him of wine and fruit. He was so fed up and disgusted with all these things that he preferred to die from hunger rather than to think about them.

Piero laughed at Donatello's simple ways, but in order to free Donatello from this worry he accepted the farm at Donatello's insistence, and he assigned him from his own bank an allowance of the same amount or more but in cash, which was paid to Donatello every week in appropriate installments. This made Donatello exceedingly content.

PREFACE TO PART THREE

Those excellent masters we have described up to this point in the Second part of these *Lives* truly made great advances in the arts of architecture, painting, and sculpture, adding to the accomplishments of the early artists rule, order, proportion, design, and style, and if they were not perfect in every way, they drew so near to the truth that artists in the third group, whom we shall now discuss, were able, through that illumination, to rise up and reach complete perfection, the proof of which we have in the finest and most celebrated modern works. But to clarify the quality of the improvements that these artists made, it will not be out of place to explain briefly the five qualities I mentioned above and to discuss succinctly the origins of that true goodness which has surpassed that of the ancient world and rendered the modern age so glorious.

. . . Design is the imitation of the most beautiful things in Nature in all forms, both in sculpture and in painting, and this quality depends upon having the hand and the skill to transfer with great accuracy and precision everything the eye sees to a plan or drawing or to a sheet of paper, a panel, or another flat surface, and the same is true for relief in sculpture. And then the most beautiful style comes from constantly copying the most beautiful things, combining the most beautiful hands, heads, bodies, or legs together to create from all these beautiful qualities the most perfect figure possible, and using it as a model for all the figures in each one's works; and on account of this, it is said to be beautiful style.

Neither Giotto nor those artisans did this, even though they had discovered the principles underlying all such difficulties and had resolved them superficially, as in the case of drawing, which became more lifelike than it had been before and more true to Nature, and in the blending of colours and the composition of the figures in scenes, and in many other things, about which enough has already been said. And although the artists of the second period made extraordinary efforts in these crafts in all the areas mentioned above, they were not, however, sufficient to achieve complete perfection. They still lacked, within the boundaries of the rules, a freedom which—not being part of the rules—was nevertheless ordained by the rules and which could coexist with order without causing confusion or spoiling it; and this freedom required copious invention in every particular and a certain beauty even in the smallest details which could demonstrate all of this order with more decoration. In proportion, they lacked good judgement which, without measuring the figures, would bestow upon them, no matter what their dimensions a grace that goes beyond proportion. In design they did not reach the ultimate goal, for even when they made a rounded arm or a straight leg, they had not fully examined how to depict the muscles with that soft and graceful facility which is partially seen and partially concealed in the flesh of living things, and their figures were crude and clumsy, offensive to the eye and harsh in style. Moreover, they lacked a lightness in touch in making all their figures slender and graceful, especially those of women and children, whose bodies should be as natural as those of men and yet possess a volume of softness which are produced by design and good judgement rather than by the awkward example of real bodies. They also lacked an abundance of beautiful costumes, variety in imaginative details, charm in their colours, diversity in their buildings, and distance and variety in their landscapes.

. . .

The artisans who followed them succeeded after seeing the excavation of some of the most famous antiquities mentioned by Pliny: the Laocoon, the Hercules, the great torso of Belvedere, the Venus, the Cleopatra, the Apollo, and countless others, which exhibit in their softness and harshness the expressions of real flesh copied from the most beautiful details of living models and endowed with certain movements which do not distort them but lend them motion and the utmost grace. And these statues caused the disappearance of a certain dry, crude, and clear-cut style which bequeathed to this craft.

. . .

But what matters most is that the artisans of today have made their craft so perfect and so easy for anyone who possesses a proper sense of design, invention, and colouring that whereas previously our older masters could produce one panel in six years, the masters of today can produce six of them in a year. And I bear witness to this both from personal observation and from practice, and these works are obviously much more finished and perfected than those of the other reputable masters who worked before them.

But the man who wins the palm among artists both living and dead, who transcends and surpasses them all, is the divine Michelangelo Buonarroti, who reigns supreme not merely in one of these arts but in all three at once. This man surpasses and triumphs over not only all those artists who have almost surpassed Nature but even those most celebrated ancient artists themselves, who beyond all doubt surpassed Nature: and alone he has triumphed over ancient artists, modern artists, and even Nature herself, without ever imagining anything so strange or so difficult that he could not surpass it by far with the power of his most divine genius through his diligence, sense of design, artistry, judgement, and grace. And not only in

painting and colouring, categories which include all the shapes and bodies, straight and curved, tangible and intangible, visible and invisible, but also in bodies completely in the round; and through the point of his chisel and his untiring labour, this beautiful and fruitful plant has already spread so many honourable branches that they have not only filled the entire world in such an unaccustomed fashion with the most luscious fruits possible, but they have also brought these three most noble arts to their final stage of development with such wondrous perfection that one might well and safely declare that his statues are, in every respect, much more beautiful than those of the ancients. When the heads, hands, arms, and feet they created are compared to those he fashioned, it is obvious his works contain a more solid foundation, a more complete grace, and a much more absolute perfection, executed at a certain level of difficulty rendered so easily in his style that it would never be possible to see anything better. The same things can be said of his paintings. If it were possible to place any of them beside the most famous Greek or Roman paintings, they would be held in even greater esteem and more highly honoured than his sculptures, which appear superior to all those of the ancients.

But if we have admired those most celebrated artists who, inspired by excessive rewards and great happiness, have given life to their works, how much more should we admire and praise to the skies those even rarer geniuses who, living not only without rewards but in a miserable state of poverty, produced such precious fruits? It may be believed and therefore affirmed that, if just remuneration existed in our century, even greater and better works than the ancients ever executed would, without a doubt, he created. But being forced to struggle more with Hunger than with Fame, impoverished geniuses are buried and unable to earn a reputation (which is a shame and a disgrace for those who might be able to help them but take no care to do so).

STUDY QUESTIONS

1. Did Donatello gain more from his relationship to his patrons Cosimo and Piero de Medici than they received from him?
2. Does Vasari claim that artists in his day can surpass the achievements of the Greeks and Romans?

12.10 BENVENUTO CELLINI, *AUTOBIOGRAPHY*, 1558–1563

Benvenuto Cellini (1500–1571) was a Florentine sculptor and goldsmith whose *Autobiography* is one of the great literary treasures of the Renaissance. As the following passage makes clear, he found himself in one sort of trouble after another throughout his life, and somehow always felt that his excellence as an artist gave him right to do whatever he wanted.

Now we turn to Pietro Torrigiani, who said to me one day while holding a drawing of me in his hand, "[Michelangelo] Buonarroti and I, when we were kids, used to go to the church of the Carmine in order to study Masaccio's chapel and Buonarroti would always make fun of everyone who was there to make sketches. One day he was really bothering me; I got much more annoyed than usual, clenched my fist, and gave him such a punch in the nose that I could feel the bone and cartilage in his nose shatter like a wafer. He'll carry the mark of that punch for the rest of his life!"

These words made me feel nothing but hatred for him, for I was then in the habit of examining the works of the divine Michelangelo almost every day, and the result of this hatred was that I no longer had any desire to travel to England with him [as we had previously planned]. I could hardly bear the sight of him, in fact.

The whole time I was in Florence I set myself to studying Michelangelo's beautiful style, a style from which I have never since strayed. At this time I also met and became close friends with a fine young man about my age—another goldsmith. His name was Francesco and he was the son of that superb painter Filippo di Fra Filippo. We worked together, which created so strong a bond of friendship between us that we were hardly ever apart, day or night. His home held many beautiful sketches drawn by his talented father and gathered together in several volumes, mostly depicting the great antiquities of Rome. When I saw these studies I fell completely in love with them. Francesco and I worked together for about two years. It was at this time that I created a bas-relief in silver, about the size of a toddler's hand. This piece was ultimately used as a man's belt buckle, for in those days large buckles were in fashion. The piece was carved in the ancient style with foliage, cherubs, and some lovely masks. I finished it in Francesco Salimbene's workshop. When several members of the goldsmith's guild saw it, they praised me as the most talented youngster then at work in the craft. Another fellow—a woodcarver of my age named Giambattista Tasso—began to say that if ever I wanted to go to Rome he would gladly come with me. One day we were discussing this idea, just after our mid-day meal. At the time I had just been arguing with my father (the usual reason: my music-playing), and so I said to Tasso, "You're the type who always talks of doing things but never does them." To which he replied, "Listen, I'm angry too—at my mother. If I had enough money to get to Rome, I wouldn't even take the time to go around to lock up that wretched little shop of mine." That's when I offered that if lack of money was the only thing keeping him in Florence, I had enough of it set aside to get both of us to Rome. We were walking as we were talking, and found ourselves unexpectedly at the San Pietro Gattolini Gate. "Tasso, my friend," I said,

Translation by Clifford Backman.

"this is God's handiwork, our arriving at this gate! Neither of us was planning it, but now that we're here it seems to me that we're half on our way!" He agreed, so we continued on, saying, "Oh, what will our parents say this evening!" We promised each other that we wouldn't give them another thought until we reached Rome, and so it was that with our aprons tied behind our backs and with scarcely another word between us, we soon reached Siena.

When we arrived there Tasso complained that his feet hurt and he could go no further and didn't even want to. He asked to borrow enough money for a ride back home. I answered, "You should have thought about this before leaving Florence! If I loaned you the money, I wouldn't have enough to continue on by myself. You say that you can't go on because your feet hurt. Well then, let's find a horse that is making a return trip to Rome! That way you won't have an excuse for not coming with me." So we hired a horse, and since Tasso made no reply, I turned the horse onto the road towards Rome. Seeing that I was determined, Tasso limped along after me as best he could, never letting up with his complaints. He was slow and fell some distance behind. By the time we reached the gate that led towards Rome I felt sorry for him and halted, and then I lifted him into the saddle. "What on earth would our friends say if they heard us declare that we were leaving for Rome but couldn't make it past Siena!" Then the good Tasso declared that what I had said was true, and since he was fundamentally a happy person he began to laugh and sing. In this way, laughing and singing together, we made our way to Rome. This happened when I was exactly nineteen years old, the same age as the century we now live in.

Once arrived in Rome, I immediately found work in the shop of a master smith called Firenzuola. His name was Giovanni and he came from the village in Lombardy called Firenzuola. He was a talented goldsmith who worked mainly on trays, dishes, and other large items. He was deeply impressed when I showed him a model of the belt buckle I had made at Salimbene's shop in Florence, and turning to his apprentice (a Florentine lad named Giannetto Giannotti who had been with him for several years) he said, "Here is

a Florentine who knows a thing or two! You, on the other hand, are a Florentine know-nothing!"

I recognized Giannetto, since before setting out for Rome he used to go drawing with me and we had been good friends. I wanted to speak to him, but his master's words had so offended him that he pretended not to know me and said we had never met. This hurt me, so I said, "Giannetto! We were friends, good friends! We spent time together in this place and that place, and used to sketch together, and ate and drank and slept in your home in the country. Still, it doesn't matter if you vouch for me or not to this honest master of yours, because I intend to let the work of my hands show him the kind of man I am. I don't need your help!"

. . .

It happened one day that I was leaning against the wall of one of the Roman goldsmith's shops, and he began to yell at me in a reproachful, threatening manner. I retorted that if everyone working there had treated me honorably I would have nothing to say except how worthy and honest they were; but since they had done just the opposite, they should direct their criticism at themselves instead of at me. So I just stood there and chatted. Then one of them—a cousin, named Gherardo Guasconti, goaded by the others—bided his time until a packhorse carrying a load of bricks happened by. Gherardo then shoved the beast into me with great force. The pain was terrible. I spun around to face him—he was laughing—and drove my fist into his temple so hard that he fell unconscious to the ground, looking for all the world like a dead man. Then, turning to his cousins, I shouted, "That's how I deal with thieving good-for-nothings like you!"

Now there was a bunch of them and they were angry and ready to spring into action, so I drew my knife and said, "If anyone leaves this shop, it had better be to find a confessor, for he'll have no need of a doctor!" My words scared them so that no one moved to help his cousin. The second I left the shop all the men and boys ran to the magistrates and said I had attacked them with a weapon in their shop—something that was unheard of in Florence. The magistrates had me summoned and

I subsequently appeared before them. They gave me a harsh reprimand and scolding, for unlike the Guascontis (who had dressed in fancy mantles and hoods) I wore only a simple cloak. Moreover, the Guascontis had already pleaded their case, in private, at the magistrates' own homes, whereas I had naively trusted in the fairness of the system and had not tried to win the magistrates over beforetimes. I testified that I had indeed given Gherardo a slap in anger but only on account of the enormous and offensive injury he had done to me, and consequently I had done nothing to merit so strong a chastisement. No sooner had I spoken the word slap when one of the magistrates, Prinzivalle della Stufa, shouted, "You punched him; you didn't slap him!" Then the bell rang and we were all dismissed. While we were out, Prinzivalle spoke in my defense to his colleagues, saying, "My lords, consider how naïve this poor fellow is. He says he gave only a slap, thinking it less serious than a punch. But the penalty for a slap in the Mercato Nuovo is twentyfive scudi, whereas that for a punch is nothing, or practically so. Undoubtedly he is a very talented artist and does his best to support his family by his work. I wish to God our city had more, not fewer, young men like him!"

Some of the other magistrates were followers of Savonarola (I could tell by the cut of their cowls), and because were part of that gang and had been persuaded by all the pleadings and lies put forth by my enemies, they were only too happy to toss me into a prison cell and mete out the harshest of punishments. Fortunately, though, good Prinzivalle was there to make everything all right, and so I was hit only with a small fine of four bushels of flour that I was to donate to the Convento della Murata. After he summoned me back inside, Prinzivalle was quick to tell me not to say another word lest I risk the other magistrates' displeasure, and to obey the terms of my sentence right down to the letter. And so the full panel of magistrates gave me a proper scolding and ordered me to see the chancellor. "It was still only a slap, not a punch," I muttered under my breath—which made all eight of them laugh.

The chancellor formalized the orders on behalf of the magistracy and officially sentenced me alone to pay the four bushels of flour. I felt I had been treated unfairly. Not long afterwards I asked my cousin M. Annibale the surgeon (and father of the honorable Librodoro Librodori) to serve as my guarantor. When Annibale refused to appear in court I became indignant, puffed myself up like an asp, and decided to take a desperate measure. How clear it is, in relating all of this, how the stars not only influence us but actually drive us into certain courses of action! My anger was great, for I knew well how much this Annibale owed to my family, and being hot-blooded by nature I made a rash choice: once the magistrates had withdrawn to their dinner and I was alone (the guards had stopped paying any attention to me), I left the courthouse in a rage, ran to my workshop, grabbed a large dagger, and raced to where my enemies lived and worked. I came upon them as they were at table. Young Gherardo, the cause of all my troubles, hurled himself at me. I reacted by thrusting my dagger at his chest; it pierced his tunic and vest, and even went through his shirt, although it never touched his flesh or did him the slightest harm. But to judge from the sound his clothes made and the feeling in my hand, I was certain I had wounded him badly. When he fell to the floor, looking terrified, I shouted, "Traitors! Today I will kill you all!"

Thinking the Last Judgment had arrived, Gherardo's father, mother, and sisters all fell to their knees and cried out for mercy at the top of their lungs. Seeing that they were defenseless and Gherardo was stretched out on the floor like a dead man, I thought attacking them would be a cowardly thing to do, so instead I ran down the stairs, still in a rage, and when I got to the street I found the rest of their clan—all twelve or more of them. One held an iron shovel, another a large iron pipe. Still others were lugging hammers, anvils, and cudgels. I attacked them all like a furious bull, throwing four or five of them to the ground. I rushed at them thrusting my dagger at this one and that one. Those still on their feet did their best to strike me with their hammers, cudgels, and anvils, but since God in His mercy often intervenes in our actions, He saw to it that none of us harmed each other in any way. The only thing I left at the scene was my hat, which my enemies (who had previously run away at the sight of it) kept as a prize and which they took turns striking with their weapons. When they finally stopped and looked around to tend to their dead and wounded, they found that no one had been harmed at all.

STUDY QUESTIONS

1. What picture of Florentine and Roman artistic circles emerges from Cellini's description? Does this picture differ from the way artists are usually depicted?
2. How do networks play a role in Cellini's professional life?

CHAPTER 13

WORLDS OLD AND NEW

13.1 BARTOLOMÉ DE LAS CASAS, A *SHORT ACCOUNT OF THE DESTRUCTION OF THE INDIES*, WRITTEN 1542; PUBLISHED 1552

A Dominican friar, Bartolomé de Las Casas (ca. 1484–1566) wrote his *Short Account* to open the eyes of King Philip II of Spain to the atrocities committed upon the native peoples in newly discovered Latin America. For this early devotion to the protection of what would be called "human rights," de Las Casas was appointed "Protector of the Indians." The text itself can be difficult to read—the crimes against the Indigenous populations are recounted with a matter-of-fact tone that seems at odds with the level of horrific detail provided. De Las Casas argues that this inhumane activity must cease for two reasons: first, because "Indian" souls cannot be saved through conversion if the people continue to be murdered first, and second, because Spain will suffer God's wrath as a result of these sins.

PREFACE

The Americas were discovered in 1492, and the first Christian settlements established by the Spanish the following year. It is accordingly forty-nine years from now since Spaniards began arriving in numbers in this part of the world. They first settled the large and fertile island of Hispaniola, which boasts six hundred leagues of coastline and is surrounded by a great many other large islands, all of them, as I saw for myself, with as high a native population as anywhere on earth. Of the coast of the mainland which, at its nearest point, is a little over two hundred and fifty leagues from Hispaniola, more than ten thousand leagues had been explored by 1541, and more are being discovered every day. This coastline, too, swarming with people and it would seem, if we are to judge by those areas so far explored, that the Almighty selected this part of the world as home to the greater part of the human race.

God made all the peoples of this area, many and varied as they are, as open and as innocent as can be imagined. The simplest people in the world—unassuming, long-suffering, unassertive, and submissive— they are without malice or guile, and are utterly faithful and obedient both to their own native lords and to the Spaniards in whose service they now find themselves. Never quarrelsome or belligerent or boisterous, they harbour no grudges and do not seek to settle old scores; indeed, the notions of revenge, rancor, and hatred are quite foreign to them. At the same time, they are among the least robust of human beings: their delicate constitutions make them unable to withstand hard work or suffering and render them liable to succumb to almost any illness, no matter how mild. Even the common people are no tougher than princes or than other Europeans born with a silver spoon in their mouths and who spend their lives shielded from the rigours of the outside world. They are also among the poorest people on the face of the earth; they own next to nothing and have no urge to acquire material possessions. As a result they are neither ambitious nor greedy, and are totally uninterested in worldly power. Their diet is every bit as poor and as monotonous, in quantity and in kind, as that enjoyed by the Desert Fathers. Most of them go naked, save for a loincloth to cover their modesty; at best they may wrap themselves in a piece of cotton material a yard or two square. Most sleep on matting, although a few possess a kind of hanging net, known in the language of Hispaniola as a hammock. They are innocent and pure in mind and have a lively intelligence, all of which makes them particularly receptive to learning and understanding the truths of our Catholic faith and to being instructed in virtue; indeed, God has invested them with fewer impediments in this regard than any other people on earth. Once they begin to learn of the Christian faith they become so keen to know more, to receive the Sacraments, and to worship God, that the missionaries who instruct them do truly regard them men of exceptional patience and forbearance; and over the years I have time and again met Spanish laymen who have been so struck by the natural goodness that shines through these people that they frequently can be heard to exclaim: "These would be the most blessed people on earth if only they were given the chance to convert to Christianity."

It was upon these gentle lambs, imbued by the Creator with all the qualities we have mentioned, that from the very first day they clapped eyes on them the Spanish fell like ravening wolves upon the fold, or like tigers and savage lions who have not eaten meat for days. The pattern established at the outset has remained unchanged to this day, and the Spaniards still do nothing save tear the natives to shreds, murder them and inflict upon them untold misery, suffering and distress, tormenting, harrying and persecuting them mercilessly. We shall in due course describe some of the many ingenious methods of torture they have invented and refined for this purpose, but one can get some idea of the effectiveness of their methods from the figures alone. When the Spanish first journeyed there, the indigenous population of the island of Hispaniola stood at some three million; today only two hundred survive.

. . .

One God-fearing individual was moved to mount an expedition to seek out those who had escaped the Spanish trawl and were still living in the Bahamas and to save their souls by converting them to Christianity, but, by the end of a search lasting three whole years, they had found only the eleven survivors I saw with my own eyes. A further thirty or so islands in the region of Puerto Rico are also now uninhabited and left to go to rack and ruin as a direct result of the same practices. All these islands, which together must run over two thousand leagues, are now abandoned and desolate.

On the mainland, we know for sure that our fellow-countrymen have, through their cruelty and wickedness, depopulated and laid waste an area which once boasted more than ten kingdoms, each of them larger in area than the whole of the Iberian Peninsula. The whole region, once teeming with human beings, is now deserted over a distance of more than two thousand leagues: a distance, that is, greater than the journey from Seville to Jerusalem and back again.

At a conservative estimate, the despotic and diabolical behaviour of the Christians has, over the last forty years, led to the unjust and totally unwarranted deaths of more than twelve million souls, women and children among them, and there are grounds for believing my own estimate of more than fifteen million to be nearer the mark.

. . .

[The *conquistadores*] spared no one, erecting especially wide gibbets on which they could string their victims up with their feet just off the ground and then burn them alive thirteen at a time, in honour of our Saviour and the twelve Apostles, or tie dry straw to their bodies and set fire to it. Some they chose to keep alive and simply cut their wrists, leaving their hands dangling, saying to them: "Take this letter"—meaning that their sorry condition would act as a warning to those hiding in the hills. The way they normally dealt with the native leaders and nobles was to tie them to a kind of griddle consisting of sticks resting on pitchforks driven into the ground and then grill them over a slow fire, with the result that they howled in agony and despair as they died a lingering death.

It once happened that I myself witnessed their grilling of four or five local leaders in this fashion (and I believe they had set up two or three pairs of grills alongside so that they might process other victims at the same time) when the poor creatures' howls came between the Spanish commander and his sleep. He gave orders that the prisoners were to be throttled, but the man in charge of the execution detail, who was more bloodthirsty than the average common hangman (I know his identity and even met some relatives of his in Seville), was loath to cut short his private entertainment by throttling them so he personally went round ramming wooden bungs into their mouths to stop them making such a racket and deliberately stoked the fire so that they would take just as long to die as he himself chose. I saw all these things for myself and many others besides. And, since all those who could do so took to the hills and mountains in order to escape the clutches of these merciless and inhuman butchers, these mortal enemies of human kind trained hunting dogs to track them down—wild dogs who would savage a native to death as soon as look at him, tearing him to shreds and devouring his flesh as though he were a pig. These dogs wrought havoc among the natives and were responsible for much carnage. And when, as happened on the odd occasion, the locals did kill a European, as, given the enormity of the crimes committed against them, they were in all justice fully entitled to, the Spanish came to an unofficial agreement among themselves that for every European killed one hundred natives would be executed.

. . .

CONCLUSION

I, Bartolomé de Las Casas, or Casaus, a brother in the Dominican Order, was, by the grace of God, persuaded by a number of people here at the Spanish court, out of their concern for the Christian faith and their compassion towards the afflictions and calamities that befall their fellow-men, to write the work you have before you in order to help ensure that the teeming millions in the New World, for whose sins Christ gave His life, do not continue to die in ignorance, but rather are brought to knowledge of God and thereby saved. My deep love of Castile has also been a spur, for I do not wish to see my country destroyed as a divine punishment for sins against the honour of God and the True Faith. It has always been my intention to pen this account, although it has been long delayed by my being taken up with so many other tasks. I completed it in Valencia on the eighth day of December 1542, at a time when the violence, the oppression, the despotism, the killing, the plunder, the depopulation, the outrages, the agonies and the calamities we have described were at their height throughout the New World wherever Christians have set foot. It may be that some areas are worse than others: Mexico City and the surrounding territories are a little better than most, for there, at least, outrages cannot be committed so publicly, as there is justice of a sort, despite the crippling taxation unjustly imposed on the people. Yet I do see hope for the future, for, as the Emperor and King of Spain, Charles V (whose person and whose Empire may God preserve), learns of the crimes committed against his will and against that of God by his servants in the New World and of their treachery towards the people of the continent (for, until now, there has been an effective conspiracy of silence about what has really been happening), he will, as one wedded to the concept of justice and avid to see it prevail, put a stop to the wickedness and undertake a total reform of the administration of this New World that God has bestowed upon him and will do so for the greater glory of the Holy Catholic Church and for the salvation of his own royal soul. Amen.

STUDY QUESTIONS

1. In what terms does de Las Casas argue for the humanity of the Native Americans?
2. Is his principal interest in their souls, which can be converted if they are reached in time and by the right agents?

13.2 NICOLAUS COPERNICUS, DEDICATION OF *THE REVOLUTIONS OF THE HEAVENLY BODIES* TO POPE PAUL III, 1543

Nicolaus Copernicus's (1473–1543) heliocentric theory upset centuries of Western scientific tradition—a tradition that appeared to have the authority of the Bible behind it, since the Scriptures refer repeatedly to the sun's rising and setting. He knew that his theory would confront resistance, which is why he delayed the publication of his work for so long. In this preface he explains his work to the pope.

I can easily conceive, most Holy Father, that as soon as some people learn that in this book which I have written concerning the revolutions of the heavenly bodies, I ascribe certain motions to the Earth, they will cry out at once that I and my theory should be rejected. For I am not so much in love with my conclusions as not to weigh what others will think about them, and although I know that the meditations of a philosopher are far removed from the judgment of the laity, because his endeavor is to seek out the truth in all things, so far as this is permitted by God to the human reason, I still believe that one must avoid theories altogether foreign to orthodoxy. Accordingly, when I considered in my own mind how absurd a performance it must seem to those who know that the judgment of many centuries has approved the view that the Earth remains fixed as center in the midst of the heavens, if I should, on the contrary, assert that the Earth moves; I was for a long time at a loss to know whether I should publish the commentaries which I have written in proof of its motion, or whether it were not better to follow the example of the Pythagoreans and of some others, who were accustomed to transmit the secrets of Philosophy not in writing but orally, and only to their relatives and friends, as the letter from Lysis to Hipparchus bears witness. They did this, it seems to me, not as some think, because of a certain selfish reluctance to give their views to the world, but in order that the noblest truths, worked out by the careful study of great men, should not be despised by those who are vexed at the idea of taking great pains with any forms of literature except such as would be profitable, or by those who, if they are driven to the study of Philosophy for its own sake by the admonitions and the example of others, nevertheless, on account of their stupidity, hold a place among philosophers similar to that of drones among bees. Therefore, when I considered this carefully, the contempt which I had to fear because of the novelty and apparent absurdity of my view, nearly induced me to abandon utterly the work I had begun.

My friends, however, in spite of long delay and even resistance on my part, withheld me from this decision. First among these was Nicolaus Schonberg, Cardinal of Capua, distinguished in all branches of learning. Next to him comes my very dear friend, Tidemann Giese, Bishop of Culm, a most earnest student, as he is, of sacred and, indeed, of all good learning. The latter has often urged me, at times even spurring me on with reproaches, to publish and at last bring to the light the book which had lain in my study not nine years merely, but already going on four times nine. Not a few other very eminent and scholarly men made the same request, urging that I should no longer through fear refuse to give out my work for the common benefit of students of Mathematics. They said I should find that the more absurd most men now thought this theory of mine concerning the motion of the Earth, the more admiration and gratitude it would command after they saw in the publication of my commentaries the mist of absurdity cleared away by most transparent proofs. So, influenced by these advisors and this hope, I have at length allowed my friends to publish the work, as they had long besought me to do.

But perhaps Your Holiness will not so much wonder that I have ventured to publish these studies of mine, after having taken such pains in elaborating them that I have not hesitated to commit to writing my views of the motion of the Earth, as you will be curious to hear how it occurred to me to venture, contrary to the accepted view of mathematicians, and well-nigh contrary to common sense, to form a conception of any terrestrial motion whatsoever. Therefore, I would not have it unknown to Your Holiness that the only thing which induced me to look for another way of reckoning the movements of the heavenly bodies was that I knew that mathematicians by no means agree in their investigations thereof. For, in the first place, they are so much in doubt concerning the motion of the sun and the moon, that they cannot even demonstrate and prove by observation the constant length of a complete year; and in the

second place, in determining the motions both of these and of the five other planets, they fail to employ consistently one set of first principles and hypotheses, but use methods of proof based only upon the apparent revolutions and motions. For some employ concentric circles only; others, eccentric circles and epicycles; and even by these means they do not completely attain the desired end. For, although those who have depended upon concentric circles have shown that certain diverse motions can be deduced from these, yet they have not succeeded thereby in laying down any sure principle, corresponding indisputably to the phenomena. These, on the other hand, who have devised systems of eccentric circles, although they seem in great part to have solved the apparent movements by calculations which by these eccentrics are made to fit, have nevertheless introduced many things which seem to contradict the first principles of the uniformity of motion. Nor have they been able to discover or calculate from these the main point, which is the shape of the world and the fixed symmetry of its parts; but their procedure has been as if someone were to collect hands, feet, a head, and other members from various places, all very fine in themselves, but not proportionate to one body, and no single one corresponding in its turn to the others, so that a monster rather than a man would be formed from them. Thus, in their process of demonstration which they term a "method," they are found to have omitted something essential or to have included something foreign and not pertaining to the matter in hand. This certainly would never have happened to them if they had followed fixed principles; for if the hypotheses they assumed were not false, all that resulted therefrom would be verified indubitably. Those things which I am saying now may be obscure, yet they will be made clearer in their proper place.

Therefore, having turned over in my mind for a long time this uncertainty of the traditional mathematical methods of calculating the motions of the celestial bodies, I began to grow disgusted that no more consistent scheme of the movements of the mechanism of the universe, set up for our benefit by that best and most law-abiding Architect of all things, was agreed upon by philosophers who otherwise investigate so carefully the most minute details of this world. Wherefore I undertook the task of rereading the books of all the philosophers I could get access to, to see whether anyone ever was of the opinion that the motions of the celestial bodies were other than those postulated by the men who taught mathematics in the schools, and I found first, indeed, in Cicero, that Niceta perceived that the Earth moved; and afterward in Plutarch I found that some others were of this opinion, whose words I have seen fit to quote here, that they may be accessible to all:—

"Some maintain that the Earth is stationary, but Philolaus the Pythagorean says that it revolves in a circle about the fire of the ecliptic, like the sun and moon. Heraklides of Pontus and Ekphantus the Pythagorean make the Earth move, not changing its position, however, confined in its falling and rising around its own center in the manner of a wheel."

Taking this as a starting point, I began to consider the mobility of the Earth; and although the idea seemed absurd, yet because I knew that the liberty had been granted to others before me to postulate all sorts of little circles for explaining the phenomena of the stars, I thought I also might easily be permitted to try whether by postulating some motion of the Earth, more reliable conclusions could be reached regarding the revolution of the heavenly bodies, than those of my predecessors.

And so, after postulating movements, which, farther on in the book, I ascribe to the Earth, I have found by many and long observations that if the movements of the other planets are assumed for the circular motion of the Earth and are substituted for the revolution of each star, not only do their phenomena follow logically therefrom, but the relative positions and magnitudes both of the stars and all their orbits, and of the heavens themselves, become so closely related that in none of its parts can anything be changed without causing confusion in the other parts and in the whole universe. Therefore, in the course of the work I have followed this plan: I describe in the first book all the positions of the orbits together with the movements which I ascribe to the Earth, in order that this book might contain, as it were, the general scheme of the universe. Thereafter in the remaining books, I set forth the motions of the other stars and of all their

orbits together with the movement of the Earth, in order that one may see from this to what extent the movements and appearances of the other stars and their orbits can be saved, if they are transferred to the movement of the Earth. Nor do I doubt that ingenious and learned mathematicians will sustain me, if they are willing to recognize and weigh, not superficially but with that thoroughness which Philosophy demands above all things, those matters which have been adduced by me in this work to demonstrate these theories. In order, however, that both the learned and the unlearned equally may see that I do not avoid anyone's judgment, I have preferred to dedicate these investigations of mine to Your Holiness rather than to any other, because, even in this remote corner of the world where I live, you are considered to be the most eminent man in dignity of rank and in love of all learning and even of mathematics, so that by your authority and judgment you can easily suppress the bites of slanderers, albeit the proverb has it that there is no remedy for the bite of a sycophant. If perchance there shall be idle talkers, who, though they are ignorant of all mathematical sciences, nevertheless assume the right to pass judgment on these things, and if they should dare to criticize and attack this theory of mine because of some passage of Scripture which they have falsely distorted for their own purpose, I care not at all; I will even despise their judgment as foolish. For it is not unknown that Lactantius, otherwise a famous writer but a poor mathematician, speaks most childishly of the shape of the Earth when he makes fun of those who said that the Earth has the form of a sphere. It should not seem strange then to zealous students, if some such people shall ridicule us also. Mathematics are written for mathematicians, to whom, if my opinion does not deceive me, our labors will seem to contribute something to the ecclesiastical state whose chief office Your Holiness now occupies; for when not so very long ago, under Leo X, in the Lateran Council the question of revising the ecclesiastical calendar was discussed, it then remained unsettled, simply because the length of the years and months, and the motions of the sun and moon were held to have been not yet sufficiently determined. Since that time, I have given my attention to observing these more accurately, urged on by a very distinguished man, Paul, bishop of Fossombrone, who at that time had charge of the matter. But what I may have accomplished herein I leave to the judgment of Your Holiness in particular, and to that of all other learned mathematicians; and lest I seem to Your Holiness to promise more regarding the usefulness of the work than I can perform, I now pass to the work itself.

STUDY QUESTIONS

1. What argument does Copernicus offer to the pope in defense of his new theory?
2. How does Copernicus use reason to support his heliocentric theory?

13.3 GALILEO GALILEI, LETTER TO DON BENEDETTO CASTELLI, DECEMBER 21, 1613

An Italian astronomer, physicist, and mathematician, Galileo Galilei (1564–1642) made many significant contributions to science—such as improvements to the telescope and work with sunspots—but is remembered primarily for his support of a heliocentric model of the solar system. His conviction led him into conflict with the Catholic Church; he was accused of heresy and finished his days under house arrest. Aside from his astronomical texts, Galileo also corresponded with leading figures of his day. This letter, to the Benedictine mathematician Benedetto Castelli, addresses one of the main articles of the problem with Galileo's heliocentrism: how to reconcile observable scientific fact with the words of the Bible, held to be literal and inviolable in seventeenth-century Italy.

Very Reverend Father and most worthy Signore,

I received a visit yesterday from Signor Niccolò Arrighetti, who brought me news of your Reverence. I was delighted to hear what I never doubted, namely the high opinion in which you are held by the whole university, both the governors and the teachers and students of all nations. . . . But what set the seal on my pleasure was hearing his account of the arguments which you were able to put forward, thanks to the great kindness of their Serene Highnesses, first at their dinner table and later in Madame's drawing-room, in the presence of the Grand Duke and the Archduchess and the distinguished and excellent gentleman Don Antonio and Don Paolo Giordano and other excellent philosophers. What greater favour could you wish for than that their Highnesses should be pleased to hold conversation with you, to put their doubts to you, to hear you

Galileo Galilei, *Selected Writings*. Translated by William R. Shea and Mark Davie. Oxford: Oxford University Press, 2013, pp. 55–61. By permission of Oxford University Press.

resolve them and finally to be satisfied with your Reverence's replies?

The points which you made, as Signor Arrighetti reported them to me, have prompted me to think afresh about some general principles concerning the citing of Holy Scripture in disputes on matters of natural science, and in particular on the passage in Joshua which was put forward by the Dowager Grand Duchess, and to which the Archduchess offered some rejoinders, as evidence against the motion of the Earth and the fixed position of the Sun.

As regards the first general question raised by Madame, it seems to me that both she and you were entirely prudent when she asserted and you agreed that the Holy Scripture can never lie or be in error, but that its decrees are absolutely and inviolably true. I would simply have added that, although Scripture cannot err, nonetheless some of its interpreters and expositors can, and in various ways. One error in particular, which is especially serious and frequent, is to insist always on the literal meaning of the words, for this can lead not only to many contradictions but also to grave heresies and blasphemies; for it would mean attributing to God feet and hands and eyes, not to mention physical human affectations such as anger, repentance, hatred, and sometimes even forgetfulness of past events and ignorance of the future. So, since Scripture contains many statements which, if taken at their face value, appear to be at variance with the truth, but which are couched in these terms so as to be comprehensible to the ignorant, it is up to wise expositors to explain their true meaning to those few who deserve to be set apart from the common herd, and to point out the particular reasons why they have been expressed as they have.

Given, then, that Scripture in many places not only admits but necessarily requires an interpretation which differs from the apparent meaning of the words, it seems to me that it should be brought into scientific disputes only as a last resort. For while Holy Scripture and nature proceed alike from the divine Word—Scripture as dictated by the Holy Spirit, and nature as the faithful executor of God's commands—it is agreed that Scripture, in order to be understood by the multitude, says many things which are apparently and in the literal sense of the words at variance with absolute truth. But nature never transgresses the laws to which it is subject, but is inexorable and unchanging, quite indifferent to whether its hidden reasons and ways of working are accessible to human understanding or not. Hence, any effect in nature which the experience of our senses places before our eyes, or to which we are led by necessary demonstrations, should on no account be called into question because of a passage of Scripture whose words appear to suggest something different, because not every statement of Scripture is bound by such strict rules as every effect of nature.

. . .

I believe that the purpose of the authority of Holy Scripture is solely to persuade men of those articles and propositions which are necessary to their salvation and which, being beyond the scope of human reasoning, could not be made credible to us by science or by any other means, but only through the mouth of the Holy Spirit himself. I do not consider it necessary to believe that the same God who has endowed us with sense, and with the power of reasoning and intellect, should have chosen to set these aside and to convey to us by some other means those facts which we are capable of finding out by exercising these faculties. This is especially the case with those sciences of which only a tiny part is to be found in scattered references in Scripture, which as astronomy, of which Scripture contains so little that it does not even mention the planets. For if the sacred writers had intended to persuade the people of the order and motions of the heavenly bodies, they would not have said so little about them—almost nothing compared to the infinite, profound, and wonderful truths which this science contains.

So you can see, Father, if I am not mistaken, how flawed is the procedure of those who, in debating the questions of natural science which are not directly matters of faith, give priority to verses of Scripture—often verses which they have misunderstood.

. . .

To confirm this, I come now to the particular case of Joshua, about which you presented three statements to their Highnesses; and specifically, to the third of these, which you rightly attributed to me, but to which I now want to add some further considerations, which I do not believe I have yet explained to you.

So let me first concede to my adversary that the words of the sacred text should be taken in exactly their literal sense, namely that God made the Sun stand still in response to Joshua's prayers, so that the day was prolonged and Joshua was able to complete his victory. But let me claim the same concession for myself, lest my adversary should tie me down while remaining free himself to change or modify the meanings of words; and I will show that this passage of Scripture clearly demonstrates the impossibility of the Aristotelian and Ptolemaic world system, and on the contrary fits perfectly well with the system of Copernicus.

I ask first, does my adversary know in what ways the Sun moves? If he does, he must perforce reply that it has two motions, an annual motion from west to east, and a daily one in the opposite direction, from east to west.

My second question then is, do these two different and almost contrary motions both belong to the Sun, and are they both proper to it? To this the answer must be no: only the annual motion is specific and proper to the Sun, while the other belongs to the highest heaven or Primum Mobile, which draws the Sun, the other planets, and the sphere of the fixed stars along with it, making them complete a revolution around the Earth every twenty-four hours, with a motion which is, as I have said, contrary to their own natural and proper motion.

So to the third question: which of these two motions of the Sun produces day and night, the Sun's own real motion or that of the Primum Mobile? The answer has to be that day and night are the result of the motion of the Primum Mobile, and that the Sun's own motion produces not day and night but the changing seasons, and the year itself.

Hence it is clear that, if the length of the day depends not on the motion of the Sun but on that of the Primum Mobile, in order to prolong the day it is the Primum Mobile which must be made to stop, not the Sun. Indeed, anyone who understands these first elements of astronomy will realize that if God had stopped the motion of the Sun, the effect would have been to shorten the day, not to lengthen it. The motion of the Sun being in the opposite direction to the daily revolution of the heavens, the more the Sun moved towards the east, the more its progress towards the

west would be held back; and if the Sun's motion were diminished or stopped altogether, it would reach the point where it sets all the more quickly. This effect can be clearly seen in the case of the Moon, whose daily revolution is slower than the Sun's by the same amount as its own proper motion is faster than the Sun's. So it is simply impossible, according to the system of Ptolemy and Aristotle, to prolong the day by stopping the motion of the Sun, as Scripture says happened. It follows therefore that either the motions of the heavens are not as Ptolemy says, or we must change the sense of the words of Scripture and say that, when Scripture says that God stopped the Sun, what it meant was that God stopped the Primum Mobile.

. . .

However, since we have agreed that we should not change the meaning of the words of Scripture, we must have recourse to another arrangement of the world to see whether it agreed with the plain meaning of the words, as indeed we shall see that it does.

I have discovered and rigorously demonstrated that the globe of the Sun turns on its own axis, making a complete revolution in all the space of roughly one lunar month, in the same direction as all the other revolutions of the heavens. Moreover, it is very probable and reasonable to suppose that the Sun, as the instrument and the highest minister of nature—the heart of the world, so to speak—imparts not only light (as it clearly does) but also motion to the planets which revolve around it. So if we follow Copernicus in attributing first of all a daily rotation to the Earth, it is clear that, to bring the whole system to a stop solely in order to prolong the extent and time of daylight without disrupting all the other relations between the planets, it was enough that the Sun should stand still, just as the words of Holy Writ say. This, then, is how the length of the day on Earth can be extended by making the Sun stand still, without introducing any confusion among the parts of the world and without altering the words of Scripture.

I have written much more than my indisposition allows, so I close by offering myself as your servant, kissing your hand and praying our Lord that you may have a joyful festive season and every happiness.

In Florence, 21 December 1613, your Reverence's devoted servant, Galileo Galilei.

STUDY QUESTIONS

1. How does Galileo, with specific reference to the story of Joshua making the sun stand still, illustrate the danger of reading Scripture in *literal* terms?

2. How does he contrast the various purposes of Scripture and science in this respect?

13.4 JOHN DONNE, SERMON, DECEMBER 12, 1626; "TO HIS MISTRESS GOING TO BED," 1633

John Donne (1572–1631) was a Catholic-turned-Anglican priest, poet, and satirist. Donne spanned the literary scale, writing hundreds of texts ranging from erotic love poems to sermonic meditations on God. After love pushed him into an economically ruinous marriage (that ultimately yielded twelve children), Donne endured fourteen years of destitution and depression—during which time he wrote some of his most poignant poetry. The sermon included here explores the lofty topics of true knowledge and change, whereas the almost bawdy poem revels in the exploration of his lover's body.

FROM A SERMON PREACHED 12 DECEMBER 1626

[THE STATE OF KNOWLEDGE]

How imperfect is all our knowledge? What one thing do we know perfectly? Whether we considered arts, or sciences, the servant knows but according to the proportion of his master's knowledge in that art, and the scholar knows but according to the proportion of his master's knowledge in that science; Young men mend not their sight by using old men's spectacles; and yet we look upon nature, but with Aristotle's spectacles, upon the body of man, but with Galen's, and upon the frame of the world, but with Ptolemy's spectacles. Almost all knowledge is rather like a child that is embalmed to make a mummy, than

that is nursed to make a man; rather conserved in the stature of the first age, than grown to be greater; And if there be any addition to knowledge, it is rather new knowledge, than a greater knowledge; rather a singularity in a desire of proposing something that was not known at all before, than an improving, an advancing, a multiplying of former inceptions; and by that means, no knowledge comes to be perfect. One philosopher thinks he is dived to the bottom, when he says, he knows nothing but this, That he knows nothing; and yet another thinks, that he hath expressed more knowledge than he, in saying, That he knows not so much as that, That he knows nothing. St. Paul found that to be all knowledge, To know Christ; And Mahomet thinks himself wise therefore, because he knows not, acknowledges not Christ, as

John Donne, *The Major Works, Including Songs and Sonnets and Sermons.* Edited by John Carey. New York: Oxford University Press, 2008, pp. 12–13, 372–4.

St. Paul does. Though a man knew not, that every sin casts another shovel of brimstone upon him in Hell, yet if he knew that every riotous feast cuts off a year, and every wanton night even years of his seventy in this world, it were some degree towards perfection in knowledge. He that purchases a manor, will think to have an exact survey of the land: But who thinks of taking so exact a survey of his conscience, how that money was got, that purchased that manor? We call that a man's means, which he hath; But that is truly his means, what way he came by it. And yet how few are there, (when a state comes to any great proportion) that know that; that know what they have, what they are worth?

. . .

[MUTABILITY]

I need not call in new philosophy, that denies a settledness, an acquiescence in the very body of the earth, but makes the earth to move in that place, where we thought the sun had moved; I need not that help, that the earth itself is in motion, to prove this, That nothing upon earth is permanent; The assertion will stand of itself, till some man assign me some instance, something that a man may rely upon, and find permanent. Consider the greatest bodies upon earth, The monarchies; Objects, which one would think, destiny might stand and stare at, but not shake; Consider the smallest bodies upon earth, the hairs of our head, objects, which one would think, destiny would not observe, or could not discern; And yet destiny, (to speak to a natural man) and God, (to speak to a Christian) is no more troubled to make a monarchy ruinous, than to make a hair gray. Nay, nothing needs to be done to either, by God, or destiny; a monarchy will ruin, as a hair will grow gray, of itself. In the elements themselves, of which all sub-elementary things are composed, there is no acquiescence, but a vicissitudinary transmutation into one another; air condensed becomes water, a more solid body, And air rarified becomes fire, a body more disputable, and in-apparent. It is so in the conditions of men too; a merchant condensed, kneaded and packed up in a great estate, becomes a Lord; And a merchant rarified, blown up by a perfidious factor, or by riotous son, evaporates into air, into nothing, and is not seen.

And if there were anything permanent and durable in this world, yet we got nothing by it, because howsoever that might last in itself, yet we could not last to enjoy it; If our goods were not amongst moveables, yet we ourselves are; if they could stay with us, yet we cannot stay with them.

. . .

ELEGY: TO HIS MISTRESS GOING TO BED

Come, Madam, come, all rest my powers defy,
Until I labour, I in labour lie.
The foe oft-times, having the foe in sight,
Is tired with standing though they never fight.
Off with that girdle, like heaven's zone glistening,
But a far fairer world encompassing.
Unpin that spangled breastplate, which you wear
That th'eyes of busy fools may be stopped there:
Unlace yourself, for that harmonious chime
Tells me from you that now 'tis your bed-time.
Off with that happy busk, which I envy,
That still can be, and still can stand so nigh.
Your gown going off, such beauteous state reveals,
As when from flowery means th'hill's shadow
    steals.
Off with your wiry coronet and show
The hairy diadem which on you doth grow.
Off with those shoes: and then safely tread
In this love's hallowed temple, this soft bed.
In such white robes heaven's angels used to be
Received by men; thou angel bring'st with thee
A heaven like Mahomet's paradise; and though
Ill spirits walk in white, we easily know
By this these angels from an evil sprite,
They set our hairs, but these our flesh upright.
    Licence my roving hands, and let them go
Behind, before, above, between, below.
O my America, my new found land,
My kingdom, safeliest when with one man
    manned,
My mine of precious stones, my empery,
How blessed am I in the discovering thee.
To enter in these bonds is to be free,
Then where my hand is set my seal shall be.
    Full nakedness, all joys are due to thee.
As souls unbodied, bodies unclothed must be,

To taste whole joys. Gems which you women use
Are like Atalanta's balls, cast in men's views,
That when a fool's eye lighteth on a gem
His earthly soul may covet theirs, not them.
Like pictures, or like books' gay coverings made
For laymen, are all women thus arrayed;
Themselves are mystic books, which only we

Whom their imputed grace will dignify
Must see revealed. Then since I may know,
As liberally as to a midwife show
Thyself; cast all, yea, this white linen hence,
Here is no penance, much less innocence.
    To teach thee, I am naked first: why then
What needest thou have more covering than a man?

STUDY QUESTIONS

1. Does Donne seem to believe that perfect knowledge of anything can exist?
2. What do his references to "Mahomet" and "America" reveal about his time and place?

13.5 RENÉ DESCARTES, *A DISCOURSE ON METHOD*, 1637

René Descartes (1596–1650) has been called the Father of Modern Philosophy because of his work in philosophy, metaphysics, theology, and mathematics. Perhaps best known for the groundbreaking maxim "I think, therefore I am," Descartes lays out a method for creating solid foundations on which he can build theoretical arguments—an epistemology known as Cartesianism. The *Discourse* moves from autobiography to philosophical tract and recounts how Descartes came to the thoughts and processes that redefined philosophy.

PART ONE

Good sense is, of all things among men, the most equally distributed; for every one thinks himself so abundantly provided with it, that those even who are the most difficult to satisfy in everything else, do not usually desire a larger measure of this quality than they already possess. And in this it is not likely that all are mistaken the conviction is rather to be held as testifying that the power of judging aright and of distinguishing truth from error, which is properly what is called good sense or reason, is by nature equal in all men; and that the diversity of our opinions, consequently, does not arise from some being endowed with a larger share of reason than others, but solely from this, that we conduct our thoughts along different ways, and do not fix our attention on the same objects. For to be possessed of a vigorous mind is not enough; the prime requisite is rightly to

René Descartes, *A Discourse on the Method of Rightly Conducting the Reason, and Seeking Truth in the Sciences.* Translated by John Veitch and available via Project Gutenberg.

apply it. The greatest minds, as they are capable of the highest excellences, are open likewise to the greatest aberrations; and those who travel very slowly may yet make far greater progress, provided they keep always to the straight road, than those who, while they run, forsake it.

For myself, I have never fancied my mind to be in any respect more perfect than those of the generality; on the contrary, I have often wished that I were equal to some others in promptitude of thought, or in clearness and distinctness of imagination, or in fullness and readiness of memory. And besides these, I know of no other qualities that contribute to the perfection of the mind; for as to the reason or sense, inasmuch as it is that alone which constitutes us men, and distinguishes us from the brutes, I am disposed to believe that it is to be found complete in each individual; . . .

I will not hesitate, however, to avow my belief that it has been my singular good fortune to have very early in life fallen in with certain tracks which have conducted me to considerations and maxims, of which I have formed a method that gives me the means, as I think, of gradually augmenting my knowledge, and of raising it by little and little to the highest point which the mediocrity of my talents and the brief duration of my life will permit me to reach. For I have already reaped from it such fruits that, although I have been accustomed to think lowly enough of myself, and although when I look with the eye of a philosopher at the varied courses and pursuits of mankind at large, I find scarcely one which does not appear in vain and useless, I nevertheless derive the highest satisfaction from the progress I conceive myself to have already made in the search after truth, . . .

. . .

My present design, then, is not to teach the method which each ought to follow for the right conduct of his reason, but solely to describe the way in which I have endeavored to conduct my own. . . .

From my childhood, I have been familiar with letters; and as I was given to believe that by their help a clear and certain knowledge of all that is useful in life might be acquired, I was ardently desirous of instruction. But as soon as I had finished the entire course of study, at the close of which it is customary to be admitted into the order of the learned, I completely changed my opinion. For I found myself involved in so many doubts and errors, that I was convinced I had advanced no farther in all my attempts at learning, than the discovery at every turn of my own ignorance. And yet I was studying in one of the most celebrated schools in Europe, in which I thought there must be learned men, if such were anywhere to be found. I had been taught all that others learned there; and not contented with the sciences actually taught us, I had, in addition, read all the books that had fallen into my hands, treating of such branches as are esteemed the most curious and rare. I knew the judgment which others had formed of me; and I did not find that I was considered inferior to my fellows, although there were among them some who were already marked out to fill the places of our instructors. And, in fine, our age appeared to me as flourishing, and as fertile in powerful minds as any preceding one. I was thus led to take the liberty of judging of all other men by myself, and of concluding that there was no science in existence that was of such a nature as I had previously been given to believe.

I still continued, however, to hold in esteem the studies of the schools. I was aware that the languages taught in them are necessary to the understanding of the writings of the ancients; that the grace of fable stirs the mind; that the memorable deeds of history elevate it; and, if read with discretion, aid in forming the judgment; that the perusal of all excellent books is, as it were, to interview with the noblest men of past ages, who have written them, and even a studied interview, in which are discovered to us only their choicest thoughts; that eloquence has incomparable force and beauty; that poesy has its ravishing graces and delights; that in the mathematics there are many refined discoveries eminently suited to gratify the inquisitive, as well as further all the arts an lessen the labour of man; that numerous highly useful precepts and exhortations to virtue are contained in treatises on morals; that theology points out the path to heaven; that philosophy affords the means of discoursing with an appearance of truth on all matters, and commands the admiration of the more simple;

that jurisprudence, medicine, and the other sciences, secure for their cultivators honors and riches; . . .

. . .

I was especially delighted with the mathematics, on account of the certitude and evidence of their reasonings; but I had not as yet a precise knowledge of their true use; and thinking that they but contributed to the advancement of the mechanical arts, I was astonished that foundations, so strong and solid, should have had no loftier superstructure reared on them. On the other hand, I compared the disquisitions of the ancient moralists to very towering and magnificent palaces with no better foundation than sand and mud: they laud the virtues very highly, and exhibit them as estimable far above anything on earth; but they give us no adequate criterion of virtue, and frequently that which they designate with so fine a name is but apathy, or pride, or despair, or parricide.

. . .

. . . But after I had been occupied several years in thus studying the book of the world, and in essaying to gather some experience, I at length resolved to make myself an object of study, and to employ all the powers of my mind in choosing the paths I ought to follow, an undertaking which was accompanied with greater success than it would have been had I never quitted my country or my books.

. . .

PART FOUR

. . . but as I then desired to give my attention solely to the search after truth, I thought that a procedure exactly the opposite was called for, and that I ought to reject as absolutely false all opinions in regard to which I could suppose the least ground for doubt, in order to ascertain whether after that there remained aught in my belief that was wholly indubitable. Accordingly, seeing that our senses sometimes deceive us, I was willing to suppose that there existed nothing really such as they presented to us; and because some men err in reasoning, and fall into paralogisms, even on the simplest matters of geometry, I, convinced that I was as open to error as any other, rejected as false all the reasonings I had hitherto taken for demonstrations; and finally, when I considered that the very same thoughts (presentations) which we experience when awake may also be experienced when we are asleep, while there is at that time not one of them true, I supposed that all the objects (presentations) that had ever entered into my mind when awake, had in them no more truth than the illusions of my dreams. But immediately upon this I observed that, whilst I thus wished to think that all was false, it was absolutely necessary that I, who thus thought, should be somewhat; and as I observed that this truth, I think, therefore I am (COGITO ERGO SUM), was so certain and of such evidence that no ground of doubt, however extravagant, could be alleged by the sceptics capable of shaking it, I concluded that I might, without scruple, accept it as the first principle of the philosophy of which I was in search.

In the next place, I attentively examined what I was and as I observed that I could suppose that I had no body, and that there was no world nor any place in which I might be; but that I could not therefore suppose that I was not; and that, on the contrary, from the very circumstance that I thought to doubt of the truth of other things, it most clearly and certainly followed that I was; while, on the other hand, if I had only ceased to think, although all the other objects which I had ever imagined had been in reality existent, I would have had no reason to believe that I existed; I thence concluded that I was a substance whose whole essence or nature consists only in thinking, and which, that it may exist, has need of no place, nor dependent on any material thing; so that "I," that is to say, the mind by which I am what I am, is wholly distinct from the body, and is even more easily known than the latter, and is such, that although the latter were not, it would still continue to be all that it is.

After this I inquired in general into what is essential to the truth and certainty of a proposition; for since I had discovered one which I knew to be true, I thought that I must likewise be able to discover the ground of this certitude. And as I observed that in the words I think, therefore I am, there is nothing at all which gives me assurance of their truth beyond this, that I see very clearly that in order to think it is necessary to exist, I concluded that I might take, as a general rule, the principle, that all the things which we very clearly and distinctly conceive are true, only observing, however, that there is some difficulty in rightly determining the objects which we distinctly conceive.

In the next place, from reflecting on the circumstance that I doubted, and that consequently my being was not wholly perfect (for I clearly saw that it was a greater perfection to know than to doubt), I was led to inquire whence I had learned to think of something more perfect than myself; and I clearly recognized that I must hold this notion from some nature which in reality was more perfect. As for the thoughts of many other objects external to me, as of the sky, the earth, light, heat, and a thousand more, I was less at a loss to know whence these came; for since I remarked in them nothing which seemed to render them superior to myself, I could believe that, if these were true, they were dependencies on my own nature, in so far as it possessed a certain perfection, and, if they were false, that I held them from nothing, that is to say, that they were in me because of a certain imperfection of my nature. But this could not be the case with the idea of a nature more perfect than myself; for to receive it from nothing was a thing manifestly impossible; and, because it is not less repugnant that the more perfect should be an effect of, and dependence on the less perfect, than that

something should proceed from nothing, it was equally impossible that I could hold it from myself: accordingly, it but remained that it had been placed in me by a nature which was in reality more perfect than mine, and which even possessed within itself all the perfections of which I could form any idea; that is to say, in a single word, which was God. And to this I added that, since I knew some perfections which I did not possess, I was not the only being in existence (I will here, with your permission, freely use the terms of the schools); but, on the contrary, that there was of necessity some other more perfect Being upon whom I was dependent, and from whom I had received all that I possessed; for if I had existed alone, and independently of every other being, so as to have had from myself all the perfection, however little, which I actually possessed, I should have been able, for the same reason, to have had from myself the whole remainder of perfection, of the want of which I was conscious, and thus could of myself have become infinite, eternal, immutable, omniscient, all-powerful, and, in fine, have possessed all the perfections which I could recognize in God.

STUDY QUESTIONS

1. How does Descartes account for the general perception of equal knowledge among people?
2. How does he find enlightenment through introspection, rather than through trusting conventional authorities of wisdom?

13.6 *THE JESUIT RELATIONS*, FRENCH NORTH AMERICA, 1649

The Jesuit Relations are the most important set of documents attesting the encounter between Europeans and native North Americans in the seventeenth century. These annual reports of French missionaries from the Society of Jesus document the conversions—or attempted conversions— of the various native peoples in what is today the St. Lawrence River basin and the Great Lakes

Paul Ragueneau, *Relation of 1648–49*. In *The Jesuit Relations: Natives and Missionaries in Seventeenth-Century North America*, edited by Allan Greer. New York: Bedford/St. Martin's, 2000, pp. 112–15.

region. When they arrived on the banks of the St. Lawrence in 1625, French Jesuits were entering a continent still very much under the control of First Nations peoples, who were divided by their own ethnic and linguistic differences. Even the catch-all terms "Huron" and "Iroquois" masked the existence of confederacies, composed of several distinct nations, who had joined together prior to the arrival of Europeans.

When the Jesuits made headway with one group, they usually lost initiative with the group's rivals—and sometimes found themselves in the midst of a conflict that they could barely understand or appreciate. This section of one of the *Relations* concerns the torture and murder of Jean Brébeuf, who had lived among the Hurons at various points from the 1620s through the 1640s, observing their culture and systematically attempting to convert them to Catholicism. However, when an Iroquois raiding party invaded his settlement, the depth of the Hurons' Christian commitment—and his own—would be tested.

The sixteenth day of March in the present year, 1649, marked the beginning of our misfortunes—if an event, which no doubt has been the salvation of many of God's elect, can be called a misfortune.

The Iroquois, enemies of the Hurons, arrived by night at the frontier of this country. They numbered about a thousand men, well furnished with weapons, most of them carrying firearms obtained from their allies, the Dutch. We had no knowledge of their approach, although they had started from their country in the autumn, hunting in the forests throughout the winter, and had made a difficult journey of nearly two hundred leagues over the snow in order to take us by surprise. By night, they reconnoitered the condition of the first place upon which they had designs. It was surrounded by a pine stockade fifteen or sixteen feet in height, and a deep ditch with which nature had strongly fortified this place on three sides. There remained only a small space that was weaker than the others.

It was at this weak point that the enemy made a breach at daybreak, but so secretly and promptly that he was master of the place before anyone could mount a defense. All were then sleeping deeply, and they had no time to recognize the danger. Thus this village was taken, almost without striking a blow and with only ten Iroquois killed. Part of the Hurons—men, women, and children—were massacred then and there, while the others were made captives and were reserved for cruelties more terrible than death.

. . .

The enemy did not stop there, but followed up his victory, and before sunrise he appeared in arms to attack the town of St. Louis, which was fortified with a fairly good stockade. Most of the women and the children had just gone from it upon hearing the news which had arrived regarding the approach of the Iroquois. The people of greatest courage, about eighty persons, being resolved to defend themselves well, courageously repulsed the first and the second assaults, killing about thirty of the enemy's boldest men, in addition to many wounded. But finally, the larger number prevailed, as the Iroquois used their hatchets to undermine the palisade of stakes and opened a passage for themselves through some considerable breaches.

About nine o'clock in the morning, we perceived from our house at St. Marie the fire which was consuming the cabins of that town, where the enemy, after entering victoriously, had reduced everything to desolation. They cast into the flames the old, the sick, the children who had not been able to escape, and all those who, being too severely wounded, could not have followed them into captivity. At the sight of those flames, and by the color of the smoke which issued from them, we understood sufficiently what was happening, for this town of St. Louis was no more than a league distant from us. Two Christians who escaped the fire arrived about this time and confirmed this.

In this town of St. Louis were at that time two of our fathers, Father Jean de Brébeuf and Father

Gabriel Lalemant, who had charge of a cluster of five towns. These formed but one of the eleven missions of which we have spoken above, and we call it the mission of St. Ignace.

Some Christians had begged the fathers to preserve their lives for the glory of God, which would have been as easy for them as for the more than five hundred persons who went away at the first alarm, for there was more than enough time to reach a place of safety. But their zeal could not permit such a thing, and the salvation of their flock was dearer to them than the love of their own lives. They employed the moments left to them as the most previous which they had ever had in the world, and through the heat of the battle their hearts were on fire for the salvation of souls. One was at the breach, baptizing the catechumens [native converts who had not yet been baptized], and the other was giving absolution to the neophytes [recently baptized Christians]. Both of them urged the Christians to die in the sentiments of piety with which they consoled them in their miseries. Never was their faith more alive, nor their love for their good fathers and pastors more keenly felt.

An infidel, seeing the desperate situation, spoke of taking flight, but a Christian named Etienne Annaotaha, the most esteemed in the country for his courage and his exploits against the enemy, would never allow it. "What!" he said. "Could we ever abandon these two good fathers, who have exposed their lives for us? Their love for our salvation will be the cause of their death, for there is no longer time for them to flee across the snows. Let us then die with them, and we shall go together to heaven." This man had made a general confession a few days previously, having had a presentiment of the danger awaiting him and saying that he wished that death should find him disposed for Heaven. And indeed he, as well as many other Christians, had abandoned themselves to fervor in a manner so extraordinary that we shall never be sufficiently able to bless the guidance of God over so many predestinated souls. His divine providence continues lovingly to guide them in death as in life.

STUDY QUESTIONS

1. How well do the Jesuits seem to have understood the conflicts among native peoples in this region?
2. How was Ragueneau's reporting of the battle designed to highlight the "success" of the mission, despite an apparent setback?

13.7 THOMAS HOBBES, "ON NATURAL LAW," *LEVIATHAN*, 1651

Thomas Hobbes (1588–1679) was an English political philosopher who examined the idea of a "social contract" existing between a ruler and society. Although he upheld absolutism as a political system, his liberal ideas—such as the belief in natural equality for all men and the idea that

From Thomas Hobbes, *Leviathan*. Edited by J. C. A. Gaskin. New York: Oxford University Press, 2010, pp. 82–6, 132–3, 138–9, 141–3.

rule should emerge from the needs of society—helped frame early American political thought. His massive work *Leviathan*, named for the biblical sea beast, explores and explains this theory of social contract during the English civil war that challenged traditional monarchy. This selection outlines Hobbes's views on natural law and the liberties it demands.

CHAPTER XIII: OF THE NATURAL CONDITION OF MANKIND AS CONCERNING THEIR FELICITY, AND MISERY

NATURE hath made men so equal, in the faculties of the body, and mind; as that though there be found one man sometimes manifestly stronger in body, or of quicker mind than another; yet when all are reckoned together, the difference between man, and man, is not so considerable, as that one man can thereupon claim to himself any benefit, to which another may not pretend, as well as he. For as to the strength of body, the weakest has strength enough to kill the strongest, either by secret machination, or by confederacy with others, that are in the same danger with himself.

And as to the faculties of the mind, (setting aside the arts grounded upon words, and especially that skill of proceeding upon general, and infallible rules, called science; which very few have, and but in few things; as being not a native faculty, born with us; nor attained (as prudence,) while we look after somewhat else,) I find yet a greater equality amongst men, than that of strength. For prudence, is but experience; which equal time, equally bestows on all men, in those things they equally apply themselves unto. That which may perhaps make such equality incredible, is but a vain conceit of one's own wisdom, which almost all men think they have in a greater degree, than the vulgar; that is, than all men but themselves, and a few others, whom by fame, or for concurring with themselves, they approve. For such is the nature of men, that howsoever they may acknowledge many others to be more witty, or more eloquent, or more learned; yet they will hardly believe there be many so wise as themselves; for they see their own wit at hand, and other men's at a distance. But this proveth rather that men are in that point equal, than unequal. For there is not ordinarily a greater sign of the equal distribution of any thing, than that every man is contented with his share.

From this equality of ability, ariseth equality of hope in the attaining of our ends. And therefore if any two men desire the same thing, which nevertheless they cannot both enjoy, they become enemies; and in the way to their end, (which principally their own conservation, and sometimes their delectation only,) endeavor to destroy, or subdue one another. And from hence it comes to pass, that where an invader hath no more to fear, than another man's single power; if one plant, sow, build, or possess a convenient seat, others may probably be expected to come prepared with forces united, to dispossess, and deprive him, not only of the fruit of his labour, but also of his life, or liberty. And the invader again is in the like danger of another.

And from this diffidence of one another, there is no way for any man to secure himself, so reasonable, as anticipation; that is, by force, or wiles, to master the persons of all men he can, so long, till he see no other power great enough to endanger him: and this is no more than his own conservation requireth, and is generally allowed. Also because there be some, that taking pleasure in contemplating their own power in the acts of conquest, which they pursue farther than their security requires; if others, that otherwise would be glad to be at ease within modest bounds, should not by invasion increase their power, they would not be able, long time, by standing only their defence, to subsist. And by consequence, such augmentation of dominion over men, being necessary to a man's conservation, it ought to be allowed him.

Again, men have no pleasure, (but on the contrary a great deal of grief) in keeping company, where there is no power able to over-awe them all. For every man looketh that his companion should value him, at the same rate he sets upon himself: and upon all signs of contempt, or undervaluing, naturally endeavours, as far as he dares (which amongst them that have no common power to keep them in quiet, is far enough to make them destroy each other,) to extort a greater value from his contemners, by damage; and from others, by the example.

So that in the nature of man, we find three principal causes of quarrel. First, competition; secondly, diffidence; thirdly, glory.

The first, maketh men invade for gain; the second, for safety; and the third, for reputation. The first use violence, to make themselves masters of other men's persons, wives, children, and cattle; the second, to defend them; the third, for trifles, as a word, a smile, a different opinion, and any other sign of undervalue, either direct in their persons, or by reflection in their kindred, their friends, their nation, their profession, or their name.

Hereby it is manifest, that during the time men live without a common power to keep them all in awe, they are in that condition which is called war; and such a war, as is of every man, against every man. For WAR, consisteth not in battle only, or the act of fighting; but in a tract of time, wherein the will to contend by battle is sufficiently known: and therefore the notion of *time*, is to be considered in the nature of war; as it is in the nature of weather. For as the nature of foul weather, lieth not in a shower or two of rain; but in an inclination thereto of many days together: so the nature of war consisteth not in actual fighting; but in the known disposition thereto, during all the time there is no assurance to the contrary. All other time is PEACE.

Whatsoever therefore is consequent to a time of war, where every man is enemy to every man; the same is consequent to the time, wherein men live without other security, than what their own strength, and their own invention shall furnish them withal. In such condition, there is no place for industry; because the fruit thereof is uncertain: and consequently no culture of the earth; no navigation, nor use of the commodities that may be imported by sea; no commodious building; no instruments of moving, and removing such things as require much force; no knowledge of the face of the earth; no account of time; no arts; no letters; no society; and which is worst of all, continual fear, and danger of violent death; and the life of man, solitary, poor, nasty, brutish, and short.

It may seem strange to some man, that has not well weighed these things; that nature should thus dissociate, and render men apt to invade, and destroy one another: he may therefore, not trusting to this inference, made from the passions, desire perhaps to have the same confirmed by experience. Let him therefore consider with himself, when taking a journey, he arms himself, and seeks to go well accompanied; when going to sleep, he locks his doors; when even in his house he locks his chests; and this when he knows there be laws, and public officers, armed, to revenge all injuries shall be done him; what opinion he has of his fellow-subjects, when he rides armed; of his fellow citizens, when he locks his doors; and of his children, and servants, when he locks his chests. Does he not there as much accuse mankind by his actions, as I do by my words? But neither of us accuse man's nature in it. The desires, and other passions of man, are in themselves no sin. No more are the actions, that proceed from those passions, till they know a law that forbids them: which till laws be made they cannot know: nor can any law be made, till they have agreed upon the person that shall make it.

It may peradventure be thought, there was never such a time, not condition of war as this; and I believe it was never generally so, over all the world: but there are many places, where they live so now. For the savage people in many places of America, except the government of small families, the concord whereof dependeth on natural lust, have no government at all; and live at this day in that brutish manner, as I said before. Howsoever, it may be perceived what manner of life there would be, where there were no common power to fear; by the manner of life, which men that have formerly lived under a peaceful government, use to degenerate into, in a civil war.

But though there had never been any time, wherein particular men were in a condition of war one against another; yet in all times, kings, and persons of sovereign authority, because of their independency, are in continual jealousies, and in the state and posture of gladiators; having their weapons pointing, and their eyes fixed on one another; that is, their forts, garrisons, and guns upon the frontiers of their kingdoms; and continual spies upon their neighbours; which is a posture of war. But because they uphold thereby, the industry of their subjects; there does not follow from it, that misery, which accompanies the liberty of particular men.

To this war of every man against every man, this also is consequent; that nothing can be unjust. The notions of right and wrong, justice and injustice have there no place. Where there is no common power, there is no law: where no law, no injustice. Force, and fraud, are in war the two cardinal virtues. Justice, and injustice are none of the faculties neither of the body, nor mind. If they were, they might be in a man that were alone in the world, as well as his senses, and passions. They are qualities, that relate to men in society, not in solitude. It is consequent also to the same condition, that there be no property, no dominion, no *mine* and *thine* distinct; but one that to be every man's, that he can get; and for so long, as he can keep it. And thus much for the ill condition, which man by mere nature is actually placed in; though with a possibility to come out of it, consisting partly in the passions, partly in his reason.

The passions that incline men to peace, are fear of death; desire of such things as are necessary to commodious living; and a hope by their industry to obtain them. And reason suggesteth convenient articles of peace, upon which men may be drawn to agreement. These articles, are they, which otherwise are called the Laws of Nature: whereof I shall speak more particularly, in the two following chapters.

. . .

CHAPTER XX: OF DOMINION PATERNAL, AND DESPOTICAL

A COMMONWEALTH *by acquisition*, is that, where the sovereign power is acquired by force; and it is acquired by force, when men singly, or many together by plurality of voices, for fear of death, or bonds, do authorize all the actions of that man, or assembly, that hath their lives and liberty in his power.

And this kind of dominion, or sovereignty, differeth from sovereignty by institution, only in this, that men who choose their sovereign, do it for fear

of one another, and not of him whom they institute: but in this case, they subject themselves, to him they are afraid of. In both cases they do it for fear: which is to be noted by them, that hold all such covenants, as proceed from fear of death, or violence, void: which if it were true, no man, in any kind of commonwealth, could be obliged to obedience. It is true, that in a commonwealth once instituted, or acquired, promises proceeding from fear of death, or violence, are no covenants, nor obliging, when the thing promised is contrary to the laws; but the reason is not, because it was made upon fear, but because he that promiseth, hath no right in the thing promised. Also, when he may lawfully perform, and doth not, it is not the invalidity of the covenant, that absolveth him, but the sentence of the sovereign. Otherwise, whensoever a man lawfully promiseth, he unlawfully breaketh: but when the sovereign, who is the actor, acquitteth him, then he is acquitted by him than extorted the promise, as by the author of such absolution.

But the rights, and consequences of sovereignty, are the same in both. His power cannot, without his consent, be transferred to another: he cannot be punished by them: he is judge of what is necessary for peace; and judge of doctrines: he is sole legislator; and supreme judge of controversies; and of the times, and occasions of war, and peace: to him it belongeth to choose magistrates, counselors, commanders, and all other officers, and ministers; and to determine of rewards, and punishments, honour, and order. The reasons whereof, are the same which are alleged in the precedent chapter, for the same rights, and consequences of sovereignty by institution.

. . .

So that it appeareth plainly, to my understanding, both from reason, and Scripture, that the sovereign power, whether placed in one man, as in monarchy, or in one assembly of men, as in popular and aristocratical commonwealths, is as great, as possibly men can be imagined to make it. And though of so unlimited a power, men may fancy many evil consequences, yet the consequences of the want of it, which is perpetual war of every man against his neighbor, are much worse. The condition of man in this life shall never be without inconveniences; but there happeneth in no commonwealth any great inconvenience, but what proceeds from the subject's disobedience, and breach of those covenants, from which the commonwealth hath its being. And whosoever thinking sovereign power too great, will seek to make it less, must subject himself, to the power that can limit it; that is to say, to a greater.

The greatest objection is, that of the practice; when men ask, where, and when, such power has by subjects been acknowledged. But one may ask them again, when, or where has there been a kingdom long free from sedition and civil war. In those nations, those commonwealths have been long-lived, and not been destroyed but by foreign war, the subjects never did dispute of the sovereign power. But howsoever, an argument from the practice of men, that have not been sifted to the bottom, and with exact reason weighed the causes, and nature of commonwealths, and suffer daily those miseries, that proceed from the ignorance thereof, is invalid. For though in all places of the world, men should lay the foundation of their houses on the sand, it could not thence be inferred, that so it ought to be. The skill of making, and maintaining commonwealths, consisteth in certain rules, as doth arithmetic and geometry; not (as tennis-play) on practice only: which rules, neither poor men have the leisure, nor men that have had the leisure, have hitherto had the curiosity, or the method to find out.

. . .

But as men, for the attaining of peace, and conservation of themselves thereby, have made an artificial man, which we call a commonwealth; so also have they made artificial chains, called *civil laws*, which they themselves, by mutual covenants, have fastened at one end, to the lips of that man, or assembly, to whom they have given the sovereign power; and at the other end to their own ears. These bonds in their own nature but weak, may nevertheless be made to hold, by the danger, though not by the difficulty of breaking them.

In relation to these bonds only it is, that I am to speak now, of the *liberty of subjects*. For seeing there is no commonwealth in the world, wherein there be rules enough to set down, for the regulating of all the actions, and words of men; (as being a thing impossible:) it followeth necessarily, that in all kinds of actions, by the laws praetermitted [passed over], men

have the liberty, of doing what their own reasons shall suggest, for the most profitable to themselves. For if we take liberty from chains and prison, it were very absurd for men to clamour as they do, for the liberty they so manifestly enjoy. Again, if we take liberty, for an exemption from laws, it is no less absurd, for men to demand as they do, that liberty, by which all other men may be masters of their lives. And yet as absurd as it is, this is it they demand; not knowing that the laws are of no power to protect them, without a sword in the hands of a man, or men, to cause those laws to be put into execution. The liberty of a subject, lieth therefore only in those things, which in regulating their actions, the sovereign hath praetermitted: such as is the liberty to buy, and sell, and otherwise contract with one another; to choose their own abode, their own diet, their own trade of life, and institute their children as they themselves think fit; and the like.

Nevertheless we are not to understand, that by such liberty, the sovereign power of life, and death, is either abolished, or limited. For it has been already shown, that nothing the sovereign representative can do to a subject, on what pretence soever, can properly be called injustice, or injury; because every subject is author of every act the sovereign doth; so that he never wanteth right to any thing, otherwise, than as he himself is the subject of God, and bound thereby to observe the laws of nature. And therefore it may, and doth often happen in commonwealths, that a subject may be put to death by the command of the sovereign power; and yet neither do the other wrong: as when Jeptha caused his daughter to be sacrificed: in which, and the like cases, he that so dieth, had liberty to do the action, for which he is nevertheless, without injury put to death. And the same holdeth also in a sovereign prince, that putteth to death an innocent subject. For though the action be against the law of nature, as being contrary to equity, (as was the killing of Uriah, by David;) yet it was not an injury to Uriah, but to God. Not to Uriah, because the right to do what he pleased, was given him by Uriah himself: and yet to God, because David was God's subject; and prohibited all iniquity by the law of nature. Which distinction, David himself, when he repented the fact, evidently confirmed, saying, *To thee only have I sinned.* In the same manner, the people of Athens, when they banished the most potent of their commonwealth for ten years, thought they committed no injustice; and yet they never questioned what crime he had done; but what hurt he would do: nay they commanded the banishment of they knew not whom; and every citizen bringing his oystershell into the market place, written with the name of him he desired should be banished, without actually accusing him, sometimes banished an Aristides, for his reputation of justice; and sometimes a scurrilous jester, as Hyperbolus, to make a jest of it. And yet a man cannot say, the sovereign people of Athens wanted right to banish them; or an Athenian the liberty to jest, or to be just.

The liberty, whereof there is so frequent, and honourable mention, in the histories, and philosophy of the ancient Greeks, and Romans, and in the writings, and discourse of those that from them have received all their learning in the politics, is not the liberty of particular men; but the liberty of the commonwealth: which is the same with that, which every man then should have, if there were no civil laws, no commonwealth at all. And the effects of it also be the same. For as amongst his neighbor; no inheritance, to transmit to the son, nor to expect from the father; no propriety of goods, or lands; no security; but a full and absolute liberty in every particular man: so in states, and commonwealths not dependent on one another, every commonwealth, (not every man) has an absolute liberty, to do what it shall judge (that is to say, what that man, or assembly that representeth it, shall judge) most conducing to their benefit. But withal, they live in the condition of a perpetual war, and upon the confines of battle, with their frontiers armed, and cannons planted against their neighbours round about. The Athenians, and Romans were free; that is, free commonwealths: not that any particular man had the liberty to resist their own representative; but that their representative had the liberty to resist, or invade other people. There is written on the turrets of the city of Lucca in great characters at this day, the word LIBERTAS; yet no man can thence infer, that a particular man has more liberty, or immunity from the service of the commonwealth there, than in Constantinople. Whether a commonwealth be monarchical, or popular, the freedom is still the same.

STUDY QUESTIONS

1. Does Hobbes see war as a natural and even necessary experience for humanity?
2. How does he contrast the "freedom" of the individual with the freedom of the commonwealth as a whole?

CHAPTER 14

THE WARS OF ALL AGAINST ALL

14.1 JOHN FOXE, *FOXE'S BOOK OF MARTYRS*, TRIAL OF ANNE ASKEW

John Foxe (1517–1587) authored this martyrology that especially focuses on the martyrdoms of sixteenth-century Protestants at the hands of Catholic inquisitors. This selection recounts the trial against Anne Askew, an Englishwoman who became actively involved in propagating Protestant beliefs—even being rejected by her husband as a result of her zeal. As in medieval inquisitions, the questions asked to Anne are aimed at clarifying where the error arises; here, she rejects the doctrine of transubstantiation and challenges the authority of "improper" priests. Her answers are logical and coherent as she unwittingly condemns herself. Anne was tortured in the Tower of London and burned at the stake in 1546 at the age of twenty-five.

To satisfy your expectation: good people (saith she) this was my first examination in the year of our Lord 1545 and in the month of March.

First Christopher Dare examined me at Sadler's Hall; being one of the quest, and asked if I did not believe that the sacrament, hanging over the altar, was the very body of Christ really. Then I demanded this question of him: wherefore Saint Stephen was stoned to death, and he said, he could not tell. Then I answered that no more would I assoil his vain question.

Secondly, he said that there was a woman, which did not testify that I should read, how God was not in temples made with hands. Then I showed him the seventh and seventeenth chapters of the Acts of Apostles, what Stephen and Paul had said therein. Whereupon he asked me how I took those sentences? I answered, "I would not throw pearls among swine, for acorns were good enough."

Thirdly, he asked me wherefore I said that I had rather read five lines in the Bible, than to hear five masses in the temple? I confessed, that I had said no less: not for the dispraise of either the epistle or the gospel, but because the one did greatly edify me, and the other nothing at all. As Saint Paul doth witness in the fourteenth chapter of his first epistle to the Corinthians, whereas he saith, "If the trumpet giveth an uncertain sound who will prepare himself to the battle?"

John Foxe, *Foxe's Book of Martyrs: Select Narratives*. Edited by John N. King. New York: Oxford University Press, 2009, pp. 22–35.

Fourthly: he laid unto my charge that I should say: "If an ill priest ministered, it was the devil and not God."

My answer was, that I never spake any such thing. But this was my saying: that whosoever he were that ministered unto me, his ill conditions could not hurt my faith, but in spirit I received nevertheless, the body and blood of Christ. ·

He asked me what I said concerning confession? I answered him my meaning, which was as Saint James saith, that every man ought to acknowledge his faults to other, and the one to pray for the other.

Sixthly, he asked me what I said to the King's Book? And I answered him, that I could say nothing to it, because I never saw it.

Seventhly, he asked me if I had the spirit of God in me? I answered, "If I had not, I was but a reprobate or castaway." Then he said he had sent for a priest to examine me, which was here at hand.

The priest asked me what I said to the sacrament of the altar, and required much to know therein my meaning. But I desired him again, to hold me excused concerning that matter. None other answer would I make him, because I perceived him to be a papist.

Eighthly he asked me, if I did not think that private Masses did help souls departed? I said it was great idolatry to believe more in them, than in the death which Christ died for us.

Then they had me thence unto my Lord Mayor, and he examined me, as they had before, and I answered him directly in all things I answered the quest before. Besides this my Lord Mayor laid one thing to my charge, which was never spoken of me, but of them: and that was, whether a mouse eating the host, received God or no? This question did I never ask, but indeed they asked it of me, whereunto I made them no answer but smiled.

Then the bishop's chancellor rebuked me and said, that I was much to blame for uttering the scriptures. For Saint Paul (he said) forbade women to speak, or to talk of the word of God. I answered him that I knew Paul's meaning as well as he, which is in 1 Corinthians 14, that a woman ought not to speak in the congregation by the way of teaching. And then I asked him, how many women he had seen go into the pulpit and preach? He said he never saw none.

Then I said he ought to find no fault in poor women, except they had offended the law.

Then the Lord Mayor commanded me to ward, I asked him if sureties would not serve me, and he made me short answer, that he would take none. Then was I had to the Counter, and there remained eleven days, no friend admitted to speak with me. But in the meantime there was a priest sent to me, which said that he was commanded of the bishop to examine me, and to give me good counsel, which he did not. But first he asked me for what cause I was put in the Counter, and I told him, I could not tell. Then he said it was great pity that I should be there without cause, and concluded that he was very sorry for me.

Secondly, he said, it was told him, that I should deny the sacrament of the altar. And I answered again that, that I have said, I have said.

Thirdly he asked me if I were shriven, I told him, so that I might have one of these three, that is to say, Doctor Crome, Sir Guillam, or Huntington. I was contented because I knew them to be men of wisdom, "as for you or any other I will not dispraise, because I know you not." Then he said, "I would not have you think, but that I, or another that shall be brought to you, shall be as honest as they, for if we were not, you may be sure the kind would not suffer us to preach." Then I answered by the saying of Solomon: "By communing with the wise, I may learn wisdom, but by talking with a fool, I shall take scathe." Pro[verbs, ch. 1].

Fourthly he asked, "If the host should fall and a beast did eat it, whether the beast did receive God or no?" I answered, "Seeing you have taken the pains to ask the question, I desire you also to assoil it yourself: for I will not do it, because I perceive you come to tempt me." And he said, "It was against the order of schools that he which asked the question should answer it." I told him [that] I was but a woman and knew not the course of schools.

Fifthly he asked me, if I intended to receive the sacrament at Easter, or no? I answered, that else I were not Christian woman, and thereat I did rejoice, that the time was so near at hand, and then he departed thence with many fair words.

The twenty-third day of March, my cousin Brittain came into the Counter unto me, and asked me whether I might be put to bail or no? Then went he immediately unto my Lord Mayor, desiring of him to be so good unto me. That I might be bailed. My Lord answered him, and said that he would be glad to do the best that in him lay. Howbeit he could not bail me, without the consent of a spiritual officer: requiring him to go and speak with the chancellor of London. For he said, like as he could not commit me to prison without the consent of a spiritual officer, no more could he bail me without consent of the same.

. . .

On the morrow after, the Bishop of London sent for me, at one of the clock, his hour being appointed at three, and as I came before him, he said he was very sorry for my trouble, and desired to know my opinion in such matters as were laid against me.

. . .

In the mean while he commanded his archdeacon to common with me, who said unto me: "Mistress wherefore are you accused and thus troubled here before the bishop?" To whom I answered again and said: "Sir, ask I pray you my accusers, for I know not as yet." Then took he my book out of my hand, and said: "Such books as this, have brought you to the trouble you are in. Beware," (saith he), "beware, for he that made this book and was the author thereof, was an heretic I warrant you, and burnt in Smithfield." Then I asked him, if he were certain and sure, that it was true that he had spoken. And he said he knew well the book was of John Frith's making. Then I asked him if he were not ashamed for to judge of the book before he saw it within, or yet knew the truth thereof. I said also, that such unadvised and hasty judgement is a token apparent of a very slender wit. Then I opened the book and showed it to him. He said he thought it had been another, for he could find no fault therein. Then I desired him no more to be so unadvisedly rash and swift judgement, till he thoroughly knew the truth, and so he departed from me.

. . .

Then brought he forth this unsavoury similitude: that if a man had a wound, no wise surgeon would minister help unto it before he had seen it uncovered. "In like case," saith he, "can I give you no good counsel, unless I know wherewith your conscience is burdened." I answered, that my conscience was clear in all things: and for to lay a plaster unto the whole skin, it might appear much folly.

. . .

Then said my Lord unto me, that I had alleged a certain text of the scripture. I answered that I alleged none other but Saint Paul's own saying to the Athenians in the eighteenth chapter in the Apostle's acts, that God dwelleth not in temples made with hands. Then asked he me what my faith and belief was in that matter? I answered him, "I believe as the scripture doth teach me."

Then enquired he of me, "What if the scripture do say that it is the body of Christ?" "I believe," said I, "as the scripture doth teach me." Then asked he again, "What if the scripture do say that it is not the body of Christ?" My answer was still, "I believe as the scripture informeth me." And upon this argument he tarried a great while, to have driven me to make him an answer to his mind. Howbeit I would not: but concluded this with him, that I believe therein and in all other things as Christ and his holy apostles did leave them.

Then he asked me why I had so few words? And I answered, "God hath given me the gift of knowledge, but not of utterance. And Solomon saith: "That a woman of few words is a gift of God." Proverbs nineteen.

. . .

"Be it known," (saith he), "of all men, that I Anne Askew do confess this to be my faith and belief, notwithstanding my reports made afore to the contrary. I believe that they which are houseled at the hands of a priest, whether his conversation be good or not, do receive the body and blood of Christ in substance really. Also I do believe, that after the consecration, whether it be received or reserved, it is no less than the very body and blood of Christ in substance. Finally I do believe in this and in all other sacraments of holy church, in all points according to the old Catholic faith of the same. In witness whereof I the said Anne have subscribed my name."

There was somewhat more in it, which because I had not the copy, I cannot not remember. Then he read it to me and asked me if I did agree to it. And I said again, "I believe so much thereof, as the holy scripture both agree unto: wherefore I desire you, that ye will add that thereunto." Then he answered, that I should not teach him what he should write. With that, he went forth into his great chamber, and read the same bill before the audience, which inveigled and willed me to set to my hand, saying also, that I have favour showed me.

. . .

"The true copy of the confession and belief of Anne Askew, otherwise called Anne Kime, made before the Bishop of London, the twentieth day of March, in the year of our Lord God after the computation of the Church of England, 1545, and subscribed with her own hand, in the presence of the said bishop and other, whose names hereafter are recited, set forth and published at this present, to the intent the world may see what credence is now to be given unto the same woman, who in so short a time hath most damnably altered and changed her opinion and belief, and therefore rightfully in open court arraigned and condemned," *Ex. Registrum*.

"Be it known to all faithful people, that as touching the blessed sacrament of the altar, I do firmly and undoubtedly believe, that after the words of consecration be spoken by the priest, according to the common usage of this Church of England, there is present really the body and blood of our saviour Jesus Christ, whether the minister which both consecrate, be a good man, or a bad man, and that also whensoever the said sacrament is received, whether the receiver be a good man or a bad man, he doth receive it really and corporally. And moreover, I do believe, that whether the said sacrament then received of the minister, or else reserved to be put into the pix, or to be brought to any person that is impotent or sick, yet there is the very body and blood of our said saviour: so that whether the minister or the receiver be good or bad, yea whether the sacrament be received or reserved, always there is the blessed body of Christ really.

"And this thing with all other things touching the sacrament and other sacraments of the church, and all things else touching the Christian belief, which are taught and declared in the king's majesty's book lately set forth for the erudition of the Christian people, I Anne Askew, otherwise called Anne Kime, do truly and perfectly believe, and so

here presently confess and knowledge. And here I do promise that henceforth I shall never say or do anything against the promises, or against any of them. In witness whereof, I the said Anne have subscribed my name unto these presents. Written the twentieth day of March, in the year of our Lord God 1545." *Ex Registrum*.

By me Anne Askew, otherwise called Anne Kime.

. . .

Here mayest thou note gentle Reader in this confession, both in the bishop and his register: a double sleight of false conveyance. For although the confession purporteth the words of the bishop's writing, whereunto she did not set her hand, yet by the title prefixed before, mayest thou see that both she was arraigned and condemned before this was registered, and also that she is falsely reported to have put to her hand, which indeed by this her own book appeareth not so to be, but after this manner and condition: "I Anne Askew do believe all manner things contained in the faith of the Catholic Church, and not otherwise." It followeth more in the story.

Then because I did add unto it the Catholic Church he flang into his chamber in a great fury. With that my cousin Brittain followed him, desiring him for God's sake to be good Lord unto me. He answered that I was a woman, and that he was nothing deceived in me. Then my cousin Brittain desired him to take me as a woman, and not to set my weak woman's wit to his lordship's great wisdom.

Then went in unto him Doctor Weston, and said, that the cause why I did write there "the Catholic Church," was that I understood not "the church" written afore. So with much ado, they persuaded my Lord to come out again, and to take my name with the names of my sureties, which were my cousin Brittain, and Master Spilman of Gray's Inn.

This being done, we thought that I should have been put to bail immediately according to the order of the law. Howbeit, he would not suffer it, but committed me from thence to prison again, until the next morrow, and then he willed me to appear in the Guildhall, and so I did. Notwithstanding, they would not put me to bail there neither, but read the bishop['s] writing unto me, as before, and so commanded me again to prison.

Then were my sureties appointed to come before them on the next morrow in Paul's Church: which did do indeed. Notwithstanding they would once again have broken off with them because they would not be bound also for another woman at their pleasure, whom they knew not nor yet what matter was laid unto her charge. Notwithstanding at the last, after much ado and reasoning to and fro, they took a bond of them recognizance for my forthcoming. And thus I was at the last delivered.

Written by me Anne Askew.

. . .

Hitherto we have entreated of this good woman. Now it remaineth that we touch somewhat as concerning her end and martyrdom. After that she, being born of such stock and kindred, that she might have lived in great wealth and prosperity, if she would rather have followed the world, than Christ, now had been so tormented, that she could neither live long in so great distress, neither yet by her adversaries be suffered to die in secret: the day of her execution being appointed, she was brought into Smithfield in a chain, because she could not go on her feet, by means of her great torments. When she was brought unto the stake, she was tied by the middle with a chain that held up her body. When all things were thus prepared to the fire, Doctor Shaxton who was then appointed to preach, began his sermon. Anne Askew hearing, and answering again unto him, where he said well, confirmed the same: where he said amiss, there said she, "He misseth, and speaketh without the book."

The sermon being finished, the martyrs standing there tied at three stakes ready to their martyrdom, began their prayers. The multitude and concourse of the people was exceeding, the place where they stood being railed about to keep out the press. Upon the bench under Saint Bartholomew's Church, sat Wriothesley Chancellor of England, the old Duke of Norfolk, the old Earl of Bedford, the Lord Mayor with diverse other more. Before the fire should be set unto them, one of the bench hearing that they had gunpowder about them, and being afraid lest the faggots by strength of the gunpowder would come flying about their ears, began to be afraid, but the Earl of Bedford declaring unto him how the gunpowder was not laid under the faggots, but only about their bodies to rid them out of their pain, which having vent, there was no danger to them of the faggots, so diminished that fear.

Then Wriothesley Lord Chancellor, sent to Anne Askew letters, offering to her the king's pardon, if she would recant. Who refusing once to look upon them, made this answer again: that she came not thither to deny her lord and master. Then were the letters likewise offered unto the other, who in like manner, following the constancy of the woman, denied not only to receive them, but also to look upon them. Whereupon the Lord Mayor commanding fire to be put unto them, cried with a loud voice, "*Fiat justitia.*"

And thus the good Anne Askew with these blessed martyrs, being troubled so many manner of ways, and having passed through so many torments, having now ended the long course of her agonies, being compassed in with flames of fire, as a blessed sacrifice unto God, she slept in the Lord, anno 1546, leaving behind her singular example of Christian constancy for all men to follow.

STUDY QUESTIONS

1. How does Anne Askew appeal to her own reading of the Bible throughout her interrogation?
2. Why were her interrogators so insistent on the point of transubstantiation, and how does this reflect the larger goals of Henry VIII's Church of England in the 1540s?

14.2 OGIER GHISELIN DE BUSBECQ, "THE COURT OF SULEIMAN THE MAGNIFICENT," 1581

Ghiselin (1522–1592) was a Flemish ambassador who represented the Austrian Habsburgs at the court of Suleiman the Magnificent (1520–1566) in Istanbul. In 1581, he published an account of his time among the Ottomans as *Itinera Constantinopolitanum et Amasianum* (*Travels in Constantinople and Asia Minor*). A polymath, a sensitive observer of court politics, and an adventurous intellectual, Ghiselin also discovered a nearly intact copy of the autobiography of the Roman emperor Augustus that had been inscribed at Ankara, and he publicized the contents of this *Monumentum Ancyranum* for scholars around the world—and up to the present day. However, in this segment of his travel narrative, he draws attention to the personal habits and behaviors of a contemporary emperor—and one who saw himself as the heir to the Romans as well as to the other monarchs who had held Constantinople/Istanbul.

The Sultan was seated on a very low ottoman, not more than a foot from the ground, which was covered with a quantity of costly rugs and cushions of exquisite workmanship; near him lay his bow and arrows. His air, as I said, was by no means gracious, and his face wore a stern, though dignified, expression. On entering we were separately conducted into the royal presence by the chamberlains, who grasped our arms. . . . After having gone through a pretense of kissing his hand, we were conducted backwards to the wall opposite his seat, care being taken that we should never turn our backs on him. The Sultan then listened to what I had to say; but the language I held was not at all to his taste, for the demands of his Majesty breathed a spirit of independence and dignity . . . and so he made no answer beyond saying in a tetchy way, "Giusel, giusel," i.e. well, well. . . .

. . .

With all this luxury great simplicity and economy are combined; every man's dress, whatever his position may be, is of the same pattern; no fringes or useless points are sewn on, as is the case with us. . . . They were quite as much surprised at our manner of dressing as we were at theirs. They use long robes reaching down to the ankles, which have a stately effect and add to the wearer's height, while our dress is so short and scanty that it leaves exposed to view more than is comely of the human shape; . . .

I was greatly struck with the silence and order that prevailed in this great crowd. There were no cries, no hum of voices, the usual accompaniments of a motley gathering, neither was there any jostling; without the slightest disturbance each man took his proper place according to his rank. The Agas, as they call their chiefs, were seated, to wit, generals, colonels (*bimbashi*), and captains (*soubashi*). Men of a lower position stood. The most interesting sight in this assembly was a body of several thousand Janissaries, who were drawn up in a long line apart from the rest; their array was so steady and motionless that, being at a little distance, it was some time before I could make up my mind as to whether they were human beings or statues; at last I received a hint to salute them, and saw all their heads bending at the same moment to return my bow.

. . .

Wayne S. Vucinich, *The Ottoman Empire: Its Record and Legacy*. Princeton: Van Nostrand, 1965, pp. 127–9. Wayne S. Vucinich, *The Ottoman Empire: Its Record and Legacy*, Krieger Publishing Company, Malabar, FL © 1979.

When the cavalry had ridden past, they were followed by a long procession of Janissaries, but few of whom carried any arms except their regular weapon, the musket. They were dressed in uniforms of almost the same shape and colour, so that you might recognize them to be the slaves, . . . There is only one thing in which they are extravagant, viz., plumes, head-dresses, etc., and veterans who formed the rear guard were specially distinguished by ornaments of this kind. The plumes which they insert in their frontlets might well be mistaken for a walking forest.

STUDY QUESTIONS

1. Why were order and discipline apparently so important at Suleiman's court?
2. Why might Ghiselin have found the Janissaries particularly impressive?

14.3 FROM CHRISTOPHER MARLOWE, *THE MASSACRE AT PARIS*, CA. 1593

Christopher Marlowe (before 1564–1593) was an Elizabethan poet and playwright, historically connected with Shakespeare's work. Until his mysterious assassination, Marlowe was England's most celebrated dramatist—a title Shakespeare then inherited. His play *Massacre at Paris* describes the horrific event known as the Saint Bartholomew's Day massacre (beginning on August 23, 1572), in which the ruling Catholic majority arranged the simultaneous assassination of the leaders of the dissenting Protestant (Huguenot) party. The surviving manuscript is most likely reconstructed from the memory of the play's actors, but nonetheless gives a glimpse into how deadly religious disagreement could become in early modern France. These scenes show the Catholic Duke of Guise's attempts to limit Huguenot survivors, attitudes toward "heretical" corpses, and concerns about inheritance of the French throne in this era of dramatic turmoil.

GUISE: My Lord of *Anjoy*, there are a hundred
    Protestants.
Which we have chased into the river rene,
That swim about and so preserve their lives:
How may we do? i fear me they will live.

DUMAINE: Go place some men upon the bridge,
    With bows and darts to shoot at them as
    they flee,   510
    And sink them in the river as they swim.
    Guise.

Christopher Marlowe, *The Massacre at Paris.* Oxford: The Malone Society Reprints, 1928, lines 504–42, 578–633.

GUISE: Tis well advice *Dumaine*, go see that it be done.
And in the meantime my Lord, could we devise
To get those pedants from the King *Navarre*, that
are tutors to him and the prince of *Condy*.

ANJOY. For that let me alone, Cousin stay you here,
And when you see me in, then follow hard. *He
knocks, and enter the King of* Navarre *and Prince of*
Condy, *with their schoolmasters.*

How now my Lords, how fare you?   521

NAVARRE: My Lord, they say that all the Protestants
are massacred.

ANJOY: I, so they are, but yet what remedy: I have
done what I could to stay this broil.

NAVARRE. But yet my Lord the report does run, That
you were one that made this Massacre.

AN: Who I, you are deceived, I rose but now.

ENTER GUISE. HENCE.

GUISE: Murder the Hugonets, take those
pedants   530

NA: Thou traitor *Guise*, lay off thy bloody hands.

CONDY: Come let us go tell the King. *Exeunt.*

GUISE: Come sirs, I'll whip you to death with my
Dagger's point.   *He kills them.*

AN: Away with them both.   *Exit* Anjoy.

GUISE. And now sirs for this night let our fury stay.
Yet will we not that the Massacre shall end,
Gonzago posse you to Orleance, *Retes* to Deep,
Mountsorrell unto Roan, and spare not one that
you suspect of heresy.   540
And now stay that bell that to the devils Mattins
rings.

                    Now.

                    . . .

Enter two with the Admirals *body.*   *sc. vii*

1. Now sirra, what shall we do with the
    Admiral?   580
2. Why let us burn him for a heretic.
1. O no, his body will infect the fire, and the fire
    the air, and so we shall be poisoned with him.
2. What shall we do then?
1. Let's throw him into the river.
2. Oh it will corrupt the water, and the water the
    fish, and by the fish ourselves when we eat them.
1. Then throw him into the ditch.   590
2. No, no, to decide all doubts, be ruled by me, let's
    hang him here upon this tree.

1. Agreed.   *They hang him.*

Enter the Duke of Guise, and Queen Mother, *and the*
Cardinal.

GUISE: Now Madame, how like you our lusty
Admiral?

[B 5]   *Queen.*

QUEEN: Believe me *Guise* he becomes the place so
well, As I could long before this have wished
him there.   600
But come let's walk aside, the air is not very sweet.

GUISE: No by my faith Madam.
Sire, take him away and throw him in some ditch.
carry away the dead body.
And now Madam as I understand,
There are a hundred Hugonets and more,
Which in the woods do horde their synagogue:
And daily meet about this time of day,
And thither will I to put them to the sword.

QU: Do so sweet *Guise*, let us delay no time,   610
For if these stragglers gather head again,
And disperse themselves throughout the Realm of
France,
It will be hard for us to work their deaths.
Be gone, delay no time sweet *Guise*.

GUISE: Madam I go as whirl-winds rage before a
storm.   *Exit* Guise.

QU: My Lord of Loraine have you marked of late,
How *Charles* our son begins for to lament: For
the late nights work which my Lord
of *Guise*   620
Did make in Paris amongst the Hugonites?

CARD: Madam, I have heard him solemnly vow, With
the rebellious King of *Navarre*, For to revenge
their deaths upon us all.

QU: I, but my Lord let me alone for that, For *Katherine*
must have her will in France: As I do live, for
surely he die.

                    And

The Massacre

And *Henry* then shall wear the diadem.
And if he grudge or cross his Mothers will,
I'll disinherit him and all the rest: 630
For I'll rule France, but they shall wear
the crown:
And if they storm, I then may pull them down.

Come my Lord lets us go.   *Exeunt.*

STUDY QUESTIONS

1. What seems to be motivating Guise, Anjou, and the Queen Mother Catherine in their deliberations about the impending massacre?
2. How might this play have appealed to Elizabethan English audiences, who had not experienced the French Wars of Religion in the 1570s and 1580s?

14.4 JOHANNES JUNIUS, LETTER TO HIS DAUGHTER AND TRIAL TRANSCRIPT, 1628

Johannes Junius (1573–1628), the mayor of Bamberg, Germany, was accused of witchcraft during the craze of 1628. Before his tragic execution, Junius wrote a moving letter to his daughter Veronica so that she would understand the charges brought against him and the torture he endured. Amid prayers to keep him in God's care, Junius describes false witnesses brought against him, his sufferings, and the lies that he finally "confessed" to no avail. The transcript of his trial has survived as well and permits a glimpse into the terrifying machinery of the witch-hunts.

A hundred thousand Good Nights, my darling Veronica, my daughter. Innocent have I been imprisoned, innocent have I been tortured, and innocent must I die—for whoever comes into this place must become a witch, or else he will be tortured until he invents something (may God have mercy) and confesses to it. I will tell you everything that has happened to me. The first time I was brought before the court Doctor Braun, Doctor Kötzendorffer, and two other doctors whom I did not know were there [SEVERAL WORDS MISSING] Then Doctor Braun asked me from the gallery, "How did you end up here, brother?" "Bad luck," I answered. "Listen!" he said, "You are a witch! Will you confess it freely? If not, they will put witnesses and the executioner in front of you." I said, "I've been betrayed! My conscience is clean. Even if they bring a thousand witnesses, I'm not worried. I'll gladly listen to their witnesses." Then the Chancellor's son was brought forth. I asked him, "Herr Doctor, what do you know about me? I have never seen you before in all my life, whether for good or for bad." And he gave me in answer, "Friend, I know you from the district court. I asked you for a pardon when I appeared before you in court." "Yes, but so what?" He said nothing. So I asked the Lord Commissioner to question him under oath. Doctor Braun said that "he need not do what he does not wish to do; it is enough that he has stated he saw you. Step down now, Herr Doctor!" I said, "My lords, what kind of evidence is that? If that is how this process goes, then how can you be any more sure it was me [he saw] than some other honest man?" But no one would listen to me. Then the Chancellor came up and said that he too, just like his son, had seen me [at a witch-gathering]. But he knew me only by reputation, nothing more. Then came Hopfen-Else, who said she had seen me dance on the Hauptmoor. "With whom?"

From Johannes Junius, "Letter from Prison." Bamberg, 1628. Translation by Clifford Backman.

I asked. She replied that she didn't know. I then swore on oath to the lord justices that what they had heard was all pure lies, so help me God, and that they should ask these witnesses of theirs to be truthful and honest. But they did not wish to know the truth, or else they would have said so; instead they wanted me to confess freely, or else the executioner would drag it out of me. I answered, "I have never renounced God and will never do so. May God in His grace keep me from such a thing! I would rather suffer anything, than that." And that was when—O God in Highest Heaven have pity!—in came the executioner, who tied my hands together and twisted thumbscrews on them until blood flowed out from my nails and all over; for four weeks I couldn't use my hands, as you can see by my writing. I thought about the five Holy Wounds suffered by God and said, since as far as the name and glory of God was concerned I had not renounced them, I would commend my innocence and all my agony and suffering to His Five Wounds. He would ease my pain, so that I could endure any amount of it. But then they hauled me up, hands bound behind my back, and lifted me in the hanging torture. I thought then that heaven and earth were ending. Six times they hoisted me up in this way, and then let me fall. The pain was horrible.

All of this happened while I was stark naked, since they had stripped me and left me that way. Since no one but Our Lord God could help me, I called out to Him, saying, "Forgive them. O God, for they are hurting an innocent man! They care nothing for my life and soul! They only want to seize my wealth and possessions!" Then Doctor Braun said, "You are a devil!" I answered, "I'm no devil or any such thing. I'm as innocent as any one of you! And if anyone doubts me, then no honest man in all of Bamberg is safe—not you, not me, not anyone else!"

The Doctor then cried out that he would not be challenged by a devil. "Neither will I!" I shouted. "But these false witnesses are the devil, and so is this wretched torture of yours—for it lets no one go free, and no one can endure it."

All of this occurred on Friday, 30 June, when I was forced to endure, with God's help, the torture. Throughout that entire time I was strung up and could not use my hands, but suffered pain upon pain despite my innocence. When the executioner

finally led me back to my prison cell he said to me, "I beg you, sir! For God's sake, confess to something, whether it's true or not! Invent something—for you won't be able to survive the torturing they plan for you. Even if you do survive, you'll never go free. Not even if you were an earl. It will just be one torture after another, until you confess and say that you are a witch. Only then will they let you go free. That's how all these trials go, each one just like the other."

Sometime after this, Georg came and told me that the Commissioner had declared he wanted to make such an example of me that people would talk about it for a long time. They had already brought in several more torturers, just for me. Georg too pleaded with me, for God's sake, to confess to something, for even if I were entirely innocent I would never again go free. The candle-maker, the lamplighter, and a few others, too, told me the same thing. Since I was in such a sad plight, I asked to be granted a day to think things over and consult with a priest. They denied me a priest but allowed me some time to think.

So now, dear daughter, what do you think about the danger I was in, and still am in? I have to confess to being a witch even though I am not one, and must do for the first time something that I have never before considered—renounce God. I wrestled with myself day and night over this, until finally an idea came to me one night as I was praying, showing how I need not be troubled: since I was denied a priest, with whom I could take counsel, I would simply invent something and say it. How much better it would be to simply confess something by the words of my mouth even though it was not actually true. I could confess my lie later, and the fault would be on those who had forced me to do it. I could explain that I had asked to see a priest from the Dominican cloister but had been refused. And so, here follows my sworn statement—the entire thing a lie. Dearest child, what follows is the affidavit I made on account of the horrible pain, the cruel torture, I suffered and could endure no longer.

In 1624 or 1625 I had gone on city business to the town of Rottweil, and had to carry about six hundred florins with me in order to conduct some legal affairs on behalf of Doctor Braun and the city—which is why I had taken counsel with so many honest people who had helped me out. Everything that follows appears in my affidavit, but is nothing but a pure lie—a lie I told in light of the horrible, monstrous torture that compelled me, and for which I now must die. In my affidavit it says that I went into my field at Friedrichsbrunnen, and was so troubled that I had to sit down. While I was there a peasant girl approached and asked, "What's wrong, sir? Why are you so sad?" "I don't know," I replied. She drew closer to me and did several things to me that resulted in my lying with her, and no sooner was this done than she turned into a goat and said, "Behold, now you can see who you've been dealing with." Then he grabbed me by the throat and said, "You must be mine now, or else I'll kill you!" "God save me!" I cried. He disappeared suddenly, then just as suddenly he reappeared with two women and two men at his side. I was forced to renounce God, which I did, and at the same time I renounced the Lord of Heaven. After this, he baptized me—and the two women he had brought became my godmothers. Then they gave me a gold coin as a token, but it was really just a potsherd. It seemed to me that I had survived, for they then led me to stand alongside the executioner. Where was I during the dances? I confessed then and there, after giving it some thought, what I had heard from the Chancellor, his son, and Hopfen-Else, and all the elders of the court, the council-room: the Hauptmoor—just as I had heard in the reading of the initial charges against me. So that was the name of the site that I gave.

Next I was told to identify the people I had seen there. I said that I had not recognized anyone. "You devil! I'll put the executioner at your throat! Tell us! Wasn't the Chancellor there?" I said he was. "Who else?" I said I hadn't recognized anyone else. So he said, "Take one street after another; start at the market then go up one street and down the next." I had to name a few people at least. Then came the long street—I had to name at least one person there. Next the Zinkenwörth—one person more. Then over the upper bridge to both sides of the Bergtor. I knew nobody. Did I recognize anyone from the castle, anyone at all? I should speak without fear. They carried on this way for street after street, but there was nothing more I could or would say, so they handed me over to the executioner, saying that he should strip me, cut off all my hair, and start to torture me again. "This devil knows someone in the market, sees him every day, and yet refuses to identify him!" They meant Dietmeyer—so I had to identify him too.

Then they made me tell what evils I had committed. "None," I replied, "the Devil had wanted me to do something, but I had refused, and so he beat me." "Haul the fellow up!" So I said that I was supposed to murder my own children, but I had killed a horse instead. That didn't help, though, [so I said that] I had also taken a piece of the Host and had desecrated it. Once I had said this, they left me in peace.

Dear child, you now have my entire confession and the reasons for which I must die. They are nothing but lies and imaginings, so help me God. I said all these things out of fear of the wretched torture that was threatened beyond what I had already suffered; they never stop with the torturing until one confesses something. No matter how pious a man might be, he will confess to being a witch. No one escapes, not even a lord. If God allows no remedy that would let the light of day shine through, the whole family is done for. One has to denounce other people, even if one knows nothing at all about them, as I have had to do—and God in Heaven knows that I know next to nothing about [the people I accused]. I die an innocent man, like a martyr. Dearest child, I know that you are every bit as devout as I am, but even you have told a few lies in your time, and if I may be permitted to give you some advice: take all the money and letters you have [SEVERAL WORDS MISSING] and devote half a year to a holy pilgrimage, and do everything you can, in that time period, to [SEVERAL WORDS MISSING]. I recommend doing this until it becomes clear that your resources have run out. This way, at least, there will be some honest men and women in Bamberg, both in the church and in the world of business—people who do not know evil and who have clean consciences, as I once was (as you know) before my arrest. Nevertheless, they very well may find themselves in the witch-prison; for all it takes is for a rumor about an individual to go around, no matter if he is honest or not. Herr Neudecker, the Chancellor, his son, the candle-maker, the daughter of Wolff Hoffmeister, and Hopfen-Else have all testified against me, all at the same time. Their testimony was all false, drawn out of them by force, as they all told me later when they begged my forgiveness in God's name before they were executed. Their last words to me were that they knew nothing but good of me. They had been forced to lie, just as I was. I am done for, for sure. That's how it is for many people now, and will be for many more yet to come, if God does not shine a path out of this darkness. I have nothing more to say.

Dear child, hide this letter so that no one ever sees it. Or else I will be tortured yet again, and piteously; more than that, my jailers would be beheaded—so strongly is it forbidden [to smuggle out letters]. Herr Steiner, my cousin, is familiar to you—you can trust him and [SEVERAL WORDS MISSING] him read it. He is a discreet man.

Dear child, pay this man a Reichstaler [SEVERAL WORDS MISSING].

It has taken me several days to write this, since my hands are broken. I am in a wretched state. I beg you, in the light of Judgment Day, to keep this letter safe, and to pray for me, your father, as you would for a true martyr. After my death, do as you wish but be careful not to let anyone see this letter. Please ask Anna Maria also to pray for me. You can swear it on oath that I was not a witch but a martyr, and that I died as such.

A thousand times Good Night. Your father, Johannes Junius, will never see you again. 24 July 1628.

STUDY QUESTION

1. Why does Junius fail to convince his accusers of his innocence of witchcraft?

CHAPTER 15

FROM WESTPHALIA TO PARIS: REGIMES OLD AND NEW

15.1 ANNE OF FRANCE, *LESSONS FOR MY DAUGHTER*, 1560–1600

"Madame la Grande," as she was called, was the daughter of King Louis XI of France and briefly the regent for her brother Charles VIII. Anne (1461–1522) was an able stateswoman who managed royal lands and the ducal territories of her husband and oversaw the education and raising of aristocratic offspring. In this vein, Anne wrote a handbook for her only daughter, Suzanne, guiding her through the courtly gauntlet. Like Dhuoda's handbook to her son (Document 8.6), Anne here attempts to help her daughter avoid the pitfalls of courtly life—but in this case, a woman's worst enemies are frivolity, immodesty, and a quick tongue. The Dr. Lienard referred to several times in this passage cannot be identified.

And so, my daughter, devote yourself completely to acquiring virtue. Behave so that your reputation may be worthy of perpetual memory: whatever you do, above all, be truly honest, humble, courteous, and loyal. Believe firmly that if even a small fault or lie were to be found in you, it would be a great reproach. As Doctor Lienard writes in his argument about lying, it is the worst of all the vices, foul and dishonest to God and the world. Now then, my daughter, if you would like to be numbered among worthy women and to have a good and honest reputation, be very careful to avoid it. And as Socrates says, do not be like those foolish idlers who, in their idiocy, think themselves wise and worthy when they deceive and abuse many people with their evil and venomous cunning, which is detestable to God and abominable to the world. And as the aforementioned Doctor Lienard says, no man or woman of great rank who has good judgment wants to have such a reputation. And he also says there are many dishonest and evil nobles in the world today who come from good families and have a large following, but, to speak frankly and truthfully, those who follow them are either fools or have business with them. Be assured, as the aforesaid doctor says, that if their followers flatter them to their faces, they damn them behind their backs. Finally, as Saint Ambrose says, whatever pretenses they make and however long it takes, in the end such people are neither loved by

Translation by Clifford Backman.

God nor by the world. Wise men say you should fly from them as if they were poison no matter how pleasing their greetings and no matter how charming their pastimes— in the end, associating with them is too perilous. And so, my daughter, protect yourself from them and their deceptive company.

. . .

And so, my daughter, because virtues and good works are as well praised, loved, and valued in this world as they are in the next, you should take great pains to be virtuous; to this end, make sure that your conversation is always honest and good, that you are courteous and amiable in all things, and that you are pleasant to all and loved by all. And, truly, when it comes to love, the Philosopher says honesty must be its foundation because any other "love" is only false treachery and hypocrisy—with all the authority and power that a mother can and should have over a daughter, I command you to flee from such love. It is important to control your bearing, your expressions, your words, your sentiments, your thoughts, your desires, your wishes, and your passions. As Saint Paul says, of all the temptations and subtle deceptions in the world, this is one of the worst, and from such "love" comes great evil, so dishonestly is it practiced today. As many doctors agree, there is no man of worth, however, noble he may be, who does not use treachery, nor to whom it does not seem good sport to deceive or trick women of rank from one good family or another, it doesn't matter which. And Doctor Lienard says there is no man so perfect who, in matters of love, is truthful or keeps his word, however firm or fervent—which I certainly believe. One time I heard a noblewoman of great rank tell about a knight she knew who, in such a situation, took a solemn oath of his own free will, on his honor as a gentleman, on the altar and on a missal where Mass is said everyday—and this knight did not keep his oath for more than four hours! And, as she told me, the oath was very reasonable and, with all respect to his honor and conscience, he had no excuse whatsoever for breaking it except his own lust, weak will, and sudden change of heart. Therefore, my daughter, whatever flattering speeches or great signs of love that someone may make you, trust none of them. As Doctor Lienard says, those who are wisest and think they are following the right path are often

the first to be misled. . . . Although, certainly, it must be said that when those of virtuous character come together, by one means or another, love can be marvelously great and, in the end, good and honest. But when this does happen, as Doctor Lienard says at the end of his argument about true love, the enemy, who is full of venomous subtlety, uses his power to break and distance such love because of the great goods and honors that result from it. . . . Therefore, for the greatest certainty in such situations, I advise you to avoid all private meetings, no matter how pleasant they are, because, as you have seen, many an honest beginning comes to a dishonest and harmful end. And even when it seems all is for the best, you must also fear the foolish and the irresponsible opinions others often express, to the prejudice of women and at their expense. As Doctor Lienard says, in this situation and in others, the world is so vile and so corrupt that true love is hardly understood or recognized.

. . .

For this reason, my daughter, heed this example and, wherever you are, avoid making any unpleasant faces and shaking or turning your head this way and that, and do not stare, peer around you, or let your eyes wander. Also, make sure you do not laugh too much for any reason because it is very unbecoming, especially for young noblewomen, whose manners should be more solemn, gentler, and more controlled than the manners of others. Nor should you talk too much or too sharply like many foolish and conceited women who want to attract attention and, to be more admired, speak boldly and in a flighty way, responding to everyone and on all topics, which is very unbecoming in all women, whatever their state, but especially so for young virgins, rich and poor alike, who must protect their reputations. Because of their careless talk, many young women are judged to be foolish and unchaste; as one philosopher says, the way a woman minds her eyes and her tongue is an indication of her chastity. For this reason, my daughter, always use your eyes and tongue cautiously and carefully; that is, know when to speak and where your eyes belong, never be the first or the last to talk, and do not be a tale-teller, especially of anything unpleasant or prejudicial. Also, be slow and cool in all your responses because, as wise men say, on some subjects a reply cannot be avoided. Also, take care not to run or jump, and do not pinch or hit anyone. Likewise suffer no man to touch your body, no matter who he is, no holding of hands or pressing of feet. In conclusion, my daughter, remember those three aforementioned daughters who were the cause of their mother's death, and do not behave so that your bad conduct is the cause of mine.

. . .

I do not wish to say that . . . in hearing, speaking, and responding to honest questions and proposals you might not sometimes encounter the bad as well as the good. But, suppose a castle is beautiful and so well-guarded that it is never assailed—then it is not to be praised, nor is a knight who has never proven himself to be commended for his prowess. To the contrary, the thing most highly commended is that which has been in the fire yet cannot be scorched (or worse) or that which has been in the terrible depths of the sea yet cannot be drowned or that which has been in the mire of this world yet cannot be soiled in any way. Worthy of being praised, therefore, are women who in this miserable world know to live in purity of conscience and chastity; they are worthy of eternal glory because by their steadfast chastity and good virtue they redirect fools, disordered in their carnality, to the good road. As the saying goes, the habit does not make the monk, and sometimes those you think are the biggest deceivers and the most worldly are easiest to convert and are then greatly to be commended. Nevertheless, in this situation there is no certainty, and I counsel more doubt than surety. As Saint Paul says, the assaults and stings of this world are hard to endure except with the help of God, with which nothing is impossible.

STUDY QUESTIONS

1. Is it even more essential for women to channel their thoughts and words into virtuous paths than for their male counterparts?
2. How can a woman avoid scandalous talk, even if standards of behavior are applied unequally to females?

15.2 MOLIÈRE, *THE MISANTHROPE*, FIRST PERFORMED 1666

An actor who abandoned social prestige for the stage, Jean-Baptiste Poquelin (1622–1673), better known as Molière, numbers among the greatest comedy playwrights. His plays incorporated traits of *commedia dell'arte* while poking fun at the foibles of humankind—such as the hypochondriac obsessions of the main character in his popular *The Imaginary Invalid*. *The Misanthrope*, another comedy of manners, centers around the plight of Alceste, who adores the flirtatious Célimène while simultaneously condemning her for blindly obeying social niceties, such as politeness toward strangers. When he ultimately discovers that Célimène has led him on, Alceste decides that self-imposed exile from society is the only solution to his misanthropic loathing.

Molière, *The Misanthrope, Tartuffe, and Other Plays.* Translated by Maya Slater. Oxford: Oxford University Press, 2009, 1397w from pp. 209–13. By permission of Oxford University Press.

ACT I, SCENE 1

ALCESTE, PHILINTE

PHILINTE: Oh, what's the matter? What's wrong now?

ALCESTE: Leave me alone.

Go away.

PHILINTE: But why must you adopt this angry tone? . . .

ALCESTE: Oh, leave me here, I said. Go, run away and hide.

PHILINTE: Alceste, don't lose your temper. Listen, then decide.

ALCESTE: I want to lose my temper, and to make a stand.

PHILINTE: I find your angry rantings hard to understand.

Although we're still good friends, I really must insist . . .

ALCESTE: What? Me, your friend? Why don't you cross me off your list?

It's true I've always made a show of liking you;

But now I've witnessed your behaviour, we're through.

I tell you, I don't want your friendship any more—

I hate you, now I know you're rotten to the core.

PHILINTE: You seem to have decided I'm the one to blame . . .

ALCESTE: That's right. Why don't you crawl away and die of shame?

I'm telling you, there's no excuse for what you've done—

Your antics must seem scandalous to everyone.

You met a man, you treated him as your best friend,

You were all over him, you hugged him without end,

You said he mattered to you, swore by Heaven above

That what you felt for him was liking, even love.

I asked you for the fellow's name, when he had gone,

And you scarcely remembered who he was—come on!

No sooner had he turned his back on you, I swear,

You spoke of him to me, as if you didn't care.

Good grief! The way you carry on is a disgrace.

You worthless coward, must you really be so base?

If I had done what you've just done, do you know what

I'd do? I'd go and hang myself, right on the spot.

PHILINTE: Come on, it's not a hanging matter, so don't tease.

I beg leave to appeal against my sentence, please.

It's time you showed some mercy. Don't be quite so hard.

What, make me hang myself for that? What a charade!

ALCESTE: Oh, very funny! That was typical of you.

PHILINTE: But, seriously, what am I supposed to do?

ALCESTE: You should be honourable, honest, without art,

And everything you say should come straight from the heart.

PHILINTE: But when a stranger rushes up and hugs you tight,

You have to hug him back—it seems only polite;

You can't keep him at arm's length, you must play the game,

And if he swears you're his best friend, you do the same.

ALCESTE: No. Your hypocrisy disgusts me, and that's flat.

You fashionable types, you all behave like that.

I tell you, I can't stand the phoney posturing

Of men who claim they like you more than anything,

And fling their arms around you, kiss you on the cheek,

Insist that they adore you, every time they speak.

They've perfect manners, and they obey the rules,

But decent men are treated on a par with fool.

Look, I mean, what's the point of someone kissing you,

And swearing he appreciates and loves you too,

Proclaiming to the world that you're the only one,

Then rushing off to do the same to everyone?

No. If a man who has the slightest self-respect

Is faced with such hypocrisy, he must object.

For very little's added to our sense of worth

If we're the same as all the others on this earth.

If you respect a man, believing he's the best,

Don't put him on an equal footing with the rest.

Now you're no different from the other fellows, so,

Damn it, you're not the sort of man I want to know.

I can't value a friend who puts himself about,

And doesn't see why merit should be singled out.

I want to be distinguished from the rest, you see:
The friend of all humanity's no friend to me.

PHILINTE: But, in polite society, you have to do
Your bit, or people won't think very well of you.

ALCESTE: Nonsense! I say, the time has come to make
a stand
Against these hypocrites. I want them to be
banned.
I want us to be proper men, and when we meet,
To show our secret, inner thoughts, without
deceit.
We must speak from the heart, lay bare our
sentiments,
Not hide the truth with empty, formal
compliments.

PHILINTE: It won't work. There are times when total
frankness would
Be idiotic, totally misunderstood.
And sometimes, even if we find it an ordeal,
It's better to suppress the truth of what we feel.
Truth can be inappropriate; most people shrink
From telling everyone precisely what they think.
What if we know someone we hate, or find
uncouth—
Are we supposed to tell the whole, unvarnished
truth?

ALCESTE: Yes.

PHILINTE: What, you want to go to poor old Emilie,
And tell her she's too old to dress so prettily—
With all that make-up, she looks like a painted
whore?

ALCESTE: That's right.

PHILINTE: Should we tell Dorilas he's a great bore?
The courtiers hate the way he shows off endlessly,
And boasts about his courage, and his pedigree.

ALCESTE: We should.

PHILINTE: You must be joking.

ALCESTE: Joking? not at all.
I tell you, we must spare nobody, great or small.
My eyes are never spared, at court or in the town:
I'm always shaving to see sights that make me
frown.
It puts me in a rage, to see what I detest:
The way men treat each other makes me so
depressed.
Hypocrisy is everywhere, and flattery,

And crude self-interest, and even treachery.
I've had enough. Mankind's an absolute disgrace.
I'll make a stand, alone against the human race.

PHILINTE: Your grim philosophy is too morose by half.
Your fits of black depression simply make me
laugh.
It strikes me we resemble, in a curious way,
The brothers in *The School for Husbands*, Molière's
play,
Who . . .

ALCESTE: Good God! Some comparison. Please, let
that drop.

PHILINTE: Fine. Let's be serious. I'm asking you to stop
This madness. You won't change the world with
what you do,
And since this frankness seems to have such
charms for you,
I tell you, frankly, you've become so querulous,
That, nowadays, the world finds you ridiculous.
You turn your nose up, claim our modern
manners shock,
But everyone around thinks you're a
laughingstock.

ALCESTE: Well, good, damn it! Yes, good! I ask for
nothing more.
I'm quite delighted, that's what I've been hoping
for.
Since everyone I know seems hateful in my eyes,
I'd be disgusted, if they thought that I was wise.

PHILINTE: Why blame the human race? You're eaten
up with hate.

ALCESTE: It overwhelms me totally—I'm desperate.

PHILINTE: You say you loathe us all, without excep-
tion, and
There's not a single human being you can stand?
Can't you imagine any situation when . . .?

ALCESTE: No. My disgust is general. I hate all men—
Hate some of them because they are in an evil
crew,
And others for condoning what the villains do,
Instead of treating them with loathing and
contempt,
As they deserve. They might at least make an
attempt
To judge that fellow who's no better than he
ought,

I mean the filthy beast who's taken me to court:
His wickedness shines out behind his bland façade,
And everybody knows his manner's a charade.
He sighs and rolls his eyes, and mouths his platitudes,
But no one's taken in, save idiots or prudes.
Confound him! He's got his flat foot in every door.
He gets on in the world by dirty tricks, what's more.
He does so well, living off his ill-gotten gains,
Ironically, he's rewarded for his pains—
He has some sort of title, which he likes to use,
But all his posturing can't alter people's views.
Call him confounded liar, no one will object;
Say he's a fraud, and nobody will contradict.
Yet, with his smirking face, he gets himself received
In the best circles, though his hosts are not deceived.
He knows all the right people, so he always wins.
He beats his rivals, though he can't conceal his sins.
Yes, curse him, every time! It cuts me to the quick
To see him get away with every dirty trick.
Sometimes, it overwhelms me. I feel mortified
By all mankind, and long to run away and hide.

STUDY QUESTIONS

1. How does Alceste skewer the phoniness and hypocrisy of "polite society"?
2. What does he believe will happen, even if the essentially fraudulent nature of this society is exposed?

15.3 CARDINAL RICHELIEU, "THE ROLE OF THE KING," *POLITICAL TESTAMENT*, CA. 1638, FIRST PUBLISHED 1688

Armand Jean du Plessis (1585–1642), the Duke of Richelieu and a Catholic bishop, became the first minister for King Louis XIII. He worked to centralize the French state at the expense of the nobility and factions; this included curtailing the political liberties of the Huguenots but supporting them in the Thirty Years' War (1618–1648) to limit Austrian and Spanish power before a strong French king. His *Political Testament*, one of many works, would have served as a guide for the young Louis XIII in case Richelieu fell victim to one of his frequent illnesses—which explains its hasty, jotted-down feel. This selection outlines the proper role of the king in Richelieu's vision of a strongly centralized France.

God is the principle of all things, the sovereign master of kings, and the only one who can make their reigns happy. If the devotion of Your Majesty were not known to all, I would begin this chapter, which is concerned with your person, by stating to you that should you not follow the wishes of your Creator and submit to His laws you could not hope to have yours observed by subjects obedient to your orders.

But it would be a superfluous gesture to exhort Your Majesty in the matter of devotion. You are so bent toward it by inclination and so confirmed in it by virtuous habit that there is no reason to fear you might turn away from it. It is because of this that in place of showing you the advantage religious principles have over others I will content myself with observing that although devotion is necessary for kings, it ought to be devoid of all over-scrupulousness. I say this, Sire, because the sensitiveness of Your Majesty's conscience has often made you fear to offend God in reaching even those decisions which you cannot abstain from making without sin.

I well know that faults of such a nature in a prince are much less dangerous for a state than those which lean in the direction of presumption and disrespect toward that which a monarch should revere. But since they are faults, it is necessary to correct them, as it is most certain that they have resulted in many inconveniences prejudicial to the interests of the state. I beseech you, in this matter, to try to fortify yourself against your scruples, reminding yourself that you can never be guilty in the eyes of God if, on occasions involving difficult discussions of matters of conscience, you follow the advice of your council, confirmed by that of several competent theologians not suspected of having an interest in the question.

The basic problem recognized, there remains nothing else of a personal nature intrinsically necessary to the successful conducting of your affairs save the preservation of your health, and I cannot go on without giving it special emphasis. Long, thorough, and persistent observation of your conduct in all sorts of circumstances emboldens me to say that nothing is more important than the proper direction of your will, which otherwise can be a most powerful enemy, as it so often is with princes who cannot be prevailed upon to do not only what is useful but

what is even absolutely necessary. Your Majesty's mind so completely dominates your body that the slightest emotional upset affects your whole being. Many occurrences of this have made me so certain of the truth of my diagnosis that I am convinced I have never seen you ill in any other way.

God has seen fit to give Your Majesty the force of character necessary to act with firmness when confronted with business of the greatest importance. But as a balance to this noble quality He has often allowed you to be sensitive to matters so small that no one in advance would suspect they might trouble you and thus try to protect you from their bothersome quality. So far, time alone has provided the only remedy for these overwhelming experiences of which the inward consequence has always been a bodily indisposition. You are, in this regard, much like those whose great courage makes them disdain the blows of a sword but who cannot, because of a certain natural antipathy, stand the puncture of the scalpel. It is impossible for many men to anticipate the surprises which will come from their emotions. I do not think, however, that such is the case with Your Majesty, who has many excellent qualities most people do not have. I believe that, in all likelihood, the first ebullience of your ardent youth having passed, the stability of a greater maturity will help you protect yourself by forethought in the future from an enemy which is all the more dangerous because it is internal and domestic, and which has already caused you misfortune serious enough on two or three occasions to have brought your life in jeopardy.

Just as this is a matter of great importance for your health, so is it also for your reputation and glory, for which it should always appear that reason prevailed over your emotions. I cannot help repeating again a plea that I have made many times before to Your Majesty, begging you to apply yourself to the matters of greatest importance to your country, disdaining the little ones as beneath your thought and interest. It would be useful and inspiring for you to dwell often upon the vast prospects of the trend of events. If you preoccupy yourself with the small matters, you will not only fail to gain benefit therefrom, you will even bring misfortune upon yourself. Not only does such a preoccupation divert you from a better one.

Just as little thorns are more capable of pricking than larger ones, which are more easily seen, so it would be impossible for you to protect yourself from many unpleasant happenings inconsequential for public business and bad for your own health.

The great emotional outbursts to which you have been subject on several occasions urge me to tell you here, as I have earlier done more than once, that while there are certain public charges necessary to the furtherance of state affairs which you must perform, there are others the performance of which can do no less than destroy the good disposition of whoever plunges into them. This in turn so adversely affects those charged with carrying out decisions that they too are less able to do what is expected of them. The experience of governing that Your Majesty has acquired from a reign which thus far has lasted twenty-five years makes you well aware of the fact that the outcome of large undertakings rarely confirms directly with the orders initially given. It also teaches you that you might better have compassion for those charged with the execution of your commands when their efforts do not succeed, rather than to blame them for the poor results for which they may not be responsible. It is only God whose acts are infallible, and yet His goodness is such that, letting men act as their weakness directs, He even so overlooks the gulf between their deeds and His standards. This should teach kings to tolerate with patient reasonableness what the Creator endured assuredly because of His benevolence.

Your Majesty being by nature delicate, with a weak constitution, and a restless, impatient disposition, particularly when you are with the army where you always insist on taking the command, I believe it would be committing a crime if I did not beseech you to avoid war in the future in as far as it is possible. This plea I base upon the fact that the frivolousness and unreliability of the French can generally be overcome only by their master's presence and that Your Majesty cannot, without endangering your health, commit yourself to a program of long duration with the hope of success. You have made the valor and strength of your arms well enough known to entitle you in the future to think only of how to enjoy the peace your efforts have brought to the realm, while ever being on the alert to defend it against all those who might break their pledge and attack it again.

Although it is common enough with many men to act only when driven by some emotion, so that one may conceive of them as being like incense which smells sweet only when it is being burned, I cannot help reminding Your Majesty that such a character trait is dangerous in any kind of person, and it is particularly so in kings, who more than all others should be motivated by reason. If emotion once in a while does in fact bring good results, it is only a matter of luck, since by its very nature it misleads men so much that it blinds those who are possessed by it. If a man so deprived of sight occasionally does find the proper course, it is a marvel if he does not stray and get lost completely. And if he does not fall down he will certainly need the best of good fortune not to falter many times. Often indeed have evils befallen princes and their countries when they have been more inclined to follow their emotions than their minds, especially when guided by their whims rather than by considerations of the public interest. Because of this is it impossible for me not to beg Your Majesty to reflect frequently on this matter in order to confirm more and more in yourself your natural tendency to do the right thing.

I also plead with you to think often of how I have reminded you many times that there is no prince in a worse position than he who, not always able to do those things by himself which it is nevertheless his duty to perform, finds it even harder to let others do them for him. The capability of allowing himself to be served is not one of the least qualities a great king should have. Without this quality, opportunities are often quickly and senselessly lost when favorable action could be taken in settling matters for the advancement of the state.

The late king, your father, being in dire extremity, paid with kind words those who served him, accomplishing with caresses what his lack of funds would not permit him to encourage by other means. Your Majesty is unable to follow the late king in this practice, not being of the same make-up, having instead a natural dryness which you inherited from your mother the Queen, who herself has told you this in my presence several times. I cannot help reminding you that the public interest requires that you treat with consideration those who serve you, and at the least it is wise for you to be particularly careful not to say anything that would offend them.

Since I am going to deal later with the subject of the liberality princes should exercise I will say no more about it here, but I will dwell a bit on the bad effects which result from the remarks of those who speak too loosely about their subjects. The blows from a sword are easily healed. But it is not the same with blows of the tongue, especially if they be from the tongue of a king, whose authority renders the pain almost without remedy unless it be provided by the king himself. The higher a stone is thrown, the greater its striking force when it returns. There are many who would give no thought to being cut to pieces by the enemies of their master but who cannot suffer the slightest scratch from his hand. Just as flies do not constitute the diet of the eagle, so the lion is contemptuous of all animals with less than his strength. Likewise, a man who attacked a child would be blamed by everyone. In similar fashion, I make bold to say, a great king should never insult his subordinates since they too are relatively weak. History is full of the unfortunate episodes which have resulted from the excessively free rein great men have given to their tongues, causing the unhappiness of those they considered beneath them.

God has seen fit to so endow Your Majesty as to make it natural for you not to do evil, and such being the case, it is only reasonable that you should carefully guard what you say, so that even your words will give no offense. I am sure, in this matter, that you will not by intent speak offensively, but it is difficult for you not to act impulsively, and sudden waves of emotion occasionally overtake you when you least expect them. I would not be your loyal servant if I did not warn you that both your reputation and your interests require that you have a particular care with regard to them, because such looseness of the tongue, while it may not disturb your conscience, can do much harm to your affairs. Just as to speak well of your enemies is an heroic virtue, so also a prince cannot speak offensively about those who would lay

down their lives a thousand times for him and his interests without committing a great fault against the laws of Christianity, to say nothing of those of political wisdom.

A king who has clean hands, a pure heart, and a gentle tongue is not of little virtue, and he who has the first two qualities so eminently as Your Majesty, can with great facility acquire the third. As it is part of the grandeur of kings to be so reserved in their speech that nothing comes out of their mouths which could give offense to their subordinates, so too it is prudent to say nothing derogatory about the principal governmental agencies. Indeed, they should be so spoken of as to give occasion for the belief they are held in high regard. The most important undertakings of state so frequently require that they be thwarted, that prudence itself indicates they should be pampered in lesser matters.

It is not enough for great princes to resolve never to speak evil of anyone. Good sense requires that they also close their ears to slander and false information, pursuing and even banishing authors as most dangerous plagues, often capable of poisoning the hearts of princes, as well as the minds of all those who approach them. All those who have free access to the ears of kings, without meriting it, are dangerous, and those who possess their hearts out of pure favoritism are even more so, for in order to preserve such a great treasure it is necessary to have recourse to artifice and malice, in default of the true virtues which invariably are lacking in such people.

I am compelled to say further in this matter that I have always been more apprehensive about the power of such influences over Your Majesty than of the world's greatest kings, and you have more need to guard yourself from the artifice of a valet who wants to take you by surprise than of all the factions the high nobles might form within your realm, even if they should have a common goal. When I first entered your service, I learned that those who previously had the honor of serving you were absolutely convinced you were easily persuaded to suspect them, and having such a conviction their principal care was ever to keep their agents close to you to counteract the suspected evil. The fact of the firmness of Your Majesty in supporting me obliges me to recognize either that this judgment was without foundation or else that mature reflection has erased your youthful weakness. Even so, I cannot help beseeching you to strengthen this trait in your character so that the attitude you have been pleased to take toward me will be the one naturally expected by anyone who may succeed me. In addition, I must also say to you that just as the ears of princes ought to be closed to calumny, so also should they be open to all truths useful to the state, and in like manner just as their tongues should never give utterance to words prejudicial to the reputation of others, so they should be able to speak freely and boldly when questions of public interest are at stake.

STUDY QUESTIONS

1. How does the cardinal mix flattery with sound advice?
2. Did Richelieu have an interest in warning the king against listening to gossip about his subordinates?

15.4 JEAN DOMAT, *THE CIVIL LAW AND ITS NATURAL ORDER*, 1689

Jean Domat (1625–1696) was a lawyer and legal scholar who served as royal prosecutor in the city of Clermont from 1655 to 1683, after which he retired to his study and dedicated himself to compiling his massive legal code. Apart from reordering the bulk of the Roman law tradition, Domat's work is significant for its concern to emphasize natural law as the basis for civil law—that is, the idea that law arises from, and represents, the innate moral values of a society. Although he accepted the then-popular idea of the divine right of kings to rule, Domat presents law as an organic system over which the king presides but which does not emanate from him.

I t is well-known that human society forms a kind of organic body, of which each person forms a part—and this truth, as the Bible has shown and the light of reason makes clear, is the foundation upon which all the duties and obligations that govern all men's actions toward one another individually and toward the body as a whole is based. These duties, moreover, are nothing less than the prescribed functions expected of each person, whatever his position in society. In this principle we find the origin of those laws that determine the duties of those who govern and of those who are governed. . . . As the Lord commands everyone to faithfully obey the precepts of His law that pertain to everyone, so does He command every person to faithfully obey the precepts that pertain to whatever specific condition or status

Jean Domat, "Le droit public, suite des lois civiles dans leur ordre naturel." In *Oeuvres completes, nouvelle edition revue corrigée*, vol. 3, edited by Joseph Remy. Paris: Firmin-Didot, 1829, pp. 1–2, 15–21, 26–7, 35, 39, 40, 44–5. Translation by Clifford Backman.

he holds in the body politic. . . . But since, in their fundamental nature, all men are equal simply by virtue of being human, nature does not decree that any one person is subject to another. . . . Within this state of natural equality, however, individuals are differentiated by various qualities that result in their being of unequal status, and thus people must develop relationships and dependencies that determine their duties toward each other. Thus, government is made necessary.

And since government, as established by God, is necessary for the good of society, it is therefore also incumbent upon all who are subject to it to submit to it and obey it—for if not, they would be resisting God Himself, and government (which ought to be the guarantor of peace and unity and the mainstay of the public good) would become the cause of division and conflict, and thus bring about its own downfall. . . .

To obey a government entails accepting its laws as laws, not attempting any action that runs counter to them, performing whatever action they require, avoiding all that they forbid, shouldering the public responsibilities they assign—whether in terms of serving in office or in payment of taxes—and in general to accept the obligation not to disturb public order but to endorse and assist it as one's circumstances allow.

Such obedience being necessary to maintain the harmonious order that should unite the head and other members that make up the state, it remains an essential duty for all subjects to obey without question the ruler's commands, without presuming to judge which orders they will or will not obey. For if everyone had the right to determine what is or is not justice, then every person would in effect be his own master—and sedition would arise. . . .

Among the rights given to the sovereign by the law is the right to possess and display whatever accoutrements of grandeur and majesty he needs to make known the tremendous authority and dignity of the all-encompassing power he possesses, in order to impress upon the minds of his subjects a proper attitude of veneration. . . . For it is by God's grace that He invests His power in sovereigns, and He permits rulers to adorn the authority He gives them with whatever seems to them to be appropriate, as a means of assuring the people's respect. This can be best achieved by having an aura of splendor radiate from their magnificent palaces, amid other visible signs of that splendor. . . .

The primary and most absolute of all the duties owed by those to whom God has entrusted the power of government is this: to acknowledge that they hold all of their power from God Himself, that it is His place they are taking, that it is through Him that they govern, and that it is God to Whom they should turn for guidance and wisdom in the matter of governing. May these truths form the foundation of all their conduct, and guide all of their actions in the performance of their duties. . . . [duties which include]: maintaining public order throughout the state, the peaceful lives of his subjects and the peace of mind of their families, care for every matter that pertains to the common good, the selection of capable ministers who love justice and truth, the appointment of worthy men to all public offices. . . . the discreet application of either severity or mercy in cases where the strong hand of justice may perhaps be restrained. . . . the good administration of public finances, prudence in relations with foreign states—in all, everything that can make government a blessing to good people, a terror to the wicked, and a worthy exemplar to Heaven's mandate to govern.

STUDY QUESTIONS

1. What metaphor does Domat use to present natural law?
2. How would Louis XIV—who ruled France when Domat composed *Civil Laws According to the Natural Order*—have responded to Domat's view of law as an organic system over which the king presides but which does not emanate from him?

15.5 FRANÇOIS FÉNELON, *THE ADVENTURES OF TELEMACHUS*, 1699

A Catholic priest and writer, François Fénelon (1651–1715) was enlisted by the church to preach to French Protestants (Huguenots) to bring them back to orthodox belief. His bestseller work, *The Adventures of Telemachus*, adds to the story of the *Odyssey* (see Document 3.2) by describing the travels of Odysseus's son, Telemachus. Guiding Telemachus is his tutor, simply called Mentor (but later revealed as Diana, goddess of wisdom), who explains the tenets of a truly good society—one that abolished government, upheld the brotherhood of citizens, and looked back to ancient Greece as a model. Thus, Telemachus served as a fierce criticism of the rule of the Sun King, Louis XIV of France (1638–1715).

The bark now touched the dominions of Pluto, and the shades ran down in crowds to the shore, gazing, with the utmost curiosity and wonder, at the living mortal who stood distinguished among the dead in the boat; but, the moment Telemachus set his foot on the shore, they vanished like the darkness of night before the first beams of morning. Then Charon, turning towards him, with a brow less contracted into frowns than usual, said to him: "O favored of heaven, since thou art permitted to enter the realms of darkness, which to all the living, besides thyself, are interdicted, make haste to go whithersoever the Fates have called thee; proceed by this gloomy path to the palace of Pluto, whom thou wilt find sitting upon his throne, who will permit thee to enter those recesses of his dominion, the secrets of which I am not permitted to reveal."

Telemachus, immediately pressing forward with a hasty step, discovered the shades gliding about on every side, more numerous than the sands on a seashore; and he was struck with a religious dread to perceive that, in the midst of the tumult and hurry of this incredible multitude, all was silent as the grave. He sees, at length, the gloomy residence of unrelenting Pluto: his hair stands erect, his legs tremble,

and his voice fails him. "Tremendous power!" said he, with faltering and interrupted speech, "the son of unhappy Ulysses now stands before thee. I come to inquire whether my father is descended into your dominions, or whether he is still a wanderer upon the earth?"

Pluto was seated upon a throne of ebony: his countenance was pale and severe, his eyes hollow and ardent, and his brow contracted and menacing. The sight of a mortal still breathing the breath of life was hateful to his eyes, as the day is hateful to those animals that leave their recesses only by night. At his side sat Proserpine, who was the only object of his attention, and seemed to soften him into some degree of complacency. She enjoyed a beauty that was perpetually renewed but there was mingled with her immortal charms something of her lord's inflexible severity.

At the foot of the throne sat the pale father of destruction, Death, incessantly whetting a scythe which he held in his hand. Around this horrid spectre hovered repining Cares and injurious Suspicions; Vengeance, distained with blood and covered with wounds; causeless Hatred; Avarice, gnawing her own flesh; Despair, the victim of her own rage; Ambition,

From François Fénelon, *The Adventures of Telemachus*. Translated by Dr. Hawkesworth. New York: Hurd and Houghton, 1872, pp. 450–8.

whose fury overturns all things like a whirlwind; Treason, thirsting for blood, and not able to enjoy the mischief she produces; Envy, shedding round her the venom that corrodes her heart, and sickening with rage at the impotence of her malice; Impiety, that opens for herself a gulf without bottom, in which she shall plunge at last without hope; Spectres, all hideous to behold; Phantoms, that represent the dead to terrify the living; frightful Dreams; and the horrid Vigils of disease and pain. By these images of woe was Pluto surrounded: such were the attendants that filled his palace. He replied to the son of Ulysses in a hollow tone, and the depths of Erebus remurmured to the sound: "If it is by fate, young mortal, that thou hast violated this sacred asylum of the dead, that fate, which has thus distinguished thee, fulfill. Of thy father I will tell thee nothing; it is enough that here thou art permitted to seek him. As upon the earth he was a king, thy search may be confined, on one side, to that part of Tartarus where wicked kings are consigned to punishment, and, on the other, to that part of Elysium, where the good receive their reward. But, from hence thou canst not enter the fields of Elysium till thou hast passed through Tartarus. Make haste thither, and linger not in my dominions."

Telemachus instantly obeyed, and passed through the dreary vacuity that surrounded him with such speed that he seemed almost to fly; such was his impatience to behold his father and to quit the presence of a tyrant equally the terror of the living and the dead. He soon perceived the gloomy tract of Tartarus at a small distance before him: from this place ascended a black cloud of pestilential smoke, which would have been fatal in the realms of life. This smoke hovered over a river of fire, the flames of which, returning upon themselves, roared in a burning vortex with a noise like that of an impetuous torrent precipitated from the highest rock, so that in this region of woe no other sound could be distinctly heard.

Telemachus, secretly animated by Minerva, entered the gulf without fear. He first saw a great number of men, who, born in a mean condition, were now punished for having sought to acquire riches by fraud, treachery, and violence. Among them he remarked many of the impious hypocrites, who,

affecting a zeal for religion, played upon the credulity of others and gratified their own ambition. These wretches, who had abused virtue itself, the best gift of heaven, to dishonest purposes, were punished as the most criminal of men. Children who had murdered their parents, wives who had sold their country in violation of every tie, were punished with less severity than these. Such was the decree pronounced by the judges of the dead, because hypocrites are not content to be wicked upon the common terms; they would be vicious, with the reputation of virtue; and by an appearance of virtue, which at length is found to be false, they prevent mankind from putting confidence in the true. The gods, whose omniscience they mock and whose honor they degrade, take pleasure in the exertion of all their power to avenge the insult.

After these appeared others, to whom the world scarcely imputes guilt, but whom the divine vengeance pursues without pity—the liar, the ingrate, the parasite who lavishes adulation upon vice, and the slanderer who falsely detracts from virtue—all those who judge rashly of what they know but in part, and thus injure the reputation of the innocent.

But, among all who suffered for ingratitude, those were punished with most severity who had been ungrateful to the gods. "What!" said Minos, "is he considered as a monster who is guilty of ingratitude to his father or his friend, from whom he has received some such benefits as mortals can bestow, and shall the wretch glory in his crime who is ungrateful to the gods, the givers of life and of every blessing it includes? Does he not owe his existence rather to the authors of nature than to the parents through whom his existence was derived? The less these crimes are censured and punished upon earth, the more are they obnoxious in hell to implacable vengeance, which no force can resist and no subtlety elude."

Telemachus, seeing a man condemned by the judges, whom he found sitting, ventured to ask them what was his crime. He was immediately answered by the offender himself. "I have done," said he, "no evil; my pleasure consisted wholly in doing good. I have been just, munificent, liberal, and compassionate; of what crime, then, can I be accused?" "With respect to man," replied Minos, "thou art accused of none; but didst thou not owe less to man than to the gods? If so, what are thy pretensions to justice? Thou hast punctually fulfilled thy duty to men, who are but dust; thou hast been virtuous, but thy virtue terminated wholly in thyself, without reference to the gods who gave it: thy virtue was to be thy own felicity, and to thyself thou wast all in all. Thou hast, indeed, been thy own deity. But the gods, by whom all things have been created, and who have created all things for themselves, cannot give up their rights: thou hast forgotten them, and they will forget thee. Since thou hast desired to exist for thyself, and not for them, to thyself they will deliver thee up. Seek, then, thy consolation in thine own heart. Thou art separated forever from man, whom, for thy own sake, thou hast desired to please, and art left to thyself alone, that idol of thy heart. Learn now, at least, that piety is that virtue of which the gods are the object, and that without this no virtue can deserve the name. The false lustre of that which thou hast long dazzled the eyes of men, who are easily deceived, will deceive no more. Men distinguish that only from which they derive pain or pleasure, into virtue and vice, and are, therefore, alike ignorant both of good and evil: but here the perspicacity of divine wisdom discerns all things as they are; the judgment of men, from external appearance, is reversed; what they have admired is frequently condemned, and what they have condemned, approved."

These words, to the boaster of philosophic virtue, were like a stroke of thunder, and he was unable to sustain the shock. The self-complaisance with which he had been used to contemplate his moderation, his fortitude, his generosity, was now changed to despair. The view of his own heart, at enmity with the gods, became his punishment. He now saw, and was doomed forever to see, himself by the light of truth. He perceived that the approbation of men, which all his actions had been directed to acquire, was erroneous and vain. When he looked inward, he found every thing totally changed; he was no longer the same being, and all comfort was eradicated from his heart. His conscience, which had hitherto witnessed in his favor, now rose up against him, and reproached him even with his virtues, which, not having deity for their principle and end, were erroneous and illusive. He was overwhelmed with consternation and trouble, with shame, remorse, and despair.

The Furies, indeed, forbore to torment him; he was delivered over to himself, and they were satisfied; his own heart was the avenger of the gods, whom he had despised. As he could not escape from himself, he retired to the most gloomy recesses, that he might be concealed from others: he sought for darkness, but he found it not; light still persecuted and pursued him: the light of truth, which he had not followed, now punished him for neglect. All that he had beheld with pleasure became odious in his eyes, as the source of misery that could never end. "O fool!" said he, "I have known neither the gods, men, nor myself; I have, indeed, known nothing, since I have not known the only and true good. All my steps have deviated from the path I should have trodden; all my wisdom was folly and all my virtue was pride, which sacrificed, with a blind impiety, only to that vile idol, myself!"

The next objects that Telemachus perceived, as he went on, were the kings that had abused their power. An avenging Fury held up before them a mirror which reflected their vices in all their deformity. In this they beheld their undistinguishing vanity, that was gratified by the grossest adulation; their want of feeling for mankind, whose happiness should have been the first object of their attention; their insensibility to virtue, their dread of truth, their partiality to flatterers, their dissipation, effeminacy, and indolence; their causeless suspicions; their vain parade and ostentatious splendor, an idle blaze, in which the public welfare is consumed; their ambition of false honor, procured at the expense of blood; and their inhuman luxury, which extorted a perpetual supply of superfluous delicacies from the wretched victims of grief and anguish. When they looked into this mirror, they saw themselves faithfully represented; and they found the picture more monstrous and horrid than the Chimera vanquished by Bellerophon, the Lernaean hydra slain by Hercules, and even Cerebus [Cerberus] himself, though from his three howling mouths he disgorges a stream of black venomous blood, that is sufficient to infect the whole race of mortals that breathe upon the earth.

At the same time another Fury tauntingly repeated all the praises which sycophants had lavished upon them in their lives, and held up another mirror, in which they appeared as flattery had represented them.

The contrast of these pictures, widely different, was the punishment of their vanity. It was remarkable that the most wicked were the objects of the most extravagant praise; because the most wicked are most to be feared, and because they exact, with less shame, the servile adulation of the poets and orators of their time.

Their groans perpetually ascended from this dreadful abyss, where they saw nothing but the derision and insult of which they were themselves the objects—where every thing repulsed, opposed, and confounded them. As they sported with the lives of mankind upon the earth, and pretended that the whole species were created for their use, they were, in Tartarus, delivered over to the capricious tyranny of slaves, who made them taste all the bitterness of servitude in their turn. They obeyed with unutterable anguish, and without hope that the iron hand of oppression would lie lighter upon them. Under the strokes of these slaves, now their merciless tyrants, they lay passive and impotent, like an anvil under the hammers of the Cyclops, when Vulcan urges their labor at the flaming furnaces of Mount Aetna.

Telemachus observed the countenance of these criminals to be pale and ghastly, strongly expressive of the torment they suffered at the heart. They looked inward with a self-abhorrence, now inseparable from their existence. Their crimes themselves had become their punishment, and it was not necessary that greater should be inflicted. They haunted them like hideous spectres, and continually started up before them in all their enormity. They wished for a second death, that might separate them from these ministers of vengeance, as the first had separated their spirits from the body—a death that might at once extinguish all consciousness and sensibility. They called upon the depths of hell to hide them from the persecuting beams of truth, in impenetrable darkness; but they are reserved for the cup of vengeance, which, though they drink it forever, shall be ever full. The truth, from which they fled, has overtaken them, an invincible and unrelenting enemy. The ray which once might have illuminated them, like the mild radiance of the day, now pierces them like lightning—a fierce and fatal fire, that, without injury to the external parts, infixes a burning torment at the heart. By truth, now, an avenging flame, the very soul is

melted, like metal in a furnace; it dissolves all, but destroys nothing; it disunites the first elements of life, yet the sufferer can never die. He is, as it were, divided against himself, without rest and without comfort; animated by no vital principle, but the rage that kindles at his own misconduct, and the dreadful madness that results from despair.

Among these objects, at the sight of which the hair of Telemachus stood erect, he beheld many of the ancient kings of Lydia who were punished for having preferred the selfish gratification of others, which, to royalty, is a duty of indispensable obligation.

These kings mutually reproached each other with their folly. "Did I not often recommend to you," said one of them to his son, "during the last years of my life, when old age had given weight to my counsel, the reparation of the mischiefs that my negligence had produced?" "Unhappy father!" replied the son, "thou art the cause of my perdition; it was thy example that made me vain-glorious, proud, voluptuous, and cruel. While I saw thee surrounded with flattery, and relaxed into luxury and sloth, I also insensibly acquired the love of pleasure and adulation. I thought the rest of men were to kings what horses and other beasts of burden are to men—animals wholly unworthy of regard, except for the drudgery they perform and the conveniences they procure. This was my opinion, and I learnt it of thee. I followed thy example, and share thy misery." These reproaches were mingled with the most horrid execrations: mutual rage and indignation aggravated the torments of hell.

Around these wretched princes there still hovered, like owls in the twilight, causeless Jealousies and vain Alarms, Mistrust and Dread, which revenge upon kings their disregard of mankind; Avarice, insatiable of wealth; False-Honor, ever tyrannical and oppressive; and effeminate Luxury, a deceitful demon that aggravated every evil, and bestows only imaginary good.

Many kings were also severely punished, not for the mischief they had done, but for the good they had neglected to do. Every crime that is committed by the subject in consequence of laws not enforced, is the crime of the kings, for kings reign only as ministers of the law. To kings also are imputed all the disorders that arise from pomp, luxury, and every other excess which excites irregular and impetuous passions that cannot be gratified but by the violation of the common rights of mankind. But the princes who, instead of watching over their people as a shepherd watches over his flock, worried and devoured them like the wolf were punished with the most exemplary severity.

In this abyss of darkness and misery, Telemachus beheld, with yet greater astonishment, many kings who had been honored for their personal virtues upon earth, but were, notwithstanding, condemned to the pains of Tartarus for having left the administration of government to wicked and crafty men. They were punished for mischiefs which they had suffered to be perpetrated under the sanction of their authority. The greater part of them, indeed, had been by principle neither virtuous nor vicious; supinely taking the color impressed upon them from without, they did not shun the truth when it presented itself, but they had no relish for virtue, no delight in doing good.

When Telemachus left Tartarus, he felt himself relieved, as if a mountain had been removed from his breast. This relief, so sudden and so great, impressed him with a strong sense of the misery of those who are confined there without hope of deliverance. He was terrified at having seen so many kings punished with much greater severity than any other offenders. "Have kings, then," said he, "so many duties to fulfill, so many difficulties to surmount, and so many dangers to avoid? Is the knowledge that is necessary to put them upon their guard, as well against themselves as others, so difficult to be acquired? and, after all the envy, tumult, and opposition of a transitory life, are they consigned to the intolerable and eternal pains of hell? What folly, then, to wish for royalty! How happy the peaceful private station, in which the practice of virtue is comparatively easy!"

STUDY QUESTIONS

1. How are the tribunals and monarchs of Hades modeled on those of Louis XIV's France?
2. Does the document serve as a warning to kings against the powers of sycophants and the long-term consequences of poor decisions?

15.6 DANIEL DEFOE/CAPTAIN CHARLES JOHNSON, "THE LIFE OF ANNE BONNY," 1724

The popular *General History of the Pyrates,* credited in its title page to Captain Charles Johnson, has long been thought to be the pseudonymous work of the English novelist Daniel Defoe (1667–1731), the author of *Robinson Crusoe* (1719) and *Moll Flanders* (1722). Defoe, who was frequently in legal trouble for his political stances and many debts, is known to have used nearly two hundred pseudonyms in his lifetime. The question of the book's authorship continues to be debated. The *General History* consists of thirty-nine short biographies of the most notorious pirates who sailed in the Caribbean during the so-called "Golden Age" of piracy. Some of the pirates, including the one treated below, may have been wholly fictional. The text is complete.

As we have been more particular in the Lives of these two Women, than those of other Pyrates, it is incumbent on us, as a faithful Historian, to begin with their Birth. Anne Bonny was born at a Town near Cork, in the Kingdom of Ireland, her Father an Attorney at Law, but Anne was not one of his legitimate Issue, which seems to cross an old Proverb, which says, that Bastards have the best Luck. Her Father was a married Man, and his Wife having been brought to Bed, contracted an Illness in her lying in, and in order to recover her Health, she was advised to remove for Change of Air; the Place she chose, was a few Miles distance from her Dwelling, where her Husband's Mother liv'd. Here she sojourn'd some Time, her Husband staying at Home, to follow his Affairs. The Servant-Maid, whom she left to look after the House, and attend the Family, being a handsome young Woman, was courted by a young Man of the same Town, who was a Tanner; this Tanner used to take his Opportunities, when the Family was out of the Way, of coming to pursue his Courtship; and being with the Maid one Day as she was employed in the Household Business, not having the Fear of God before his Eyes, he takes his Opportunity, when her Back was turned, of whipping three Silver Spoons into his Pocket. The Maid soon miss'd the Spoons, and knowing that no Body had been in the Room, but herself and the young Man, since she saw them last, she charged him with taking them; he very stifly denied it, upon which she grew outragious, and threatned to go to a Constable, in order to carry him before a Justice of Peace. These Menaces frighten'd him out of his Wits, well knowing he could not stand Search; wherefore he endeavoured to pacify her, by desiring her to examine the Drawers and other Places, and perhaps she might find them; in this Time he slips into another Room, where the Maid usually lay, and puts the Spoons betwixt the Sheets, and then makes his Escape by a back Door, concluding she must find them, when she went to Bed, and so next Day he might pretend he did it only to frighten her, and the Thing might be laugh'd off for a Jest.

As soon as she miss'd him, she gave over her Search, concluding he had carry'd them off, and went directly to the Constable, in order to have him apprehended. The young Man was informed, that a Constable had been in Search of him, but he

regarded it but little, not doubting but all would be well next Day. Three or four Days passed, and still he was told, the Constable was upon the Hunt for him, this made him lye concealed; he could not comprehend the Meaning of it, he imagined no less, than that the Maid had a Mind to convert the Spoons to her own Use, and put the Robbery upon him.

It happen'd, at this Time, that the Mistress being perfectly recovered of her late Indisposition, was returned Home, in Company with her Mother-in-Law; the first News she heard, was of the Loss of the Spoons, with the Manner how; the Maid telling her, at the same Time, that the young Man was run away. The young Fellow had Intelligence of the Mistress's Arrival, and considering with himself, that he could never appear again in his Business, unless this Matter was got over, and she being a good-natured Woman, he took a Resolution of going directly to her, and of telling her the whole Story, only with this Difference, that he did it for a Jest.

The Mistress could scarce believe it, however, she went directly to the Maid's Room, and turning down the Bed Cloaths, there, to her great Surprize, found the three Spoons; upon this she desired the young Man to go Home and mind his Business, for he should have no Trouble about it.

The Mistress could not imagine the Meaning of this, she never had found the Maid guilty of any pilfering, and therefore it could not enter her Head, that she designed to steal the Spoons her self; upon the whole, she concluded the Maid had not been in her Bed, from the Time the Spoons were miss'd, she grew immediately jealous upon it, and suspected, that the Maid supply'd her Place with her Husband, during her Absence, and this was the Reason why the Spoons were no sooner found.

She call'd to Mind several Actions of Kindness, her Husband had shewed the Maid, Things that pass'd unheeded by, when they happen'd, but now she had got the Tormentor, Jealousy, in her Head, amounted to Proofs of their Intimacy; another Circumstance which strengthen'd the whole, was, that tho' her Husband knew she was to come Home that Day, and had had no Communication with her in four Months, which was before her last lying in, yet he took an Opportunity of going out of Town that

Morning, upon some slight Pretence. All these Things put together, confirm'd her in her Jealousy.

As Women seldom forgive Injuries of this Kind, she thought of discharging her Revenge upon the Maid. In order to this, she leaves the Spoons where she found them, and orders the Maid to put clean Sheets upon the Bed, telling her, she intended to lye there herself that Night, because her Mother-in-Law was to lye in her Bed, and that she (the Maid) must lye in another Part of the House; the Maid in making the Bed, was surprized with the Sight of the Spoons, but there were very good Reasons, why it was not proper for her to tell where she found them, therefore she takes them up, puts them in her Trunk, intending to leave them in some Place, where they might be found by Chance.

The Mistress, that every Thing might look to be done without Design, lyes that Night in the Maid's Bed, little dreaming of what an Adventure it would produce. After she had been a Bed some Time, thinking on what had pass'd, for Jealousy kept her awake, she heard some Body enter the Room; at first she apprehended it to be Thieves, and was so fright'ned, she had not Courage enough to call out; but when she heard these Words, Mary, are you awake? She knew it to be her Husband's Voice; then her Fright was over, yet she made no Answer, least he should find her out, if she spoke, therefore she resolved to counterfeit Sleep, and take what followed.

The Husband came to Bed, and that Night play'd the vigorous Lover; but one Thing spoiled the Diversion on the Wife's Side, which was, the Reflection that it was not design'd for her; however, she was very passive, and bore it like a Christian. Early before Day, she stole out of Bed, leaving him asleep, and went to her Mother-in-Law, telling her what had passed, not forgetting how he had used her, as taking her for the Maid; the Husband also stole out, not thinking it convenient to be catched in that Room; in the mean Time, the Revenge of the Mistress was strongly against the Maid, and without considering that to her she owed the Diversion of the Night before, and that one good turn should deserve another; she sent for a Constable, and charged her with stealing the Spoons. The Maid's Trunk was broke open, and the Spoons found, upon which she was carry'd before a Justice of Peace, and by him committed to Gaol.

The Husband loiter'd about till twelve a-Clock at Noon, then comes Home, pretending he was just come to Town; as soon as he heard what had pass'd, in Relation to the Maid, he fell into a great Passion with his Wife; this set the Thing into a greater Flame, the Mother takes the Wife's Part against her own Son, insomuch that the Quarrel encreasing, the Mother and Wife took Horse immediately, and went back to the Mother's House, and the Husband and Wife never bedded together after.

The Maid lay a long Time in the Prison, it being near half a Year to the Assizes; but before it happened, it was discovered she was with Child; when she was arraign'd at the Bar, she was discharged for want of Evidence; the Wife's Conscience touch'd her, and as she did not believe the Maid Guilty of any Theft, except that of Love, she did not appear against her; soon after her Acquittal, she was delivered of a Girl.

But what alarm'd the Husband most, was, that it was discovered the Wife was with Child also, he taking it for granted, he had had no Intimacy with her, since her last lying in, grew jealous of her, in his Turn, and made this a Handle to justify himself, for his Usage of her, pretending now he had suspected her long, but that here was Proof; she was delivered of Twins, a Boy and a Girl.

The Mother falling ill, sent to her Son to reconcile him to his Wife, but he would not hearken to it; therefore she made a Will, leaving all she had in the Hands of certain Trustees, for the Use of the Wife and two Children lately born, and died a few Days after.

This was an ugly Turn upon him, his greatest Dependance being upon his Mother; however, his Wife was kinder to him than he deserved, for she made him a yearly Allowance out of what was left, tho' they continued to live separate. It lasted near five Years; at this Time having a great Affection for the Girl he had by his Maid, he had a Mind to take it Home, to live with him; but as all the Town knew it to be a Girl, the better to disguise the Matter from them, as well as from his Wife, he had it put into Brecches, as a Boy, pretending it was a Relation's Child he was to breed up to be his Clerk.

The Wife heard he had a little Boy at Home he was very fond of, but as she did not know any Relation of his that had such a Child, she employ'd a Friend to enquire further into it; this Person by talking with the Child, found it to be a Girl, discovered that the Servant-Maid was its Mother, and that the Husband still kept up his Correspondence with her.

Upon this Intelligence, the Wife being unwilling that her Children's Money should go towards the Maintainance of Bastards, stopped the Allowance. The Husband enraged, in a kind of Revenge, takes the Maid home, and lives with her publickly, to the great Scandal of his Neighbours; but he soon found the bad Effect of it, for by Degrees he lost his Practice, so that he saw plainly he could not live there, therefore he thought of removing, and turning what Effects he had into ready Money; he goes to Cork, and there with his Maid and Daughter embarques for Carolina.

At first he followed the Practice of the Law in that Province, but afterwards fell into Merchandize, which proved more successful to him, for he gained by it sufficient to purchase a considerable Plantation: His Maid, who passed for his Wife, happened to die, after which his Daughter, our Anne Bonny, now grown up, kept his House.

She was of a fierce and couragious Temper, wherefore, when she lay under Condemnation, several Stories were reported of her, much to her Disadvantage, as that she had kill'd an English Servant-Maid once in her Passion with a Case-Knife, while she look'd after her Father's House; but upon further Enquiry, I found this Story to be groundless. It was certain she was so robust, that once, when a young Fellow would have lain with her, against her Will, she beat him so, that he lay ill of it a considerable Time.

While she lived with her Father, she was look'd upon as one that would be a good Fortune, wherefore it was thought her Father expected a good Match for her; but she spoil'd all, for without his Consent, she marries a young Fellow, who belong'd to the Sea, and was not worth a Groat; which provoked her Father to such a Degree, that he turn'd her out of Doors, upon which the young Fellow, who married her, finding himself disappointed in his Expectation, shipped himself and Wife, for the Island of Providence, expecting Employment there.

Here she became acquainted with Rackam the Pyrate, who making Courtship to her, soon found Means of withdrawing her Affections from her Husband, so that she consented to elope from him, and go to Sea with Rackam in Men's Cloaths. She was as good as her Word, and after she had been at Sea some Time, she proved with Child, and beginning to grow big, Rackam landed her on the Island of Cuba; and recommending her there to some Friends of his, they took Care of her, till she was brought to Bed. When she was up and well again, he sent for her to bear him Company.

The King's Proclamation being out, for pardoning of Pyrates, he took the Benefit of it, and surrender'd; afterwards being sent upon the privateering Account, he return'd to his old Trade, as has been already hinted in the Story of Mary Read. In all these Expeditions, Anne Bonny bore him Company, and when any Business was to be done in their Way, no Body was more forward or couragious than she, and particularly when they were taken; she and Mary Read, with one more, were all the Persons that durst keep the Deck, as has been before hinted.

Her Father was known to a great many Gentlemen Planters of Jamaica, who had dealt with him, and among whom he had a good Reputation; and some of them, who had been in Carolina, remember'd to have seen her in his House; wherefore they were enclined to show her Favour, but the Action of leaving her Husband was an ugly Circumstance against her. The Day that Rackam was executed, by special Favour, he was admitted to see her; but all the Comfort she gave him, was, that she was sorry to see him there, but if he had fought like a Man, he need not have been hang'd like a Dog.

She was continued in Prison, to the Time of her lying in, and afterwards reprieved from Time to Time; but what is become of her since, we cannot tell; only this we know, that she was not executed.

STUDY QUESTIONS

1. What are the circumstances that led to Anne becoming a pirate?
2. How would you describe Anne's relationship with Rackham?

15.7 THE ABSOLUTIST REGIMES

Four families—the Bourbons (France), Hohenzollerns (Brandenburg-Prussia), the Habsburgs (Austria and Spain), and the Romanovs (Russia)—ruled over much of Europe during the Old Regime. A web of intermarriages connected the royal families to one another.

The Absolutist Regimes

Habsburg Austria	Hohenzollern Brandenburg-Prussia	Bourbon France	Romanov Russia	Bourbon Spain
Leopold I 1658–1705	Friedrich Wilhelm 1640–1688	Louis XIII 1610–1643	Alexis 1645–1676	Felipe IV (*) 1621–1665
Josef I 1705–1711	Friedrich III 1688–1713	Louis XIV 1643–1715	Theodore II 1676–1682	Carlos II (*) 1665–1700
Karl VI 1711–1740	Friedrich Wilhelm I 1713–1740	Louis XV 1715–1774	Ivan V 1682–1689	Felipe V 1700–1746
Maria Theresa 1740–1780	Friedrich II the Great 1740–1786	Louis XVI 1774–1792	Piotr I the Great 1689–1725	Ferdinando VI 1746–1759
Josef II 1780–1790	Friedrich Wilhelm II 1786–1797		Katerina I 1725–1727	Carlos III 1759–1788
Leopold II 1790–1792	Friedrich Wilhelm III 1797–1840		Piotr II 1727–1730	Carlos IV 1788–1808
Francis II 1792–1835			Anna 1730–1740	
			Ivan VI 1740–1741	
			Lizaveta 1741–1762	
			Piotr III 1762	
			Katerina II the Great 1762–1796	
			Pavel 1796–1801	
			Aleksandr I 1801–1825	

(*)= last two Habsburg kings of Spain

Printed in the USA/Agawam, MA
November 2, 2023

854139.006

"Wisdom is supreme;
Therefore, get wisdom.
Though it cost all you have,
get understanding."

Proverbs 4:7 NIV

5,000 Years of Wisdom

Published in the United States of America
Published by CLC Publishing

Cover Design by Paul Roden

ISBN-13: 978-1719442367

ISBN-10: 1719442363

For more information visit

5000YearsOfWisdom.org

Endorsements

"One of my favorite sayings is *"There's no substitute for knowledge"*. To read of the wisdom and knowledge of all these people over the age of 100, is priceless. This book is a must read for all who want to learn from the accomplishments and disappointments of the real pioneers."

Gene Stallings
Author, Speaker
Former NFL Head Coach, Phoenix Cardinals
Former Head Football Coach, University of Alabama

"Paul Roden has given the world a priceless treasure with 5,000 Years of Wisdom. By putting pen to paper in this way, he has built a living, breathing, and interactive bridge to our past and we can walk it anytime we wish. For those who have longed for a time machine, you need only pick up this fantastic book and begin turning the pages."

Duane Cummings
CEO of Leadercast
Speaker and Author of
The Sensational Salesman

Table of Contents

Dedication

To my father, Paul Gene Roden Jr.
and my grandfather, E.L. Kuykendall,
two of the wisest men I have ever known.

Acknowledgments

"You should write a book," they said. *"It'll be easy,"* they said. If I had known how much work it was going to take to write this book, I probably never would've started it. I am so thankful to all the people who have given so much help and support to this project. Thank you to my mothers, Jackie Foster and Anita Roden for your support and encouragement and for scouring newspapers to find people for me to interview. Thanks to Kathy Floyd for proofing, editing and for all your advice. Thank you to Melissa Wilson for transcribing so many interviews, Cole Feix for your formatting skills, Kody Larsen for editing, to Shannon Whittington for your wisdom, guidance and encouragement, and to Nic Bittle for your friendship and for kicking me in the seat of the pants when I needed it. And to my beautiful bride, Kate, for countless hours of transcribing, editing, and encouraging me throughout this entire process. You are my world. And finally, to the incredible individuals that shared their lives, their stories and their wisdom to make this book possible, I am humbled and grateful. You have changed my life, and I hope that through this book, you change many more.

Introduction

It was a Sunday afternoon when my parents called my sister and me into the living room. What they said would affect me for the rest of my life. They had decided to divorce. That day, my eleven-year- old world shattered into a million broken pieces. I spent the rest of my childhood and adolescence coping with the ongoing issues that resulted, in addition to the typical teen challenges. Later, after graduating college and meeting the love of my life, I found myself afraid to make a commitment. After all, if the two people I loved and respected the most couldn't make marriage work, what chance did I have? Eventually the pain of living without her won over the fear of commitment, and I made the leap, but I knew I couldn't make it work all on my own. I knew I would need some help, however, I foolishly vowed not to seek marital advice from either of my parents, after all, they had failed.

Sometime during that first year of my marriage I read a quote that would have a profound impact on my life. It said, *"If any of you lacks wisdom, he should ask God, who gives generously to all without finding fault, and it will be given to him"* (James 1:5 NIV). It seemed like a risk-free proposal to me. So, I said, *"OK God, give me wisdom,"* expecting him to miraculously download Wisdom 2.0 directly into my brain, but nothing happened. I did, however, still have an intense desire to make my marriage work, and as a paramedic, I had the occasional opportunity to visit with some of my older patients. I began to ask them how long they had been married, and I would frequently get responses of 50 and even 60 years. Then I would ask, *"So, what is the secret to a good marriage?"* As they opened up and poured out their wisdom, I soaked up all I could.

I began to put their advice into practice. I tried not to be selfish. I began to put my wife's needs and desires ahead of my own. I tried to openly communicate and make decisions based on what is best for my marriage, not what is best for me. Gradually, quietly, subtly, He was doing it. God was giving me wisdom. As I opened my

heart and my mind, I began to see that my parents were not failures at marriage. Both had since remarried and had wonderful marriages with wonderful spouses. I had just been too foolish and blind to see what was right in front of me.

As I continued my search for wisdom, I began to develop a hunger to read and seek out people who could help me learn and grow. The book of Proverbs became my favorite book. I would read it over and over, each time picking up something new that made me a better husband, a better son, a better person. Wisdom had impacted every area of my life and I was hungry for more. Then I read it, *"Wisdom belongs to the aged, and understanding to those who have lived many years"* (Job 12:12 NLT). That was it; that was the secret. Those who have lived the longest lives have the most wisdom, and who has lived longer than people over 100?

That is the genesis of this book. And so, I started a quest to meet and interview 100 people all over the age of 100. The following pages contain more than just wisdom, they contain the life stories of some of the most beautiful people I have ever met. Their stories tell of their joys and heartaches, struggles and victories, good times and bad. Their wisdom is not some untested theory, it has been earned and paid for by their own blood sweat and tears. I am honored to have sat at the feet of these great teachers. I have laughed with them, cried with them and prayed with them. I have shared in their lives and I have attended their funerals. And though their memory may fade and some of them may not remember me, they have permanently impacted my life in a profound way. So sit back, open your heart and your mind, and learn from the masters.

Chapter 1
Wisdom 101

Why Wisdom?

Lots of people ask me, "Why did you write this book?" It's a fair question. Webster's Dictionary summarizes wisdom as: *knowledge, understanding and good judgment gained through experiences* - So who wouldn't want that?

If I have knowledge, understanding and good judgment I can make better decisions. If I make better decisions, I'll make fewer mistakes. If I make fewer mistakes, I'll have better results. If I have better results, my wife will be happier. If my wife is happier.......

So here is why I wrote this book.

I want fewer mistakes, fewer problems, fewer regrets, less worry, less stress, less anxiety,

More solutions, more efficiency, more productivity, more growth, more victories, more happiness, more joy,

A better marriage, a better family, better children, better relationships, better health, better finances, better results, a better present, a better future.

I want a better life, a fuller life, a life with meaning, a life with purpose, a life that matters, a life of joy and happiness.

That's it. I want a better life. Maybe that's selfish, but if I can improve the lives of others through my life and my wisdom, maybe it's not so selfish.

The interesting thing about wisdom is that its principles apply to every area of your life, from your personal life to your family life to your business or career. Think about it: good families require

good management and leadership skills, just like a Fortune 500 company.

Wisdom can improve every area of your life. You're going to learn many of these lessons anyway. You can either learn them the hard way, or the *wise* way. It's your choice. Choose wisely.

Education Does Not Equal Wisdom

By most standards, I'm a reasonably educated guy. I was a good student, I have a college degree, and numerous professional licenses, certifications and accomplishments, but still there was something missing. As I entered adulthood, life began throwing problems at me that I couldn't solve. All of my college and professional degrees did a great job of preparing me for an occupation, but they didn't prepare me for life.

In contrast, many of the people in this book have less than an eighth-grade education, but what they may lack in formal education is more than made up for by the centuries of wisdom they collectively possess. It's not something they read in a book; it's not a theory from some college professor. It is hard core wisdom and experience that they *earned* the hard way, through their own blood, sweat and tears.

H.D. McCarty once said, *"The man with a theory will always be at the mercy of the man with an experience."* The result of that experience is wisdom, and there are only two ways to get it: go learn it yourself through trial and error, or learn it through someone else's trial and error. Personally, I prefer the second choice, but I wasn't always that smart.

When I was a teenager, I was an idiot. Like every other teenager, I thought I knew everything, but, in reality, I knew nothing. Then in my 20's and 30's, I slowly realized that I knew a lot, but I really didn't know *everything*. And now in the stage of life referred to as "middle age", I've come to the conclusion that I don't know *anything*, and in that realization.... lies wisdom.

Socrates once said, *"The only true wisdom is in knowing you know nothing."* Profound but true. My one regret is that I wish I had learned this lesson earlier in life. How much pain could I have avoided? How much money could I have saved? How much better could my life be right now?

The Theory of Wisdom

I've made a lot of mistakes in life, and I've paid for them.... dearly. Think of all the mistakes you have made in your life. What if you could have avoided all those mistakes and their consequences? Now think of all the problems that you've had. What if you had known the solution to the problem... *before you had the problem?*

I have a theory; I call it "The Theory of Wisdom." It says: *Every problem you will ever have has already been solved by someone else.* Think about it. What problem have you ever had that no one else has ever experienced? Money problems? Marriage problems? Relationships? Health issues? Job issues? Parenting? Addictions? Tragedy? Death? It's all been done before. Ecclesiastes says, *"What was will be again, what has happened will happen again. There's nothing new on this earth..."* (Ecc 1:9, MSG)

So why do we repeatedly try to go it alone and battle our problems the old-fashioned way, with our own blood, sweat and tears? Wouldn't it be easier to find someone who has already experienced what we are going through, and ask them for advice? Maybe we think we can handle it ourselves. Maybe we think no one will understand. Maybe we're too proud to admit our weaknesses. *"Pride cometh before the fall, shame cometh after"*, a little piece of wisdom from Ethel Brocklebank, age 101.

All of our decisions and mistakes come with consequences. Wouldn't it be easier and safer to make decisions when you know what the consequences will be? That's what wisdom does. It lets you know the end results before you make the decision.... or the mistake.

Again, Webster's Dictionary defines wisdom as: *Knowledge, understanding and good judgment gained through experiences. Knowledge of the best ends and the best means.* To put it another way, wisdom is the ability to foresee the end result and to then use the simplest, most efficient means to achieve the best outcome.

When I was in high school, I wasn't very good in math. Sometimes, while doing my homework, I had trouble figuring out how to work the problem. Our text books had the answers to the homework problems listed in the back of the book. So, I would look up the correct answer, and work the problem backwards to learn how the equation worked. I wasn't cheating, I was learning to solve the problem backwards. That's how wisdom works; It gives you the end results so you can work through the problem backwards and make the right decisions.

So, then the question becomes, where do you get wisdom? There are many answers:

Confucius said, *"By three methods we may learn wisdom: First, by reflection, which is noblest; Second, by imitation, which is easiest; and third by experience, which is the bitterest."*

The Bible says, *"If any of you lacks wisdom, he should ask God, who gives generously to all without finding fault, and it will be given to him."* (James 1:5 NIV) It also says, *"Wisdom belongs to the aged, and understanding to those who have lived many years."* (Job 12:12)

And Publilius Syrus said, *"From the errors of others, a wise man corrects his own."*

But what I tell audiences is, *"Experience is the process of learning from your mistakes. Wisdom is the process of learning from the mistakes of others."*

So, it's really your choice. Life *IS* going to present you with wave after wave of problems and challenges, but *YOU* get to decide how you will solve them. You can grind it out all by yourself, spending

needless time, effort and money, or you can find someone who has already navigated that minefield to guide you through. When you think about it, it's really a no-brainer.

The following pages contain more wisdom than you can imagine. If you're looking to solve a problem, if you're looking for direction, if you're looking for a better life, then this is the right place. Relax, open up, and receive.

A SPECIAL NOTE TO YOUNG READERS:

When I was a teenager, like most teenagers, I thought I knew everything. I thought that my parents had no idea what it was like to be a teenager. How could they relate to my problems? They didn't know anything about the challenges or temptations that I faced. They tried to tell me what to do, but I didn't listen. They were clueless - or so I thought.

Looking back, I was the one who was clueless. My parents knew exactly what I was going through. They knew all the problems, challenges, and temptations that I was facing. More importantly, they knew the consequences that I would face if I made the wrong decisions. They had been through it all themselves. They did their best to guide me through this swamp called the "teenage years," but I was an idiot, and I refused to listen. I insisted on doing things *my* way.

What a fool I was. I didn't know anything, but I was too wrapped up in myself to see the truth. It's clear to me now. I see all the heartache and pain that I could have avoided. I see all the problems that would have been much easier to solve if I had only listened to them. Don't make the same mistakes I did. One of my biggest regrets is that I didn't ask for the wisdom of my parents, teachers and others. I shudder to think what I could have accomplished in life if I had only sought their guidance earlier.

Another regret was not seeking out the wisdom of my grandparents

when I had the chance. I don't have that opportunity anymore; they are all gone, but I won't let that opportunity slip by with my parents. I may have wasted my opportunities to gain wisdom as a young man, but I don't have to make the same mistake again. I can start right now. I can seek out people who have already solved the problems I am facing. I can read books, I can talk to and listen to people who are smarter than I am. I still have a lot to learn, but I'm tired of being educated by the "school of hard knocks." There is a better way; it's called wisdom.

If you are a young person reading this, remember this one thing; life is a harsh teacher who forces us to solve problems. If you get it wrong, the results can be brutal, even fatal. But if you seek out and listen to people who have already solved these problems successfully, your education and your life will be much easier and much less expensive. Wisdom is there waiting to help you. All you have to do is ask.

"When I was a boy of fourteen, my father was so ignorant I could hardly stand to have the old man around. But when I got to be twenty-one, I was astonished at how much the old man had learned in seven years."

Mark Twain

Berle Arthur Swagerty

Berle Swagerty at college graduation July 28, 1938

At first glance, Mr. Swagerty appeared to be a gruff, grumpy old man. As I introduced myself, he said "Well what do you want?" I explained how I wanted to interview him about the wisdom and experiences of his life. He just grumbled something under his breath. At that moment, a young nurse walked through the door to see if he needed anything. In a loud, grouchy tone he told her he just wanted to be left alone. Shocked and visibly upset, she left. Then, looking at me, he commented, "Oh, you're still here?" Looking downward, he watched for my reaction out of the corner of his eye. Then I saw it; a mischievous little grin appeared. I was being tested. I stated that I just wanted to visit with him about his life, or he could sit there by himself all day.... his choice. "Well, I guess you can stay," he replied. I had passed the test.

Berle Swagerty was born on February 5, 1908 in Rocky, Oklahoma. Together, he and his wife, Fredia, had two children, Jeanne and Jim. Fredia passed away in 2000. Berle worked as a public-school teacher for 46 years, teaching industrial arts, and attended college during his summer breaks to further his education.

After 13 years, he earned a bachelor's degree in education from Oklahoma State University, and four more years of part-time college earned him his master's degree. He was the first in his family to ever attend college.

After being a teacher for 46 years, what do you think about education?

I believe that education is important, but then, I'm a teacher. Education helps to prepare you for not only for your career, but also for life. Back in my day, most people didn't go to college. You were lucky if you even got to finish high school. Maybe that's why those were such hard times. These days, a good education is necessary. If you're not educated, an employer won't even look at you. It may be the only difference between a good job and minimum wage.

How much education do you think you need?

Well I guess it depends on what you want to do. Education is a lifelong process. You never really stop learning, and you don't get it all at once. I went to school each summer for 13 years to get my college degree, and four more to get my master's. It was that important to me. It helped me be a better teacher, and it helped me to provide better for my family. Sure, it took me a long time.... but I got it. Now days you've got to keep learning. Things are changing so fast, technology and such. If you stop learning, the whole world will just fly right past you and leave you behind. I think these days, education is more important than ever. One thing about knowledge, it's the best investment you can ever make, and it's the only thing that no one can take away from you.

How long were you married to your wife, Fredia?

Sixty-five years.

So, what was your secret?

If you want a good marriage, you have to love each other. If you love each other that means you'll take care of each other. We got married for better or worse. Sometimes marriage isn't easy, but life isn't easy. When my wife got sick, I took care of her. I had to; I loved her. It wasn't easy, but I loved her. That's what you're

supposed to do, take care of each other. That's the promise you make. People don't take that seriously enough. If you take those vows and say, "*I do*", you'd better live up to it.

Tell me about how you managed your money.
Well for one thing, we worked hard to make ends meet. We had to. Sometimes I had to get a second job, or three jobs. I had to provide for my family; it was my responsibility. I had to do whatever was necessary to put food on the table. They were depending on me.

Another thing was, we never spent more than we made. That gets people in trouble. If we couldn't afford it, we didn't buy it. If something's paid for, they can't come and take it away.

And I always tried to save money. Each month I would take a little bit out of each check and put it in savings. You never know when you're going to need it. My wife *(laughing)* used to get mad at me because I would put money in the bank instead of letting her go out and buy things. But then when she got sick, we had the money we needed to take care of her. We didn't have to go into debt to pay her medical bills. I sure was glad that I had saved all those years. One day *(crying)*, not long before she died, she took my hand and she smiled at me and told me that now she knew why I had saved all that money. I don't know what I would've done if I hadn't been able to take care of her. You never know what life's gonna throw at you; you'd better be prepared.

What is the greatest lesson you ever learned?
The biggest lesson I ever learned was to respect your elders. By that I mean listen to them and learn from them. They have been where you are and they know how to handle the problems that you're going through. I wish I had listened more. It would've saved me a lot of trouble. That lesson applies to your whole life. There's always someone older and wiser than you that has already been through what you're going through. You need to find those people and listen to them. Most young folks think that us old folks don't know what we're talking about. They think they know it all, so they don't need to listen to anyone else. I was like that. I sure

wished I had listened more. My life would've been a whole lot easier.

Do you ever think about dying?
Yeah, I think about dying a lot. I'm sure my days are numbered here. You never know what's going to happen, whether it will be easy or hard, but that's the way life is, sometimes it's easy, sometimes it's not. That's life. I'm not afraid of it, that doesn't matter, it's going to happen anyway.

What do you think happens after we die?
I don't know what will happen after I die, nobody does I guess. Sometimes I think I've got things figured out, but the more I think about it, the more I don't know. Just make sure your life counts for something. Because someday, it'll be too late.

What do you think your life counted for?
Well I think it counted for my family, my wife and my boys. And I think I mattered to some of my students. I had a lot of students over 46 years. I'd like to think that I made a difference to a few of them. I'm sure I could've done a lot more good than I did, but it's too late now. Maybe I should've worked harder at that.... I don't know. Everybody wants their life to count, but it's not gonna happen by accident.

Berle Swagerty's life counted, to me personally, and to countless students and teachers over his 46-year career. Mr. Swagerty was the first interview I did when I started this book project. I didn't know what to expect from him or the others I would interview. I certainly wasn't prepared to cry with him as he told me about his wife dying. The gruff old man that I initially greeted changed into one of the most beautiful human beings I've ever met when he opened his heart and shared with me the most intimate moments of his life. I came for an interview; I left with a friend and a mentor.

Shortly after this interview, Berle Swagerty died on January 14, 2008, just 22 days before his 100th birthday. It was my intention to

only include people over 100 years old in this book. However, because of his proximity to 100 years, his practical wisdom, and the way he captured my heart during our visit, I simply couldn't exclude him. After all, true wisdom is ageless.

"Everybody wants their life to count, but it's not gonna happen by accident. "

Berle Swagerty

Greta Heslet

Greta Cottrell was born on December 16, 1905. The last of five children, she was the youngest by 11 years, *"I was quite a surprise"*. After graduating high school, she attended one year of college earning her teaching certificate and taught in a one room school house. She quit one year later to marry Herb Woodson at age 19. After divorcing Herb three years later, she began singing with a 12-piece orchestra and was soon discovered by the recording industry. Greta recorded six albums during the roaring 20's. She traveled the U.S. by train, singing in speak-easy's and nightclubs during prohibition, and in a touring variety show for RKO records. Greta was married a total of five times, outliving all her husbands but the first. All totaled, she was married for 68 years. She never had children.

You've been married for a total of 68 years; how did you make it work?
Well, I've had five husbands. I was married to Herbert for three years before we divorced, then Ernie....it was love at first sight with Ernie as far as I was concerned. We only knew each other six weeks but we were married for 33 years. When Ernie died, I married Harry, he had a heart attack and died in his sleep 20 months after we got married. We went to a football game one day and the next morning he was gone. It was just awful. I was a widow again

for two years and then I married Frank and we were married for almost five years before he died of cancer. I was a widow again for two years I guess, then I married Dale Heslet. We were married when we were 70 years old and we had 25 good years together.

The secret to a good long marriage is trust. It requires some give and take and being able to communicate. And love.....lots of love. I don't have any children, I had two step-sons. We thought we were going to adopt twins but by the time we heard about them, they had been adopted by another family. It would have been nice to have had children; right now, I wish I did, but I don't regret it. I was just so busy all my life.

You've outlived four husbands; how do you deal with losing a spouse?
Actually, the worst thing that ever happened to me was losing my mother. I didn't lose her 'til after I lost Ernie. It's difficult losing a spouse, it makes you feel absolutely abandoned. When Ernie died I had friends that really took care of me. You just have to make up your mind to get through it. I developed the ability to put it behind me and look forward instead of mourning forever. I've known people that set the table for their departed husbands like he was going to be there for supper. That is just feeding on misery and doesn't do any good. That doesn't mean that I forget them, but I quit mourning and think about the wonderful times we had together instead. You have to look at it like it's a page in a book and you've turned that page.... a page in the book of life. I miss them and I pray for them every night.... all of them. It's given me a completely different view of dying to where I have no fear of it anymore.

Do you ever think about dying?
Sure, I think about dying...I wish I would. I don't want to live forever. I'd just like to go before I run out of money *(laughing)*. I don't want to outlive my finances and I don't want to live so long that I lose my mind. I see that here at the nursing home. I see these people in wheel chairs that don't know where they are, they don't know what they've eaten, they don't know anything. They're just kept alive by medication, and I don't want that. I just want to go.

I'd rather go in my sleep if I had my druthers.... just go to sleep and never wake up When I was diagnosed with cancer, I thought that was it. I was scared. Now, I don't fear dying. I just feel like I'm going on to a better place. I believe what the Bible says, that we'll have eternal life.

So, you believe in the Bible?
Oh yes, God is my best friend. I have conversations with Him. I don't get many answers from Him but I pray that He leads me in doing what He wants me to do. I believe that He has steered and guided my life, and I've had a *wonderful* life. I've had sorrow too, but that's just part of life. I think God had His hand in the middle of it all. I think He pulled me through all the sorrow.

What has 100 years of life taught you?
Life has taught me patience more than anything. Patience is a virtue. Everything will happen in its own time. Learn to be patient and learn to forgive. Don't hold grudges. Be quick to say, "I'm sorry" and quick to forgive.... whether they apologize or not. And forgiveness in a marriage is especially important. You know, they always said if you're married, don't go to bed mad; make up before you go to bed. Well, I think that's true.

So, being a cancer survivor yourself, what advice do you have for someone battling cancer?
I've had cancer; I've had a breast removed, but I was lucky they got it all. They took 16 lymph nodes and they got it in time. It didn't spread anywhere else, but I never had to take chemo or radiation. Some people aren't so lucky.

When they told me I had cancer, I thought that was the end, and I was scared. There's nothing you can do but face it and accept it....and fight. I'd tell them to pray a lot. Fight and pray.... that's the only thing you can do. I just told myself, if that's what I've got, then that's what I've got. What will be, will be. There's nothing else you can do about it. Fight and pray, that's what I did....and I'm still here! The Lord's been with me through it all and He kept me here for some reason. It's all up to the Lord.

If you had just one piece of advice to give someone, what would you say?

Be true to yourself. By that I mean be yourself... love yourself. Believe in what you're doing and live while you've got the chance, I mean *really* live. Believe me, 100 years goes by *fast!* I wish I was 80 again. I was dancing and having a good time. I wouldn't do a thing different than I did. I enjoyed life to the hilt. I played golf; I went to church, and I danced and sang. I just loved life. Life is meant to be lived. Live it well.

Greta Heslet certainly lived life well. In the 1920's, Greta sang with famed jazz conductor Jean Goldkette and his orchestra. She was also a part of two popular female singing trios, Three Shades of Blue as well as Wynken Blynken and Nod. She has recorded six record albums, starred in the widely seen short film "Wildflowers," was named one of the top female jazz singers of all time and at age 102, she is the oldest recording artist alive. Greta has even had a play written about her life, and her music is still available on Amazon.com.

At the end of our interview as Greta was walking me out, an old man was playing the piano in the nursing home lobby. Greta's face lit up and she asked me to dance with her. Of course, I accepted. How could I refuse such a lady? While we danced and laughed, other residents sat in wheelchairs, smiling, laughing and clapping. Though they were no longer able to dance, their faces were filled with the joy and memories of days gone by. It was a beautiful sight. That's what Greta did; she filled people with joy. Thank you for the dance Greta, it was my pleasure.

Greta Heslet passed away May 22, 2009 at the age of 103. You can hear Greta on several of her albums at the links below. I promise it will bring a smile to your face.

http://www.youtube.com/watch?v=NHRmLfxkQnY
http://www.youtube.com/watch?v=mALOu_NdOZM
http://youtu.be/XRDuluuk5uo

*"Life is meant to be lived.
Live it well."*

Greta Heslet, 102

Ora Holland

Ora Holland and her daughter Ruth

Ora Reed was born December 24, 1900 to Nathan and Stella Reed of Rosebud Missouri who recorded the event in the family Bible. *"That's the way we did it back then. I never had a birth certificate."* The third of twelve children, Ora attended school in a one room school house and suffered numerous health problems as a young girl. *"They told me I wouldn't live to age 10, but look at me now!"* At age 22 she married Thomas Holland and had two children; one died at birth. After 18 years of marriage, she and Thomas divorced and she never remarried. As a single mother with only an eighth-grade education, she worked at a shipyard during World War II to make ends meet stating, *"I was Rosie the Riveter, but that was a long time ago"*. Later she started and ran her own beauty shop for 12 years and then started her own childcare business which she operated for ten years. *"It was a lot of work, but I did alright."*

Ora celebrated her 100th birthday by buying a new car, which she used to drive herself to the store and to church each week until age 108. *"A policeman gave me a speeding ticket last year and I decided it was time for me to stop driving. Besides, I can't see like I used to."*

At the time of this interview, Ora was 108 years old. Strong physically, mentally and fiercely independent, she was still living

by herself in her own home, doing her own cooking, cleaning and even mowing the lawn! *"I plan on doing for myself as long as the Lord will let me."*

You were a single mother and business owner with an 8th grade education. How did you learn to manage your money?

Well, I just learned, just like you learn. Somebody didn't *poke* it down you, did they? You learn it by doing it. That's how everybody learns. When I left my husband, I got out without anything. That was way back when salaries wasn't much and we didn't have much either. My parents never helped me with a dime, but I was used to hard work; I was raised on a farm. So, I went and found a job in the shipyards and finally started making some money. It wasn't much, but it was enough to get by. Then once you get it, just don't spend it. You best start saving it. You know, when salaries were good, people thought their money was going to last forever. They spent it instead of putting it in the bank and saving it for a rainy day. That's why so many people today are in trouble and wondering if they're going to lose their homes, because they didn't save their money.

I've got a couple of grandchildren that's doing the same thing and I'm having to help them. My granddaughter and her husband own three cars. That's not necessary.... not necessary at all. Then my grandson bought a new car and then bought this great big television. They need that like I need a hole in the head! They need to learn to save their money instead of just blowing it on everything that they see and want. They don't need all of those things.

What are they going to have in the future? They're going to be in trouble and need help and Grandma's going to be gone. You've got to learn to save money 'cause you never know what's going to happen or when you might need it. Trust me, I know!

After 108 years of living, what advice can you give me about making my life count?

Help others. That's what our Bible says, help others. Everybody needs a little help every now and then. It doesn't necessarily have

to be money. During the depression, some folks needed food and clothing and such. Sometimes people just need someone to talk to. I've been helping for a good many years. I guess is what I'm here for. We should all be willing help each other. That's what God says for us to do. If you want to live a good life, go find somebody to help.

You mentioned God. Do you believe in God?
I sure do. I *know* there's a God and Jesus is His son. He means everything to me. He's taken care of me my whole life. I guess when I was young I didn't think too much about God, not like I do today. I depend on Him. I'll tell you something, if you don't believe in God and believe that Jesus is His son, there's no use you do anything else. That is a must, to believe in God and Jesus, because if you don't, nothing else matters.

I don't think I've made it all these years by myself. I think He's there taking care of me. I think that as long as we do what He says for us to do, that He's going to watch out for us and take care of us until He's ready to take us home. He says none of us are perfect. I try to be honest with everybody but I know I haven't been perfect *(laughs),* but He loves me anyway. God's been helpful to me my whole life. He's helpful to everybody.... if they *want* help.

If you believe in God, then do you ever think about heaven?
Sure, I think about it. Heaven's on my mind a lot of times. I'm not afraid of the hereafter, but just going through that death stage kind of worries me. I can't say that I'm really afraid of it, I just kind of dread going through the misery and all that stuff, but God will take care of me; He always has. One things for certain; we all die. There's no gettin' around it. It might be a long time from now and it might be a short time. We just don't know.... but you'd better be ready.

*Recently (May 2013), I was able to go visit Ora Holland again at the retirement center where she now lives. She is now 113 years old. "I can't be that old.... I don't feel that old." **"How old do you feel?"**, I ask. She replied, "I only feel about 105!" Her daughter,*

Ruth, is now gone, along with the rest of her family. Her grandson looks after her and visits often, but it is obvious that she longs for the old days. "I'm the only one left," she states. It is sad to see her lonely, living in a place she'd rather not be. At 113, she still gets around be herself, but like her eyesight, her memory is fading. "I can't remember things like I used to," she says, struggling to recall her husband's name.

Ora Holland passed away February 11, 2015 at the age of 114 years and 49 days. At the time of her death, she was the ninth oldest living American, and the 15th oldest person in the world.[1]

It is hard to grasp the concept of living 114 years. To put it in perspective, out of 108 billion (108,000,000,000) people ever to be born over the course of human history, she was one of the 100 longest living people ever.[2] She was born before either radio or TV was invented, before Henry Ford produced the first automobile, before the Wright brothers flew the first airplane, and she was a teenager when World War I broke out. Ora saw lot of changes in the past 114 years. It makes me wonder about the changes we'll see.

You can learn more about Ora Holland at the links below. God bless you Ora, you were truly one of a kind.

http://www.sliceok.com/November-2014/Memories-of-a-Lifetime-The-Oldest-Oklahoman/
https://en.wikipedia.org/wiki/List_of_supercentenarians_from_the_United_States

---

[1] Gerontology Research Group

[2] http://www.sliceok.com/November-2014/Memories-of-a-Lifetime-The-Oldest-Oklahoman/

Dawson Gorman

Walter Dawson Gorman was born May 6, 1907 on a farm on part of the Choctaw Nation in Indian Territory; a region which would later become the state of Oklahoma. He was the third of eight children born to an Irish father and a mother who was *"full blood Choctaw Indian."* Her parents had been relocated there on the infamous "Trail of Tears." Growing up on a 320-acre family farm, he and his brothers did their share to help out the family. *"We plowed the fields by hand behind a mule, picked cotton by hand; it was hard work but I wouldn't trade it for nothing."* As a boy, he rode a horse seven miles each day just to attend school and farmed his own cotton on a 30-acre plot for several years, earning and saving $6,000 to attend college. Three months into his college education, his bank went bankrupt losing all his money, and that of many others. He returned home finding work in the coal mines and oilfield, and in 1928, he married *"the love of my life,"* Mary. Together they had two sons, Bill and Don.

At the onset of World War II, following the Japanese attack on Pearl Harbor, Dawson and his brothers joined the military. *"We all felt like we had to do our part."* Dawson enlisted in the U.S. Navy and served two years in the southern Pacific, seeing action at both Iwo Jima and Okinawa. *"We had close calls four different times. Four*

times I thought we were going to die." Dawson and his brothers all survived the war and returned home safely.

After the war, Dawson worked in the hardware and lumber business later owning his own hardware store. In 2000, his wife, Mary, passed away after 72 years of marriage. *"I've never loved anyone so much,"* he said choking back tears. At age 102, he faced another battle, defeating colon cancer with the same strength and grit that's carried him for over a hundred years.

Tell me about your marriage.
Mary and I got married when I was 23 years old. We were young and broke and life was hard. She was my high school sweetheart. That's where we started from. When she said she would wed me, that shook me up quite a bit, because I didn't know a lot about marriage, and she didn't know anything about marriage.... We were both so innocent. We didn't know *anything!* She had to learn to cook, and how to do sex and everything else! *And me too, you know, 'cause I didn't know anything either!* Then, first thing we knew, she was pregnant. Now *that* was a big surprise, and scary too! And that's the way life started out for us.

So, after 72 years of marriage, what is the secret to making it work?
I didn't know how we were going to make it work, but we didn't know anything else except to just *make* it work. There wasn't any other choice. Oh, we made lots of mistakes over 72 years, but we loved each other and you learn from the mistakes and you keep moving forward. Love goes a long way, you know. If you love someone you forgive them. Lord knows I needed forgivin' plenty of times. But that's what love does, it forgives. Another thing, you can't give up. When times get hard....and they will.... you've got to keep going. You've got to be able to count on each other and you can't give up on each other. Love doesn't give up. Sooner or later, things will get better if you just don't give up.

Do you have any regrets?
Just going off to war. I left my wife and my two young sons at

home, but I felt like it was my duty. They sent me to Iwo Jima and Okinawa out in the southern Pacific. There were Japanese submarines everywhere, I mean *everywhere*. We had close calls four different times. I didn't think we were going to make it. We saw a lot of fighting, especially in Iwo Jima. I saw a lot of men die. Sometimes I'd think, "God, what am I doing killing these men over here? They're human beings just like me." But I know they'd kill me if they could've. That's the only excuse I had.

When the battle for Iwo Jima was finally over, we started loadin' up wounded Marines. We had a whole shipload *full* of Marines. There were dead soldiers everywhere, thousands of them. I had to walk over them. I had to step over all these dead Marines *(eyes beginning to water)*. Blood was everywhere, running down the deck. I think that hurt me worse than the war.... I still think about it. It's still right here *(clutching his chest)*, all those Marines.... and I had to take care of some of 'em. I thought about their families never seeing them again, or knowing where they were. That like to have got me. But all I could think about was getting home alive to my wife and sons. I was a nervous wreck when we finally got to the island and unloaded all of those wounded Marines. I still think about them. There are a lot of things that you think about when you're killing people. I don't like the idea of killing. War really is hell.

Do you think about dying?

Yeah, I've thought about dying. I spent two years out in the Pacific during the war, and every night I didn't know whether I was going to be alive the next morning or not. The Japanese had submarines all over that place. I had four close calls, and several times I got to worrying about it. I'd pray, "God, my wife is young and I got two young sons at home," and I'd say, "I've *got* to get back home. I can't be killed here." And God saw me through it…. somebody sure saw me through it because we almost didn't make it. God had to have been in it 'cause I come out of it and I didn't get a scratch on me. I thought for sure I was going to die, but I didn't.

One night, before my wife died, she asked me, *"Am I going to die?"* How do you answer that? I looked at her and said, *"Everything on this earth that's alive, has got to go."* I said, *"What you do tonight, you ask God to forgive all your sins and if you're honest about it, and truthful about it, He'll do it."* You've got to be truthful with God if you want His forgiveness. If you're not truthful, there's no use asking for it.

One night I was lying in bed, and I couldn't sleep, and I thought, *"God, why am I still alive? I'm so tired and I'm so tired of suffering. Why don't you just go on and take me?"* Well, I didn't really get an answer, but I'm still here. And there's plenty of people in worse shape than me. I guess I should be thankful, and I am. I've had a great life. I guess He has His reasons for keeping me here. I guess He's still got something left for me to do.

On June 22, 2011, God took Dawson Gorman home at the age of 104. I've interviewed a lot of people for this book, and several of them have impacted my life in a deep and profound way. Dawson Gorman is one of those. He may be gone from this world, but his love and humor and wisdom live on in his family, and hopefully in this book. Thank you, Mr. Gorman, for sharing your laughs, your tears, and your life with me.

"When times get hard.... and they will.... you've got to keep going."

Dawson Gorman, 103

Delmar Hopkins

Delmar Hopkins was born May 13, 1908 to Henry and Amanda Hopkins of Honey Grove, Texas. The youngest of nine children, Delmar grew up on the family farm *"picking and chopping cotton"* along with all the other chores that come along with farm life. At age nine, he enrolled in school where he completed the fifth grade before going back to work. Throughout life, Delmar held a wide variety of jobs, doing whatever he needed to do to make ends meet. *"I always took the jobs that nobody else wanted. Some didn't pay much but I always had a job, even when other people didn't"*. Delmar has been married three times for a total of 73 years. Together, he and his first wife had his only son, Kenneth, before separating after eight years together. He and his second wife, Mazella, shared 47 years before breast cancer took her, and he and his third wife, Ardee, were married for 18 years before her death in 2008. Today, Delmar lives independently, is in good health, takes no medications, and still works two jobs, five days a week because, *"It keeps me young"*.

You're 105 years old and still working two jobs. Why?
(Laughing) That's what keeps me going! I love it. It keeps me

healthy. I always took the jobs nobody else wanted. When I go to work, I go in at five or six o'clock and I work from six until midnight or 1am, 'til I get through cleaning up, and by the time I get home it's sometimes 2 am! If I'm sitting around for a day or two, I can feel my age creeping up on me. I've got to keep going. Work's good for the body, and the mind. It gives me a purpose; you've got to have a purpose. It keeps me going. I've retired three times, but I'm just not happy unless I'm out there working and meeting new people.

You said you've always taken whatever job you could find, for all your life. How did you manage your money?
I just made up my mind I was never gonna be broke. I've never made a lot of money. Sometimes only $3 or $4 a day, but I started saving when the depression hit back in the 30's. I'd put my little bit aside and I give the rest to my mother for groceries or whatever else we needed, and it just kept building up and building up. I always paid cash for whatever I needed. I never borrowed much money; didn't really need to. Any time I got some money, I just put it in the bank.

My wife Mazella never could save nothing. She was too free hearted. People was always asking her for money, her brother and such. When we moved here from Denver, we had quite a bit of money from selling our house. We had over $100,000 in the bank! One day the bank statement came in and said the account had dropped down to $7000, and I said, "*Oh my God, she can't save no money!*" So, I went and made me a bank account of my own. I started up a money market fund and from there started putting money into mutual funds, and that's what I'm in now. I think it's important to learn investing. I started investing my money and made it grow and now I ain't got nothing to worry about.

What was it like growing up as a black man in the 1930's and 40's?
Man, I had it all. I've had the white folks run us out of town. I had the white folks run us out of the field. We've had our problems out there. One time, when I was younger, we'd gone uptown and was

walkin' around the streets and three white boys come walking up behind us and started meddlin' with us. One of them kicked one of my friends and I told him *"You put your foot on me and you're a dead man, I'll kill you"*. And he didn't, he didn't kick me. So, there was a black guy working in the bakery shop and we went into the bakery shop and went out the back door to keep from having any more problems. So then, whenever we'd see problems, we'd always turn and go the other way. You have to learn to shun problems sometimes. You learn not to be so brave, but to shun trouble. And that's what we did. You gotta learn to stay out of trouble and just walk away, and that's what I did. Most times it's just not worth it.

But people mistreated you just because of the color of your skin. Doesn't that make you angry?
Tell me about it! But I don't hold no grudges against them; they're just ignorant. I just tell them, *"You're ignorant"*. I've been turned away hundreds of times, all because of the color of my skin. I had my days. Back in the 30's, I walked into a beer joint to get a pack of cigarettes and the guy said, *"Hey boy, you can't come in here. You go around to the back door."* And I said *"It ain't worth it,"* and left. They're just ignorant. I wonder sometimes how people can have so much hate in their heart just 'cause I've got different colored skin. There's still some out there that still hate us, but I don't have much trouble anymore. Every now and then you find someone like that. I just look at 'em and laugh at 'em. I say, *"You've got a lot to learn, boy"*

What's been the biggest lesson you've learned in life?
Be happy.... and laugh. Anybody that laughs will have a long and happy life. It builds your life up. To laugh and be happy makes your life longer. That's the most important thing in life. It's not the money or the stuff. It's just that I can live and be happy and try to make somebody else happy out there. I want them to feel good about themselves. I'm looking to make other people happy like me.

So, what's the key to being happy?
It's all in your attitude. I'm happy with my life. I tell people I am the luckiest man alive....*and I believe that!* I am the luckiest man

alive. I wouldn't trade my life for no one. I don't care how much money they got or how good they look, I wouldn't trade my life for all the money in China. I love my life just like it is. I don't need money; I have everything I need. I just want to be happy.

Another thing, treat people like you want to be treated. Don't say or do something to nobody that you don't want them to do to you. Treat people like you want to be treated. That's the Golden Rule...and that's my life. I tell people all the time, "*I love you.*" It's the law of sowing and reaping, If I love them, they'll love me back. Whatever I do is going to come back on me one way or another; so it might as well be good. So, I just try to treat people right and make everybody as happy as I can and let them know I love 'em. And that way I don't have no fear that something bad is going to come back and happen to me.

You've lost two wives. How did you get over their deaths?
The only way to do that, you've got to let them go. You can't bring them back. I don't care if it's your mother, father, sister or brother, they're put here on earth to die, and you've got realize that you've got to let them go. Sure, it hurts. It takes a lot out of you but you've got to put it behind you and keep on with your life.

May (Mazella) and I talked about that because she had cancer and she said "*I want you to keep on with your life when I'm gone. I don't want you to give up.*" And that's what I did, I kept going with my life. Yeah, it's hard. You better believe it's hard! It takes you a while. It took me three, maybe four years to get over my wife. I wasn't ready to give her up. Many nights I laid in the bed wondering why should I go on. And I said well, she would want me to. And the same way with her life. If I had died, I wouldn't want her to give up. I'd want her to go on and have the best life she could. So, I kept on going.

Do you ever think about dying?
Never. I'm healthy. I figure I can live another 20 years if I want to.

Why are you so healthy?
'Cause I talk to the Man upstairs *(pointing upward)*. I pray, I talk to The Man. I believe in God; I do. When I'm out there on my job, I'm talking to the Lord a lot of the time, thanking him, not begging him, but thanking him for my health and strength. Not asking for nothing, because I've already got everything I need. I don't have to ask for it. I just thank him for my health and my strength and the things that come my way.

My mother was a praying woman. She prayed hard for all her kids, all her life. One day a long time ago, my wife and I were talking about God, and I said, *"If there's a God, I'd like for him to let me know one way or the other"*. I said, *"If there's a God, how come I can't go out there and find me a pocket full of money"*? And that night I went out, and when I got out of the car and kicked something under a pile of leaves, I picked it up; it was ladies pocketbook with *$600 in it*! That let me know there *must* be a God, and I thanked him right then and there. And I still thank him every day I live.

Delmar Hopkins is truly a remarkable man. His attitude and happiness are so contagious, you can't help but feel better after being around him. It seems almost divinely ironic how a poor black man with a fifth-grade education, who has been discriminated against, hated and rejected, could be so full of love, happiness and wisdom. Perhaps there's a lesson here.

At the time of publishing, Delmar Hopkins is 110 years old and still happy. You can learn more about Delmar and his incredible attitude at the links below.

https://www.youtube.com/watch?v=1N7oNeZNjCw
http://dc.library.okstate.edu/cdm/ref/collection/hundred/id/17
http://www.news9.com/story/22229498/norman-man-celebrates-105th-birthday-at-work
http://newsok.com/article/3909472

"I just made up my mind I was never gonna be broke. Any time I got some money, I just put it in the bank."

Delmar Hopkin, 105

Marguerite Beard

Marguerite Beard was born on January 2, 1908, the third of seven children to William Love and Eudora Bradley Beard of Paris, Texas. Marguerite graduated from Paris High School in 1922 and attended one year at Paris Junior College. She later attended a commercial college before taking a job as a legal secretary, making $9 a week. Marguerite continued working as a legal secretary for over 68 years before finally retiring at age 88. She never married and has no children. *"Some people say that's why I lived to be 100."* Marguerite still lives independently in her own home, and is actively involved in her church and with her family.

How did you manage your money?
I never made a lot of money, no one did back then, but you learned to live within your means, always. I think the problem is kids don't save anymore. When I started working, I saved some of what I made every paycheck. I made $9 a week and I'd save $2 or $3 of it. I think you need to save some of what you make; you can do it...you just *don't* it. Some people don't ever care about paying off anything. They just think about how much have I got to pay each month. They don't think about paying it off. Then they get in over their heads and end up losing it all. There's people out there worrying about whether the bank is going to come and take their house away.... they had no business buying it in the first place.

They didn't have enough money. They didn't even have the down payment! They didn't even have to put any money into the deal. They shouldn't have ever been in those houses. Now the government wants to come in and bail them out. I don't agree with that. It was their judgment that got them into that mess.

Another thing, you need to save something for retirement because it's bad when you're old and you don't have any money and you don't have a place to live and you can't pay for your medicine. What are you going to do at my age, go get a job? You'd better start saving your money while you can. When I was growing up we were all taught to live within our means, and as long as you do that you'll get along alright.

What are you most thankful for?
My family!

Why family?
Because they just mean more to me now days. Family gets more important as you get older, but then it's always been important to me. You have to invest in family; family is all you really have in the end. If you don't have family you're in a bad fix. Now days people don't think as much about family; they don't do as much with the family as we did. We got together for lots of things.... you have to do that. If you're not around them, you don't know them. Friends come and go, but family is always there for each other.... and I've got a good family. If you invest time into it, it comes back to you.

Do you have any advice about growing old?
As far as getting old, I haven't dreaded it or anything. It's not so much what you do, you're just here and it happens. You have to accept that you can't do certain things anymore. I think being healthy and able bodied is more important than just growing old.... regardless of your age. I think that you have to exercise if you expect to get around, and you have to keep at it. That's what you do. You can always think of an excuse of why you don't want to. You have to make yourself get up and go and stay with it. Some

say, "Well I don't have time." *Hell, if you're old then you don't have anything but time* (laughing)! You know?   If you don't do that, then you're not gonna be able to get around and do anything. You have to work at it just like you do everything else. Being old's not bad. Being old and cripple is terrible. You can't think of it as getting' old. It's just there, it happens. But as long as you're alive, you've got to take care of yourself.

Do you have any regrets about your life?
Regrets? No, not really. I've had a happy life.

Do you regret not getting married and having kids?
I don't regret not getting married. I don't. There's more to life than being married and having kids. I've got nothing against it, but I've had a good life. I've had fun and I've traveled.   I always had somebody to do things with and always had somebody to do something for, and I've got a good family. Life has been good to me. I liked it all. I really liked it when I got to be about 50. That's kind of a time when you can just be you, and there you are, you got the rest of your life to live and people aren't all after you about things. Everybody says 50's getting old. I say Lord.... the 50's was a *good* time!

What is the most important lesson you've learned?
Well I think the most important lesson is to try to be satisfied with what you've got. I just never envied anybody anything they had. Be happy with what you have. I think it makes your life happier. Enjoy your life as you go on. Life is good, and you ought to enjoy it.... 'cause I enjoyed all mine. And people would say *"How could you? You're just sitting there an ol' maid?"* (laughing). You can.... if you want to. I've had a good life.... I'm happy.... and I've been happy all along. I've had good friends.... and their all gone now.

Marguerite Beard passed away on June 1, 2015 at the age of 107.

"Everybody says 50's getting old. I say Lord.... my 50's was a good time!"

Marguerite Beard, 106

B. J. Slothower

Belden J. Slothower was born on September 21, 1912 in Osborne, Kansas, the second of seven children. Growing up on a farm, his father, Joe, provided for the family by farming and working odd jobs while his mother, Etta, *"raised us kids"*. While attending school, B.J. worked at a neighbor's dairy *"milkin' cows twice a day and peddlin' milk."* After graduating high school, he took a job in California driving trucks and at age 25, married his *"sweetheart,"* Esther. Together they had one son. Upon returning to Kansas, B.J. went to work on a farm where one day, *"I heard the voice of God, he said 'I want you to preach.'"* So, at age 38, he quit his farming job, sold all his livestock and enrolled in Bethany College to major in ministry. After three semesters, he was asked to pastor his first church which led to a 26-year career in the ministry pastoring churches in Hutchison, Salina and Gaylord, Kansas.

At age 65, B.J. retired from preaching and took a job as a custodian at his alma mater, Bethany College. *"The college was part of my life and I just wanted to be part of the college."* In 1996, Esther, his wife of 59 years, died after a lengthy illness. Two years later at the age of 86, B.J. married Maxine Lewis, a longtime family friend.

That same year he retired for the second time from Bethany College following 20 years of service. After 11 *"joyful years"* of marriage, Maxine passed away in 2009. Today, at the time of this interview, B.J. lives alone in a retirement home and still reads his Bible twice every day.

You were married for a total of 70 years. With half of all marriages ending in divorce, what made your marriages work?
Falling in love. I fell in love with the girl. She was my neighbor back in Kansas. We had a good marriage because I loved her and she loved me. You just fall in love with them and you don't fall out of love. Your faithful to them and honest with them. She's the only one. There's nobody else, in all that time I had no desire looking around for anyone else. She was my honey.

When we were married, we were both innocent and pure. I mean we had saved ourselves for each other. We had rented this little house for $18 a month, but they had to do some work on it, and we couldn't get in it for two weeks. We lived in a hotel room for two weeks after we were married, before we could move into that little house. We never even had sex that first two weeks of marriage. That's not what we got married for. I loved her and she loved me. There's more to marriage than sex life. The Bible says we're to save our bodies for marriage. We're supposed to stay innocent and pure and that will make our marriage pure and two will become one. It's more than giving your bodies to each other, it's giving your life to each other. I wanted to be part of her life and I wanted her to be part of my life. That's what call you real love.

A couple years after Esther died, there were two ladies that we had been friends with, and after while I messed around and fell in love with one of them. I was 86 when we got married and we had 11 good years together 'til the Lord took her home. We had a wonderful time together. We enjoyed one another so much. Now both of 'em are up there waitin' on me. I still love them both.

But what made your marriage work?
Well, we loved one another to start with. We never had any

disagreements. We just didn't argue. You're not always gonna be right and she's not always gonna be right, but don't argue about it. You've got to get along. We'd talk things over. You don't have to agree on everything, but you don't have to fuss and fight about it. People get so they can't talk to one another and then they have problems. As long as you can sit down and talk with one another, you can thresh things out. When you start fussin' and fightin' that's when you divide and have problems. Remember, the Bible says a husband and wife are supposed to become one. Don't let an argument divide you. That's my preachin' point.

Do you have any advice about growing old?
It doesn't seem possible that I'm 100 years old. I'm healthy, I'm not on any medication, I don't take any pills. My biggest problem is this brain up here, I can't remember anything. I have a hard time remembering everything. When you get to be 100, *you can't remember nothing!*

Do you ever think about dying?
I've thought about it, but I don't waste any time on it.

Does the thought of dying scare you?
No. It doesn't scare me one bit because I'm ready to go. I'm gonna die one day anyway. I don't know when that time's gonna be, whether its 100 years or 50, but I'm ready to go. I got one sister still living in Colorado and the rest of my family is all gone. Why I'm still here at 100 years old, I don't know. What good am I doing down here anyway? I guess He has a reason because I pray every day *"Lord Why am I still here? Come and take me home."*

So how do you prepare to meet the Lord?
You put yourself in His hands. You ask Jesus to come into your heart, into your life. You have to realize that you're a sinner; you were born a sinner, and you have to pray and ask Him to forgive you for your sins and ask Him to save you. He always has an open ear and He'll hear you and He'll come into your life and be part of your life. Everyone should be prepared, because you never know your time.

One last question, after living 100 years, what is your best advice on living a good life?

The Bible, read your Bible. I read my bible every morning and every night. It's my guide for how to live my life. It's God word. It's God speaking to me *through* His word. You won't understand it all, but it's the truth because it's the word of God. It's food for your soul. You've got to feed your soul just like your body. That's the spiritual side of life. You see, God is love. The presence of God in a person's life creates love, and when you love people, you can't love 'em and hate 'em at the same time. You love 'em and you get along with 'em. When you have Jesus in your heart, that kind of love penetrates into other people's hearts. The love of Jesus shines through you into other people's lives. And one more thing, pray every day. I pray every morning and every night. I pray for my family and friends, and I pray that whenever He's ready to come take me.... I am ready to go home.

B.J. Slothower went home on October 7, 2015. He was 103 years old.

Lillie Seager

Lillie Louise Phillips was born March 9, 1908 in Meadowvale, Ontario to English immigrant parents just eight months after they had settled in Canada. Growing up poor in a family of eight children, Lillie's childhood was difficult. *"We would walk along the railway tracks, picking up pieces of coal just to heat our home."* Lillie attended school through the sixth grade before dropping out to go to work and help care for the family and her sick mother. In 1927 she met Art Seager, whom she dated for eight years before marrying him at age 27. Together they had two children, Richard and Arthur Lyn. Life continued to be a struggle for the family, but through hard work and determination, they managed to survive. After losing a leg and a foot to diabetes, Art died in 1974 after 39 years of marriage. Lillie continued to work until retiring at age 69, but remained active in various civic groups and social activities.

You said life was hard?
Life *was* hard. When I was a little girl, we didn't even have enough blankets on our beds to keep us warm, so we'd cover up with newspapers. Sometimes we would go to the Stuart Street coke ovens and pick up coke in potato sacks to drag home. Coke is kind of like coal, we used it to heat our home. My brother Richard and

I had to walk two miles just to get water to drink, and in the winter, we would have to pull it home on a sleigh. One winter my brother made a harness for the dog and the dog would pull the sleigh home with the copper boiler pot full of water. But the toughest thing was when my brother Richard died. He was only 18. It broke my heart so much. When we laid the casket I said to myself, "If I ever get married and I have a little boy I'd name him after my brother," and I did. My son's name is Richard.

So how did you deal with all those struggles?
We just did what we had to do to survive. We didn't have any money, so whatever we needed, it was up to us. If we needed coal for heat, we walked the railway tracks until we found enough. If we needed water, we'd walk two miles to the well to get it. When my mother took sick, I quit school to take care of her and the family. After I got married, we worked as janitors looking after eight apartments and two stores, scrubbing stairways and hallways on my hands and knees. It was hard, we never really had much money, but we managed. We just did whatever we had to do to make it.

So how did you manage your money?
I never had any money *to* manage. My friends would say "Lillie, let's sit and have a cup of tea." I wouldn't spend ten cents for a cup of tea; I couldn't afford it. I didn't have a car; I walked everywhere I went. I wouldn't even take the bus because it cost money. All I ever got was minimum wage. I didn't save. I didn't have any money *to* save.

What would you tell your grandchildren about money?
First of all, get a good education. Education is very important. And you've got to be willing to work hard. I worked hard all my life. I started working at age 15 for .25 cents an hour and worked until I was 69. Today kids get far too much without having to work for it; it spoils them. When I was little, we had one toy and we would take off our stockings from our feet and hang them for Santa. We'd get an apple and an orange and Daddy would always put a lump of coal in our stockings. I still have it! I never threw it away! Children

today don't know what it means to work hard and go without things.

You said education is important. Why?

I was so cross-eyed that mother kept me home so I didn't start school 'til I was seven. Later when I was 13, mother took sick and I missed a lot of schoolin' to take care of her and keep house. When I was 15 I quit school to go to work and go to a technical school one day a week. They asked me what I wanted to take, hairdressing or typewriting. I said, "What's typewriting?" I would've loved to have taken typewriting but I didn't know what it meant! I was dumb.

My kids would come home with homework and I couldn't help them. I didn't know the answers myself. I never learned nothin' in school, but I had a hunger to learn and I taught myself everything I know. I joined the Knights of Pythias, and that is what educated me. When they initiated me, the President stood up and spoke, and she didn't even look at her book! She recited it all from memory. I said to myself, if I could do that I'd give a million dollars. From that day every office I took, I memorized every book I had. The Pythian Order educated me. Everything I know I owe them, and I still belong today. I wish I had gotten a good education. I think if I had gotten an education, I could have gone a lot further in life.

What's the most important thing in life?

Helping other people. I'd want somebody to help me if I couldn't do it myself. After I got married, I took care of my mother for 23 years. There were eight of us kids and none of the others would take her. They wouldn't even help with her expenses. My brother Jack took my sisters to court to try to make them pay towards her keep but they appealed and the judge said at that time girls don't have to pay to keep their mother, only boys had to pay. But none of them ever paid, not even Jack. I didn't have any money but I did the best I could. As we left court that day, Mom cried to think that out of eight kids none would take care of her. I said, "Mom I'll do it." I had to do it.

What is your best piece of advice about life?
Treat others like you'd like to be treated. People aren't born all the same. Some people are born thoughtful and other people are born thoughtless, but I always give them the benefit of the doubt. Many times, they were *so* wrong, but I just kept my mouth shut. I never fight with anybody. Nobody wins an argument.

Do you think about dying?
I don't mind if the Lord took me tomorrow. I just pray that the Lord takes me before the old devil gets me! I'm not afraid of dying. We all gotta die sometime. I hope the Lord can take me without there being any suffering, that's all. That's all I pray for.

The Lord took Lillie Seager on November 19, 2010 at the age of 101. She left behind 2 children, 4 grandchildren, 3 great-grandchildren, and countless others whose lives she had touched. Her mantra was, "Never sit when you can stand, stand when you can walk, and walk when you can dance." She was still dancing, albeit with her walker, just two months before she died. God bless you Lillie. You are missed.

"I never fight with anybody. Nobody wins an argument."

Lillie Seager, 101

Lawrence Mason

Lawrence Lowell Mason was born November 26, 1906 to a family of farmers in Arcadia, IT (Indian Territory) which would later become the state of Oklahoma. Growing up with seven brothers and sisters, Lawrence worked on the family farm and attended a small country school where he met his sweetheart and future wife, Cecille, who grew up just down the road. *"That first morning I got on that bus she said, 'That's the boy for me!'"* After completing the eighth grade, Lawrence dropped out of school and went into farming full time. *"We farmed corn, wheat, oats, cattle and hogs, so I didn't know anything but farming. My daddy left us 160 acres when he passed away, so we just kept farmin'."* Lawrence and Cecille married in 1928 and together they had one daughter. They continued working the family farm, and living in the same house in which Lawrence was born. On May 14, 2003 Cecille passed away after seventy-six years of marriage.

You've had a long life. What are you most thankful for?
I am thankful for Cecile mostly. She was a good girl. Her name was Cecile but I called her Shorty. She had a good family; they was nice folks, and I'm thankful for 76 years of wonderful marriage. We had

a good life together. She passed away about five years ago, but I'm thankful for my daughter and that she's still with me and that she takes care of me. And my health, I'm thankful for my health.

Is your health important?
Your health is everything! When I was seven years old I got sick with appendicitis. My dad had to go a mile and a half up the road to call the doctor 'cause we didn't have no telephone. The doctor came out in a horse and buggy and they loaded me up in the buggy on my mother's lap and we road into town. From there we took a streetcar to the city and they put me in the hospital. I was there 30 days. I thought I was going to die. Otherwise I haven't had any other major health problems.

I'm very fortunate considering my age, but getting older is a booger! Especially in my shape, I can't walk, I can't stand, I can't get around unless somebody helps me or I'm in this wheelchair. Getting older is good and bad. I can still get around though. I can get around the house and go outside if the weather is warm enough, even go to the farm and look around. I can't go down in the field too far though, I'm afraid I'll get stuck! If a wheel falls in a cow track, well I'm stuck, they'll just sit there and spin until somebody pulls me out! But I'm doing pretty good.

How did you manage your money?
I didn't spend my money. I did without. I never mortgaged any of my land. My first loan was for $75 for a set of harnesses for my mule team. I was around 22, and my brother had to go on the note with me. I worked all that summer helpin' people harvest their wheat to earn money to pay that off. I didn't like the idea of owing somebody money.

One year some land went up for sale next to our farm and Cecile wanted me to buy it, but I didn't think we had enough money. She was so mad! But I just wasn't comfortable going that far in debt. I guess it's okay to go into debt if it's something that'll make you money, but it's best to be conservative.

Is there anything you really regret?

The worst thing I ever done was....my wife had an aunt and we would go down there every month to be with her and take her places. We left one time to come home and, bless her heart, she was just standin' out there cryin'. Why did I do that? I didn't have to come home. All I had to do was call and say I wasn't coming home. I hated leaving her there crying. She passed away before we ever went back. I still feel terrible about that.

What did you learn from that?

You'd better do good things for people and tell them you love them while you've got the chance, 'cause someday, all your chances will run out.

What is your favorite memory?

Watching my grand-kids grow up. One thing I remember was back on the farm when I let the grand-kids drive my brand-new pickup. We had an oil well drilling in the field and they drove the truck right into a slush pit. They ramped that truck up, got it airborne and landed it right in that pit *(laughing)!* They had to climb out the windows and onto the hood. Cecile and I were in the house watching, just laughing! I had to get the tractor and pull it out.... never said a harsh word to those kids. They made my day *(laughing)!* When you get to be my age, all you've got left is your memories. Better make a lot of 'em.

What was your darkest moment in life?

When my wife passed away.... I had a cancer growth and I was at the hospital, they were removing it when my wife passed away. It was awful, I wasn't there when she died. I wish I could've been there. I should've been there, but what can I do? I miss her so much.

Another dark day was when my half-brother drowned. Me and some other boys were all at my father's house and we decided to go swimming in the pond. The youngest, Lloyd, wanted to come with us. He asked me if he could and I told him to ask his mother, and his mom said he could go. We went over to the pond and jumped

in the water and before we knew it, Lloyd was gone. We looked for him but couldn't find him. I was getting on my horse to ride home and tell my dad, when they said, "Here he is" .... so, we put him on my horse and rode back home. It was about two miles back to the house. My father and his mother put him in the buggy and they went up the road and called the doctor. He didn't survive; he was only twelve.

How did you get through all of that?
I don't know how I got through all that, it was pretty rough. You just take it day by day and keep moving forward, I guess.

What's the biggest lesson life has taught you?
Life is a pretty good struggle, but you've got to make the most of it. Don't leave any regrets. There's nothing I can think of that I wish I had done, that I didn't do.

What one piece of advice would you give me about life?
I think one of the keys to living a good life is to treat others like you'd like to be treated. I always did that. It may not happen overnight, but it'll come back to you.

On June 8, 2008, Lawrence Mason passed away in the same house, on the same farm on which he was born. He was 101 years old.

"When you get to be my age, all you've got left is your memories. Better make a lot of 'em."

Lawrence Mason, 101

Ernie and Dorothy Weeks

Frederick Ernest (Ernie) Weeks was born April 5, 1911 in the village of Bouctouche, New Brunswick, Canada. At age eight, he and his family moved to Ontario where Ernie graduated high school and attended the University of Toronto. However before graduating, he dropped out of college to enroll in St. Peter's Seminary, *"I wanted to become a priest."* But before completing seminary, he again dropped out to begin a career in aviation. Ernie earned his commercial pilot rating and began flying supplies and equipment to remote sites throughout northern Canada. In 1941, he married his first wife, Pauline; together they had one son, Vince. In 1942, Ernie enlisted in the Royal Canadian Air Force and was immediately assigned as an instructor pilot. Later, with years of experience as a bush pilot, he was assigned to fly survey crews throughout the Canadian arctic to map the area. *"We were afraid Stalin was going to try and invade from the north."* After leaving the military in 1945, Ernie returned to Ontario, working in the family's general store for $30 a week. He sold the store and retired in 1972 to travel world. In 1999, Pauline, his wife of 58 years,

passed away.

Dorothy Alton was born December 26, 1912 in Nelson Township, Ontario, the only child to a family of farmers. After graduating high school, she earned her teacher's certificate and began teaching school. In 1936 she married Vern Stetler and had three children. After 17 years of marriage, Vern *"Left me with three children for another woman."* After several years as a single mother, Dorothy met and married Don Scott for 34 years, until his death. Several years later, in 2000, she ran into an old school friend, Ernie Weeks. *"We went to high school together in the 1920's. He was my cousin's boyfriend. As soon as I laid eyes on him.... that was it."* Ernie and Dorothy were married in 2001, 80 years after first meeting. She was 88, he was 90.

Ernie, you have a total of 71 years of marriage, and Dorothy, you have 64. So, what's the secret?
Ernie: You have to know one another and know what each other needs and you do your best to meet those needs. You have to look out for one another and take care of each other, and balance each other out....and be willing to listen to the other person's point of view.

Dorothy: You just have to understand the person your living with, their needs and their wants and their ideas and all this kind of stuff. You have to live *with* people and understand them. You can't be selfish. You have to put the needs of other people above your own. With my first husband, we knew each other so well that we used to finish each other's sentences. We knew what each other was thinking.... at least I thought I did 'til I found out he was seeing somebody else.

What went wrong with your first marriage?
Dorothy: There was no falling apart. Everything seemed fine to me, then all at once, he was seeing somebody else. Nobody else knew about it.... or so I thought. Turns out *everybody knew about it*, but nobody told me. I knew her. I even went and talked to her about it because I had three kids to think about, what effect it would

have on them. I did my best to keep the family stable but it takes two to make a marriage. I cried like crazy when he left. Finally, I thought *"This is stupid. Stop the tears and get on with your life,"* and that's when I started to smoke. I didn't take to drinking.... but I did start smoking....and I haven't hardly cried since. Eventually you learn that sometimes things happen and there is nothing you can do about it, and I just learned to accept it and move on.

What is marriage like at 100 years old?
Ernie: It's the same I guess.... except we don't have the distractions that we used to have. I was working a lot then and wasn't home much, and now the children are grown and gone and you can focus on each other more.

Dorothy: Marriage is great. It's more stable now, but romantically it's different.

How?
Dorothy: Well.... you can take the *sex* out of it! *(laughing)* But other than that, we're still romantic. We still hold hands and kiss, and he always waits on me. I can't walk as fast as he can, so he waits on me and looks out for me. You learn to take it day by day. You live today and you look forward to what's going to happen tomorrow, because you don't know how many days you're going to get. So, we forget about what's happened in the past and we look forward to tomorrow and what we're going to do together.

Ernie: I guess you could say she's my soul mate.

Do you have any regrets?
Dorothy: I did a lot of stupid things that if I could do over again, I'd do differently. Five or six years after Vern left me, I met Don. We got along together, but I never really loved him.... but we got married, which was *stupid.* It lasted for 34 years, but in that time, I put up with a heck of a lot more than I did with Vern, but I don't want to talk about that part of my life anymore. I made my mistakes and I accept that, but I don't want to relive those mistakes anymore. I learned from them and I've moved on.

Ernie: I don't have any regrets. I never drank or smoked. I always thought it was a waste of time, so I didn't bother. Oh, I've made a few bad investments, but I don't think I'd change anything about my life.

You mentioned investments, how have you managed your finances over the years.
Ernie: Most of our money was invested in our business. My father owned a general store that evolved over the years into a hardware store. After I got out of the Air Force, I started off working in the store for $30 a week. Whatever we made, we put back into the business. When my dad retired, I took over. And finally, in 1972, we sold the business and I retired. After that, I took the money and invested it in some mutual funds. It's tougher now to retire than when I did. I was 62 years old when I retired, but that was 40 years ago now. Back then gas was .25 cents a gallon; *now it's over $5 a gallon.* If I'd known I was going to live this long, I would've saved a lot more money!

Dorothy: As far as finances go, I never had much. Growing up on the farm, we raised what we needed, so I never really thought about money until I was married, but then it was tight. I worked as a teacher which gave me health insurance and a pension, but when I quit, I cashed it in. That was a mistake. I should've left it alone and let it build and today I would be getting monthly retirement check. Most of my mistakes were related to money. So, Ernie saved my life, really. (*Ernie laughing) And she has extended mine!*

What is the greatest lesson life has taught you?
Dorothy: I've learned to take life as it's given to me. You have to take whatever's coming and you have to deal with it. We live here in this retirement center, but I want to be in my own home.... but I can't *be* in my own home. So now, I just have to deal with it...accept it and deal with it. (*Ernie:) It's difficult to face the fact that we're not independent anymore, but you can't do anything about it, so you might as well accept it.* There are a lot of things that happen in life that you just have to grit your teeth and think, "Oh well,"

and slough it off. I've just learned to accept it and moved on.

Ernie: Treat others like you'd like to be treated yourself. I guess that's about all you can say.

You mentioned the Golden Rule. Is faith important to you?
Ernie: Yes, I think it has gotten me through a lot of these tough times.

Dorothy: I think faith has gotten me through a lot of things that has happened in our lives. I just live on faith. We never know when our time is. Someday, something's going to happen to us.

Ernie: And exactly what that is or how that works, we don't know. We just have to have faith.

Dorothy: Yes, Have faith.

Ernie Weeks passed away December 18, 2013. Dorothy still lives in a retirement center in Canada.

Ernie and Dorothy Weeks at 102 and 100 years old.

Zela Wilson

Zela Marrietta Wilson was born January 10, 1906 to William and Elizabeth Wilson of Webb City, Missouri. As a child, she had a difficult life with an overbearing stepmother who treated her as a *"servant-girl"*. After graduating from the 8th grade, she continued caring for her family until moving out and going to work at age 24. Zela later met John Hampton; together they had one son but never married and separated soon after. Zela struggled as a single mother, often working multiple jobs to make ends meet. During World War II, she worked as *"Rosie the Riveter"* building B-29 bombers. *"Life has been tough, but I've managed all these years."*

Do you have any regrets?
I wish I had gotten more schoolin'. I wish I'd been able to go on to high school, but I didn't have that opportunity. I was raised by a stepmother from the time I was nine years old, and she didn't believe that girls needed an education to cook and clean, so I was just a personal maid to her. I had to get up each morning and cook breakfast for my parents and brothers and then clean everything up. By the time I'd get through with all that, it was time to leave for school. Sometimes, I didn't even have time to change, and my stepmother would make me go to school in my old *scrungy* work

clothes. It got so bad that I finally went to her and my dad and told them I wasn't going to school anymore. Well, that tickled them to death. They didn't care whether I went to school or not. I think education is important, but I think life has a way of educating you too. So anyway, I've lived through it. There's a lot of other things that I wished I had done different, but I can't do anything about that now so why sit around and mope about it.

You said life has been tough. How did you manage?
Well you just do the best you can and make the best of what you got to do with. That's all I can say. You just do the best you can with what you've got, and learn from your mistakes. Just keep going; keep pluggin' along. I just try to take each day as it comes and make the most of it, that's it. That's all I can expect.

As a single mother, what advice do you have about parenting?
I wanted Jim *(her son)* to have a better life than I did, so I thought it was important that he learned about money. I never had too much problems with money 'cause I never had that much money to manage. I tried to save some, but it's awful hard sometimes when you're living on a fixed income and you have to try to make it go as far as it'll go. I always lived on a budget. If I had $1.00, I had to learn to make it stretch to $1.50 in value. I had to make every penny count, but I've managed all these years. I taught my son Jim to pay his own way since he was just a kid. Even before he was old enough to hold a real job, I hired him to sack soap at the laundromat where I worked. He's always contributed what he was making to the household budget. We always had food, but we didn't buy steak. I remember one time we were at the store and this man bought some steaks and Jim said, "Mama, what's that?" He didn't even know what a steak was! It don't hurt a child to learn to work and contribute towards the family. Kids need to learn to appreciate money.

What advice do you have about growing older?
That just comes on so gradually that you just don't think about it. It just happens. There's nothing you can do about it. You just take it as it comes along. I never even dyed my hair. I figured when it

started gettin' gray that I was just old enough for it to be gray. I never tried to be younger than what I am. I just try to live a good clean life. I never did smoke. I just never cared anything for it. I never did drink.... a lot. I never was a drunkard, but I do like a can of beer every now and then. I can't deny that *(laughing)*!

Does growing old make you wiser?
I don't know. Sometimes I think I'm getting' dumber *(laughing)*! When you get past 100 you don't have brains enough to remember what you did at 30! I don't know that I've learned very much, but I always tried to learn from my mistakes.

What is the biggest lesson life had taught you?
I try to look for the best in every circumstance and I try to treat other people like I would like them to treat me. Don't hold a resentment or hard feelings toward others. If someone does something that don't like, I just try to ignore it and look beyond what they did or said. You need to forgive people, even when you don't feel like it. If somebody says something critical of you, I think it's better to just forget it than to make something out of it and hold a grudge. Life's too short to hold grudges; maybe that's why I've lived so long. Resentment and bitterness will eat you alive, and I just don't have any of that. Life's just too short for all that nonsense.

Zela Marrietta Wilson died December 22, 2008 just three weeks before her 103rd birthday. She left behind 1 son, 2 granddaughters, and 3 great-grandchildren.

Richard A. Overton

Richard Arvine Overton was born on May 11, 1906 to Gentry and Elizabeth Overton on a small farm in rural Bastrop County, Texas. As a child, Richard attended school through the eleventh grade and worked the farm with his ten brothers and sisters to help feed the family. *"We picked cotton for a white fellow. I did all kinds of work: cotton picking, raised cattle and sheep, pulling corn, shucking hay.... I did all that."* At age 18 Richard married Novella Prince, but separated after eight years. His second wife, Wilma, died of cancer after 49 years of marriage. He never had any children. In 1942, Richard joined the army serving as a Sargent with the all black 1887th Engineer Aviation Battalion throughout the South Pacific including Pearl Harbor, Palau, Iwo Jima, Okinawa and Guam. *"I saw plenty of people get shot, but I never got a scratch."* After leaving the military in 1945, Richard worked for the Texas Department of Treasury until retiring. As the oldest surviving World War II veteran, he has met and been honored by Texas

Governors Rick Perry and Greg Abbott, U.S. Senators John Cornyn and Ted Cruz, and President Barack Obama. *"Who ever thought I'd be that important?"*

Tell me about your time in the Army.
I was in the 1887th Aviation Engineer Battalion and did base security. I went to Pearl Harbor; when I got there the ships were still smoking from the Japanese attack. Then when I left Pearl Harbor, I went from island to island. I went to Iwo Jima, Okinawa, Guam, Palau.... shoot yeah, I saw action. You and I might be sitting here talking like this and a bullet's liable to hit right here in between us, and under you and over there.... and two men would've been killed standing right over there *(motioning with his hand)*. All my friends, a bunch of 'em got killed, and I didn't get a scratch on me. Yeah, I saw some bad stuff.

Like them trees over there *(pointing across the street)*, you couldn't go into them trees at all because there's liable to be 10 Japs in that tree line. So, we had three airplanes fly over and drop bombs. If that didn't do it we'd get three more, and open that whole space up, 300 yards so you could see everything. Then we would go through it. That's when you'd have hell 'cause some of 'em are laying in holes. But you've got to take that tree line. You've got to go through there shootin' and you don't know where they're at. You might see some over yonder and you look, and some 'em might be behind you. Sometimes we'd throw a grenade and kill one or two. Sometimes they might throw it back at you and you don't have time to shoot 'em, you ain't even got time to turn around; just throw it back at them. That's where the danger's at, but it was a lot of fun looking back.... a lot of fun.

Were you ever scared?
What does it matter? If it was my time to go, I'm going. If it ain't your time, God ain't gonna let you go. When I was in the army and people were shootin' at me, and bullets were flying all over the place.... it wasn't my time! That's the reason I didn't get hit! I went through all that and I didn't get a scratch on me. If it ain't your time to go....

So, you believe in God?
I got to! I've always believed in God. That's the One that brought you here. God's taken care of me my whole life. Man wasn't takin' care of me.... God was! Man ain't helping you, that's God helping you.

So, you think God helped you through all of that?
Man didn't.... he was the one that sent me out there! *(laughs)* Man was the one shootin' at me! Yeah, I believe in God, He's taken care of me for 109 years. He ain't let me down yet!

Having gone through the war and being 109 years old, do you ever think about dying?
I don't think about dying.... there's nothing you can do about it. When you go to bed at night, you never know whether you're gonna get up or not. It don't matter; just go on and go to sleep. I'll die when my time comes, and I'll be happy as a field lark *(laughs)*. I'm not worried about it. I ain't scared. You don't know when your gonna die, and you won't know it when it happens anyway. That's the reason I say don't worry about it. You're crazy if you worry about it.

What do you think happens to us after we die?
I don't know, I ain't made it that far yet. *(laughing)*

Do you have any regrets?
There's a lot of things in my mind but I never let 'em worry me. Lots of times I'd say, "Oh I should've done this or I should've done that," but I don't let that worry me. It don't matter anyway. Just think of something else and get on with your life. I don't worry about nothing. Nothing ever hurts me. I'm happy every time I get up in the morning and I'm happy when I go to bed.

What's the key to happiness?
I never let nothing worry me. If you let things worry you, you'll never get nowhere. When worry comes on you again and again, that the devil workin' on you.... tryin' to get you. You've got to

watch the devil. God's got to change you. Get on your knees and ask God "Can you turn me around?"

Were you ever mistreated because of the color of your skin?
You know, some people will hate you, but you don't hate everybody. Some people used to hate blacks.... some of 'em still that way. That's foolish, but I don't care. That don't bother me. I ain't scared of 'em. I ain't worried about 'em. That's their business. They don't want to treat you good, that's their bad luck. Treat 'em good anyway. I had people that wouldn't speak to me, some won't speak to you now! But that ain't your troubles, that's them. They don't want to accept it, that's their problem. Always treat people right. Sometimes they won't treat you right back... treat 'em right anyway. That's the Golden Rule. I don't care who it is, treat 'em all good.

How do you want to be remembered?
I'm gonna leave it to them. Let 'em make up their own minds. After you're dead and gone you ain't worried about it, you're going where ever you're going, hell or heaven or where ever you're supposed to go. I ain't worried about it. I ain't even worried about what people think of me now!

What is the most important thing in life?
Just keep a livin'. That's the best thing you can do, keep a livin'. Life is a good thing. It's a good thing to do. It's good. You can't find nothing any better than life. Tell me what you can find better than life?

I haven't found it.
You ain't gonna find it! Just keep livin'. Let God kill you. He brought you here, let Him take you away. You didn't know when you was comin', you ain't gonna know when you're goin'. I can't do nothing about it. Just keep goin'; that's life. God's the One that put you here. Some people say, "I wish I could live that long." Well, ask God. He might give it to you but you might have to ask Him. You have to ask things of Him, He's your friend. You ask God, will He take care of you; He's already doing it! He's taken care of me!

I've had a good life. It's just as sweet as it can be. You've got to have a happy life.

At the time of this interview, Mr. Overton is 109 years old, still in good health and still living in his own home that he bought when he returned from the war in 1945. He still does his own yard work, drives and is known for helping out people in need. As the oldest surviving U.S. World War II veteran, he's become somewhat of a celebrity with several videos posted online and his own Wikipedia page.

On May 11, 2018, at age 112, Mr. Overton also became the oldest living man in America. He celebrated on his front porch with his friends, neighbors and a few cigars. You can learn more about Richard Overton at the links below. I am honored to have known him. Thank you, Mr. Overton, for your wisdom and your service.

http://en.wikipedia.org/wiki/Richard_Arvine_Overton
https://youtu.be/aW4V6V-qnrY
https://youtu.be/ubrvCLL9X2E

What do you think happens after you die?

"I don't know;
I ain't made it that far yet!"

Richard Overton, 109

Paul Roden with Richard A. Overton, 109

Lola Bird

Lola Hurley was born to Caleb and Ada Hurley on September 20, 1907. Growing up, she attended a small, one room, country school together with her 16 brothers and sisters. Each day after school, they all pitched in to work chores on the family farm. *"We worked every day.... we had to.... even the little ones. That's how we ate.... and we had a lot of mouths to feed!"* After completing the eighth grade, Lola dropped out of school and continued working on the farm until meeting and marrying Orlie Bird in 1925. Like most families in those days, Lola and Orlie started their own farm and family, having three daughters together. Later, Orlie found work in Dallas, and moved the family to the big city. *"We were so excited! It was the first time we ever had electricity or running water. We thought we were rich!"* Following an injury and a stroke, Orlie died in 1989 after 64 years of marriage. A few years later, Lola would lose two of her three daughters.

With 16 brothers and sisters, and three kids of your own; do you have any advice on raising children?
Set them straight early. By that I mean lay down the rules early, while they're young, and let them know what you expect of them. Then hold them to it. If they start to wander off course a little, it's

your job to put 'em back in line. Parents today don't discipline their kids. Most kids don't know what discipline is. Nowadays parents just tell their kids to go sit down and think about what they've done wrong. They just sit there thinking about how they just got away with something. If my kids got out of line, I told them once, "You'd better straighten up," and if they didn't, I'd give em' a whipping. That straightened them up! Work is something else. I think hard work is good for children. All us kids worked on the farm. Every day after school there was work to be done, and we did it. We had to work so we could all eat. Ain't nothing free in this world; someone's got to work for everything you get. Children need to learn that lesson; the earlier the better. Kids now days are so spoiled; they don't have any idea what real work is. Everything I've ever had, I had to work for, but I've managed alright. Work is good for you. We worked hard.... but we played hard too (laughing).

Do you have any regrets?
Oh, I have regrets. For one, I wished I had gotten a better education. I only went to school through the eighth grade, but that's as far as our little country school went. If I wanted more schoolin', I would've had to go to a different town, but we didn't have a car, so I had no way of goin'. I think if I'd had a better education I wouldn't have had to work as hard and I probably could've gone farther in life. I made sure my daughters had the opportunity to get a good education, you need it in today's world. It's much more important now than it was been then.

You've had a lot of hard times in your life. How did you get through them?
Hard work. I never knew anything else. We lived through the depression and life was hard. Some people didn't have food or jobs, or even a place to live. We lived on a farm and managed to get by, but it was hard work! Some folks weren't so lucky. Life is hard, and the only way to get through is to work hard. Sometimes it's easy, other times not, but it doesn't really matter. All you can do is work hard to do the best you can.

How did you get through the death of your husband and daughters?

What other choice is there? There's nothing you can do about it. It wasn't easy. I didn't know what to do. I didn't know how I would make it through. You just have to take it one day at a time. You either do what you have to do, or you don't make it; it's that simple. You just learn to deal with it. Nobody ever said life was fair.

What is the most important lesson you've learned about life?

Be honest and work hard. Honesty is everything. You've got to be honest with people. Lying just leads to trouble, then nobody trusts you or wants to be around you. People respect someone who's honest; they trust them. Would you trust someone who's always lying to you? And you've got to work hard. Kids now days don't know what hard work is. Hard work never hurt nobody. I've worked hard all my life. I never knew anything different. Everything I've ever had, I worked for. We never got any handouts. We worked for everything we got. Life was hard.... but we worked hard and here I am. I've done alright.

One thing I have learned from these people is that hard work goes a long way. Like Lola, most of these people came from nothing. Many grew up on family farms growing their own food in order to survive. They learned the value of hard work at an early age, because literally, if you didn't work, you didn't eat. Most of us have to work for a living, but few of us have ever had to work to live. Anything that they wanted or needed, they had to work for. They learned early that nothing ever comes free; someone has to work for it. Too many people today have an entitlement mentality; that someone should give us things for free because we deserve it. No one ever gave Lola anything for free. She had to work for everything she ever got. She came from poverty and through hard work, has been able to support herself and her family for over 100 years. Maybe that is the secret to her long life. Maybe that is the lesson we all need to learn.

"Ain't nothing free in this world; someone's got to work for everything you get."

Lola Bird, 104

Allen Cox

Allen Cox was born December 14, 1905 in Whitefield, Indian Territory, which would later become the state of Oklahoma. He and his wife Monnie shared 72 years of marriage until her death in 1998. Together, they had two sons. Early in his career, he worked as a schoolteacher in a one-room schoolhouse teaching grades one through eight, and earning $75 per month. *"I taught everything, you name it!"* For 20 years, he attended college for eight weeks each summer to eventually earn both his Bachelor's degree, and his Master's degree. He continued working as a schoolteacher and principal for forty years until retiring in 1966.

You and Monnie were married for 72 years. What's the secret?
I think the secret to marriage is to get along with each other. We always got along. We never had any big problems. We always handled those before they got to be big problems. You've got to work things out. You can't be selfish and always have your way. How would you feel if you never got your way? You have to be willing to compromise. Another thing is to find things to do together. That's why we got married, because we liked being together. We liked to travel, so we did that a lot. Find things you both like to do and do them together. That's what marriage is about, being together.

Do you have any regrets?

One thing I would do different is I would have gotten my education faster. It took me 16 years to get my Bachelor's degree. I went to college for eight weeks each summer and tried to complete eight or ten hours each time. It took a long time, but I'm glad I did it. Then I went back and got my Master's and that took another three or four years. I wish I had done it faster. It was important to me. That's why I spent so much time getting it. I think it was worth it. Yeah, I'd do it all over again, only faster.

You said you'd lived through some hard times, how did you get through that?

During the Great Depression times got real tough. It was tough everywhere. Lots of people didn't have jobs. I was lucky 'cause I was a schoolteacher; I had a job. Sometimes we would get our paychecks but we couldn't cash it. The county would say that they didn't have the money. So, we would have to hold it and wait for them to get the money; sometimes that took a while. Sometimes the stores would let us buy food and they would take the county's check in exchange as barter. It was tough. I would take on extra jobs when I needed to… when I could. You just do what you have to. What other choice do you have.

After 100 years of living, what's your best piece of advice?

My best advice is to never quit. Always keep trying. Always keep fighting; never give up. You haven't lost as long as you're still fighting, and if you quit fighting, you've already lost. Never give up. And one more thing, always give it your best.

How can I make my life count for something?

I think it's important to help other people. People helped me when I needed it. I think you need to help others when they need it. That's how it works. Someone has probably helped you out a time or two, now it's your turn. Make someone's life a little better, a little easier. It doesn't have to be money, it might be just encouraging someone, or taking time to listen when they need a

friend. We all need encouragement now and then. I always tried to encourage my students. You never know when someone's on the verge of giving up. You just may be the person that inspires them to keep going. There's lots of people out there hurting. It's a good feeling to know you've helped someone, to have made a difference in someone's life. That's what we're here for.

Why do you think you've lived so long?
You know, sometimes I wonder why I'm still here. Why has God let me live so long? What am I supposed to be doing? I believe He has a purpose for keeping me here, I just don't know what it is. I guess He'll take me when I'm done with whatever it is I'm supposed to be doing. I believe in God and I believe there's a heaven. I think about that a lot. It seems like we spend all our life here hoping to get there, but you've got to do more than hope. If there's no heaven, what is there to hope for? Nothing. And what is life if you don't have hope? But hope alone isn't enough. You've got to live right, here; and believe, if you're ever going to make it up there.

On October 18, 2009 Allen Cox passed away at age 103.

"If there's no heaven, what is there to hope for? Nothing. And what is life if you don't have hope?"

Allen Cox, 102

Doris Mary King

Doris Mary Pocock was born June 5, 1907 to Thomas and Ellen Pocock of London, England. As a little girl, Doris grew up in an average, working class neighborhood, attending school through age 14. Upon graduating high school, she earned her teaching certificate. *"Most children left school at age 14. I was the only one on my street to go to high school."* *(stated in a proper English accent.)* After high school, she went to work for the H. J. Heinze Company as a payroll clerk. At age 25 she quit the Heinze Company and married George King; together they settled in northwest London had two sons, Richard and Eric. After 20 years of marriage, George and Doris divorced, but life was hard as a single woman and mother. *"I didn't have and job, and no home either. A very dear friend took me in for a while."* She went back to work for Heinz for a time and later worked as a receptionist, clerk, housekeeper, cook and cake decorator. *I did all sorts of work!"* In 1966, she moved to Washington DC, working as a secretary for a psychoanalyst. After retiring in 1980, Doris continued to serve others by reading to the blind, volunteering with AARP, and as a Pink Lady at the local hospital for over twenty years. As a trained vocalist, she sang with the Methodist Church choir well into her 100's. *"I had to give up singing when I couldn't see the music anymore."*

What was it like growing up in England?
I can remember the German bombing raids in World War I. The planes and the guns going off and the search lights filled the sky. It was so noisy! London was hit of course, but we didn't actually have any bombs hit in northwest London where I was living, so it wasn't particularly dangerous for us, but come World War II, it was a different picture altogether. I was there during the German blitz and the house right behind us took a direct hit. I don't know if there were any people in there or not, but it was demolished completely. It was a very scary time.

Did your husband serve in the military?
Yes, but I divorced my husband after 20 years.

May I ask why?
Yes, one day he brought a woman home to the house with her little boy and he says, *"They're here to stay, you do what you like about it."* Well the house wasn't big enough for all of us and why would I stay with my husband when he's got another woman there? I had married for better or worse and I was prepared for whatever came along, but I thought there's no way I can live like this. A couple of ministers suggested we get a separation, but I thought to myself, *"What's the point of that? Your neither one thing nor the other, your both married and not married."* I thought, that doesn't seem right. So, I read some in *The Grail Message*; it told me you shouldn't stay with somebody that you can't trust. You shouldn't stay with somebody if there isn't real true love there, 'cause it's only the love that lives. If you don't love them, it's no good and it's wrong. So, I thought that's giving me the permission to divorce him.... so, I did.

That must have been a difficult decision.
You see, really and truly I had no choice because he had this woman there. He was living with this woman in my home! I didn't have and job.... and no home either! A very dear friend took me in for a while. I went back to work for Heinz for a time. Then I went to work for Sir Irving and Lady Albery as a cook. I liked cooking. He was an Earl and they were quite wealthy. Then I went to work as a

receptionist and housekeeper for a doctor in north London. I did all sorts of work!

What did you learn from that?
Well, I think when people are looking for a partner for marriage, the one thing that you must do is keep communication going. You've got to be friends before you can be husband and wife. You've got to keep communicating with them, and if true love isn't there, you shouldn't stay with them.

How did you deal with all of that?
One thing the good Lord gives us is a sense of humor. You can get over many styles with a sense of humor. A sense of humor helps a lot. If you can laugh about something, you'll be okay.

You mentioned the Lord, tell me about Him.
God? Well, He's the Creator, and He created everything that exists. And He loves us, and of course Jesus....He let the people murder Him for our sake. So, Jesus Christ is very, very, very special. Jesus Christ told us what we should do and how we should live and if we live according to what Jesus taught us, then eventually we hope to reach our heavenly home which is the spiritual region. But of course, we've got this world to go through first, and it depends on how we behave, where we finally land. But we hope to get to heaven or paradise, or whatever you call it.

So, you believe in heaven?
Of course. Yes, the spiritual sphere, where we first started.

Do you think you'll make it to heaven?
Well I'm doing my best to get there! It's not for me to say is it? Not at all. You have to understand what you believe in, because if you don't understand it, then you can't work it. You've got to believe what faith you have. I've tried to do the best I can. I don't know exactly what I'm supposed to be here for but there must be a reason. There's surely a reason.

Do you think God has directed your life?
I've had a lot of help. I've really had a lot of help, especially here. I think the Lord wanted me in America. I don't know why He wanted me here, and I don't know how long I'm going to be here either! That's in the Lord's hands and I've nothing to do with it. I have a lot to be thankful for.

Probably because you've helped so many other people. I hope that I have. I hope that I have because that's what I want is to have helped other people. And whether I have or not is not for me to say. How far I have complimented the Lord's will, I don't know. I've done a lot of volunteer work in my life. Reading for the blind and I was a hospital pink lady for over twenty years. I was in a choir but unfortunately, I had to give that up. During the war I had the opportunity of getting four years of professional voice training. I thought at one time that I would become a professional singer, but that didn't work out. That road came to a stop.

What's it like to be 106?
There's a lot of things that I used to do that I can't do now. I can't see properly at all; I can't hear very well, and my hands don't work; they're painful to move. But put all that aside; in lots of ways I've been very, very fortunate. I haven't got a lot of money but I have enough to buy the things I need to buy. My son looks after what I need. He's been very good to me.

Do you ever think about death?
I was still living in England when my father died. He was sick and living at home and I remember something inside me saying, *"Tell you father to let go. Your mother is holding him back."* I realized he depended on her a lot at the end, and he was ready to go, but he was holding back. I felt that I had to say to him *"Dad, it's okay to let go. Let go,"* and he died the next day. Now that's a gift that I felt was given to me. And with my mother, I was still in England when my mother died. She had a sister living with her and looking after her and then she had a second stroke and I went back to England to help nurse her in her last illness and I was there for a couple of years.

So, after 106 years, do you have any regrets in life?
Yes, I do. When my first child was born, they induced and delivered him early. He weighed about five pounds, and oh did he cry! And he cried and he cried and it got so much on my nerves. I couldn't stop him crying, he was so very, very sick, and it seems to me that I didn't quite treat him that well. He was a gift and I wish that I'd had more patience with him.

That was Richard?
Yes, he still lives in England.

If you had your whole life to live over again, what would you do different?
I don't know. I really don't know.

What is the most important thing in life?
Prayer. Keeping in touch with the Lord. You do it with prayer.

Why? Because if you keep in touch with the Lord, He'll send you the help you need. After all, look at all the help I've had.

Do you think the Lord sent you all that help? Well who else? He made us...... didn't he?

Yes ma'am.
And he made the world a beautiful place, and man has messed it up quite a bit, and one day we'll probably have to pay for it. Whatever you do has a consequence. Whether in thought or deed or word.... whatever you do has a consequence. If it's kind, it's kind. If it's not kind, it's not kind. And one day we may have to face those consequences too. But even then, I think we'll get help.

What is the best piece of advice you could someone?
You've got to keep in touch with the Lord. And this is how I look at prayer. The Lord sometimes says yes and your prayer is answered. Sometimes it's no, but if the Lord says no, then it's because that isn't good for you. Then there's the one that says wait.

Sometimes you have to wait. The Lord's timing isn't the same as ours. So sometimes you have to wait. Sometimes it's very hard to wait. Sometimes you want something in a certain way, but the Lord knows a better way, and will reveal it to you. Sometimes the Lords knows a better way than the way you want it.

On August 23, 2014, Doris King left for heaven at the age of 107. As her obituary states, "She saw the end of the Victorian Era and the beginning of the Space Age, the introduction of electricity and automobiles, and the invention of the telephone, television, rocket ships, and computers." Though she didn't state it, she seemed to view life as a grand adventure with many places to see and many things to do. At age seventy she learned to drive. At age fifty, she recorded an album and continued to sing until she was 107. She has been the subject of numerous articles and interviews. A YouTube video of one of her interviews is located at the link below. Watch it and smile. God bless you Doris, you sure blessed me.

https://youtu.be/busMq6qxAgM
http://dc.library.okstate.edu/cdm/ref/collection/hundred/id/51

"One thing the good Lord gives us is a sense of humor.... If you can laugh about something, you'll be okay."

Doris King, 106

Edgar Newby

Edgar "Ed" Lee Newby was born July 2, 1914 to Rewel and Effie Newby of Waurika Oklahoma. Like most children of that period, Edgar worked the family farm along with his three brothers and three sisters in order to feed the family. He also attended school through the eighth grade, which was as far as most country schools went in that day and age. After finishing school, Ed continued to work on the farm. *"You couldn't get a job; it was during the Depression years."* At age 19, he decided to go into the ministry for the Assemblies of God church. On September 12, 1934 Ed married Margaret Edwards of Greenville, Texas. She was 17, he was 20. Together they had two sons, Bill and Edgar Jr. Ed served as the pastor of First Assembly of God in Roswell, New Mexico from 1956 until 1981. He also pastored churches in Seminole and Enid Oklahoma, Gallup New Mexico, and Levelland and Alvord Texas until finally retiring in 1981. In 2000, Margaret passed away after 66 years of marriage. *"She was my sweetheart."*

How did you make it through the Depression era?
Any way you could really. I thought I was going to be a mortician, but I didn't like that. I went home and told my dad, *"Well, I quit*

my job." He said, *"What are you gonna do then?"* I didn't have the slightest idea. My dad said, *"If I was you I'd spend a lot of time prayin'. Just talk to the Lord about it."* So that's what I did. One night while I was praying, I was alone, and it was really clear to me. You're gonna be a minister. I said, *"Whoa, that'd put me in front of a lot of people."* I was a timid sort of a person, but the thought wouldn't leave. That same night three guys came lookin' for me and said, *"We want you to speak at a revival."* When we got out to where the revival was gonna be, it was in the fork in a road. I was really disappointed. They had cleared the place and sawed a bunch of logs for people to sit on. There were Coca Cola bottles with kerosene and a wick in 'em about every ten feet; that was the lighting system. I thought, *"I'll speak tonight but this is the whole shebang for me."* I don't have the slightest idea what I spoke on, but there were three or four guys converted that night. I thought, *"Well maybe I can come back."* We did that for three weeks and we had 65 conversions. I never did stop after that. I was nineteen.

Tell me about your marriage.
I got married to Margaret when I was 20. She was everything that a man would dream about in a wife. She was wonderful. We were together for more than 60 years until she died. She had dementia; I was taking care of her. She was the greatest person I ever knew. She was absolutely perfect with me. She was a wonderful mother to our two boys. She was beautiful and she was good. It's funny, as a pastor I would always advise people that lost a companion *"don't sit around and feel sorry for yourself. Find someone that you enjoy and move forward with your life."* I couldn't do it. The very thing I had advised a bunch of people to do, I couldn't do it. I've never seen anybody in my life like she was. She was ideal. I couldn't have had a better wife.

Why weren't you able to find someone else and move forward?
She was my one and only and I just couldn't see myself being with anyone else. She was perfect, and I didn't want to place somebody in a position of trying to live up to what this woman was.

You were married over 60 years, what's the secret?
We were sweethearts. We looked out for each other. I took care of her and she took care of me. There wasn't one time that I needed her that she wasn't available. She was always there for me.

How did you get through her death?
It was terrible, but it didn't destroy me. There were times I thought it would, but I made it through it.

Can you look back at your life and see God's hand on you?
Yes. I believe everything is by design, even in the hard times. I made it through the hard times better than I thought I could. I have been a little boy in God's hands from the beginning. When I became a Christian and went into the ministry I was led all the time. I didn't do things until I felt a strong feeling that God was leading me. I lived my whole life like that.

If you could go back, is there anything in your life you'd change?
Yeah, I'd spend more time with Margaret. I would treasure those moments more. I wouldn't take things for granted.... you know.... the little things like holding hands and kissing her cheek. If I could go back I would do more of those things.... they're priceless now.

What are you most thankful for?
I'm thankful I became a Christian. My whole life has been directed by the Lord. He's guided me and taken care of me the whole time. I can't imagine what my life would be without Him.

You're 100 years old. Do you ever think about dying?
You know you're not gonna live forever. I know I'm gonna die.... *unless the Lord comes tomorrow!*
I'm not afraid of dying. I've had a very wonderful relationship with the Lord. I was 17 when I became a Christian. I'm not afraid. I know He'll take care of me; He always has. There's not one person that could have arranged my life better than the Lord.

If you could give me one piece of advice what would it be?
I would advise you like I did my boys; learn everything you can about the Lord and embrace Him because He is the whole program. I look back at my life and I was a nothing, I was nobody and every good thing that happened to me in my life, the Lord has done it. Anything that was of any importance to me in my life, I prayed about it. and I committed it to the Lord. I let Him be the head man. It's not difficult to be a Christian. The Lord knows everything and when He's running the controls, it'll be good. It's gotta be good because He loves you. The hard part is letting go and letting Him take over. I don't give myself any credit for anything. I know I'm mud, but I've had the most wonderful life and I take it right back to that night when I was down on my knees talking to Him. He did it. I didn't do anything.... He did it *all.*

Talking with Ed was more of a visit than an interview. He spent over two hours telling me stories about hunting and fishing, and about his horses and mules. It was fun to see the way his eyes would light up as he relived so many memories of his past. We looked at old pictures and talked a lot about his Margaret. It is obvious that he is still very much in love with her, even 15 years after her death. They say that love is eternal. I guess Ed and Margaret Newby are proof of that.

Edgar Lee Newby was reunited with Margaret on March 9, 2015 at the age of 100. He left behind two sons, two grandchildren, six great-grandchildren, and two siblings. Thank you, Ed, for sharing your life and your wisdom with me, and give Margaret my best.

If you could go back, is there anything in your life you'd change?

"I wouldn't take things for granted.... you know.... the little things, like holding hands and kissing her cheek. If I could go back I would do more of those things.... they're priceless now."

Edgar Newby, 100

Vetus VanDerWiele

Vetus Angeline Hovey was born Feb 9, 1908 to Clement and Mary Hovey of Whitechurch, Kansas. Her parents later divorced while she was still very young leaving her, and her three sisters to be raised by her grandmother and uncle, John. After graduating high school, Vetus met and married James (Jim) VanDerWiele in 1928 and had two children, James Milton and Carol. Vetus worked at the Kansas City Star newspaper, quitting to raise her children, then going back to work when they entered school. She continued working various jobs throughout her life until finally retiring in 1978. In August of 1982, Jim suffered a heart attack and died after 54 years of marriage. After his death, Vetus spent her retirement years volunteering at the local hospital and spending time with her two children, three grandchildren, ten great-grandchildren and eight great-great-grandchildren. *"I taught them all how to sew and knit."*

Tell me about your husband.
I was 20 when I married Jim. He worked for Elko Company and was a pioneer in the photo finishing industry. He worked with the

process of developing film and printing pictures back when Eastman Kodak came out with their cameras and film processing. He died in 1982 of heart attack.

1928 to 1982, so you were married 54 years. What's the secret?
We had a good marriage. You have to learn to give and take. You can't always have it your way. Don't be selfish. Nobody wants to be around someone who's selfish all the time. You have to learn that it's not all about you. And you have to learn to forgive mistakes, 'cause you're both going to make a lot of 'em.

What about raising good kids?
My kids grew up well in spite of me.... not because of me! You have to love them and discipline them. Teach them the rules and teach them there will be consequences if they break the rules.

What were the consequences?
I'd smack 'em with a rolled-up newspaper! *(laughing)* You know, if they got in trouble at school, I'd talk to them. Kids are going to misbehave every now and then, but they've got to learn that if you break the rules, there will be consequences. It's better for them to learn that lesson while they're young rather than later on. Later on, the consequences may be a lot bigger.

Do you think education is important?
Education is very important. Back in my day most people didn't get more than an eighth-grade education, but I did well in school. I was president of my senior class and belonged to the National Honor Society. I think getting through high school helped me get a better job. After high school, I worked at the Kansas City newspaper in the circulation department, and then the advertising department. The more education you can get, the better job you can get, and the better you can live and provide for your family. Education is a must.

Did Jim have a good education?
No, he didn't have that advantage. He came from a big family, they went through the eighth grade and that was as good of an education

as they got. But he was self-motivated and he educated himself in the business world.

How did you two manage your money?
We spent it! *(laughing)* We tried to save some but weren't real good at it! We had a little savings and had a broker that invested some for us, but we went through the Depression years so we had very little. We couldn't save much but we managed to get by.

Did that teach you any lessons?
Probably not as much as it should have!

You're 106. Most people don't prepare for 40 years of retirement. Were you able to prepare?
Well, I thought I had plenty of money to see me through my life, but I lived too long! That's true. I lived too long and my money didn't last as long as I thought it would. I had a good savings and I thought it was plenty, but it wasn't.

What would you do differently if you could go back?
I would probably save more. I'd prepare better for retirement. Save more and invest more. It costs a lot of money to grow old.

What's it like to be over 100 years old?
I'm content. I've grown more patient. My health is real good. I take vitamins, and I haven't had any major health issues. I eat well, don't smoke, and I don't drink.... much!

Tell me about your parents. Did they live to an old age?
My father was Alfred Clement. He died when he was 75. My mother's name was Mary Angeline, I don't remember how old my mother was when she passed.

Why do you think you've lived so long?
I'm an optimist, I always think things will go well. I go to church every Sunday, even now. My faith is very important to me. I joined the Methodist church when I was 10 years old and I got baptized. I've been a Christian most of my life. I haven't always succeeded. I

kind of fell short for a few years and didn't participate much, and then I came back. I wasn't happy with my life back then, so I got back into church.

Why weren't you happy with your life?
Well, I wasn't satisfied with my life where I was going, and I wanted to get back to my faith. I had just drifted away. Getting back to church made me realize what I didn't have and what I needed. I needed God in my life, so my husband and I joined the church.

Can you look back and see how God directed your life?
Oh Yes, I can. There have been times when God took care of me when I couldn't even take care of myself.

You've had some hard times in your life. What's the hardest thing you've dealt with?
My husband's death. He had a heart attack. He lived a week, but I was thankful he didn't go through a long painful thing like cancer. God helped me through that. It was hard, but I decided to make the rest of my life worthwhile. I haven't always succeeded, but I keep at it. One thing I did was work as a volunteer at St. Francis hospital for several years. I love my grandchildren and enjoy spending time with them. I taught them all how to sew and knit.

Most important thing in life?
Faith in God. He's always there to help you when you ask for it.

At 106, do you think about dying?
I suppose. At my age, I know I can't live forever, but It doesn't scare me. Dying is a part of living. When your time is up, God calls you home. I just hope I can die peacefully like my sisters did. They faced death with joy; they knew it was their time. My oldest sister knew her time was up and she faced it with grace and love. I hope I can be like that.

How do you want to be remembered?
That I faced life and dealt with it as it came with faith. We all waste

some of our life, but we've all got a chance to do better. Don't blow it.

Vetus VanDerWiele passed away on Wednesday, April 29, 2015 at the age of 107.

"We all waste some of our life, but we've all got a chance to do better. Don't blow it."

Vetus VanDerWiele, 107

Edna Sims

Edna Greenway was born to Edmund and Lela Greenway on September 17, 1912 in Ashdown, Arkansas. Growing up with two sisters and one brother, she got the best education she could. *"Back in my day we didn't have no school; they just taught you what they knew at home. We didn't have a schoolhouse for colored people in Ashdown 'til 1923. I got to the sixth grade, that's all I got."* In those days, life was hard for black people, especially in a southern state. *"Lord have mercy honey.... We were poor! Every child that lived with a black family had to work. We did everything that poor people had to do.... cookin', sweepin', picked cotton, chopped cotton, and everything else.... whatever we had to do to make a livin'."* In 1928, she married Leonard Owens. Together they had one son before he left in 1929. In 1931 she had a daughter, and in 1933 married Tommy Sims. They were married 52 years when he died in 1985.

Edna had a hard life, *"I was lonely, hungry, and homeless.... And then I got with the Barbee's."* Edna took a job as a cook, housekeeper and nanny for the Barbee family. They had a profound impact on her life. *"The Barbee's took me in like I was one of them. They treated me like a human being. I learned all my education from the Barbee's... mmm hmm...they taught me everything I know. I love them white people 'cause they was good to me!"* She

continued to work, throughout her life, doing whatever was needed to make ends meet. *"I even worked for Bonnie and Clyde...the gangsters.... did some house cleanin' for 'em.... and them suckers didn't even pay me!"* Today, Edna still lives by herself in her own home, *"still raisin' hell!"*

Tell me what life was like when you were a little girl.
Ashdown was a little ol' bitty place. Everybody raised cotton...picked cotton... chopped cotton. They'd raise their own garden; they raised their own meats and things. They had slaves. I remember slavery times back down there where I was raised.

They still had slavery when you were a little girl?
Mmm hmm. I went through it. They had slavery down there where I lived. I had an uncle that worked with some of them people, and there was three families of poor people that had never been to town. They *couldn't* come to town. They had a homestead, they had a church, and they had a graveyard. And all them black folks stayed on it, and they worked in the fields, and they all wore the same kind of clothes. Children didn't go to school and all that stuff. That was slavery.

Then when the war broke out, the depression started, and that's when a lot of people lost their money and the banks and all that. And that's when they let the black folks be free and go where they wanted to go.

So, you're saying those three black families were still owned by someone?
Yeah! That's what I'm talkin' about! They were owned! Everybody!

But I thought slavery ended in the 1800's after the civil war.
No, no. That war didn't mean a thing. They were just like they was before it changed. When I come in the world, it was still the same.... it was harder. Some of the people had owners that was good to 'em, and some owners weren't. They'd beat you to death and all that bit. When I was a girl in Ashdown, you couldn't even walk on the sidewalk. If a white person was coming down that side.... you'd

best get in the ditch.

So, you didn't grow up in slavery, but you had family that did?
Mmm hmm. They didn't get set free 'til I come up here in '31. All them white people, they had horses and cows and all that stuff, and when the banks failed there was a lot of poor folks and poor white folks too. That's when we got more friendly with the white people. It changed 'cause the white people were just like us, tryin' to find 'em a job anywhere.

So, you've seen a lot of injustice in your life.
Yeah....I've been there. I've seen things happen that sometimes make me wanna cry. We had a hard life. Black people had a long, hard life when I was coming up. It was terrible. Some of them white people were real cruel to you, some of 'em were nasty. It's the same thing today, some good people and some bad. They was just that'a way.

When the black school got started, two girls come to town, just young teachers, just got out of school themselves. They didn't know nothin' about our town. And one day they was walkin' down the sidewalk and these white girls told 'em to get off the sidewalk and pushed 'em.... knocked 'em down. And the police come down there and beat them girls, and they left and never did come back. That's what I lived through. You feared for your life, but yet you had a good life in a way. We had a hard life. We didn't have the freedoms that they got now, and I think if they'd had the freedoms they got now it would've been a better place. It was bad, it was really bad. They just had hate in 'em. There was some mean ones, some mean white ones and some mean black ones..... all races. I think some of that still goes on today, but it's different today than it was then.

I'm gonna tell you something. I hate it, but I'm gonna tell you. When I was a little girl, two white men come and raped my auntie in front of my uncle all night....and he couldn't say a word. They wouldn't do nothing anyway! A lot of that went on back then. They were just mean people, just mean.... *just mean!*

How do you forgive people for things like that?
Well... Say you hate me 'cause your white and I'm black. You don't
know any more about me than I know about you, but you might do
something to me, or I might do something to you that's hateful, and
if you let that linger inside you, it'll eat you up. But if you and I get
together and we talk it over, or if you go your way and I go mine,
it's over. That's it. Let it go. I've had things happen to me, and I go
over it and think about what I'd done and how I'd treated them.
Then I'd ask the Lord to forgive me for what I did, and I let it go.

How do you let something like that go?
As long as they didn't put their hands on you or nothing.... it didn't
hurt you. I might get mad, and I think about it for a while.... then
something inside tells me to pray over it and forget it and get on
with life. It'll hurt a while, but finally, it'll go away from you. He
(pointing upward) won't let it come back to you. He'll stay with
you. If you think through it and see what you did wrong and what
they did wrong, He'll show you if you're right or not, and that's it.
I'm fine, you ain't done nothin' to me. You the one hurtin'; I ain't.
I've had people do things to me, and I laugh about it; I don't care. I
just go on 'bout my business. That's just how I feel about it.

Did you go to school?
Back in my day, we didn't have no school like they do now. We
didn't have a schoolhouse for colored people in Ashdown 'til 1923.
I had an uncle and an auntie that was teachers and they just taught
you what they knew at home. Later on, they taught us at the church.
My uncle and another lady was teachin' us and that's all the school
I had. We got to the sixth grade; that's all I got. I learnt myself, and
the Barbee's learnt me. I learned all my education from the
Barbee's... mmm hmm...they taught me everything I know. When I
come I was lonely, hungry, and homeless. And Ms. Barbee's
momma, she hired me and she taught me a lot. I kept house,
cooked, cleaned, and looked after all them white children. To them,
I wasn't black or white.... I was Edna.

So, you've got a sixth-grade education and you've been poor most all your life.
Mmmm hmmm.

How did you manage your money?
I worked whatever job I needed to, to make ends meet. I even worked for Bonnie and Clyde...*the gangsters*.... did some house cleanin' for 'em..... *and them suckers didn't even pay me!* But I was honest. Didn't nobody have to run me down to pay a bill. If I owe my bills, I pay my bills. Out of all my money, even if I don't have nary a dime left, I'm gonna pay my bills, and I'm gonna be free. If you owe somebody, you're gonna be worried.... I don't want to go through that kind of stuff.

I got through all these hard times by working hard.... doing whatever you had to do, and by being honest. That made people trust you, so they would give you credit, or they would help you out, or they would hire you because they trusted you with their children and everything else. I could get a job anytime I wanted one. I never did borrow more than I could pay back. I never was one of these kind that would take my money and go buy something else when I know I owed you. I'm gonna pay you first. I'm gonna pay anybody I owe!

One day I decided I wanted to buy a house, so I went to savin' a little bit at a time. Before you knew it, I'd saved up $650, and I used it on a down payment on this little ol' house. That's how I got a home.

What are you most thankful for?
There's a lot of things.... a lot of things. I thank Ms. Barbee. I thank them white people. I *love* them white people, 'cause they was good to me. They treated me like a human being. I had a good life. The Barbees took me in like I was one of them.

Do you have any regrets?
No, I don't guess so, 'cause I always did what I wanted. If I had it

in my mind to do it, I did it. If it takes me two or three days or a year, if I had a mind to do it, I did it. I stayed by myself, and I did things for myself to please me. I didn't try to please other people. There's no sense in that. But there's a whole lot I wished I didn't do! (laughing).

Like what?
I've been bad, I've been bad. I did sin and I did things that I didn't have no business doin',

So, you believe in God?
My life is with God.

What's it like being 100 years old?
Ooh honey.... you don't wanna be old! It's hard. You don't ever wanna be old, not this kinda old. I can't do what I want to. When I was 60, I was goin' and doin' whatever I wanted to. I was doin' alright 'til I got 99 years old. I broke down when I got to 99. I was doin' fine! Whenever I wanted to do something I'd just get up and do it, I ain't got time to be sittin' 'round lookin' ugly! Do 'til you can't, and I just did 'til I couldn't anymore.

Do you ever think about dying?
Yeah! (laughing) I was thinking about that today! Lord, *"How come I'm still livin'?" (laughing)* I do. I think about dyin'.

Does it scare you?
Uh uh. (no) I'm not scared. When I was younger I was scared of dead people, but when I got older I saw so many people dyin' and I seen how death is and now I just live to die. That's what they tell you, live to die. I hope He comes and gets me and be good to me.

What is your best piece of advice?
Be happy. Love the folks that hate you. Take care of 'em. Be good to 'em.

It's hard for me to comprehend the kind of hate and discrimination Edna and others had to endure. What's even harder to understand is how Edna not only forgives those people, she loves them! ***"Love the folks that hate you. Take care of 'em. Be good to 'em."*** *That almost makes no sense to me. People hate you, look down on you, discriminate against you, abuse you.... and in return.... you love them? It makes no logical sense, but then again, love is not logical. It amazes me that in a self-centered world of experts, diplomats and scholars, a poor black woman with a sixth-grade education is the one who's got it all figured out. Maybe we've got the wrong people running things. God bless you Edna*

Edna Sims died May 8, 2017 at the age of 104.

"Love the folks that hate you. Take care of 'em. Be good to 'em."

Edna Sims, 103

Ruby McConnell

Ruby Joy Thatcher was born January 27, 1905 in Hamilton, Ontario, the youngest of twelve children. *"My dad was Canadian and my mother was from England. Bless her heart, she had a baby every two years! There were only three of us at home when I came along, all the others were married and had children."* While Ruby was still a little girl, her mother died, leaving her to be raised by two of her older sisters. *"They were absolutely wonderful. They were just like a mother to me."* After completing the eighth grade, Ruby dropped out of school began working. She later enrolled in night school to learn typing and office work. In 1925, she married James McConnell and together they had two children, Jim and June. James died of cancer in 1972 after 47 years of marriage. Later her son, Jim, would also die from the same disease. *"That was the darkest moment of my life."*

Did you ever think you'd live to be 100?
No, I never think about my age. Age has nothing to do with me. I do a lot of other things. I don't dwell on my age, I don't dwell on being older. Nothing like that bothers me. I don't see it as a limitation. I just do whatever I want to do.... but I can't do the things

I did before, and that bothers me. I used to go dancing. I would like to keep on with my dancing and do all the things I used to do, but I just can't do that anymore. Sometimes now I just dance with my wheels *(laughing and moving her wheelchair back and forth)*! But I try to keep my mind active. I play word games in my mind; just all the time I work on my mind. I can't read anymore, but I think a lot. I remember all the good times, my family, friends, the old neighbors. Always remember this: never think of your age, just turn your mind on something you like doing. I think my attitude toward life might be a reason on why I lived so long..... but I think my genes may have something to do with it too.

Tell me about your marriage.
I married Jim McConnell in August 1925. He was a wonderful husband; we always got along. He was my best friend. He's been dead many years now; he died of a brain tumor in 1972, so we were married 47 years. I idolized that man; he was so good to me. We were a happy family together. He was an incredible man and a great father, and the grand kids just loved him.

It sounds like you had a great marriage.
Oh yes!

What would you say is the key to a great marriage?
Companionship. We always went together. We did everything together. We were best friends. We had our tiffs once in a while like everybody else but nothing to speak of. No big calamities. I'll tell you about one incident. He was standing with his arms folded and I was mad about something and I was pointing at him, you know *(shaking her finger back and forth)*, *"Don't you ever do that again,"* and all the rest of it. He just stood there and looked down at me. He was a big, tall man, and said, *"Are you finished?"* I said *"Yes,"* and I felt about *that* big *(holding her fingers an inch apart)*. So, he picked me up in his arms and kissed me and settled me down and said, *"Now that's the last of that then, it's all settled."* He was awfully good to me. My marriage was more important than anything else. I couldn't have wished for a better man.

Tell me about your education.

I worked in retail and really loved it, but came a time I had to give it up. I went into the first year of high school and didn't care for it, so I left and went to work. I guess I could have gone on if I wanted to, but it was my own decision. I didn't want to. I went to night school to learn typing and office work. If I had known then what I know today, I think I would've gone on farther. I think education is important but my life was different because my mother died when I was just a little girl, and of course, when she died, everything changed. I was raised by two older sisters and they were absolutely wonderful. They were just like a mother to me. Two lovely sisters.

What is your greatest accomplishment?

I guess I'm proud of a lot of things I've done in my life. I tried to be a good mother; that was an accomplishment. Let me tell you something funny, when June *(daughter)* was a little girl, she came and told me that she was adopted. I said, "You're adopted?" She said, "Yes I am I just never told you." I said, "Well very well then, go and pack your things and go to your mother. If I'm not your mother then go to your mother." My husband slipped out around the back where she couldn't see him but he could watch her when she came out the door. She packed all her things and put them in a little suitcase and out the door she went. It was dark. She went out on the street, and my husband followed. She didn't see him, but he followed. She started to cry, *"Mom I don't want to stay out here anymore, I guess you're my mother. I don't know where she is."* I said, *"Oh, you'll find her! It was nice having you here."* We had put up with that for several weeks, that she was adopted. She came back that night and there was never another word about it *(laughing)*.

What are you thankful for?

I'm thankful for my children and my grandchildren.... and I'm grateful that God looked after me and brought me this far. I don't know where it's gonna end! I never thought that I would live this long.

Do you have any regrets?
I regret getting older, that I can't do the things I did before. I still want to do things, like dance. One time, I came down to the States with a bunch of dancers. I went and sat down because I was dancing so long; I was tired. A girl came over and she said, "What are you sitting here for?" I said, "I'm awfully tired, I've been dancing half the night." She called a young fella over and he said, "We don't sit in this place, we dance." So, he picked me up bodily and put me on a table and he turned to the orchestra and they started to play. There I was, sitting on the table dancing (laughing)! I'll never forget that as long as I live!

What is the secret to managing your money?
When we were married, we both handled the money. Jim didn't say to me, *"I'm going to do so and so."* We sat and talked about it; what was the best thing to do. We made the decisions together. We saved a lot. A part of our money was invested in stocks and bonds.

What advice would you give your grandchildren about money?
I wouldn't. I wouldn't interfere in their life. If I saw that they were getting into trouble maybe I would, but they've got to learn their own lessons.

Were there some hard times in your life?
Oh yes. It was when the Depression was on. That was a terrible thing. My husband only worked three days a week. That's when I went back to work for a while. But he'd borrow his mother's car and go out to the farms and pick things the days he was off. He never fiddled around. He used to go and do things so we'd be able to eat. I used to say, 'I've never done potatoes so many ways in my life' (laughing). We managed; we came through it. We did the best we could. I can't complain.

What was your darkest moment?
When I lost Jim and my son. That was terrible. Jim had a brain tumor. One night he tried to commit suicide. I'll never forget that in my life. I was in the kitchen and I heard an odd noise in the

bedroom. I ran across the living room and up the hall to the bedroom. There he was, God love him, trying to pull himself out of bed to get hold of the pills. He said, "If you've ever loved me, you would let me do this." I said "Jim, I can't. They'd swear that I'd killed you. You can't do a thing like that. I'm sorry." So, he just laid back in the bed exhausted. That was a terrible moment in my life. Before he got too bad he'd sing this song to me, *"Please release me, let me go. I can't stand this pain anymore."* It was pretty hard. He didn't know me for two years while he was in the hospital. Going all the way to the hospital and he didn't even know me. That was darkest moment of my life, when my son went. He died of cancer. Those were the hardest things in my life to get over.

How do you get past that?
You have to think about them. You have to deal with it. Don't ever put them out of your mind. Just think about them and what they went through. Imagine yourself going through that. No, you never get over it. To me, he's still with me. I think of them nearly every day. Jim is always on my mind, in my thoughts. It leaves a big whole in your heart and you have to make a new life. I wondered how am I gonna do it without them?

When Jim died my son took over. He was so good to me. He had an education in music. He loved it. He played the drums and he'd call and say "Mom, I'm playing at so and so, I'll come and get ya, I want to have some dances with you." He was awfully good to me. I'm a very fortunate person to have a husband and children be as good to me as anything in this world could be. I have had a good life. I don't regret my life with the ups and downs and whatnot. I don't regret it because I think you have to have some ups and downs to get along, to learn the other side. If it were good all the time or bad all the time it would get monotonous to me. The bad times make us grow. They give us an understanding of another side. They never leave you. I think about my father; his birthday is coming up. I think about my mother, I didn't know her that well but there's a lot of questions I'd like to ask her about her family, her sisters....

Do you ever think about dying?

I don't really think about dying. I'm not afraid. When my time comes I'll go. I can't be afraid. I've got to live. Keep myself going while I *am* alive. You can't just lay back and say *"Yeah, yeah, one day I'm gonna die."* I don't do that sort of thing. I'm too busy living. Lots of times I just wish I was out of some pain, but other than that... I'm just living until I die. That's all I can do! Don't dwell on it. I never dwell on my age. Think that your 40, and if you're 40 you're gonna have a heck of a good time! Don't think about dying and pain and whatnot... you don't do those things.

What is the one piece of advice you could give me about life?

Behave yourself. Don't drink. Don't smoke. Think of your life and what it's going to lead you into. Take care of yourself. Don't do the things you shouldn't do. Don't upset your wife. Have a happy life, like I did. Family becomes very important as you get older. I have so many friends, *but I can't remember their names!* My life was very happy. My husband and I got along. I think this is all the main things in your life. Always tell your children the truth. Play with your children; we always played games together. Encourage them in things. Get acquainted with them. Don't let them go out of your life.

Ruby McConnell died February 2, 2011 at the age of 106. She left behind one daughter, four grandchildren, nine great-grandchildren and one great-great-grandson. If you knew her, you could see that she was full of life, and, as her obituary stated, "She lived life to the fullest and danced 'til the music stopped playing." God bless you Ruby. Thanks for the wisdom.

"The bad times make us grow. They give us an understanding of another side."

Ruby McConnell, 105

Herman Thompson

Herman Thompson was born February 22, 1913 to Irvin and Ida Thompson of Damascus Virginia. Growing up with his six brothers and sisters, he attended school until the eighth grade before dropping out and going to work. *"I thought I knew more than the teacher, so I quit and never went back."* At the onset of World War II, Herman enlisted in the U. S. Army, serving as an MP throughout Europe. *"Four of us went in, my older brother and two younger brothers, and we all came home."* After the war ended, he returned home to marry his *"sweetheart"*, Dorothy Campbell, at the age of 32. Together they had three children; two died at birth. Herman and Dorothy later divorced after twenty years of marriage. *"I never got married again. I just didn't want to. I dated a lot of women but never wanted to marry any of 'em."* Herman worked numerous jobs in the automotive and manufacturing industry before retiring.

After 100 years of living, what really matters in life?
I think most people are chasing the wrong thing in life. The Lord is what matters. I think the Lord has looked after me all my life. I was in the Army and fought in the Battle of the Bulge. We went

into France after D-Day. We were supposed to be the first ones to land on the beaches of Normandy, but somehow the orders got all mixed up and another group went instead of us. They all got killed but one. Ever since then, I believed in the good Lord (crying). It was terrible. We went in the next day and pushed up through France fighting the Nazis and the Germans all the way to Berlin. I was an MP (Military Police). We would come and set up law in the towns that had been liberated after the front had moved ahead. I wasn't in any of the big battles, but we had plenty to watch out for.... snipers, enemy resistance and all that stuff. I saw *too* much. I believe that I survived because the good Lord was with me; I just have that feeling. So now I live for Him...that's what matters.

What's one of your best memories?
Once when we were over in Europe during the Battle of the Bulge, we were standing guard at a crossroads near the front. The snow was up above our waist; *man, it was cold! B*ut we couldn't leave our post. Then we noticed some smoke coming out the chimney of this little farm house nearby. I told my buddy, *"I'm going to that farmhouse to warm up."* He said, *"Man are you crazy? Those might be German's!"* I said, *"I don't care! I can't just stand here and freeze to death!"* So, I went and this family fed me some soup and let me warm up. A little later I came back, and my buddy said, *"Man, I thought you was dead!"* I laughed and told him to go warm up, that they were nice people and would take care of him.

Do you have any regrets? Would you do anything differently?
Oh, there's plenty I would do over if I could. I saw too much in the war, but I don't like to talk about it. You see injured guys laying on the ground and they can't get up; you don't even want to *think* about it. People haven't seen what I've seen. I hope they never see what I've seen. War is terrible. It tears families apart, tears up the generation, tears up the towns. It tears up everything. It was terrible.

Another thing is I should've stayed in school but I didn't. I only went through the eighth grade. I thought I knew more than the teacher, so I quit and never went back. I wish I went on through

college, but I didn't have sense enough to do that. But I can't do anything about that now.

What's it like growing old?
You can't tell no difference. I feel just as I did when I was 14, but there are some things I don't like about being old. I can't get around like I did when I was young, I can't drive, I can't live in my own house. I like being independent. I don't like my daughter telling me what to do!

Do you ever think about dying?
It never enters my mind. I know I'm gonna die one day. I know the good Lord is going to take me away, but what day and what minute, I don't know. He could come and take me right now, two months from now or year from now. I don't think about it. It doesn't scare me because I'm right with the Lord, and I believe in heaven; so, what is there to be scared of?

What is your best piece of advice about living life?
Live for the Lord. Live *with* Him. After D-Day is when I started believing in the Lord. When I asked Christ into my heart, it changed my life. It made me stop doing the things that I shouldn't of been doing. God made me *want* to change.... but I had to do the changing.

I used to drink a little. You do things when you're drinking that you wouldn't do if you had a clear mind, but that was before I was baptized. When I got baptized, I quit all that. Back then you was baptized in the river, and two preachers had me out in the middle of the river about chest deep, and a rattlesnake came floatin' by. One of 'em got scared and ran, but the other preacher stayed with me, and I got baptized anyway *(laughing)*.

Now days I do the things that *He* wants me to do *(pointing upward)*, live clean and clear, attend church regular, pray. I didn't do those things before the war, but that changed my life. If you'd seen what I did back then, you'd change too.

The old saying goes, "There's no atheist in foxholes." Herman Thompson is proof of that. He passed away on March 14, 2016, just one month after his 103rd birthday. He leaves behind one daughter, five grandchildren and twelve great-grandchildren.

"God made me want to change.... but I had to do the changing."

Herman Thompson, 102

Eunice Ford

Eunice Ione Ellis was born March 23, 1912, the only child of Arthur and Zela Ellis. As a young girl, she attended public schools and worked on the family farm. *"I milked cows, chopped cotton, plowed fields; you name it, I did it."* After graduating high school at age 17, she married Lloyd Ford by eloping with him late one night. *"I finished my chores and*

Lloyd and Eunice Ford and children.

knew he'd be coming for me that night." Together they snuck off to the preacher's house and said, I do. *"I left my daddy a note under his breakfast plate, telling him that when he read it, I'd be Mrs. Lloyd Ford. He wasn't happy about losing his best farm hand."* Lloyd and Eunice settled down on their own 100-acre farm and had two children, Gary and Norma. In 1943 the US government bought them out to build a military camp for German prisoners of war. Lloyd and Eunice used the money to start their first small grocery

store. Through the years they bought and sold several stores, eventually retiring in 1979, back on their own small farm. On April 9, 2012 Lloyd and Eunice celebrated their 83rd wedding anniversary at the ages of 102 and 100, respectively. Lloyd died on October 12, 2012.

Tell me what it was like being married for 83 years.
When I was a little girl, my grandparents lived up the hill from Loyd's family, and I got acquainted with his sister when I came to visit. Later on, me and him started dating. After about a year, his mother started encouraging us to get married. Then one day she went with him to get a marriage license. They said if they got the license they'd come by and honk the horn. That afternoon, I was out in the pasture bringing up the cows to milk, and I heard the horn. I went ahead and did my chores, and I knew when he come that night we was gonna get married. So later that night, we snuck off to the preacher's house and got married. We didn't tell my parents. I wrote a note and told my daddy when he read that letter I'd be Mrs. Lloyd Ford, and I put it under his breakfast plate. So later the next day, daddy had to go somewhere, but we didn't have a car, so he caught a ride with the preacher. He told the preacher he was going to have it annulled, but when the preacher finally got through talking to him, he decided he wouldn't. Daddy liked Lloyd alright but he wasn't too happy about losing his best farm hand. I was the boy of the family! *(laughing)* I plowed and hoe'd and cut wood.... *I did everything!*

So how did your marriage start out?
When we got married, we didn't have *nothin',* but we were happy. We lived with his mother and daddy for a while and I helped them until we rented our own house and we started farming the land that it was on. We had two children together, Gary and Norma. We raised our own food, we had a couple of cows, and we grew tomatoes, watermelon and cantaloupe, and sold the produce. That was during The Depression. We didn't have anything, but we didn't know any different. Then in 1939, our house burned down, and we lost everything. We had nothing but the clothes on our back, but people would give us canned goods, and clothes.... We didn't have

any money, but it didn't matter. I didn't know nothing different. Marriage wasn't about the stuff; it was about each other.

So, after 83 years of experience, what's the secret to a happy marriage?
You got to make your own happiness. It doesn't just happen by itself; you've got to work at it. Be good to your mate. Don't try to be the boss. You've got to keep in mind that you *belong* together. We were always together. We worked on the farm together, then we had the stores. We were together nearly every day. It don't go peaceful all the time. Every now and then you're going to disagree, but we didn't fuss or quarrel; we just let it go. We didn't think it was that important. If it *was* important, we worked it out. Some people tend to get selfish, and that has no place in a marriage. It's ridiculous how some people get mad and fuss and talk ugly to each other if they don't get their own way. That's just being childish. You've got to give a little and take a little. Lloyd and I always talked things through. We talked about the pros and cons, and we settled on what was best. Sometimes his was the best way and sometimes mine was, but there's no sense in quarrelin' about it.

Lloyd died last year. After 83 years of marriage, how do you cope with that?
It was hard.... it's still hard. He got down sick for several days and I thought he was going to be alright, but he wasn't. It's lonesome; I get lonesome for him. He was a big part of my life. We were together all the time. We worked together, we lived together.... You just have to accept that they're not gonna come back. You just got to go on and keep livin'. I wish Lloyd lived longer.... but he was here a long time.

What's it like being over 100 years old?
I don't think about it. I don't think about how old I am. I don't feel that old.

How old do you feel?
Maybe in my 90's!

What are you most thankful for?
My health. I've been sick, but I've never been near death. I've always eaten good; we grew all our own vegetables. I never drank or smoked. My husband used to make his own wine, home brew he called it. I tried it once, but I didn't like it. It had a kick to it! I'm thankful for my family, my home....and being able to stay at home.

Eunice Ford died at her home on May 21, 2015 at the age of 103. At the time of her husband's death in 2012, they had been married for 83 years, 191 days which is the 19th longest marriage ever. You can read more about it at the link below.

https://en.wikipedia.org/wiki/List_of_people_with_the_longest_marriages

"Some people tend to get selfish; that has no place in a marriage.
Marriage wasn't about the stuff, it was about each other."

Eunice Ford, 102, married 83 years

Ida Mae Wilson

Ida Mae Woody was born December 24, 1907 to a family of cattle ranchers on the Pen Elm Ranch near the Texas, Oklahoma border. The oldest of three, Ida Mae went to school and worked the family ranch with her brother and sister. *"We raised white-faced beef cattle then shipped them to the stockyards at Kansas City because the prices were higher there."* After graduating high school, she attended Oklahoma University where she met Paul Wilson whom she later married in 1937. Ida Mae worked for Southwestern Bell for 45 years until her retirement at the age of 65. In 1986, her husband, Paul, died after 49 years of marriage. *"He was a wonderful man and a wonderful husband."* In 2007, Ida Mae was named OU's biggest fan for attending OU football games for more than 80 years.

You were married for almost 50 years. What advice do you have for a good marriage?
The main thing is love. You have to love each other and treat each other like you love them. Love each other, love and kindness, that's the main thing...love. I had a wonderful husband. He was real good to me.... maybe because I was so good to him *(laughing)*. If your good to them, they'll be good to you. It's like sowing and reaping.

If you sow love, you'll reap love. That's what we did. Our marriage was built on love.

Another thing, don't argue. If something comes up and you don't agree, I think you should sit down and work it out. We always worked everything out, and we had a happy marriage. It's not that hard to be happy and not argue about a lot of things, you know. He died a number of years ago now.

How did you get thru that?
It was hard. I was real lonesome, but my friends and neighbors got me through it.

Do you have any advice on managing money?
Always save money. I always had money because I always saved it. I always had a savings account. When I started to work for the telephone company in the 1930's, I put one dollar a week in savings, and I was only making seven dollars a week. Seven dollars a week! Isn't that something? I think younger people spend too much. They see something they want and just go buy it instead saving it. One day, they are going to need it, and they aren't going to have it. I think they should save more because they make so much more now than I did when I went to work. As I said, I just made seven dollars a week. Back then, that was good wages you know. I could have saved a lot more, but I didn't. I should have; I wish I had, but I didn't. Most young kids don't. They don't save. But you don't learn that until after it's too late.

What's it like to be 106 years old?
It's wonderful. It's beautiful. It's just beautiful. I'm having the time of my life. I'm in good health. I try to take care of myself and eat the right food. And I think happiness and a good attitude helps. I haven't regretted a year I've lived, and I'll be a 107 Christmas Eve this year. *Who would have thought it?*

Having a good attitude helps. I try to be happy all the time. It's all in the way you think about life. Unhappy people make themselves unhappy. It's just as easy to be happy instead. You know, you can't

worry about everything because you're going to have ups and downs all through life. That's just the way life is. Take it from me, I'll be 107, and I know.

Do you have any regrets?
I regret never having children. We couldn't have children. We thought about adopting, but my husband never could make up his mind whether he wanted to or not, and I wasn't going to adopt a child if he wasn't willing....and he never was willing. I wanted to adopt, but sometimes it's not up to me; it's up to Him *(pointing upward)*.

You mentioned the Bible. Do you believe in God?
Oh Yes. I believe in Him.... I do. I believe that he takes care of us, but He expects us to take care of ourselves too.... and each other. I was raised in a Christian home, and so, I've been a Christian all my life. I don't think anybody could have a happy life without God. There's just too much happening. He's you're life. He takes care of us, but He expects us to take care of ourselves....and other people too. I think the world would be much better off if children were taken to church to learn about God. That's why so many people are not happy, because they don't know about God. I don't see how people can be happy if they don't know God.

What is your best advice for living a good life?
My best advice? Live a good Christian life. Live a good Christian life. What I mean by that is treat everybody like you want to be treated yourself. The Golden Rule, I've always lived that. Treat everybody like you want to be treated yourself. Love other people. I know it's hard to do sometimes, but do it anyway. And you have to forgive. It's awful hard to forgive some people, but you still have to forgive them. You have to forgive in order to live a happy life. And pray. You can't get through bad times without prayer. That's the best thing.... that's the only thing that can get you through those bad times, you know, is prayer, through prayer. I think God helps us through those times; I know He did me. Live a good Christian life and pray. Stay in your church and treat everybody like you want to be treated. Don't you think that's good advice?

Yes ma'am.
Well, that's about the best advice I can give you.

Ida Mae Wilson passed away on November 20 2016 just one month before her 109th birthday. God bless you Ida Mae. You are a treasure.

"It's all in the way you think about life. Unhappy people make themselves unhappy. It's just as easy to be happy instead."

Ida Mae Wilson, 106

Millie Feaster

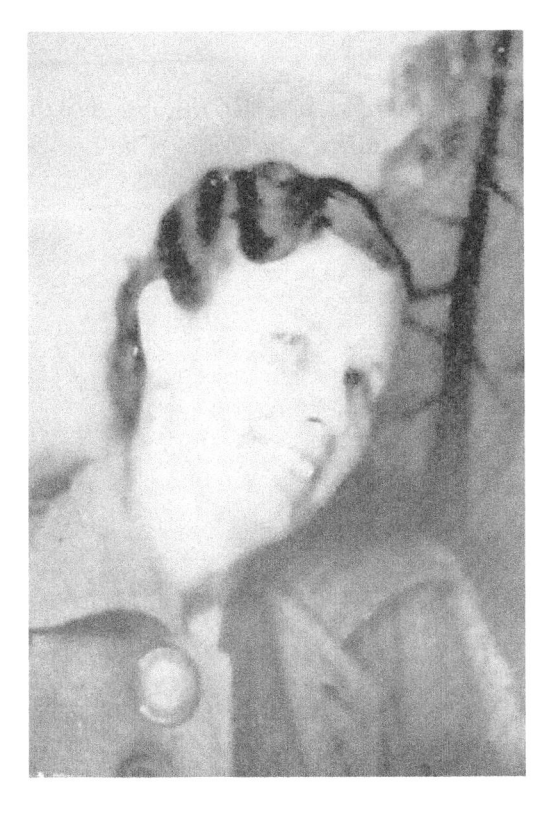

Millie Mae Maughon was born July 28, 1911 in Atmore, Alabama to a Pentecostal preacher and his wife. She was the third of six children. As a child, Millie and the family moved several times throughout Mississippi and Alabama as her father was assigned to new churches. Millie attended public schools but dropped out after the fifth grade to work. At age 16, she married Leroy Feaster, and together they had two sons, Harvey and Hodges. Hodges would later die at age 27, and Millie and Leroy divorced after 31 years of marriage. *"Two weeks after I married him he got to running around on me. Finally, I told him, 'Man I've had enough of you,' and I've been single ever since!"* Millie worked many years as a seamstress and in the public sector, working well into her 80's, retiring only after her sight began to fail. She never remarried.

What was the biggest mistake you ever made?
I made a mistake when I married my husband, but I loved him. His name was Leroy and I was only 16. Two weeks after I married him, he got to runnin' around on me. That went on for a while. He kept promising me he'd change, but he never did. We had two boys

together. Finally, I told him, *"Man I've had enough of you,"* and I filed for divorce. He come back and wanted me to remarry him and I said *"Nope."* I never did remarry. I never even dated anymore; I didn't want to. I had chances, but I didn't do it. You couldn't give me enough. After my husband run around on me like he did, I didn't know what the others would do. I didn't trust them. I never did love another one, and I didn't think you should marry someone you didn't love. But I always did believe that God had a purpose in it some way or another.

What advice would you have if someone else was in the same situation?
Leave 'em, because you can't trust 'em no more. Leroy kept tellin' me he would change, but he never did. He'd just turn around and do it again. I guess if they really changed you could work it out, but there would sure have to be a change in 'em to trust 'em any more. I didn't ever trust him anymore.

Sounds like you had some tough times. How did you get through them?
Whatever I needed, mostly I went to the Lord. I've had mistakes in my life, but He's always been there. So far, He has been pretty good to supply my needs all my life. I didn't have nobody else looking after me, just the good Lord taking care of me. Oh, my God's been good to me. I call on Him and he helps me. God is my refuge. Whatever I need, I have to trust the Lord with it cause that's all I have is Him.

Don't you ever worry about anything?
Worry doesn't do you any good. I used to worry about whether my boys were saved or not. My baby, boy, he's been gone awhile now, and my oldest, I don't know. I don't hear from him anymore. I try not to worry about him. I just pray for him, that he'd be ready to meet the Lord when he leaves here. That's the most important thing, to know God. He's liable to come anytime. I believe God will honor my prayers about my boys, but you have to give your life yourself. So, he's gonna have to do it. I can't do it for him. I can pray for the Lord to send it upon him, but I can't save him. So, I just turned

them over to the Lord. I can't do nothing about it.... *but I can pray.*

What's it like to grow old?
It's just like any other day if you've got God. If Jesus is dwelling in you, 100 years old don't bother you. Don't bother me anyway. It's good to realize that you're all this old. It's exciting to think that you're goin' home. When He gets ready for me I'll be ready to go. I'm ready right now. I don't know when He's gonna call me, maybe tonight, maybe tomorrow, I don't know. Just because I'm a little over 100 years old doesn't mean he won't keep me here a few more years if He has something for me to do here on this earth. If I can win a soul, I'm willing. *Here I am Lord (laughing).*

What would you say is the most important thing in life?
Living for the Lord, and have Him within you. Have Him dwell within you.

What do you mean?
Live for God. Have God dwelling within you. Nothing else matters if you don't have God. What does it matter if you don't have God? Hell matters if you don't have God. We all make mistakes, but if we don't ask forgiveness for them, we're gonna reap what we sow. God's a forgiving God. He's not gonna hold it against you if you get down and pray and be earnest with Him. If you ask Him to forgive you, He will, but you've got to ask for it. Then He'll forgive you and dwell within you. Then you've got stay close to God. He'll use you, if you're dependable, but you have to do that yourself. You've got to be *ready* for him to do these things. You can't just be running around doing as you please and think God's gonna use you. You have to live a clean life for the Lord. The only way you're gonna get to heaven is to live a clean life. No sin's gonna enter in up there.... no. You've got to be right with God. *Hallelujah!*

So, you believe you'll go to heaven when you die?
Oh yes, I'm ready! Heaven's gonna be a beautiful place. *Glory, hallelujah!* He's gonna take me home. Yes, I'm ready. I'm gonna get to go home. Lord any day now! *(laughing excitedly)* I've got a mother there. I look forward to that day. I get to meet my momma.

We're gonna be shouting on the hills of glory *(Starts singing)*.
Shoutin' on the hills of glory
Shoutin' on the hills, yes, Shoutin' on the hills
There'll be shoutin' on the hills of glory
Shoutin' on the hills of God.
Woooooo! *(Laughing and excited)*. I just wonder if I'm gonna be able to sing up there with my mother!

Aren't you afraid of dying?
I'm not afraid of dying. What's there to be scared of? It's that other place you ought to be scared of! I'm not scared about going. It'll be a wonderful place. Any day now the trumpets will sound! *Woo hoo!* I'm ready. Praise the Lord! Hallelujah! *"Be ye also ready, for such a day ye think not, the Son of Man cometh,"* *(quoting Matthew 24:44)*. So you'd better stay ready. Glory Hallelujah! *(laughing, crying)* It's gonna be wonderful, but that other place.... Lord, have mercy. Are you saved? **Yes ma'am, I am**.

Do you talk to God?
I pray every day. I've talked to him since I was a little bitty girl. When I call on him, He answers. I don't always pray outwardly, sometimes I pray within. I can pray anywhere. Anytime I call on Him, He always hears me. He'll never leave you; You have to do the leaving. You go out and do the things you shouldn't do, that's leaving. Give your life to the Lord. Stay prayed up and ready to go up. People will know you're saved by the way you act. And if you don't act like it, they *sure* can tell. You better be ready when He calls you. The most important thing in anybody's life is God. Oh, what a joyful time that will be. Hallelujah! Are you prepared? He's coming! *(Starts singing again)*.

My trials here will soon be o'er someday, some happy day
My pain on earth shall be no more, someday, some happy day
Someday, some happy day, from sin I will be free
I'll live with God eternally, someday, some happy day (laughing).
Hallelujah!

I'm not sure what to say about Millie Feaster. I don't think I've ever met anyone so passionate about God. I can't describe the glow on her face or the gleam in her eye as she would cry and laugh simultaneously while singing and praising God. It was nothing short of beautiful. It was as if she was actually in the presence of the Almighty.... and who's to say she wasn't.

Millie Feaster passed away on February 15, 2014 at the age of 102. She is survived by one son, six grandchildren, eighteen great-grandchildren, and two great-great-grandchildren.

Although some people may question the concept of heaven, I can promise you one thing.... wherever she is, she's still singing.

"Whatever I need, I have to trust the Lord with it, cause that's all I have is Him."

Millie Feaster, 102

Millard Gaddie

Millard Wesley Gaddie was born June 8, 1902 in Campbellsville, Kentucky to Thomas and Cora Gaddie. *"My father was a farmer and my mother raised us kids."* He had a normal upbringing for children of that period, attending school and working on the farm after school and in the summers. When Millard was 13, his father bought a Model T Ford, and packed up everything the they could fit in it and moved the family to Sherman, Texas. *"There weren't any highways in those days, so we had to use a guidebook and compass to navigate our way on the dirt roads."* In the evenings, they would pull up to an old farmhouse and ask to spend the night in their barn. *"Folks would always welcome us in and feed us dinner."* The next morning, they would wake up, pack up the car, and off they'd go again. *"It took us 10 days to get there! Folks sure were a lot nicer back in those days."*

Were you ever married?
Oh yeah! I was married for a long time.... but not all of it to the same woman. My first wife's name was Ruth. She was a good woman and we had three daughters together, Nadine, Mildred and Lavita. We were married for 51 years when she died of a heart attack. That was tough. I really loved her. I never thought I'd get married again, but then I met my second wife. Her name was Leola. She was a good woman too until she died. We were

married for 33 years.

So, you were married a total of 84 years?
Yep.

What's the secret?
Well, it's not really a secret. You see, when it comes to marriage, the first thing you do is find out that you're not the boss *(laughing)*. Marriage is a two-way street you see. You have to give and let give. You can't always have your way all the time. The other person has needs and wants too, you know. You've got to respect other people's rights. That's what I did. It takes two people getting along to make a marriage work. One person can't make it work all by themselves. It doesn't work like that. It takes two to make it work. If you're selfish all the time and she's selfish all the time, what kind of marriage is that? But if you work to take care of her, and she works to take care of you, then you've got something good. That's what marriage is, two people working to take care of each other. And believe me, it's work! But it's all worth it. My marriages were the best years of my life.

You mentioned that life was tough back then. How did you deal with it?
Well you see, we went through The Great Depression, and times were hard. I worked as a barber, and we got 35 cents for a haircut, and 20 cents for a shave. Well, when the depression hit, we got down to 15 cents for a shave and 25 cents for a haircut. It was hard to make a living, so I had to go out and get second job. I learned how to hang wallpaper, and lots of people wanted some wallpaper hung in those days. So, I'd cut hair all day, then I'd go out at night and hang paper. Then along about the late '20s, cured meat come in, you know, home-cured hams and such. I lived in a small town, and so nearly everybody had a cow or a chicken or a hog to kill, you see, so I did that. I cured a lot of meat. I did a lot of things like that. I did whatever I had to do to make ends meet. I had to; I had a family to feed. Later I owned my own barber shop, and that was a lot of work too! It was a lot of work, but you do whatever you've got to do to provide for your family. I never asked the government

for anything, and I never owed anyone I didn't pay, and even today, I don't have any debts.

So how did you manage your money?
If we didn't have money to pay for something, then we just didn't get it. We had to do without a lot of things, but we made it alright. Some people just can't imagine doing without things. Now days if they want something, they go buy it and they'll figure out how to pay for it later. Problem is, sometimes they can't pay for it, and they get into trouble. Have you seen all these people losing their houses here lately? They bought things that they couldn't afford, and now they're losing it all. They need to learn how to say no and start saving their money. Sure, there was lots of nice things that I would've liked to have had, but I didn't just go out and buy it all. How are these people ever going to retire if they never save any money? You'd better start saving. Believe me, retirement is expensive. And if you're not prepared for it, then how are you ever going to retire? I guess they're all going to expect the government to take care of them. But sooner or later, they'll regret it.

One last question. After 105 years of living, what is the most important thing life?
You see that picture *(pointing to a photo of a young woman in a white dress)*? That was my wedding day, and that's my Ruthie. She was so beautiful. It was the happiest day of my life. And you see that one *(pointing to another photo)*? Those are my three girls. That must have been around 1930. And that one over there *(pointing to yet another photo)*?

Mr. Gaddie pointed out every photo hanging on the walls and told me a short story about each one. As he rambled, I began to think that he had forgotten my question, but he had a big smile on his face as he talked about the past. Then he said:

You asked me what the most important thing in life is? It's simple. It's the memories you make and the people you love. No one can ever take that away from you.

Millard Gaddie died February 10, 2008 at the age of 105, just four months after this interview. It's strange how someone you barely know could have such a lasting impact on your life. I am forever changed. God bless you Mr. Gaddie, you have certainly blessed me.

"You asked me what the most important thing in life is? It's simple. It's the memories you make and the people you love. No one can ever take that away from you."

Millard Gaddy, 105

Emma Hoggle

Emma Sophonia Funderburk was born June 26, 1913 to Doug & Minnie Funderburk of Vinita, Oklahoma. Along with her six brothers and three sisters, Emma went to school and helped work the family farm to make ends meet, and *"Every Sunday mother saw to it that we were in church."* Upon graduating high school, Emma attended Northeast Oklahoma Junior College before beginning a lifelong career in fashion and business. Along the way she married Warren Hoggle and had four girls, Sonya, Nancy, Marilyn and Carolyn. After 65 years of marriage, Warren died of a stroke. Emma continued working at her dress shop until eventually retiring to spend more time with family and grandchildren.

Tell me what makes a good marriage.
I haven't been married in so dang long that I've forgotten about it. My husband passed away a long time ago. He had a stroke.

Was that difficult?
Yeah.

How did you get through that?
Well, life is not easy. There are certain conditions that you pass through in your life whether you want to or not. Think of your own life; you've had things in your life that have happened to you. That's just nature. When we're born, we all have conditions that we hate to have to pass through, but we do. We still pass through certain conditions in our lives whether we want to or not.

But how do you get through those conditions?
Well, talk to the good Lord about it first, and with His help, your own conversation with Him, you find out a lot of things in life. Like whether or not you're really living the life that Jesus wants you to live or whether you're not. That's the main thing we have to make up our mind about.

Do you think He uses those conditions to point those sorts of things out?
Yes, I sure do. I think if we're Christians and know the Lord is our savior, He takes care of us a lot of the time when we don't even know it. The Lord has helped me many times because I always call on Him for help. I go to my knees and pray and ask the good Lord to help me to come through my problems when I have them. I've had plenty of problems in my life, and He's always come through for me, but it hasn't always been easy.

Who is God to you?
God is a holy God; He is a helper. I call on Him anytime I get in trouble. Everyone has some sort of trouble once in a while, and the good Lord is always present to help you if you so desire. I think a lot of us don't think about it enough, you know, we all think we're Christians and we all go to church and we all do this or we do that and we all just float along. But if you really, really stop and think, *"Why am I here, why am I a Christian, why have I chosen the Lord as my savior? Do I really know why, or do I just play like it?"* Answer that.

Wow...tough question! For me, I tried to run my own life and I messed it up. I can't do it alone, I need help, some direction, something bigger than just me.

The devil is active every minute of our life practically. You've been tempted off and on all your life, and we all make mistakes. And all of us....at least most of us come to the place in our life where we're sorry and sad because we made those mistakes. And I know that the good Lord knows your feelings whether you know it or not, and He also knows how to correct you when you don't even know whether or not your being corrected. But the good Lord does.... He knows. He corrects us because He loves us.

Do you have any regrets?

No, not really. Any real regrets that I had, I've resigned and turned them over to the Lord and asked for forgiveness, so I'm no longer carrying that burden because I've asked for forgiveness. I'm a Christian and I've really and truly tried to live a Christian life. When you have really tried, as young as I am, to live a good life and accept the Lord as your savior, it's a chore, but then we can live without regret. I live very happily. I know that He's alive and that He's my savior. I've always depended on the Lord to help me when I needed him. The Lord is a big part of my life. Do you know the Lord as your savior?

Yes ma'am.

Well good. The Lord is willing to give you a good life, a better life, a more secure life, because He loves you, if you call on Him, He'll be there. Think about it.

What's the biggest lesson you've learned in 100 years?

Live for Him. If you know the Lord, I think that you become a better person. You try to serve Him and you begin to do things differently in your life. The more we love and serve Him, the more we love and serve others. It becomes natural to you. Sometimes you don't even realize it.

What are you most thankful for?

I really and truly thank God for my upbringing. Sometimes I kneel

and pray and tell Him how thankful I am that I had a Christian mother and father and that they both cared for their children enough to teach us to love Jesus. I'm just thankful that I had a Christian mother and father, because that has affected every area of my life ever since. God has been the center of life since I was a little girl. Every Sunday mother saw to it that we were in church. There were four of us girls, and every Sunday we sat with Momma in church; it was just a normal thing. I still go to church every Sunday, and you know, it just becomes a part of your life.

If you could only give me one piece of advice, what would you say?
Well, I think you probably know the answer to that *(smiling)*.

At the end of our visit, Mrs. Hoggle asked me if I was married and about my wife. She then asked me if she could pray for us, so we held hands and this beautiful, selfless woman whom I'd only known for 45 minutes, prayed for me and my wife. Now if that's not a living example of God's love, I don't know what is. Thank you Ms. Hoggle.

Emma Hoggle passed away April 16, 2015 at the age of 101. She leaves behind four daughters, 11 grandchildren, 17 great grandchildren, six great, great grandchildren, and legacy to live for the Lord.

"I haven't been married in so dang long that I've even forgotten about it!"

Emma Hoggle, 101

Estelle Thompson

Ora Estelle Mazy was born September 27, 1910 in Wichita Falls, Texas. When she was two years old, her family moved to a farm in Lamar County, Texas where she and her two brothers walked three miles to school every day. *"We grew up chopping cotton, milking cows, and whatever else chores needed to be done."* At age nine, her father died leaving only her mother to provide for the family. After completing the 10th grade, Estelle took a job at Woolworth's department store to help with the family's finances.

In 1928, at age 18, she married Gordon Thompson and together they raised three children. *"We lived five or six miles out in the county and had to walk into town whenever we needed something."* Later they started their own business which they worked together until his death in 1979. They were married 51 years. After his death, she continued to run the business with the help of her son until finally retiring.

You were married for 51 years. What's the key to making it work?
You have to find the right person, someone you can live with, someone with patience, kindness.... dependability. And you have to be able to depend on each other.

When two people get married they're going to have disagreements at some time or another. Sometimes you get two people together that were raised differently. You might be on one side of the fence and he might be on the other, but you've got to learn how to meet in the middle, and sometimes you just make it up as you go.

What does it take to be a good parent?
I wasn't raising my family by myself. There was two of us and we would always have a talk about how we would raise the kids. Sometimes we'd disagree, but we never let the kids know that.

We didn't show any favoritism to our children; we loved them all equally. We told them over and over that if they had a problem they could come to us with their problems. We would all get together, sit down and talk, and try to make the best decision. We would work it out together. We took care of our family. When we told the kids to jump, they jumped. We didn't have any trouble with them. They minded us. They knew when I said something to them I meant it, and they minded me. And if they didn't, I paddled them. I had a switch hid behind the kitchen door. They knew where that switch was hid! *(laughing)* I'd spank them and make them be on their way.

I raised my kids to love the Lord and obey me when I told them something. I took them to church every Sunday, and then Monday, it was back to work in the fields. That's the way I raised my kids, in church. I depended on a lot of help from God. I'm thankful for the strength He gave me to raise my family.

I raised my kids to be adults.... then they got to *be* adults. It's hard for a parent to give up their child. I worried for about a year and then I just decided, they're on their way. Their life was in their own

hands now. I tried to be the best mother I could, then I depended on them to raise their own families, and they've each got good families of their own. We had some good kids and they're good people now.

Do you think of yourself as old?
I never did grow old. I haven't grown old yet.... because I love life. I love my life, from the day I was born to the day I'm going to die. I don't know when that's going to be.... but not any time soon! I love what was in my life, my family, friends, my business. I just love life and I enjoy it. Life is what you make it, I think. You have to have a good attitude and keep your spirits up and think good thoughts. You can find something good in everything that happens to you, or you can find something bad. It's your choice.

Are you afraid of dying?
I'm not afraid to die. I think about dying.... but I don't have any fear of it because when I die I know where I'm going. I know I'm going to a better place and God will take care of me. I think everyone should think about it and have their life prepared to go because when God gets through with you on this earth, you'll be judged for what you've done and not done. I really think that. Make sure you live the kind of life that God will appreciate. If you've lived the right kind of life now, you're going to be alright, but if not, you better watch out. There's a lot of people that aren't going to go to heaven.

What was one of the hardest times of your life?
We went through the Great Depression. We didn't really know what the Depression was but we knew hard times were ahead of us.

How did you get through it?
We learned to make our own food on the farm. We made a lot of our own food. We grew vegetables and raised pigs and made jellies and preserves.... We didn't waste food. You wouldn't let the kids just take and eat all they wanted, you watched them and were careful. We knew we had to save 'cause if we didn't we wouldn't have anything to eat that winter. We always had plenty to eat.... but we had people in our neighborhood come to our house a number of

times 'cause they didn't have anything to eat. We didn't give them money but we gave them food. They made it all right. I'm glad we could help them. I think you get the best feeling in the world when you were helpful that day and you went to bed that night and said your prayers and you were talking to God and God was talking to you and that was what God wanted you to do.

On April 13, 2013, Estelle Thompson passed away at the age of 102. She was a beautiful lady, inside and out. Her humor and attitude made it obvious that she loved life and loved people. She is survived by 2 living children, 10 grandchildren, 21 great-grandchildren and 4 great-great-grandchildren. I hope her words will inspire them as they have me.

"You can find something good in everything that happens to you, or you can find something bad. It's your choice."

Estelle Thompson, 102

Fay L. Hudson

Fay Leon Hudson was born February 27, 1914 on a farm staked and claimed by his grandfather in the Oklahoma Land Run. His parents, William & Edith Hudson, were farmers by trade, and along with the help of the children, in 1919, they produce 12,000 bales of cotton....... by hand. As a child, Fay attended school in a one-room schoolhouse along with his two sisters and two brothers. *"Back then, we didn't have school buses. It was five miles to school each day on horseback."* When Fay was 16, his father left, forcing him to work the farm to help support family. After graduating high school in 1932, he attended East Central College, Oklahoma University and Stanford University earning his bachelor's degree and two master's degrees in education and two life-time teaching certificates. Fay began his teaching career at age 19, also in a one-room schoolhouse making $50 a month. *"I taught everything, all grades, all subjects. I was the teacher, janitor, cook.... I even cut their hair and pulled their teeth."*

In 1936, Fay met Blanche Keslerage, *"She was the best lookin' girl in the country."* He was 22, she was 13. Two years later they eloped and got married on April 23,1938. Together they had two daughters, Martha & LaSaundra. When WWII broke out, both Fay and Blanch moved to California to work as welders in a shipyard building troop transport ships. After the war ended, Fay and Blanche moved back home and went back to teaching school. Fay

worked for 40 years in education, serving as a teacher, principle and eventually, superintendent. In 1979, Fay retired at age 65 only to take another job with the county as the Director of Retired Senior Programs. After 17 years there, he retired again at age 85, only to continue working on his 1300-acre ranch.

You've been married for over 75 years. What's the secret?
We've talked about that, and really, we just respected each other. Problems come along, but we just solved them and went on. We never did let it get to a divorce situation. Whatever she needed, I tried to provide. Most divorces are over money problems, and we didn't have any money problems, *because we didn't have any money.* We just respected each other, still do. Divorce never entered our minds. I still love her because she loves me, and she took care of me. I worked all the time. I worked two jobs, farming and teaching. She took care of me, and I took care of her. We never had any arguments that ever amounted to anything, just some little love spats.

Got any advice for young folks thinking about marriage?
Get your money problems solved before you get married.

With three degrees and 40 years of teaching, you must think education is real important.
Education *is* important because it gives you a broader perspective on what's going on around in the country. If you don't go to school you're just losing out on a lot of things. If you're farming and you need some education on agriculture; you get it through biology, and it can help you cultivate your plants. Every time I went to a meeting, I learned something. I'm still looking to learn today....no use quitting now. I never did go for dropouts. Dropouts are caused by the education system. I didn't have dropouts. I *brought* them school, either physically or through the district attorney. Kids didn't drop out; they shouldn't drop out now. Get as much education as you can, as young as you can. It's worth it; it'll pay off. If you want more money, you need to get more education because people that hire want someone with an education. My education did more than qualify me to teach, it helped me earn more money which let me

save a little bit. Then when land came for sale, I could buy it for an investment. It paid off. It helped me in my marriage, raising kids, it helps out in every area of life, even with us now, education helps.

As a teacher, what advice would you give to kids now days?
Stay in school. Don't smoke. Don't drink. Stay away from dope. Stay away from the people that use it; they'll get you in trouble, get you thrown in jail or get you killed. Dope is the number one enemy of the human race.

You mentioned money. How did you manage and invest your money?
I put it all in interest. They would pay us with certificates for teaching instead of a cashier's check, and we would take that to the bank where we'd get a little more interest. In 1919, banks all around the country were going broke, and that scared me. I had $180 that I'd saved up, and that was a lot of money back then! So, I took the money out of the bank and put in a savings company. Then the bank went broke. Then I took the money out of the savings company and they went broke. So, I put it in government bonds at the post office. Then when I worked in the shipyards, I put the money in deposit and accumulated a little bit, and when stuff would come up cheap, I'd buy it.

What kind of stuff?
Mostly real estate and land. We own about 1300 acres now. I'd raise mule colts and sell them for $100. Back then that was pretty good money. That's how I went to college was on the money from the mules I'd sell. Always look ahead. I never bought any stocks or anything like that.

We were poor growing up. We had to save money because we didn't make much. A bale of cotton was only $25. That's a lot of cotton to pick for only $25. When I was six years old, I'd get up and milk the cows and go to the fields and work picking cotton. Then when we'd get ready to go to the house for supper, we'd fill our sacks up with cotton bowls. After we ate our supper, we'd pick the cotton out of the bowls, so we'd put in a full day. I was 16 when my father

left. I've been working hard all my life, everyday.... but God looked after us.

If you could go back and do it all again, what would you do different?
I'd do the same thing. I wouldn't change anything.

Why?
I like to work...and I had a lot of fun along the way.... *a lot of fun!*

But you probably had some pretty hard times along the way.
Yeah....but I wouldn't change it. They had their purpose. That's what makes you who you are. I don't regret anything.

You said God has looked after you?
Yeah, every step of the way. I pray and He answers my prayers. The first prayer He ever answered for me was when I was 16 years old. I was plowing corn, and my mother was going to be operated on. My dad was mean to her, and I fell down own my knees and prayed that her surgery would come through....and it did. And I've believed in prayer ever since. I pray for rain.... I pray for a lot of things. Some come, some don't, but He's been just to me. The good Lord's been with me all the way through. I don't know where I'd be without God. It wouldn't be too good.

How do you want to be remembered?
Just an everyday person. No fancy, no nothing, just a common everyday person. Recognized as a good educator. I have lots of students still come and see me.

Do you think you made a difference in any of their lives?
Oh yeah. They tell me that. I had one student come to me one day, I didn't know who he was. He came up and threw his arms around me and said, *"I want to thank you."* I said, *"I don't know you,"* and he said, *"I'm Ted Booth's kid, and when I was in the fourth grade you called the sheriff down on me and made me go to school."* He said, *"If it hadn't been for you I never would have gone to school."*

What is the one piece of advice that you would tell me about life?

Study your Bible. All of life revolves around that in one way or another.

Fay Hudson died January 28, 2015, just one month shy of his 101st birthday. At the time of his death, he and Blanche had been married for over 76 years, which places them as one of the top 50 longest married couples in America.

Fay is remembered as much more than "Just an everyday person." He was actively involved in several community organizations and received numerous awards for his lifetime of work as an educator. You can impact and influence a lot of young lives over 40 years of teaching. What greater legacy is there, than to make a difference in lives of others? Fay Hudson made a difference.

You can read another great interview of Fay at the link below.

http://dc.library.okstate.edu/cdm/ref/collection/hundred/id/59

"Study your Bible. All of life revolves around that in one way or another."

Fay Hudson, 100

Lt. Col. Richard E. Cole

Crew of the Number 1 Bomber: Lt. Richard Cole right front,
Lt. Col. James Doolittle left front.

Richard E. (Dick) Cole was born September 7th, 1915 to Fred and Mable Cole of Dayton, Ohio. The fifth of six children, Dick graduated from Steele High School and completed two years of study at Ohio University. He studied aviation at Whittenberg College, earning his pilot's license before enlisting in the Army in 1940. In July 1941, he was commissioned as a Second Lieutenant in the Army Air Corps and assigned to the 34th Bombardment Squadron, 17th Bombardment Group where, in February 1942, he volunteered for a combat mission just two months after the Japanese attack on Pearl Harbor. On April 18, 1942, the 16 B-25's, known as the "Doolittle Raiders" took off from the deck of the USS Hornet and bombed Tokyo in response to Japan's attack.

Following the Tokyo raid, Lt. Cole remained in southeast Asia flying bombing and supply missions over "The Hump" (Himalayan mountains), from 1942 to 1943. It was a dangerous assignment in which over 600 aircraft and crews were lost. In late 1943 he volunteered for the 1st Air Commando Group and participated in the aerial invasion of Burma from 1943 to 1944.

In 1943, Dick met Martha Harrell at the airport in Tulsa, Oklahoma. *"We got married two weeks later."* Together they had three boys and two girls. He continued his military service, eventually retiring as a Lieutenant Colonel in 1967.

After retiring, Dick and Martha moved to Alamo, Texas and started their own business growing oranges and citrus fruits. In 2003, Martha died after a lengthy battle with Parkinson's disease. Today, Lt. Col. Dick Cole is an active member of the Doolittle Tokyo Raiders Association and is one of the last two surviving Raiders. He continues to travel the nation raising money for the General James H. Doolittle Scholarship Fund and representing the Doolittle Raiders at airshows, museums and other events.

Tell me about the Tokyo Raid.
I was flying B-25's with the 17th Bombardment Group out of Columbia, South Carolina and they needed volunteers for a mission, so I volunteered, our whole group volunteered. The mission called for 16 airplanes, so it took a whole squadron of the 17th Group. They sent us down to Eglin Field in Florida for some training and a Navy Lieutenant taught us how to take off in less than 500 feet; a loaded B-25 normally needs about 3,000 feet to take off.

So, did that tip you off as to the mission?
We thought we were going to the south Pacific, but we didn't know any details. They kept us confined to base and we were told not to talk to anyone about our training. After about a month of training, we flew to Alameda Naval Air Station in California where they loaded our planes (16) onto the USS Hornet and we started sailing west. After a few days sailing, we met up with the USS Enterprise and her task force. That's when they told us we were going to Tokyo. On the morning of the 18th (April 1942) we spotted a Japanese patrol boat; one of the ships opened-fire on it and sunk it, but they had already sent a radio warning, so they decided to launch us immediately.

How far out were you?

The Navy had said they would try to take us in to 400 miles, but we were about 650 miles when we were intercepted.

Did you know you wouldn't have enough fuel to reach your final destination?

No, we didn't know if we would, but we hoped we would. They added 10, five-gallon cans of fuel when we had to launch early.

Tell me about the takeoff and flight?

The carrier was doing about 20 to 30 knots into the wind, plus a wind of another 20 to 30 knots, so the takeoff wasn't a problem. I was in the Number 1 Bomber with Col. Doolittle. We took off and flew the whole mission low to avoid detection. We tried to maintain 200' above sea level, and 168mph. We didn't fly in formation, we didn't have enough fuel for that. We only saw one other plane the whole time, the Number 2. After about four hours we shored in north of Tokyo. I remember seeing people on the beach, but they didn't seem to care. I think they thought we were one of their airplanes. We turned south and headed toward Tokyo.

What was your target and your bomb load?

Our target was northwest Tokyo. We had incendiary bombs and we were to light up Tokyo. After dropping the bombs, we dropped back down on the deck and headed southwest toward China. The plan was to land and refuel at Chuchow (Zhuzhou) and continue to western China, but several hours past Tokyo, the navigator told us we weren't going to have enough fuel. Fortunately, we caught a tailwind and that helped us.

What happened?

We were at about 9,000 feet at night when we ran out of fuel. It was raining; we bailed out, one at a time. I landed in a pine tree and spent the night there. The next morning, I climbed down and started walking West.

So, you're alone, behind enemy lines; what's going through your mind?
Trying to keep away from the Japanese. It was occupied territory. If you walk East, you're going to walk right into their hands. The only thing to do was walk west and stay the hell away from everything. So, I elected to take the high ground and go up and down the hills and mountains rather than look for a road or look for somebody for help. I walked all day and only saw a woodcutter and two students. I didn't see anybody else. It wasn't really scary. As long as you didn't see anybody, what is there to be afraid of? We were in a pretty isolated area. We didn't ever go to the place we were supposed to go to because we drifted over another range of mountains.

So how did you get out?
The next day, I made contact with some Chinese guerillas. They took me to an outpost where Col. Doolittle was. The rest of our crew made it there within a few days. From there, we traveled by foot, horse, bus and seating chair until we arrived at a large river where we were smuggled aboard a river boat and eventually made it to a gathering place at Heng Yang which was a place where the Flying Tigers had a flight of P-40s. From there a C-47 flew us to the capitol of Chungking (Chongqing).

What about the rest of the crews?
All of the planes made it to China, except one that was low on fuel; they landed in Vladivostok, Russia and were held for 13 months. The other crews bailed out or crash-landed. Three died, eight were taken prisoner by the Japanese; three of those were executed. The rest eventually made it to Heng Yang, thanks to the Chinese. We wouldn't have made it without their help. They say the Japanese killed over 250,000 Chinese for helping us escape.

They say that the Doolittle Raids led to the Japanese's decision to attack Midway, which was the turning point of the war.
That's what they say.

So, you guys changed history.
I don't know about that. I think he changed it (Doolittle); I didn't change it. We were just part of the big picture.

Did you ever have any close calls?
If I did, I didn't know about it. Never took any hits; never even shot a gun.

Did you ever have to bail out again?
Nope.

That was your only jump?
Yep.

Did you like it?
I didn't particularly like it.... but it was necessary at the time.

As a Lieutenant Colonel, what have you learned about leadership?
That's one thing we all learned from Col. Doolittle. He was the individual that really brought out the importance of being a team. Everybody was a team member; he was a team member. He would take any question or help you out in any way. There was no rank separation. Everybody was on equal footing. The only exception was if you didn't do something right, then you were messing up the *team-ship*, and that's when he would talk to you or discipline you. Fortunately, he didn't have to do that due to the way he handled people. We couldn't have done this (the Tokyo raid) alone. The pilots, the crews, the mechanics, the Navy, Lt. Miller teaching us how to take off from a carrier, the Chinese, it took all of us to pull it off. You couldn't have done that by yourself. The team only succeeds when everyone is working together and pulling for the same goal. That's why we succeeded. I tried to take those same principles to my teams.

You have a lot of respect for Col. Doolittle.
Hell yeah.

Tell me about your wife.
I met my wife at the airport in Tulsa, Oklahoma. Her name was Martha Harrell. I was about to take a B-25 up to about 30,000 feet to test out a new radar system. She pulled up on a bicycle and said she'd been taking flying lessons and wanted to go up in big plane. I told her she couldn't go up in this one, and she left, or so I thought. So, we took off and at about 12,000 feet, she stuck her head in the cockpit! Well, I had to scrub the mission right there, but I didn't want to say anything because I didn't want to get her fired. The other pilot was a little older than me and handed her a book of matches and asked for her phone number. Well, she wrote down her phone number on the book of matches, but she gave it back to me! (laughing). It took me about a week to get up the nerve to call her....*and we got married two weeks later!* That was on October 11, 1943.

And was it a good marriage?
I guess so. We were in our 60th year when she passed away in 2003. She had Parkinson's disease.

What's the secret?
Like I said, it's teamwork. The two of you are in this together. You can't make it work all on your own; it takes both of you. You have to love and respect each other and be able to count on each other. Otherwise you'll never succeed.

So, leadership principles work in marriage too.
Absolutely! They work everywhere.

Do you have any regrets?
Regret's a pretty big word. Now if you were to ask me if I'd any mistakes...! (laughing)

Did you make any mistakes?
There were a lot of missed opportunities (still laughing), but there's none that I would do anything drastic about.

Is there anything you would have done differently? Actually, I would like to have gone and tried to finish college. I only had two years. There's nothing that would have had a major effect on my being satisfied with life.

What's the biggest lesson you learned in life?
I don't know, maybe I haven't learned it yet! (laughing)
There's a lot of lessons in life.... just like flying. You've got to have a lot of lessons or else you'll end up in the ground. The biggest thing for me is to take things as they come and do the best you can, and don't worry about the rest.

What the toughest thing you've been through in your life?
The loss of Martha and the loss Christina, (daughter) and the loss of Andrew (son).

How did you get through that?
Just like I said, you take everything as it comes and you do the best you can, but don't let it affect your outlook on life. Sometimes things happen that you can't do anything about, and you just have to learn to deal with it. In the case of someone's death, they wouldn't want you to be remorseful for the rest of your life. You've got to carry on. It takes you some time though.

Do you ever get over it?
No, you don't get over it.... you learn to live with it.

What matters most in life?
Life itself is a gift, okay? And you should treat it as such. It's your responsibility to appreciate and to take that gift and do the best you can with it. That would include all the facets of living.... you could write a book almost, on all the requirements. I just think you accept the work and the fun and the responsibilities of life and enjoy it.

At the time of publishing, Lt. Col. Cole is the only remaining survivor of the Doolittle Raiders, and at age 102, he continues to travel, representing the Raiders at airshows throughout the U.S.

For his bravery and service, Col. Cole was awarded three Distinguished Flying Crosses with 2 Oak Leaf Clusters, the Air Medal with 1 Oak Leaf Cluster, the Bronze Star, the Air Force Commendation Medal, and Chinese Army-Navy-Air Corps Medal, Class A, 1ˢᵗ Grade, the Presidential Unit Citation and the Congressional Gold Medal which was awarded to all the Doolittle Raiders. "But," he states, "all they do is collect dust!"

A simple online search produces dozens of articles, interviews and videos of Dick Cole and the Doolittle Raiders. I have included a few links below that are worth viewing.

Thank you for your service Col. Cole, and thank you for the wisdom. You truly are one of "The Greatest Generation."

https://youtu.be/-yXzYxUC93A
https://en.wikipedia.org/wiki/Doolittle_Raid
www.doolittleraider.com
https://en.wikipedia.org/wiki/The_Hump
https://youtu.be/sAmbQaC4a7c

The Number 1 Bomber taking off from the USS Hornet, April 18,1942

Mary Tankersly

Mary Pearson was born February 21, 1901 in the community of Caviness, Texas. One of nine children, her brother Alfred died as an infant. *"That wasn't too uncommon back in those days."* Her father Edmund, owned a coffectionary near downtown Paris, Texas while her mother Laura Ellen raised the family. In 1916, Mary recalls sitting on top of a hill outside of town and watching the city of Paris burn. After graduating from Paris High School in 1918, Mary attended Paris Commercial College, graduated in 1920, and went to work as a stenographer and secretary. At age 20 she moved to Dallas to work and met Onnie Tankersly whom she married two years later in 1923. Together they had 2 daughters. In 1934, Mary and her family moved back to Paris, into the same house she grew up in. In 1968, Onnie C. Tankersly died after 45 years of marriage. After his death Mary continued to work and live in Paris, she never remarried. She continued to be an active member of her church and in 2006, at age 105, she left her home to move in with her daughter after 99 years of living there.

You've been through some hard times.
Oh yeah. We went thru the depression way back then. You've heard about that haven't you? We had to give up a lot of things and cut here and there. We even lost the house we were living in because money was so tight, but we pulled through. I remember I had been working and I decided I would quit because I wanted a young man to take my place. My boss didn't want me to quit, but I told him I had to take care of my child. That was during the depression days, and that young man had a family to provide for. I figured he needed it worse than me. My husband had a job, but there were a lot of people that didn't have jobs. That was a tough time

What did you learn from living through the depression?
I learned to save money. I told myself I'd put five dollars away every payday. You never know when you're going to need it. But I left the finances up to someone who was smarter than me. Things aren't as bad now as they used to be, but if things keep going the way they are, we could see it get that way.

What would you say is the secret to living such a long and healthy life?
I wish I knew. God's just been good to me I guess. The doctors told me to eat well and exercise, and I tried to do that. I never went to a gym to exercise, I just worked, and I walked to work.   I am still very healthy; I try to eat right. I haven't had much sickness in my life because I took care of myself.   I try to stay busy, but I can't do as much as I used to. My daughter does so much for me now; I think I'm spoiled.   I remember one time in 1977, the doctors told me I had cancer. They removed my colon and I stayed in ICU four days, but that was the only surgery I ever had. I didn't have to have chemotherapy or radiation; the surgery took care of it all. But even when they say it's gone, there's still no guarantees. I'm just glad to be here still and I'll stay here just as long as God says so. When He's ready, I'm going to try to be ready too. But for now, I'm still here.

You've been through a lot, the Depression, your husband died, colon cancer.... What would you say was your biggest challenge?
Well, all of them were tough.... but my husband passing away...that was bad.... that really was.

How do you get through something like that?
You just have to go on, and keep going. Take it one day at a time. That's all you can do. It's hard sometimes, but God's not going to put more on you than you can do at any one time.

You have 30 great-grandchildren. If you could only give them one piece of advice about life, what would you tell them?
Always do the right thing. I have an idea that you can live your life like you want as long as you do the right thing. You know what is right and wrong, and I hope you're going to do what it right. Just do what's right as much as you can, as long as you can. If you do right to other people, they'll do right to you. That's how I've tried to live and I think things have worked out pretty well for me.

Visiting with Mrs. Tankersly was especially enjoyable for me because she had been a friend of my grandmother's. She is somewhat of a legend in my hometown. At age 99 she insisted on crawling underneath her house with a contractor to assess some foundation problems. She drove until age 102 and at age 105, she finally left the home she grew up in to move in with her daughter. She had lived there for 99 years.

Mary Pearson Tankersly died peacefully on December 28, 2011 at the age of 110 at her daughter's home. She left behind 2 daughters, 8 grandchildren, 30 great-grandchildren and 2 great-great-grandchildren. "And that's enough!" God bless you Mrs. Tankersly. Please tell my grandmother I miss her.

*"I don't think about dying much.
Why should I? I'm too busy living."*

Mary Tankersly, 108

Louise McCaleb

Bessie Louise Busey was born January 21, 1908 into a family of six children. Her father owned a grocery store and later worked as a vice-president of a local bank. Louise graduated high school and attended two years of college before dropping out to marry Oscar Dever in 1925. *"It was a mistake, dropping out of school, but I loved him so much."* Together they had two sons, Jack and Bill. Oscar died in 1936. Louise then enrolled in business college to complete her degree and got a job at the local electric company making $90 a month. She later married Burt McCaleb and inherited four stepchildren, but later in life, both Burt and her son, Jack, would die of cancer. *"It was the hardest thing I ever went through; it almost killed me...but I'm tough."*

What's it like being 100 years old?
I never thought anything about age. Gosh, I'm over a hundred years old! That's a century, and I'm still here! Age has never bothered me, I've never worried about it. I'm very fortunate. I'm in good health, and really there's nothing wrong with me except old age. Oh, my back hurts a little but I don't complain about it. I never complain.... ever. It doesn't do you any good. At this age, I could have a million things wrong with me like some people do, but I'm just very fortunate. 100 years.... I don't know if I'm any smarter, but you *sure*

get a lot wiser.

You said you went to business college after Oscar died. Why?
Because education is *so* important! I was just so young when he died. I was only in my 30's, and there I was left with two little boys to look after and only $2000 worth of insurance; that was it. That's why I had to go to business college, so I could get a good job and provide for my boys. I remember sitting at the typewriter learning to type with the tears falling. I just went ahead and cried and typed. It wasn't easy but I had to be strong. I think it's more important today than when I was then. Kids now, if they don't have an education, they can't get any type of a job and I don't know what they would do. I think parents should really do all they can to see that their children get a good education.

How did you get over your husband's death?
You don't get over it. You never get over it. It's always with you. But there's nothing you can do about it. You can't just sit around and grieve. You've got to be strong. You've got to go on. It's not easy, but you've got to.

The worst thing that's ever happened in my life was losing my son. It about killed me when Jack died. I've always heard and read that the worst thing that can happen to a woman is to lose a child because that child is part of you. You carry that child in your body for nine months and its part of you, but Jack's gone. It's hard when you lose a child, but you know you can't just sit down and grieve about it. You can't do that. You just have to be strong and go on. I may not look like it but I am a very strong person. I'm tough.

Where do you get your strength from?
God. He helped me through all that. I did a lot of praying. Like I said, I'm a very fortunate person.

So, you believe in God?
Of course I believe in God, and I think that God has helped me. I've been through a lot, losing two husbands and a son, and I think He helped me get through those times.

The first time I had to be strong for my children, they couldn't see me crying. You just have to be strong, but He's the one that gives you the strength.

Do you ever think about dying?
Well I know I'm going to but I don't worry about it. I've always taken good care of myself and that's the reason I think I'm so old. After all, I'm over a hundred years old. I'm not afraid of it, I know it's going to happen, but what can you do? You can't prevent it, you just have to face it. All my family's gone except me. I've lived longer than any of them. I know I'm going to die; I just hope that I die before I get so old and cripple that I can't get around or don't have a good mind. That would be terrible.

If you could only give me one piece of wisdom, what would you say?
Believe in God. Be a good person and be good to people. You know anybody can be mean and ugly, but it's just as easy to be nice. Be nice to people, it does you more good. I always try to be nice, and I never, never, ever complain. It doesn't do any good and it makes you very unpopular.

Louise Dever McCaleb died on October 24, 2008, just six months after our meeting. She left behind her son, Bill, three stepchildren, four grandchildren, five great-grandchildren, and one great-great-grandchild.

"I never complain.... ever.
It doesn't do you any good
and it makes you very unpopular."

Louise McCaleb, 100

Ethel Brockelbank

Ethel Zamba was born in Lyndora, Pennsylvania on June 17, 1906. Her mother and father were shopkeepers at a local merchandising store. *"There were eleven of us kids. Mom was too busy at the store to deal with us, so we had to learn how to work out our own problems."* In 1917, at age 11, she began knitting blankets for American soldiers in World War I which began a lifelong love of sewing. In 1927, she married Garnet Brockelbank. Together they had two daughters, and were married for 42 years before his death in 1970. Ethel continued to work various jobs as a professional seamstress and upholsterer until retiring. At age 99, she decided to join her church's choir. *"It was something I'd always wanted to do."*

With 42 years of marriage, what's the secret to a good marriage?
Well, I was married for 42 years, but they weren't good years. We didn't have a good marriage. We had lots of problems, but money was our biggest problem. We lived paycheck to paycheck. That's why being smart with your money is so important. If you live check to check, you don't have a good time.

If it was a bad marriage, why did you stay for 42 years?
If you're not happy in a situation, sometimes you have to stay anyway and you just have to make the best of it some way. Even though the marriage wasn't right, I'm thankful that I had two children who love me. If you select somebody that doesn't love the Lord, and you do, you're in trouble. And I was in trouble, hoping it would change, hoping that it would get better. And you live on that hope, one day at a time, always waiting for the next day. That was our marriage.

So what advice would you have for someone who's in a bad marriage?
Being in a marriage that wasn't good, you have to have somebody; I had the Lord. We had some hard times and that's how I got through them.... on hope.

There should be harmony in the home so that you both know what you're doing. There has to be compatibility. You should be able to converse with each other. If you don't have that you don't have anything. There has to be a give and take situation. It can't be one sided or it won't work. In a marriage two people have got to pull the wagon the same direction, but it wasn't that way with us.

So, what is the biggest lesson you learned about marriage?
Don't try to make anybody over. By that I mean, don't try to change people. Just accept them the way they are. The only person you can change is yourself; the rest is up to God. I always thought people ought to do this or do that, but if they don't understand or don't want to do it.... they don't do it. And if you're married, you have to love them anyway....and that's not easy!

After forty-two years of marriage I finally learned that I couldn't make people do *anything*.... I don't even try anymore. So, let it go. Finally, the last two years of his life, my husband gave his heart to the Lord. So, if I didn't save anybody else from going to hell.... I saved one.

But you seem so happy. What is the key to your happiness?
You have to find happiness in life, and without the Lord I don't think you can really find happiness. That's where you'll find your peace. I really believe that. It's simple to me now. For 42 years I didn't have peace, now I do. That's Him, only Him. I know that without Him I can't do anything. He is *"giving back what the locusts have eaten."* If you don't read the Bible, you don't know what's in it. The Bible is full of His promises. I know the Lord and I know His promises. I've gone through the Bible every year of my life. I read it through and through, one end to the other and start all over again, and I still find new stuff in it! It's been my guide to life.

So why do you think you're still here?
He has put me here, He has kept me here 'cause He needs me here. He put us here for something. I know what the Lord wants of me and I'm busy doing all those things. Some don't find their purpose but I found my mine. He tells me what to do and I do it and if I fail then I try again some other way. I feel I could go on a long time if He keeps me here. I've lived a long life and knowing that He gave me all this extra time, which a lot of people don't have.... I should appreciate that and appreciate that I feel as good as I do. And when he calls me, I'll go. I'm not afraid, I know where I'm going.

Although she didn't talk about it much, Ethel was quite renowned for her talent of sewing and quilt design at one point working personally for famed WWI fighter ace Eddie Rickenbacker. Today, several of her quilts are on display in various museums and archives. In her later years she continued to sew, knitting stocking caps for premature babies at the local hospital saying, "It keeps me busy."

On February 27, 2010, God called and Ethel went at the age of 103. She left behind two children, six grandchildren, seven great-grandchildren, and five great-great-grandchildren.

Frank Hurst

Francis John Hurst was born May 16, 1914 in Paris, France, two months before the outbreak of WWI. Following the war, Frank and his family led a normal life, working and attending school. He graduated high school in 1932 and attended one year of college before going to work as a pilot, surveying and mapping western Africa. *"I caught malaria and was pronounced dead two times!"*

In 1934, he moved to England where he met and married his wife Lila. When WWII broke out in 1939, Frank enlisted in the British army and was assigned to the British Army Intelligence Corp. Due to his knowledge of the French language, culture and landscape, Frank became an aid to General Dwight Eisenhower and was instrumental in the planning and execution of the D-Day invasions. Several days after D-Day, he parachuted into France to continue planning the allied invasion and the liberation of Paris. *"I'm not a hero. I wasn't in combat, but I like to think that I helped save a few lives."* Following the war, Frank went to work at Kodak Ltd. In 1957, the company transferred him to Canada, where he continued

to work until retiring. In 2010, his wife Lila died after 76 years of marriage.

You seem to be in a very good mood?
I've had a happy life. I've been very, very lucky. I don't think anyone could have had a better life than mine. I've had adventure, joy, sorrow; I've had everything. It's been good, and I'm so happy with my life now. I'm very, very fortunate, and I have quite a good philosophy of life I think.

What is that philosophy? Contentment. Taking things one day at a time and not getting too serious about unfortunate mishaps.

But a lot of people aren't happy with their life. What makes you so happy?
Because I accept life as it comes. I realize that I can't always be happy, but I try to make the best of it. I've always made the best of every circumstance I've been in, whether I've been in danger, or in personal situations or what have you. I've always tried to make the best of it. I've always taken the view that things could always be worse than what I'm in, but I don't worry about it. I take care of what I can, and what I can't take care of, to hell with it. (laughs) My philosophy is pretty simple. Take life as it comes, and enjoy it for what it is. And it's been the story of my life.

Did that philosophy help you when you wife died?
Oh very much so. When my wife passed away, that was hard. I didn't realize how much I was in love and how much I'd missed her. When she passed away, there was an immense void *(pointing to his heart)*. I remember going to the funeral; that was terrible. I thought that was the end of everything. When I kneeled in front of her coffin, to me, it was the end of the world. I thought that was the end of my life. Then, the day after, I realized it wasn't.

How did you get through that?
I just took it one day at a time. It took me awhile, but gradually I adjusted. I began to realize that I was still around, and I had to make the best of my life. That's always been my attitude. I take the view

that I am very fortunate to be alive. What has happened, has happened and there's nothing I can do about it....and what's going to happen, will happen. Like today, if something happens, I take the best that I can out of it. I don't dwell on the past and groan about my misfortune. What's the point of that? It is what it is. If I die tomorrow I've had a good life, if I live on, I'll still have a good life.

Do you have any regrets?
I've never consciously tried to do the wrong thing. I've never been cruel by intention, but I have unintentionally hurt people and I regret that. I had a very good marriage, but I was unfaithful. It was just a passing thing, you know. That was it, but I regret that now. I was ashamed because my wife was a very, very decent woman. She knew something was going on, but she never played around. Eventually, she forgave me and we had a very good relationship, but if I could go back, I wouldn't do it. I'd be faithful because I hurt her. All that did was hurt people.

To what do you attribute your long life?
I think what's kept me going is my attitude about life.... otherwise I'm sure I'd be dead by now. I'm a very fortunate man in every way. I've got my wits, I've got my health, I've got good friends, I've got a nice girlfriend, my two daughters stay in touch with me.... I've got good relationships. I'm enjoying life. Philosophically, I take a positive look on life. You know, I've had some very happy moments and some very, very sad moments but they're part of life. I accept what comes and do the best I can with it. I'm very content with what's happened to me and what's coming to me. My health has been really good. I don't drink much, but I do like the odd nip. I think I was drunk once back in the army, and I was so sick I swore I'd never do it again. I'm very moderate with everything I do. I used to smoke, but not heavily. I eat what I like, but I don't eat things that are bad for me. My father lived to 102, and my mother lived to 97, so I've got good genes. I'm not worried about being sick. If I die tomorrow, I've had a good life. If I live another ten years, that's fine. I'm not worried about it. Que sera, sera...What will be, will be. Tomorrow is tomorrow. Today is today. All in all, I would be described as a very contented person. I'm happy up

here. (pointing to his head) That's more important than down here (pointing to his heart), but I'm quite happy here too. Mental attitude is what does it.... I think that's what keeps me going.

Do you ever think about dying?
Oh no. Not at all. I'm going to live forever (laughing). No....I never think about dying. Sometimes when I'm ill I feel concerned, but that's it. I've never thought about actually croaking. I think that's what's keeping me alive. I'm not worried what's going to happen to me tomorrow. Today is today, period. What happened yesterday, happened. Some was good, some not so good, but that's that, it happened and I can't change it. I'm fortunate to still be here, but if I drop dead tomorrow, I'll be smiling five minutes before *(laughing)!* Life has been good, and it continues to be good.... right down to the last minute.

Are you afraid of dying?
Nope! If I die tomorrow, I die tomorrow. That's it. Honestly, I've had a very good life, and I'm very happy and I'm contented. I never think about either going to heaven, or down there (pointing downward). To me it will be just a termination, but I won't be thinking about where I'm going.

So, do you believe in God?
Oh yeah. I don't consider myself a religious person but I have beliefs. I'm not a church goer per say.... but I'll go now and again.... but I'm not registered as a member. I think you can be faithful without being religious. I think faith is God-made while religion is man-made. I've done some good things and some bad things but by and large I think I lived a very very good, interesting, happy life and I think I'll make it for a few more years *(smiling)*.

Today, Frank lives in a retirement center in southern Ontario. "I have two daughters, three grandchildren and one great grandchild. I'm a very, very fortunate man." Of all the people I have interviewed, I don't think I have ever met another person with such a positive mental attitude. His philosophy on life has

fundamentally changed the way I view events in my own life. Let's face it, life happens.... and many times, there is nothing we can do about it. The best we can hope for is to change the things we can, and accept the things we can't. Sometimes life is unfair, I can't change that, so all I can do is look for the best in each situation and move on. I know it sounds simpler than it really is, but Frank Hurst is proof that it works. Thank you, Frank, for the wisdom. You have changed my life.

Below is a link to an audio interview of Frank talking about World War II. It is definitely worth listening to.

http://www.thememoryproject.com/stories/1022:frank-j.-hurst/

"My philosophy is pretty simple. Take life as it comes, and enjoy it for what it is... and it's been the story of my life."

Frank Hurst, 102

Testing the Theory

I've written and re-written this chapter a hundred times in my head and on paper. This quest for wisdom and the people who have shared it with me have certainly been life altering, but I was totally unprepared to *"test the theory"* myself.

It was around 4pm, June 24th, 2013 when the phone rang. It was my sister, Kathy, telling me my father had collapsed and was in an ambulance enroute to the ER. The paramedics were performing CPR. As a paramedic of almost 20 years myself, I knew the grim reality of the situation. Then the adrenaline hit and my mind raced, but I found the composure to stop and pray for God to give wisdom and skill to the medics, nurses and doctors that were caring for my father. I prayed for his survival, but I didn't really believe it. I had seen it; I had lived it too many times before.

After throwing some clothes in a bag and calling my brothers, Kathy called again, crying, "He didn't make it." The words were short and piercing, but clear and final. "I know" I replied. "I love you and I'll be there in three hours."

As I started on that long trip back home, the adrenaline began to subside and my racing thoughts seemed to slow. And then the words began to come back, like they were always there, but unable to penetrate through the noise and chaos of the situation.

They were the words of wisdom spoken to me by all these people, telling me again how they had coped with their own losses of parents, spouses and children. I've already explained my theory that every problem we will ever face has already been experienced by someone before us; that the whole premise of wisdom is to learn from how others have dealt with these problems. But it never occurred to me that God would use *me* as the test subject for my own theory.

As the words flowed through my mind, the voice of Frank Hurst

seemed the loudest and clearest; *"What has happened, has happened, and there's nothing I can do about it. When my wife passed away, I thought that was the end of my life, then the day after, I realized it wasn't. I realized that I was still around and I had to make the best of my life."*

And Delmar Hopkins; *"You've got to let them go. You can't bring them back. I don't care if it's your mother, father, sister or brother, they're put here on earth to die, and you've got to realize that you've got to let them go. Sure, it hurts. It takes a lot out of you but you've got to put it behind you and keep on with your life."*

And so many others....

I can't say the words were comforting, but they were calming. I realized that if these other people could survive this tragedy, then I could too. It wouldn't be easy, but all I had to do was follow in their footsteps.

In hindsight, it's interesting to note that while, at the time, I thought I was totally unprepared for the sudden loss of my father, in reality, I had been prepared for precisely such an event by every person I had interviewed.

I realized that wisdom doesn't just help us solve problems we are currently experiencing; it *prepares* us to face the challenges that lie before us. Wisdom not only guided me through the darkness of my father's death; it gave me peace and confidence that I can overcome the next obstacle that life throws at me.

None of us know what the future holds for us. Maybe it's better that way. One thing is for sure, there will be challenges to face, but I feel a certain comfort in knowing that someone out there has already faced that challenge before me, and if they made it, I can make it.

Life's journey will have its share of mountains and valleys, and though we may feel abandoned and alone in our struggles, we're

not. There are many who have gone before us, who have faced the same challenges and conquered the same obstacles, who have blazed a trail for us to follow.

Our job is to find those people and learn from their mistakes, their experiences.... their wisdom, and with each new challenge that we face and conquer, we gain our own experience and wisdom. It is then our duty to share it with those who follow.

"I don't dwell on the past and groan about my misfortune. What's the point of that? It is what it is. If I die tomorrow I've had a good life, if I live on, I'll still have a good life."

Frank Hurst, 102

"In this world you will have trouble. But take heart! I have overcome the world."

John 16:33 NIV

Agnes K. Hahn

Agnes Katherine Hahn was born June 6, 1906 in Jeannette, Pennsylvania; the fourth of 10 children. As a child, she attended school through high school before dropping out to care of her ill mother, manage the household and raise the other children. *"I sure missed going to school."* Agnes later completed her high school education by correspondence course, and continued to live at home while taking care of her mother and siblings until she met Walter Hahn. They married just three weeks later. *"The first night I went out with him I knew we were going to get married!"* Together they had one son, James. After 35 years of marriage, Walter was killed in a traffic accident by a drunk driver. Agnes continued to work and raise James as a single mother and never remarried. At age 97, she was diagnosed with cancer but refused chemotherapy. *"The doctor threw me a birthday party when I turned 98 because he thought it would be my last. When that didn't work, he threw a 99th birthday party a year later!"* At the time of this interview Agnes is 102.... and cancer free.

You said you've worked all your life, what do you mean?
There was 10 of us children; five boys and five girls. The oldest was born in 1900 and the youngest in 1923. I was in the middle so

I had to help take care of the younger ones. My mother had her last baby while I was still in high school and was pretty ill for a few years afterward so I quit school to stay home and help her. I missed most of high school but I studied and read a lot of books from the public library and graduated by taking correspondence courses.

I've always worked. I mostly did what other people didn't want to do, mainly odd jobs. My father worked in a glass factory, and we owned a restaurant that I ran when I was just 16 years old. I ran it by myself. We served hamburgers and chili and stuff like that. I cooked and mother baked pies for me to sell the next day.... if she felt good enough. When she didn't, I'd stay up at night and make them myself. All the customers knew us but some of them cheated me. I thought they were my friends and I expected them to pay, but I should have known better. Later, we had a sewing machine shop and I got my certificate of teaching for sewing from a correspondence course, so I taught sewing classes.

What was the secret to your and Walter's marriage?
You have to be able to agree on things. If you can't agree, there's nothing else to a marriage. Compromise and working things out together, that's what marriage is all about. When I was a kid and we had arguments, my mother never let us go to bed mad. She'd make us stay up and talk it over. When you finally got tired and sleepy enough, you'd finally agree on something. I think that was a pretty good idea! You've got to learn to get along; otherwise, there's no use being together. My husband and I always got along good. In fact, we married when I was 30.... *three weeks after we met!* The first night I went out with him I knew we were going to get married. I don't know why, but I did.

What's the biggest lesson life has taught you?
Don't expect anything, by that I mean don't make big plans. I had my life all mapped out, but life has a way of changing things. When you make all kinds of plans about what you're going to do, they depend on too many other people. Sometimes those people don't come through for you. I've had a lot of people let me down, but you've got to learn to roll with the punches.... and there's *lots* of

punches. Whenever something comes along you just take care of it. Don't expect somebody to do it for you.

Do you have any regrets?
When I left home for the first time, I worked for the government, and I hated that job.
I was a telephone operator, and I reported everything I heard people say on the telephone.
I was spying. That's one thing I regret, that I ever told on anybody. I just don't believe in spying on people. If the government has to do it, let them do it themselves.

You said you managed a restaurant at age 16. How did you learn to handle money?
We lived through the depression and it was hard. My father was a spendthrift. He loaned money to anybody that wanted it. But they'd spend the money on stuff they didn't need and a lot of times, couldn't afford to pay him back.... and when he did get paid back, he'd turn around and loan it right back to them again! I learned to be very careful about loaning money.... *especially* to family.

At one point we owned a store, and then my brother-in-law took over and he ran it into the dump. He lost all the money on gambling. We really could have had a good time of it, but he lost it all. We were broke. We didn't even have money to pay for the next day's food; we were as low as you can go. It took a while, but finally we paid the bills, and paid all the debts off. I learned from that, not to let anybody else handle the cash. I took care of it after that.

What have you learned about growing old?
Getting old is very inconvenient. You don't feel like doing anything. It's hard getting around, and it's hard asking someone to do everything for you. I finally gave up driving the car when I was 95. I was smart enough to realize that it was time. Then when I was 97, and I was told I had cancer. The doctor wanted me to take all kinds of treatment. I had two other sisters that died of cancer.... *died during treatment!* I told the doctor I wasn't going to go through all that stuff; I'm just going to live the rest of my life. The

doctor threw me a birthday party when I turned 98. because he thought it would be my last. When that didn't work, he threw a 99th birthday party a year later! You've got to be tough to live to a hundred!

Do you believe in God?
I believe in God, but I don't believe in most churches because I think they tend to do more harm than good. It's great to have a choice, but if people can't agree on one religion and one church.... something's wrong. There's only supposed to be one God, but each church tells you something different; you can't do this or you can't do that and then some other church says go ahead and do that, it's alright. It's not up to them to tell me what I should or shouldn't do. It's between me and God.

Agnes Hahn passed away on August 1, 2008 at the age of 102.

Bertie Lee Bolton

Photo of Bertie Lee, her parents and younger sister.

Bertie Lee Frye was born to a family of cotton farmers on May 25, 1904 in the small community of Rockford, Texas. She attended school in Burnet, Texas where she completed the 10th grade before marrying her high school sweetheart, Clyde Bolton in December 1925. Together they had five children, two of which died at birth. Bertie and Clyde were married for 69 years before his death in 1995. Together they raised cotton and corn on their Texas farm using a mule-drawn plow until buying their first tractor in 1948. Bertie was 40 years old before she had electricity in her home, and 52 before she had indoor plumbing. *"A lot of things have changed since those days."*

What's the biggest lesson you've learned in the past 100 years?
I'd say to just take things as they come and try to do what is right. Life is going to throw a lot of different stuff at you and you just have to deal with it as it comes. There's not much you can do to prevent it, most of it anyways. You just have to learn to deal with it. You just do what you have to do.

I remember living through the depression. We didn't have much so we had to do what we could to survive. We farmed our land; we had a crop every year. We had cotton, corn and potatoes. We had

cows and horses. We had a garden; we killed hogs...we just did what we could to get by. We'd plant corn so we'd have roastin' ears and what we didn't need, we'd sell. We picked the cotton and sold it too. It was hard times. You just do what you have to do. Money was tight. We had to know where every penny went. We had to work hard. I don't think kids nowadays know how to work hard, not like we did.

You said money was tight, how did you manage your money?
When you get it, you save it. You buy what you need and nothing else, and you save your money. You don't go around spending it foolishly on things that you end up throwing away. You buy what you need and you take care of what you buy, and save the rest. Someday you're going to need it. Getting old is expensive! Can you imagine working at my age? You'd better start saving your money! Put it in the bank and save it for when you get old so you won't have to work.

If you could go back, is there anything you would do differently?
I'd get a better education. I went to school through the 10th grade, but if I had it to do again I'd get more education and go to college. Education is important, above anything else. Now days you've got to have a good education if you want to make anything of yourself. My life would have been a lot easier if I'd had a better education. I wish I'd had more of it, that way I'd have come out better than I did.

What is the hardest thing you've had to deal with in your life?
My daughter, Mary Lee's death. That was something. It was awful for her to be taken away from me. I almost never got over that.

How did you get over it?
I don't think you get over something like that as much as you just seem to get through it. I just kept asking the Lord to help me. It wasn't overnight, but gradually, day by day, I got through it. Some days it was all I could do to just get out of bed. But what can you do? You can't quit; you just have to go on and keep living. You've got to think about all the reasons you still have to live. Finally, one

day, I just came to the realization that she's gone and there's nothing I can do about it. I still think about her but I can't change what's already done.

You mentioned asking the Lord for help. What do you think about God?
I love God. I try to live right do right by Him and I say my prayers every day. Looking back, I see how God has directed my life all these years....and I've had a pretty good life. And someday when my time comes, I'll go. When the Lord wants to take you, He'll take you...It don't matter. I'm proud of my life. I've lived right, I've done the best I could and I'm satisfied with that. I'm ready to go when the Lord calls me.

The Lord called Bertie on November 3, 2009. She was 105 years old. She left behind two children, nine grandchildren, eighteen great-grandchildren and five great-great-grandchildren. She was an amazing woman and left an amazing legacy.

"Getting old is expensive!"

Bertie Bolton, 104

Dorothy Wilson

Dorothy Stewart was born January 18, 1914, to Fred and Anna Stewart of Muskogee Oklahoma. By her accounts, Dorothy had a normal childhood, attending school and playing with her two brothers, Paul and Fred. *"I was the only girl and I never let anybody forget it either."* After graduating high school, Dorothy went to work at the local drugstore and on November 14, 1932 she married Merle Wilson at the age of 18. Together they had three children, Don, Nancy and Mike. Dorothy later took a job with Sears Roebuck, where she continued to work for many years. In 1965 her husband, Merle, died after thirty-three years of marriage.

It sounds like you raised a good family. What was your secret?
It all starts with the parents. When Merle and I got married, we married for love, but once we were married it was just work, work, work. We were so busy, it never occurred to us to get a divorce. We didn't quarrel a lot, but I could tell when he was mad. We would fight, then kiss and make up. We always

tried to work things out between us; I think that's important. You've got to be willing to compromise and work things out. I wasn't much for blasting anybody with a bunch of words when I got mad, so I didn't have a lot to be pardoned for later on.

As far as the kids go, my parents weren't overly strict and I wasn't either. We raised 3 great kids together. We loved them and treated them all the same. We went to church, they never drank or caused any trouble....at least none that I know of! If they had ended up in prison I would've disowned them!

When the war (WWII) broke out, Merle joined the Navy and went to the South Pacific and so I had to do everything without his being there. That was a tough one. I had to take care of the house and the kids *and* I was working full time. I was more or less a single parent. But as the war was ending, they started sending the men with families' home, and that was a good step for me 'cause Merle came home after that. They all went on to have good lives and good families. I'm proud of my kids and I'm thankful that they're still around. They're getting up there in age too, but they're all healthy.

What's it like getting old?
I never thought about growing old, all of a sudden when I got to be about 95 I thought *"I'm old!"* But I feel very fortunate. I am pretty healthy, I have my memory, I have my family and I am really blessed by the Lord that I can still get around. I've always been independent. I try to a stay positive. There's people that you're afraid to ask how they are because they're always grumblin' about something. I don't want to be like that. I think your attitude is everything.

What's your best piece of advice?
Think of other people and not just yourself. Have respect for

other people and try to help them.

What was the one thing that caused you the most trouble in your life?
Tryin' to help other people *(laughing)!* Relatives that were out looking for a job and a place to live probably caused me the most problems, 'cause we'd take 'em in. We didn't have room for 'em but we'd take 'em in. That's just the way people were when I was growing up. You wouldn't turn a relative away. If someone needed something and they couldn't help themselves, we'd do what we could to help, but if they can help themselves it's important to let them do it themselves, otherwise they'll just keep comin' back askin' for more and more. Some people need to learn to grow up and take responsibility.

Do you have any regrets?
Looking back, life goes by fast. You'd better live it while you can. I've led a plain vanilla life. Marriage, work, kids; God has played an important part in my life too. He watches over me all the time. He's helped with my problems and all.... but there's nothing I would do different.

Do you ever think about dying?
I don't think about dying much. I'm not afraid of it, but there's nothing I can do to head it off. I don't want to go.... but I will. There's nothing I can do about it, so why worry about it? Instead I try to think about living. Life is all about living, and I'm happy for every day I get.

Dorothy Wilson died June 10, 2014 at the age of 100.

Beulah Mae Winter

Beulah Mae Winter was born on June 15, 1904 to a family of cotton farmers in Denmark, Mississippi. Along with two brothers and a sister, she grew up going to school and helping out on the family farm, planting, chopping and picking cotton in order to make ends meet. After finishing school, she went on to teach public school for one year and children's Bible school for more than 40 years. In 1923, at the age of 19, she married Howard Winter; together they had one son, Quitman. Beulah Mae and Howard were married for 44 years until his death in 1967. Afterward, Beulah Mae continued in her love of education by teaching English to foreign university students, using the Bible as a text book.

After 44 years of marriage, what do you think is the secret to a good relationship?
Cooperation, that's the secret to a good marriage. When Howard and I got married, we didn't have indoor plumbing, electricity, nothing. Well, after a number of years I was gettin' tired of that because I wanted a bathroom and indoor plumbing, *but Howard*

thought it was too expensive! But we compromised and we scratched and saved up $300 to install that bathroom and plumbing.... that was a lot of money back then! That was two months of salary to us! Maybe he was right, it was expensive.... but it was worth it.

You see, you're gonna have differences, but you've got to be willing to cooperate and work things out. Some people are so selfish, and they think they always have to be right. Well, everybody has different opinions about things, and you can't always argue that my way is right and yours is wrong. Would you want to be married to someone like that? I guess it comes back to the Golden Rule; treat others the way you'd like to be treated.

Tell me what it takes to be a good parent and raise good children.
Oh, I know lots about children. I only have one son, but I taught children for over 40 years, and now I've 4 grandchildren, 14 great grandchildren, and 1 great-great grandchild. I've been around a *lot* of children.

You see, when it comes to children, you've got to let them know who is boss, but you've got to let them know in the right way. You have to love them while you're bossing them. Children have got to have discipline, I don't necessarily mean punishment, I mean discipline, you know, rules. But when they break those rules, you've got to discipline them, otherwise they keep on breaking them. But when you discipline them, you must discipline them out of love, not anger. Discipline is not about you being mad at them for disobeying, it's about teaching them that there's consequences for not obeying.

I remember one morning as my son started to school, he disobeyed me and I was reprimanding him and spanking him and I said, "Now, I'm not doing this because I'm mad. I just want to you to think about what you did and remember not to do it again." I think he remembered.

Do you think things are different for kids today than it was for you when you were a little girl?
Oh heaven's yes! Now days children seem to have so many temptations. Maybe they don't have any more than I had, but it sure seems like they do. When I was a little girl, we didn't have time to get into much trouble. My daddy was a farmer, a small-time farmer, and when we came home from school, we put on our work clothes and headed out to the cotton patch. We all had to pitch in and help, that's just how it was. Nowadays, children don't want to do anything but rip, romp and play. I think you should teach them how to work. I think that would be good advice. But of course, the work children do now, it's so easy. It's just like going uptown and buying a piece of candy. It won't hurt a child to learn to work some. It's good for them and it keeps them out of trouble.

It sounds like things were hard back in those days.
Things *were* hard back in those days. At least we thought it was hard times because we had to chop cotton and pick cotton and all of those kinds of things, but for some is was a lot worse. We had it tough but we never went without food. We did what we had to do to get by. We grew cotton for money, but all everything else was just part of growing up on the farm. We grew vegetables in the garden and I would spend the summer canning them so we'd have something to eat in the winter. That was my job. We'd raised cows for the milk and chickens for the eggs, and we raised pigs. In the fall daddy would butcher a hog so we'd have some meat for the winter.

In those days, we didn't have electricity or none of that stuff; we used oil lamps and cooked on a wood burning stove. We didn't have indoor plumbing until I was married and moved to town. When I was little my mother would be in the kitchen cooking and I'd be outside playing and she'd say, "Beulah Mae, run and get me a bucket of water." That ended my playing right there. I would have to go down to draw water out of the well down by the creek. We all pitched in and did our part; we had to. Sometimes people are counting on you to do your part, just like you're counting on them.

Everyone's got to do their part, otherwise everything breaks down. It wasn't a glorious life, but we scrambled through. Of course, we didn't have money just to blow to the four winds, but we lived. Looking back, I guess really, we had it pretty good.

If you could give me just one piece of advice, what would it be? Do the right thing. Live a decent life and go to church. Be honest, tell the truth, do what you say you're going to do, and treat people the way you'd like to be treated. That's the Golden Rule and it's a good rule to live by. But there is nothing more important in life than knowing who God is and having Him in your life.

At the time of this interview, Beulah Mae was 103 years old and still teaching conversational English to her foreign college students who affectionately referred to her as "Mommy". Beulah Mae Ellen Winter died June 12, 2008, four months after this interview and four days before her 104th birthday.

Rev. Otis Clark

Otis Grandville Clark was born February 13, 1903, the son of a former slave. He grew up on the black side of segregated Tulsa where he went to school and worked as a drugstore delivery boy. In 1921, Otis narrowly escaped harm in the infamous Tulsa race riots. *"I got shot at. They killed my step-father; we never found his body. They killed my dog and burned our home down."* The Red Cross estimates that close to 300 were killed and over 10,000 left homeless by the riots. Shortly after, Otis hopped a train for California where he found work as a movie extra and served as a butler to Hollywood celebrities such as Clark Gable, Charley Chaplain and Joan Crawford. While serving a jail sentence in Los Angeles for bootlegging whiskey, Otis converted to Christianity which began a 90-year career in ministry. He served at the well-known Azusa Street Mission and became officially ordained as a minister in 1946.

"I was about 21 when I married my first wife, Martha. I was married four times... 35 years in all. They all died. I had just one daughter; she died a while back. I never had no grandchildren"

What it was like growing up in a time of so much racial tension.
See we had in our little Tulsa town, we had trouble there, what you might call a little race riot. The whites just run the colored folk out of Tulsa. That was about 1921. I was about 18 and I was living with my grandparents. My father was in Kansas City, Missouri. I remember I went to visit my friend, Jackson, and I was standing behind him when he got shot. I had to run off and leave him; I was just trying to save my own life. They killed my step-father; we never found his body. They killed my dog and burned our home down. I tried to leave after that, but the white folks stopped me on the way out of town and made me get out of the car. They didn't shoot me; they just took my gun. I went to stay with my aunt, and later we heard that the Salvation Army and the Army folks came in and stopped the killing.

I don't know how to ask this, but how did you live in a world where people hated you just because of the color of your skin?
Tulsa was more or less an oil city... really the oil capital of the world at one time, and a lot of colored folks worked for them 'oil' folks and we got along nicely on our side of town, which was the north side, and the whites was on the south side. And to be perfectly honest with you, we got along nicely, up until the Klu Klux Klan and some others got jealous of us coloreds getting along as well as we was. That's when they started the race riots, and they burnt up our part of the city. Lots of folk were killed.

How did you deal with that? Weren't you angry?
No, see we was young and didn't have sense enough to be angry *(laughing)*. We didn't have that kind of sense. We couldn't do nothing 'bout it anyways. Things was different back then. We just had to run and get out of the way and keep from getting killed.

Looking back, how can you forgive those folks for what they did?
I don't think we should look back. All we can do is just forgive one another and try to straighten up whatever wrongs we have. I ain't perfect; I've messed up too, you know, and folks have forgiven me. That's what we've got to do, learn to forgive one another.

So, what did you do after that?

My grandmother got a letter from my father that said he done gone to California. So, me and my friend hopped on a train to Los Angeles and found my father was working for the movie folks. And that's how I got started with the movie folks. I started working for Joan Crawford and got acquainted with all the movie folks. I worked as a butler for Clark Gable, Charlie Chaplin too. They was what I called the sportin' folks. They was big time into dancin' and having fun, and I was pretty popular with 'em 'cause I was a *whiskey* maker.... a moonshiner you see. That was back during Prohibition and I'd supply 'em with whiskey for all their parties. Some of them parties was $7000; they was big timers. Joan Crawford was what you might call one of the leading stars back then and she had a theater behind her home, and Clark Gable and Charlie Chaplin would come to her home for movies and parties and such. So, I was working for the folks that had something, and so I got along nicely. The movie folks treated me real good. I worked there until I finally got converted.

What do you mean by "converted"?

I got arrested and put in jail for makin' moonshine whiskey. That was a dangerous deal. Back in the prohibition days, they'd give folks five and six years for a makin' a little whiskey, but the judge had mercy on me and gave me only 20 days in jail. On Saturdays, the Salvation Army folks would come out and some of these white preachers would preach and sing to us prisoners. The first Saturday I didn't pay no mind 'cause I was looking for my gang, but my gang didn't show up! The next Saturday, the Salvation Army folks came out, and they preached and they sang, and I made up my mind that I'd get on God's side. I got converted in jail in Los Angeles. I was in my twenties. That was my first opportunity of actually hearing folks talk about God. I found out He's the boss of this *whole* thing.

So how do you get on God's side?

Repent. You have to repent for the wrongs you've done and be converted. That's what we call it in the Baptist Church. Repent and be converted and change from wrong to right. Quit your wrongs;

quit your sins and get on God's side, and live right. But we Baptist folks allowed you to drink a little, we didn't make it too serious for you. You could do a little wrong and repent and it would be alright and so a lot of us followed that line.... that you were on God's side if you just belonged to a church. But I found out later that ain't right. See, the Devil comes along somehow or another and makes us feel like it's alright to do wrong and a little wrong won't hurt us. And to tell the truth about it, we follow that line of the Devil more than the line of God. And I did that myself a long time; I followed the folks that thought it was alright to do a little wrong. But see, God's Bible tells us to repent and *believe... "He that believes and is baptized shall be saved."* But you got to *believe.* See, we was baptized, but didn't believe. In other words, we did as we pleased in the Baptist church. But God has a written word which is the Bible and you *got* to go by it. See, we had the Bible and didn't go by it in the Baptist church. They would think you was crazy if you talked about being saved and sanctified. I learned that you got to believe and repent and follow God's word. We would talk it, but we didn't live it. Nobody really talked about living no sanctified life. But you got to really do it to be saved. I found that out after God really baptized me for real when I was in jail. That changed my life. It stopped me from doing the things I used to do. I tried to come back and tell the folks in the Baptist church about it and they thought I was crazy.

So how did you go about becoming a preacher?
I got with the leadin' folks of the Azusa Street Church down there in Los Angeles. They talked about baptism in the Holy Ghost, and I made up my mind that was the right way to go, and the Lord called me to go and tell other people. See, the Devil puts it in folks to cuss, tell lies, cheat and steal. He tells us it's alright to have a little of that and have a little bit of God. The whole world practices that. But God is *pleading* with us all the time to come to him. *"Come to me the heavy laden and I will give you rest."* But in the world, you can do as you please and you can say your holy and sanctified but you're really not. You have to love God more than you love the world. But the Devil has a lot of power in this world.

Do you think God directs our way through life?
In a way He does, but in another way, He lets us have our own way. He tries to tell us what's right, but He leaves us to do whatever we want to do. We can follow right if we want to, or we can follow wrong, but He encourages us to do right. I did that myself a long time. I followed the folks that thought it was alright to do a little wrong. See the Devil comes along and makes us feel that a little wrong won't hurt us. But those 20 days in jail changed my whole life when them little Salvation Army folks came and told me about gettin' on the right side of God. See, God can even take the bad things in your life and turn 'em around into good.

Tell me how you've managed to live such a long, healthy and productive life.
That just slips up on ya! *(laughing)* I don't know why I'm living so long. I think it's because God wants me to tell the younger folk about being on His side. God is the one able to make you healthy and wealthy but the Devil tries to steal it from you and makes it hard for you. You gotta learn to stand firm. Wealth in God's way of thinking is more than money, it's good health, the ability to do what you want to do, to be physically wealthy.... and mentally wealthy..... able to think right and do right. Think right. God wants you to think on the good things.

You've got over 100 years of life experience. *(Yeah).* **How can I make the most out of my life?**
Live Holy. Holiness is righteousness in the heart, not just in the head. It's right to do right. *"And none but the righteous shall see God."* If the Lord gets in your *heart,* you gonna do right because God is right. You can't help it; it becomes a part of you. Love others. Love is a great attribute. God wants us to love one another. You are God's child and He wants you to have what He has for you. Love is a mystery that the Devil hides even from the church. The Devil has cheated us out of the real love. The real love of God would make you treat one another right at any time, in any kind of condition. God *is* love, and we're supposed to show the love of God to others. Think right, live right and do right....... and love.

Otis Clark certainly made the most out of his life. As he sat in my living room during this interview, he filled our home and lives, not only with incredible stories and wisdom, but with love and life. This man was full of life, and he was contagious, spreading it into every life he touched. At ages 103 and 104, Otis traveled twice on mission trips to Zimbabwe, Africa. After this interview, Otis was leaving immediately, traveling to San Antonio to preach.... at 105 years old! At age 107 he traveled to the West Indies to change lives and at age 109 he went to Canada to continue spreading the Word. And, at the time of his death on May 21, 2013, at the age of 109, Otis Clark was planning a trip to preach the gospel in the country of Nigeria. Now that is optimism.

Otis' life has been the subject of numerous newspaper and magazine articles and TV interviews. He even has his own Wikipedia page. Below are some links to a couple of these interviews. They are well worth viewing.
http://www.youtube.com/watch?v=GZ2380UTX4A
http://voicesofoklahoma.com/otis_clark.html

Lucille Larkin

Ester "Lucille" Paden was born October 24, 1914 to R.H. and Mary Paden on a farm near Cooper, Texas where she grew up with one sister and three brothers, one of which died at age six. Lucille attended school through the eighth grade after which she stayed to work on the family farm. *"We chopped cotton, churned our own butter and canned food in the summer.... We picked green beans, okra and stuff out of the garden."* She later moved to Commerce, Texas to work. In 1943, Lucille married Emerson "Bill" Clay, together they had two children, Billy Jr. and Phyllis. Bill and Lucille farmed and worked various jobs throughout their marriage. *"Farming didn't make much money."* Lucille retired in 1979 at age 65. In 1991, Bill passed away after a long battle with Parkinson's Disease. Today, Lucille *(her friends call her Mrs. Mack)* still lives alone in her own house out in the country.

Tell me what it was like growing up 100 years ago.
Life was hard back then. I grew up on a farm with my brothers and sister. We all went to school and each day I had to come home and do chores. There was always some kind of work that needed done. I only went through the eighth-grade cause that's as far as they taught in our town. I had a little brother that died when he was six

and Momma about had a nervous breakdown. She went to her folk's house in Oklahoma to stay a while, so we had to take care of things, cookin' and cleanin' and such. We picked green beans, okra and stuff out of the garden. We would clean it and then had to build a fire in the cook stove, 'cause that's all we had was a wood stove.

My dad drank a lot. We didn't know where he got it from but he kept it out in the barn. We told Momma when she came home, that he drank a lot. Momma asked him about it and he said, *"Well a sober man couldn't eat their cookin'."* (laughs)

After I finished school, we had two or three neighbors that got sick and I took care of their kids for a while. Then I went to Commerce and worked in a grocery store that had a little cafe. This cafe was right there by the train station. The people that owned it lived upstairs. I worked all night because the trains kept coming every night during the war. The train would come through with a bunch of soldiers and they always wanted to buy something.

Tell me about your marriage.
My husband's name was E.C.... Emerson Clay.... but everyone called him Bill. He was my cousins' boyfriend. He was datin' us both at the same time. He'd pick me up and put me on one side of the movie theater and her on the other side. I finally told him he needed to make a decision. We were married in 1943. He was 32 and I was 28. I was working at Proctor and Gamble.... I ran the label machine.

How many children did you have?
We had two children, my son Billy Jr. and Phyllis.

How long were you married?
We were married 48 years. He passed away in 1991, he had Parkinson's and shook a lot. He was sick a long time. It was a terrible disease. I don't want to ever have Parkinson's.

How did you get through that?
You just did the best you could, that's all you could do. I took care of him a long time. I didn't like seein' him suffer like that. Before

he died I never had stayed a night by myself.... but at least he wasn't suffering anymore. It was hard, but you just take it one step at a time.... and prayer.... I prayed a lot.

So, you were married 48 years, what's the key?

Just doing things with your husband. We got married because we liked spending time together. Agreein' with each other is important. You don't have to win every argument. If something was important to him, we'd do it his way and if something was important to me....... And bein' nice to each and pleasing each other, doin' nice things for one another. He cooked breakfast for us every morning. I also think it's important to be on the same page. I was a Christian when we married but he wasn't, but he became one. My momma and daddy didn't go to church so me and my sister started to go by ourselves. We went to a little Baptist church there in Brookston until I got to where I can't go anymore.

Sounds like God is pretty important in your life?

Oh, He sure is! I depend on Him. He's my savior and He answers prayer. I think God has guided me my whole life. I've been faithful to Him and I've tried to live as honest as I can live. I pray to the Lord all the time.... for everybody. Every night when I go to bed, I pray for my kids, my grandkids and my sick neighbors. I don't know what my life would have been like without God. I don't know how I would've made it without Him.... I *wouldn't* have made it without Him.

I got saved when I was a little girl.... well, I went up to the alter by myself at prayer meeting and I prayed.... and at that church, when anybody went to the alter, all the women and men all come up to the alter with you! Everybody prayed with you.... out loud. Nobody prayed to themselves. I prayed, *"Lord, how will I know when I get saved?"* All of sudden it was like I became an angel and I flew all over that church. When I came to, they were all still praying over me and I *knew* I was saved. I'll never forget it as long as I live.

So, I was told that you have never had a driver's license?
I had a wreck and went through the windshield when I was 16. My sister hadn't been driving very long and we went to my aunt's house. We got there and they said they needed some ice so we went to get some ice. We went around this blind corner, we were on the right side but the car that was coming the other way, wasn't. They run straight into us and I went through that windshield. It was terrible. Nobody else was hurt. I think the good Lord saw me through that wreck. I've driven since then but I never got my license. I walked wherever I needed to go. I walked all the time. No matter it was raining, sleet, snowing, freezing.... I'd put bread wrappers around my feet and walk out in the meadow. I was afraid I'd slip.

What's it like being 100?
It's good 'til you get sick.

What's the secret to living that long?
I have oatmeal and prunes for breakfast every day. For 40 years I've had the same thing. I never said a cuss word in my life. I Never smoked.... never tasted a beer.... no caffeine.... I try to eat healthy. I read my bible every day, but I can't see to read anymore. I used to write in a diary every day for a lot of years, from when I was a little girl 'til I was about 98 when I couldn't see anymore.

Do you have any regrets?
I regret not gettin' more schoolin'. I think it's important. I'd liked to have been a teacher but things didn't work out that way. I'm proud that my kids went to college and got a good education. That's important now days.

What would you say is the most important thing in life?
Health. You can't be happy if you don't have good health. No matter what all you had, if you don't have good health you can't enjoy it. Stay healthy.

Do you ever think about dying?
No.... I think I'm just gonna keep on living.

What is your best piece of advice about life?
Always trust in the Lord. Learn about the Bible, it has all of life's answers. It teaches you how to live and how to be a good person.... How to live right and treat your fellow man right... that's what I've done.... it's worked all right for me.

"Learn about the Bible.
It has all of life's answers."

Mrs. Mack, 103

Martha Biglow

Graduation, St. Mary's School of Nursing, 1931.

Martha Ellen White was born on November 22, 1914 to Dr. Thomas Charles White and Lina Mitchell Worth White in Canute, Oklahoma. "I had one brother, William, and two sisters." The family moved to Bobo, Mississippi where her father died from tuberculosis a few years later. Her mother then moved the children to Amarillo Texas where Martha graduated high school and attended junior college. She then moved to Rochester Minnesota and attended St. Mary's School of Nursing, graduating in 1931. *"I came back to Amarillo after I got my nursing diploma and was a nurse for 42 years, if my numbers are right."* Martha later moved to Salida, Colorado to work where she met Walter Leroy "Roy" Biglow. Martha and Roy dated about six months before marrying on April 9, 1939. Roy joined the U.S. Navy at the beginning of World War II with Martha following him to bases in California and Texas, working as a nurse. After the war, they returned to West Texas to resume their lives. Roy died on July 7, 2004 after 65 years of marriage. They never had any children.

You said you and Roy never had any children, why not?
No, we never did. I couldn't have any. It's a sad thing when you can't have children but you work that out. My husband especially was sorry we couldn't have children. We thought about adopting but that didn't work out either. I think there's a closeness that develops between you when you don't have children, that you don't have otherwise. All you have each is each other.

Do you and your wife have any children?
No ma'am, we don't.

Then you know what I'm talking about, don't you?
Yes ma'am, I do.

I had other children that I kept at times and they've been very dear to me. Nieces and nephews, and another boy that isn't a nephew that is very dear to me. I've known him since he was ten years old and he's in his 70's now.

Tell me about your husband.
Well I called him Roy. He was the cutest guy I'd ever met. We went swimming and I thought he was so cute. He was younger than I was, 4 years younger. Roy was going overseas and he wanted to know if I'd wait for him and I said, I would. He was in the Navy and went to Samoa. The war ended while he was over there.

Did you marry when he got back?
We married before he left. He was special. He was a very loving person. We were married for 65 years.

Sixty-five years? What's the secret?
Well, if you have a problem, just work it out together. You have to talk out your problems and make it work. Communicate and be willing to compromise. We had to work things out, all we had was each other. One time I told him "I'm going to Hereford (Texas) to take a job opening as a nurse." He said, "Now Martha, you're not going to do any such thing," and I thought, you know he's right. I

just hadn't even thought about what Roy might think. It seemed like a good idea at the time but I hadn't given any consideration to him. You've got to consider the other person's thoughts and feelings too. You two are in this together, and what you do affects them too. That's what I mean when I say work things out together.

What happened to Roy?
He got ill. I took care of him for years, being a nurse, I could do that, but he started losing weight and I finally couldn't take care of him anymore. So, I finally had to put him in a nursing home and they took good care of him. I bought a house nearby so I could be near him. He was the one man in my life. I was in my eighties when he passed away. We spent 65 good years together.

Was it hard?
It was hard, but I was ready for him to go when he passed away. I'd seen him become so thin and so ill, and I was ready for him to die. You know, you don't want 'em to suffer, they're not the same people that you had loved. I guess you could say I loved him enough to let him go.

How did you deal with that?
Well I'd been going up to the nursing home every day for a couple years until he died. One lives, one doesn't die, and I had to make a new life for myself. So, I just kept on living.... one day at a time. Now it's one year at a time. He's been dead 12 years now. I dream about him *(smiling)*. He was my life for many, many years. You know, I dreamed the other night that he fell and broke his leg, and I called the nurse...I mean, it was so real I *actually* called the nurse *(laughing)*.

What's it like being 101?
Well it's just like it was before... it's like being 80... it's like being 60. I'm the same person, just older. I like the same things, I do the same things, I think the same things. I'm just the same person that I always was.

It sounds like you're in pretty good health. How do you stay so healthy?
I always exercised, even today I try to do a certain amount of walking. I try to eat decently. I used to smoke but I quit that a long time ago, when I was 50. I hate to see an old lady smoke. I had to pray to quit. I tried several times to quit and I'd start smoking again. Finally, I thought, well I can't do this by myself, so I prayed and asked God to help me. So, I woke up one morning, I ate breakfast and started to light a cigarette and looked at it and said, "You're not as big as I am." I knew God was helping me. I never touched another cigarette after that.

What about your mind? How do you keep your mind healthy?
I always liked to read, I'm careful what kind of books I read. I tried to read books that were good for me.... I don't read trash. If they don't benefit me in some way, I don't read them. Of course, 'cause of my eyes, I don't read now. I read history and a lot of books on people, biographies and such.... now I play bridge on the computer. You have to exercise your mind as well as your body.

Do you have any regrets?
Only that I didn't have children... But nothing that I kept on worrying about. I don't believe in worrying. I just don't think you should worry, it's detrimental to your health. There's no sense in that. You should just put it aside, there's not much you can do about it anyway. The things that you usually worry about seem to turn out to be the things you don't need to worry about. I have a pretty positive attitude about things.... and that's important.

What are you most thankful for?
For my health... my mental health. I watch CNN sometimes, but with all the bad news in the world, I think that you're crazy to watch it... but I like to keep my mind alert about what's going on.

Are you happy?
Well.... I'm content.

What's the difference?
I'm satisfied. I wish a few things were different.... but there's nothing I can do about that, so I have to be satisfied with the way things are.

Why do you think you've lived so long?
'Cause God's not ready for me yet. I'm a firm believer in God. He's in control of everything. He's been with me my whole life, and he still with me.... and when he's ready, I'm ready.

What is one piece of advice you would give to someone about life?
Don't worry. God is in control. He is alive and He's got everything planned out....and everything will be OK.

Martha Biglow died June 8, 2016 at the age of 101. She was a beautiful woman with a beautiful smile with an air of compassion that touched the lives of not only her patients, but all those that knew her. I am fortunate indeed. Though Martha and Roy never had children of their own, they both left behind numerous nieces and nephews. God bless you Martha. Thank you for touching my life.

"I don't believe in worrying.... it's detrimental to your health."

Martha Biglow, 100

Gloria Jane Mitchell

Gloria Jane Hubbard, age 4, standing on the running board.

Gloria Jane Mitchell was born December 29, 1908 in St. Jo, Missouri to Edward and Grace Hubbard. When Jane's father came down with tuberculosis her parents moved her and her sister, Grace, to Silver City, NM. There, they had a simple life, riding a burro back and forth to town to attend school or fetch groceries. After high school, Jane moved to Kansas City, Missouri where she worked as a bookkeeper. She married Fred Davenport in 1929 and had twins, Carl and Jack, and a daughter, Jane Ann.

While Fred was in the Navy, Jane went to work at Pratt Whitney as lead lady on the conveyor line inspecting small parts. She and Fred divorced after 15 years of marriage. Jane went back to work as a bookkeeper for the US government in the War Assets Administration, the IRS, and the General Services Administration. Jane married again, however, it was short-lived and no one knows his name *"Honey, that's been 100 years ago, that's hard to remember!"* Jane remarried a third time, to Dean Ray Mitchell in

1959. Dean died in 2005 after 46 years of marriage. On September 21, 1951, Jane's son, Marine Cpl. Jack A. Davenport, was on the front lines of the Korean war when he threw himself on top of a live grenade to shield and protect the lives of his fellow Marines. He was posthumously awarded the Congressional Medal of Honor for his act of bravery and sacrifice. Jane spent the rest of her life as an active member of the Gold Star Society representing Jack and other Gold Star mothers at various events throughout the U.S.

You see like you have a really good attitude. Why?
Why not have a good attitude? It's just as easy to have a good attitude as a bad attitude. Attitude is a choice, it's a state of mind. You just have to decide to be happy. You have to decide to have a good attitude. Why shouldn't I be happy? I'm still alive. I'm here another day. God's given me another day. (Starts singing.)

Do you ever have a bad day?
Oh, sometimes things happen that try to ruin my day, but I try not to let it. It's up to you what kind of day you have. Most people let circumstances dictate whether they'll be happy or not. They've got that all backwards. You have to decide to be happy first, *then* you deal with whatever problems come up. It's all up to you. Happiness is a choice.

But you've been through some hard times...
Oh yes. My father died of TB when he was in his twenties. My daughter, Jane, passed away, and my son Jack was killed in the Korean War. He was a Marine. The enemy threw a grenade into his foxhole and Jack covered it with his body to save his buddy, Bob (Smith). Bob still keeps in touch with us after all these years. I had 3 children and two of them died. I've had nine grandchildren and three of those are dead; two died of an overdose and one was a suicide. So yes, I have seen plenty of hard times.

How do you get through things like that?
By the good Lord's grace. He will never give you more than you can handle. You just have to take it all one day at a time. That's all you can do. I used to pray, *"God just help me make it through*

today", and He did. He'd give me just enough strength to make it through that day, then the next day, I would ask Him again. I talk to God every day. I never wouldn't have made it without Him. God promises that He'll take care of us. If you need help, ask Him.... He'll see you through it.

How do you feel about getting older?
It's good. Life's good. I feel good. I'm healthy, I'm happy. God's good to me. He's always been good to me. He's taken care of me for a lot of years, and I guess I'll be here until He's ready to take me home.

Why do you think you have lived so long?
Because God's still got something He needs me to do. As long I can still be here and be a blessing to other people, then I'll be here.

What do you think He wants you to do?
Love people. Help people, and make people happy.... make them smile and tell them about Him. He puts us here to help each other. Sometimes when people get into trouble or have problems, they pray *"God, please help me"*. So, if I can help those people out...make them smile, make them happy or whatever... then they go to bed that night and thank God for His blessing. That's why I'm still here. That's what I'm supposed to do, be a blessing to other people so they thank God.

It sounds like God is pretty important to you.
He's everything to me. He's been with me my whole life. He's gotten me through a lot. I never would've made it without Him. If you don't have God in your life, I don't know how you'd ever make it.

Do you have any secrets about staying healthy?
I like to exercise. I used to have to walk a long way to work every day. I think that is a key to me being so healthy. You have to *take* care of yourself. I don't take any medications, I guess overall, I'm in pretty good health.

Do you ever think about dying?
No, I don't think about it. Why should I? God's still got me here. As long as I'm here living His purpose, He'll keep me here. And when He's done with me, He'll take me. So, I don't have to think about it. It's not up to me. I can't do anything about it anyway.

What piece of advice would you give your grandchildren about life?
Be happy. Just take one day at a time. Keep putting one foot in front of the other. Do what you can. Love people. Help people.... and know what God wants you to do...... and go do it.

Jane Mitchell died August 26, 2014, at the age of 105. She is survived by her son, Carl, six grandchildren and numerous great and great-great grandchildren.

Jane dedicated a large portion of her life to the memory of her son, Cpl. Jack A. Davenport, USMC. To honor her dedication and his heroism, I've included the following links detailing his story.

http://themedalofhonor.com/medal-of-honor-recipients/recipients/davenport-jack-korean-war

http://www.homeofheroes.com/moh/citations_1950_kc/davenport_jack.html

https://en.wikipedia.org/wiki/Jack_A._Davenport

Troy Perkins

Troy Perkins was born Jan 20, 1915 in a tent on the shores of the Pease River near Matador, Texas, to Jessie Dudley Perkins and his wife Ester. Troy's father, "J.D.", ran a team of mules and performed dirt work for the construction of the Pease River Bridge while his mother cooked and took care of Troy, his two older sisters and younger brother. *"My father was a horse trader. He couldn't read or write.... but he wasn't dumb, he was actually pretty smart."* After graduating high school, Troy attended Texas Tech University and majored in mathematics until graduating with his bachelor's degree in 1938. After that, he began teaching math and coaching football in several small west Texas towns. Troy married Evelyn Moore on June 1, 1942; together they had two boys and one girl. Later in 1942, following the Japanese attack on Pearl Harbor, Troy enlisted in the U.S. Navy and was stationed at the National Navy Medical Research Institute in Bethesda, Maryland where he did research teaching pilots how to safely bail out of planes at high altitude. Troy left the Navy in 1945 and returned to teaching until his retirement in 1977. *"They asked me if I wanted to do substitute teaching and I said absolutely not!"* In 2009, Evelyn passed away after almost 68 years of marriage; she was 89.

So, tell me about your time in the Navy.

Well, I was coaching in Aspermont, Texas.... I wasn't much of a coach, but I coached the football team. It was a small team, I didn't have but about 14 or 15 boys. I made a mistake, I should have asked how many seniors they had down there, but I didn't. Anyway, I stayed there that year, and it was an awfully wet year. The army came in there to do maneuvers. They put those soldiers in those little old pup tents, and I said, *that's not for me.* So, I applied to the Navy. Of course, back then, if you had a college degree, you could apply for what we called, "The 90 Day Wonder" program. You may not be old enough to remember, but they would take you and give you training for 90 days and then they'd usually put you in PT boats, like what JFK was in.... or they would put you in these amphibious landing boats where you would be landing on some shore somewhere.... either in Europe or the South Pacific. You'd take the landing boat in full of Marines and you'd let 'em off and you'd come back and get another load.... and you kept it up until you either got killed or you got 'em all ashore. So, I was in Dallas, Texas getting sworn in the Navy in 1942 and my wife called and said my commission had come through. I was just a hospital apprentice and they asked me if I had any other education. I told them I had a bachelor's degree in mathematics and few days later they promoted me up to second class and sent me to work at the National Navy Medical Research Institute in Bethesda, Maryland. I did research to teach military pilots how to safely bail out at altitude. Back then if they had to bail out, they had to crawl out on the wing to keep from getting tangled up and they learned early that if they bailed out at 35,000 feet with a parachute they would be dead when they got to the ground; they'd freeze to death. So, I worked in a pressure chamber and we taught the pilots to free fall 18,000 feet before deploying their parachutes. I spent the whole war right there in Bethesda, some may say it's cowardice, but I went where the Navy sent me. I think that probably saved my life. I made $96 a month, that was pretty good pay back then. I got out of the Navy October 1945 and not long after I was back to teaching.

Tell me about your wife.

Her name was Evelyn Moore and we got married June 1, 1942. We had 3 children, 2 boys and one girl. It was a good marriage but she passed away in May 2009. She was 89. We loved each other.... I still love her. We were married almost 68 years.

So, what's the secret to having such a good marriage?

That's not an easy question. Both of our parents were married a long time. My mother and father celebrated their 64th anniversary. I guess were setting an example set for us before we even got married. We just stayed married. Divorce wasn't a thing a lot of folks did back then. It just wasn't an option, that was the way we looked at it. We never even talked about divorce. We had lots of fusses and quarrels, but we always made up. If divorce isn't an option, there's no other choice but to work out your problems and get along with each other....at least that's how we saw it. We just loved each other, that's all you can do. I still love her today. We were married almost 68 years when she died.

How do you deal with losing someone you were married to for 68 years?

I didn't have any choice. You've got to get through it. You just try to get through one day at a time for a while, then it's one week at a time. Eventually you learn to live with it. Don't get me wrong, I still miss her, but I've learned to live with it. That's all you can do.

Did you ever think about getting married again?

Evelyn always said that I would get married again; I thought about it. There was a woman that lived here, she was one of the first people that we got acquainted with when we moved here. I thought, well, I might just tie it up with her, but the more I got to thinking about it, I wouldn't put this old broken body of mine up with anybody. One or two of 'em made advances toward me, one of them even wanted to get *intimate!* I told her I don't want to be intimate with *anybody....* I still love my wife.

Any advice about raising good children?

You just love 'em and do the best you can. You're gonna make

mistakes, but you just do your best. My daughter is the one that takes care of me and tells me what I can do and what I can't do. I got a boy that's still living. We had a cabin in the mountains that we built ourselves and we had a little squabble about it and he decided he doesn't want to talk to me anymore. I still love him but he just doesn't want to talk to me. I can't do anything about it. I've tried to reach out to him but he won't talk to me. I arranged a meal here for the family but he didn't come.

Yeah, my family has some of the same problems.
All kids eventually grow up and become their own person. They start to make their own decisions and start living their own lives. Whether you agree with it or not, doesn't really matter, it's their life. All you can do is keep loving them the best you can and be there when they're ready. You just have to forgive them and hope they'll forgive you. I wish things were better between us.... I wished we talked more, but there's nothing I can really do about it now. It's hard, but you've got to learn to love people even when they don't love you back.

What do you think about politics and our government now days?
Well, I have participated in politics in the past but I got to where I can't hardly tend to my own business. I don't know what's gonna happen to these Untied States. This president we've got (Obama) has put us into such enormous debt that our great-great grandchildren won't be able to pay it off. Last count I had it was about seventeen trillion dollars; do you know how much a trillion dollars is?

That's a lot of zeros.
Yeah, that's a lot of zeros and I don't know where it's gonna come from. In WWII in the European countries, money got to where it was worth very little. That may happen to us if we don't get this thing fixed.

Do you think it's a Democrat problem or Republican problem, or what?
Well, it's Democrat, it's Republican.... whoever's in charge. Obama's there, the Republicans are there.... but none of 'em seem to care. Their just worried about raising more money and gettin' reelected. Those guys up there that's opposed to Obama, they still write me and call me wantin' me to give 'em more money.... but they're not gonna do anything different. I've got to where I don't even read their letters anymore, I just throw 'em in the waste basket. The system's broke, but I'm not sure how to fix it. One thing's for sure, you can't keep spending money you don't have. Sooner or later, someone's gonna have to pay the bill.

What would you say is the key to living a successful life?
Be honest. If somebody were to ask me who's the most honest man I ever seen, I'd say, well.... Jess Perkins *(his father)*. He was honest to the core. People would come from everywhere and trade with him. They'd say, whatever Jess tells you, you can depend on it. We lived through the Depression and President Franklin Roosevelt declared a moratorium on debt. That's what saved my father. He owed the bank at Matador quite a bit of money and there was lots of other farmers just like him, they had everything all mortgaged up, and they just told the bank to come and get it. Not my father, he didn't. He lived to pay off every debt he owed. I guess I got some of my characteristics from him. I want to be honest with myself, and I want to be honest with God, and I want to be honest with my neighbor.... like in the Bible, the good Samaritan that come along.... he was a good neighbor. Everybody that I met was my neighbor. I would think that would be part of my philosophy.

So besides that, what is your philosophy for life?
I was afraid you'd ask me that! I'm not sure I've ever had a course in Philosophy, but it's the way you live. Just be honest. Be honest with your neighbor. Be honest with God. That's it. I didn't always tell the truth. I've lied a lot, *(laughs)* and it always came back to bite me.

You mentioned the Bible, so you believe in God?
I believe in God, always have. I taught the bible over 50 years. I try to live right, I do my best to be a good person, but understand that being good or bad doesn't take you to heaven. Faith in Jesus Christ is what brings you to heaven. You can't do good deeds in order to get right with God.... first you get right with God, then *He* does good deeds *through* you.

So how do you get right with God?
Ask God for forgiveness and trust Him with your life. I grew up in this little community with Methodists and Baptists. The Baptists always said, "once you're saved, you're always saved." and the Methodists thought you could be saved and then lose it. That's not true. All He wants from you and from me is our life. I tell Him *"Here's my life, God, take it.... I belong to You. Do with me whatever You want, and I hope You get all the honor and glory out of it."*

Do you think your life has brought Him honor and glory?
I think my sins are so great, that it's not nearly enough, but He says, *"It's all right, My grace is greater than all your sins."* Grace is good.

Troy Perkins passed away on May 8, 2018 at the age of 103.

"Grace is good."

Troy Perkins, 103

Chary Jean-Pierre

Charitable Jean-Pierre, who goes by the name Chary (pronounced Shah-ree), was one of six children born to Jean Roc Pierre Matthieus (father) and Lamercie Innocent Saint Jean (mother) near the village of Gressier, Haiti, approximately 25 miles west of the capital city of Port-au-Prince, Haiti.

As you might expect in a third-world country, there are no records of her birth. Although she doesn't remember her exact birth date, she knows she is well over 100 years old and her grandson states that she was born in May 1903 which would make her 112 at the time of this interview. Other senior villagers tell stories of Chary as an old woman when they were all still children. Living to such an old age is a remarkable feat in anywhere, but the fact that the average life expectancy in Haiti is 63 makes Chary an extraordinarily remarkable case.

Chary never learned to read or write but managed to provide for her family by making and selling charcoal. She never married, which was common in her culture at the time but she had a total of five children, three have since passed away and two are still living.

Chary lives in a meager one-room house, there is no bathroom, no

running water and no electricity. Her home's furnishings consist of two beds, one chair, and a small shelf. Chary is blind and at age 112, spends most of her days lying on a mattress supported by concrete blocks where she is cared for by her family.

Author's Note: Chary does not speak English and this interview was conducted on October 13, 2016 by a Christian missionary, Kathy Floyd, and her interpreters Martellus, Frantz and Fritz. Chary was laying on her bed when we arrived, but when she knew she had company, she sat up and tied a pretty scarf around her head.

Miss Chary, thank you for talking to me today. I want to ask you some questions about your life. How many children did you have?
I had five children, but three of them have now died.

What advice would you give me about raising children?
Children are a blessing from God. A man can't give you children. Only God can give you children. My advice would be you need to be ready for a baby! *(laughing)*.

How did you make a living to support and feed your family?
I was a seller, a saleswoman. Mostly I made and sold charcoal. I was also a farmer and I sold sweet potatoes. I learned to plant and I learned to sell.

That sounds like a hard way to make a living.
I've worked hard all my life. I never learned to read or write, so I didn't have a lot of other choices.
It was hard, but I did what I had to do to feed my children.

It sounds like you've had a hard life.
It has been a hard life. I've had many sicknesses and sufferings. I've lost three of my children. I'm old and blind, but God has taken care of me my whole life.

How did you get through all those hard times?
I talked to my God. He's been working in me all my life.

Tell me about God and His work in your life.
I have been serving God and Jesus became my passionate Savior, even before I became blind. I thank Him that I am still alive. I am under His grace. I am under His mercy. Otherwise, He would take me. He has done many things in my life. Since I was a child, God raised me. I used to go to church at Joy House but I can't go now because I'm blind and I can't make it up the hill *(laughing)*.

You seem really happy.
I am happy. You can be happy or you can be sad. You might as well be happy!

So, what is the secret to having a happy life?
When God is inside . . . no one can see what makes you smile, only Jesus in your heart. Jesus is the only thing that can truly bring happiness *(smiling)*.

Is there anything you regret about your life?
Nothing.... because I gave my life to God, I know everything will be okay.

What is the biggest lesson you've learned in your life?
I need Christ in my life...this is the biggest lesson I've learned. *(Chary then recited Psalm 23 in Creole)*

"The Lord is my shepherd; I shall not want. He makes me to lie down in green pastures; He leads me beside the still waters. He restores my soul; He leads me in the paths of righteousness For His name's sake. Yea, though I walk through the valley of the shadow of death, I will fear no evil; For You are with me; Your rod and Your staff, they comfort me. You prepare a table before me in the presence of my enemies; You anoint my head with oil; My cup runs over. Surely goodness and mercy shall follow me All the days of my life; And I will dwell in the house of the Lord Forever."

Author's note: The beauty of a 112-year-old, uneducated, poor, blind woman reciting the 23rd Psalm in Creole is indescribable. It was truly a moment of worship.

If you could give your grandchildren one piece of advice, what would you tell them?
I would tell them to seek the Lord as their passionate Savior! Accept God as Savior because He is coming soon. He is *everything!* If you are away from God, become close.

What is your secret to living such a long successful life?
I told you already.... have God in your life. *(stated with a little bit of attitude!)*

Mesi (thank you), Miss Chary, for talking to me today.
I thank God that you talked to me. I thank Him for His mercy and grace. I ask Him to keep you in His Word and His mercy and His grace. I would want you to come see me again if I am still here when you come back. I don't know if I'll still be alive when you come back, but would you come see me again and shake my hand?

I would love to come see you again.
If I am not still here, I will see you in Heaven.

It's hard for me to describe my thoughts and feelings about Chary. Here is a 112-year-old blind woman who can't read or write, living in a state of poverty that most of us can't begin to imagine. She has practically no possessions, no money, no security, and is dependent on others to care for her, and yet she is as happy and joyful as a child. She literally has nothing..... except God, and if you ask her, she'll tell you in no uncertain terms that God is all she needs.

Most of us tend to think of the poor and uneducated as unfortunate and unable to live a full, purposeful and productive life, but people like Chary makes me wonder if we're not the unfortunate ones. Our society is obsessed and distracted by the pursuit of success, recognition, status and worldly treasures, yet we remain depressed and empty inside. While Chary has literally nothing, and yet she is

full of love, joy, happiness and life..... at 112 years old, Chary Jean-Pierre is full of life! And if you ask her why, she'll tell you, **"Because my heart is full of Jesus"!** *God bless you Chary, for showing me how to truly be happy.*

"Blessed are the poor in spirit: for theirs is the kingdom of heaven." Mt. 5:3 KJV

What is your secret to living such a long successful life?

***"I told you already....
have God in your life."***

Chary Jean-Pierre, 112

Ida Roselius

Ida Ethel Walcher was born February 26, 1914 in Panhandle, Texas. She was one of eight children born to Mr. and Mrs. Z.L. Walcher. Ida graduated high school in 1931 and soon after, she met Ernest Roselius at a street dance. He was nine years her senior. The two were married in 1934 and together they had three children, Dale Joe, Carol Ann, and Jay Bob. Ida worked at several of the small businesses on Main Street in the small town of Panhandle. *"I worked in the variety store, the hardware store, the drugstore, and the soda fountain. I liked that the least, I didn't like fixin' food for people."* Together, She and Ernest led a simple life, living in the same house their entire married life. They were married 65 years until his death in 1999.

Tell me about life with Ernest.
Ernest was a barber and he was a fine man. He was well received and he really enjoyed that barbershop. We bought a lot in downtown Panhandle with two brick walls and I helped him fix it up and we had a good lookin' building when we were through. We made it into the barbershop. We ordered one of those store-bought fronts. We borrowed money from the bank and then I borrowed money from a friend for the fixtures. Ernest wouldn't have asked for the money but I did. And we paid all of our debt down.

You're 100 years old, how do you think you made it this long?
I had family that drank but I wouldn't have anything to do with that. I know that had something to do with it. I've been around a bit of everything, but I didn't do any of it. Some things just aren't good for you, and you've got to stay away from those things.

What's it like to be a 100?
It's good. Life's good. I've enjoyed it. It doesn't feel like I'm 100. There's nothing wrong with me. I've never had any surgery. I'm just as happy as I can be.

Did you ever have any hard times?
Of course. My husband passed away in 1999, and my daughter, Carol, died from Leukemia. She didn't tell me about it until just before she died. Carol kind of tuned me out. It was hard when she died, it didn't seem like it was real. Now it consoles me to think that she's up there with my husband. I miss him but I just gotta keep on. What other choice do you have? My son, he was the sweetest, but his wife just wanted him all the time. It's been a big issue in my life 'cause I could've used his help.

Would you have done anything different?
I might have gone to college. You can't do anything without it now. I didn't let it keep me back though.

What are you most thankful for?
My husband. We had a good marriage. We traveled some. My kids have been everywhere. He did what he thought was best for us. He was a good man and we had a good life together.

Do you believe in God?
Sure I do. I pray every night, it's like I'm talkin' to Him. He helps me along.... always has. He's taken care of me since day one.

Do you think about dying?
Sure, and I don't mind it a bit. I mean, what can you do? It's gonna happen and there's nothing you can do about it, so why fret it? I

think about it but I don't dwell on it. I'm ready whenever He's ready *(pointing up)*. My husband is up there, my daughter is up there, someday I will be too.

Do you have one piece of advice that you would give people?
Love everybody. Everybody wants to be loved. Everybody needs to be loved. If everybody loved everybody else, we'd have a lot less problems in this world. One other thing..... life passes fast.

As of the date of publishing, Ida Roselius is 104 years old and lives in a retirement center in Amarillo, Texas with five other women all over the age of 100.

"Life passes fast."

Ida Roselius, 103

Noline Long

Allie Noline Rutledge was born November 10, 1915 in a little farm house near Camel Hill in Franklin County, Texas. Her parents, Felix and Maude Rutledge, worked as sharecroppers to scratch out a living. *"I was the youngest.... I had a younger brother, but he died when he was 18 months old."* Along with her brothers and sisters, Noline attended school and worked on the farm in order to feed the family. *"I walked three miles to school and three miles home, that was 6 miles a day. I didn't have much energy by the time I got home, but we still had to help with the chores."*

After graduating high school Noline took a job at a convenience store and then in a small cafe. *"Back then you were happy just to have a job.... that was during the time of the Depression."* When she was 24 years old, Maurice Penn "MP" Long accepted a bet and asked her out on a date. They were married on December 24, 1941, just before MP left to fight in World War II. After his return, Noline and MP moved to Dallas and where they started their own family with two daughters and a son. They lived a happy life together for 74 years until his death on February 1, 2016.

Tell me about growing up in the Depression. It sounds like you had some tough times.

It was tough. I went to school and did chores every day when I got home. My chores were kind of small because I was younger than the rest of 'em.

So, you had it easy?

Not easy, the depression years were rough! You don't have any idea! You didn't have money for anything, you traded whatever you had. There just wasn't any money to be exchanged. We traded off butter or eggs or whatever else we had to get what whatever we needed. My daddy always had three hogs and butchered them in November so we had meat to eat. We didn't have any refrigerator so we had to cure all the meat. In the summer we had a garden and grew vegetables which we canned to eat in the winter. Like I said, it was rough!

How did you make it through all that?

Well, we never did go hungry but you just never did have any money for anything. Some folks weren't so lucky, especially the ones that lived in town that didn't maintain a farm and raise their own food. My granddaddy ran a little hamburger joint there in town, you could get a hamburger for nickel, if you *had* the nickel. After I graduated high school I worked at a convenience store and then I worked in a little cafe, back then you were happy just to have a job.... that was during the time of the Depression.

So, how did you manage your money?

I tell you how we got our money, we had chickens.... laying hens. We got so many dozen eggs a week and daddy would bring those eggs to town and sell 'em and that's how I got spending money. Later when I got married, we learned to saved money. We didn't invest really. My husband would say he'd need a tractor on the farm and I'd say yes. We bought land and had mineral rights and raised cattle.... He couldn't see the big picture, but I could, I think land is as good an investment as you can get. We still have a farm, 335 acres. So, I guess we really did invest, just in a different way.

Sounds like investing to me. You just invested in farmland and cattle instead of the stock market or CD's.
I guess so. We made it work for us.

How did you and Maurice meet?
We moved to a community where they lived. He's seven years younger than I am.

You're kind of robbing the cradle, aren't you?
Yeah.... *(laughing)* that's what they all said! I met him in Majors, Texas. Majors had a big grocery store.... there were about 20 young men that sat around, do nothings, and they bet him one evening that he couldn't get a date with me. He took the bet up and he came over bare footed, scared to death and asked me to go the chuck wagon games, with him. I said, *"Yeah, I'll go."* I couldn't get rid of him then! *(laughing)*

So, he won the bet?
Yeah, he won. That's been 74 years ago. I was 24 years old.

So, tell me about your marriage.
We got married December 24th, 1941. All those years I never knew if I got a Christmas present or an anniversary present! After we got married and loaded up and went to Dallas.... we didn't have a house, didn't have a job.... didn't have anything! When we got there, he got on a streetcar and went down to a bakery, he knew the man that ran the bakery.... it's still in business. He told the man he needed a job and he got one. It was a pretty good paying job at the time. Then he went off to the service with the war going on and all. They sent him to China where he flew the hump (over the Himalayan mountains) to deliver supplies... men... ammunition into China. He served over there for five years. We had six dollars between us when he went to the army, *of course he took it with him!* He didn't get paid for 3 months because they messed up his paperwork. I got $50 a month while he was gone. You could live on that then. When he got back home they'd filled his job in Dallas, so he went to work delivering bread on the bread route, then he had a radio shop, then

he was an electrician.... Later He became the Post Master here in Mt. Vernon and the fire chief for 40 years. Maurice could do anything he set his mind to. He wasn't lazy.

After 74 years of marriage, what's the secret?
You've got to be honest about everything, you can't have any secrets. We didn't agree on everything, but when it came to important things, we both agreed. All the serious things you have to work out together. If they want to do something, let them do it. We supported each other. We worked together.

Did you have any children?
We had two daughters, Linda and Marilyn, then eight years (1953) later we had a son, Kevin. The hardest thing was when Maurice went to the army and I had two little girls to raise.

How did you handle that?
You do what you have to do. Whatever needed to be done, I did it.

What's the secret to raising good children?
They said I was rough on them. I wanted them to make good decisions. I just wanted them to do what was right. They stayed within the boundary lines most of the time, when they didn't, I corrected them. I think that's missing now. You've got to be their support and tell them what to do.... not *them* telling you. When they didn't do what I told them to do, they just had to suffer the consequences. I didn't bail them out, I let them go through their consequences. I think another thing today is that so many parents are so quick to bail out their kids and get them out of trouble instead of letting them live through those life lessons. How are they ever gonna learn if you keep bailing them out?

What's it like being 100 years old?
You really can't tell any difference. It's just any other day. I get dressed every day, I go exercise, I play bingo and cards. I like to stay active, physically and mentally, but it's hard being in a retirement center, there's not much stimulation. So, I read the paper every day from cover to cover. You've got to keep the mind active.

If your brain goes, everything else follows. I have my aches and pains. Some people mention their ailments every day, I try not to do that, no one wants to hear it.

I see you have two devotionals and a Bible here on your table, so I take it that you believe in God?
I sure do. I think God had a hand in my marriage, He sent me Maurice. When Maurice went to China in the service, he flew The Hump (Himalayan mountains). A lot of planes didn't make it back, but God brought him back safe. God has guided me every day of my life. As a wife and a parent, you have to make decisions every day and you need wisdom to make the right decisions. God gives us the wisdom we need to make the right decision for our lives and for our families. I've always tried to do what's right. I pray every day, it may not be a long prayer but I pray for guidance and wisdom and what I need for the day. I was baptized 84 years ago and He hasn't let me down yet.

What do you think is the most important thing in life?
I think the choices you make. Choices have consequences- choose wisely.

Do you have any regrets about your life?
When I grew up you took life one day at a time. I walked everywhere I went, we didn't have a car, we had a wagon and a team of mules. We didn't have running water, we didn't have lights, we didn't have nothing, but I don't regret growing up that way. I grew up without money; we didn't have the money to do much of anything, and at that time, everyone was in the same shape. People are money crazy these days. They never get enough. You've got to be content. You've got to learn to be satisfied with what you've got. Do something for somebody else every day. It keeps you mind off your situation. It helps you get along, and it helps them too.

What's the greatest lesson life has taught you?
You never know what's going to happen today or tomorrow, but you've got to face whatever it is.

At the age of 100, do you ever think about dying?
Oh, I think about it from time to time.

Are you afraid?
No, I'm ready. When it's my time to die, I'm ready. When the time comes it'll be alright; the good Lord will take care of it. Being afraid won't do you any good; you can't do anything about it anyhow, it's out of your hands. The only thing you can do is be ready.

How do you get ready?
Live a life that you're not ashamed of. Do what's right, treat other people right and believe in God.

What do you tell people that don't believe in God?
There's one lady here, more than one I'm sure. She works at it to say that there's not any God, but I've seen the results in my own life. He took care of me during the Depression, He took care of me while Maurice was at war... He has taken care of me my entire life..... He's still doing it.

If you could only give me one piece of advice, what would you say?
Believe in God and do what's right.

That's it?
That's all you need.

Allie Noline Long died June 28, 2016 at the age of 100, just five months after her husband of 74 years. She left behind her son, two daughters, seven grandchildren, 16 great-grandchildren, and 6 great-great-grandchildren. "Noline was a strong woman of God who lived her life by following her faith in Him. She leaves a legacy of love, dedication, and devotion for those she leaves behind."

"Choices have consequences....
Choose wisely."

Noline Long, 100

Marion Howard

Marion Jeannes was born January 20, 1912 to Warren and Dolly Jeannes in the U.S. Indian territory near what would become Duncan, Oklahoma. Marion was the middle child of five children. She had three brothers and one sister, all of whom have now passed away. Growing up, the family lived in the small town of Halliburton where her father worked in the oil fields.

After Marion graduated high school, she attended Hill's Business college and learned to use a typewriter and do secretarial work. She moved to Oklahoma City and went to work at Wilson Foods as the secretary to the traffic manager. While working at Wilson Foods she met her husband, Domer Lawton Howard, and they were married on June 13, 1937. Domer had four children from a previous marriage, however, Marion and Domer never had any children of their own.

Marion continued to work at Wilson Foods for 42 years, retiring in 1975. *"After that I got to studying genealogy and that took up a lot of time. I try to keep my mind active. I read anything I can get my hands on."* Domer passed away in 1986. They were married 49

years.

Tell me about your husband, Domer.
He was from Montana and worked for the Russell Products Company; they made mayonnaise, jelly, salad dressing. We met through our jobs and got married in 1937, when I was 25 years old. Domer had four children from a previous marriage and we thought that was enough, so we decided we didn't want to have any more. We were married 49 years until he died.

So, is there a secret to a happy marriage?
That's hard to say. We were happy for the most part. We had some rough times but when bad things happen you just get over it and let it roll. Times were tough back then. The Dust Bowl was the worst. We went through the Depression too. We just barely got through that, but you just keep pluggin' along until it goes away. Somehow, we made it. I was working through the Depression but lots of people didn't have a job. I guess we were lucky. But as far as a secret to marriage.... Always be happy, do the best you can. Don't let things get you down....and keep pluggin'.

What's the biggest lesson you've learned?
That time goes by awful fast. You've got to take the time to enjoy the important things in life, but don't take too long or you'll miss everything else! Time keeps movin' on. It doesn't stop. One minute the kids are small, the next minute they're grown with kids of their own and you're standin' there wonderin' *"What happened?"* Learn to enjoy life while you've got it. Go do all things you want to do, 'cause one day you'll be old like me and you would be able to do them anymore.

Do you have any regrets about your life?
I don't know, maybe I should have had children. Domer had four children from his previous marriage, but I didn't have any of my own. Three of 'em have died and I only have one step child left...and I don't get to see her much 'cause she doesn't drive anymore. I don't get to see my grandchildren much either because they are in school or busy working and living their own lives. It's

lonely when you get this old. But it's nice when someone comes to see you and take care of you. It makes you feel good.

You're over 100 years old. When it comes down to the end, what really matters in life?
That you were happy with your life, with what you did and what you did with it. That you led the kind of life that you can be happy about. I think that happiness is a decision, it's up to you. Are you gonna live the kind of life that you want to be remembered for? Happiness is about living the life you want to live and being the kind of person you want to be. It's about what you *do* with it, not about what happens *to* you. You're gonna have some good things in life and your gonna have some bad things, but what you do with it is up to you. You can choose to be happy or you can choose to be sad. There's lots of sad people, but they choose to be sad. They could just as easily choose to be happy. It's your choice.... you might as well be happy.

Marion Howard passed away on April 30, 2016 at the age of 104. She is survived by 11 grandchildren (through her step-children), 4 nieces and nephews, 12 great grandchildren and 14 great-great-grandchildren. That's a pretty good family for a woman who never had children of her own. I guess that just proves that sometimes it takes more than blood to make a family.

"You can choose to be happy, or you can choose to be sad. There's lots of sad people, but they choose to be sad."

Marion Howard, 103

Jack Henry Jackson

Jack Henry Jackson was born on August 14, 1913 to John Henry and Elizabeth Jackson in the town of Sutton, Oklahoma. Growing up with his three brothers and three sisters, Jack attended school through the eighth grade before going to work on the family farm where he raised cotton and cattle. With the onset of World War II, Jack was drafted by the U.S. Army at age 29 and sent to the south Pacific. At the close of the war, Jack left the Army in 1945 and returned to Haskell, Oklahoma where he went back into farming cotton and raising cattle on a forty-acre plot. In 1958, Jack married Evelyn Chaplin and together they had five daughters and three sons. Jack continued farming until retiring at age 80, and continued to work as a foster grandparent for 26 years until retiring again at age 90.

So, you were in the war?
Yep, World War II.... went in on January 17, 1942 when the war broke out, right after Pearl Harbor. The army drafted me and sent me to the South Pacific. I was in 'til December of '45.

Where all were you stationed?
I spent most of my time in Cebu City in the Philippines.

Were you in any big battles?
I got one battle star but I didn't see any action. I was assigned guard duty at an airbase. One day a little Filipino boy said "Joe, Joe, peace, peace!!" He called everybody Joe. That's how I found out the war was over.

What did you do after the war?
I went back to farmin'.... raised cotton, corn and cows. I retired from farming when I was 80 and sold my cows to my son-in-law. Then I was a foster grandparent at the local school and retired from that at 90.

What was it like to grow up black back in those days?
Oh yeah, back then, yeah...it was hard. Nobody ever really treated me bad, but there was some bad people back then. People back then might hate you just because of the color of their skin. Not everybody was like that, but there were some. Time changes things though... Now I got a grandson gettin' married to a white girl.

How do you feel about that?
I feel good. I ain't got no problem with it.

Some people still have a problem with that.
They need to get over it. We live in an age where time changes things. Forget about it, throw it in the trash. Forget about it. I ain't no preacher but I could sure preach to a bunch of them folks.

What do you think about it?
I think it's shameful.

My grandson showed me a picture of him and his girlfriend together before I ever seen her, and when I met her she was just as happy to see me as I was to see her. She was white and I was black and I was just happy to see her 'cuz she's gonna be my granddaughter-in-law. Some people just can't live with that. That's their problem.

But how do you forgive people like that?
I forgive 'em, they didn't know no better. They come up from their pa and their grandpa, and their great grandpa.... way back. They just didn't know better. They believed in that sort of hate and it stayed in their heart. They treat you like you're some kind of varmit or something.... but if you're raised nowadays, you should know better.

What do you think about it?
Who am I to judge? My God made you just like He made me. I'm no better or worse than anybody.
Mmm Hmm. That's right.

So, you've been married for 56 years, what's the secret?
Treat her right, like you do everybody else. You got to live by the Golden Rule, *"Do unto others like you'd like done to you."* If you treat her right, she'll treat you right.

You had eight kids. What the secret to raising good kids?
Raise 'em the right way...go by the Bible. And send 'em to school so they can get a better education than you got.

You went to school through the 8th grade?
Yeah, but that was the Depression era. We didn't have the opportunity to get a good education like now days. Now days, you'll never make it without a good education. Education means opportunity, and I wanted my kids to have better opportunities than I had.

What's the hardest thing you've been through?
1930 was the hardest year. I remember 1930, it started raining one night, that next morning it was snowing. Snowed all day long, it snowed, and snowed...we went up the hill to get firewood to keep warm, that was my job. It snowed for 30 days... that's the truth! We couldn't get no water; the pond froze over.... those were tough times.

How did you get through those tough times?
You trust in the Lord.... do things right. The Lord has *always* provided.... nobody else. By the grace of God, I can look back and see the Lord took care of me all my life. I'da been dead and gone otherwise. I wouldn't be a 100 years old.

Was there ever a time you didn't trust in God?
What did I say? I've always trust in the Lord! My father would trust in the Lord and he wanted me to come up in the right way like he did.

So, he set the example?
Yeah, he set the example, and I go by it, and now my children go by it.

I guess that's the secret to being a good father?
Yes sir, trust in the Lord....and teach your children to do the same. My dad raised a good kid.... I raised good kids and they're raising good kids.

Do you have any regrets?
No....no regrets. No sense in regrettin' something you can't change.

What would you say is the most important thing in life?
The most important thing in life is to live right.... to treat everybody right. Just live right. Remember that Golden Rule, *"Do unto others like you'd like done to you."*

You're 100 years old, do you ever think about dying?
How can you ask that? Of course I think about dying.... how long am I here for? Yeah, I think about that.

You know anything about dying?
Yes sir. My dad died a few months ago; he was 75, so I think about it a lot lately.
Look son, we all die. It ain't nothin' to be scared of. I look forward to that day. God'll come get me and take me on the chariots and take me on in. I'm ready. I'll be ready when He comes. Better make

sure your ready too.

How do you get ready?
Pray. Trust in God, and turn your life over to Him. It's not what you do that gets you right with God, it's what you *let* Him do with your life. Turn your life over to God, He'll make a lot better use of it than you can. I know where I come from, and I know where I'm going.... and that's why I ain't scared of dying.

If you could give your grand kids just one piece of advice, what would you tell them?
The Lord knows your heart; He knows every move you make, so be truthful. Trust in God.... look to Him. Do right...always, always do right. Treat people right and they'll treat you right.

It has been said that "The truth is best delivered, plain and simple." *Jack Jackson is the embodiment of that saying. He made no attempt to soften his words. He left no room to debate his positions, and even if you had tried, you would've lost. He just spoke wisdom and truth.... cold hard truth. It's hard to argue with that. Jack Jackson only had an eighth-grade education, and while some would consider him uneducated, I learned more from that man than from most of the college professors I've had. Thank you, Mr. Jackson, for my education.*

Jack Henry Jackson died May 20, 2015 at the age of 101. He leaves behind Evelyn, his beautiful wife of 57 years, as well as five daughters, three sons, 19 grandchildren, 13 great-grandchildren, and 18 great-great-grandchildren. A great legacy is left only by a great man.

Paul Roden with Jack Jackson, 101.

"Do right...always, always do right."

Jack Jackson, 101

Clara Peterson

Clara Peterson, seated front right

Clara A. Ritersdorf was born on February 15, 1908 to William and Emma Edgerly Ritersdorf of Bleding, Michigan. *"My grandparents had a large family, 11 children, and my mother was the oldest, and my daddy was a machinist in Michigan.* In 1930 she married Swedish immigrant Hans Almroth. *"He was born in Sweden and came to this country to visit his sister and intended to go back.... well, he didn't."* Hans served as a Chief Warrant Officer in the U.S. Air Force for 18 years, including World War II. He was stationed around the world in locations including China, Puerto Rico and Okinawa. *"As long as he was enlisted, I had an apartment near the base so we could be together."* Hans died on October 3, 1954 while still serving in Okinawa. He was 47. After Hans' death, Clara returned to the states, settling in Santa Fe, New Mexico.

"I applied to nursing school but I was told I was too old; I was 48." Instead, she applied as a licensed practical nurse (LPN) and worked in nursing until 1964. In 1959, Clara moved to La Veta, Colorado where she met and married August Peterson in 1964. They were married for 18 years until his death on August 16, 1982. At the time of this interview she was living at the Colorado State Veterans Nursing Home in Walsenburg, Colorado.

What was it like growing up 100 years ago?
Oh my goodness.... I saw everything. I remember my first automobile ride! I was with my grandparents, I was probably 6 years old. I was in Michigan when the Lusitania was sunk. I was taking violin lessons as a child and my music teachers' wife was on that. I have so much to remember. People wonder how I don't get lonesome, well I don't. I have a photographic memory. These things are so clear to me, so clear I could just paint a picture of it.

You know, I was so interested in science, I wish there was just some way that I could record all those memories and I think that's one of the things that's going to happen in the next 100 years. I've seen so many changes in this century, I'm sure there are gonna be changes that we can't even imagine.

What's the biggest change you've seen over your 100 years?
Oh, probably the trip to outer space, the rocket, the way we're cooperating with Russia by putting them in space. There's going to be a lot of development in that. We had telephones when I was young, I think probably the videos, electronics... there's gonna be big improvements in that too. It's gonna be really interesting. The dress code (fashion industry) is so different than it was. There is such a change in that.

In the past 100 years I've seen so many, many changes. When I was a little girl, there was still a Civil War veteran in the July 4th parade. I've seen so many wars, World War I, World War II. During the second world war, my husband was in the Air Force. As long as he was enlisted, I had an apartment near the base so we could be together. We traveled all over the world. We were in Puerto Rico, China, Okinawa.... and one thing I discovered in all these countries, you talk to the people individually, and they're are all the same. The world over, regardless of the language, they're all nice people. They're all just trying to raise their families and children and make it through life.... just like us.

Do you regret not having children?
Well yes and no. When I see the trouble that young people have

with children now days, part of me is glad I never had any. But one of my sisters had three boys and I spoiled her children, and my younger sister, one of her sons, he comes to visit me; He's like a son to me. I even helped with his education. I have 35 or 40 nephews and nieces from my grand-mom's family, and now it's grand-nephews and nieces. So, in a way, I had plenty of children. They are all so good to me.

What is your best memory?
Oh, I have so many, but the best memories are as a little girl with my grandparents on the farm.

What are you most thankful for?
I'm thankful for my health, and my friends and my family. It's important to have good friends.... someone to be there for you when you need them. I don't have anyone left that's my age but the younger people are so good to me. Family and friends are important, especially as you get older.

What would you say were the hardest moments in your life?
Losing someone you love. I've lost so many people, my mother, father, sisters.... and my husbands. The deaths are hard to cope with but you have to realize nothing lasts forever, you just have to go day by day. Be thankful for what you had. When something hard happens in life, prayer gets me through it.

So, you believe in God?
Oh yes! God is an image, a figure that you can't see, but He's there. I can't really explain it. He's in us, He surrounds us, He's in everything.... God *is* everything. We try to explain God and His workings with man-made terms, you know, the big bang and how the world was started, they have wonderful theories on television.... but in reality, we just can't begin to imagine the complexity of creation, or the human body, or science. We think we can, but we're just fooling ourselves.

Do you think about dying?
Oh no. What will be will be, but I'm a little curious. We just don't

know for sure what happens or how it happens. I don't fear it; it's going to happen when it happens and there's nothing I can do about it. Don't let the thought of dying ruin your living.

Do you have any regrets?
If I hurt someone, well I regret that, but I don't think I'd want to change my life, it's been very interesting.

Do you have any advice on living a good life?
Be patient. Be patient. Take advice. Don't be ashamed or afraid to ask for advice....and be more understanding. Don't judge a person when you first meet them, wait 'til you get to know them. Sometimes we meet someone and think we know them, but we really don't. And try to understand more. We get so wrapped up in our own lives that we don't take the time to listen anymore. People want to be heard and appreciated.

My grandmother had an old German bible from the 1700's. She told me she got it in Berlin, the rest of my family didn't believe her, they thought she was senile. When I was studying I made some trips to Europe and decided to check this out, and sure enough, in the old church records they had all of that information. My grandmother was right. So, if we would just listen to our grandparents more, we could learn so much more, and the same with other people's experiences. You might want to do something and they may say *"well that's not a good idea"* and you go ahead and do it anyway, and you find that they were right after all. We could save ourselves a lot of heartache if we would just listen to our parents and grandparents.

Any last piece of wisdom you'd like to give?
Live your life. Try to see the bright side of things. Enjoy life while you can. Always make the most of what you have and what you're doing and try to appreciate it.

Clara Peterson died December 30, 2008. She was 100 years old.
"It's not good bye, it's see you later."

"Don't let the thought of dying ruin your living."

Clara Peterson, 100

Wilma Ruth McDonald

Wilma Ruth Hurst McDonald was born August 18, 1917 to Isaac and Luemma Hurst on small farm near Calumet, Oklahoma. *"My parents were farmers. We grew corn, wheat, cattle, hogs.... a little bit of everything. We grew everything we ate, and sold whatever was left over."* Like most children in back in those days, Wilma attended a small country school along with her older brother Willis, eventually graduating in 1934 as valedictorian of her high school class. After graduating, Wilma moved to Oklahoma City to attend Hill's Business University where she learned typing, dictation and office skills which led to an office job with White's Auto Stores. She later met Howard McDonald "Mac" through a mutual friend and after a brief courtship, they married on September 29, 1941. In 1947, Wilma gave birth to their only daughter, Janis Kay. Later, she and Mac started and operated a tax preparation business until their retirement. Mac died on May 18, 1986 after a battle with cancer. They were married for 45 years.

So, tell me about Mac.
Well, he was working for a company that had a secretary that happened to live in our apartment. He would come up to see the her and one day decided that there was another girl there that he'd like to see, so he kind of switched.

And you were that girl?
Well, he wasn't real serious about the other girl, so we didn't feel too bad about it. We dated for a while and got married in 1941. He was an accountant and had an office job for a construction company. I worked as a secretary. Later, he got cancer and died. I took care of him for a long time; it wasn't easy.

That's got to be a tough job.
Well, it's not too tough when you love somebody.

How do you get through something like that?
Well, you ask the Good Lord to help you and He usually does. I suppose you could say in a sense that it was a relief. You realize that those things happen and when he's been sick a long time, you know he's going to go, so you kind of are prepared for it.

So, you were married for 45 years. What's the secret to a good marriage?
Well, it was a good marriage. We were both older, we weren't too young. I think that maturity helps a lot, and the Golden Rule.... you know, that old thing of *"do unto others."* It works in marriage too, if you let it. Sometimes you just have to put up with each other's faults and move on.

Did he have a lot of faults?
He had a few.... but I loved him enough to put up with his faults.

Did you ever have any tough times in your marriage?
Well, not exactly tough, but they weren't exactly easy either.

What do you mean?
Well, that was back during The Depression and World War II; you had to work for everything you got. We worked hard, but we just stayed at it. There was really no other choice.

Did you and Howard ever have any arguments?
Oh, yeah.... but we never went to bed angry. I think that's pretty

good advice. We just got over it. Things just tend to smooth over after a while. Love covers a multitude of sins. That's the solution right there.

Any other big secrets to a good marriage?
I can't tell you that sort of stuff! *(laughing)*

Did you have any children?
We had one daughter, Janis. She was a good girl.... and she's a pretty good momma.... at least I think so.

So how do you raise good kids?
Be a good person yourself in the first place. Do the things that are right and honest and good. Set a good example. Your kids watch you. If you lie and cheat and everything else, then they're probably going to do the same thing. Set a good example. Be a good person yourself and then you can give advice. Good parents produce good kids usually. I had good parents and I hope I was a good parent. My daughter turned out pretty good.... and all my grand- kids are good.... great grand- kids too.

Sounds like you've created quite a legacy.
I think so.

Where do you think they learned it from?
Well, I think I learned it from my parents, about being honest and truthful and the right things to do, and that carries down to the next generation, to the next generation, to the next generation.

How do you make the most out of life?
How do I make the most? I don't know whether I made the most out of it or not. It's never been a life of luxury, but it's been pretty good. Be honest and be truthful and that goes a long way. And do unto others like you'd want them to do.

So, what's it like to be 100 years old?
Well, I don't feel any different than I did before I got here. I feel pretty good and I'm in reasonably good health.

What's the secret to being in good health?
Well, I guess live on a farm and work hard and eat good food. Get a lot of fresh air and sunshine, that's farm life. I think hard work is good for you.... if it's not overdone. It can be overdone. A lot of these kids nowadays don't know what hard work is, but they'll find out sometime in their life.

Do you miss the farm?
No. I didn't want to be a farmer's wife. That's a hard life.... too hard for me!

How do you live a happy life?
Well, just be yourself and be honest. Do all the right things. All these things are all in the Bible. I do read the Bible once in a while. It kind of comes back, I guess, to an attitude. I have a pretty good attitude about things?

You seem like you have a pretty good attitude about life.
Well, I think I do. I'm happy. I've had a happy life.... of course, like anyone, there's been ups and downs, but overall, it's been happy? I had a good life.

So, you believe in God?
Yes, I do. Ever since I was little I've believed in God. He's our Creator. He's an important part of my life.... not all of it like some people who go all out.... but an important part. When you ask the Good Lord to help you, He does. I can't really describe it to you, it just happens. He's seen me through some tough times.

Sounds like you depended on God a lot.
You should try it.

What is the most important thing in life?
Honesty. I tell my grand-kids to be honest, because I don't want them to be like those other people who are dishonest. Being dependable and being truthful is important so other people can count on you and so you can count on yourself. You've got to be honest with yourself as well as with other people.

Do you have any regrets?
No. I've had a pretty good life. I can't think of anything I'd do different.

Do you ever think about dying?
Well, yeah, I think about it, but I'm not ready yet. I'm happy living. Life is pretty good.

I have two more questions for you.
I may not answer them, but you can ask them.

What do you think the purpose of life is?
The purpose? Well, I don't know exactly. I guess to do right and raise a family and then grand kids, and teach them how to do right and how to become good people themselves.

What is your best advice about life?
Be honest and truthful. Trust God and he'll see you through. That's the whole sum and substance.

Wilma McDonald, age 100 and Paul Roden

Lillie Taylor

J.D. And Lillie Taylor

Lillie Jewel Stovall was born *June 26, 1910, the seventh of nine children born to George & Ruth Stovall of the small rural town of Mt. Calm, Texas. While Lillie was still young, her parents bought a farm and moved the family to the small town of Era, Texas where Lillie attended school with her five brothers and three sisters. After graduating high school, her father sold the farm and moved the family to Plainview, Texas where she met a man named J.D. Taylor, "I thought he was about the best-looking man I'd ever seen!"*

J.D. and Lillie were married on November 22, 1935. At the outbreak of World War II, J.D. was drafted into the army but was stationed state-side which allowed Lillie to remain with him while he served. After the war ended, Lillie and J.D. moved to Amarillo, Texas where they started and owned their own business. Later in life, J.D. was diagnosed with prostate cancer and died on June 6, 1995 after almost 60 years of marriage. They never had any children. In early 1997, an old friend named Eldon Plunk asked Lillie to lunch in early 1997. Six months later they were married. Ten years later, Eldon was also diagnosed with prostate cancer and

died on May 8, 2008.

Tell me about your marriage.

Which one? (laughing). We moved to Plainview after I graduated high school. We moved our stuff on boxcars on the railroad. Mother had to leave her organ behind and she did not like that one bit! She was a preacher's daughter and could sing like a mockingbird. One day my daddy came home at lunch and said there's a new grocery store that went in. He said the man was really handsome and had the blackest hair and the bluest eyes he'd ever seen. He said, *"You'll have to get in there and meet him."* I told my sister, *"Well, we might need to go and get groceries pretty soon."* She laughed at me. So, we went to the store and bought a lot of stuff we didn't really need, but when we went to check out he looked at me and I looked at him. I thought he was about the best-looking man I'd ever seen. He was a handsome dude. That's what we called them back then, a dude. I thought if I could go with someone that good-looking I wouldn't be hanging around any of these other guys at all. His name was J.D. Taylor and we courted for a while and then JD said he was moving to Amarillo 'cause he got offered a job with more money. He about broke my heart. I thought he'd meet somebody better, but he came back to see me every weekend and I took the train to see him. We got married in 1935, we were still in our twenties. We never had any kids; I had a miscarriage and got real sick. The doctor said I couldn't have any after that.

Do you regret not having children?

There's no use in grieving on something you can't do anything about. We helped our nieces and nephews. They didn't have money to buy material for dresses and clothes, so I bought all the material I needed to sew everything they needed. I kept them well dressed. You see, if God takes one thing away from you, He adds another. Did you know that? I love my nieces and nephews and they love me. They are as sweet as sugar, and so I've always had somebody to love.

How long were you and J.D. married?

We were married around 60 years. He died from prostate cancer. I

don't know how I got through that, but after a while I married again. I married a man from my church, Eldon Plunk in July 1997. We sang in the choir, he had a marvelous voice. He was quite wealthy. He had an irrigated farm and a horse motel in Amarillo.

A horse motel?
Yeah, you know, horse stables, but it was a swanky place! It was full all the time. He made money hand over fist. I had known Eldon for a long time. J.D. and I were active in our church and we saw Eldon and his wife other every Sunday. Not long after J.D. died, Eldon's wife died. One day he asked me out for lunch one Sunday and I went. We married six months later. We were married about twelve years before he passed away. He died of prostate cancer too. He was a good man, a real Christian.

So, you've had two husbands die. How do you deal with that?
The Lord gives you strength to keep going, so that's what you do, keep on going. What other choice do you have? I never said it was easy, it's not. It's hard.... real hard, but you've got to keep moving forward with your life. Their life on this earth has ended, but yours hasn't. God will give you whatever strength you need to get through it. All you have to do is ask. I've been a Christian all my life. The Lord has really blessed me; I've had a wonderful life. I've been blessed in about every way you can think of. Everything I started, it turned out good. You can do more with the Lord than you can without. If you belong to a church, you ought to volunteer cause the Lord will bless you more. He sure did me. God's been guiding me my whole life.

You've owned several business ventures, what's the key to running a successful business?
I've had a mind for business all my life. First, Be honest in all your dealings. Second, help people whenever you can. My husband was a good, honest, Christian man. He was always honest and always willing to help other people. We open our business and from day one God blessed us. We had a lovely home and were able to buy a car and which means we were able to help even more people. We went and picked up people every Sunday morning for church

because we had a good car. Most people didn't even have a car then. It's a blessing to be able to help people. They say God blesses those that bless others, and that sure is the truth. Giving is important. With the business, we didn't have a regular income, we gave when we could. When we got more, we gave more. God knows what you've got. You don't fool Him, honey! If there's something I can do for somebody, I'll do it. You don't lose anything when you help somebody else. If God gives you the strength and the ability to help someone, do it.

Sounds like God is very important to you.
I've had some heart-breaking times but God always gave me everything I needed. We went through the Depression and that was something else. I hope you never have to go through anything like that. There were no jobs to be had, because people had no money to pay them. A lot of people didn't have enough to eat, so mother and daddy would give them food to eat, eggs and different things from the farm. Some people didn't have a place to sleep, so Daddy fixed up a garage apartment and let people stay there.

So, you've been helping people your whole life.
When the Lord tells you to do something, don't just sit there on your fanny, get up and get to work.... and that's what we did! When we saw someone that needed help, we did our best to help them out. We knew it was the right thing to do. That's how we were raised. Besides, next time it might be you that needs help.

What's it like being 100 years old?
I think it's great that the Lord has seen fit to let me live that long. He don't do that for everybody. I don't take any medicine.... medicine will kill you. Eat good food. We had a lot of good things to eat on the farm. That's half of what's wrong with kids now; they're parents don't feed them right. I try to stay fit. I used to walk about a mile every day until I fell and cracked my spine. If I hadn't hurt my spine I could probably run you a race!

Do you have any regrets?
Only that I could've done more to help others.

What's the most important thing in life?
Joining a church and knowing Jesus as your Lord and Savior. He's still seeing me through things. Without Him I wouldn't have amounted to anything, honey. He's the most important thing in my life.

If you could only give me one piece of advice, what would you say?
I know exactly what I'd tell you. You need to know the Lord as your Savior, that's your best bet. You don't have to know much else. He'll guide you in everything you do. You'll never have a second thought. If you got something in your head and you can't figure it out, He'll help you. Oh, you'll miss it if you don't know Him. You're missing it, honey. Everything I've ever asked Him about, it might not be the answer I wanted, but He always gives me the right answer. The Lord never lets you down. People will, but God won't. We just need to learn to listen. He'll put it in your heart if you believe in Him. You won't have to worry about anything the rest of your life.

Lillie Jewel Taylor died September 16, 2017. She was 107 years old. Though she had no children of her own, she is survived by 32 great nieces and nephews, almost 50 great-great nieces and nephews, and almost 20 great-great-great nieces and nephews. As she stated, "I love my nieces and nephews and they love me. They are as sweet as sugar, and so I've always had somebody to love."

"When the Lord tells you to do something, don't just sit there on your fanny, get up and get to work...."

Lillie Taylor, 107

Life Lessons

When I speak to audiences about wisdom, I am frequently asked what I learned from this project. It's a tough question because there are so many answers. How do you compress over 5,000 years of wisdom and experience down into a two-minute answer? But still, you must answer the question, so here it goes.

For me, I've learned how to make better decisions. I've learned what's important in life. I've learned that I can survive life's hardships because *they* have survived life's hardships. I've learned how to be happy. I've learned that life is not fair. I've learned how to accept those things in life which I cannot change. I've learned that life is short, fragile and precious. I've learned that hard work and determination go a long way. I've learned how to be a better husband, a better son, a better brother.... a better person. I learned to save and invest my money. I've learned to forgive. I've learned to collect memories, not stuff. I've learned that life is not a dress rehearsal. I've learned that prayer works. I've learned that memories are the only thing I can take with me, and that love and relationships are the only enduring things I can leave. I've learned that I wish I had known this stuff 30 years ago. I've learned that everything in life will either kill you or make you stronger.... *but eventually it will kill you!* I've learned that I wish I had listened to my parents and grandparents. I've learned that these life experiences make us who we are. I've learned that wisdom is everywhere; you just have to ask. And I've learned that I have so much more to learn.

I've learned how to live life...... I mean *really live,* not just living day to day, accidentally, waiting on life to happen. I mean living intentionally.... with purpose and joy, and peace, and direction. I've learned to love life, to celebrate its highs and accept its lows.... because it's all part of the ride. I've learned that life is an adventure and it's all about the journey, not the destination. I've learned that life is what I make of it. My happiness, my joy, my peace.... it's all comes down to my decision.... and I've learned to make better

decisions.

There are a few other things I have learned as well.

Observations

There are a few observations that these individuals seem to have in common. Please keep in mind that this is not a scientific study, nor am I a scientist. These are simply a few things I have noticed throughout this project.

An apple a day.....
There are no overweight centenarians. Perhaps there are a few, but I didn't meet any. Studies show that obesity contributes to numerous health problems and all of these people seemed to be in overall good health. None of the subjects I interviewed suffered from diabetes, heart disease, stroke, Alzheimer's or other common health problems associated with old age. There were a few cancer survivors; only a handful had high blood pressure, and many were on no medication whatsoever. I'm sure genetics plays a role in living 100 years, but according to them, diet and exercise is the secret.

Age, Race and Sex
Out of more than 100 people that I interviewed for this book, the women far outnumbered the men. A Harvard University Study[3] confirms this showing that, among centenarians, women outlive men by a margin of nine to one. I also noticed a great racial divide. Of the all the people I interviewed, only 6 were African-American. A study conducted by the University of Georgia also showed that of the 248 subjects studied, only 27% were African-American. Furthermore, despite concentrated efforts, I had great difficulty locating 100-year-old individuals from other minority groups such

---

[3] http://news.harvard.edu/gazette/1998/10.01/WhyWomenLiveLon.html

as Asian, Hispanic, Middle Eastern, Native American... to the extent that no other minorities are represented in this book. Researchers point out numerous, potential social-economic causes such as access to healthcare and affordable medications, as well as multiple societal and cultural contributors such as diet and lifestyle. There is an abundance of research in this area, so I will leave further discussion to the experts.

Attitude Really is Everything!
All the people interviewed for this book had an extremely positive attitude about themselves, and about life in general. An Iowa State University study on centenarians "characterizes them as resilient with respect to mental health and life satisfaction..."[4] I think Frank Hurst said it better; *"I think what's kept me going is my attitude about life.... otherwise I'm sure I'd be dead by now. Mental attitude is what does it.... I think that's what keeps me going."*

"In the beginning...."
To me, this was one of the most fascinating observations of this project. Every person I interviewed for this book professed a faith in God.... *100% of them.* While the faith of some was certainly stronger than others, all professed a belief in a divine Creator with many stating that their faith played a major role in their lives. Please note that a concentrated effort was made to find individuals from other cultures and religious backgrounds (Hindu, Muslim, etc.) but was ultimately unsuccessful. Regardless, in my experience, there are no 100-year-old atheists.

Happiness Really is a Choice

As stated above, the overall positive attitude of these men and women is overwhelming. These people have lived through The Great Depression, war, cancer, poverty, hunger, homelessness,

---

[4] Human Development and Family Studies, Iowa State University, Ames, IA 50011-4380, USA.
Aging and Mental Health (Impact Factor: 1.75). 11/2009; 13(6):827-37.

divorce, the deaths of children and spouses, and every other tragedy you can imagine, yet their outlook on life remains positive and upbeat.

Frank Hurst summarized it well when he said, *"My philosophy is pretty simple, take life as it comes, and enjoy it for what it is. I realize that I can't always be happy, but I try to make the best of it. I've always taken the view that things could always be worse than what I'm in, but I don't worry about it. I take care of what I can, and what I can't take care of, to hell with it (laughs), and it's been the story of my life."*

And as Estelle Thompson said, *"You can find something good in everything that happens to you, or you can find something bad. It's your choice."*

So many others voiced a similar philosophy, that happiness is truly a choice, a mindset that you *choose* regardless of the circumstances life throws at you. According to every one of these individuals, life really is what you make of it, and happiness is simply a decision. Many attribute their long lives to their overall positive outlook on life, and numerous studies back up that claim. Poor mental health has been shown to contribute to a variety of physical ailments. Maybe our grandparents were right; the key to mental and physical health is really, all in our head.

Unspoken Wisdom

I was visiting with Millard Gaddy when I learned one of the most important lessons of my life. As we talked, I asked him, "What's the most important thing in life?"

"You see that picture?" he said pointing to a young woman in a white dress, *"That was my wedding day and that's my Ruthie. She was so beautiful that day. It was the happiest day of my life. And you see that one?"* pointing to another, *"those are my three girls.*

That must have been around 1930. And that one over there," he continued, pointing to yet another photo. He went on and on, telling me about each photograph, smiling as he relived the memories that they stirred. He continued to ramble, telling old stories about his past life. I was just about to ask him the question again in an attempt to get the interview back on track when he said, *"You asked me what the most important thing in life is? It's simple. It's the memories you make and the people you love. No one can ever take that away from you."* Then it hit me. The answer was all around me.

Here I was sitting in a retirement home with a little old man surrounded by his only remaining worldly possessions; a bed, a dresser, a chair, a television and some old photographs. Everything else was gone; the cars, the homes, the businesses, the clothes, the achievements. Everything.... gone. Everything he had worked his entire life for had been whittled down to what would fit into this one room.

In the twilight of his life, he was not reminiscing about the cars and the homes and all the stuff he had accumulated. He was sharing with me his most valuable assets, his memories about his wife, his family and the people he loved most. That's what he treasured. It wasn't the stuff, it was the people and the relationships and the memories.

But it wasn't just Millard Gaddy. In every interview that followed, I became very conscious of the surroundings and possessions of each person. Just like Mr. Gaddy, they all had basic furnishings, but they *all* had pictures and photographs, and all you had to do was ask about an old photo and they would smile as they drifted back in time and told you a story of their past.

The accomplishments, the success, the possessions, none of these things seemed to matter much to someone who was approaching the end of their journey. It made me realize how my life had been filled with the empty pursuit of worldly treasures. Treasures that seem to depreciate into junk as time goes on. But the simplest

memory of time with a loved one seems to appreciate into a priceless gem.

It is a lesson that I have not forgotten. I look at things differently now. I still have a house and cars and stuff.... plenty of stuff, but now I realize that it's *just* stuff. Stuff that will rot and be worthless someday. I don't focus on the stuff anymore. In 50 years, I know that my flat-screen TV will be a non-functioning antique. I know that no one will care about my accomplishments or how much money I made. But I also know that when I am dead and gone, maybe people will smile when they remember our good times we had together, or how I impacted their life.

Just stop for a minute. Think back in your life. What is it that brings a smile to your face? Is it some material possession, some achievement, or is it the people and places you've experienced in life? That is what I focus on now.... creating memories and relationships. There is only one thing we can take with us when we go, that is our memories. And there is only one enduring gift that we can leave with someone, and that is love. That is what matters, and that is how I want to live my life.

You Can't Pick and Choose

There's a lot of wisdom packed into these pages. - Advice on how to manage your finances, improve your marriage, raise children, survive life's challenges. And it's not just advice, it's wisdom, actual experience of how these people dealt with life's issues, what worked, and what they learned.

But you can't pick and choose which bits of wisdom you believe are true and which ones are not. That option is off the table. The evidence of over 5,000 years of collective life experience versus your individual opinion is just too overwhelming. You can't accept their wisdom on finances, marriage, health, life.... and ignore their thoughts on faith and God. You either have to accept it, faith and all, or reject it all as foolishness.

I can't ignore the fact how so many of these individuals, who are nearing death and eternity, clearly believe in an Almighty Creator. Is it because they fear death and afterward, an unknown eternity? Or is it because they have seen the evidence of God's existence time and time again over the last hundred years of their lives. If you read these stories, you will see that the clear majority have no fear of death or the afterlife, and many tell of how they believe God has guided and watched over them all their lives. I have no problem with those who may be skeptics, but sooner or later you have to ask yourself the question; *"Is God just some imaginary concept to make us feel better about our temporary and otherwise pointless existence.... or is it possible that these people may know something that I don't know?"* If you choose to believe that these people's wisdom can help you with your marriage, your finances, and other challenges in your life, then you *must* give equal credit to their words regarding their faith. They have nothing to gain at this point in their lives, by perpetuating a myth. These individuals *believe* in their faith, but it is more than just belief. They embody it; they live it out daily. They have felt it and seen the effects on their lives. To them the concept of God and faith is more than a belief, it is an experience. And remember, experience always trumps theory.

"The best evidence of God is in the lives that have been changed."
Anonymous

So, that's it. I've laughed with these people, and I've cried with them. I have grown to love them and wish I could spend more time with all of them. My life has been forever changed by them. As I reflect, I can't help but realize that I have been sitting in the presence of greatness. Years ago, I prayed that God would give me wisdom, and He has answered my prayers.

About the Author

Paul Roden is a husband, business owner, entrepreneur and writer who has literally devoted years of his life to the pursuit and study of wisdom in order to improve not only his life, but also the lives of others. Paul and his wife Kate have been happily married for over 25 years.

For information about Paul, speaking engagements and future projects, visit **www.5000YearsOfWisdom.org** or you can check out his Facebook page at: **https://www.facebook.com/WisdomResearchGroup**

Made in the USA
Coppell, TX
12 January 2020